D1446658

THE LEGAL CASES
IN THE BOOK OF MORMON

THE LEGAL CASES
IN THE BOOK OF MORMON

John W. Welch

Brigham Young University Press
and
The Neal A. Maxwell Institute for Religious Scholarship
Provo, Utah

Front cover: Page from the printer's manuscript of the Book of Mormon. Courtesy Community of Christ Archives, Independence, Missouri.

Back cover: *Trial of Abinadi*, by Minerva Teichert. Courtesy Brigham Young University Museum of Art.

Brigham Young University Press

The Neal A. Maxwell Institute for Religious Scholarship
Brigham Young University
Provo, Utah 84602

14 13 12 11 10 09 08   5 4 3 2 1

Library of Congress Cataloging-in-Publication Data

Welch, John W. (John Woodland)
    The legal cases in the Book of Mormon / John W. Welch.
        p. cm.
    Includes index.
    ISBN 978-0-8425-2712-5
    1. Jewish law—History—To 1500. 2. Book of Mormon—Relation to the Bible. 3. Law (Theology)—Biblical teaching. I. Title.

    KB211.W45 2008
    289.3'22—dc22   2008027191

Judge righteously between every man and
his brother, and the stranger that is with him.

Deuteronomy 1:16

See that you are merciful unto your brethren;
deal justly, judge righteously, and do good continually.

Alma 41:14

To my law students, 1981–2007,
who have motivated, challenged, and taught me

CONTENTS

Foreword and Personal Acknowledgments

⤳

Intellectually, I am a lawyer and law professor who was trained in biblical studies and Greek philosophy. At the same time, I have loved the truths of the Bible and have enjoyed a testimony of the Book of Mormon.[1] For me, these academic and spiritual interests have been mutually synergistic and reinforcing. In both personal and professional ways, I hope to share that dynamic experience through this volume, which has been taking shape for several years. Along the way, many people have contributed to this project, and I am deeply grateful for their kindness, collegial criticism, and encouragement.

In writing this book, I have tried to keep four main audiences in mind. My goals are to make the legal cases in the Book of Mormon clear to law students, convincing to practicing attorneys, interesting to ordinary readers, and respectable to academic colleagues of any faith. To make this material accessible to readers at various levels of familiarity with the law, the Book of Mormon, or the Bible, I have minimized in-group language and disciplinary jargon as much as possible. All these audiences can identify with the legal narratives in the Book of Mormon, for they involved pressing problems of ordinary people as well as technical legal elements that require close reading. In all cases, these texts generously reward careful analysis. Appreciating their subtle details and persistent patterns in light of biblical law adds new spiritual insights and practical perspectives to these significant judicial proceedings in Nephite history.

Yet for all readers, approaching the scriptures with legal issues in mind may require something of a paradigm shift. This legal approach, developed

---

1. I am grateful for the similar interests and testimonies of many scholarly colleagues, some of whose personal statements about the Book of Mormon are found in Susan Easton Black, ed., *Expressions of Faith: Testimonies of Latter-day Saint Scholars* (Salt Lake City: Deseret Book and FARMS, 1996); my chapter, entitled "Good and True," is found on pp. 231–42.

by biblical scholars and legal historians over the past fifty years, offers new perspectives on the Book of Mormon. By reading these texts as a lawyer would read them, I do not mean to imply that Abraham, Moses, and Jeremiah, or Mosiah, Alma, and Mormon, intended us to read their sacred writings the same way that we read legal handbooks or secular judicial reports. But once one sees how deeply the judicial cases and other legal materials in the scriptures are intertwined with the entire fabric of these carefully composed books, it becomes difficult to read them again without seeing legal threads running through the warp and woof of their major ideas and messages. Law and ethics, Torah and teachings, regulations and revelations, and rights and wrongs are all closely bound up together.

Indeed, law and religion were much more closely aligned in the ancient world than they are in the modern state. In antiquity, God's will was seen to reside in the judicial resolution of crucial issues. Thus the legal cases reported in the Book of Mormon, as in the Bible, are not just about crime and punishment in a secular sense. To the men and women who experienced those legal confrontations, those cases are all about the ultimate definitions of righteousness and wickedness, the open differentiation of truth from falsity, and the firm recognition of righteous authority as opposed to unjust imposition. Reading the scriptures in light of ancient laws, principles, practicalities, purposes, and sympathies enriches appreciation for issues and contexts out of which many of the plain messages of the prophetic Book of Mormon arose.

Since I would like this book to be as interesting for readers to read as it has been for me to research and write, I have chosen to begin this volume with a personal foreword. Telling how this study has developed and who has been involved in this project over the past quarter century will, I hope, get us off to a good start.

I grew up in the home of a consummate lawyer. Upon the advice of my parents, who always held out hope I would become a lawyer, I studied a fair amount of Latin in high school taught by two dedicated women. In their classes, I developed an interest in the legal orations of Cicero, the laws of the Roman Republic and Empire, and the role and development of law in ancient Greece. Then, as a college freshman in one of Professor Hugh Nibley's Book of Mormon classes at Brigham Young University in 1964, I became aware of the great extent to which the cultures of the ancient Israelites, Egyptians, Assyrians, and Babylonians, as well as the general milieu of the ancient Near East, shed light on the political and social world out of which Lehi, Nephi, and their ensuing civilization is said to have emerged. Whether Nibley was discussing the cultural context of

Laman's unsuccessful attempt to negotiate a legal acquisition of the plates of brass from Laban,[2] the social norms behind the coronation of King Mosiah by his father Benjamin,[3] or any other such topic, it became apparent that ancient legal rules and practices never stood very far in the background behind the narratives, speeches, and events reported in the Book of Mormon. Nibley's command of a wide array of ancient sources and his facility in linking diffused texts enriched his faith and moved the inert cerebral mountains of many of his students, mine included.

Three years later, in 1967, midway through my two years as a missionary for The Church of Jesus Christ of Latter-day Saints, I was stationed in Regensburg, Germany, where I learned in a theological lecture in the local Catholic seminary about chiasmus (a significant literary form in the Bible). I was led a few days later to find several excellent examples of chiasmus in the Book of Mormon.[4] Returning to Brigham Young University, I pursued that discovery in a master's thesis that compared literary structures in the Nephite record with similar patterns in other ancient writings.[5] It did not take long for legal matters to enter this picture as well, for large portions of the libraries from the ancient world are legal in nature. Ancient libraries include numerous business contracts, adoption agreements, slave manumissions, international treaties, prenuptial agreements, loans, commercial records, wills, judicial rulings, and lists of legal rules or wise counsel about potential situations.

After studying Greek philosophy for two years at Oxford University and law for three years at Duke University, I practiced law from 1975 to 1980 in Los Angeles. During this time, I edited a collection of studies entitled *Chiasmus in Antiquity*, which contains analyses of several such legal

---

2. Hugh Nibley, *An Approach to the Book of Mormon*, 3rd ed. (Salt Lake City: Deseret Book and FARMS, 1988), 95–131; see 1 Nephi 3:11–14.

3. Nibley, *Approach to the Book of Mormon*, 297–98; compare Mosiah 1:2–5.

4. This discovery was first published in John W. Welch, "Chiasmus in the Book of Mormon," *BYU Studies* 10, no. 1 (1969): 69–84. These events are explained in John W. Welch, "The Discovery of Chiasmus in the Book of Mormon: Forty Years Later," *Journal of Book of Mormon Studies* 16/2 (2007): 74–87.

5. John W. Welch, "A Study Relating Chiasmus in the Book of Mormon to Chiasmus in the Old Testament, Ugaritic Epics, Homer, and Selected Greek and Latin Authors" (master's thesis, Brigham Young University, 1970). I am grateful to J. Reuben Clark III, Hugh W. Nibley, and C. Terry Warner for serving on my committee and directing my research path. The chapter in this thesis on chiasmus in Ugaritic was published in *Ugarit-Forschungen* 6 (1974): 421–36, and the chapters on chiasmus in the writings of Greek and Latin authors and in the New Testament were published in an anthology I edited, *Chiasmus in Antiquity: Structure, Analysis, and Exegesis* (Hildesheim: Gerstenberg, 1981; Provo, UT: Research Press, 1999), 211–68. For a recent update and correction of one part of chapter 7 of my thesis, see "How Much Was Known about Chiasmus in 1829 When the Book of Mormon Was Translated?" *FARMS Review* 15, no. 1 (2003): 47–80.

texts, notably the narrative of Haman's injustice in the book of Esther, the case of the blasphemer in Leviticus 24, and the stoning of the Sabbath breaker in Numbers 15.[6] In this work, I was fortunate to collaborate with Yehuda T. Radday (a faculty member at the Technion in Haifa) on his analysis of chiasmus in the legally rich texts of the Pentateuch (the first five books of the Bible) and the book of Ruth (which reports the legal proceeding at the town gate that made it possible for Boaz to marry Ruth clear of the rights of another kinsman).[7] Professor Radday brought Professor Bezalel Porten of the Hebrew University of Jerusalem into this project. As a lawyer, I was especially intrigued by Porten's discovery of chiasmus in Aramaic legal papyri from two family archives from the fifth century BC left by Jewish soldiers who had settled on the Nile island of Elephantine (a settlement in Upper Egypt whose residents, like Lehi and Nephi, fled the Babylonian destruction of Jerusalem in 587 BC).[8] In this volume, which appeared in 1981, are also chapters on chiasmus in Ugaritic, Greek and Latin texts, and the Book of Mormon. Reading the Book of Mormon alongside this array of ancient texts yielded a number of favorable and productive literary comparisons. These convergences set the stage for a similarly detailed reading of the Book of Mormon with ancient legal principles in mind.[9]

In 1979, an invitation from Rex E. Lee, dean of the newly formed law school at Brigham Young University, to join its law faculty gave me an opportunity to combine my professional interests in law with the study of ancient scriptures. Dean Lee told me that if I would teach one business-related course, I would be free to teach anything else I wanted. Almost in jest, but testing to see if he really meant what he had just said, I asked, "How about a course on Babylonian law and the Book of Mormon?" Without a second's hesitation, he smiled and said, "That would be perfect. I can't think of anything better. That's the kind of thing we want at this law school." I was surprised at his response, but recognizing this as a chance to see where further research in this direction might lead, and with careful consideration and the concurrence of my wife and family, I accepted the

---

6. Welch, *Chiasmus in Antiquity*, 55–57, 87, 90.

7. Yehuda T. Radday, "Chiasmus in Hebrew Biblical Narrative," in Welch, *Chiasmus in Antiquity*, 50–117; and Yehuda T. Radday and John W. Welch, "Structure in the Scroll of Ruth," *Beth Mikra* 77 (1979): 180–87.

8. Bezalel Porten, "Structure and Chiasm in Aramaic Contracts and Letters," in Welch, *Chiasmus in Antiquity*, 169–82.

9. My interest in ancient law was first fueled by reading Roland de Vaux's convenient description of the main elements of the Hebrew legal system in his study of the social institutions of ancient Israel: *Ancient Israel: Its Life and Institutions* (New York: McGraw-Hill, 1965), 1:143–63.

position. Without the consistent encouragement of the deans at the law school (Rex E. Lee, Carl S. Hawkins, Bruce C. Hafen, H. Reese Hansen, Kevin J. Worthen, and associate deans J. Clifton Fleming and James D. Gordon), and but for the unfailing support of my wife, Jeannie, little of this work would have been possible.

In my first year as a law professor, I taught Business Associations, Advising Closely Held Businesses, and also an innovative course entitled "Ancient Legal Systems and the Scriptures." As far as I know, no class like the last one had ever been taught before. My students and I studied the published literature on law and legal cases in the Bible, and we broke new ground in examining the judicial proceedings in the Book of Mormon. It was not difficult for my students to detect legal elements in the Book of Mormon. We began building a biblical law collection in the law library, compiling bibliographies of books and articles about biblical law,[10] and rereading the scriptures with legal issues in mind. In teaching this course over the past twenty-five years, I have found the works of many scholars to be particularly helpful to my students: Jewish jurist David Daube (first introduced to me by his friend Professor Douglas Parker),[11] Professor Ze'ev W. Falk (of the Hebrew University of Jerusalem),[12] German scholar Hans Jochen Boecker (professor of Old Testament at Wuppertal-Barmen),[13]

---

10. In the process, we have published and updated a comprehensive bibliography of biblical law and created in the Howard W. Hunter Law Library at BYU's law school a sizable collection of biblical law materials. See *A Biblical Law Bibliography* (Lewiston, NY: Edwin Mellen Press, 1990); "Biblical Law Bibliography: Supplement through 1995," *Zeitschrift für Altorientalische und Biblische Rechtsgeschichte* 3 (1997): 207–46; and a further supplement through 2002 published in the same journal, 9 (2003): 279–318. These bibliographies have been combined and published in CD-ROM format in John W. Welch, comp., *Biblical Law Cumulative Bibliography* (Winona Lake, IN: Eisenbrauns; Provo, UT: BYU Press, 2005), listing over 5,500 entries.

11. For example, David Daube, *Ancient Jewish Law: Three Inaugural Lectures* (Leiden: Brill, 1981); *Studies in Biblical Law* (1947; repr., New York: KTAV, 1969); and *Witnesses in Bible and Talmud* (Oxford: Oxford Centre for Postgraduate Hebrew Studies, 1986). The collected works of David Daube are in the process of being published by the Robbins Collection at the University of California, Berkeley, edited by Calum Carmichael.

12. Ze'ev W. Falk, *Hebrew Law in Biblical Times: An Introduction* (Jerusalem: Wahrmann Books, 1964). Following a visit by Professor Falk to the J. Reuben Clark Law School, arrangements were made for BYU Press to publish a second edition of this work. That volume appeared after his untimely death in September 1998: *Hebrew Law in Biblical Times: An Introduction*, ed. John W. Welch, 2nd ed. (Provo, UT: Brigham Young University Press; Winona Lake, IN: Eisenbrauns, 2001), containing a complete bibliography of Falk's works on pp. 203–20 (all subsequent citations are to this edition). See also his *Introduction to Jewish Law of the Second Commonwealth*, 2 vols. (Leiden: Brill, 1972–78); and *Law and Religion: The Jewish Experience* (Jerusalem: Mesharim, 1981).

13. Hans Jochen Boecker, *Law and the Administration of Justice in the Old Testament and Ancient East*, trans. Jeremy Moiser (Minneapolis: Augsburg, 1980); and *Redeformen des Rechtslebens im Alten Testament* (Neukirchen-Vluyn: Neukirchener Verlag, 1964, 1970).

Professor Bernard S. Jackson (a barrister as well as a leading scholar in the Jewish Law Association, now Alliance Professor of Modern Jewish Studies, University of Manchester),[14] Professor Raymond Westbrook (a lawyer and ancient Near Eastern law specialist at Johns Hopkins University),[15] as well as Reuven Yaron (Hebrew University),[16] Eckart Otto (University of Munich),[17] and many others.[18]

That first year, forty very enthusiastic law students each completed a significant research paper on topics suggested to them. In most cases, we were breaking new ground. Since then, I have taught this course in the J. Reuben Clark Law School every other year, and pioneering research

---

14. For example, Bernard S. Jackson, *Wisdom-Laws: A Study of the Mishpatim of Exodus 21:1–22:16* (Oxford: Oxford University Press, 2006); *Studies in the Semiotics of Biblical Law* (Sheffield, England: Sheffield Academic Press, 2000); "Legalism and Spirituality: Historical, Philosophical and Semiotic Notes on Legislators, Adjudicators and Subjects," in *Religion and Law: Biblical-Judaic and Islamic Perspectives*, ed. Edwin B. Firmage, Bernard G. Weiss, and John W. Welch (Winona Lake, IN: Eisenbrauns, 1990), 243–61; "Susanna and the Singular History of Singular Witnesses," *Acta Juridica* (1977): 37–54; and *Essays in Jewish and Comparative Legal History* (Leiden: Brill, 1975).

15. Raymond Westbrook, "Jubilee Laws," *Israel Law Review* 6 (1971): 209–26; "Lex Talionis and Exodus 21, 22–25," *Revue Biblique* 93, no. 1 (1986): 52–69; *Studies in Biblical and Cuneiform Law* (Paris: Gabalda, 1988); "Biblical Law," in *An Introduction to the History and Sources of Jewish Law*, ed. Neil S. Hecht et al. (Oxford: Oxford University Press, 1996), 1–17; and Westbrook, ed., *A History of Ancient Near Eastern Law*, 2 vols. (Leiden: Brill, 2003).

16. Reuven Yaron, "Biblical Law: Prolegomena," in *Jewish Law in Legal History and the Modern World*, ed. Bernard S. Jackson (Leiden: Brill, 1980), 27–44; "Jewish Law and Other Legal Systems of Antiquity," *Journal of Semitic Studies* 4, no. 4 (1959): 308–31; and "The Middle Assyrian Laws and the Bible," *Biblica* 51, no. 4 (1970): 549–57.

17. To mention only a few, Eckart Otto, "Interdependenzen zwischen Geschichte und Rechtsgeschichte des antiken Israels," *Rechtshistorisches Journal* 7 (1988): 347–68; *Wandel der Rechtsbegründungen in der Gesellschaftsgeschichte des antiken Israel: Eine Rechtsgeschichte des "Bundesbuches" Ex XX 22–XXIII 13* (Leiden: Brill, 1988); and "Zur Stellung der Frau in den ältesten Rechtstexten des Alten Testament (Ex 20:14; 22:15f) wider die hermeneutische Naivität im Umgang mit dem Alten Testament," *Zeitschrift für Evangelische Ethik* 26, no. 3 (1982): 279–305.

18. Some of the studies most relevant to the judicial administration of justice in ancient Israel include the following: Pietro Bovati, *Re-Establishing Justice: Legal Terms, Concepts and Procedures in the Hebrew Bible*, trans. Michael J. Smith (Sheffield, England: JSOT Press, 1994); Enrique Nardoni, *Rise Up, O Judge: A Study of Justice in the Biblical World*, trans. Seán Charles Martin (Peabody, MA: Hendrickson, 2004); Bruce Wells, *The Law of Testimony in the Pentateuchal Codes* (Wiesbaden: Harrassowitz, 2004); Robert R. Wilson, "Israel's Judicial System in the Preexilic Period," *Jewish Quarterly Review* 74, no. 2 (1983): 229–48; G. d'Ercole, "The Juridical Structure of Israel from the Time of Her Origin to the Period of Hadrian," in *Populus Dei*, ed. I. Israel (Rome: Communio, 1969), 389–461; Donald A. McKenzie, "Judicial Procedure at the Town Gate," *Vetus Testamentum* 14, no. 1 (1964): 100–104; "The Judge of Israel," *Vetus Testamentum* 17, no. 1 (1967): 118–21; Jacob Weingreen, "The Case of the Blasphemer (Leviticus XXIV 10 ff.)," *Vetus Testamentum* 22, no. 1 (1972): 118–23; "The Case of the Daughters of Zelophchad," *Vetus Testamentum* 16, no. 4 (1966): 518–22; and "The Case of the Woodgatherer (Numbers XV:32–36)," *Vetus Testamentum* 16, no. 3 (1966): 361–64.

has remained an important part of each class. Students have always found interesting research topics, and an extensive collection of valuable student research papers has been created. Most of them are now available in the Howard W. Hunter Law Library at Brigham Young University.[19] I am indebted to these wonderfully engaging students at the J. Reuben Clark Law School who have challenged, stimulated, and motivated me in my research, analysis, and writing.

In addition, scholarly resources and collegial associations outside the law school have proved invaluable. In 1979 FARMS (the Foundation for Ancient Research and Mormon Studies) began to assemble a unique group of dedicated scholars who pooled their wisdom and energies in efforts to discover more about the ancient backgrounds of the Book of Mormon. John L. Sorenson, Stephen D. Ricks, Gordon C. Thomasson, Robert F. Smith, Paul Y. Hoskisson, Hugh W. Nibley, Noel B. Reynolds, S. Kent Brown, Donald W. Parry, and soon several others combined their efforts to explore, among many other things, the Israelite backgrounds of the Book of Mormon. I owe a deep debt of gratitude to these colleagues for their stimulating conversations, insights, and critiques.

In 1982 I presented a paper entitled "Ancient Near Eastern Law and the Book of Mormon" at the regional meeting of the Society of Biblical Literature (SBL) in Denver, Colorado.[20] This conference was an important turning point for me, giving me an opportunity to test this fledgling research in front of a skeptical and erudite audience. After vigorous discussion and questioning, the response was very favorable and encouraging. One significant concession came from a critical Lutheran scholar from Kansas who, as a result of my presentation, disclosed to me that he now felt he had not read the Book of Mormon as carefully as he should have and that he intended to study it more before passing judgment on the book again. His confession was probably true of everyone in the 1980s; we all had need to examine this scripture much more thoroughly. At this same time, serious Book of Mormon study received its greatest impetus from the exhortations of Ezra Taft Benson, president of The Church of

---

19. For a list of these titles, see John W. Welch, "Bibliography of Hebrew Law in the Book of Mormon," *Studia Antiqua: The Journal of the Student Society for Ancient Studies* (Summer 2003): 181–86, in a special issue copublished with FARMS. Recent papers are available online through the J. Reuben Clark Law School's electronic reference library.

20. John W. Welch, "Ancient Near Eastern Law and the Book of Mormon" (paper presented to the regional meeting of the Society of Biblical Literature in Denver, Colorado, and published as a FARMS Preliminary Report, 1981).

Jesus Christ of Latter-day Saints.[21] The FARMS organization soon began making preliminary Book of Mormon research available in the form of "Preliminary Reports," among which was this SBL presentation and several of my law students' papers.[22]

Also in the early 1980s, I joined the recently organized Biblical Law Consultation, a new program unit within the SBL. Along with significant strides forward in the biblical law discipline generally, this group soon grew from a consultation to a section within the SBL, reflecting a significant rise in interest concerning the study of law in the ancient world. My participation in this group, composed of scholars interested in both law and religion, helped pave the way for my involvement in a conference held in 1984 at the University of Utah and cohosted at Brigham Young University. This conference, organized principally by University of Utah law professor Edwin B. Firmage, featured distinguished scholars from Israel, England, and the United States who came together to discuss religion and law from Judaic, Christian, and Islamic perspectives.[23]

Interactions with scholars in settings such as these afforded opportunities to test my ideas and to benefit from current research and feedback from experienced scholars. For instance, discussions with Professor Moshe Greenberg of the Hebrew University of Jerusalem about the biblical limitations on royal and governmental power made me more aware of the legal postulates behind the so-called Paragraph of the King in Deuteronomy 17:14–20[24] and the striking relevance of that text to King Benja-

---

21. For a convenient collection of his main speeches on the Book of Mormon, see Ezra Taft Benson, *A Witness and a Warning: A Modern-day Prophet Testifies of the Book of Mormon* (Salt Lake City: Deseret Book, 1988).

22. For example, Fred Essig and H. Daniel Fuller, "Nephi's Slaying of Laban: A Legal Perspective," FARMS Preliminary Report (Provo, UT: FARMS, 1981); Roy Johnson, "A Comparison of the Use of the Oath in the Old Testament and the Book of Mormon," FARMS Preliminary Report (Provo, UT: FARMS, 1982); Richard McGuire, "Prophetic Lawsuits in the Hebrew Bible and Book of Mormon," FARMS Preliminary Report (Provo, UT: FARMS, 1982); Mark J. Morrise, "Simile Curses in the Ancient Near East, Old Testament and Book of Mormon," FARMS Preliminary Report (Provo, UT: FARMS, 1981); James L. Rasmussen, "Blood Vengeance in the Old Testament and the Book of Mormon," FARMS Preliminary Report (Provo, UT: FARMS, 1981); and David Warby, "The Book of Mormon Reveals the Forgotten Law of False Prophecy," FARMS Preliminary Report (Provo, UT: FARMS, 1981).

23. The papers from this conference were published in *Religion and Law: Biblical-Jewish & Islamic Perspectives*, ed. Edwin B. Firmage, Bernard G. Weiss, and John W. Welch (Winona Lake, IN: Eisenbrauns, 1990).

24. Moshe Greenberg, "Biblical Attitudes toward Power: Ideal and Reality in Law and Prophets," in *Religion and Law*, 101–12.

min's analogous words and political policies (Mosiah 2:12–14), similarly limiting the king's status and wealth.[25]

On another occasion, I enjoyed a dinner conversation with Professor James H. Charlesworth, from whom I had taken a class in the Divinity School while I was attending law school at Duke University and who now is at Princeton Theological Seminary. Our discussion of the trial and death of Jesus turned to comments about the practice of crucifixion in antiquity. I mentioned the rules given both in the Talmud and by Maimonides that required an executioner to chop down the tree or to take away the post on which a person had been hanged or crucified, in order to remove from the face of the earth the memory of the person who had been so ignominiously put to death. I asked Professor Charlesworth if he was aware of any other text in world literature, besides in Jewish law, that required the felling of the tree on which a culprit had been hanged. He was not. Charlesworth was intrigued, however, when I told him about the execution of Zemnarihah in 3 Nephi 4:28 and the chopping down of the tree on which he had been hanged.[26]

While exploring the biblical law of excusable (unintentional) homicide with English barrister and Jewish law scholar Bernard S. Jackson, who has lectured at BYU's law school on two occasions, we turned attention to the Book of Mormon account of Nephi's slaying of Laban.[27] Professor Jackson had made the point that the biblical concept of premeditation was different from the Anglo-American definition, which has come to require much less than the deliberate preplanning and lying in wait for one's victim mentioned in Exodus 21:13–14. In American law, the requirement of premeditation is satisfied as long as the killer is conscious of what he is willfully doing merely the instant before the deed is accomplished. Jackson felt that he could prove his interpretation of the biblical concept of premeditation in Exodus 21:13–14 from a linguistic analysis of its Hebrew text, but he regretted the lack of an actual instance from antiquity confirming his interpretation. What he needed was an account in which a person had not been lying in wait and whose victim was delivered by God into his hands, and in which the slayer, when the killing occurred, was fully aware of what was happening and yet the deed was viewed as

25. Discussed at several points in *King Benjamin's Speech: "That Ye May Learn Wisdom,"* ed. John W. Welch and Stephen D. Ricks (Provo, UT: FARMS, 1998), 34, 60, 173, 188, 248, 520.

26. John W. Welch, "The Execution of Zemnarihah," in *Reexploring the Book of Mormon,* ed. John W. Welch (Salt Lake City: Deseret Book and FARMS, 1992), 250–52. See pp. 352–56 below.

27. This case is analyzed in detail in John W. Welch, "Legal Perspectives on the Slaying of Laban," *Journal of Book of Mormon Studies* 1/1 (1992): 119–41. This topic is explored further in John W. Welch, "Introduction," *Studia Antiqua* (Summer 2003): 9–12.

falling between a homicide that was committed with malice aforethought and a death that was purely accidental. Jackson found it very interesting that the slaying of Laban might provide something like the kind of case he was looking for, but he figured it would be difficult to find a way in which he might use it.[28]

My associations over the years with Bernard Jackson and his scholarship have been particularly rewarding for me. While in Oxford to attend his Speaker's Lecture series in 1985, I read his 1972 treatise on theft in early Jewish law,[29] which sharply distinguished between the concepts of theft and robbery in the ancient world; it struck me that his analysis could be applied directly to the Gadianton robbers in the Book of Mormon and to the legal concepts of theft and robbery in Nephite society.[30] My subsequently inviting Professor Jackson to lecture at Brigham Young University led to a generous reciprocal invitation in 1993 for me to make a presentation on the trial of Jesus to the British Association of Jewish Studies in Liverpool.

Jackson's kindness was such that he agreed to spend a week one summer during his years at the University of Kent at Canterbury reading and discussing various legal texts in the Book of Mormon. I am very grateful to Professor Jackson for this time we spent together exploring Sherem's accusations against Jacob (Jacob 7:1–21), the trial of Abinadi (Mosiah 12:19–17:1), the blasphemy of Korihor (Alma 30), and many of the other legal proceedings in the Book of Mormon discussed in the chapters below. As we read, he pulled books I had never seen before off the shelves in his library for comparison. His comments about these cases were riveting as we walked together from campus to his Canterbury home and as we sat in the shade of a large willow tree overlooking the Canterbury Cathedral tower and the English landscape below.

I returned home to present papers at various conferences at Brigham Young University in the late 1980s and early 1990s on such topics as Lehi's last will and testament (in which I took an innovative legal approach to

---

28. For his latest thinking on the law of homicide in Exodus 21:12–14 and the legal question presented if a "killing is neither premeditated, nor accidental," see Jackson, *Wisdom-Laws*, 124–30, quotation on p.124.

29. Bernard S. Jackson, *Theft in Early Jewish Law* (Oxford: Clarendon, 1972). Jackson's treatment of theft and robbery on the occasion of the Speaker's Lecture at Oxford now appears as chapter 9 in his recently published *Wisdom-Laws*, 291–312.

30. John W. Welch, "Theft and Robbery in the Book of Mormon and Ancient Near Eastern Law," FARMS Preliminary Report (Provo, UT: FARMS, 1985); and Welch, "Legal and Social Perspectives on Robbers in First-Century Judea," *BYU Studies* 36, no. 3 (1997): 141–53.

Lehi's final blessings to his sons and posterity in 2 Nephi 1–4),[31] the law of war in the Book of Mormon (explaining the rules of martial law that applied under the law of Moses and evidently regulated Nephite military conduct),[32] and the law and the temple (examining the law of Moses as it apparently would have been observed in the temples of the Nephites in the cities of Nephi, Zarahemla, and Bountiful up until the time when the law of Moses was finally fulfilled with the death and coming of Christ as described in 3 Nephi 8–11).[33] These studies appeared in volumes published by the BYU Religious Studies Center, as brief FARMS Updates (often coauthored) in the FARMS newsletter, or in compilations in the 1990s. Those studies shed light on additional links between the Book of Mormon and legal materials from the ancient world, such as Hebrew legal terminology, kingship and lawgiving, inheritance law, legally required holy days, the laws of apostasy and false prophecy, rules of evidence, various crimes and punishments, military law, collective responsibility, legally established weights and measures, and the speechlessness of an opposing litigant.[34]

At the same time, correspondence with various scholars invariably enriched my studies. I became a member of the Jewish Law Association and, in 1990, presented a paper titled "Chiasmus in Biblical Law" at the biannual meeting of the association in Boston. That paper discussed several texts, including the marvelous use of chiasmus in the case of the blasphemer in Leviticus 24:13–23, which literarily depicts the concept

31. John W. Welch, "Lehi's Last Will and Testament: A Legal Approach," in *The Book of Mormon: Second Nephi, the Doctrinal Structure*, ed. Monte S. Nyman and Charles D. Tate (Provo, UT: Religious Studies Center, Brigham Young University, 1989), 61–82.

32. John W. Welch, "Law and War in the Book of Mormon," in *Warfare in the Book of Mormon*, ed. Stephen D. Ricks and William J. Hamblin (Salt Lake City: Deseret Book and FARMS, 1990), 46–102.

33. John W. Welch, "The Temple in the Book of Mormon: The Temples at the Cities of Nephi, Zarahemla, and Bountiful," in *Temples of the Ancient World: Ritual and Symbolism*, ed. Donald W. Parry (Salt Lake City: Deseret Book and FARMS, 1994), 297–387.

34. For example, in *Reexploring the Book of Mormon*, see chapters on "Statutes, Judgments, Ordinances, and Commandments," 62–65; "Kingship and Temple in 2 Nephi 5–10," 66–68; "Jacob's Ten Commandments," 69–72; "Seven Tribes: An Aspect of Lehi's Legacy," 93–95; "Abinadi and Pentecost," 135–38; "Joseph Smith: 'Author and Proprietor,'" 154–57; "The Destruction of Ammonihah and the Law of Apostate Cities," 176–79; "Exemption from Military Duty," 189–92; "The Case of an Unobserved Murder," 242–44; "Thieves and Robbers," 248–49; and "The Execution of Zemnarihah," 250–52. See also my article "Weighing and Measuring in the Worlds of the Book of Mormon," *Journal of Book of Mormon Studies* 8, no. 2 (1999): 36–46. See also more recent FARMS Updates in the *Insights* newsletter entitled "Better That One Man Perish" (vol. 18, no. 6, June 1998, p. 2); "Sherem's Accusations against Jacob" (vol. 11, no. 1, January 1991, p. 2); "Unintentional Sin in Benjamin's Discourse" (vol. 16, no. 4, April 1996, p. 2); "The Laws of Eshnunna and Nephite Economics" (vol. 18, no. 12, December 1998, p. 2); and "Cursing a Litigant with Speechlessness" (vol. 18, no. 10, October 1998, p. 2).

of reciprocity that is so fundamental to the ancient Israelite concept of justice. That paper also pointed out the very creative use of chiasmus by Alma in Alma 41, which similarly represents the aspect of reciprocity, or restoration, that undergirded the Nephite concept of justice. Several of the Jewish scholars at the Boston conference were fascinated, others were puzzled, and some were quite bemused that a Gentile could show them something they had overlooked in their own Hebrew Bible.[35]

In 1995 I focused attention on ancient legal deeds. The prophet Jeremiah tells briefly of an interesting sixth-century BC property transaction (Jeremiah 32:6–15) in which one of Jeremiah's cousins challenged him to put his money, as it were, where his prophetic mouth was: if Jeremiah truly believed that the Lord would bring the Jews back to their ancestral lands, then Jeremiah should pay his cousin good money for a piece of family land near the village of Anatoth. To consummate this purchase, Jeremiah used a two-part deed having an open portion and a sealed portion. He rolled up the deed and hid it up in a clay pot for long-term preservation. I wanted to learn more about these doubled, sealed, witnessed documents because it seemed that the Book of Mormon plates had been constructed in accordance with this same ancient pattern, with one part open and the other sealed. On the way to a conference of the Society for the Study of Ancient Law at the University of Leiden in Holland that summer, I consulted with scholars in England and looked for examples of these double deeds in the British Museum and at the libraries at Oxford, but to little avail. Not finding what I was looking for, I put the matter aside and went on to Holland. The conference meetings were convened in the library of the Papyrological Institute in Leiden. As it would turn out, we met around a conference table with books surrounding us on all four sides, and right next to where I sat were books containing exactly the information and facsimiles of double deeds for which I had been searching. The librarians there were very helpful, and out of this grew a lengthy paper describing this ancient legal practice, involving not only papyrus scrolls but also Roman bronze plates with considerable parallels to the Book of Mormon plates.[36] Ten years later, in August 2005, I was involved in putting together a group of donors to acquire a matching set of two such Roman bronze military diplomas from

---

35. John W. Welch, "Chiasmus in Biblical Law: An Approach to the Structure of Legal Texts in the Hebrew Bible," *Jewish Law Association Studies* 4 (1990): 5–22. On the legal significance of Alma 41, see pp. 340–46 below.

36. John W. Welch, "Doubled, Sealed, Witnessed Documents: From the Ancient World to the Book of Mormon," in *Mormons, Scripture, and the Ancient World: Studies in Honor of John L. Sorenson,* ed. Davis Bitton (Provo, UT: FARMS, 1998), 391–444.

the year AD 109, in excellent condition, for donation to and display in the Harold B. Lee Library at Brigham Young University.[37]

In 1997 Noel Reynolds organized a three-day conference sponsored by the Liberty Fund to study the concept of justice in the Book of Mormon.[38] As a result, a dozen first-rate scholars (most of whom were reading the Book of Mormon in depth for the first time) found significant jurisprudential ideas "bubbling up off the page again and again," as one of the participants expressed it.

On February 24, 2001, this momentum continued to build as FARMS sponsored a daylong conference on Hebrew law in the Book of Mormon, the proceedings of which were published in the summer 2003 issue of *Studia Antiqua* as a copublication with FARMS. The occasion prompting that conference was the publication of the new edition of Zeʾev Falk's *Hebrew Law in Biblical Times*, which easily constitutes the most convenient introduction to the study of Israelite law during the pre-exilic period, the time period most relevant to the world of Lehi preceding the destruction of Jerusalem by the Babylonians. Falk's book is highly recommended as a companion to all explorations of law in the Book of Mormon. Speakers at that conference included BYU professors Douglas H. Parker, Noel B. Reynolds, Stephen D. Ricks, Donald W. Parry, S. Kent Brown, myself, and seven of my law students. The topics covered legal studies on the sources of law, crime and punishment, slavery and social justice, God and the law, and family law.[39]

In 2004 David R. and Jo Ann H. Seely and I collaborated in producing a book entitled *Glimpses of Lehi's Jerusalem.*[40] Nineteen contributors and

37. John W. Welch and Kelsey D. Lambert, "Two Ancient Roman Plates," *BYU Studies* 45, no. 2 (2006): 55–76.

38. Described in Noel B. Reynolds, "The Coming Forth of the Book of Mormon in the Twentieth Century," *BYU Studies* 38, no. 2 (1999): 6–47.

39. The papers presented at this conference are published in a special issue of *Studia Antiqua* (Summer 2003), a journal of the Student Society for Ancient Studies at Brigham Young University.

40. John W. Welch, David Rolph Seely, and Jo Ann H. Seely, eds., *Glimpses of Lehi's Jerusalem* (Provo, UT: FARMS, 2004). This book serves as a counterweight for readers who might see the Book of Mormon as historically anachronistic. In this regard it is fundamental to harbor a correct perception of the nature of pre-exilic Israelite religion. In seeing the Book of Mormon as stemming from the spiritual milieu of Jerusalem before 600 BC, Margaret Barker made a significant statement at the Joseph Smith Bicentennial Conference, "The Worlds of Joseph Smith," held at the Library of Congress in Washington, D.C., in May 2005. Barker, a former president of the prestigious Society for Old Testament Study, argues that the First Temple era was a dynamic time of ongoing revelation and visions, of seers in direct communication with God and angels, of competing bodies of scripture, and of sacred texts with multiple meanings. Of concern in that age was not only the law of Moses but a "law for all generations," with decrees given on heavenly tablets featuring the Son of Man figure and inviting deification through the white fruit of the

several editorial assistants combined efforts to reconstruct the world of Jerusalem around 600 BC in order to help modern readers imagine what it would have been like to live in that time and place. Ways in which Jerusalemite legal procedures left deep impressions on the culture and jurisprudence of the Nephites are discussed in my chapter about the trial of Jeremiah (reported in Jeremiah 26) as a legal legacy of Lehi's Jerusalem.[41]

Opportunities such as these have opened interesting doors and have led to rewarding experiences in the study of ancient Israelite law. Beginning in 1995, my students and I have provided the abstracts of biblical law articles for the survey of current literature in the *Jewish Law Annual.* For five years I was on the executive committee of the Jewish Law Section of the American Association of Law Schools and for six years on the steering committee of the Biblical Law Section of the Society of Biblical Literature, associating with such exemplary scholars as Bernard M. Levinson, William S. Morrow, Raymond Westbrook, Pamela Barmash, Richard E. Averbeck, Cheryl Anderson, Rachel F. Magdalene, and Bruce Wells. My main responsibility was to compile for the Biblical Law Section a comprehensive bibliography of the rapidly expanding list of scholarly publications on law in the Bible.

The culmination of two decades of this bibliographic work came in 2005 with the publication *Biblical Law Cumulative Bibliography* on CD-ROM, copublished by Eisenbrauns and BYU Press.[42] This reference tool is organized by key subjects and is electronically searchable, making it easy to locate numerous books and articles on various legal topics pertinent to understanding a wide array of passages in the Bible, many of which are used or discussed in this volume. Beyond the sources cited in the footnotes in this volume, many more studies listed in this bibliography shed further light on the legal backgrounds of the Book of Mormon, and hopefully will stimulate further research for years to come.

In all of this, the adventure of exploring law in the Book of Mormon has far exceeded my intellectual and spiritual expectations. Over and over again, I have found the Book of Mormon to be a rich source of legal material. In numerous ways texts from the ancient Near East, the Bible,

---

tree of life and the guiding rod of the temple. Barker concludes, "The original temple tradition was that Yahweh, the Lord, was the Son of God Most High, and present on earth as the Messiah. Thus finding Christ in the Old Testament is exactly what we should expect." The same factors, she points out, also characterize the Book of Mormon. See Margaret Barker, "Joseph Smith and Preexilic Israelite Religion," *BYU Studies* 44, no. 4 (2005): 69–82, quotations on pp. 72, 79.

41.   John W. Welch, "The Trial of Jeremiah: A Legal Legacy from Lehi's Jerusalem," in *Glimpses of Lehi's Jerusalem,* 337–56.

42.   See note 10 above for publication details.

and the Book of Mormon prove relevant to each other. The interconnections between these bodies of materials are extremely thought provoking. Not only has the world of biblical law prompted and furthered my research concerning law in the Book of Mormon, but legal circumstances and textual materials in the Book of Mormon have equally guided and enlightened my understanding of law in ancient Israel. All of this has led to a greater appreciation of the complexity and profundity of the Book of Mormon as a truly remarkable religious record.

I appreciate the many students, research assistants, and colleagues who have been interested in and have contributed to this ongoing work. Several have worked on each chapter in this book. Especially noteworthy is the research and writing assistance of Robert Eaton, James Garrison, Claire Foley, Robert Hunt, Alan Moore, and John Nielsen, to name only a few, as well as the editorial expertise of Don Brugger, Alison Coutts, Paula Hicken, Kelley Konzak, Jacob Rawlins, Sandra Thorne, Shelsea Vanornum, and others at the J. Reuben Clark Law School, the Neal A. Maxwell Institute for Religious Scholarship, and the Foundation for Ancient Research and Mormon Studies.

This field of research is not yet exhausted. New insights keep coming up,[43] and this gives positive assurance that this line of inquiry is on a productive track that will lead to even more discoveries in the future.

---

43. See generally John W. Welch, "A Steady Stream of Significant Recognitions," in *Echoes and Evidences of the Book of Mormon*, ed. Donald W. Parry, Daniel C. Peterson, and John W. Welch (Provo, UT: FARMS, 2002), 331–87.

PART ONE

Background Considerations

CHAPTER ONE

Entering the Ancient Legal World

The interdependence of law and society complicates the analysis of any legal system, be it the law in modern America or in the ancient world of the Bible, the Near East, or the Book of Mormon. As one biblical scholar has correctly stated, "All judicial systems are an integral part of the societies in which they are found."[1] This reality manifests itself in various circularities that are quickly confronted by every first-year law student. On the one hand, laws govern the choices that people make; but on the other hand, laws are the results of choices made by people. Similarly, laws are norms or pronouncements that judges use in forming their opinions, but those judicial decisions in turn become laws that will be used as precedents in the next round of pertinent cases. Further, any body of law generally reflects the highest ideals and the timeless values embraced by a community or civilization, yet at the same time individual laws are based on the prevailing policies or needs of that time and place and are expedient solutions to immediate, temporal problems. For reasons such as these, law is sometimes called a "seamless web,"[2] whose threads are so interwoven that it is impossible to discover where they begin or end.

---

1. Robert R. Wilson, "Israel's Judicial System in the Preexilic Period," *Jewish Quarterly Review* 74, no. 2 (October 1983): 231, has set forth the following agenda for understanding the legal system in pre-exilic Israel: "Any adequate reconstruction of Israel's judicial system must satisfy two important requirements. First, the reconstruction must take into account all of the Biblical evidence in an acceptable way. Second, the reconstruction must be compatible with what we know of the structure of ancient Israelite society. This is so because all judicial systems are an integral part of the societies in which they are found. The political, economic, social, and religious organization of a society does not necessarily determine the nature of its judicial system, but social factors do limit the types of judicial systems that can function effectively within the society. This interrelation between the judiciary and the overall social structure means that the judicial system cannot be studied in isolation but must be seen in a larger social context." The same considerations apply to the study of the legal system in the Book of Mormon.

2. The expression "The law is a seamless web" is of uncertain origin, but the general idea is often attributed to English legal historian Frederic W. Maitland, who used the phrase "seamless

Thus no single door leads into an open chamber in which any student of the Nephites, Lamanites, or other groups that populate the pages of the Book of Mormon can readily comprehend the full meaning and operation of law in that world. To understand law in Nephite civilization fully is to understand virtually everything about Nephite society, values, religion, government, morals, economy, customs, and practically every other aspect of their personal, family, and collective life. But in order to grasp all that, one must also understand the law, the legal rules, regulations, policies, and institutions that shaped and controlled those very elements of Nephite life. Given this circularity, the question is obviously a bit perplexing: Where do we best begin a systematic study of law in the Book of Mormon?

First, it helps to see the workings of the law as an ongoing process. Beginning students of American law soon learn that law is a complicated process that moves from legislative debates to constitutional rights, statutes, private choices, administrative rulings, police enforcement, political opinion, public policy, economic efficiency, moral duties, individual cases, judicial decisions, jury verdicts, appellate jurisdiction, criminal sanctions, equitable remedies, civic concerns, and back again to more legislative debates, whereupon the process of legislation, enforcement, and adjudication is repeated over and over again. To enter the flow of this cycle, one must dive in at some point and try to swim along.

Second, to understand the root nature of the law—that which drives the legal system at crucial points when push comes to shove—it is probably best to do as most legal educators advise: begin with the case method. For more than a century, the study of law in American law schools has begun with the careful study of individual cases, their findings of fact, and judicial opinions as issued by various prominent courts resolving significant issues or controversies. Experience has shown that the case method is more instructive than other points of departure, such as digesting statutes or treatises on separate topics such as property, contracts, torts, or tax. Only individual, real-life cases reveal the actual inner workings of a particular legal system. One learns more about how the law operates—how conflicts are abstracted, formulated, presented, and analyzed as legal issues; how parties work their way through a judicial trial; how judges and other adjudicators think of the law; and what the law ultimately means—by studying individual cases than by pursuing any other method.

web" to refer to the "unity of history" in a law-related context. Frederic W. Maitland, "A Prologue to a History of English Law," *Law Quarterly Review* 14 (1898): 13–33; also Frederick Pollock and Frederic W. Maitland, *The History of English Law*, 2nd ed. (Cambridge: Cambridge University Press, 1899).

And so it seems best to begin studying law in the Book of Mormon by examining the Nephite legal cases. This choice becomes even clearer when we recognize that while the Book of Mormon has not preserved any copy of any Nephite law code, it contains excellent detailed accounts of several significant legal disputes. Because these reports contain not only a statement of the final decision but also a considerable amount of information about the unfolding of the case, studying the Nephite legal cases provides a good idea of how the law was understood and enforced in that society.

Not Thinking Like a Modern Person

A challenge inherent in this kind of study is to reconstruct the Nephite legal system, so far as possible, as the Nephites themselves might have understood and experienced law in the context of their own world. Thinking like an ancient person, whether in Lehi's Jerusalem in the seventh century BC or in any other ancient setting, is not a simple undertaking.[3] Dallin H. Oaks, a former law professor and president of Brigham Young University, has said that a lawyer "is a student of meaningful differences among apparently similar situations, and meaningful similarities among situations of no apparent connection."[4] It is difficult enough to spot such differences or similarities in a modern context, to explain their importance or unimportance, or to describe the current state of a law in federal court; it becomes all the more challenging to reconstruct an understanding of law in pre-exilic Israel, under the pharaohs of Egypt, or during the Nephite reign of the judges in first century BC in the land of Zarahemla. Even in cuneiform studies, a field that presents students with numerous legal records in various languages, many technical legal questions remain unanswerable concerning the meaning and administration of the law in Mesopotamian societies.

In this light, it is crucial for modern readers to step back from their own world, leave behind their modern experiences, and make an effort, however incomplete, to think like an ancient Israelite, Egyptian, Babylonian, or Nephite. In order to do this, modern (or postmodern) people

---

3. For a broader example of an effort to transport oneself back into the cultural setting of ancient Jerusalem, see John W. Welch and Robert D. Hunt, "Culturegram: Jerusalem 600 B.C.," in *Glimpses of Lehi's Jerusalem*, ed. John W. Welch, David Rolph Seely, and Jo Ann H. Seely (Provo, UT: FARMS, 2004), 1–40, together with the sources cited there, discussing such topics as ancient travel, foods, clothes, health, family, daily routines, housing, employment, politics, and religion in the daily lives of people in pre-exilic Israel and in the ancient Near East.

4. Dallin H. Oaks, "Opening Remarks," August 27, 1973, posted at http://www.law2.byu.edu/law_school/foundingdocumentsnew/index.php (accessed March 12, 2008).

must divest themselves of a host of presuppositions and expectations conditioned by the modern concept and practice of law.

Even though we cannot always know exactly how the law operated in
these ancient civilizations, we do know of many things that surely did *not*
exist in their legal systems two or three thousand years ago.[5] Thus appreciating in general what the ancient world was like is a useful way to begin
any study of how law developed and was practiced over the thousand-
year history of the Nephite people. Consider the following representative
observations.

Most legal systems in the ancient world operated without enforcers
comparable to police officers or FBI agents as we know them. Judicial proceedings or legal disputes were initiated as private lawsuits; there were no
district attorneys, public prosecutors, or state-appointed public defenders.[6] Accordingly, the distinction between public criminal law and private
civil law had not yet developed in any formal sense.

In many societies, there were no paid professional judges, at least in
any modern sense. Instead, in most parts of the ancient world, town elders, priests, and leading citizens of the village served as citizen-judges
hearing lawsuits that were initiated quite spontaneously and were usually
argued, deliberated, decided, and concluded within a fairly short period
of time.[7] Occasionally, officials were appointed by the king to hear certain
kinds of cases, but we do not know how they were paid or how much of
their time was spent in judging cases. No lawyers served as advocates for
paying clients before the fourth century BC, when professional forensic
orators appeared mainly in Athens. There were very few officially reported

5. For discussions of the daily life and society of ancient Israel, see, for example, Roland de Vaux, *Ancient Israel* (New York: McGraw-Hill, 1965); Philip J. King and Lawrence E. Stager, *Life in Biblical Israel* (Louisville: Westminster John Knox, 2001); Victor H. Matthews and Don C. Benjamin, *Social World of Ancient Israel, 1250–587 B.C.E.* (Peabody, MA: Hendrickson, 1993); Shunya Bendor, *The Social Structure of Ancient Israel: The Institution of the Family from the Settlement to the End of the Monarchy* (Jerusalem: Simor, 1996); Philip R. Davies, *In Search of "Ancient Israel"* (Sheffield, England: JSOT Press, 1992); Frank S. Frick, *The City in Ancient Israel* (Missoula, MT: Scholars Press, 1977); Frank S. Frick, *The Formation of the State in Ancient Israel: A Survey of Models and Theories* (Decatur, GA: Almond, 1985); and Raphael Patai, *Family, Love and the Bible* (London: MacGibbon and Kee, 1960).

6. See generally Pietro Bovati, *Re-Establishing Justice: Legal Terms, Concepts and Procedures in the Hebrew Bible*, trans. Michael J. Smith (Sheffield, England: Sheffield Academic Press, 1994), 62–92, 217–25.

7. See Samuel Greengus, "Law: Biblical and ANE Law," in *The Anchor Bible Dictionary*, ed. David Noel Freedman (New York: Doubleday, 1992), 4:244–45, discussing both royal and local judicial bodies and also the town elders, priests, and officials who served in judicial capacities. On the judicial responsibilities of the head of the household, see C. J. H. Wright, "Family," in *Anchor Bible Dictionary*, 2:764.

decisions; wisdom, customs, and common sense rather than strict adherence to controlling statutes or binding precedents usually formed the basis for judgment by judges.[8] Enforcement mechanisms were few and relatively simple. A pit, cistern, or dungeon might be used occasionally for temporary restraint, but long-term imprisonment was rarely an option.[9]

In the world of the ancient Near East and eastern Mediterranean, there existed no state-creating constitutions, no popularly elected law-making legislatures, no true separation of powers between branches of government, and little formal distinction between church and state or between the temple estate and the king's palace. Government was fairly unsystematic. There were no organized political parties, universal suffrage, paid professional judges, or career lobbyists; and except to a limited degree in a few places such as classical Greece, people did not have representative legislatures or bureaucratic administrative agencies, and even in Greece public officials were selected by lot rather than by campaigning for office.[10] The concept of legal rights was scarcely developed, let alone the idea of a bill of rights. Duties and obligations, together with honor and shame,[11] formed a greater part of the legal consciousness among ancient peoples than they do in modern Western societies, which have come to focus more on rights than on duties.

We know of no legal treatises, hornbooks (scholarly explanations of the law), or law manuals from the ancient world, and it is doubtful that the so-called law codes of the Bible and the ancient Near East functioned

---

8. Bernard Jackson argues that the biblical concept of adjudication was fundamentally guided by the idea that "justice is divine," making the judicial process more "charismatic" than "rational." Bernard S. Jackson, *Wisdom-Laws: A Study of the Mishpatim of Exodus 21:1–22:16* (Oxford: Oxford University Press, 2006), 411–12.

9. For a survey of the uses of prisons in ancient Israel, see Karel van der Toorn, "Prison," in *Anchor Bible Dictionary*, 5:468–69. Also, for a brief discussion of imprisonment in the broader context of punishment, see Ze'ev W. Falk, *Hebrew Law in Biblical Times: An Introduction*, ed. John W. Welch, 2nd ed. (Provo, UT: Brigham Young University Press; Winona Lake, IN: Eisenbrauns, 2001), 73–75.

10. For a detailed description of the organization of the government in Athens, see Aristotle, *The Athenian Constitution*, trans. Frederic G. Kenyon (Adelaide: eBooks, 2004). For a general discussion of governmental institutions in Israel, see de Vaux, *Ancient Israel*, 1:92–99, 127–38.

11. See, for example, Lyn M. Bechtel, "Shame as a Sanction of Social Control in Biblical Israel: Judicial, Political, and Social Shaming," *Journal for the Study of the Old Testament* 49 (1991): 47–76; and David A. DeSilva, "The Wisdom of Ben Sira: Honor, Shame, and the Maintenance of the Values of a Minority Culture," *Catholic Biblical Quarterly* 58 (1996): 433–55. "Unlike our Western guilt-oriented society, the pivotal value of the Mediterranean society of the first century was honor-shame." Bruce J. Malina and Richard L. Rohrbaugh, *Social-Science Commentary on the Synoptic Gospels* (Minneapolis: Augsburg Fortress, 1992), 76.

in that world in the same way as do statutes in the modern world.[12] No specialized schools of law existed, although the scribal tradition prepared people to record legal agreements and to advise others involved in legal transactions in the use of traditional manners of documentation.[13] A systematic sense of jurisprudence was still centuries away, and no attempts to rationalize decisions in individual cases appear to have been made. Legal decisions proceeded on a case-by-case basis, and while rules were significant, ancient evidence is scanty that express principles or broad policies were theoretically advocated or officially adopted.

A modern person can scarcely imagine running a courtroom or law office without telephones, computer technology, libraries, faxes, and copy machines. In antiquity, messengers were occasionally used and some legal matters could be reduced to writing on papyrus, parchment, or clay tablets; but few other resources were available as tools of the infant legal profession. While customs regarding property law, family law, and personal injury law were relatively well established, no one had even begun to dream of such things as intellectual property rights, class actions, or Internet access.

Life in the ancient world revolved around different instruments and institutions than are known in the modern world. With no cars, trucks, or tractors, speeding laws were not needed. Because foot travel and draft animals played crucial roles in society, laws dealing with oxen that gored pedestrians were of greater importance then than now. National and municipal borders were much less distinct, with large areas of unoccupied land lying between villages and towns. Consequently, no standard passports existed, border crossings were very difficult to regulate, and even the concept of a nation or state with territorial boundaries held little meaning. Village security and the need to be able to mobilize a citizen army for defense posed constant challenges. Obviously, there was no United Nations to keep the peace. Other cultural institutions, such as reliance on the gods to guarantee treaties, were customary.

---

12. See Greengus, "Law: Biblical and ANE Law," in *Anchor Bible Dictionary*, 4:243–44, affirming that writing played a fairly minor role in ancient legal systems. In antiquity, nothing close to a complete collection of written laws or prescriptions for any society ever existed.

13. Anne Fitzpatrick-McKinley, *The Transformation of Torah from Scribal Advice to Law* (Sheffield, England: Sheffield Academic Press, 1999), 146–77. For general discussions of education in ancient Israel and the ancient Near East, see Piotr Bienkowski, "Education," in *Dictionary of the Ancient Near East*, ed. Piotr Bienkowski and Alan Millard (Philadelphia: University of Pennsylvania Press, 2000), 101; Miguel Civil, "Education: Education in Mesopotamia," in *Anchor Bible Dictionary*, 2:301–4; de Vaux, *Ancient Israel*, 1:48–50; and André Lemaire, "Education: Ancient Israel," in *Anchor Bible Dictionary*, 2:305–12.

There were no sophisticated banks, insurance companies, or stock markets. To a large extent, temples provided the storehouses of gold and silver that supplied needed capital and resources in many societies.[14] The king (with his palace and officers) and the temple (with its priests and sacred structures) were closely affiliated in most kingdoms, and virtually all local residents in an area accepted and revered the same principal patron god or religious system. The people feared their gods, and oaths sworn in the name of a god were taken extremely seriously.[15] A person would usually rather die than break a sworn oath and thereby incur the wrath of a god who could inflict famine, disease, plagues, and other disasters upon a person, his family, or his people—all of which were fates more fearful than death.

In the absence of anything like a land survey and a county recorder's office, property boundaries were often indistinct, and therefore moving a boundary stone was a serious offense (Deuteronomy 27:17). Deeds were duplicated and sealed up to preserve them against breakage or damage (Jeremiah 32:11–14). Without a standardized system of currency or money in place, prescribed weights and measures were generally used instead of coins.[16] Accordingly, a merchant who had bogus weights in his bag was not only despicable but also very hard to apprehend and punish.

In daily life, families and workers had to be largely self-sufficient. No permanent employees worked for corporations or employers. Slaves, debt servants, indentured servants, or day laborers were regularly used, but there was little or no job security for anyone. Workers had no long-term employment contracts, no workers' compensation, no employee benefit plans, and no unemployment insurance.

The tools of life were relatively simple in the absence of electricity, gas, machinery, or other complex equipment. From what we can tell, there was little in the way of long-term food storage or refrigeration, and families faced a constant risk of famine, a regular theme in the Bible

---

14. William A. Ward, "Temples and Sanctuaries: Egypt, Economic Functions of the Temple," and John F. Robertson, "Temples and Sanctuaries: Mesopotamia, Social Role of the Temple," in *Anchor Bible Dictionary*, 6:371, 375–76.

15. See Raymond Westbrook, "Evidentiary Procedure in the Middle Assyrian Laws," *Journal of Cuneiform Studies* 55 (2003), 87–97, examining the role of oaths and ordeals in evidentiary procedure. On the importance of oaths and ordeals and the differences between them, see Karel van der Toorn, "Ordeal," in *Anchor Bible Dictionary*, 5:40–42. See generally Manfred R. Lehmann, "Biblical Oaths," *Zeitschrift für die alttestamentliche Wissenschaft* 81 (1969): 74–92.

16. John W. Betlyon, "Coinage," in *Anchor Bible Dictionary*, 1:1076–89; de Vaux, *Ancient Israel*, 195–96, 199–209; and Falk, *Biblical Law in Hebrew Times*, 90–91.

(Genesis 12:10; 26:1; 41:27; 47:13; Ruth 1:1).[17] By modern standards, markets were mainly small, local, and inefficient; the producers of goods usually took their own wares to market. If the rain did not fall and the year's crops did not grow, immediate disaster was imminent. There was no little way to insure against that risk. These economic conditions had direct bearing on legal concerns such as contracts, debt collection, interest rates, and care for the poor and needy.[18]

At home, women spent most of their time cooking and weaving and caring for children. With no real indoor plumbing, villages of even moderate size experienced serious problems with sanitation. Homes were typically small, and several members of the family shared the same bedroom and kitchen. Privacy was not the norm in antiquity; suspicions were probably aroused whenever doors were closed. Family conditions generally influenced the concepts of justice pertinent to family law.

Since social security was nonexistent, if a woman did not have a husband or son to care for her in her older age, her life became extremely impoverished and difficult. No orphanages, hospitals, or other formal charitable organizations existed. As one might expect under these conditions, life expectancy was fairly short. Ordinary people could not expect to live beyond the age of forty-five or fifty. If a priest happened to live beyond the average number of years, the mandatory retirement age from temple service in ancient Israel, which involved the heavy work of making sacrifices, was fifty: "And from the age of fifty years they shall cease waiting upon the service thereof, and shall serve no more" (Numbers 8:25). In ancient Greece, seventy was considered an extraordinarily full lifetime. Solon, the great lawgiver-poet of Athens around 600 BC, ended his lyrical lines about the ages of a man's life with these two lines: "But if he completes ten ages of seven years each, full measure / death, when it comes, can no longer be said to come too soon."[19]

---

17. William H. Shea, "Famine," in *Anchor Bible Dictionary*, 2:769–73.

18. For an in-depth treatment of the socioeconomic conditions that served as the setting for laws regarding debt-collection, debt-slavery, and the poor, see Gregory C. Chirichigno, *Debt-Slavery in Israel and the Ancient Near East* (Sheffield, England: JSOT Press, 1993); see also Falk, *Hebrew Law in Biblical Times*, 93–97; Bruce V. Malchow, *Social Justice in the Hebrew Bible* (Collegeville, MN: Liturgical Press, 1996); Léon Epsztein, *Social Justice in the Ancient Near East and the People of the Bible*, trans. John Bowden (London: SCM Press, 1986); and Richard D. Patterson, "The Widow, the Orphan, and the Poor in the Old Testament and the Extra-Biblical Literature," *Bibliotheca Sacra* 130 (July–September 1973), 223–34.

19. Solon, "The Ten Ages of Man," in *Greek Lyrics*, trans. Richard Lattimore, 2nd ed. (Chicago: University of Chicago Press, 1960), 23.

No professional organizations, bar associations, or medical associations existed. Health and medicine were scarcely understood.[20] The brain was thought simply to be the marrow of the skull. The circulation of blood had not been discovered. Causes of death were not well understood, and partly for such reasons the laws pertaining to homicide or tort focused on issues different from the medical or technical concerns that can consume so much of the time and attention in modern lawsuits involving wrongful deaths.

When common people died, no professional morticians took care of the burial. Relatives buried their dead, taking care to ensure minimal sanitation and to protect burial sites.[21] The ancients were much more immediately familiar with death than are most modern people, who have sanitized, institutionalized, and impersonalized death and dying in most respects. Tombs were protected places, and enduring legal institutions arose to honor and serve the dead.

Although we cannot know exactly how such factors played themselves out in the Nephite world, we can be fairly sure that Nephite civilization was not dramatically different from other pretechnical societies around the world.[22] Inhabitants of the Book of Mormon world found ways within their means to address their needs, their concerns, their exposure to risks and problems, and their societal challenges, many of which are no longer problematic in a modern age. Ancient legal systems served those respective purposes sufficiently, and in many cases with sophistication and durable success. Some of the challenges confronting ancient societies, of course, reflect universal human conditions and struggles with which all people can readily identify; but most of their legal problems were by necessity addressed and resolved in terms of social policies and practicalities that were unique to their age and circumstances.

Thinking of Law in the Ancient World

A primary purpose of this book is to discover the legal world of the Nephites. Once their legal concepts, rules, and decisions are understood

---

20. For an anthropological approach to the health care systems of ancient Greece, Mesopotamia, and Israel, see Hector Avalos, *Illness and Health Care in the Ancient Near East: The Role of the Temple in Greece, Mesopotamia and Israel* (Atlanta: Scholars Press, 1995); and Avalos, *Health Care and the Rise of Christianity* (Peabody, MA: Hendrickson, 1999). See also Howard Clark Kee, "Medicine and Healing," in *Anchor Bible Dictionary*, 4:659–64.

21. For further discussion on burial practices in ancient Israel, see Elizabeth Bloch-Smith, "Burials," in *Anchor Bible Dictionary*, 1:785–89; and de Vaux, *Ancient Israel*, 56–61.

22. For an excellent archaeological and anthropological discussion of the main elements of Book of Mormon culture in the New World, see John L. Sorenson, *Images of Ancient America: Visualizing Book of Mormon Life* (Provo, UT: FARMS, 1998).

in their own context, we may then be able to extrapolate from those specific elements a collection of legal doctrines, teachings, principles, and policies that can be carried across cultural boundaries and made relevant to a modern world. But that end result must follow a careful reading of the Book of Mormon text on its own terms.

In general, we know that law was extremely important to the ancient Nephites, as well as to the Israelites and all ancient Near Eastern peoples. Modern people can scarcely fathom the degree to which law was venerated and respected by people in the ancient world. Lehi's blessing to his son Jacob gives us insight into the importance of law in Nephite religion and society. In describing the very purposes of God, Lehi reasons: "If ye shall say there is no law, ye shall also say there is no sin," and thus no righteousness, nor happiness, nor punishment, nor misery; "and if these things are not there is no God" (2 Nephi 2:13). Without law, the virtues of righteousness, the conditions of happiness, and even the existence of God himself were logically unimaginable in Lehi's world. Contrast this prevailing Nephite attitude—which Lehi presents as irrefutable and self-evident—with the general attitude of modern people about the law as a whole, to say nothing of modern perceptions of specific laws, such as the Internal Revenue Code. Can we imagine a prophet today saying that if there were no Internal Revenue Code or even no Constitution, there would be no God? Clearly, much has changed over the past two thousand six hundred years in what societies mean by "law."

Most people in the ancient world believed that their laws had in some significant sense come from divine sources.[23] The book of Exodus presents Moses as establishing laws that he received directly from Jehovah on Mount Sinai. The prologue to the laws of King Hammurabi affirms that he was commissioned by Marduk, the god of Babylon, and that he was obedient to Shamash, the god of justice, in establishing his laws.[24] King Lipit-Ishtar said that he acted by the command of the god Enlil in establishing justice in his lands in Mesopotamia.[25] In the Greek world, Plato consid-

---

23. For more on the divine origin of law, see Joseph P. Schultz, "Max Weber and the Sociological Development of Jewish Law," *Diné Israel* 16 (1991–92): 71–82.

24. The text appears in English translation in James B. Pritchard, *Ancient Near Eastern Texts Relating to the Old Testament*, 3rd ed. (Princeton: Princeton University Press, 1975), 164–65.

25. The text appears in English translation in Martha T. Roth, *Law Collections from Mesopotamia and Asia Minor*, ed. Piotr Michalowski (Atlanta, GA: Scholars Press, 1995), 25. "The date-formula for his second year, 'The year he enacted the law of the land,' indicates that he promulgated his famous lawcode at the very beginning of his reign." James B. Pritchard, *The Ancient Near East: An Anthology of Texts and Pictures* (Princeton: Princeton University Press, 1958), 138.

ered it axiomatic that "no mortal man frames any law,"[26] and Heraclitus, another Greek philosopher, once said, "All human laws are nourished by a divine one. It prevails as it wills and suffices for all and is more than enough."[27] In Roman times, worshippers of Isis believed that the goddess "established laws for humans, and created legislation which no one has the power to change, . . . invented marriage contracts, . . . delivered the person plotting unjustly against another into the hands of the person plotted against, [to] inflict punishment on those acting unjustly."[28] Even in the late Roman period, the emperor Justinian saw Deity as necessarily involved in the legal process: "Justice is an unswerving and perpetual determination to acknowledge all men's rights. Learning in the law entails knowledge of god and man, and mastery of the difference between justice and injustice."[29] Accordingly, in the ancient world, law was much more than a matter of pragmatic policy or economic regulation. Law was an expression of the divine will, the highest ideals of a civilization, the necessary order of life, and the fundamental substance of justice and reality.

For these reasons, people in the ancient world held their laws in the highest esteem possible. Heraclitus moralized, "People should fight for their law as for a city wall."[30] Similar expressions of reverence for the value of law are found in the Bible. The book of Deuteronomy asks, Who else has "statutes and judgments so righteous as all this law?" (Deuteronomy 4:8). All Israelites were commanded to talk about the law when at home, when walking down the street, "when thou liest down, and when thou risest up" (6:7; see Joshua 1:8). C. S. Lewis marveled, at first, how mysterious and strange it seemed to him that the ancient Israelites could speak of the law as being so exhilarating and delicious, even "sweeter than honey"; but then he came to understand how deeply these people valued the law: "[The psalmist] felt about the Law somewhat as he felt about his poetry; both involved exact and loving conformity to an intricate pattern."[31]

In particular, three "torah-psalms," as James Mays has classified them, give modern readers important insights into the prominence of law, the

---

26. Plato, *Laws*, 709a.

27. Heraclitus frag. 30, as cited in Charles H. Kahn, *The Art and Thought of Heraclitus: An Edition of the Fragments with Translation and Commentary* (Cambridge: Cambridge University Press, 1979), 43.

28. From an inscription in Memphis, Egypt, in front of a temple to Hephaistos, in Mary Beard, John North, and Simon Price, *Religions of Rome* (Cambridge: Cambridge University Press, 1998), 2:297–98.

29. Justinian, *Institutiones* 1.1.

30. Heraclitus frag. 65, as cited in Kahn, *Art and Thought of Heraclitus*, 179.

31. C. S. Lewis, *Reflections on the Psalms* (London: Fontana Books, 1961), 49–51.

instruction of the Lord, in the minds of pious members of the ancient house of Israel. In Psalm 1, which sets an important tone for the whole collection of biblical psalms, "the torah of the Lord replaces wisdom and its human teachers."[32] The first verses of Psalm 1 read: "Blessed is the man . . . [whose] delight is in the law of the Lord; and in his law doth he meditate day and night. And he shall be like a tree planted by the rivers of water, that bringeth forth his fruit in his season; his leaf also shall not wither; and whatsoever he doeth shall prosper" (vv. 1–3). The law (broadly understood) defines the way that allows a person to be planted in righteousness as a tree of life.

Second, Psalm 19 places law prominently in the eternal landscape of God's creation. Here "the heavenly order praises God, and the psalmist praises the instruction [torah] of the Lord."[33] The body of "law [*torah*] of the Lord is perfect," exclaims the psalmist (v. 7). Indeed, Psalm 19, which appears even to have been "part of the liturgical structure of the day of the king's enthronement,"[34] praises and extols the virtues of the law in magnificent terms. The law (the *torah*) was potent, "converting the soul," and the written law (*edut*) of the Lord was "sure, making wise the simple." The law's precepts are upright, the commandment of Jehovah is pure, and his judgments are true and righteous (vv. 7–9).

Third, Psalm 119 is a masterful composition that, from beginning to end, blesses those who "walk in the law of the Lord" (v. 1). In this torah-psalm, "line by line, all the various situations and moods that belong to the relation between the Lord and the servant of the Lord are dealt with, always with one of the torah terms as medium of the relationship."[35] Its point is that "torah applies to everything: . . . to the basic narrative that runs from the fathers to the land, . . . to the offices of priest and king, . . . to Israel's future, . . . to the life of every person, . . . even to the Lord's creating and ordering the elements of the world."[36] This psalm concludes: "Great peace have they which love thy law," and thus "I do not forget thy commandments" (vv. 165, 176). In this world, the law deeply touched and influenced almost every part of life, ranging not only from worship to sacrifice but also from torts to property.

---

32. James Luther Mays, "The Place of the Torah-Psalms in the Psalter," *Journal of Biblical Literature* 106, no. 1 (1987): 4.
33. Mays, "Torah-Psalms," 5.
34. Nicolas Wyatt, "The Liturgical Context of Psalm 19," *Ugarit Forschungen* 27 (1995): 592.
35. Mays, "Torah-Psalms," 6.
36. Mays, "Torah-Psalms," 8–9.

The conventional wisdom of ancient Israel held that "the law of the wise is a fountain of life" (Proverbs 13:14), and Israel was commanded to "do all the words of this law . . . because it is your life" (Deuteronomy 32:46–47). Written law provided the basis for ethical training; it was more than a mere manual for the administration of justice.[37] Folk wisdom in early Judaism similarly held that "the Law is the tree of life for all who study it, and everyone who observes its precepts lives and endures as the tree of life in the world to come."[38]

The Book of Mormon contains similar expressions indicative of the high value placed on law. The rod of iron symbolized "the word of God" (1 Nephi 15:24), which certainly included all the statutes and commandments that one must obey in order to come to the tree of life and partake of its fruit. The strong image introduced by Psalm 1:1–3 compares closely with the words in Alma 32:41–42, where Alma promises that the "word" will "take root in you" and will become as "a tree springing up unto everlasting life." In the spirit of Psalms 19 and 119, wisdom-law terms of all kinds relating to law, justice, equity, statutes, ordinances, judgments, commandments, customs, principles, and so on appear throughout the Book of Mormon. As in Jerusalem, law in Zarahemla related to mundane affairs and human justice as well as to revealed law, divine justice, the atonement of Christ, or types and shadows of his salvation. Ultimately, Alma states, without justice "God would cease to be God" (Alma 42:25).

Precisely how these words and concepts were understood by the ancient Israelites is a topic for another discussion; but for present purposes, it is clear that people in the ancient world deeply valued their laws, and they did so for many reasons. Without national flags, Olympic teams, famous artists, or other cosmetically distinguishing characteristics, various groups thought of their laws as the greatest force that unified and defined them as a people. Though many ancient civilizations had their own distinguishing features, including costume, language, and religion, their sense of social cohesion and public order was created mostly out of formless human chaos by virtue of law, strong legal expectations, effective regulations, and cherished legal customs.

37. Bernard S. Jackson, "Ideas of Law and Legal Administration: A Semiotic Approach," in *The World of Ancient Israel: Sociological, Anthropological and Political Perspectives,* ed. R. E. Clements (Cambridge: Cambridge University Press, 1989), 188, states that "both Deuteronomy and 2 Chronicles also tell us about a written text of law. . . . In both sources, written law has a didactic function; it is not the basis of adjudication."

38. Palestinian Targum on Genesis 3:24, discussed in Martin McNamara, *Targum and Testament: Aramaic Paraphrases of the Hebrew Bible: A Light on the New Testament* (Grand Rapids: Eerdmans, 1972), 121.

Indeed, civilization in the ancient world was precariously fragile. Cultures would cease to exist if, for whatever reason, the stabilizing language, norms, and rules were not successfully transmitted from one generation to the next.[39] Much that was of social importance hinged upon the preservation and perpetuation of the law. The law was not self-perpetuating or self-enforcing. It defined the social order, and it implemented the divine order. No ancient person would doubt the axiom that a nation without law would dwindle and perish in unbelief and disarray (compare 1 Nephi 4:13; Mosiah 1:5). The same is actually true in the modern world, but our legal systems are so much more entrenched, self-perpetuating, verbally established, and massively rooted in modern society through libraries, bureaucracies, buildings, and businesses that we take the stability of law simply for granted. For an ancient city, however, nothing was more important or more vulnerable than its walls and its laws.

Goals and Objectives

Accordingly, the main objective of this volume is to focus on the legal cases in the Book of Mormon in order to gain a better sense of Nephite judicial process in the context of biblical law traditions. Other studies have dealt or will deal further with additional legal topics relevant to the Book of Mormon, such as its many sources of law (ancient Israelite or otherwise), its substantive definitions of crimes and punishments, policies of law and social justice, applications of civil and commercial law, and intersections of law and religion. Many of these subjects will be mentioned in passing in connection with their relevance to the Nephite judicial cases, but more systematic and thorough coverage of those topics will be left for another day.

The goal of understanding the Book of Mormon through the channel of legal research into its judicial procedures will necessarily take us into uncharted territory. No similar attempt has ever been made to examine the Nephite legal system in operation. Consequently, this study is necessarily experimental, probing, and inquisitive. Like any other form of scholarly investigation in its early stages, the following chapters are sometimes tentative in nature, setting forth and testing hypotheses and drawing possible conclusions or leaving further questions for later study. A degree of adventure is involved in this enterprise, and certain detective skills are necessary. Sometimes we seem to be hot on the trail, and the clues seem remarkably fresh and indicative. Other times, the tracks seem

---

39. Consider, for example, the sudden disappearance of the great ancient cities of Ebla and Ugarit.

to fade out, but when they reemerge, we have some reassurance that we are still pointed in the right direction.

While this effort may seem conjectural in some respects, I prefer to see it not as a speculative venture exposed to unreasonable risks, but similar to speculating for oil or mineral deposits with the help of geological surveys. In Latin, the word *specula* means "hope" and can also mean "watchtower."[40] A speculator is a scout or investigator who *hopes* to find good results, or a guard who watches out for new arrivals, and it is in that spirit of alert investigation and observation that we hope, through study and faith, to understand the Book of Mormon better by achieving a clearer understanding of its important legal dimensions. As the legal policies and precedents embedded in the text are brought to the fore, the logic, coherence, internal consistency, and fundamental values of Nephite law can be seen in sharper relief.

Of course, this is not the only way to read the Book of Mormon. For example, it can and should be read as scripture, as literature, as prophecy, as a witness of the Messiah, as a guide to daily religious life, as a moral text, as a lineage history, and in many other ways.[41] However, readers can uniquely find the heart of many important religious and social concepts in the Book of Mormon—including such legally foundational concepts as agency and accountability, warning and confession, error and revelation, justice and mercy, equality and charity—by studying it from a legal point of view.

Thus this study has the following goals and objectives:

- To examine the literary and historical backgrounds of the legal narratives in the Book of Mormon
- To compare the laws in the Nephite world with those in the Hebrew Bible and the ancient world in general
- To understand in detail the relevant facts and specific legal issues raised by each legal case in the Book of Mormon
- To utilize all available tools of textual analysis, word studies, archaeology, and scripture study in illuminating these legal passages
- To appreciate the judicial procedures and outcomes involved in these cases

40. *Specula* is the diminutive of *spes* ("hope"), hence "a small hope"; *specula* also means "watchtower," and the meaning of the Latin *speculator* includes "lookout," "scout," "spy," "observer," or "investigator."

41. Similarly, it is said of the Bible, "Within the one text, there was room for both popular and more specialised audiences." Jackson, "Ideas of Law," 196.

- To highlight the roles of logic, persuasion, testimony, and divine intervention in the determination of those legal results
- To extract legal and ethical value from each of these precedents by determining what these cases meant to the Nephites as their own political and religious history unfolded and why these cases were eternally important enough for Mormon to include them in his abridgment of what he considered the sacred records of his people

Finally, this project has spiritual aspirations as well, working to provide and assay evidence of the authenticity of the Book of Mormon as a record of a people of ancient Near Eastern origins. The task facing Joseph Smith simply of translating the Book of Mormon in such a miraculously short period of time is impressive enough,[42] but when one considers that he accomplished everything else involved in that process while at the same time managing to produce a record that keeps so many details, including all its legal technicalities, coherently straight, the product is simply staggering. The coming forth of the Book of Mormon is all the more impressive when one realizes that the comprehensive study of biblical law as an academic specialty is itself only a relatively recent development in biblical scholarship. Despite all such hurdles, the following outcome on close examination becomes apparent: the Nephite legal system is internally coherent and organically consistent with pre-exilic Israelite jurisprudence. The legal system in the Book of Mormon makes abundant sense as an ancient legal system. Its legal elements are at home in an ancient legal setting and are consistent with the explanation given within the book itself that Nephite law and civilization originated in the legal world of the ancient Near East and then developed logically and distinctively over its thousand-year history.

---

42. Neal A. Maxwell, "'By the Gift and Power of God,'" in *Echoes and Evidences of the Book of Mormon*, ed. Donald W. Parry, Daniel C. Peterson, and John W. Welch (Provo, UT: FARMS, 2004), 5–12; John W. Welch, "The Miraculous Translation of the Book of Mormon," in *Opening the Heavens: Accounts of Divine Manifestations, 1820–1844*, ed. John W. Welch with Erick B. Carlson (Provo, UT: Brigham Young University Press; Salt Lake City: Deseret Book, 2005), 77–213.

CHAPTER TWO

QUERIES AND PROSPECTS

Judging righteously involves asking broad policy questions, requesting answers to specific interrogatories, spotting significant issues, and exposing and examining presumptions, all while being patiently optimistic that something good will be accomplished in the process. Before we turn to the legal cases in the Book of Mormon, it will be helpful to lay similar groundwork by addressing some preliminary questions and exploring a few basic methodological issues. By so doing, I hope to clarify the basic assumptions and methods I have used in seeking to understand the legal system that operated in the Nephite world and to establish certain limitations and bearings to aim this research toward attainable conclusions.

How Do Lawyers Think?

First, lawyers recognize that it is difficult, even under the best of circumstances, to give an accurate and persuasive opinion concerning the state of "the law" at any given time in any society. Modern attorneys find it challenging and often controversial to determine what the law truly is on a particular subject, even though innumerable volumes of cases, statutes, regulations, and law review articles have been written and a host of other resources are available to assist in legal research. The problem of ascertaining the law becomes even more perplexing when one tries to determine what the law was in an ancient society and how it might have functioned, especially where only scant information pertaining to the legal system in question has survived. Despite the numerous excellent books and articles that have been written about biblical law in recent decades, one may still agree with the sentiments expressed by popular Jewish writer George Horowitz: "About the early Hebrew law as about the beginnings of Jewish history, we know little that is certain."[1] Similarly, Arthur Hoyles warns,

---

1. George Horowitz, *The Spirit of Jewish Law* (New York: Bloch, 1953), 8. See Robert R. Wilson, "Israel's Judicial System in the Preexilic Period," *Jewish Quarterly Review* 74 (October 1983): 229, 231.

"The attempt to discover what the Bible has to say on any particular subject is likely to be frustrating."[2] If biblical scholars encounter difficulties such as these in their study of biblical law, where extensive sections of legal materials are available in the Bible and cognate literatures to shed light on numerous jurisprudential topics, readers of the Book of Mormon should expect to encounter at least as many questions in connection with legal matters in the Nephite record.

These problems, however, should not dissuade us. A degree of indeterminacy is simply in the nature of the law. In the face of these difficulties, lawyers have developed conventional practices to analyze legal situations and to form acceptable professional judgments. Biblical law scholars likewise have developed methods by which to evaluate and qualify their findings. Good legal analysis involves spotting issues, formulating justiciable claims, marshaling all available relevant evidence, and weighing alternatives. Applying the techniques of legal analysis, it is possible for a reader to think like a lawyer when approaching the narratives in the Book of Mormon, just as legal scholars have done with respect to the Bible.

For readers who have not studied or practiced much law, let me sketch generally what lawyers mean by the phrase "thinking like a lawyer." Legal analysis in all legal systems and especially in the United States tends to be built on what might be called substantive rules, procedural practices, the formulation of legal issues arising out of individual cases, and the resolution of those issues by the imposition of appropriate remedies.[3]

Substantive rules. Lawyers usually begin their analysis by identifying rules of substantive law. These rules deal with relations between human beings. They may define rights and duties regarding property, personal injury, contracts, commerce, criminal conduct, and other such subjects. They may be particular and specific, or they can be broad and general. Some of these rules are clear authoritative statements, while others emerge from precedents, customs, moral principles, or societal norms.

---

2. J. Arthur Hoyles, *Punishment in the Bible* (London: Epworth, 1986), vii.

3. See generally Oliver Wendell Holmes, *The Path of the Law* (Bedford, MA: Applewood Books, 1996); David S. Romantz and Kathleen Elliott Vinson, *Legal Analysis: The Fundamental Skills* (Durham, NC: Carolina Academic Press, 1998); Patrick M. McFadden, *A Student's Guide to Legal Analysis: Thinking Like a Lawyer* (Gaithersburg, MD: Aspen Law & Business, 2001); Sarah E. Redfield, *Thinking Like a Lawyer: An Educator's Guide to Legal Analysis and Research* (Durham, NC: Carolina Academic Press, 2002); and Irvin C. Rutter, "Law, Language, and Thinking Like a Lawyer," *University of Cincinnati Law Review* 61 (1993): 1303–60. For an effort to relate biblical principles to the process of thinking like a lawyer in understanding pleadings, detecting verbal traps, negotiating dispute resolutions, and proceeding fairly, see Alfred R. Light, "Civil Procedure Parables in the First Year: Applying the Bible to Think Like a Lawyer," *Gonzaga Law Review* 37 (2001–2002): 283–313.

Accordingly, a lawyer's mind notices in the record of King Benjamin's speech (Mosiah 1–6), the case of Seantum (Helaman 9), or the discourse of Amulek (Alma 34) rubrics or maxims that reflect substantive rules of law that would have been known to those speakers and their audiences. For example, Amulek's theological argument about the atonement in Alma 34 reflects an absolute and well-known prohibition in Nephite criminal law against vicarious punishment in cases of capital homicide: "Now, if a man murdereth, behold will our law, which is just, take the life of his brother? I say unto you, Nay" (v. 11). Ancient Nephites or Israelites did not formulate legal concepts or rules into positive laws, nor did they articulate binding judicial instructions or follow legal precedents as judges do today, but certainly substantive rules existed in some form and can be discerned in their writings that shed light on their legal systems and cultures.

Procedural practices. Secondly, lawyers think in terms of judicial procedure. Just because a law is on the books does not mean that it will or can always be enforced; or if it is to be enforced, it is not always apparent how or by whom it will be administered. Laws of civil procedure and administrative practice define jurisdictional powers, rules of evidence, and other practices essential to the administration of justice. Lawyers learn to think in terms of the legal options that are open to members of society, how the legal system works, and how to implement in a practical manner the substantive legal rules in the living context of their particular judicial system. Accordingly, a lawyer cannot read the experiences and trial of Abinadi in Mosiah 11–17 without wondering about such matters as what modern diction would call the jurisdiction of the priests, the absence of a right against self-incrimination, the use of various forms of dispute resolution, and the scope of judicial discretion open to the priests as judges.

Individual cases and conflicts. Next, while legislators and jurisprudential philosophers think of law in the abstract, lawyers work with law in terms of individual cases. Each case begins with a story that tells of the situations, relationships, circumstances, and motivations of each of the parties involved in the action. Each story is somewhat unique, and thus each case poses a distinct and different conflict. Not all social conflicts, of course, amount to legal conflicts, but when a case or controversy involves subjects that are typically or exclusively resolved by judicial intervention, or when the consequences of the case are so dramatic or irreconcilable that the individual parties or the society cannot afford to have the issue settled by the parties privately, the matter presents what lawyers call a justiciable controversy—one that can and ought to be decided by a court. Lawyers think in terms of identifying these justiciable legal issues and refining their meaning so that the issues can be analyzed in terms of discrete, somewhat abstract legal principles, while at the same time never forgetting that doing justice in a particular case requires meticulous attention to the particular details of the case.

Thinking like a lawyer requires readers to understand the nature and origin of the conflicts or controversies between parties, their unique factual circumstances, and the key legal issues evoked by each case. Accordingly, while Alma's religious problems with the people in Ammonihah may, at one level, be understood simply as a theological dispute, at another level numerous legal issues and justiciable controversies immediately surfaced when that heated discussion escalated to include issues of jurisdiction, civil disobedience, apostasy, imprisonment, expulsion, and execution. The hostility that erupted may certainly have had something to do with the fact that, eight years earlier, Alma had been the very judge who had convicted and executed Nehor, the religious hero of the people of Ammonihah (Alma 16:11).

Deciding cases and fashioning remedies. Finally, lawyers and judges ultimately think of ending each case by assessing the strengths and weaknesses of the parties' cases and then by demanding, finding, and fashioning appropriate punishments or remedies. For example, if a law prohibits a person from "stealing," it becomes important for a lawyer to examine how the law defines theft (as distinguished, perhaps, from taking something by mistake or failing to return something legitimately borrowed). In drawing such lines, lawyers often must make fine distinctions and in some cases will place high value on the letter of the law. At the same time, the spirit of the law is important in every legal system, and lawyers must think in terms of balancing competing values, protecting the interests of highest social value, making trade-offs, judging righteously, reaching negotiated settlements, and so on when trying to resolve or settle a case. Likewise, as lawyers examine the legal cases reported in the Bible or in the Book of Mormon, they can detect indications of things that mattered most to those people and the relative abilities of those people to assert their positions even in the most trying of forensic circumstances.

Above all, thinking like a lawyer, in a modern setting, demands reasoning, explaining, justifying one's position, and appealing to the strongest authorities in support of a particular result. While legal reasoning in antiquity valued logic, the ancient jurist or litigant placed greater weight on reaching immediate practical outcomes, making efforts to please God, and following a more amorphous sense of doing justice while still showing mercy. Thus, while the reasons given for judicial outcomes may vary from one civilization to another, thinking like a lawyer requires all people to reach practical outcomes while simultaneously remaining true to more general feelings or policies valued by their society.

In reading the Bible or the Book of Mormon like a lawyer, it is not necessary to think that everything in those books is legal in nature. Lawyers are sometimes tempted, almost irresistibly, to see everything in legal terms. As is often said, to a man with a hammer in his hand, everything looks like a nail. To my mind, however, it does not invalidate or weaken the primary purpose of sacred texts for their readers to notice their secondary characteristics, purposes, or features, such as its literature, culture, geography, or law. Almost every story in the Bible or Book of Mormon tells readers something about the society, rules, ethics, jurisprudence, statutes, judgments, and laws, both of God and of those people. One of the strengths of the Book of Mormon is the fact that its writers could weave into their records so many accurate and consistent details about their legal and political institutions without diverting the reader's attention from the main religious purpose of the book. Indeed, a close examination of the secondary features of the Book of Mormon may prove to enhance its self-stated purpose of convincing readers of the validity of its primary message. As Elder B. H. Roberts once wrote, "Secondary evidences in support of truth, like secondary causes in natural phenomena, may be of firstrate importance."[4]

Can the Narratives in the Bible or Book of Mormon Be Read as Legal Cases?

The present study turns on close readings of cases in the Bible and Book of Mormon. The primary source for jurisprudential information regarding Israelite law is the Bible itself, and the authoritative source for understanding Nephite law is the Book of Mormon. The analysis of each topic must rise or fall by carefully ferreting out each bit of legal information possible.

This effort requires—and often rewards—a closer reading than people usually give to these books, which are usually read for other purposes. But legal cases need to be analyzed step by step, even word by word; and narratives involving the commissions of crimes or the instigation of legal actions need to be dissected point by point. In reading these texts, I try to discern the legal significance of each element. Sometimes the meaning

4. Brigham H. Roberts, *New Witnesses for God* (Salt Lake City: Deseret Book, 1909), 2:viii; quoted and discussed in John W. Welch, "The Power of Evidence in the Nurturing of Faith," in *Echoes and Evidences of the Book of Mormon*, ed. Donald W. Parry, Daniel C. Peterson, and John W. Welch (Provo, UT: FARMS, 2002), 25.

may be obvious; other times the legal content is more subtle, found in circumstantial evidence and the implications of contextual patterns or interrelationships. A strong reading of any text strives to give that text the best and fullest reading possible, to draw out of the text all the meaning with which it may be saturated. Perceiving the legal nuances behind the otherwise generally plain prose of the historical or legal materials in the Bible or Book of Mormon requires attention to detail. Otherwise, readers may not spot even the most basic legal issues, let alone fully assess their import.

Of course, neither the records of the Book of Mormon nor the books of the Bible were written as legal texts per se. Those scriptures were written for religious and ethical purposes that pertain to a different sphere than does the law. The linguistic and literary conventions used today in drafting well-defined legislation, in writing bureaucratic regulations, and in reporting judicial decisions with exhaustively reasoned opinions are, for the most part, modern inventions. No one in the ancient world spoke or wrote about law in such modes as we do today, but embedded in the narratives, instructions, prophecies, orations, and poems from any ancient society are reflections of that culture's legal principles and judicial practices, from which many interesting conclusions about the law in that civilization can be derived.

Since legal cases in the Bible and Book of Mormon are reported as stories, an initial challenge is to extract legal data from these narratives. Fortunately, several techniques have been developed and used by biblical scholars, such as David Daube, Bernard Jackson, Pamela Barmash, and Pietro Bovati, for drawing legal insights out of ancient Israelite narratives.[5] For example, Daube strives to "reconstruct ancient Hebrew law

---

5. See, for example, David Daube, *Some Forms of Old Testament Legislation* (Oxford: Oxford Society of Historical Theology, 1945); Daube, *Studies in Biblical Law* (Cambridge: Cambridge University Press, 1947; New York: KTAV Publishing House, 1969); Bernard S. Jackson, "Reflections on Biblical Criminal Law," *Journal of Jewish Studies* 24 (1973): 8–38; Jackson, "Review of *The Laws of Deuteronomy*," *Journal of Jewish Studies* 27 (1976): 84–87; Pietro Bovati, *Re-Establishing Justice: Legal Terms, Concepts and Procedures in the Hebrew Bible* (Sheffield, England: Sheffield Academic Press, 1994); and Pamela Barmash, "The Narrative Quandary: Cases of Law in Literature," *Vetus Testamentum* 54, no. 1 (2004): 1–16. While acknowledging that "literature is only incidentally about law" and that narratives may not always accurately portray legal subjects, Barmash makes a strong appeal for the claim that "narrative texts are indispensable for the study of biblical law. The analysis of literary texts is necessary for reconstructing legal practice and the perception of how law operated. Statutes only tell us so much" (p. 2). See the recent dissertation of Assnat Bartor, "Reading Law as Narrative—a Study in the Casuistic Laws of the Pentateuch" (PhD diss., Tel Aviv University, 2005), building on the law and literature approaches of scholars such as Robert Cover, Peter Brooks, Martha Nussbaum, and Stanley Fish, some of which was reported by Bartor at the annual meeting of the Society of Biblical Literature, 2006, in a paper entitled "The Representation of Speech in the Casuistic Laws of the Pentateuch—the Phenomenon of 'Combined Discourse.'"

with the help of the sagas and annals preserved in the Bible."[6] He typically begins with legal texts and then highlights legal language and circumstances found in the narratives that correspond with those legal texts. His reading of the story of Jacob's sons presenting Jacob with Joseph's torn and bloodied coat is enriched by connections with the shepherd laws in Exodus 22:10–13 that would absolve the sons of any legal responsibility for Joseph's death and disappearance. Both the law and the narrative are better understood by reading both together.

Emphasizing the point that ancient laws were not technically defined rules, Jackson seeks to determine instead the "typical image(s) . . . the words of [a] rule evoke."[7] He uses narratives to substantiate interpretations for laws by fleshing out the contexts in which the laws were intended to apply.

Barmash uses legal narrative to recover an expansive view of the law by placing the law in the comparative contexts of the societies in which laws operated. Narrative situations that have no counterparts in the legal texts are especially interesting in filling in gaps in our understanding of those legal systems.

Bovati extracts information about judicial procedures from the patterns of simple vocabulary words, such as *take*, *move*, or *stand*, in narratives about actions before judges. Thus narrative accounts of the execution of Naboth by wicked King Ahab (1 Kings 21), of the proceeding initiated by Boaz at the town gate against his kinsman (Ruth 4), and of the indictment of Jeremiah by the priests and princes in Jerusalem for false prophecy (Jeremiah 26)[8] have been profitably studied by biblical historians from a legal perspective—even though none of these stories found their way into the Bible for the purpose of serving as a handbook of legal instructions.[9]

Similar techniques can be applied successfully to the narratives of the Book of Mormon. Following Daube's illuminating approach, we see that the ancient Near Eastern laws concerning the duties of shepherds say something about the story of Ammon defending the flocks of King Lamoni (Alma 17), and the laws concerning blasphemy and false prophecy shed

---

6. Daube, *Studies in Biblical Law*, 3 (in 1969 reprint edition).

7. Bernard S. Jackson, *Wisdom-Laws: A Study of the Mishpatim of Exodus 21:1–22:16* (Oxford: Oxford University Press, 2006), 24–25.

8. See, for example, John W. Welch, "The Trial of Jeremiah: A Legal Legacy from Lehi's Jerusalem," in *Glimpses of Lehi's Jerusalem*, ed. John W. Welch, David Rolph Seely, and Jo Ann H. Seely (Provo, UT: FARMS, 2004), 337–56.

9. For a lucid statement of methodological procedures and terminological issues, see James K. Bruckner, *Implied Law in the Abraham Narrative: A Literary and Theological Analysis* (Sheffield, England: Sheffield Academic Press, 2001), 51–123.

light on the cases of Sherem (chapter 5 below) and Abinadi (chapter 6 below). Employing the semiotic tools that generated many of Jackson's insights, readers of ordinary narratives in the Book of Mormon may begin to get a feel for the typical meanings of certain legal obligations or of civil rights and duties in Nephite or Lamanite or Nehorite mindsets. Using comparative and cultural analyses as Barmash does, we find that the narratives about Alma and Amulek's treatment in Ammonihah (Alma 9–14) or about the Gadianton robbers (Helaman 1–2, 6; 3 Nephi 3–4) can fill in our understanding of how criminal law operated in Nephite society. Following Bovati's lead, we notice patterns of particular words such as *take*, *bind*, and *carry* in the accounts of the legal cases of Abinadi, Nehor, Alma and Amulek, or Korihor, which raise significant prospects and possibilities for reconstructing Nephite law in general and reading these narratives in particular.

Once a reader becomes aware of the legal dimensions of these narratives, it is difficult to read these accounts again as simple stories. For example, consider the cry against the people of Sodom in the Abraham narrative. As James Bruckner skillfully demonstrates, an abundance of legal referents in the narrative regarding the inquest against the Sodomites shows, among other things, the existence of "a juridical process of inquiry and decision between competing jurisdictions and rights" in Genesis 18:16–19:38.[10] He also shows that a legal reading of Genesis 20:1–18 clarifies the legal, moral, and cosmological issues in the conflict regarding Sarah's residence in Abimelech's tent.[11] Once their legal backgrounds are clarified, these stories make much better sense to the modern reader. Likewise, in reading the stories of Joseph in Egypt in the book of Genesis, a lawyer may readily wonder about the Egyptian legal circumstances involved in binding Joseph and throwing him into prison (39:20), the execution of the baker but the release of the butler (40:21–22), the nature of the agency powers given to Joseph by Pharaoh (41:40),[12] the conventional punishments that would have been applied to someone convicted as a spy in a foreign land (42:14), or the fate of one who was discovered to possess the silver cup of another in one's own sack under strongly suspicious circumstances (44:12). Stories such as

---

10. Bruckner, *Implied Law in the Abraham Narrative*, 124.

11. Bruckner, *Implied Law in the Abraham Narrative*, 171–98.

12. For the legal text installing the Vizier of Egypt under Thutmose III, about 1490–1436 BC, approximately the era of Joseph in Egypt, see James B. Pritchard, ed., *Ancient Near Eastern Texts Relating to the Old Testament*, 3rd ed. (Princeton: Princeton University Press, 1975), 212–14.

these in the Abraham narratives and in the Joseph cycle are more than fictional folktales; they reflect legal and historical realities.

As we will see, the same can be said of the accounts in the Book of Mormon. The abundance of legal terms and referents in its narratives bespeaks the existence of a traditional judicial system and suggests that the events reported arose in real-life settings, with high stakes, in powerful legal places. These texts can be seen through a legal lens, and once their legal layers are uncovered, these texts spring vividly to life.

How Else Has the Study of Biblical Law Been Approached?

In light of the complex and often difficult nature of biblical law, it is not surprising that scholars have attempted many other approaches to enhance the understanding of law in biblical times. Because no single approach has dominated or controlled the field of biblical law, and because many approaches have valuable insights to contribute, I have made use of various methodologies used by biblical scholars, and I have found that each of these can be applied profitably to the Book of Mormon as well as to the Bible.

Consider the richness of this collection of approaches. Beginning with Albrecht Alt,[13] some biblical scholars have used literary tools to study the formalistic and structural composition of bodies of biblical law, and such tools elucidate legal formulations in the Book of Mormon.[14] Other scholars, such as Reuven Yaron,[15] approach biblical law using historical tools, carefully analyzing various periods in legal history and the importance of time factors in evaluating comparative legal information. David Daube,[16] Victor Matthews,[17] and others explore such social dimensions of the law

---

13. Albrecht Alt, "The Origin of Israelite Law," in *Essays on Old Testament History and Religion* (London: Oxford University Press, 1996), 79–132.

14. For a correlation of the legal topics found in the Code of the Covenant and also in the various law lists in the Book of Mormon, see chart 127 in John W. Welch and J. Gregory Welch, *Charting the Book of Mormon* (Provo, UT: FARMS, 1999). Apodictic ("thou shalt not . . .") and casuistic ("if a man . . .") legal formulations were integral not only to legal language in biblical law but also in the Book of Mormon. See 2 Nephi 26:32 for a Nephite law list in the apodictic form, and see Alma 30:10 and 34:11 for the Nephite use of casuistic formulations.

15. Reuven Yaron, "Biblical Law: Prolegomena," in *Jewish Law in Legal History and the Modern World* (Leiden: Brill, 1980), 27–44.

16. For example, David Daube, *The Scales of Justice* (London: W. Green & Sons, 1946); *The Culture of Deuteronomy* (Ibadan, Nigeria: University of Ibadan, 1969); and *Civil Disobedience in Antiquity* (Edinburgh: Edinburgh University Press, 1972).

17. For example, Victor H. Matthews, *Manners and Customs in the Bible* (Peabody, MA: Hendrickson, 1991), and two papers he presented at meetings of the Society of Biblical Literature: "The Social Context of Law in the Second Temple Period" (*Biblical Theology Bulletin* 28 [1998]: 7–15) and "Kings of Israel: A Question of Crime and Punishment" (*SBL Seminar Papers* [Baltimore: Scholars Press, 1988], 517–26).

as economics, power structures, liminality of marginal groups, and the use of shame or other values implicit in legal systems. Writers such as Zeʾev Falk,[18] Dale Patrick,[19] and Eckart Otto[20] have much to say about theology, philosophy, and the moral dimensions of biblical law.[21] Raymond Westbrook[22] and Bernard Levinson[23] are among those who have explored the oral, scribal, social, and archetypal features of biblical law.[24] Bernard Jackson, Calum Carmichael, James Watts, and others have developed tools to help readers understand how biblical law worked narratively,[25] semiotically,[26] sapiently,[27] literarily,[28] didactically,[29] practically,[30] and politically;[31] these laws gave legal warnings, social exhortations, judicial

18. For example, Zeʾev W. Falk, "Testate Succession in Jewish Law," *Journal of Jewish Studies* 12 (1961): 67–77.

19. For example, Dale Patrick, "Studying Biblical Law as a Humanities," *Semeia* 45 (1989): 27–47.

20. Eckart Otto, *Theologische Ethik des Alten Testaments* (Stuttgard: Kohlhammer, 1994).

21. See also David Noel Freedman, *The Nine Commandments: Uncovering a Hidden Pattern of Crime and Punishment in the Hebrew Bible* (New York: Doubleday, 2000); Frank Crüsemann, *The Torah: Theology and Social History of Old Testament Law* (Minneapolis: Fortress, 1996); J. G. McConville, *Law and Theology in Deuteronomy* (Sheffield, England: Sheffield Academic Press, 1984); and Rousas John Rushdoony, *The Institutes of Biblical Law* (Phillipsburg, NJ: Presbyterian and Reformed Publishing, 1973).

22. For example, Raymond Westbrook, "Biblical Law," in *An Introduction to the History and Sources of Jewish Law*, ed. N. S. Hecht et al. (Oxford: Oxford University Press, 1995), 1–17.

23. For example, Bernard M. Levinson, "'The Right Chorale': From the Poetics of Biblical Narrative to the Hermeneutics of the Hebrew Bible," in *"Not in Heaven": Coherence and Complexity in Biblical Narrative*, ed. Jason P. Rosenblatt and Joseph C. Sitterson (Bloomington: Indiana University Press, 1991), 129–53; and Levinson, "The Case for Revision and Interpolation within the Biblical Legal Corpora," in *Theory and Method in Biblical and Cuneiform Law*, ed. Bernard M. Levinson (Sheffield, England: Sheffield Academic Press, 1994), 37–59.

24. See also Joe M. Sprinkle, *"The Book of the Covenant": A Literary Approach* (Sheffield, England: Sheffield Academic Press, 1994); and Jay W. Marshall, *Israel and the Book of the Covenant: An Anthropological Approach to Biblical Law* (Atlanta: Scholars Press, 1993).

25. Jackson, *Wisdom-Laws*, 23–39.

26. For example, Bernard S. Jackson, *Studies in the Semiotics of Biblical Law* (Sheffield, England: Sheffield Academic Press, 2000); Jackson, "Towards an Integrated Approach to Criminal Law: Fletcher's Rethinking Criminal Law," *Criminal Law Review* (1979): 621–29; Jackson, "Structuralism and the Notion of Religious Law," *Investigaciones Semióticas* 2, no. 3 (1982–83): 1–43; and Jackson, *Semiotics and Legal Theory* (London: Routledge, 1987).

27. Calum Carmichael, *The Spirit of Biblical Law* (Athens, GA: University of Georgia Press, 1996); and Anne Fitzpatrick-McKinley, *The Transformation of Torah from Scribal Advice to Law* (Sheffield, England: Sheffield Academic Press, 1999).

28. Discussed in Jackson, *Wisdom-Laws*, 16–24.

29. James W. Watts, *Reading Law: The Rhetorical Shaping of the Pentateuch* (Sheffield, England: Sheffield Academic Press, 1999).

30. For example, Anthony Phillips, *Essays on Biblical Law* (Sheffield, England: Sheffield Academic Press, 2002).

31. For two very different approaches, see Moshe Weinfeld, *Social Justice in Ancient Israel and in the Ancient Near East* (Jerusalem: Magnes Press, 1995); and Harold V. Bennett, *Injustice*

guidance, as well as ritual regulations. As recently as 1980, Yaron could rightly state, "There are very few legal historians who specialize in the field of biblical law."[32] In the intervening decades, however, that situation has changed, with contributions being made by many scholars very profitably employing a wide variety of techniques and approaches.[33]

Each of these approaches offers tools that help identify ways in which laws functioned in the ancient world; and if the law functioned in a certain way in ancient Israel, the possibility can be readily entertained that the law functioned in a similar manner among the Nephites. As the following analyses of the legal cases in the Book of Mormon show, each of these approaches to biblical law opens new prospects for reading and understanding the legal issues, legal vocabulary, and legal precepts in the Book of Mormon. Many of these investigators have placed me in their debt.

Comparisons between the Bible and Book of Mormon, however, should not be taken too far. A comparison is only a comparison. Similarities do not constitute identity. Each legal system will be to some extent unique. The laws of neighboring states within the United States have points of uniqueness even though they share many broad features. I assume that biblical law was, to some degree, unique among the legal systems in the ancient world, although perhaps not as unique as some people may have uncritically assumed. I also assume that Nephite law was somewhat unique and distinct from Israelite law, although its general dependence on biblical law is explicit and lineal. Thus, as in any other endeavor of comparative law, comparison of biblical law with other ancient Near Eastern laws, and also comparison of law in the New World with law in the Old World, requires a careful balance between noting similarities and realizing differences. As Jonathan Z. Smith rightly observes, the postulation of some difference between biblical and ancient Near Eastern law is, in fact, ironically necessary in order to make comparison of similarities at all possible and "interesting (rather than tautological)."[34] Indeed, as he

---

Made Legal: Deuteronomic Law and the Plight of Widows, Strangers, and Orphans in Ancient Israel (Grand Rapids, MI: Eerdmans, 2002).

  32. Yaron, "Biblical Law: Prolegomena," 31.

  33. For three excellent assessments of approaches taken in the study of biblical law, see "The History of Research on the Covenant Code," in John Van Seters, *A Law Book for the Diaspora: Revision in the Study of the Covenant Code* (Oxford: Oxford University Press, 2003), 8–46; "Some Recent Approaches to Old Testament Law," in Fitzpatrick-McKinley, *The Transformation of Torah*, 23–53; and Raymond Westbrook, "The Laws of Biblical Israel," in *The Hebrew Bible: New Insights and Scholarship*, ed Frederick E. Greenspahn (New York: New York University Press, 2008), 99–119.

  34. Jonathan Z. Smith, *Imagining Religion* (Chicago: University of Chicago Press, 1982), 35.

says, a bit of "magic" and not just "science" exists in any process of comparison as we draw the various legal systems close enough to each other to make them relevant in illuminating each other, while at the same time methodologically maintaining some distance between the two in order to then bridge that "gap in the service of some useful end."[35]

How Relevant to the Bible and Book of Mormon Are the Laws of the Ancient Near East?

The practice of comparative law has been another major area of interest for biblical law scholars, and although to a lesser degree than for biblical law, the laws of the ancient Near East also aid in the understanding of the legal milieu that stands behind the cases in the Book of Mormon. The laws of the Babylonians, Hittites, Assyrians, and many others arose in lands that were not far from the Levant, and they use several cognate legal terms and address many of the same subjects that one also finds in the Bible.[36] Moreover, a fair degree of consistency among the ancient Near Eastern laws shows the considerable legal stability that often prevailed even in the midst of social upheavals spanning the course of many centuries. All of these points of commonality and continuity lend credence to the assumption that insights gained by studying one ancient Near Eastern legal system may shed light on another. Such benefits may come in the form of recognizing and understanding direct borrowings of words and phrases, the meaning of shared customs, and other similarities.

The further one moves in either direction from 600 BC, however, the less probative the earlier or later materials become for Book of Mormon purposes. For example, the great Babylonian lawgiver Hammurabi lived over a thousand years before Lehi, while the Talmud was compiled or written by Jewish rabbis around a thousand years after Lehi. Nevertheless, direct dependence and identical meanings can still be seen in some cases within the Old World texts that span these two thousand years. On other occasions, direct dependence may still be evident, even though new interpretations or different applications were followed. Comparing these bodies of law, even though they span great periods of time, can be very instructive. For example, when biblical law is silent on a particular rule of

35. Smith, *Imagining Religion*, 22, 35.

36. Martha T. Roth, *Law Collections from Mesopotamia and Asia Minor* (Atlanta: Scholars Press, 1995). For an exhaustive exposition of the legal systems of the ancient Near East, see Raymond Westbrook, *A History of Ancient Near Eastern Law*, 2 vols. (Leiden: Brill, 2003), with ancient Israel covered by Tikva Frymer-Kenski, 2:975–1046. On required criteria, see Meir Malul, *The Comparative Method in Ancient Near Eastern and Biblical Legal Studies* (Neukirchen-Vluyn: Butzon and Bercker Kevelaer, 1990).

Ancient Collections of Laws outside Israel	Approximate Dates BCE
Laws of Ur-Nammu	2100
Laws of Lipit-Ishtar	1930
Laws of Eshnunna	1770
Laws of Hammurabi	1750
Hittite Laws	1650–1300
Middle Assyrian Laws	1076
Neo-Babylonian Laws	700
Laws of Gortyn (Crete)	600–400
Roman Twelve Tables	450

law, but the same principle is found in ancient Near Eastern sources and also the Talmud (such as the law of purchasing stolen goods from the thief or the rights of an absentee husband), a reasonable conclusion may be drawn that biblical law also dealt with that same principle of law and most likely conformed to the general ancient Near Eastern policies, as Yaron has cogently demonstrated.[37] Carefully applied comparisons may be useful in filling holes in our knowledge about various principles of biblical law.

Thus, in examining the legal cases in the Book of Mormon, ancient Near Eastern legal provisions are occasionally cited not because there is any possibility that Sherem or Alma was directly aware of the Hittite or Assyrian laws, but because this broad base of cultural data helps to establish the persistence and prominence of certain jurisprudential concepts and concerns throughout this sphere of civilization and its progenies. Any such comparisons, of course, can commence only after the text of the Book of Mormon has been examined on its own terms. Alexander Rofé's advice is equally applicable to the present endeavor: "Study of biblical law [or, equally, law in the Book of Mormon] should first base itself on inner, independent interpretation before it can be completed by comparison with Ancient Near Eastern laws and/or by Rabbinic sources."[38]

37. Yaron, "Biblical Law: Prolegomena," 38–41; and Yaron, "The Evolution of Biblical Law," in *La Formazione Del Diritto Nel Vicino Oriente Antico* (Naples: Edizioni Scientifiche Italiane, 1988), 77–108.

38. Alexander Rofé, "Methodological Aspects of the Study of Biblical Law," in *Jewish Law Association Studies*, ed. Bernard S. Jackson (Atlanta: Scholars Press, 1986), 2:1.

How Relevant to Biblical Law or to the Book of Mormon Are Later Jewish Laws?

Another issue that has arisen in the study of biblical law is the relevance of passages from the later texts of the Dead Sea Scrolls or the Talmud, especially when they speak on issues of law not found either in the Bible or in ancient Near Eastern law. Here it is possible that the Talmud or the Qumran scrolls alone preserve an oral or alternate tradition that extends back as far as the seventh century BC, and in that case back far enough to be helpful in understanding biblical law as it existed in Lehi's day. It is also possible, however, that such provisions are unique Essene interpretations or late Talmudic inventions. But even in those cases, the method or general principle involved in such an invention may be helpful in the quest for understanding the way in which Book of Mormon law may also have changed.

Four general observations apply to the use of Jewish law as a legal source in studying the Book of Mormon:[39]

1. Antiquity of oral law. With respect to the use of later rabbinic and Jewish traditions that were first committed to writing long after Lehi left Jerusalem, it is still possible that those rules and regulations found in the oral law dated back to the time of Lehi, even though the archaic written sources may be silent on the particular point involved.

2. Nephite corroboration. If materials found in the oral Jewish traditions are similar to factors found in the Book of Mormon, this corroboration makes it more plausible that those oral law traditions dated back far enough for them to have been known by Lehi, although one cannot rule out the possibility that the Jewish and Nephite practices simply developed independently along parallel lines.

3. Chronological terminology. To avoid overstating or understating the possible significance of Jewish law comparisons in probing the Book of Mormon, I identify the time period from which each piece of evidence derives by using the following terms:

- The terms *biblical* and *Israelite* are used in speaking of the earliest and therefore most relevant texts and evidences, which are typically pre-exilic.

---

39. For a discussion of these principles in connection with King Benjamin's speech in the context of ancient Israelite festivals and laws relating to annual gatherings at the temple, see Terrence L. Szink and John W. Welch, "King Benjamin's Speech in the Context of Ancient Israelite Festivals," in *King Benjamin's Speech: "That Ye May Learn Wisdom,"* ed. John W. Welch and Stephen D. Ricks (Provo, UT: FARMS, 1998), 147–223.

- The word *Jewish* is used to refer to materials that come from the Second Temple period (536 BC to AD 70), Qumran (200 BC to AD 66), the Mishnah (first and second centuries AD), and Talmud (second through fifth centuries AD). Being later than Lehi, they constitute secondary evidence.
- Terms such as *Jewish traditions* or *customs* refer to sources that date to more recent times and thus are less probative, but they still may prove interesting and supportive for Book of Mormon purposes.

Readers are free to weigh these bits of information as they wish in determining the degree to which these details from Jewish law shed light on the legal practices of the Nephites.

4. Varieties of Judaism. In allowing comparisons between law in the Book of Mormon and Jewish law, one should not forget that early biblical law and Jewish law are not necessarily the same. Concerns about how many steps one may take on the Sabbath or whether turning on a light switch is "kindling a fire" are much later Jewish developments. Several varieties of Jewish law proliferated among various Jewish communities several centuries after Lehi left Jerusalem and on down to the present day. The Pharisees, Sadducees, Samaritans, and Essenes each understood the law in their own ways, and the works of Philo of Alexandria show that Hellenistic Jews understood the law in yet other ways.[40] Thus, saying that the Nephites observed the law of Moses does not mean that Lehi's views were necessarily those of a rabbinic Jew from any later time in Jewish history.

What Was the Law of Moses Like in Lehi's Day?

These chronological and comparative issues also require readers of the Book of Mormon to ask, What was the state of the law of Moses in Jerusalem in the seventh century BC? Indeed, a basic point of departure for studying law in the Book of Mormon is trying to understand the law of Moses as it existed in Lehi's day. I assume that the more we can learn about the law of Moses at that time, the more we will understand Lehi and Nephi and the branch of Israelite law that they brought with them from Jerusalem, adapted to their situation in the New World, and set in motion down through the generations that followed them. Determining the state of the law in Jerusalem in Lehi's day, however, has proven in biblical studies to be a very difficult task, to say the least; but this quest, as arduous as it might be, bears useful and enjoyable rewards.

---

40. Daniela Piattelli and Bernard S. Jackson, "Jewish Law during the Second Temple Period," in Hecht et al., *Introduction to the History and Sources of Jewish Law*, 19–56.

In terms of textual sources available to them, Lehi and Nephi would have begun any legal discussion with an examination of the law of Moses contained on the plates of brass. Knowing that Nephi had risked his life to obtain the plates of brass, and knowing of the conflicts between the Nephites and Lamanites over the possession of those plates, one may safely assume that these records would have been regularly consulted and were highly valued by the Nephites as a source of legal information and instruction. To a high degree, the Nephites labored under the specter that they would dwindle and perish in unbelief if they did not have and keep the law of Moses (e.g., 1 Nephi 5:19–22). These plates were used not only to bring people to repentance and to the knowledge of their Lord God but also to "enlarge the memory" and to "convince many of the error of their ways" (Alma 37:8, 9). Alongside the prophetic texts found on the plates of brass, the legal texts also functioned in didactic and inspirational settings, helping people to remember important principles and correcting errors by delineating right from wrong.

The plates of brass contained "the five books of Moses" (1 Nephi 5:11). Accordingly, Nephite jurists, judges, and elders had at their disposal not only the Ten Commandments (Mosiah 12:33–36; 13:12–24) but also the law "codes" as they existed at that time embedded within the books of Exodus, Leviticus, Numbers, and Deuteronomy. Although we need not assume that the version of these texts on the plates of brass was exactly the same linguistically as our version of the five books of Moses (i.e., the Pentateuch, the first five books in the Bible), evidence within the Book of Mormon indicates that the Nephites' version of the legal provisions found in the five books of Moses was probably similar to the traditional text that has come down to us in the Bible. Because many paraphrases of or allusions to biblical law are found throughout the Book of Mormon, a reliable working assumption can be made that the Nephites were familiar with the basic corpus of biblical law much as it exists in the Bible today. Biblical laws, however, are rarely quoted in the Book of Mormon, the one notable exception being Abinadi's quotation in Mosiah 13 of the Ten Commandments from Exodus 20.

This discussion, of course, raises the question of when the five books of Moses, as found on the plates of brass or in the Bible, were actually written. Unfortunately, this is a general problem in biblical studies. It is unclear when any book in the Bible was originally written or when it took its final form. It is popular among scholars to date sections of the Pentateuch over a fairly wide range of centuries, even though orthodox Jewish traditions attribute the writing of all of this material personally to Moses at the time of the Israelites' exodus from Egypt and their forty years in the wilderness.

The claim of exclusive Mosaic authorship, however, is complicated by several factors. For example, significant sections of the law of Moses are typical of ancient Near Eastern laws in the second millennium BC (the broad period in which Moses is thought to have lived), which points to outside influences in the assembling of laws such as those found in the Code of the Covenant in Exodus 21–23. Moreover, several provisions and phrases found in the Pentateuch appear to have arisen well after Moses's death, during time periods after the conquest of Canaan by Joshua. Apparent contradictions, duplications, and stylistic differences have opened up arguments about possible editorial modifications and contributions. Thus one must always be alert to the possibility that any law originally given by Moses may have been edited, emended, modified, supplemented, or transformed by later Israelite leaders or writers in certain respects as time went on and as the needs of society changed.[41]

Indeed, Latter-day Saint scripture provides evidence that not all of the words in the first five books of the Bible have been preserved exactly as Moses originally gave them. As is apparent to Latter-day Saints from Joseph Smith's revision of the Bible (in which the first three chapters of Genesis, for example, receive much fuller expression in the extract known as the Book of Moses in the Pearl of Great Price), the Hebrew scriptures saw various changes and deletions (some perhaps inspired but most probably not) during the six (often apostate) centuries between Moses and the time of Lehi.

At the same time, those modifications need not have been extensive. The change or deletion of a word here or there typically would have served most needs of redactors or revisionists. Indeed, in some quite dramatic cases, close textual parallels between biblical laws and early Babylonian and Hittite laws show that those provisions in the law of Moses bear the unmistakable stamp of early antiquity (compare the ox laws in Exodus 21:28–32 with the similarly worded Babylonian ox laws of Eshnunna 53–55,[42] or the incest laws of Leviticus 18 and 20 with a similar list of

---

41. For a convenient overview of theories and evidences regarding authorship of the Pentateuch, see Richard Elliott Friedman, "Torah (Pentateuch)," in *The Anchor Bible Dictionary*, ed. David Noel Freedman (New York: Doubleday, 1992), 6:605–22.

42. Regarding the ox laws, "anyone looking at the two texts without preconceived notions will see at once how closely they resemble each other, not only concerning the actual solution laid down, but beyond that in the mode of formulation." Yaron, "Biblical Law: Prolegomena," 34. Sections 53–55 of the law of Eshnunna (ca. 1770 BC) read, "If an ox gores an(other) ox and causes (its) death, both ox owners shall divide (among themselves) the price of the live ox and also the meat of the dead ox. If an ox is known to gore habitually and the authorities have brought the fact to the knowledge of its owner, but he does not have his ox dehorned, it gores a man and causes

prohibited relationships in the Hittite Laws 187–195). An effective and inspired lawgiver such as Moses, who led Israel for forty years, certainly had the time and ability to bring together all of the essential legal materials found in the Pentateuch; some provisions could have been initially written during the early years of the exodus, and others could have been formulated near the end of those years in the wilderness, thus accounting for many of the stylistic differences.

For Book of Mormon purposes, however, many of the text-critical issues conventionally associated with the so-called Documentary Hypothesis are somewhat moot. This is because many of the textual uncertainties that biblical scholars argue about deal with possible layers of editing and redacting that would have occurred, in any event, before the time of Lehi. Whatever the very ancient history of the emergence of the textual units of the Pentateuch may have been during the six hundred years between the time of Moses and the time of Lehi,[43] most of the Hebrew text of the core legal codes was probably in place by the years 620–610 BC, when by my reckoning the plates of brass were fashioned.[44]

The subject of dating the laws in Exodus 21–23 has been hotly debated, especially in the last forty years, with several scholars tracing the Covenant Code to very early times[45] and others dating its composition to the time of the exile of the Jews in Babylon.[46] With regard to the Covenant Code, I find Bernard Jackson's coverage of the issues most impressive. He demonstrates that modern scholarship "overwhelmingly favors" the view that the Covenant Code existed as a written text before it was

---

(his) death, then the owner of the ox shall pay two-thirds of a mina of silver. If it gores a slave and causes [his] death, he shall pay 15 shekels of silver."

43. I remain impressed by the arguments advanced by U. Cassuto, *The Documentary Hypothesis and the Composition of the Pentateuch* (Jerusalem: Magnes Press, 1983), raising doubts about source criticism in pentateuchal studies.

44. My reasons for this are given in "Authorship of the Book of Isaiah in Light of the Book of Mormon," in *Isaiah in the Book of Mormon*, ed. Donald W. Parry and John W. Welch (Provo, UT: FARMS, 1998), 430–32.

45. For example, on the early, more traditional side, arguing that the Sinai documents in the legal corpus of the Bible "have an indubitable fourteenth/thirteenth century [BC] format," see K. A. Kitchen, *On the Reliability of the Old Testament* (Grand Rapids, MI: Eerdmans, 2003), quotation on p. 289.

46. On the far edge of the revisionist side, arguing that the Covenant Code was written by a single author during the captivity of Judah in Babylon during the sixth century BC, see Van Seters, *A Law Book for the Diaspora*. This strident book and several others in this field have provided grist for the academic mill as the relevant textual and historical details have been ground, reground, sifted, and evaluated. See further entries in the CD-ROM publication of John W. Welch, comp., *Biblical Law Cumulative Bibliography* (Winona Lake, IN: Eisenbrauns; Provo, UT: BYU Press, 2005).

"incorporated into its present narrative context"[47] and that although "both the dating and function of the earliest written redactions must necessarily remain speculative,"[48] there is ample evidence of scribal activity in the seventh and eighth centuries BC, during which time, at the latest,[49] various biblical law collections, such as not only the *mishpatim* in the Covenant Code in Exodus 21:1–22:16 but also the Holiness Code in Leviticus 17–27 and other legal and prophetic scrolls, could well have been compiled essentially into their nearly final forms.[50]

Similarly, materials underlying the book of Leviticus are traced by many scholars to pre-exilic times[51] and thus would have been known in some form to Lehi, even though debates still exist over the dating of various parts and also the final form of that book. Portions of the Priestly Code dealing with the descendants of Aaron and Levi, of course, would have been considered largely inapplicable among the Nephites, in whose party there were no Levites. The Nephite priesthood looked back beyond Aaron and Moses to Melchizedek in the days of Abraham for the paragon of their priestly order (Alma 13:14–19).[52] Nevertheless, legal precedents and ceremonial instructions concerning the Day of Atonement (Leviticus 16), blasphemy (Leviticus 24), the jubilee (Leviticus 25–26), and other passages in the book of Leviticus seem to have been adequately familiar to Lehi's posterity.[53]

With the discovery (or production) of a scroll of the law during the renovation of the temple in Jerusalem at the beginning of the reign of Josiah (640–609 BC) (2 Kings 22:1–23:30; 2 Chronicles 34:8–33), the book of Deuteronomy either entered or reentered the corpus of ancient Israelite

---

47. Jackson, *Wisdom-Laws*, 9.

48. Jackson, *Wisdom-Laws*, 69.

49. See generally Jackson, *Wisdom-Laws*, 69–70, and sources cited.

50. David P. Wright dates the writing of the Covenant Code to the end of Isaiah's era, about 710 BC; see his "The Laws of Hammurabi as a Source for the Covenant Collection (Exodus 20:23–23:19)," *Maarav* 10 (2003): 50–51. Jacob Milgrom, *Leviticus 17–22* (New York: Doubleday, 2000), 1361–63, dates most of the Holiness Code in Leviticus 17–27 as "preexilic."

51. For the best examination of the terminology in Leviticus, demonstrating that the Priestly sources in that book are pre-exilic, see Jacob Milgrom's three-volume magnum opus, especially the discussions of the issues surrounding the antiquity of P in *Leviticus 1–16* (New York: Doubleday, 1991), 3–35, and of the pre-exilic dating of the Holiness writings in *Leviticus 17–22* (New York: Doubleday, 2000), 1345–67.

52. See further John W. Welch, "The Melchizedek Material in Alma 13," in *By Study and Also by Faith: Essays in Honor of Hugh Nibley on His 80th Birthday*, ed. Stephen D. Ricks and John M. Lundquist (Salt Lake City: Deseret Book and FARMS, 1990), 2:238–72.

53. Welch and Szink, "King Benjamin's Speech in the Context of Ancient Israelite Festivals," 147–224.

law around 623 BC, which was during Lehi's lifetime.[54] Many factors in the Book of Mormon indicate that certain parts of Deuteronomic law and theology profoundly influenced Nephite law on such subjects as social justice and generosity (Deuteronomy 15:13–14; compare Mosiah 4:16–23), limitations on kingship (Deuteronomy 17:14–20; compare Mosiah 2:11–14), destruction of apostate cities (Deuteronomy 13:12–16; compare Alma 16), punishment of false prophets (Deuteronomy 18:20), and rules of warfare (Deuteronomy 20).[55] These points of legal intersection do not necessarily mean that Lehi agreed with the agenda of the Deuteronomic reformers in all respects, and indeed Margaret Barker and Kevin Christensen have spelled out several reasons for thinking that Lehi may well have disagreed with certain political trajectories in Jerusalem promoted by those aggressive Deuteronomists during and after the reign of Josiah.[56] At the same time, the affinities between the Book of Mormon and the book of Deuteronomy also make it clear that Lehi was conversant with the vocabulary, the rhetoric, and the legal topics that were in vogue in Jerusalem in the last decades of the sixth century, and that Lehi and his righteous posterity followed the spirit of ethics and justice, if not all the politics and excisions, that grew out of the Deuteronomy reform movement.

Efforts to determine the original forms and purposes of these legal materials or to puzzle over the reasons and manners in which these bodies of law became incorporated into the books of the Pentateuch are fascinating academic pursuits,[57] but at least for dating purposes, these issues mainly involve developments that would have predated Lehi and Nephi. The process of archiving, compiling, narratively contextualizing, editing, supplementing, and officially canonizing the biblical legal texts

---

54. Discussed further in Marvin A. Sweeney, *King Josiah of Judah: The Lost Messiah of Israel* (Oxford: Oxford University Press, 2001), 137–77; see also Welch and Hunt, "Culturegram: Jerusalem 600 B.C.," and Margaret Barker, "What Did King Josiah Reform?" in Welch, Seely, and Seely, *Glimpses of Lehi's Jerusalem*, 32–33, 523–42. For good descriptions of the Deuteronomic movement, see Raymond F. Person Jr., *The Deuteronomic School: History, Social Setting, and Literature* (Atlanta: Society of Biblical Literature, 2002).

55. Compare the discussion of these and other rules of martial law in John W. Welch, "Law and War in the Book of Mormon," in *Warfare in the Book of Mormon*, ed. Stephen D. Ricks and William J. Hamblin (Salt Lake City: Deseret Book and FARMS, 1990), 46–102.

56. Kevin Christensen, "The Temple, the Monarchy, and Wisdom: Lehi's World and the Scholarship of Margaret Barker," and Barker, "What Did King Josiah Reform?" in Welch, Seely, and Seely, *Glimpses of Lehi's Jerusalem*, 449–542. One need not subscribe to all of Barker's views in order to appreciate that Lehi probably was not in complete agreement with the Deuteronomists, for otherwise they would have been his ally and he would not have been met with such opposition from the controlling parties in Jerusalem.

57. For the most recent and best surveys of these issues in recent biblical scholarship, see Jackson, *Wisdom-Laws*, 3–74; and Fitzpatrick-McKinley, *The Transformation of Torah*, 23–53.

undoubtedly spanned several centuries; but legal systems in general are fundamentally conservative, and so those changes probably occurred incrementally, not radically. Thus the basic texts of the books of Moses that would have governed in Lehi's day are probably adequately represented by the texts of the Pentateuch as those five books have long been known and as they still exist today.

Therefore, unless a good reason exists for doubting that the Nephites knew a particular passage in the first five books of the Bible, I have assumed in the following analyses of the Nephite legal cases that the Nephite jurists had access to and felt a pious obligation to actually follow[58] their version of the law. In other words, I proceed, for purposes of investigation, on the premise that the Nephites had the five books of Moses in some form that modern readers would essentially recognize. I find confirmation of this hypothesis in the light that this approach sheds on the general legal theory and particular legal rules implicitly standing behind many passages in the Book of Mormon itself.

How Would Lehi and His Posterity Have Understood and Kept the Law?

The mere fact that Lehi had the law written on the plates of brass, however, does not answer the questions of how much of that law he and his posterity actually understood and how they interpreted it. In addition to having the words on the plates of brass, how did they understand the customs, policies, practices, and procedures of biblical law as a whole? How would Lehi and subsequently his posterity have understood and kept that law?

Ample evidence supports the general idea that Lehi and his family were deeply familiar with the world of Jerusalem. Born around 650 BC, Lehi was a mature, longtime participant in the public life of Jerusalem. As a wealthy man, apparently a merchant and landowner, he would have participated in public life, negotiated business transactions, witnessed coronations, and probably observed legal proceedings such as the one that led to the execution of Urijah ben Shemaiah (Jeremiah 26:23). He himself was accused of the crime of false prophecy under Deuteronomy 13:5 or 18:22, and so he would have had personal familiarity with the risks involved in being subjected to prosecution in Jerusalem over such a charge.

---

58. I concur with Jacob Milgrom that, in addition to being used for religious instruction, "there is every likelihood that [biblical legal precepts] were actually carried out. . . . It may be concluded that the Torah's laws, far from being [merely] a guide for behavior, were, at least in part, the living code of Israel." Milgrom, *Leviticus 17–22*, 1348.

Much comparative, biblical, and archaeological evidence indicates that Lehi was an astute observer of his surrounding world.[59] Yet one need not assume that he knew or accepted everything about the laws and legal institutions of Jerusalem, let alone of all the surrounding peoples in neighboring lands in the ancient Near East and Arabia. Indeed, he probably hoped to forget many wicked and perverse practices that he opposed in Jerusalem and may have encountered among other peoples. Nevertheless, he would have known and taught to his family and followers many things that were important to the legal legacy that he brought with him from the Old World, and he would have passed the wisdom of his civilization on to his posterity as best he could.

At the same time, we must frequently remind ourselves that the law of Moses has never been easy to understand completely. Various branches of Judaism, ancient and modern, in the center at Jerusalem and abroad in the Jewish Diaspora, have struggled mightily and in good faith, between themselves and even among themselves, to interpret and apply this extensive and detailed body of law. It is true that the priests of Noah misunderstood the law of Moses; but even the people of ancient Jerusalem could be accused of not understanding it very well either (Mosiah 13:32). And so, while one may assume that Lehi and his posterity in the New World understood the law in light of their own revealed insights and prophetic worldview, we must exercise caution, realizing that numerous views about the law certainly existed in ancient times and that the technical meanings formerly attributed to many details in the law of Moses are now lost or at least obscure to modern readers.

Above all, however, it is clear that the Nephites viewed the law of Moses as the foundation of their law and legal system. They understood that the purpose of the law was to foster obedience: "And for this intent we keep the law of Moses, it pointing our souls to [Christ]; and for this cause it is sanctified unto us for righteousness" (Jacob 4:5); "The Lord God saw that his people were a stiffnecked people, and he appointed unto them a law, even the law of Moses" (Mosiah 3:14).

Explicit statements by Nephi (2 Nephi 5:10), Jarom (Jarom 1:5), Alma (Alma 30:2–3), and others demonstrate beyond any doubt that for six centuries the Nephites saw themselves as strictly observing the judgments, statutes, commandments, and ordinances of God in all things according to the law of Moses until the coming of Christ. For example, in laying the legal foundation of his fledgling kingship, Nephi conformed to a traditional Israelite

---

59. See generally Welch, Seely, and Seely, *Glimpses of Lehi's Jerusalem.*

pattern when he assured that his people "did observe to keep the judgments, and the statutes, and the commandments of the Lord in all things, according to the law of Moses" (2 Nephi 5:10; compare the order issued by King David to his successor-son Solomon in 1 Kings 2:3). In King Benjamin's day the people "took of the firstlings of their flocks, that they might offer sacrifice and burnt offerings according to the law of Moses" (Mosiah 2:3, ca. 124 BC). In Alma's day "the people did observe to keep the commandments of the Lord; and they were strict in observing the ordinances of God, according to the law of Moses; for they were taught to keep the law of Moses until it should be fulfilled" (Alma 30:3, ca. 74 BC; see 34:13). Even the Lamanites who were converted by Nephi and Lehi a few years before the birth of Christ "did observe strictly to keep the commandments of God, according to the law of Moses" (Helaman 13:1), for which Samuel the Lamanite praised them in contrast to the less obedient Nephites: "And I would that ye should behold that the more part of them are in the path of their duty, and they do walk circumspectly before God, and they do observe to keep his commandments and his statutes and his judgments according to the law of Moses" (Helaman 15:5). Once the sign of the birth of Jesus was seen, some "began to preach, endeavoring to prove by the scriptures that it was no more expedient to observe the law of Moses" (3 Nephi 1:24); their understandable but erroneous contentions make no sense unless one presumes that the law of Moses was being followed programmatically down to that day. These emphatic statements, together with the total Nephite history until the appearance of Christ among those people, are all the more remarkable because of their prophetic knowledge of the "deadness of the law" (2 Nephi 25:27).

Indeed, the Nephites realized that the law of Moses was given by faith (Ether 12:11) and that a time would come when the purpose of the law would be fulfilled. From the outset, Nephi reported that, notwithstanding their belief in Christ, his people kept the law of Moses until it should be entirely fulfilled (2 Nephi 25:24). Likewise, Abinadi insisted to the priests of Noah in the second century BC, "If ye teach the law of Moses, also teach that it is a shadow of those things which are to come—teach them that redemption cometh through Christ the Lord, who is the very Eternal Father" (Mosiah 16:14–15). The people of God in the land of Nephi were taught by Ammon to "keep the law of Moses; for it was expedient that they should keep the law of Moses as yet, for it was not all fulfilled. But notwithstanding the law of Moses, they did look forward to the coming of Christ, considering that the law of Moses was a type of his coming, and believing that they must keep those outward performances until the time that he should be revealed unto them. Now they did not suppose that salvation came by the law of Moses; but the law of Moses did serve to strengthen their faith in Christ" (Alma 25:15–16).

The Nephites observed the law not just perfunctorily but meaningfully and meticulously. Amulek taught: "Therefore, it is expedient that there should be a great and last sacrifice, and then shall there be, or it is expedient there should be, a stop to the shedding of blood; then shall the law of Moses be fulfilled; yea, it shall be all fulfilled, every jot and tittle" (Alma 34:13).[60] Moreover, Alma affirmed that the Nephites were "*strict* in observing the ordinances of God, according to the law of Moses" (30:3; emphasis added), and Jarom stated even further that their observance of these laws was "*exceedingly* strict" (Jarom 1:5; emphasis added).

Regarding the laws of sacrifice, while the Nephites most probably would not have observed the ritual laws in the same way as did the Jews in the Second Temple period in Jerusalem, one should not imagine that they did not observe the laws of sacrifice at all. As shown elsewhere,[61] it seems probable that the Nephites offered some kind of sacrifice not only on special days, such as the holy Day of Atonement or the Feast of Tabernacles (Mosiah 2:3), but also on each regular day (13:30–31). In whatever way they understood the rules of the law of Moses, they observed them accordingly, including the laws of sacrifice. As discussed above, even though the Nephites knew the deadness of the law, which was given life only through Christ (2 Nephi 25:24–27), they still lived the law of Moses (5:10).

This blending of elements from both the old and new covenants is one of the most distinctive characteristics of the Book of Mormon. Essentially, the Nephite record bridges both Jewish and Christian backgrounds. The world of the Book of Mormon is neither Jewish nor Christian but both— if both those terms are properly understood. Unlike some Jews who looked "beyond the mark" (Jacob 4:14) or who became overly concerned about the letter of the law, the Nephites saw themselves as following in the tradition of other ancient Israelites, such as Melchizedek, who knew

---

60. The Book of Mormon further records the changing of the law as a result of Christ's atonement: 3 Nephi 9:17, "and in me is the law of Moses fulfilled"; 3 Nephi 15:2, "And it came to pass that when Jesus had said these words he perceived that there were some among them who marveled, and wondered what he would concerning the law of Moses; for they understood not the saying that old things had passed away, and that all things had become new"; 3 Nephi 15:4, "Behold, I say unto you that the law is fulfilled that was given unto Moses"; and 4 Nephi 1:12, "And they did not walk any more after the performances of the law of Moses; but they did walk after the commandments which they had received from their Lord and their God, continuing in fasting and prayer, and in meeting together oft both to pray and to hear the word of the Lord."

61. See my discussion in "The Temple in the Book of Mormon," in *Temples of the Ancient World*, ed. Donald W. Parry (Salt Lake City: Deseret Book and FARMS, 1994), 305–9.

the messianic gospel and embraced the order of the priesthood "after the order of [the] Son" (see Alma 13:7–9, 18), thus understanding and keeping the performances and ordinances of the law of Moses in light of their knowledge of Christ (2 Nephi 25:24).

The righteous Nephites knew that obedience and remembrance were among the indelible principles of the gospel (Mosiah 2:31–41; 4:30; 5:11; 3 Nephi 12:1; 18:10; 4 Nephi 1:12). They scrupulously remembered and obeyed the laws they had been given until they were fulfilled. It appears also that Jesus himself continued to observe the law of Moses in Galilee and Jerusalem until it was all fulfilled.[62] Of course, the manner in which Jesus observed every provision of the law is unknown; moreover, it is clear that he disagreed with some interpretations of the law advocated by other people in his day. But Jesus kept every jot and tittle of the law (Matthew 5:18), however he understood those provisions. By suggesting that the Nephites were true to their word and were strict to observe the law of Moses, I mean to imply that the Nephites were no more or less committed to the traditions of Israel than was Jesus himself.

To be sure, the law of Moses was a high-principled schoolmaster. It taught, at its root, such important virtues as sacrifice, obedience, modesty, chastity, holiness, generosity, and gratitude. Indeed, the law of Moses was profoundly based on important eternal principles. The underlying purpose of the law of Moses was to make the faithful "an holy people" (Deuteronomy 7:6; see Exodus 22:31; Leviticus 19:2) and to prefigure the coming of Christ through various patterns and concepts such as the scapegoat and the city of refuge. The law of Moses contains some of the greatest commandments and principles ever revealed by God. It contains much of the spirit of moral judgment and practical wisdom. When Jesus was asked about the greatest commandment (Matthew 22:36–40), he turned to the Pentateuch for his answer: "Thou shalt love the Lord thy God with all thy might, mind, and strength," which is based on Deuteronomy 6:5, and "Thou shalt love thy neighbor as thyself," found in Leviticus 19:18. Laws or teachings regarding doing good to one's enemy (Exodus 23:4), obeying and taking care of one's parents (20:12), and showing kindness to the widow and fatherless child (22:22–24) teach powerful lessons of generosity, social justice, and pure religion undefiled. In some ways, my favorite commentary on the book of Deuteronomy is Hugh Nibley's essay entitled

---

62. Welch, "Temple in the Book of Mormon," 313–14, see pp. 309–19 for a similar discussion of surrounding materials in this section.

ironically "How to Get Rich."[63] Nibley shows that the book of Deuteronomy, a quintessential restatement of the law of Moses, is essentially an
exposition of and elaboration on the law of consecration. The book of
Deuteronomy presents us with celestial precepts that are in many respects
highly relevant to contemporary society and the restored gospel in the
dispensation of the fulness of times.

At the same time, the law of Moses is often a misunderstood schoolmaster. Even the much-maligned biblical law formula "an eye for an eye"
may convey eternal values. While this expression's exact meaning in antiquity is unknown, it may well have meant something to the effect of "be
fair" or "let the punishment suit the crime." Biblical scholars have pointed
out that this talionic formula may have been a limiting factor (in other
words, no more than an eye for an eye), and the rabbinic tradition explained that it really meant money, or in other words "the value of an
eye for an eye" (see chapter 13 below). Be that as it may, in the Book of
Mormon the principle of divine justice is clearly understood as one of
"restoration" as taught in Alma 41:13–15 and elsewhere. The concept of
divine justice there teaches that people will receive from God as they have
imparted (Mosiah 4:21–22), will be forgiven as they forgive (3 Nephi
13:14–15; compare Matthew 6:14–15), and will be judged as they have
judged (3 Nephi 14:2; compare Matthew 7:1). Thus even God restores justice for justice, mercy for mercy, goodness for goodness, as well as evil for
evil, carnal for carnal, and devilish for devilish (Alma 41:13)—in principle, an eye for an eye.

In other words, people should not think that the law of Moses is just
a religious system of "thou shalt nots," as Christians are often inclined
to do. This law also calls for positive righteousness. Consider the inward
morality required by the curses expressed in Deuteronomy 27 that place
woes on people who do evil in secret and who think they will not get
caught. The law of Moses is much more than the law of sacrifice. Given
the comprehensive coverage of the law of Moses, its long-standing value
in applied practice, and its divine origins, it is easy to see why the prophet
Lehi would have thought so highly of the law and why he risked so much
to have a copy of it for his people. In sum, law loomed large in Nephite
life as that civilization changed from generation to generation, as had also
been the case in pre-exilic Israel. The ancient concept of law was broader
than is the modern concept of law. Modern society tends to view law in a
positivist way, assuming that laws are only those specific commands given

63. Hugh W. Nibley, "How to Get Rich," in *Approaching Zion*, ed. Don E. Norton (Salt Lake
City: Deseret Book and FARMS, 1989), 178–201.

by a sovereign body coupled with a specific remedy or punishment. Federal and state constitutions also act to limit the scope of governmental authority, and hence to limit the breadth of the concept of law itself. The Nephites, however, like most other ancient peoples, understood law in broad cultural terms. They spoke of laws, statutes, ordinances, customs, commands, and teachings, giving to all of these norms and practices the moral imprimatur or sanction of law. The word *torah* itself comes from the Hebrew word meaning "to teach" and may be loosely defined as simply "the right way to live."[64] Little distinction was made between civil law and religious law in ancient societies, and the distances between the modern domains of politics, statecraft, commerce, morals, family, and purity were scarcely noticeable. Indeed, many other elements of the modern worldview, such as an understanding of the physical laws of cause and effect, the physiology of sickness or well-being, and notions about human responsibilities and divine intervention, were understood in completely different terms by ancient peoples. Thus one should not assume that a narrow, modern concept of law operated in ancient Nephite jurisprudence.

Did the Nephites Change or Adapt the Law of Moses in the Course of Their History?

While most parts of the law of Moses would have readily applied to life in the New World, some parts of that law probably did not. Laws for the designation of specific towns in Israel as cities of refuge, for example, would obviously have been in need of modification in order for them to make any sense in the new world of the Nephites, or perhaps they were simply ignored. But most provisions in the law of Moses speak to generic human situations and cover a full spectrum of what lawyers call civil, criminal, religious, political, and administrative legal issues. Because of its broad scope to social and personal life, the law of Moses would easily have applied to most parts of Nephite life and civilization.

However, no legal system remains completely static over time. Biblical law in the tenth century BC was not exactly the same as biblical law in the seventh century BC.[65] Lehi undoubtedly made certain legal adaptations at the outset, as his new circumstances mandated. For example, Lehi significantly forbade polygamy and concubinage among his sons (Jacob 2:27, 34; 3:5),

---

64. *Reexploring the Book of Mormon*, ed. John W. Welch (Salt Lake City: Deseret Book and FARMS, 1992), 62–63.

65. Giuseppe D'Ercole, "The Juridicial Structure of Israel from the Time of Her Origin to the Period of Hadrian," in *Populus Dei: Studi in onore del Card. Alfredo Ottaviani per il cinquantesimo di sacerdozio: 18 Marso 1966*, ed. Henri Cazelles (Rome: Communio, 1969), 389–461.

even though Deuteronomy clearly allowed such practices (Deuteronomy 21:15), if not done to excess (17:17). Lehi's ruling must have made especially good sense in a very small society that would have been short on women and where Lehi did not want his sons marrying women from Arabia or elsewhere from outside the clan unless God specially commanded it (Jacob 2:30). Moreover, Nephite law developed in certain other respects over its thousand-year history. Even though we cannot know the intricacies of these developments in all respects, readers should always be alert to the possibility of cultural changes, especially when compiling and comparing the evidence in one section of the Book of Mormon with evidence about legal situations in other parts of that text.

Based on the descriptions given within the Book of Mormon itself, it appears that the major Nephite legal developments came primarily in the form of administrative changes rather than substantive law reforms. Thus, for example, even though Mosiah changed the government from a kingship to a judgeship, which consequently changed the procedural rules of Nephite legal practice dramatically, he charged the people to choose judges "that ye may be judged according to the laws which have been given you by our fathers, which are correct, and which were given them by the hand of the Lord" (Mosiah 29:25), and he held the new judges responsible to decide cases "according to the law which has been given" (v. 28). At the same time, Mosiah condemned any king who "teareth up the laws of those who have reigned in righteousness before him" and "trampleth under his feet the commandments of God" and instead "enacteth laws, and sendeth them forth . . . after the manner of his own wickedness" (Mosiah 29:22–23). Accordingly, although the legal system in Nephite civilization developed to some extent, it appears that the underlying substantive Nephite law was essentially conservative, staying as close to the pentateuchal laws as possible.

As a general matter, particularly important moments in the history of any people are marked by fundamental changes in their legal system.[66] Thus, in reconstructing the legal history of the Book of Mormon, I have assumed that every time a law was introduced, modified, or significantly challenged, Nephite jurists were required to revisit many basic questions regarding the impact of these new developments on their overall legal system.

Legal changes create profound problems not only as people think through the meaning of a new legal provision itself but also as they

---

66. For a succinct and insightful summary of this history by political scientist Noel B. Reynolds, see "Government and Legal History in the Book of Mormon," in *Encyclopedia of Mormonism*, ed. Daniel H. Ludlow (New York: Macmillan, 1992), 1:160–62.

contemplate its relevance to situations that were probably not imagined at the time of enactment. From a legal point of view, much of what is happening in the trials of Nehor and Korihor, and much of what stands behind the questions of religious independence raised by the members of the apostate order of Nehor in Ammonihah, reflect this precise problem: How would the law reforms of King Mosiah (enacted in Mosiah 29) actually be construed in the society, and what were the implications of that new law with respect to old religious regulations? It should come as no surprise that the law reforms of Mosiah, constituting the largest law reform in the history of Nephite civilization, were immediately followed by the most intense period of judicial action recorded in the Book of Mormon. Nor should it be surprising that the outcomes were all conservative.

Throughout the Book of Mormon, evidence shows that the Nephites placed a high value on retaining the integrity of their basic legal system while accommodating only a moderate degree of change. The preservation of the status quo was a fairly standard Nephite attitude toward the law. They revered, read, studied, and even memorized their primary legal texts. For example, Nephi's account of the slaying of Laban in 1 Nephi 4:6, 11 shows that he knew well the specific criteria and precise language of the legal code in Exodus 21:13–14.[67] Benjamin's paraphrase in Mosiah 2:12–14 of material from the "Paragraph of the King" in Deuteronomy 17:14–20 shows that he knew and followed the law on the plates of brass, which he expressly affirms he had taught his sons to read and to appreciate (Mosiah 1:2–7).

While certain things changed as Lehi and his posterity applied the law of Moses in the New World, many other things stayed the same, preserving an overriding legal presence. Modern readers often skip over the legal sections of the Pentateuch, scarcely reading the book of Leviticus, but these legal texts would have loomed much larger on the religious landscape for the Nephites. Much of the Old Testament and all of the New Testament, to say nothing of the Doctrine and Covenants and other scripture in our possession today, were unknown to the Nephites. Children growing up as Nephites had far less scripture to learn than do the youth of today. The percentage of ancient scripture dedicated to the law that a person such as Benjamin taught his sons was far higher than a modern reader might casually assume.

---

67. John W. Welch, "Legal Perspectives on the Slaying of Laban," *Journal of Book of Mormon Studies* 1, no. 1 (1992): 119–41; and Welch, "Introduction," *Studia Antiqua* (Summer 2003): 9–12.

What Analytic Problems Arise from Layers of Authorship, Abridgment, and Translation?

Questions of authorship, of course, have plagued the study of biblical law. Theories about when, why, and by whom the Covenant Code, the Holiness Code, or virtually any other part of the Hebrew Bible was originally written and subsequently revised have been strenuously debated.

As with the Bible, the compositional history of the Book of Mormon is also complicated by the fact that many authors have contributed to the record, but in different ways. For one thing, the Book of Mormon is much more self-conscious about its multiple authorship, keeping track of various records, sources, and abridgers contributing to the final text. Although Nephite culture reflects broad interest in the law generally, some Book of Mormon writers spoke more directly and extensively on legal topics than others did. For example, Alma, who served professionally as the chief judge in Zarahemla for eight years, provides a considerable amount of legal detail in his narratives and speeches, while Nephi and Jacob give less attention to legal matters. Those two earlier Nephite writers lived in a smaller, clan-based community that was far less regulated by legal institutions than was Alma's world in the land of Zarahemla, and they wrote their records not on the large political plates as did Alma but on the small plates that were dedicated to select sacred topics. Nephi expressly states his theological reasons for saying little about the law: he and his people placed greater emphasis on belief in the Messiah and less weight on the eternal efficacy of the law of Moses (2 Nephi 25:24–27).

In addition to the words spoken or written by various original authors, several intermediary compilers also influenced and shaped the texts of the Book of Mormon as we have them. Consider, for example, the textual history of the account of the trial of Abinadi found in Mosiah 11–17. How many people might have influenced or contributed to the speaking, writing, recording, compiling, structuring, editing, or abridging of this account? (1) Abinadi, (2) the people, (3) Noah, and (4) the priests all spoke as the case developed. (5) Alma, one of the priests, who was expelled from the court because he favored acquitting Abinadi, went into hiding where he wrote "all the words which Abinadi had spoken" (17:4). However, Alma was not present in court during the final day of this trial, and he "went about privately among the people, and began to teach the words of Abinadi" (18:1), presumably putting himself in contact with (6) other people who could have told him about the final events in Abinadi's life. Additionally, (7) a royal record of the trial was kept by the government and shared with Ammon (8:5), perhaps conveying additional information about this trial. (8) King Limhi, the son of Noah, might have brought this record with him or might have told this story when he and his people returned to Zarahemla. Eventually, of course, (9) someone sat down to write the book of Mosiah. Alma the Younger is a leading candidate as the architect of this book, which features prominently the conversion of Alma's father during the trial of Abinadi. Finally, four centuries later, (10) Mormon found the book of Mosiah on the large plates of Nephi, which he abridged, perhaps supplementing the book with additional sources that he had at his disposal. The textual history of most cases is not as complicated as this one, but in order to reach sound legal conclusions, each report of any legal proceeding in the Book of Mormon must be approached astutely, considering to the extent possible how and why the record was shaped as it was.

Overarching the textual history of the Book of Mormon are Mormon's purposes in compiling and editing the final form of the book. Certain objectives guided his abridgment and thus add another layer of selection through which modern analysts must filter the underlying data that he included. Mormon's abridgment was not done for legal purposes. He and his son Moroni abridged and wrote the Book of Mormon for the three stated purposes of (1) showing the great things the Lord had done for the house of Israel (2) teaching people the covenants of the Lord and (3) convincing all peoples that Jesus is the Christ (Book of Mormon title page). Thus readers should assume that Mormon included these legal accounts because he saw them, in some fashion, as promoting one of these purposes, not because they were primarily of some detached historical or legal interest. Indeed, Mormon may not have understood (or cared about) the legal rules or conventions used five hundred years earlier by the righteous judge Alma in the city of Zarahemla (Alma 1), let alone the policies or legal strategies employed by the wicked priests in the courts of Noah (Mosiah 11) or the overreaching lawyers of Ammonihah (Alma 11–14). The law of Moses, under which those courts putatively, to some extent, operated, had been abrogated by the words of Jesus Christ at the temple in Bountiful when he explained, "I am he that gave the law, and I am he who covenanted with my people Israel; therefore, the law in me is fulfilled, for I have come to fulfil the law; therefore it hath an end" (3 Nephi 15:5). Thus "they did not walk any more after the performances and ordinances of the law of Moses" (4 Nephi 1:12). Accordingly, Mormon would have little motivation to dwell in any detail on the particulars of the law in his telling of or inclusion of the Nephite legal cases.

One should not assume, however, that just because Mormon did not give extensive information about a subject, the subject was not important to the earlier Nephites or uninteresting to Mormon as historian. The Book of Mormon as it now exists is not an all-encompassing record. Other important records existed in Nephite times, but space limitations on the plates and the particular purposes for his prophetic abridgment led Mormon to include certain things and to exclude others. In leaving out many details, including those touching on the law of Moses and the legal practices of the Nephites, Mormon and his son Moroni may simply have assumed that their modern readers would have the Old Testament and other records of the Jews (Mormon 7:8; Ether 1:3) from which to draw background information, including legal principles and their implications and correspondences.

More problematic for this investigation than Mormon's influence as an abridger is the fact that the Book of Mormon exists only in English and its subsequent translation into other modern languages. This is not the case with the Bible. But just as biblical scholars wrestle endlessly over the technical meanings of many cryptic words and legal phrases in Hebrew and other ancient languages, no translator, including Joseph Smith, could be expected to represent completely in English many important legal nuances exactly as they were understood in Nephite culture. Thus modern readers are handicapped by not having access to the paleo- or proto-Hebrew language of Jacob in early Nephite days,[68] the reformed Egyptian script used in Nephite archives,[69] the dialect spoken by Alma in the days when Nephite civilization had merged with the Mulekites, or the final vernacular spoken by Mormon, which again had undergone changes from earlier centuries (Mormon 9:13).[70]

While this language barrier does not pose significant problems to readers in sections of the Book of Mormon text that deal with common human experiences, technical vocabulary becomes a matter of great concern in conducting specific legal analysis. Fortunately for purposes of textual analysis and argumentation, recent examinations of the original manuscript of the Book of Mormon have yielded evidence that Joseph

---

68. For informative discussions of Israelite language at the time of Lehi, see Dana M. Pike, "Israelite Inscriptions from the Time of Jeremiah and Lehi"; and William James Adams Jr., "Nephi's Written Language and the Standard Biblical Hebrew of 600 B.C.," in Welch, Seely, and Seely, *Glimpses of Lehi's Jerusalem*, 193–244 and 245–58.

69. See the various insights of John S. Thompson, "Lehi and Egypt," of John Gee, "Egyptian Society during the Twenty-Sixth Dynasty," and of Aaron P. Schade, "The Kingdom of Judah: Politics, Prophets, and Scribes in the Late Preexilic Period," in Welch, Seely, and Seely, *Glimpses of Lehi's Jerusalem*, 267, 282–83, and 318, with accompanying notes.

70. For a philological and comparative discussion of stylistic evidences of this change, see Adams, "Nephi's Written Language," 245–58.

Smith's dictation came forth "word for word and even letter for letter."[71] As I have discussed elsewhere, "several factors indicate that [Joseph's process brought forth] quite a precise translation," although not slavishly literalistic; several textual details "strongly suggest that the meaning of something on the plates gave rise to each element of meaning in the translation."[72] Fortunately, in this process the translation drew upon the English vocabulary of the King James Bible, which is typically quite closely aligned with the underlying ancient Hebrew and Greek vocabularies, although several Elizabethan expressions were more commonly used and understood in Joseph Smith's day than they are today.[73] For this reason I have used the King James Version in the discussions below unless that translation is legally imprecise, in which cases I offer my own translations.

This utilization of recognizable King James phraseology allows modern readers of the Book of Mormon to hypothesize that when English words are used in comparable settings in both the Book of Mormon and the King James Old Testament, those translated words probably derive from a common Hebrew word or idiom. This hypothesis is especially plausible in legal settings, for legal language tends to be very conservative and slow to change in most cultures. Over the centuries in the ancient Near East, for example, certain terms have remained constant in legal usage; and over the centuries in Jewish law, key words have persisted without great modification. As Nephite history moves further away from its roots in Jerusalem, of course, one must allow some latitude for the development of independent Nephite legal terminology, vocabulary, and meanings. But in most cases—as I believe the following case studies will bear out—when the Book of Mormon uses such terms as *blasphemy* or *robbery*, we may learn much about their meanings in that context by studying their biblical Hebrew counterparts, even though verbal nuances are never identical from one context to the next.

A Word of Caution about Things We Do Not Know

In spite of our best efforts, many things in the study of ancient law will always remain beyond our reach. While Nephite law was largely

---

71. Royal Skousen, "History of the Critical Text Project," in *Uncovering the Original Text of the Book of Mormon*, ed. M. Gerald Bradford and Alison V. P. Coutts (Provo, UT: FARMS, 2002), 18.

72. See the chapter on Joseph Smith and the translation of the Sermon at the Temple, in John W. Welch, *Illuminating the Sermon at the Temple and Sermon on the Mount*, 2nd ed. (Provo, UT: FARMS, 1999), 179–98, quotations on pp. 189 and 190.

73. Royal Skousen, "Towards a Critical Edition of the Book of Mormon" (FARMS paper, 1990); see generally Skousen, "Translating the Book of Mormon: Evidence from the Original Manuscript," in *Book of Mormon Authorship Revisited: The Evidence for Ancient Origins*, ed. Noel B. Reynolds (Provo, UT: FARMS, 1997), 61–93.

autonomous and independent, since the Nephites rejected the wickedness of the people in Jerusalem, one should not assume that they rejected everything they left behind. But how much they drew on their northern Israelite backgrounds, as members of the tribes of Manasseh and Ephraim, is unknown.

While knowing more about the rules, words, and concepts of biblical law proves helpful in understanding the Book of Mormon, the meaning of Hebrew legal terminology is not always apparent. When the law prohibits "murder" or "bearing false witness," exactly what was meant? When the biblical text speaks of situations in which "mischief [would] follow" (Exodus 21:23) or gives prohibitions not to "seethe a kid in [its] mother's milk" (23:19), exactly what did the ancient lawgivers have in mind? Definitive meanings are often lost in the distant past.

Modern readers must be especially sensitive to legal euphemisms. For example, phrases such as "contend with," "come near to," or "be in the way with" may or may not signify the commencement of a legal action. In addition, the meanings of words may have changed from one era to another. The terms *robber* and *lawyer*, for instance, have definite meanings in modern society, but they presumptively meant something quite different in the ancient world in which robbers had no guns and lawyers were not advocates for individual clients.

Moreover, biblical law rarely explains who is to carry out these rules and what punishments should apply. Sometimes the text, as is the case in Exodus 22:1–4 dealing with theft, states what the punishment should be, but how should we understand, in a legal sense, the prohibition "Thou shalt not covet" when no penalty is mentioned? It is often difficult to tell what really happened in ancient legal proceedings, and it is frequently impossible to know how rules were actually enforced. No original judicial records have survived from ancient Israel.[74]

How are modern readers to understand ancient legal formulas such as "thou shalt not . . ." or "if a man . . ."? Were these rules promulgated as ideals binding on all people, as covenant obligations applicable only to people who voluntarily assumed these responsibilities, as binding instructions to judges, or as guiding principles for judges to apply in their discretion? Are they describing individual outcomes of specific cases intended to serve as precedents in future cases? Or do they reflect individual out-

74. Jackson, *Wisdom-Laws*, 52; Jackson, "Ideas of Law and Legal Administration: A Semiotic Approach," in *The World of Ancient Israel: Sociological, Anthropological and Political Perspectives*, ed. R. E. Clements (Cambridge: Cambridge University Press, 1989), 185; and Robert R. Wilson, "Israel's Judicial System in the Preexilic Period," 230.

comes of prior experience that are interesting for judges or elders but not compelling in the sense of modern legal precedent? Raymond Westbrook and others have promoted a legal model, seeing biblical laws essentially in the positivist legal tradition, in which these laws are to be seen as laying down rules to be followed by judges in resolving legal disputes.[75] Bernard Jackson argues that biblical laws should be understood as narrations of wisdom values aimed at teaching people to avoid judicial controversies by drawing on divine mediation at the outset.[76] Each of these views may be, in some important sense, correct. Regardless of how these legal statements originated, all of them came to be used in ancient times to meet a variety of needs that inevitably arose in many contexts over greater ranges of application.

In light of these difficulties, I have found it best to proceed by placing the Book of Mormon and the Bible on an equal footing. Each may shed needed light on the other. While biblical texts often illuminate the sense of a passage in the Book of Mormon, the Book of Mormon may also be vital in bringing the essence of the law of Moses to life.

Where Might This Study Lead?

Finally, I hope that studying the principles of biblical law and the legal cases in the Book of Mormon will serve many constructive purposes for several kinds of people.

For readers who may not know very much about the Book of Mormon, these case studies can provide a portal of entry. Reading the Book of Mormon for the first time can be somewhat intimidating, even (as it was put by one prominent Old Testament scholar on an SBL panel) "bamboozling." It is a complicated book in many respects, with names, wars, prophets, dates, and records that are otherwise unfamiliar. But with a bit of explanation, this book becomes personally engaging. After discussing chiastic structures in the Book of Mormon with me and then reading Alma 36 with its impressive literary composition in mind, David Noel Freedman turned to me and thoughtfully said, "Mormons are very lucky. Their book is very beautiful." Similarly, understanding the legal substructure of Nephite society can help modern readers to grasp and appreciate many of the basic societal concerns and worldviews propounded and promoted by the Book of Mormon.

---

75. For instance, Raymond Westbrook, "Cuneiform Law Codes and the Origins of Legislation," *Zeitschrift für Assyriologie* 79 (1989): 202; and his "Biblical and Cuneiform Law Codes," *Revue Biblique* 92 (1985): 256.

76. Jackson, *Wisdom-Laws*, vii, 23–36.

For readers who may have read the Book of Mormon many times, a new look at the Book of Mormon through the lens of the law illuminates the significance of numerous details that might otherwise have appeared irrelevant or tangential or might have gone unnoticed altogether. By striving to think more like an ancient Israelite or a Nephite, readers of the Bible and Book of Mormon can see consequences, implications, problems, values, mores, and norms implicit in the religious and doctrinal teachings of these scriptures. For example, appreciating the legal connotations that words such as *covenant, property, witness,* or *redeem* would have communicated in ancient times sheds light on metaphors used by writers in the Bible and Book of Mormon in communicating important theological messages. God meets people on their own terms. Latter-day Saints believe that he spoke to the Nephites in their own language and culture, as he does to all peoples (2 Nephi 29:11–12; Doctrine and Covenants 1:24).

For all readers, another payload comes in the form of literary criticism. Examining legal themes helps in the analysis of literary genres and compositional organization of the Book of Mormon. A good example of this comes from the book of Alma, which abruptly and stunningly begins with the trial of Nehor (discussed in chapter 7 below). By giving such attention to the trial and execution of this popular challenger to the Nephite order, the authors and abridgers of the book of Alma send a conspicuous signal that the overriding leitmotif of the book of Alma will be the Nephite struggle against dissenters and opponents during the initial years of the reign of judges. Throughout the book of Alma, one encounters the repeated legal attempts of the Nephites to deal with the dissensions of Nehor and the Nehorites, the Ammoniahites (chapter 8 below), the Zoramites, Korihor (chapter 9 below), the Amalickiahites, and others. In a similar fashion, the book of Helaman, right after the book of Alma, begins with the rebellion of Paanchi (chapter 11 below), ushering in the next era in Nephite history, a period characterized by social banditry, the Gadianton robbers, violence, insurrection, and political instability in the land and capital city of Zarahemla.

For those who are interested in the historical origins of the Book of Mormon, the study of its legal materials can help to assess and, I believe, to affirm the historical core of the records that stand behind Mormon's abridgment and the English translation of the Book of Mormon, which was published in upstate New York in 1830. The Nephites' extensive use of biblical law is consistent with the claim, made at the outset by the Book of Mormon itself, that Lehi and his people left Jerusalem around 600 BC. In large principles and small details, their legal system is technically accurate, legally plausible, and consistent with that point of departure. Even though Joseph Smith had at his disposal biblical texts from the King James translation, perceptively using those legal materials presumes a level of comprehension and familiarity with biblical law that exceeded the articulated knowledge of biblical scholars in the nineteenth century, let alone the comprehension of the young Joseph Smith. Most ancient Near Eastern legal materials were unknown or unavailable to him, for the Laws of Hammurabi, the Hittite Laws, the Middle Assyrian Laws, and so on were first discovered by archaeologists in the twentieth century, and most of Jewish law materials were not translated and published in English until the end of the nineteenth century or later. And yet, whoever wrote the Book of Mormon appears to have been intimately familiar with the workings of ancient Israelite law as well as with the Nephite legal system that putatively derived from it.

Personally, my effort to bridge the gap between the ancient world and our day is impelled by a belief that Lehi, Nephi, Benjamin, and Alma were real people who lived in a real world. This conviction is strengthened when their words and experiences fit understandably into an ancient legal setting.

Admittedly, the study of law in the Book of Mormon remains explorative. Much remains to be examined. Still, I hope that the conclusions advanced in this book are cogent and that this approach will inspire people to think more about what it means to judge righteously. In the Bible and Book of Mormon, readers find strong examples of successes and failures of righteous judgment by judges, rulers, litigants, and ordinary people. By pondering the legal cases in these scriptures, people can grasp contours of righteous judgment in principle as well as in practice.

CHAPTER THREE

THE IDEAL OF RIGHTEOUS JUDGMENT

Every legal system, so it would seem, is founded on a set of theoretical ideals or ultimate values that are recognized by its culture as essentially constituting its concept of justice. Sometimes such ideals are articulated very succinctly in a prologue or preamble, as in the prologue to the Laws of Hammurabi or the Preamble to the Constitution of the United States. Other times these judicial values are embedded more symbolically in the founding epics of the civilization, as is the case with the crystallization and inculcation of civic ideals in Homer's *Iliad*, in Virgil's *Aeneid*, in the Vedic literature, or in Germanic, Celtic, or Norse sagas. Most civilizations that become self-reflective eventually produce philosophical expositions about the meaning of justice, as we find in ancient Greece in Plato's *Republic* and Aristotle's *Ethics* and *Politics*, in China with Confucius, in medieval Catholicism with Thomas Aquinas, or in Reformation Protestantism with Thomas Hobbes. Occasionally a society sets forth in a founding document its vision of what it means to do justice, as we find in the English Magna Carta or the American Bill of Rights.

Among the laws issued on Mount Sinai and recorded in Exodus 19–23 is a passage that may appropriately be called "Jehovah's Code of Civil Justice."[1] It embodies *in nuce* the ideal qualities of justice as far as biblical law traditions are concerned, and in it are found the fundamental values that inspired and guided the administration of justice in ancient Israel. Similar to how lawyers in the United States are held accountable to the standards of professional conduct established by the Code of Professional Responsibility and adopted by the judiciary and bar associations of the various states, in ancient Israel all judges and litigants were similarly expected to conduct themselves in accordance with high ethical principles—namely, those distinctively set forth in the latter part of

---

1. John W. Welch, "Jehovah's Code of Civil Justice," *Clark Memorandum* (Spring 2005): 12–20.

the Covenant Code of Exodus 21–23. These verses in Exodus 22:18–23:19 may well contain the earliest code of professional responsibility in the history of the world. Not only do these standards tell us the rules of ethics and judicial conduct that governed Israelite legal cases, they also establish the foundational rules that would have operated in the judicial system of the Nephites as well. The legal narratives and ethical teachings of the Book of Mormon confirm that this set of ideals and judicial values in fact defined the essence of what it would have meant in Nephite legal minds to judge righteously, and thus this set of judicial ideals provides a fundamental theoretical background for understanding the legal cases in the Book of Mormon.

Beyond the Ten: Three More Sets of Apodictic Commandments

Familiar to all readers of the Bible is the issuance of the list of ten "thou shalt not" commandments in Exodus 20, commonly known as the Ten Commandments. Following this decalogue in Exodus 20 is found a body of "if a man" rulings, known as the Covenant Code, in Exodus 21–22. The Covenant Code then culminates in a further series of "thou shalt not" provisions dealing with religion and society in general and with the legal system in particular. In the midst of these apodictic provisions, one Old Testament scholar, J. W. McKay, counts ten judicial commandments in Exodus 23:1–3 and 6–8 and has called those ten a "decalogue for the administration of justice in the city gate."[2] These rules applied to all judges and officials in Israel, but also to any plaintiffs and witnesses involved in legal disputes. Nowhere else in scripture or in ancient law codes can one find a comparable cluster of judicial mandates stated so succinctly.

Furthermore, other biblical scholars are convinced that behind or alongside this series of ten judicial guidelines in Exodus 23 there once stood in ancient Israel actual formalized sets of instructions that were given to, or were expected of, all who participated in the legal process.[3] Frank Crüsemann has stated that "like no other texts, the instructions regarding behavior in a trial, which we find in [Exodus 23:1–2, 7–8], give us a picture of legal procedure during the monarchic period" in pre-exilic Israel.[4] By easy extension, one may also see these commandments as

---

2. J. W. McKay, "Exodus XXIII 1–3, 6–8: A Decalogue for the Administration of Justice in the City Gate," *Vetus Testamentum* 21, no. 3 (1971): 311–25.

3. See the contributions of S. R. Driver, Roland de Vaux, and others, discussed in McKay, "Exodus XXIII 1–3, 6–8," 322–25.

4. Frank Crüsemann, *The Torah: Theology and Social History of Old Testament Law* (Minneapolis: Fortress, 1996), 189.

constituting the theoretical ideal of what it meant to do justice in Lehi's Jerusalem and among his righteous descendants.

Less noticed even by regular readers of the Bible is the fact that if one begins counting at Exodus 22:18, the Covenant Code actually ends with an even longer series of twenty-five "thou shalt not" prohibitions, appearing in Exodus 22:18–23:19. As a distinct stylistic cluster, these twenty-five requirements can be broken into three sets of apodictic commandments. The rules in the first set of ten (Set A) deal with the creation of a just society. These commandments are addressed to all people of the covenant and set forth legal conditions that define the conditions of social justice that should prevail among the people at large. The second set (Set B) is basically McKay's ten, dealing with the operation of a just legal system. These prohibitions are directed more specifically toward those involved in the judicial process. A final group of five (Set C) ends in Exodus 23:19. These five pertain to religious duties, shifting attention to the articulation of obligations toward God. All together, these twenty-five "thou shalt not" injunctions can be seen as setting forth responsibilities toward one's neighbor, one's government, and God.

These twenty-five rules set forth in Exodus 22–23 are briefly explained as follows:

Set A: Ten Commandments for Righteousness at Large
   Thou shalt not allow a witch to live (22:18)
   Thou shalt not vex or mistreat a resident alien (22:21)
   Thou shalt not oppress a resident alien (22:21)
   Thou shalt not afflict or take advantage of a widow or orphan (22:22)
   Thou shalt not loan money (silver) to the needy (22:25)
   Thou shalt not charge interest to the needy (22:25)
   Thou shalt not revile or blaspheme God (22:28)
   Thou shalt not curse a ruler over the people (22:28)
   Thou shalt not delay to offer the first of thy ripe fruits (22:29)
   Thou shalt not eat of torn flesh in the field (22:31)

Set A is aimed at the general population. These commandments strive to regulate and direct general citizens in their civic dealings with each other. The so-called motive clause, "ye shall be holy men unto me" (Exodus 22:31), which stands at the conclusion of these provisions and explains their overriding purpose, points the general community to the ultimate purpose and benefit of keeping these commandments. In this ideal, a just society is grounded in the conduct of the general populace.

Set B: Ten Commandments of Jehovah's Code of Legal Justice
    Thou shalt not bring up a false rumor or report (23:1)
    Thou shalt not be in cahoots with a wicked person as a false wit-
        ness (23:1)
    Thou shalt not follow the crowd with intent to do evil (23:2)
    Thou shalt not speak against the majority with intent to pervert
        justice (23:2)
    Thou shalt not be partial toward the poor in a lawsuit (23:3)
    Thou shalt not deny justice to the poor in a lawsuit (23:6)
    Thou shalt stay away from lies (23:7)[5]
    Thou shalt not execute the innocent or righteous (23:7)
    Thou shalt not take a bribe (23:8)
    Thou shalt not oppress a resident alien (23:9)

Set B is concertedly aimed at those involved in the administration of justice, although in principle these ethical mandates can also be applied to all human conduct. All people involved in the legal process, especially those who act as judges, are to be honest, independent, impartial, careful, and compassionate. In particular, under this theoretical model of justice, those who officiate or function within the legal system must be beyond any reproach of spreading hearsay, colluding with the guilty, caving into group pressure, obstructing justice, favoring the rich, telling lies, killing the innocent, accepting bribes, or abusing their power over the vulnerable.

Set C: Five Provisions for Ritual Obligations
    Thou shalt not invoke the name of other gods (23:13)
    Thou shalt not speak the name of other gods (23:13)
    Thou shalt not offer blood sacrifice together with leavened bread
        (23:18)
    Thou shalt not leave the fat of my sacrifice until morning (23:18)
    Thou shalt not seethe a kid in its mother's milk (23:19)

The focus of Exodus 23:10–19 is on the observance of religious obligations to God, specifically observing the Sabbath and other holy days and offering sacrifice of the firstfruits. This section includes five final "thou shalt not" provisions. It is prohibited to speak in the name of any other gods, and sacrifices may not be offered in an improper or unseemly

---

5. In this one case, the command is stated in the form of a positive command. McKay and others believe that it may have originally been expressed as a command not to listen to or utter lies (McKay, "Exodus XXIII 1–3, 6–8," 317–18). In Exodus 20, two of the ten are also formulated as positive commands, "Remember the sabbath day" and "honour thy father and thy mother."

fashion. According to this view, justice is a divine virtue that cannot become a reality without the support of God, whose presence and guidance in the judicial process is made possible only by the worthiness and purity of the hearts and minds of those who strive to do justice and have "clean hands and a pure heart" (Psalm 24:4).

From this overall arrangement it is clear that, from the biblical perspective, the actualization of justice requires social, legal, and religious confluence. Without a sense of social justice among the populace at large, legal enforcement will never bring about a just society. Without a judicial system that functions with impeccable integrity, written norms will never be effective. And without reverence to God, people will not be deeply committed and motivated to judge as God does.

Perceptively, Thomas Leclerc has found a similar threefold configuration in the construction of the book of Isaiah that confirms the depth of this conception of justice throughout the law and the prophets in ancient Israel. Leclerc has argued that, first, the concept of justice in Isaiah 1–39 is grounded in social settings, such as defending the weak, the widows and orphans, resident aliens, and the poor; second, in Isaiah 40–55 justice is centered in the procedural administration of justice; and third, in Isaiah 56–66 the idea of law and justice is associated with God and covenant obligations.[6]

Thus, in biblical law traditions, justice happens when these twenty-five commandments are followed. Injustice happens when they are not. This is true of the legal narratives and prophetic exhortations in the Bible; the same is true of the legal cases and ethical teachings in the Book of Mormon, as the following discussion of each of these twenty-five principles demonstrates.

Righteousness at Large: Creating a Just Society

A1. Thou shalt not allow a witch to live (22:18). Perhaps curious to modern readers, the Bible's code of justice begins with the injunction "Thou shalt not allow a witch to live." At the foundation of any ancient legal system was the assumption that justice could be achieved in court only if the god's or some divine influence was directly present in the proceeding. This assumption operated not only in the ancient Near Eastern laws generally[7] but specifically in the Bible and also in the Book of Mormon.

---

6. Thomas L. Leclerc, *Yahweh Is Exalted in Justice: Solidarity and Conflict in Isaiah* (Minneapolis: Fortress, 2001).

7. Raymond Westbrook, "Witchcraft and the Law in the Ancient Near East," in *Recht gestern und heute*, ed. Joachim Hengstl and Ulrich Sick (Wiesbaden: Harrassowitz, 2006), 45–52.

Just and righteous people are to stay away from sorcery or divination precisely because, first and foremost, God and not some oracle or astrologer is to be the source of true guidance and revelation.[8]

For example, the divine will was consulted in the case of the blasphemer in Leviticus 24 and in the detection of Achan in Joshua 7. Properly consulting the will of the true God was essential, but any other form of augury, divination, oracular consultation, or conjuring up spirits would fundamentally deny the sole jurisdiction of the true God over the case and would render it impossible for his spirit to produce a just result. Accordingly, allowing a witch to live would effectively deny God's jurisdiction over the justice system.

The Book of Mormon is fundamentally in accord with this basic premise. Beyond the examples of divine manifestations during the cases of Sherem, Abinadi, and Korihor (discussed in chapters 5, 6, and 8 below), the hand of God was essential in detecting the criminality of Seantum (see chapter 12 below). The Book of Mormon also strongly denounces priestcraft, which is another form of false priesthood or lack of loyalty to the true source of justice. It was due to priestcrafts that the trial of Jesus could result in the death of a God (2 Nephi 10:5); and for this reason the prophet Nephi issued a commandment that "there shall be no priestcrafts" (26:29), but rather that "all men are privileged the one like unto the other, and none are forbidden" (v. 28), in order that equal justice and welfare in Zion could be established. Because the inauguration of priestcraft threatened the fledgling reign of the judges so deeply, Alma was all the more justified in taking drastic action against Nehor in an albeit unsuccessful effort to prevent "the spreading of priestcraft through the land" (Alma 1:16), which indeed threatened the very establishment of this new system of justice among the Nephites. At the end of Nephite history, of course, the justice system collapsed. Not only did Gadianton robbers "infest the land, insomuch that the inhabitants thereof began to hide up their treasures in the earth" (Mormon 1:18), but also it soon "came to pass that there were sorceries, and witchcrafts, and magics; and the power of the evil one was wrought upon all the face of the land" (v. 19). With the loss of individual security and the lack of protection of property, the total fabric

---

Westbrook concludes: "Amateur, opportunistic acts of sorcery tended to be treated as a serious crime analogous to homicide or adultery, which gave the right of revenge or ransom to the victim, while creating some pollution which might have public repercussions. The work of professional sorcerers, typically women, was a source of public concern and could lead to repressive measures analogous to the treatment of polluting crimes like incest and bestiality" (p. 51).

8. Moshe Weinfeld, *Social Justice in Ancient Israel and in the Ancient Near East* (Jerusalem: Magnes, 1995), 20–23, 179–214.

of Nephite civilization came unraveled, so that "no man could keep that which was his own" (2:10). This situation was apparently due not only to crimes against persons and property but also to the people's tolerance for "the magic art and the witchcraft which was in the land" (v. 10). While the presence of thieves, robbers, and murderers indicates the deterioration of the social order, the presence of priestcraft, witches, and magic gives even deeper evidence of the corruption of the judicial order away from the correct spirit of God and of true, righteous justice.

A2 and A3. Thou shalt not vex or mistreat a resident alien (22:21). Thou shalt not oppress a resident alien (22:21). The ideal biblical code of justice is also concerned with the fair treatment of strangers, or resident aliens, people from other lands or nations living within the local boundaries. Biblical law emphasized this social value because the Israelites themselves were once "strangers in the land of Egypt" (Exodus 22:21); and for that reason followers of the law of Moses were frequently reminded that "ye know the heart of a stranger, seeing that ye were strangers in the land of Egypt" (23:9). To fail in sympathizing with strangers would, in effect, be tantamount to forgetting the deliverance of God in rescuing the Israelites from their condition as strangers in a foreign land. Sympathizing with the plight of these resident aliens did more than extend the niceties of civil courtesy. Judges operating under the judicial code of the Bible have need to extend justice to other people in order to retain the favors and blessings of their redeeming and saving God.[9]

For this same essential reason, the writers of the Book of Mormon were likewise sensitized to the demands of social justice that prohibited any mistreatment of strangers. Seeing themselves as "wanderers in a strange land" (Jacob 7:26; Alma 13:23; 26:36), the Nephites understood that treating all people hospitably was a necessary condition for being treated favorably by God themselves. For example, the Ten Commandments proscribed work on the Sabbath day by any member of the society, including the "stranger that is within thy gates" (Exodus 20:10). Abinadi quoted this text to the priests of Noah at a time when the members of that Nephite colony were aliens in the sense of being subjects to the Lamanite king even in their own ancestral lands (Mosiah 13:18). Several decades later, when the sons of Mosiah traveled to the land of Nephi, they were likewise considered strangers and suffered imprisonment and judicial mistreatment (see Alma 21:13), showing the vulnerability of foreigners in places where people were highly suspicious of outsiders. On yet another

---

9. See generally Christiana van Houten, *The Alien in Israelite Law* (Sheffield, England: Sheffield Academic Press, 1991).

occasion, in reminding his inhospitable audience in Ammonihah that they all were "wanderers in a strange land" (13:23), Alma hoped their injustice might be tempered by greater sensitivity to his own plight as an outsider among them.

Perhaps for this reason, in particular, the Nephites welcomed wholeheartedly, as fellow citizens, the foreigners who migrated into their land as converts of Ammon (Alma 26:36). Knowing of this judicial principle to treat strangers equitably that theoretically prevailed in the land of Zarahemla, Ammon confidently said to the king of the displaced Ammonites, "I will go and inquire of the Lord, and if he say unto us, go down unto our brethren, will ye go?" (27:7). When the king even offered that he and his people would become slaves in the land of the Nephites, Ammon assured him further with an additional provision of social justice among the Nephites that "it is against the law of our brethren, which was established by my father, that there should be any slaves among them; therefore let us go down and rely upon the mercies of our brethren" (v. 9). The outcome of the humble willingness of the Ammonites is well known: neither God's justice nor the Nephites' sense of fundamental fairness disappointed them in any way. The chief judge sent forth a proclamation treating the Ammonites as brethren and giving to them the land of Jershon "for an inheritance" (v. 22). In reciprocation, these people of Anti-Nephi-Lehi were themselves "perfectly honest and upright in all things" (v. 27), becoming models of justice and loyalty to God, as their expulsion of Korihor (30:19–21) and their obedience to their oath of nonviolence (56:6–8) demonstrate.

This principle of justice was reestablished and reinforced among the Nephites gathered at the temple in the land of Bountiful when the resurrected Lord gave them the concluding words of the prophet Malachi: "And I will come near to you to judgment; and I will be a swift witness against the sorcerers, and against the adulterers, and against false swearers, and against those that oppress the hireling in his wages, the widow and the fatherless, and that turn aside the stranger, and fear not me, saith the Lord of Hosts" (3 Nephi 24:5). This passage from Malachi actually confirms seven of the provisions in the biblical code of judicial justice in Exodus 23: God will come near to his people in the judicial process (a desirable thing); but in that setting he will not be tolerant of those who worship other gods or spirits, those who are secretively deceptive or untrustworthy (such as adulterers or perjurers), those who oppress the weak (including day workers, widows, and orphans), and, ultimately, those who "turn aside the stranger," for they also are children of the Lord of Hosts.

A4, A5, and A6. Thou shalt not afflict or take advantage of a widow or orphan (22:22). Thou shalt not loan money (silver) to the needy (22:25). Thou shalt not charge interest to the needy (22:25). People in a just society must avoid taking advantage of the weak, the poor, or the vulnerable (specifically mentioned are widows, orphans, the impoverished, and people from other lands).[10] The prohibitions against oppressing widows, orphans, children, the weak, the poor, or the needy are pervasively present in Nephite ethics and jurisprudence from beginning to end. For example, the words of the prophet Isaiah, well known to the early Nephites, sharply condemned those who were not generous and merciful to the widows and orphans. Because of their hypocrisy and evildoing, the Lord will reciprocate by having no "mercy on their fatherless and widows" (Isaiah 9:17; 2 Nephi 19:17). At the waters of Mormon, the righteous followers of Alma committed to "bear one another's burdens" (Mosiah 18:8). Meanwhile, back in the city of Nephi, faced with a problem because of the "great number of women, more than there was of men," King Limhi issued a royal edict "that every man should impart to the support of the widows and their children" (21:17). The importance of protecting such individuals as a basic purpose of civilization is reflected to the end in the Nephites' awareness of the deep suffering of "many widows and their daughters" who in the final hours of Nephite depravity suffered in the extreme, being "carried away and left to wander whithersoever they can for food; and many old women do faint by the way and die" (Moroni 9:16).

In the Book of Mormon, aversion to oppression is connected with the just conduct of government. Among the evils and iniquities of King Noah and his priests, who are prime examples in the Book of Mormon of the miscarriage of justice, was the fact that they "oppressed" people and held them "in bondage" (Mosiah 23:12). Further, in the sixty-first year of the reign of the judges, the Nephites lost half of their lands because of wickedness and abomination among their own people. In particular, the record tells us that, among other breaches of righteousness and justice, they oppressed the poor specifically by "withholding their food from the hungry, withholding their clothing from the naked, and smiting their humble brethren upon the cheek" (Helaman 4:12). Hitting poor people on the cheek may well be a euphemism for turning them aside from the judicial process, not granting them a hearing, or even accusing them wrongly of having transgressed the law, because elsewhere in the Book of Mormon

---

10. See generally Bruce V. Malchow, *Social Justice in the Hebrew Bible: What Is New and What Is Old* (Collegeville, MN: Liturgical Press, 1996); and Leon Epsztein, *Social Justice in the Ancient Near East and the People of the Bible*, trans. John Bowden (London: SCM, 1986).

we see people being smitten upon the cheek precisely in a judicial context of accusation and humiliation (Alma 14:15).

Extending generosity to the poor, for Book of Mormon prophets, meant more than simply allowing them access to the judicial system. Affirmative assistance to the poor was required by King Benjamin as a condition for being worthy to accept the generosity and support of God (Mosiah 4:16–21), and Amulek makes it clear that if a person turns away the needy and does not impart of his substance to them, God will be perfectly fair in ignoring that person's prayers, which avail nothing (Alma 34:28).

A7 and A8. Thou shalt not revile or blaspheme God (22:28). Thou shalt not curse a ruler over the people (22:28). Jehovah's code of judicial conduct also makes a strong point of prohibiting any reviling against God or his rulers. In order for a religiously based judicial system to operate, the people subject to the decisions of their leaders must hold their rulers in high esteem. Reviling leaders who represent God is tantamount to blasphemy against God himself, and hence these two problems are linked in Exodus 22:28.

The judicial sense of Book of Mormon writers accords with this sentiment precisely. Reviling and blasphemy go hand in hand, as they do in the case of Korihor: he not only reviled against the priests and teachers (Alma 30:31) but he went on to "revile even against God" (v. 29) and, a small step later, to "blaspheme" (v. 30). According to Nephi, the Israelites in the wilderness "did revile against Moses, and also against God" (1 Nephi 17:42). Amulek was accused of reviling against the laws in the land of Ammonihah (Alma 10:24), and Alma accused Zeezrom of plotting to "revile us and to cast us out" (12:4), referring to his plan to reject and expel Alma himself as high priest over the land of Zarahemla. The leaders in Zarahemla challenged the people, asking why they would suffer Nephi to "revile against us" (Helaman 8:5). In these and several other similar passages in the Book of Mormon, it is evident that reviling against leaders, against the truth, against the prophets, and especially against God was a terribly indicative symptom of injustice and corruption in society.

A9 and A10. Thou shalt not delay to offer the first of thy ripe fruits (22:29). Ye shall be holy men unto me: Thou shalt not eat of torn flesh in the field (22:31). The final two "thou shalt not" provisions of this set of public virtues are not directly evidenced in the Book of Mormon. Nevertheless, the Nephite record extols the virtue of having "holy men in the land" (Words of Mormon 1:17) and of being "just and holy men" (Alma 13:26).

If a moral or legal lesson may be drawn from the need for promptness, it can be pointed out that combating the problem of delay was of considerable ethical and religious concern to the Nephite leaders. Stern warnings against procrastinating "the day of [one's] repentance" were commonly issued (Alma 13:27; 34:33–35; Helaman 13:38). Being "quick to hearken unto the words of the Lord" was seen as a powerful virtue (Helaman 7:7; see Alma 5:28–29), while its opposite, being "quick to do iniquity" (Mosiah 13:29; Alma 46:8; Helaman 12:4), was a strong indicator of wickedness. Delay in making thank offerings to God or in obtaining forgiveness from God increased the likelihood that these essential oblations would be neglected, leaving people impure and unfit to stand individually and collectively as a holy people (Exodus 22:31) and as a justly righteous community.

Doing Judicial Justice

B1. Thou shalt not bring up a false rumor or report (23:1). Leading the list of prohibitions in Exodus 23 is "Thou shalt not raise a false report" (v. 1). Spreading rumors and misunderstandings is the first step in churning up false litigation and abusing the judicial system. Gossip and rumors almost always damage reputations and the standing of people in the community. Hearsay and talebearing are off-limits for all people, a fortiori those who work in the justice system (Leviticus 19:16). Lawyers are in a particularly strong position to have inside information and to have reason to accuse or disparage their opponents. People who spend all day trying to judge cases, advocate causes, or criticize opponents must exert special efforts to stop judging others in ordinary social settings. Especially because judges and lawyers are often influential and powerful people in the community, rumors or false reports started by them are likely to be given much higher credence than information coming from those without insider information. With this high degree of potency comes a high level of responsibility. Thus the biblical code of legal conduct requires its agents to be especially scrupulous in respecting confidences and in guarding against the dissemination of false information. The Hebrew speaks literally of "spreading" or "carrying" any false report: one should simply drop such matters. Particularly, one should not carry such things "up," that is, to the temple or to the city gates, where judgment takes place. The Septuagint Greek adds the connotation that one should not "accept" or "welcome" any such rumors either. The Hebrew *shemaᶜ* can refer to any hearing, report, rumor, news, evidence, or witness. Truth is to be promoted. To be avoided is anything that is *shavʾ*: false, empty, lying, vain, worthless, destructive, or deceitful.

The Book of Mormon peoples were certainly sensitive to the enormity of this problem. In one of the most suspense-filled judicial moments in

the Book of Mormon, when believers were waiting to see if the prophecy
of Samuel would be fulfilled by the sign of Christ's birth coming within
five years after the prophecy was given, the legal system itself was controlled by corrupt judges. Even though preliminary indications were given
that the scriptures were beginning to be fulfilled, people explained these
occurrences away and rationalized them so that most of the people remained "in their pride and wickedness" (Helaman 16:10). They went so
far as to set a day on which those who believed in the prophecies of Samuel "should be put to death except the sign should come to pass" (3 Nephi 1:9). It is conceivable that these people could have been legally put to
death on the grounds that they continued to believe in a prophet who had
been shown to be a false prophet. In other words, if the sign predicted by
Samuel did not come to pass, then he was clearly a false prophet who, accordingly, should be put to death (Deuteronomy 18:20). At the same time,
those who continued to believe in his words should receive that same reward, so to speak. But only an extreme court could go so far as to exact
such a toll, and so it is significant that the Book of Mormon establishes
the perversion and injustice that reigned in the hearts of these would-be
accusers at this time. Several elements preventing justice are mentioned.
The people made false assumptions and jumped to unjust conclusions,
and they went around spreading rumors and initiating arguments, dissension, and probably legal actions throughout the land: "And many more
things did the people imagine up in their hearts, which were foolish and
vain; and they were much disturbed, for Satan did stir them up to do iniquity continually; yea, he did go about spreading rumors and contentions
upon all the face of the land, that he might harden the hearts of the people
against that which was good" (Helaman 16:22). Having set the stage with a
dire judicial tone, the book of Helaman closes and the record glides seamlessly into the seriousness of the judicial threat hanging over the believers
at the beginning of 3 Nephi.

B2. Thou shalt not be a malicious witness to help a wicked man (23:1).
Righteous conduct is inimical to malicious prosecution. Suborned witnesses, revengeful plaintiffs, and compliant counsel who use the legal system to promote unjust causes wield power and manipulate the judicial
process wrongfully. The legal system is a tool. Like any other tool, it can
be used either to build up or to tear down. Those who sit in seats of power
must be careful at all times to use that power to promote just and right
causes. The Hebrew concept behind the word *maliciousness* in this context
involves greedy desire, ill will, exploitation of the socially helpless, or even

hatred. Fallacious and overreaching use of legal process is to be abhorred. Kindness must be cultivated.

Bearing false witness is also strongly condemned in the Book of Mormon, as one would expect. At the heart of any legal system stands the absolute dependence on people telling the truth. The book of Deuteronomy, especially, condemns the false witness and imposes on him the same punishment that would have befallen the victim if the false testimony had been accepted: "Then shall ye do unto him, as he had thought to have done unto his brother" (Deuteronomy 19:19). In addition to appearing in the Ten Commandments recited by the prophet Abinadi, the prohibition against perjury is strongly stated by Nephi, the son of Helaman, as he spoke to the people in the city of Zarahemla from his tower. Among the crimes that he alleges against the people are murdering, plundering, stealing, and bearing false witness against one's neighbor (Helaman 7:21).

B3. Thou shalt not follow the crowd with the intent to do evil (23:2). Judicial morals require individuals to stand up courageously for what is right, regardless of peer pressure or the prevailing consensus. The Hebrew word for "follow" here includes the connotations of submitting to or answering to those who would pervert justice. The pressures on judges and lawyers are no less potent today. The majority is often swayed by wicked desires. Anyone involved in defending or advocating justice must always guard against being intimidated by unjust influences.

Although the prohibition against following the crowd to do injustice is not specifically mentioned in the Book of Mormon, the force of social pressure is evident as a negative social quality on several occasions. For instance, the independent vote of Alma the Elder in favor of acquitting Abinadi in the Book of Mormon is a classic example of one who did not follow the crowd (Mosiah 17:2). A generation later, in the beginning of the book of Alma the Younger, when the people forgot their commitment to the word of God, Alma bore down against those popular pressures in "pure testimony against them" (Alma 4:19).

B4. Thou shalt not speak against the majority with intent to pervert justice (23:2). Interestingly, biblical justice requires people not only to oppose the majority when it is wrong, but also to be careful not to speak out *against* the majority with intent to obstruct justice. Minority views need to be heard, but special interests can become just as tyrannical as majority domination, especially if their advocates lack the intent of doing principled justice or wish to pervert, literally to "turn aside," the course of justice. Cooperation is crucial to civic-mindedness and collective well-being. The repeated, prominent concern in the Book of Mormon about the minority voices or "dissensions" (Mosiah 26:5; Alma 51:16; Helaman 3:3) of "dissenters" (Alma 31:8; 47:35–36; 51:15; 61:17; Helaman 4:4) who "dissented from" and left the main body of the community (Alma 43:13; 46:7; Helaman 5:35) reflects the attitude toward justice found in this biblical precept.

B5. Thou shalt not be partial (hidor) *toward the poor* (dal) *in a lawsuit (KJV: "Neither shalt thou countenance a poor man in his cause") (23:3).* It has always been the case since the beginning of civilization that the rich have had easier access to the law. In addition, judges and lawyers are inclined to favor the rich, for many reasons. The briefs of rich clients are usually better written than those of poor people. The rich may appear more credible. The effects of this bias must be overcome (see, for example, commandment B6). The focus of commandment B5, however, prohibits people also from bending over too far in the opposite direction. The main question in interpreting this provision is, What does the Hebrew word *hidor* ("partial") mean? This word may actually mean that one should not give "undue honor" to the poor, to the weak, or to anyone. In other words, the text prohibits partiality of any kind, whether to the rich or to the poor (Leviticus 19:15, "thou shalt not respect the person of the poor [*dal*], nor honor the person of the mighty [*gadhol*]"). The Septuagint Greek goes so far as prohibiting the judge from showing too much mercy to the poor or from being swayed by pity.

Impartiality was also an ideal of Nephite justice and jurisprudence. God himself, being no respecter of persons, has commanded men to avoid a long list of injustices, including malice and contention (2 Nephi 26:32), "for none of these iniquities come of the Lord; for he doeth that which is good among the children of men; . . . and he inviteth them all to come unto him and partake of his goodness; and he denieth none that come unto him, black and white, bond and free, male and female; and he remembereth the heathen; and all are alike unto God, both Jew and Gentile" (v. 33). Impartiality toward both the rich and the poor is also reflected in the Nephite sense of judicial justice at the beginning of the reign of judges, at which point the record states positively the prosperous circumstances in which the Nephites thrived when they did not turn away the poor and the needy but were "liberal to all, both old and young, both bond and free, both male and female, whether out of the church or in the church, having no respect to persons as to those who stood in need" (Alma 1:30). Accordingly, Alma and Amulek also "did impart the word of God without any respect of persons, continually" (16:14). Likewise, in his discussion about the justice of God that does not require infant baptism, Mormon argues that if God were to require the baptism of little children, he would be "a partial God, and also a changeable God and a respecter to persons; for how many little children have died without baptism!" (Moroni 8:12). Curiously, to a modern mind, it might appear that God is "partial" if he has one rule for children and another rule for adults, but to the ancient mind the argument did not seem to run that way. Instead, God is partial and a respecter of persons if he does *not* come to the defense of the weak and the helpless children, for the lack of such affirmative defense would disadvantage them, which would in turn benefit the strong and the advantaged.

B6. *Thou shalt not deny justice to the poor in a lawsuit (KJV: "Thou shalt not wrest the judgment of thy poor in his cause") (23:6).* In this commandment, readers must wrestle with the meaning of the word *deny* or *wrest.* The Hebrew words here are broad in meaning and application but suggest that if a poor person asserts a claim of right, the legal process should not make it difficult for that person to obtain the entitled benefit. The poor are granted several rights under biblical law: the right to glean in the fields of local farmers, the right to redeem sold property, the right to be given start-up capital upon release from servitude, and other such rights. If a poor person comes forward and claims these benefits, the law should not stand in the way. This commandment is related to the earlier commandment (A4) not to take advantage of a widow or orphan (Exodus 22:22).

Justice in the biblical tradition is indeed not blind. It makes a difference who the parties are. The weak need protection. Widows and orphans are especially vulnerable because they lack a husband or father who in biblical society would have advocated and defended their interests. Negotiating one's way through the legal system requires knowledge and experience. Widows and orphans in their loneliness are sometimes prone to making weak decisions; they may be in special need of counsel and advice. Just as a football game between a championship college team and a regular high school team would be inherently unfair, even though the football field is exactly the same size for both teams and even if the referees blow the whistle evenhandedly on both sides, the contest could in no way be thought of as a fair competition. Similarly, for the judicial code of the Bible, human law *should* be a respecter of persons, in the sense of looking out for proper interests. People are required to administer justice in a manner that is suitable to the parties. Indeed, if lawyers and judges do not fashion justice in a fitting way, God will apply a fitting reciprocal punishment: "Your wives shall be widows, and your children fatherless" (Exodus 22:24). In the book of Mosiah, King Benjamin similarly required his people to give to the poor and the needy who asked for sustenance;

and the reciprocal consequence of failing to give to the poor was that God would deny their petitions that they put up to him and cause their remitted sins to return (Mosiah 4:22, 26).

B7. *Thou shalt stay away from lies (23:7).* In the better-known Ten Commandments, one reads, "Thou shalt not bear false witness" (Exodus 20:16). Applied to broad society, this means "don't lie." But in a judicial context, this commandment requires judges and lawyers to avoid any form of deception, misrepresentation, misleading omission, and perjury. Biblical law was especially hard on perjury. Deuteronomy 19:19 requires the judges to impose on a perjurer the following penalty: "Then shall ye do unto him, as he had thought to have done unto his brother." In other words, in a capital case the penalty for perjury was death. Lying under oath was especially problematic in ancient Israel where God was a presence in the legal process. Plaintiffs and witnesses verified their claims and assertions in the name of God. Defendants certified their innocence by solemn oaths and vows pledged before God or in his sanctuaries. Both taking the name of God in vain and swearing a false oath by the name of God were forms of blasphemy. Thus the Hebrew law code requires the judge or participant to be "far away from, be distant from, to depart from, or to withdraw from" anything that approaches perjury. One should not get even close to this line.

Any form of lying is also strongly decried in the Book of Mormon, but especially in the context of lawsuits. Those who lied were punished (Alma 1:17). Korihor lied as a witness (30:44). Abinadi was accused of lying about King Noah (Mosiah 12:14). Amulek was accused of lying to people in Ammonihah (Alma 10:28). Indeed the devil is identified as "the father of all lies" (2 Nephi 2:18), making it all the more important for those involved in the judicial process to "keep thee far from a false matter" (Exodus 23:7).

B8. *Thou shalt not execute the innocent or righteous (23:7).* Biblical law requires a righteous legal system to take special precautions to prevent the miscarriage of justice. The innocent, literally "those who are free from liability," are explicitly entitled to protection. The judicial system must particularly see that those people are never executed. Those who break this commandment are themselves guilty of a serious infraction of the law, not just an excusable or unfortunate error (Deuteronomy 19:16–21).

Executing the innocent receives particular opprobrium and condemnation in the Book of Mormon. The trial of Abinadi, whose innocent blood was demanded by the wicked court of King Noah, epitomizes the miscarriage of justice in the Book of Mormon (Mosiah 17:10). For their gross injustice, Noah and his priests were burned to death in fulfillment of the curse placed upon them by the dying prophet Abinadi (vv. 14–18; 19:20; Alma 25:7–12).

B9. *Thou shalt not take a bribe (KJV "gift")(23:8)*. Next, the code of judicial conduct in the ancient Israelite law prohibited any judge from taking gifts or bribes that would blind the wise or pervert justice. Any kind of bribery or financial influence on judicial decision should be eschewed. Jewish law went so far as to prohibit any judge from accepting money from any party to a lawsuit, whether before, during, or after the lawsuit.[11] Even an expectation that a wealthy or influential person might sometime in the future give favors to a judge in return for a favorable verdict or judgment was eschewed under Jewish law. The biblical code prohibits even a "gift" or "donation" (*shachad*) of any kind to judges. Any such influence, according to the biblical command, will "twist, pervert, or overturn" the words of even an otherwise righteous man.

Therefore, when Zeezrom offered to give Amulek six onties of silver if he would only "deny the existence of a supreme being" (Alma 11:22; see chapter 8 below), it would be particularly obvious to any ancient jurist operating under the biblical code that even such a "gift" (Zeezrom uses the words "will I give thee") was indeed a bribe and not an acceptable form of inducement. Any use of money by gift or otherwise to influence or affect testimony or the resolution of the case against Alma would have been considered deeply offensive and unjust under this code of judicial conduct.

B10. *Thou shalt not oppress a resident alien (23:9)*. Returning to commandments A2 and A3 found near the top of Set A, Set B ends with the requirement that the legal system not be used to mistreat or take advantage of foreigners living in the land. This point, made applicable to the general population in Set A, is now directed also at those involved in the administration of justice, and for good reason. Oppression of foreigners is especially easy because of language barriers and a lack of familiarity with the local judicial and governmental systems. Biblical law makes this mistreatment of foreigners especially odious because the people of Israel themselves were foreigners who were oppressed in a distant land. The law requires all participants in the judicial process to empathize with these disadvantaged parties; and just as God was kind to Israel in liberating them from bondage, so it is becoming of all lawyers to emulate this divine characteristic in promoting fairness in the interest of resident aliens. In this vein, it is particularly commendable that King Benjamin extended

---

11. Discussed below, particularly in chapter 8.

full justice to "all the people who were in the land of Zarahemla" (Mosiah 1:18), even though there were cultural groups and some language differences among them (Omni 1:17).

Righteousness before God

C1, C2, C3, C4 and C5. Thou shalt not invoke the name of other gods (23:13). Thou shalt not speak the name of other gods (23:13). Thou shalt not offer blood sacrifice together with leavened bread (23:18). Thou shalt not leave the fat of my sacrifice until morning (23:18). Thou shalt not seethe a kid in its mother's milk (23:19). Finally, idolatry or any corruption of the proper form of worshipping God was prohibited, for reasons discussed under A7 above. The seriousness of performing unauthorized sacrifices is unmistakably represented in the case of Aaron's sons, Nadab and Abihu, who were devoured by fire (Leviticus 10:1–2). In the Book of Mormon, the archetype of judging unrighteously was King Noah, who for apparent reasons was characterized mainly as an idolater (Mosiah 11:6) and corrupter of the temple and its priestly order (vv. 10–11). In the end, King Noah also suffered death by fire (19:20).

Instructions to Judges to Follow These Ideals

Whatever their shortcomings, many of the ancient Israelites made conscious efforts to honor these rules of judicial conduct. As mentioned above, scholars strongly suspect that behind or alongside the series of judicial rules in Exodus 22–23 there once stood in ancient Israel specific sets of instructions that were given to or expected of those who participated in the legal process.[12] We see evidence to support this suspicion in several places. To begin with, judges in Israel were charged with the general duty of judging righteously, and these charges reflect the provisions of this judicial code of conduct.

For example, in 2 Chronicles 19:7 and 9, King Jehoshaphat installed judges and sent them to do justice. As he did so, he reportedly charged them to observe certain standards that bespeak his familiarity with the Covenant Code: shun "iniquity" (A1, A7, A10, C1–4), avoid "respect of persons" (B3–5), and refuse the "taking of gifts" or bribes (B9).

Further, several classic formulations of judicial ethics are found in Deuteronomy: "Judge righteously between every man and his brother, and the stranger that is with him [A2, B10]. Ye shall not respect persons in judgment [B3–5]; but ye shall hear the small as well as the great [B6]; ye shall not be afraid of [or be intimidated by] the face of man [B3]"

---

12. Discussed in McKay, "Exodus XXIII 1–3, 6–8," 322–25.

(Deuteronomy 1:16–17); "judge the people with just judgment. Thou shalt not wrest judgment [B4]; thou shalt not respect persons [B3, 5], neither take a gift [B9]" (16:18–19); "they shall justify the righteous, and condemn the wicked [B2, 8]" (25:1).

This ideal of righteous judgment was also projected onto God. People in pre-exilic Israel expected that God would "judge the people righteously" (Psalm 67:4). He was addressed as the "Lord of hosts, that judgest righteously, that triest the reins and the heart" (Jeremiah 11:20). And he promised exaltation only to those who walked accordingly: "He that walketh righteously, and speaketh uprightly; he that despiseth the gain of oppressions, that shaketh his hands from holding of bribes, that stoppeth his ears from hearing of blood, and shutteth his eyes from seeing evil, he shall dwell on high" (Isaiah 33:15–16).

Conversely, the violation of these rules of judicial conduct would call down the wrath of divine disapproval and justice. Amos condemned these particular abuses: "For I know your manifold transgressions and your mighty sins: they afflict the just, they take a bribe, and they turn aside the poor in the gate from their right" (Amos 5:12). The prophet Zechariah demanded, "Execute the judgment of truth and peace in your gates: and let none of you imagine evil in your hearts against his neighbor; and love no false oath: for all these are things that I hate, saith the Lord" (Zechariah 8:16–17). The violation of these ideals would bring upon the people the fearful judgment of God, and for this reason "the fear of the Lord" is listed in Psalm 19 as one of the six defining, operative components of Hebrew law, namely the Torah, the testimony, the statutes, the commandments, the fear, and the judgments of the Lord (Psalm 19:7–10).

When these expectations of appropriate judicial conduct are laid against the Book of Mormon, it is evident that the Nephite sense of societal and judicial justice corresponded very closely with the ideal profile of justice found in the biblical code of judicial responsibility articulated in Exodus 22–23. As devoted followers of the laws of Moses found on the plates of brass, Nephite jurists would have had every reason to perceive and administer justice in the light of the concepts set forth in the Covenant Code. The following chapters confirm that this was precisely the case. In every instance, Nephite judicial sensitivities align congruently with the requirements of the code of judicial conduct set forth in the law of Moses. Nephite prophets, judges, leaders, and the people at large understood and perpetuated this code of justice throughout their one-thousand-year history. Nephite judges were held accountable to judge righteously. During the Nephite reign of judges, the chief judge was obligated, first and foremost, "to judge righteously, and to keep the [social justice of] peace and the freedom of the people, and to grant unto them [ritual justice respecting] their sacred privileges to worship the Lord their God, yea, to support and maintain the cause of God all his days, and to [establish legal justice by] bring[ing] the wicked to justice according to their crime" (Alma 50:39). In theory, a number of lower judges reflecting the will of the people at large would judge the higher judges if the "higher judges do not judge righteous judgments" (Mosiah 29:29). Presumably, those cases of judicial misconduct would be judged according to the ideals embodied in this foundational cluster of 25 apodictic laws that supported the concept of social justice, legal process, judicial fairness, and righteous judgment in the biblical law tradition.

CHAPTER FOUR

Judicial Procedures in Biblical Times

It is one thing to talk of righteous judgment. It is another thing to put the rules of law and justice into practice. The code of civil justice found in Exodus 22–23 gives readers a good idea, in theory, of law and equity in ancient Israel. Reports of actual cases, however, can give careful readers an idea of how those ideals worked in real practice. Of course, in all legal systems, gaps will be found between the theory and the practice of justice. This disparity is visible in the legal cases reported in the Bible as well as in the Book of Mormon, some of which are presented as paragons of righteous judgment while others are examples of the miscarriage of justice.

Over a dozen legal proceedings are found in the books of the Old Testament. Some involve private complaints between family members, such as a grievance raised by a father-in-law against his son-in-law for theft and abduction. Others involve the execution of people who had committed blasphemy, had violated the Sabbath law, had hidden booty taken in battle instead of turning it over to the military commander for consecration to God, or had conspired against the king. Two cases deal with the inheritance rights of daughters in a case where their deceased father had no sons; another proceeding involves a complicated real estate transaction by one kinsman, extinguishing any interests that another kinsman might claim in the property. Cases showing how the legal system was readily vulnerable to abuse include two petitions of women before King Solomon, a trumped-up charge of cursing God and the king, several accusations against prophets claiming that they prophesied falsely, and one near stoning of a virtuous woman maliciously accused of adultery.

These cases have been studied by translators, historians, and legal scholars. Full texts of these cases appear below in appendix 1. These biblical cases feature a variety of judicial procedures, making it difficult, if not impossible, to generalize completely about what constituted a typical

Legal Proceedings in Biblical Times

Laban against Jacob . . . . Genesis 31:25–55

Trial of the Blasphemer . . . . Leviticus 24:10–23

Trial of the Sabbath Breaker . . . . Numbers 15:32–36

Inheritance of the Daughters of Zelophedad . . . . Numbers 27:1–11

Marriages of the Daughters of Zelophedad . . . . Numbers 36:1–13

Trial of Achan . . . . Joshua 7:1–26

Boaz at the town gate . . . . Ruth 4:1–12

Trial of Ahimelech . . . . 1 Samuel 22:6–23

Petition of the Woman of Tekoa . . . . 2 Samuel 14:4–11

Petition of the Two Harlots . . . . 1 Kings 3:16–28

Trial of Naboth . . . . 1 Kings 21:1–16

Trial of Micah the Morasthite . . . . Jeremiah 26:18–19; Micah 3:12

Trial of Urijah ben Shemaiah . . . . Jeremiah 26:20–23

Trial of Jeremiah . . . . Jeremiah 26:1–24

Trial of Susanna . . . . Daniel 13:1–64 (LXX)

judicial procedure in ancient Israel, let alone how Hebrew practices compared with legal procedures in surrounding cultures.

But this variety itself is significant. In analyzing judicial procedure in biblical times, one must recognize that several models of judicial conduct and practice prevailed in ancient Israel. No single set of rules of civil or criminal procedure regulated the administration of justice in that culture.

In much the same way, the Book of Mormon reports a variety of judicial procedures. In the Nephite record are found relatively detailed reports of seven legal actions that were commenced and brought to conclusion. The first involved three complaints raised by one person against the reigning high priest in the city of Nephi; subsequent cases involved charges of lying, false prophecy, blasphemy, reviling the king, slander, sedition, conspiracy, and homicide. Some were private actions; others were of public concern. Some were heard by a single judge, others by bodies of judges or priests. On various occasions, these cases involved the king, public officials, or the general populace.

These seven main legal cases in the Book of Mormon, as the chapters below demonstrate, can be compared successfully and informatively with the same types of legal cases reported in the Old Testament. The legal cases in the Book of Mormon compare favorably with judicial procedures in biblical times, both on individual points of law and in terms of their overall ranges of substantive issues, their approaches to ascertaining the law, the variety of personnel they involved, the forms of procedures they followed, and the judicial and societal results that occurred.

Before turning to the seven legal cases in the Book of Mormon, it will be helpful to survey in general the judicial procedures in ancient Israel. The Hebrew cases provide the best legal backdrop against which the Book of Mormon cases can be compared and understood.

Justice and Injustice

In the biblical cases, justice is sometimes done and sometimes not. The standard against which the success or failure of these actual cases can be judged, in the biblical mind, is always the set of high expectations for judicial conduct set forth in Exodus 23.

Injustice. The execution of Naboth (1 Kings 21:1–16) is the most salient example of the miscarriage of justice in the Old Testament. A convincing case can be made that the entire story of Ahab and Jezebel's scheming actions, which led to the wrongful execution of the innocent and unsuspecting owner of an attractive vineyard, is told in such a way as to let readers know that the king and his queen violated virtually every one of the apodictic commandments found in Exodus 23:1–3, 6–9.[1] Desiring to own Naboth's ancestral land near the king's palace and not being able to convince Naboth to accept a reasonable offer to sell or trade his land for another, more valuable property, King Ahab became despondent. His queen came up with a plan to get Naboth executed so that his property would escheat to the king. Her plan succeeded, but in so doing she broke every rule in the Israelite book of justice. She raised a false report, sending letters in the king's name that contained false accusations and that proclaimed a fast, apparently on some kind of false or odd pretense. She put her hand together with two wicked men who stood as false witnesses, and the crowd was swayed to do evil by the queen's influence. Naboth was given little or no opportunity to defend himself, and justice was wrested in favor of the high and the mighty. Compared to the king,

---

1. This argument has been successfully developed by Debra Peck in "The Trial of Naboth as a Violation of the Covenant Code" (2006), available in the Howard W. Hunter Law Library, J. Reuben Clark Law School, Brigham Young University.

Naboth was a poor, ordinary citizen who was wrongfully accused and disadvantaged. The witnesses against him lied, and no one stayed far from this false matter. In the end, an innocent man was executed. While the trial of Naboth raises several interesting legal issues regarding property law, sealed documents, royal authority, and offenses against the king, the dominant legal purpose of this narrative is to illustrate the abuse of judicial process. This outrageous case led Elijah to prophesy against Ahab that "in the place where dogs licked up the blood of Naboth shall dogs lick thy blood" (1 Kings 21:19), and the precise fulfillment of that curse (22:38) attested that divine justice eventually prevailed.

In a similar way, two of the legal cases in the Book of Mormon illustrate the evils and risks of injustice that result when the ideals of Exodus 23:1–3, 6–9 are not put into practice. For example, in the trial of Abinadi, a group of self-interested priests and a wicked king wrongfully execute a lone, righteous man of God; and in the case of Alma and Amulek, group pressure and bribery exemplify injustice. In both cases, divine justice was shown to prevail where human justice had failed.

Justice. At the same time, many righteous cases in the Hebrew Bible set the standard for proper conduct in administering justice. Seeking divine wisdom always undergirds righteous judgment, either implicitly or explicitly, as is displayed in the case of the blasphemer (Leviticus 24) and in the case of Achan (Joshua 7). Unforgettable examples of judging righteously are found in the unselfish legal action of Boaz in obtaining the right to marry Ruth the Moabitess and in protecting her inheritance of the property of her mother-in-law, Ruth's previous husband and Naomi's husband and sons all having died (Ruth 4); and in the courageous and innovative action of Daniel in separately cross-examining the witnesses against Susanna and exposing them in their perjury (Daniel 13 in the Greek Septuagint and Catholic Bible).

Likewise, in the Book of Mormon most of the legal cases are examples of successful righteous judgment. Divine factors are determinative in the cases of Sherem, Korihor, and Seantum. The unselfish sacrifice of Amulek in standing up as a second witness in defense of a falsely accused Alma (Alma 10, 14) and the courageous and innovative rulings handed down by the judge Alma in the case of Nehor (Alma 1) are powerful, formative instances of the proper conduct of justice in the biblical tradition as well.

Justice without Judges

Underlying the entire biblical tradition of justice is the assumption that having no court is often better than having any court at all. Initially, it was expected in the biblical system of justice that every man would simply do that which was right "in his own eyes" (Deuteronomy 12:8), which becomes a major theme of the book of Judges: "In those days there was no king in Israel: every man did that which was right in his own eyes" (Judges 17:6; 21:25). While there is an upside and a downside to the idea that doing justice is essentially the task of all individual members of society, and while governmental institutions assumed increasing responsibility for administering justice as Israelite civilization became more established and politically regulated, the principle of individual responsibility for creating a just society remained a strong feature of Israelite law and wisdom. One of the Proverbs requires individuals to rise above their own superficial personal prejudices and to do right instead in the depths of the heart: "Every way of a man is right in his own eyes: but the Lord pondereth the hearts. To do justice and judgment is more acceptable to the Lord than sacrifice" (Proverb 21:2–3; see 1 Samuel 16:7).

So interwoven are the private and public concepts of justice in the Bible that, as Moshe Weinfeld has said, "One cannot always determine whether a biblical passage which speaks of justice and righteousness applies to acts performed by the government (= monarchy) and its leaders, or whether the intention is of good deeds carried out by the individual."[2] The duty of doing justice oscillates between the obligations of the king and the tasks of the people. As the appointed task of the people (Isaiah 5:1–7; Jeremiah 7:5–6; Ezekiel 18:7–8), justice and righteousness should happen without the need for the judicial enforcement of morals.[3] The words of Jesus, that a person should settle legal disputes "quickly, whiles thou art in the way with him" (Matthew 5:25), reflects this long-standing biblical value that trespasses should be resolved "between thee and him alone" (18:15).

Thus legal disputes are often handled in the biblical world without involving judges. Pietro Bovati has denominated these legal cases as "juridical" to distinguish them from "judicial" actions, in which judges are involved. Juridical (or pre-judicial) crises were serious legal clashes that used recognizable verbal expressions and followed customary rules of accusation, defense, and peaceful resolution.

The confrontation between Laban and Jacob (Genesis 31) is one of the very best examples in the Hebrew Bible of such a legal controversy (*rîb*) between two parties who settled their dispute without the mediation of a

---

2. Moshe Weinfeld, *Social Justice in Ancient Israel and the Ancient Near East* (Jerusalem: Magnes, 1995), 215.

3. Weinfeld, *Social Justice in Ancient Israel*, 222–30.

judge or judges.[4] This account gives a detailed view of the informal and unstructured way in which many legal disputes would have been resolved in biblical society.

Laban's sons were upset and accused Jacob of taking too much of the family's property (Genesis 31:1). From Laban's countenance, Jacob could tell that he had fallen into disfavor and that Laban would side with his sons in this matter. Thus, after having labored for Laban for twenty years, Jacob took his two wives, children, flocks, and household goods and left in secret. Jacob's legal justification for this unilateral termination of his relationship with Laban and for his departure with household properties was that Laban had changed Jacob's wages ten times (v. 7). The angel of God confirmed Jacob's decision to him in a dream, recalling to Jacob a vow that he had made to God after setting up a pillar back home in Bethel and then telling him to return to the land of his kindred (v. 13).

Rachel and Leah agreed with Jacob's decision (vv. 14–16). They asserted an additional legal point, claiming that they had never received a dowry from Laban and lamenting that their father had "sold" them to Jacob and "hath quite devoured also our money." (It violated custom, but not law, for a father not to give his daughters a dowry.) When they left, Rachel secretly took Laban's household "gods" (figurines that Laban worshipped in the belief that they protected his house).

Laban learned of Jacob's departure three days later and pursued his son-in-law, overtaking him in seven days. The two men met to lodge and discuss their respective complaints against each other. In the tent where they worked out their differences, no judges or lawyers were present. The two men argued their cases personally, passionately, and honorably and reached a legal resolution and personal reconciliation.

Laban's legal and personal claims against Jacob were that Jacob had (a) departed in secret, (b) taken Laban's daughters like captives taken by a robber, (c) deprived Laban of the opportunity to send them off with ceremony and affection, and (d) stolen Laban's gods (vv. 26–30).

Jacob (a) counterclaimed that he had feared Laban would take his daughters back by force (v. 31), and he (b) offered to kill anyone who had the household gods. After searching, Laban did not find the gods, because Rachel was sitting on them (vv. 32–35). Feeling vindicated, Jacob (c) denied that he had wronged Laban in any way, (d) complained that Laban had wrongfully pursued him, (e) averred that Laban had been given open access to search among Jacob's camp and goods, (f) affirmed that he had served

---

4. Charles R. Mabee, "Jacob and Laban: The Structure of Judicial Proceedings (Genesis XXXI 25–42)," *Vetus Testamentum* 30, no. 2 (1980): 192–207.

Laban faithfully for twenty years, (g) pointed out that he had borne the loss of Laban's torn cattle and thus went beyond that which was legally required of ordinary herdsmen (compare Exodus 22:10–13), and (h) counterclaimed that Laban had unilaterally changed Jacob's wages often (Genesis 31:36–42).

Jacob and Laban settled their dispute and mutually restored their honors (v. 43). Laban's honor was restored when he was allowed to assert ownership of all of Jacob's wives, children, and property (v. 43) and when he obtained concessions that benefited his daughters and grandchildren (v. 50).

The two men then made a covenant to solemnize their settlement. The covenant was memorialized by a "pillar" (v. 45), a monument symbolizing that in the future the parties could call on heaven and earth to witness that the covenant had been made between Laban and Jacob. Each man named the stone separately: Laban called it "Jegarsahadutha" ("the heap of witness" in Aramaic); Jacob called it "Galeed" ("the heap of witness" in Hebrew). The parties promised that they would not cross over the monument to harm each other and that God was their witness and the enforcer of this agreement (vv. 51–53). Jacob agreed that if he were to mistreat Laban's daughters or if he were to take more wives, the agreement would be nullified (v. 50).

To consummate their resolution, Laban swore an oath by "the God of Abraham, and the God of Nahor," and Jacob swore an oath "by the fear of his father Isaac" (v. 53). Jacob offered a sacrifice and provided food for a covenantal meal, and he invited all to celebrate together the entire night. In the morning, Laban kissed and blessed his children and departed in peace (v. 55).

The way in which this controversy between Laban and Jacob was handled provides useful points of reference in analyzing many other instances of juridical clashes in the Bible or in other texts that reflect such disputes in biblical culture. An excellent example found in the Book of Mormon, discussed in detail in chapter 5, is the controversy raised by Sherem against Jacob, the son of Lehi. Although this confrontation does not end as happily for Sherem as it did for Jacob and Laban in the hill country of Canaan, the contention between Sherem and Jacob in the city of Nephi resembles the case in Genesis 31 in many fundamental ways. Most especially, no human judges were brought into this case that instead was handled by the two parties with God as the ultimate witness, judge, and enforcer.

Who Served as Judges?

In the biblical world, if attempts at private reconciliation proved unsuccessful, people could resort to adjudication. The cases show that many people qualified and served as judges. Sometimes single judges were involved, but at other times "more than one judge would hear a case; the number may have varied."[5] Nothing was entirely typical.

At first, Moses heard all kinds of cases, but at the behest of his father-in-law Jethro, he set up a system of lower judges, "able men, such as fear God, men of truth, hating covetousness," to judge small cases but to bring the hard cases to him (Exodus 18:21–26). Accordingly, Moses heard the cases of the blasphemer,[6] the wood gatherer,[7] and the daughters of Zelophehad[8] and other matters, while routine cases were heard by lower officials. Later, in a similar fashion, King Jehoshaphat appointed subordinate judges to travel and handle cases throughout the kingdom of Judah (2 Chronicles 19:5). Comparably, in the Book of Mormon, as the political situation in Zarahemla became more complex, it became advisable to broaden the base of the judicial system; a reform instigated by the king gave a chief judge jurisdiction over the great matters, and lower judges were installed to handle the ordinary cases (Mosiah 29:28–42).

In biblical society, local elders also served as judges in various capacities and configurations. The judicial authority of the elders, the senior men in the area, can be traced back to Numbers 11:16–17, which reports the creation of another auxiliary system: "And the Lord said unto Moses, Gather unto me seventy men of the elders of Israel, whom thou knowest to be the elders of the people, and officers over them; . . . and they shall bear the burden of the people with thee, that thou bear it not thyself alone."

Extending this administrative system, the book of Deuteronomy begins with the appointment of tribal leaders to serve as judges in cases involving private disputes: "So I took chief of your tribes, wise men, and known, . . . and I charged your judges at that time, saying, Hear the causes between your

---

5. Tikva Frymer-Kenski, "Anatolia and the Levant: Israel," in *A History of Ancient Near Eastern Law*, ed. Raymond Westbrook (Leiden: Brill, 2003), 2:992.

6. Jacob Weingreen, "The Case of the Blasphemer, Leviticus XXIV 10ff," *Vetus Testamentum* 22, no. 1 (1972): 118–23; Rodney R. Hutton, "Narrative in Leviticus: The Case of the Blaspheming Son (Lev 24,10–23)," *Zeitschrift für Altorientalische und Biblische Rechtsgeschichte* 3 (1997): 145–63; "The Case of the Blasphemer Revisited, Lev. XXIV 10–23," *Vetus Testamentum* 49, no. 4 (1999): 532–41; and Jacob Milgrom, *Leviticus 23–27: A New Translation with Introduction and Commentary* (New York: Doubleday, 2001), 2101–45.

7. Jacob Weingreen, "The Case of the Woodgatherer (Numbers XV 32–36)," *Vetus Testamentum* 16, no. 3 (1966): 361–64; and Gnana Robinson, "The Prohibition of Strange Fire in Ancient Israel: A New Look at the Case of Gathering Wood and Kindling Fire on the Sabbath," *Vetus Testamentum* 28, no. 3 (1978): 301–17.

8. Jacob Weingreen, "The Case of the Daughters of Zelophchad," *Vetus Testamentum* 16, no. 4 (1966): 518–22; and Josiah Derby, "The Daughters of Zelophehad Revisited," *Jewish Bible Quarterly* 25, no. 3 (1997): 169–71.

brethren, and judge righteously between every man and his brother, and the stranger that is with him" (Deuteronomy 1:15–16). Exactly how the judicial systems described in Exodus 18, Numbers 11, and Deuteronomy 1 related to each other has been debated over the centuries,[9] yielding various interpretations and several configurations based on these precedents.

Cases involving public concerns, however, such as whether a manslayer who had sought refuge at the altar in one of the cities of refuge should be granted asylum, were heard by a local assembly composed, apparently, of groups of city elders in each city of refuge (Numbers 35:24).

On other occasions, perhaps mainly in cases concerning family and property affairs,[10] a group of ten town elders could be convened rather spontaneously at the town gate to witness and resolve legal matters (Ruth 4:2).[11] In some cases, local courts may have consisted of a single judge (Numbers 25:5; Deuteronomy 25:1–3), perhaps assisted by some of the elders; in other cases, they sat as a body (Deuteronomy 19:17).[12] In Israel, as elsewhere, ad hoc courts of various configurations were often the rule locally: "The local courts give the impression of being ad hoc assemblies. . . . 'The judges' seem to be different from the official- or council-based courts but remain shadowy figures in the sources. At all periods, it is a matter of debate whether the term designated a profession or merely a function. Certainly, they were not trained jurists in the manner of modern judges."[13] Still, these judicial bodies had great power and influence.[14]

---

9. Hanoch Reviv, "The Traditions Concerning the Inception of the Legal System in Israel: Significance and Dating," *Zeitschrift für die alttestamentliche Wissenschaft* 94, no. 4 (1982): 566–75.

10. Of Anatolia (Asia Minor) and the Levant, Israel, Frymer-Kenski notes: "The judges sat for the judgment. The number of judges is not specified, and it may be that in simple cases one judge would have sufficed. Family law procedures may have anticipated all the men of the town sitting together." "Anatolia and the Levant: Israel," 2:995.

11. Thomas Thompson and Dorothy Thompson, "Some Legal Problems in the Book of Ruth," *Vetus Testamentum* 18, no. 1 (1968): 79–99; Derek R. G. Beattie, "The Book of Ruth as Evidence for Israelite Legal Practice," *Vetus Testamentum* 24, no. 3 (1974): 251–67; Robert Gordis, "Love, Marriage, and Business in the Book of Ruth: A Chapter in Hebrew Customary Law," in *A Light unto My Path: Old Testament Studies in Honor of Jacob M. Myers*, ed. Howard N. Bream, Ralph D. Heim, and Carey A. Moore (Philadelphia: Temple University Press, 1974), 241–64; and Baruch A. Levine, "In Praise of the Israelite *Mišpāḥâ*: Legal Themes in the Book of Ruth," in *The Quest for the Kingdom of God: Studies in Honor of George E. Mendenhall*, ed. H. B. Huffmon, F. A. Spina, and A. R. W. Green (Winona Lake, IN: Eisenbrauns, 1983), 95–106.

12. Ze'ev W. Falk, *Hebrew Law in Biblical Times: An Introduction*, ed. John W. Welch, 2nd ed. (Provo, UT: Brigham Young University Press; Winona Lake, IN: Eisenbrauns, 2001), 49. See also Joachim Oelsner, Bruce Wells, and Cornelia Wunsch, "Mesopotamia: Neo-Babylonian Period," in Westbrook, *History of Ancient Near Eastern Law*, 2:919.

13. Raymond Westbrook, "Introduction: The Character of Ancient Near Eastern Law," in Westbrook, *History of Ancient Near Eastern Law*, 1:30.

14. Westbrook, "Introduction," 1:31.

In certain instances, kings would serve as judges, especially in Mesopotamia and Egypt,[15] but apparently less often in Israel.[16] Kings would
sometimes reserve the power to judge capital cases: "A capital offence
comes before the king" (Law of Eshnunna 48; compare the law in 3 Nephi
6:22 that no one could impose the death penalty "save their condemnation
was signed by the governor of the land"). Kings would naturally handle
cases of conspiracy or disloyalty against them, as occurred in King Saul's
handling of the conspiracy of Ahimelech: "And the king said, Thou shalt
surely die, Ahimelech, thou, and all thy father's house" (1 Samuel 22:16).
Border disputes and the arrival of unidentified foreigners into the land
were natural extensions of the king's jurisdiction over his lands (e.g., the
arrest of Ammon by King Limhi in Mosiah 7:6–16). The false petition before King David by a woman from Tekoa, feigning to be a widow with two
sons, one of whom had supposedly killed the other and was now about
to be killed by her clansmen (2 Samuel 14:4–11), and also the famous
vignette of the two harlots arguing before King Solomon over whose baby
had died (1 Kings 3:16–28), show that the poorest people in Israelite society could seek legal protection from the king, even should these cases be
viewed more as literary depictions than historical reports.

Priests in Israel served in various judicial capacities (Deuteronomy
17:9; 19:17; 33:10), especially in proceedings that called for the swearing
of oaths or ordeals or purification rituals. For example, the husband who
suspected his wife of adultery could take her before a priest, and her oath
and drinking of the bitter waters could exonerate her (Numbers 5:15); and
after the discovery of a slain person outside of a village, there being no witnesses to the crime, the Levitical priests would put the matter completely

---

15. "The king was everywhere the supreme judge, although his judicial activity is more in
evidence in some periods than in others. There was no formal machinery of appeal from a lower
court; rather, a subject would petition the king to redress an injustice suffered by a lower court or
official. The king could also try cases at first instance. Various law-code provisions suggest that
certain serious crimes involving the death penalty were reserved for the king, but he is also found
judging apparently trivial matters." Westbrook, "Introduction," 1:30. In Mesopotamia, in the Old
Babylonian period, "the king might deal with a case brought before him in one of three ways. He
either tried the case himself and gave final judgment, decided a point of law and remitted the case
to a local court for a decision on the facts, or remitted the entire case to a local court." Westbrook,
"Mesopotamia: Old Babylonian Period," in Westbrook, *History of Ancient Near Eastern Law*,
1:367. In Egypt, "the pharaoh himself . . . constituted the highest court." Ignacio Márquez Rowe,
"Anatolia and the Levant: Canaan," in Westbrook, *History of Ancient Near Eastern Law*, 1:739.

16. Margaret Elizabeth Bellefontaine, "Customary Law and Chieftainship: Judicial Aspects of
2 Samuel 14:4–21," *Journal for the Study of the Old Testament* 38 (1987): 47–72; and Theodore J.
Hoftijzer, "David and the Tekoite Woman," *Vetus Testamentum* 20, no. 4 (1970): 419–44.

to rest by requiring all the men in the village to swear an oath of ignorance and innocence (Deuteronomy 21:5).

Ultimately the people as a whole remained a constant force in the judicial system (Jeremiah 26:16). As Jacob Milgrom has concluded: "One factor remains unchanged. As the trials of Naboth and Jeremiah clearly demonstrate, the people, *'am*, persists as an integral element of the judiciary."[17]

The trial of Jeremiah clearly illustrates the wide array of people and officers who could get involved almost spontaneously in a lawsuit in Jerusalem in the seventh century. Shortly after the catastrophic defeat and death of King Josiah in 609 BC, Jeremiah (a contemporary of Lehi) positioned himself prominently in the court of the temple at Jerusalem and called the people of Jerusalem to repentance, their wickedness having well been the cause of God's disapproval that led to the debacle at Megiddo. Jeremiah was instructed by the Lord to deliver a certain message word for word ("diminish not a word," Jeremiah 26:2). The substance of Jeremiah's complaint against the people was that they had not conducted themselves according to the laws that God had set before them (v. 4) and that they had not obeyed the words of the prophets that God kept sending to them (v. 5). Significantly, Jeremiah required obedience to both the law and the prophets. The threat from the Lord lodged by Jeremiah against the people in Jerusalem took the form of a simile curse: "I will make this house like Shiloh" (v. 6), alluding to the destruction of the shrine at Shiloh that resulted in the loss of the ark of the covenant in the disastrous battle of Ebenezer around 1050 BC when the Philistines dealt a severe military blow to the Israelites.

Legal action against Jeremiah was immediately initiated by the priests, prophets, and all the people who heard him (v. 8). The people indicted Jeremiah with the phrase "Thou shalt surely die" (v. 8). Before matters could develop very far in the trial of Jeremiah, however, certain princes or officials (*sarîm*) from the palace arrived (v. 10). It is unclear whether they heard the commotion and came on their own accord or if they were summoned by Jeremiah's friends or other concerned citizens. It is also unclear exactly what legal authority these officials held.

---

17. Jacob Milgrom, "The Ideological and Historical Importance of the Office of Judge in Deuteronomy," in *Isaac Leo Seeligmann Volume: Essays on the Bible and the Ancient World*, ed. Alexander Rofé and Yair Zakovitch (Jerusalem: E. Rubinstein's Publishing House, 1983), 139. See Ze'en Weisman, "The Place of the People in the Making of Law and Judgment," in *Pomegranates and Golden Bells (Studies in Biblical, Jewish, and Near Eastern Ritual, Law and Literature in Honor of Jacob Milgrom)*, ed. David P. Wright, David Noel Freedman, and Avi Hurvitz (Winona Lake, IN: Eisenbrauns, 1995), 407–20.

They took their seats in the New Gate of the house of the Lord. Doing "justice 'at the gate'" was idiomatic in ancient Israel. Before these seated officials, the prophets and priests pressed their charge against Jeremiah, accusing him of having "prophesied against this city" (v. 11). In defending himself, Jeremiah simply testified that he spoke in the name of the Lord, telling the officials that he was willing to have them do what they thought was "good and meet [proper]" (v. 14), raising the specter of "innocent blood," the shedding of which would bring divine judgment upon the judges, the city, and all the people (v. 15). The earlier cases of Micah and Urijah were invoked as precedents. The officials announced their verdict fairly quickly, finding Jeremiah innocent without much difficulty, having decided that he had indeed spoken in the name of the Lord (v. 16). Ultimately, Jeremiah was defended and protected by Ahikam, an influential prince.[18]

Perhaps because Lehi came out of Jerusalem shortly after this trial (and probably other similar litigations), a similar variety of judicial functionaries greets readers in the Book of Mormon. As will be discussed below, the trial of Abinadi was conducted in the palace of King Noah, whose judicial role was significant but was limited by his council of priests who took charge in certain ways. Alma sat as a single judge in the trial of Nehor. Other judges and priests were involved in the trial of Korihor. Local elders and appointed officials participated in the trial of Alma and Amulek. And Paanchi "was tried according to the voice of the people" (Helaman 1:8).

Trials were held essentially wherever the judges could be found. In Mesopotamia, "there appears to have been no special term for courthouse before the Neo-Babylonian period. The location of the court is occasionally mentioned as a temple or temple gate, but it was by no means the universal practice and, where so situated, did not necessarily involve participation of priests in the court."[19] In Egypt, "justice was often apparently administered at a gate, forecourt, or portico, presumably of a temple."[20] In Israel, places of judgment could vary from the city gate, the palace, temple, or other places. A similar range of judicial settings is found in the legal cases in the Book of Mormon. Cases were originated or heard in the palace or temple of King Noah, as judges sat on their judgment seats, or in places open to the general populace.

---

18. Frank-Lothar Hossfeld and I. Meyer, "Der Prophet vor dem Tribunal. Neuer Auslegungsversuch von Jer 26," *Zeitschrift für die alttestamentliche Wissenschaft* 86 (1974): 30–50; and John W. Welch, "The Trial of Jeremiah: A Legacy from Lehi's Jerusalem," in *Glimpses of Lehi's Jerusalem*, ed. John W. Welch, David Rolph Seely, and Jo Ann H. Seely (Provo, UT: FARMS, 2004), 337–56.

19. Westbrook, "Introduction," 1:30.

20. Richard Jasnow, "Egypt: New Kingdom," in Westbrook, *History of Ancient Near Eastern Law*, 1:306.

What Procedures Were Generally Followed?

An interesting degree of variety is also found in the judicial procedures followed by various biblical and ancient Near Eastern courts. Again, the rules of civil, criminal, or administrative procedure do not appear to have been particularly rigid, but certain patterns seem to emerge from the surviving documents. Because these patterns add important insights into what it meant in biblical times to do justice in a given case, it is helpful to get a general sense of these customary legal procedures.

Donald McKenzie has attempted to reconstruct the procedural steps and terms used in a typical Israelite lawsuit brought before judges at a town gate. In the picture he paints, no technical term for defendant is found, but the plaintiff is variously called an "adversary," an "attacker" or "accuser" (the Hebrew word in each of these instances is *satan*; 2 Samuel 19:22; Psalm 38:20; 71:13; 109:20, 29), or a "man of quarrel." This party makes "violent accusations" against the alleged offender, who "vehemently denies them." The two decide to submit their dispute to the town elders. One of the elders announces that a trial is beginning. The accuser then presents his case, lays out the matter before the judges, and perhaps suggests or demands certain punishment. The proceeding is "entirely public," open to anyone who might be passing in or out of the city gate. Volleys of accusations and responses ensue, witnesses or advocates step forward for both sides, the elders deliberate, and eventually they rise to declare either party innocent or culpable. The onlookers may chorus their assent, and the prescribed remedy or punishment is administered immediately.[21]

Robert Wilson offers a somewhat different overview of a typical biblical trial. In his view, the elements include the following: an initial act that "emphasizes the justness of the proceedings and the fairness of the elders"; during the hearing, "litigants are encouraged to present their view of the dispute"; the elders then question the parties and "attempt to suggest a compromise that will be acceptable to both parties"; should one of the parties prove guilty, the elders invite that party "to confess his guilt" and impose a penalty in order to restore order and unity to the society.[22]

What words signaled the commencement of litigation? As Bovati points out, in the biblical world verbs of motion such as *draw/come unto*,

---

21. Donald A. McKenzie, "Judicial Procedure at the Town Gate," *Vetus Testamentum* 14, no. 1 (1964): 100–104.

22. Robert R. Wilson, "Israel's Judicial System in the Preexilic Period," *Jewish Quarterly Review* 74, no. 2 (1983): 236–37. See also Pietro Bovati, *Re-Establishing Justice: Legal Terms, Concepts and Procedures in the Hebrew Bible* (Sheffield, England: JSOT Press, 1994), part II, discussing acts and procedures preceding the debate, the accusation, the defense, bringing one or both of the parties to silence, the sentence, and execution of judgment.

draw/come near, go up, enter into, and *arise* often signaled that legal proceedings were about to begin.[23] Consider, for example, the expressions
such as "come unto judgment" (Deuteronomy 25:1), "come together in
judgment" (Job 9:32), or "let us come near together to judgment" (Isaiah
41:1; see Malachi 3:5).

Along this line, Book of Mormon usage seems to draw directly on the
active biblical mandate to "take hold of" the accused and "bring" him before the judges,[24] the words used in the King James translation to describe
an accused's apprehension and arraignment ("lay hold on him, and bring
him [to the court]," Deuteronomy 21:19). In both Nephite and Lamanite
contexts, an accused was generally said to be "taken" before the court.[25]
The comparable idea of "bringing"[26] an accused to be judged also occurs
often in the Book of Mormon. These cases of "taking" or "bringing" often
involved "binding" the accused (e.g., Mosiah 12:9; Alma 17:20; 30:20) and
"carrying" him before the decision maker (e.g., Mosiah 12:9; Alma 30:21),
whether before judges or the populace. To visualize the dramatic scenes
that these otherwise relatively bland words might ordinarily connote, consider the Sumerian instance of binding and carrying in which a husband
"strapped his wife and her lover caught in *flagranti delicto* to the bed and
brought them bed and all before the Assembly of Nippur."[27]

Many cases in the Book of Mormon also contain references to "laying
hands" on the accused.[28] "The hand," according to Bovati, "has a certain
relevance in legal testimony . . . [as evidenced by Exodus 23:1], which
seems to echo the custom of the laying of a hand on the culprit in the act
of making an accusatory declaration."[29] Thus it seems that laying hands

---

23. Bovati, *Re-Establishing Justice*, 218–21; Falk, *Hebrew Law in Biblical Times*, 64n33; Zeʾev W. Falk, "Hebrew Legal Terms," *Journal of Semitic Studies* 5, no. 4 (1960): 350–54.

24. Falk, *Hebrew Law in Biblical Times*, 58.

25. As in the cases of Ammon (Mosiah 7:16), Abinadi (Mosiah 12:9; 17:1, 13), Alma (Alma 9:33; 14:4), Ammon (Alma 17:20), Aaron (Alma 22:19), Korihor (Alma 30:20, 21), and Nephi (Helaman 9:19); and it was attempted against Samuel (Helaman 16:6).

26. As in the case of Abinadi (Mosiah 11:28; 12:18; 17:6), the capture of a Lamanite king (20:13–14), the prosecution of those accused of apostasy (26:7, 10, 11), the trial of Nehor (Alma 1:2, 10), and in the cases of Alma and Amulek (11:1–2, 20; 14:8) and Korihor (30:30).

27. Raymond Westbrook, "Judges in the Cuneiform Sources," *MAARAV, A Journal for the Study of the Northwest Semitic Languages and Literatures* 12, nos. 1–2 (2005): 34. See Samuel Greengus, "A Textbook Case of Adultery in Ancient Mesopotamia," *Hebrew Union College Annual* 40–41 (1969–1970): 33–44.

28. As in the cases of Abinadi (Mosiah 13:2–3), Alma (Alma 9:32), Ammon (Alma 17:35), Aaron and his companions in the court of Lamoni's father (Alma 22:20), and Nephi (Helaman 8:4, 10; 10:15). For a time this practice was forbidden by Lamoni's father with regard to the Ne-phite missionaries in order to assist them in their proselyting efforts (Alma 23:1–2).

29. Bovati, *Re-Establishing Justice*, 281.

on an accused not only served to keep him from fleeing but also was an integral part of the formal proceeding (tantamount to service of process), as the seized was then formally accused.[30]

Not all litigants were compelled to appear before a judicial body. Accusers often "came" of their own accord to commence a legal proceeding.[31] When the accused was brought before a presiding authority, the king or judge could either extend benevolence by raising him up[32] (apparently a practice among the Nephites and Lamanites, Alma 47:23) or simply proceed with the trial.

Contend (Hebrew *rîb*) is probably the most prominent biblical (Isaiah 50:8; Micah 6:1) and Book of Mormon term[33] connected with legal disputes, and hence the absence of contention was a distinctive sign of peace in biblical cultures (Helaman 3:1–2). As mentioned above, an accuser under Hebrew law had various titles, one of them being *satan*. This may explain why contending with "adversaries" was so strongly condemned in the Book of Mormon (Alma 1:22) and why the spirit of contention was said to be "of the devil, who is the father of contention" (3 Nephi 11:29).

Who could commence a legal action? In Israel, "when a crime was discovered, legal process began with the pronouncement of an *ʾalah*, a general imprecation that demanded that anyone with knowledge step forward. . . . A procedure could also be initiated by an accusation brought by a witness."[34] Bovati describes the accusation itself as "lay[ing] the responsibility for an illegal or forbidden act upon a particular person (or

---

30. Bovati, *Re-Establishing Justice*, 281, citing Leviticus 24:14 and Job 9:33.

31. Bovati, *Re-Establishing Justice*, 221. Language of "coming" is found in Sherem's accusation of Jacob (Jacob 7:3, 6) as well as in the questioning of Alma and Amulek (Alma 12:20; 14:14, 18, 20).

32. Bovati, *Re-Establishing Justice*, 199.

33. Nephi describes his brothers' reaction and his subsequent reply to the Lord's commandment that they build a ship as a contention (1 Nephi 17:52). Jacob uses the same word to characterize his dispute with Sherem (Jacob 7:7). So too do various authors—such as Amaleki, Zeniff, Moroni, Mormon, Alma, and Helaman—to describe Zeniff's dispute with many of his settling party (Omni 1:28; Mosiah 9:2); Gideon's arguments in favor of slaying King Noah (Mosiah 19:3); Nehor's argument with Gideon and the subsequent social debate (Alma 1:7, 22); political debate over the Amlici question (2:5); the people of Ammonihah's accusations of Alma (9:1); the Lamanite debate over Ammon upon seeing King Lamoni and his royal household lying on the palace floor (19:28); Amalekite accusations against Aaron, Muloki, and Ammah (21:5, 11); the Morianton-Lehi border dispute (50:25); arguments over the king-men question (51:9; 60:16); the succession dispute between Pahoran's three sons (Helaman 1:2–3); the argument between the five falsely imprisoned messengers immediately preceding the trial of Nephi (9:18); and the debate over the fulfillment of Samuel's prophecy (16:17).

34. Frymer-Kenski, "Anatolia and the Levant: Israel," 2:994.

group)."[35] This could take place when the accused was apprehended or at the commencement of the formal argumentative proceedings.

Similarly, the word *accuse* always arises in legal contexts in the Book of Mormon.[36] Another commonly used term is *complain*.[37] Another's wrongdoing could also be denounced by a "declar[ation]" from an accuser of a particular crime.[38] Forms of the word *say* (*said, saying, tell*, and so on)[39] or of the word *question*[40] constitute a large majority of the accusatory terminology used in a number of cases in the Book of Mormon.

How would the action move forward? In the ancient Near East, "the parties were normally responsible for marshaling their own case and bringing witnesses and other evidence. The court, however, also had inquisitorial powers: it could interrogate parties and witnesses and could summon witnesses on its own initiative. In cases of serious public interest, the proceeding was in the nature of a judicial investigation."[41] In Hellenistic Egypt "the trial itself began with a statement by the plaintiff in the case, followed by a response from the defendant. Another round of response and counterresponse followed. The judges (often members of the local priesthood) verified testimony by asking questions and also had authority

---

35. Bovati, *Re-Establishing Justice*, 62.

36. See the cases of Laman and Lemuel against Nephi (2 Nephi 1:25), King Benjamin's address (Mosiah 2:15, declaring that his purpose was not to accuse), Abinadi (12:19; 17:7, 12), the apostates brought before Mosiah to be judged (26:11), Alma and Amulek (Alma 10:12, 31), Korihor (30:31), and Nephi (Helaman 9:19).

37. This language appears in Laman and Lemuel's accusations against Nephi (1 Nephi 17:18, 22), the people's allegations to Alma and Mosiah concerning persecution of church members (Mosiah 27:1), Moroni's explanation of Nephite legal proceedings during the trial of Alma and Amulek (Alma 11:2), and the unlawful killings of prophets during the end of the judge period (3 Nephi 6:25).

38. See the case of Jacob and Sherem (Jacob 7:2, 7).

39. Forms of the word *say* appear in the accounts of Jacob and Sherem (Jacob 7:6, 11, 20), the prophetic suit brought by King Benjamin (Mosiah 2:15), the trial of Alma and Amulek (Alma 10:24, 26, 27, 28; 11:26, 36; 14:15, 21), and the trial of Korihor (Alma 30, 19 times).

40. "Questioning" an accused of allegations against him is also common, as shown in the cases of Ammon the explorer (Mosiah 7:8), Abinadi (12:18–19), and Alma and Amulek (Alma 10:13, 16, 17; 11:21; 14:18) and in the trial of Nephi (Helaman 9:19). The only time in the Book of Mormon that *question* is not used in a legal context involves Amulek's preaching to the impoverished people of Ammonihah (Alma 34:5, the "great question" concerning the coming of Christ). The sincerity of the questioning varied, of course. In the trial of Alma and Amulek, for example, the point of questioning was not to illicit responses to sincere inquiries but to "catch" them (10:13, 17), or make them contradict themselves (10:16). Ironically, this strategy backfired and resulted in the accusers themselves being "caught" (12:1). The same overtone of insincerity pervades the trials of Abinadi (Mosiah 12:20–24, when Abinadi is asked about the meaning of Isaiah's "proclaiming peace" passage) and Nephi (Helaman 9:20, when Nephi's accusers attempt to bribe him to falsely confess).

41. Westbrook, "Introduction," 1:32.

to send out investigators through the chief of police to verify facts. Both parties were responsible for marshalling and presenting their own evidence, documents, and witnesses."[42] In Israel "the parties would stand and the accuser might approach the accused (Isa. 50:8), but in Naboth's trial, he was seated at the head of the people, and the witness sat facing him and testified against him (1 Kings 21:13). The accuser would declare the particulars of his case, and the other party would then examine his statements (Prov. 18:17). The accused might have a representative (vindicator) to assist him to help him examine the witness (Isa. 50:8 and Job, throughout). Judgment would be given in the morning (Jer. 21:11–12; Zeph. 3:5)."[43]

It was necessary in making one's case to present the "evidences" against the accused (Alma 11:2), whether by physical evidence (as in the cases of Achan and Seantum), by documentary evidence (as in the letters produced in the case of Naboth), or by oral testimony (as in the cases of Susanna and Korihor).[44] "Examples of physical evidence are the bloodstained sheet that attests to a bride's virginity (Deut. 22:13–17) and the remains of a sheep that a shepherd must bring to prove that it was devoured by a wild beast (Exod. 22:13). In a Neo-Babylonian trial for the theft of two ducks, the carcasses of the stolen ducks are brought into court for examination."[45]

Oral evidence, including hearsay,[46] was the most common type of evidence, and it was supplied by witnesses. Who could stand as witnesses? "The parties were competent witnesses on their own behalf. . . . Witnesses did not initially give their evidence under oath; the court might then order them to take an oath."[47] In Deuteronomy 19:15 as well as under the Middle Assyrian laws, "a criminal conviction has to be based on the testimony of two witnesses (MAL A47)."[48] A particularly severe risk involved accusers or witnesses who committed perjury: "Prohibition of false witness is included in the Ten Commandments and the Book of the Covenant, which enjoins Israel not to enter conspiracies to be an *ʿed hamas* (Exod. 23:1). According

---

42. Joseph G. Manning, "Egypt: Demotic Law," in Westbrook, *History of Ancient Near Eastern Law*, 2:831.

43. Frymer-Kenski, "Anatolia and the Levant: Israel," 2:995.

44. On Achan, see Joshua 7:22–23; Seantum, Helaman 9:31, 37; Naboth, 1 Kings 21:8–13; Susanna, Daniel 13:36–40, LXX (Greek Septuagint); and Korihor, Alma 30:32–47.

45. Westbrook, "Introduction," 1:33.

46. Westbrook, "Introduction," 1:33.

47. Westbrook, "Introduction," 1:33.

48. Sophie Lafont, "Mesopotamia: Middle Assyrian Period," in Westbrook, *History of Ancient Near Eastern Law*, 1:528.

to Deuteronomy 19:16–20, a witness who proved false was to suffer the same penalty that the accused would have suffered if convicted."[49]

The Hebrew word for "witness" (ʿēd) can refer to one "who says (or who is able to say) publicly something of another," to an "accuser," or to one "officially present at an act."[50] The trial of Alma and Amulek illustrates all three of these uses. In the context of accusation, Alma and Amulek played the first role, "witness[ing] . . . of the things whereof [the people of Ammonihah] were accused" (Alma 10:12). On the other side, the legal authorities of Ammonihah acted as accusatory witnesses in their attempt to get Alma and Amulek to contradict themselves in front of a crowd so that the accusers "might find witness against them" and bring them up for trial (v. 16). The strategy yielded the desired accusations, which were presented (presumably publicly) "before the chief judge of the land" (14:5). Shortly thereafter, Alma and Amulek were forced to be "officially present" (as "witness[es]" of) the act of burning sacred texts, women, and children (vv. 8–10).

How would the defendant respond? The response to many accusatory questions is often characterized, appropriately, simply as an "answer." As Bovati points out, this pattern appears in the Old Testament, as there are "continual references to 'saying' and 'answering' by the disputants within the individual speeches."[51] Comparable language is also found in many places in the Book of Mormon.[52]

In answering, if he chose not to confess judgment, the accused would either (1) deny and produce his own witnesses or (2) make a counteraccusation.[53] Such responses in the Book of Mormon legal cases use verbs such as *deny*, *confound*, and *rebuke*. In the cases of Sherem, Korihor, and Nephi, for example, the accused, when responding to accusations against him, counters with predictions of false initial denials by the ultimately guilty party, which were later renounced as a result of a subsequent confession of guilt[54] or a divine manifestation.[55] Other denials from the innocent parties themselves often involve "confounding" one's accusers;[56] still others

---

49. Frymer-Kenski, "Anatolia and the Levant: Israel," 2:995.

50. J. Van der Ploeg, "Studies in Hebrew Law," *Catholic Bible Quarterly* 12, no. 3 (1950): 257.

51. Bovati, *Re-Establishing Justice*, 74, citing Job 9:14–16; 13:22.

52. See the cases of Ammon the explorer (Mosiah 7:11), Abinadi (Mosiah 12:19, 32), Alma and Amulek (Alma 11:21, 29, 34; 14:17–19), and Korihor (Alma 30:36, 38).

53. Bovati, *Re-Establishing Justice*, 31–32.

54. On Sherem, see Jacob 7:14, 19; Nephi, Helaman 8:13, 24; and Seantum, Helaman 9:30, 35–37.

55. On Korihor, see Alma 30: 41–50.

56. This occurs in the cases of Nephi (1 Nephi 2:14; 2 Nephi 4:22), Jacob and Sherem (Jacob 7:8), Abinadi (Mosiah 12:19), and the five wrongly accused messengers prior to Nephi's trial (Helaman 9:18).

may "rebuke" their accusers,[57] which was well known in biblical times as effective defense advocacy.[58] Battle metaphors were also employed,[59] as in saying that the accused withstood his accuser(s).[60]

The burden of proof quickly shifted to the accused, who needed to produce evidence in his own behalf; if a strong defense was forthcoming, the burden would shift back to the accuser, requiring him to strengthen his original allegations. An accused was not presumed innocent until proven guilty. Thus defendants such as Jeremiah, Abinadi, and Nehor all found it necessary to argue and "plead" (Alma 1:11) vigorously for themselves. In addition, cases often involved witnesses in favor of the accused. A number of cases feature outright denials of guilt voiced by third parties who "plead" for the innocent, a known ancient Near Eastern practice.[61] Ancient litigants would also at times call physical objects—such as mountains, the heavens, and the earth—as witnesses to the truth of their allegations.[62] Aside from this exception, it seems, witnesses generally testified from personal knowledge, and thus forms of the word *know* in connection with witness testimony appear in various trials in the Book of Mormon.[63] Lawyers were not present to argue the case on behalf of either side. Lawyers played small roles in ancient Near Eastern law courts. One ruling of a city assembly authorized a plaintiff, "in order to 'win his case,' to hire an 'attorney,' who could be empowered to inspect tablets or to summon and interrogate people, and could represent him in court."[64]

---

57. See examples of numerous spectators at Lamoni's palace in Alma 19:20, 21, 26, 31.

58. Bovati, *Re-Establishing Justice*, 336, citing Genesis 31:42.

59. Bovati, *Re-Establishing Justice*, 292–94.

60. For example, the prophet Abinadi being unfazed by the interrogation of Noah's priests (Mosiah 12:19), righteous Gideon standing his ground when assaulted by Nehor (Alma 1:7, 9), and the wicked people of Ammonihah resisting Alma's accusations (8:13).

61. Bovati, *Re-Establishing Justice*, 336; and Westbrook, "Introduction," 1:31. Forms of "pleading" in advocating the cause of others appear when Alma pleads the cause of Abinadi (Mosiah 17:2), the wives and daughters of the Limhites and Amulonites plead for their husbands and fathers (19:13; 23:33), the king of the Lamanites pleads for the Lehites (20:25), Zeezrom pleads for Alma and Amulek (Alma 14:7), and Lamoni offers to plead the cause of Ammon's imprisoned brothers and companions in Middoni (20:7).

62. Bovati, *Re-Establishing Justice*, 40n12 and pp. 81–82. Such also takes place in Alma's response to Korihor's accusations concerning the coming of Christ (Alma 30:41).

63. This is seen in the case of Sherem (Jacob 7:7, 9, 12), the testimony of Lamoni's servants concerning Ammon's feats in defending the king's flocks (Alma 18:3–4), the trial of Korihor (30:39, 52), and the testimony of the five messengers sent to the royal palace during the trial of Nephi (Helaman 9:15).

64. Klass R. Veenhof, "Mesopotamia: Old Assyrian Period," in Westbrook, *History of Ancient Near Eastern Law*, 2:443.

There were no established standards of proof (such as "by the preponderance of the evidence," "substantial evidence," or "beyond any reasonable doubt"). In the ancient Near East, "the law of evidence knew no standard of proof such as 'beyond reasonable doubt' because if conventional evidence failed to reveal the truth, it could be ascertained by supra-rational methods. For the same reason, and given the inquisitorial powers of the court, it is difficult to speak of a burden of proof as in modern law."[65] Making the standards of proof even lower than in modern courts, "use was made of evidentiary presumptions, where evidence of a provable state of affairs gave rise to the presumption that a second state of affairs existed."[66] For example, "a buyer is presumed a thief if he cannot identify the seller . . . : a woman is presumed to have consented to intercourse in the city (because she could have cried out) but not in the country."[67]

The presenting of evidence was aimed at convincing and silencing one party or the other. Guilt (or at least a successful refutation) was established by the opposing party's silence.[68] In the ancient world, because there was no right against self-incrimination, silence was tantamount to confession, the reason being that the accused was unable to refute the charges against him because they were true. Guilt was accompanied in some Book of Mormon cases by reports of "trembling."[69] It seems that a physical manifestation (at least in the case of Seantum) could carry as much weight as silence in determining guilt (as in Helaman 9:32–34, declaring knowledge of guilt, in part, from paleness and fear manifested by trembling).

If neither party could be brought to silence, the deadlock was broken by bringing God into the court. "The supra-rational methods were [1] the oath, [2] the ordeal, and [3] the oracle. The latter were generally administered by the priests."[70] Regarding oaths sworn in a judicial context, the court could require either party to confirm his claims or accusations by swearing an oath in the name of a god. Some oaths were assertive, affirming the truth of certain statements or documents; other oaths were declaratory or self-imprecatory. "The declaratory oath was a solemn curse that the taker called down upon himself if his statement were not true. . . . It invokes the name of a god and is taken at the temple or before a symbol of the god. . . . The oath is deemed irrefutable proof. . . . The theory was

---

65. Westbrook, "Introduction," 1:32.
66. Westbrook, "Introduction," 1:32.
67. Westbrook, "Introduction," 1:35.
68. See the case of Zeezrom in Alma 12:1 and the dispute between Moroni's followers and the king-men in Alma 51:7.
69. As in the cases of Zeezrom (Alma 11:46; 12:1, 7) and Seantum (Helaman 9:33).
70. Westbrook, "Introduction," 1:32.

that fear of divine retribution would constrain the oath-taker to speak the truth. (If later uncovered, a false oath could also lead to punishment by the court.) Indeed, so great was the fear in practice that persons sometimes refused to take the oath, or the parties reached a compromise rather than proceed with the oath."[71]

Second, sometimes judges required parties to submit to some form of ordeal. "The ordeal was not so much a means of giving evidence as a referral of the issue to a higher court—that of the gods. . . . The trial could involve one or both parties."[72] In Mesopotamia, it was common to subject litigants to the river ordeal, in which they were thrown into the river to see if they would sink or be delivered. "All the parties must go to the river. The ordeal itself, however, is undergone by a single person, chosen by the judge on the basis of his considered opinion."[73] In biblical law, the drinking of the "bitter water" can be seen as another type of ritual ordeal (Numbers 5:11–31).

Third, consulting the gods by priestly augury or divination, seeking some kind of divine sign or oracle, could also be used to bring a case to closure. For example, the "taking by the Lord" first of a tribe, then of a family, and then of a household to detect the guilt of Achan (Joshua 7:14–18) and Nephi's prophetic identification of the culprit Seantum (Helaman 8:27) are clear cases of forensic uses of oracles. While parties such as Sherem or Korihor could call for the court to consult God or to request that signs of the will of God be given or read, it remained in the discretion of the court when to use oracles, oaths, or ordeals.

Of course, at any point, a party could admit his wrong and seek to reestablish the former relationship with the accuser, or at least agree to be subject to justice.[74] When "Achan confessed after divination identified him as the culprit,"[75] no further legal action was necessary, and he and his dependents were summarily executed. Sherem's and Zeezrom's confessions demonstrate Bovati's insight that the original accuser may become the accused as a result of a successful defense by the innocent.[76]

---

71. Westbrook, "Introduction," 1:33–34.

72. Westbrook, "Introduction," 1:34.

73. Lafont, "Mesopotamia: Middle Assyrian Period," 1:529.

74. Examples of these types of confessions include Seantum (Helaman 9:35, 37), Sherem (Jacob 7:19), and Zeezrom (Alma 14:7). See Bovati, *Re-Establishing Justice*, 32, 94.

75. Frymer-Kenski, "Anatolia and the Levant: Israel," 2:996.

76. Bovati, *Re-Establishing Justice*, 114; see also McKenzie, "Judicial Procedure at the Town Gate," 101–2: "Perhaps the reason there is no special word for 'defendant' is that the accused man did not think his task consisted merely in proving his own innocence. He could also use the opportunity provided by the lawsuit to accuse his accuser (*cf.* Gen[esis 31:41])."

If an accused would not confess, recall his words, or enter into a covenant to keep the law (e.g., 3 Nephi 5:4), however, a verdict would be rendered and the appropriate punishment imposed forthwith. (When and why which punishments were used will be discussed in chapter 13 below.) In any event, legal cases in biblical times usually ended quickly. Thus the blasphemer in Leviticus 24:23, the Sabbath breaker in Numbers 15:36, Achan, and Naboth were all executed immediately; and Pachus's men in Alma 62:9–10 (62 BC), who would not take up arms in defense of their country and who fought against it, were convicted and "speedily executed." Only exceptionally would parties be granted time to produce specifically named witnesses. More important than producing further evidence was the overall character and credibility of the accuser and of the accused, which the court could judge directly.

With regard to judicial rulings in Israel, there was no appeal on the merits, although appeals were commonly available elsewhere unless the written judgment made the decision *res judicata* and barred any further litigation. In New Kingdom Egypt, for example, one could appeal a local court ruling handed down by another bench; one party litigated "four times over compensation for the same dead donkey."[77] But "a challenge to the court's decision, by the plaintiff or the defendant, was subject to severe penalties in excess of those imposed in the original decision. The court could also order the parties to take an oath not to challenge the decision in the future."[78] In Mesopotamia, "the 'King's Word' overruled any earlier decision, and thus many individuals who felt unfairly treated appealed directly to the king. . . . There were two ways to appeal to the king: either a written petition was addressed to the king or an audience was requested. In the latter case, the petitioner was led veiled into the king's presence, where he would plead his cause. The king was not only approached in matters of life and death, but also for more trivial reasons."[79] But in Israel, the only appeal seems to have been in cases where a party accused the judges of perverting justice (Mosiah 29:28–29). In such a case "the remedy is an appeal to the [judge's] superior . . . on up through the king. . . . Ecclesiastes advises that one not be shocked if the abuse continues on up the line (Eccles. 4:1). The ultimate appeal is to God."[80]

77. Westbrook, "Introduction," 1:32.

78. Kathryn Slanski, "Mesopotamia: Middle Babylonian Period," in Westbrook, *History of Ancient Near Eastern Law*, 2:493.

79. Karen Radner, "Mesopotamia: Neo-Assyrian Period," in Westbrook, *History of Ancient Near Eastern Law*, 2:887.

80. Frymer-Kenski, "Anatolia and the Levant: Israel," 2:998. Compare the unsuccessful complaint against corrupt judges in 3 Nephi 6:25–30 (AD 30), which went "up unto the land of

As is apparent for many reasons, ancient lawsuits were risky proposi-
tions. There was danger in starting a lawsuit, since accusations might fly
against the initial accuser. The rules were quite indefinite, and the evidentiary standards were vague. Who might turn out to sit that day as a judge
was rather random, how those judges might evaluate the evidence or persons involved was highly unpredictable, and the decision of the judges was
for all practical purposes final. These risks created a high cost threshold to
litigation, which must have induced many parties to settle their disputes
outside of court (Isaiah 1:18, "come now, and let us reason together"; and
Matthew 5:25, "agree with thine adversary quickly").

Turning to the Main Legal Cases in the Book of Mormon

Only a few points remain to be mentioned before analyzing the legal
cases in the Book of Mormon one by one. Although much can be said
about these cases, our view remains incomplete. It is unknown, for example, to what extent these legal cases were typical or atypical. The seven
main cases deal principally with what the modern mind would classify as
religious offenses—allegations involving blasphemy, false prophecy, causing apostasy, reviling against God or ruler, and enforcing priestcraft. One
wonders if trials involving such matters were common or rare in that society, if they followed consistent or idiosyncratic rules, and if they were
conducted in a different manner from ordinary secular cases of breach
of contract, personal injury, theft, divorce, or even capital cases such as
murder, adultery, or treason. While we know that Nephite law prohibited
murder, plunder, theft, and adultery (Alma 30:10; 51:19; 62:9–10; 3 Nephi
6:22), Mormon's abridgment gives little indication of how the Nephites
resolved cases involving delinquent debtors (Alma 11:2), ordinary business disagreements, torts, family matters, or property disputes between
two private litigants. Thus much remains uncertain.

Even if all kinds of serious legal problems were handled essentially
according to norms or customs from the biblical world, it is still likely
that considerable flexibility and discretion existed within all ancient legal
systems to allow each case to be handled on an individual basis as justice
was thought to demand. Beyond the provisions of the law of Moses found
on the plates of brass, or the general rules and customs that developed in
Nephite society, no code of civil procedure in a modern sense, or *Manual
of Discipline* in the Essene sense, or Talmud in a Pharisaical sense set forth

---

Zarahemla, to the governor." The judges were taken and brought up before the judge, but the
accused judges entered into a compact with their friends, kindreds, lawyers, and high priests "to
combine against all righteousness" (3 Nephi 6:28), thwarting the process.

Legal Cases and Procedures in the Book of Mormon

The Case of Sherem against Jacob . . . . Jacob 7:1–23

The Arrest of Ammon . . . . Mosiah 7:6–16

The Trial of Abinadi . . . . Mosiah 7:26–28; 11:20–17:20

The Trial of Nehor . . . . Alma 1:1–15

The Trial of Alma and Amulek . . . . Alma 9:1–14:29; 16:1–11

The Imprisonment of Aaron and Brethren . . . . Alma 21:12–14

The Trial of Korihor . . . . Alma 30:6–60

The Imprisonment of King-Men . . . . Alma 51:19

The Trial of Pachus's Men and the King-Men . . . . Alma 62:9–10

The Case of Paanchi . . . . Helaman 1:1–10

The Imprisonment of Lehi and Nephi . . . . Helaman 5:21–22

Gadianton Trials of Their Defectors . . . . Helaman 6:24

The Trial of Seantum . . . . Helaman 8:27–9:41

The Execution of Zemnarihah . . . . 3 Nephi 4:28–33

The Trial of Captured Robbers . . . . 3 Nephi 5:4–5

Corrupt Execution of Inspired Prophets . . . . 3 Nephi 6:20–24

Complaint against the Corrupt Judges . . . . 3 Nephi 6:25–30

for Jacob and Alma a legal glossary of detailed definitions or a mandatory digest of rigid rules governing the Nephite judicial system. Their system, like most in antiquity, tried to do justice and settle cases fairly, quickly, and unambiguously as the facts and circumstances of each case seemed to require.

But to complicate matters further, two of the seven main Book of Mormon cases may have been atypical since they were heard by corrupt courts. Although Noah and his priests openly purported to teach and observe the law of Moses (Mosiah 12:28), it is evident that they were prone to distort or interpret the law to suit their own purposes. Likewise, while the judges and legal officers in the city of Ammonihah were bound to apply the law of Mosiah—the governing law throughout the land of Zarahemla, which they themselves invoked in claiming that they were entitled to be paid for their legal services (Alma 11:1, 3, 20)—it is apparent that the trial of Alma and Amulek was in many respects retrograde and abnormal.

While these problems and shortcomings raise some interpretive obstacles in analyzing these cases, the difficulties are not insuperable. Valuable legal information can still be found in cases handled by unrighteous judges or in cases that present aberrational facts or that deal with issues of first impression. Fortunately, the writers of the Book of Mormon were sometimes careful to point out instances when corrupt judges did not follow the traditional law. For example, the briefly mentioned trials by the Gadianton robbers of their defectors in Helaman 6:24 (25 BC) used "laws of their wickedness" and did not judge according to the laws of their country. When King Noah acted contrary to the traditional rules in putting Abinadi to death by fire, the record specifically points out that this was extraordinary and irregular: "Abinadi was the first that suffered death by fire because of his belief in God" (Alma 25:11). Because Noah is accused of many things, including whoredoms, greed, laziness, idolatry, drunkenness, and not keeping and teaching the Ten Commandments (Mosiah 11:2, 3, 6, 15; 12:37; 13:25–26), one must assume that he would not have worried very much about ignoring a simple procedural rule if it worked to his advantage to do so. Nevertheless, it appears that Noah and his priests attempted to maintain the outward appearance of following the customary rules of Nephite judicial procedure—at least they claimed to keep the law of Moses. Thus, unless there is reason to believe otherwise, one should presume that Noah and his priests in most instances attempted to act legally.

Finally, one must also remember that some of these following seven cases arose in different centuries. A similar chronological challenge faces scholars in studying the administration of law and justice in the Bible, which also spans many centuries.[81] Nevertheless, while some significant legal changes occurred in the course of Israelite and Nephite history, the fundamental elements in most ancient legal systems were typically very stable over long periods of time. The early cases of Sherem (about 500 BC) and Abinadi (about 150 BC) arose under the traditional law of Moses, as that law was strictly observed in all respects by the Nephites from the beginning (2 Nephi 5:10; Jarom 1:5). About 91 BC, the changes introduced into the Nephite legal system by King Mosiah, the son of Benjamin

---

81. For more information, see John M. Salmon, "Judicial Authority in Early Israel: An Historical Investigation of Old Testament Institutions" (PhD diss., Princeton: Princeton Theological Seminary, 1968); and Herbert Niehr, "Grundzüge der Forschung zur Gerichtsorganisation Israels," *Biblische Zeitschrift* 31, no. 2 (1987): 206–27.

(Mosiah 29:11, 25–29),[82] primarily reformed procedural and administrative rules, not the substantive rules of law, and accordingly the Nephite judges in this era as in previous times were required to judge cases "according to the laws which have been given . . . by [the] fathers" (vv. 25, 28). Thus the law of Moses continued to be administered by the judges who were appointed to office pursuant to the law of Mosiah. Therefore, traditional Israelite law still formed the controlling body of law at the time of the trials of Nehor (91 BC), Alma and Amulek (82 BC), Korihor (74 BC), Paanchi (52 BC), and Seantum (about 23–20 BC), all five of which arose during the first seventy years of the reign of the judges.

Thus, while the administration of Nephite justice can and must be considered as developing over time, five of the seven principal cases come from a single era in Nephite history and yield sufficient information and points of reference to sustain several general conclusions about the Nephite legal system especially in that era, but they also allow conclusions about Nephite law as a whole, its Israelite origins, its internal developments, and its typical jurisprudence. Similarities between those five cases and the two earlier Nephite proceedings, as well as with biblical precedents, show that continuity and stability was not the exception but the rule in Nephite legal history.

Subject to these caveats, the following chapters seek to understand these seven cases in the way that an educated member of Nephite society most likely would have understood these legal cases at the time they arose. The purpose is not only to comprehend the precise legal issues involved in each proceeding and to extract from each case the prevailing legal principles and probable historical consequences, but also to allow modern readers to experience, as much as possible, these ancient episodes as if they were standing before the judge, side by side with the plaintiffs and defendants who faced these extreme moments of crisis in their lives and received profound manifestations of God's spirit in connection with these significant legal proceedings.

Much was at stake in these trials: legally, personally, socially, politically, and religiously. Most of the cases involved capital charges in unusual circumstances. In light of Israelite and Nephite law, we can reconstruct enough of the picture to see why those issues presented difficult legal problems at the time and to form opinions about what rules, statutes, or principles would

---

82. John W. Welch, "The Law of Mosiah," in *Reexploring the Book of Mormon*, ed. John W. Welch (Salt Lake City: Deseret Book and FARMS, 1992), 158–61.

have guided the strategies and tactics of the parties and would have influenced the decisions of the judges and outcomes in these cases.[83]

From this study emerges not only an appreciation for ancient legal jargon but also a sense of the remarkable judicial consistency and rational policies that existed within both the Nephite system itself and its ancient Israelite wellsprings regarding righteous judgment and the establishment of justice. As a whole, these seven Nephite legal cases manifest a high degree of coherence and sophistication. These legal narratives bespeak intimate familiarity and mature experience with an intricate body of law, and they display that law in actual operation within a vigorous cultural tradition and a vital spiritual community.

---

83. For more information on judges, see Zeʾev W. Falk, "Ruler and Judge" (Hebrew), *Leshonenu* 30 (1965–66): 243–47; F. Charles Fensham, "The Judges and Ancient Israelite Jurisprudence," *Ou Testamentiese Werkgemeenskap in Suid-Afrika* (Potchefstroom) 2 (1959): 15–22; S. Gervitz, "On Hebrew *sebet* = Judge," in *The Bible World: Essays in Honor of Cyrus H. Gordon*, ed. Gary Rendsburg and Cyrus H. Gordon (New York: KTAV, 1980), 61–66; Rolf P. Knierim, "Customs, Judges and Legislators in Ancient Israel," in *Early Jewish and Christian Exegesis: Studies in Memory of William Hugh Brownlee*, ed. Craig A. Evans and William F. Stinespring (Atlanta: Scholars Press, 1987), 3–15.

PART TWO

Cases and Controversies

CHAPTER FIVE

THE CASE OF SHEREM

Early in Nephite history, toward the end of the sixth century BC, "there came a man among the people of Nephi, whose name was Sherem" (Jacob 7:1). Sherem opposed the teachings of Jacob and sought out a confrontation with Jacob (v. 2). At this time, Jacob was well known in the city of Nephi; he was a seasoned temple official, having been ordained at a young age by his brother Nephi to be a priest and a teacher in the newly built temple in the Nephite capital city.

It is unknown where Sherem came from, but it would not appear that he was a complete outsider to the Nephite community, for he addressed Jacob as "brother" (v. 6). Nevertheless, this term is somewhat ambiguous and need not imply that Sherem and Jacob were closely related, since the Hebrew word for brother, *ʾāch*, and its Semitic cognates can mean many things, ranging anywhere from full blood brother (Genesis 4:8–11; 25:26; compare 2 Nephi 2:1) to half brother (Genesis 42:3–7; 2 Samuel 13:4) to kinsman (Genesis 14:14–16)[1] or fellow countryman (Deuteronomy 17:15; compare 2 Nephi 6:2). Moreover, "sometimes *ʾāch* is used as a polite address to strangers," but, more significantly, it was used anciently "in diplomatic correspondence between allies, as perhaps in Nu[mbers] 20:14 and certainly in 1 K[ings] 9:13 (Solomon speaking to Hiram) and 20:32 (Ahab speaking of Ben-hadad)."[2] Thus, although the word *brother* in Jacob 7:6 might

---

1. Zeʾev W. Falk, *Hebrew Law in Biblical Times: An Introduction*, ed. John W. Welch, 2nd ed. (Provo, UT: Brigham Young University Press; Winona Lake, IN: Eisenbrauns, 2001), 112–13 ("The status of the foreigner must have become a problem during the patriarchal age. A person's rights and duties were at that time dependent upon the blood relationship and upon his belonging to a family, clan, or tribe. Everybody was everybody's 'brother' and entitled to his protection and redemption in case of need").

2. Helmer Ringgren, "*ʾāch*," in *Theological Dictionary of the Old Testament*, ed. G. Johannes Botterweck and Helmer Ringgren, trans. John T. Willis, rev. ed. (Grand Rapids, MI: Eerdmans, 1974), 1:188–93, quotation on p. 191.

imply that Sherem was a member of Jacob's extended family or that he came from one of the other Nephite tribes (Nephites, Josephites, or Zoramites), it would not appear that Jacob and Sherem were very close relatives, especially in light of Sherem's lack of success in gaining an audience with Jacob (Sherem having "sought much opportunity" to speak with him, v. 3) and also in view of the very serious accusations that will follow (v. 7).

Instead of having family or tribal connections, Sherem may have addressed Jacob as a brother in their covenant community of Nephites, Jacobites, Josephites, and Zoramites.[3] Thinking along the lines of Amos 1:9–10, which speaks of the destruction that will come from God on those who break "the brotherly covenant" (*berith ʾāchim*), Sherem may have prefaced his accusations with this "brotherly" appellation in order to instill in Jacob a sense of duty to rectify what Sherem perceived to be Jacob's offenses against the Israelite or Nephite covenant community. Beyond that, the use of the term *brother* in this exchange seems to present Jacob and Sherem as being of "equal rank" professionally, in the community, or somehow as "covenant partners."[4] Be that as it may, the intensity and seriousness of the controversy that ensued between Sherem and Jacob give assurance that some previous civil bond existed between them that Sherem deemed Jacob had broken or violated.[5]

Sherem was intelligent, eloquent, and persuasive (Jacob 7:4), abilities that link him to the educated people in the small city of Nephi and probably to the royal group controlled by the kings who succeeded Nephi in the land of Nephi. Sherem's strident defense of the law of Moses as the source of righteousness would have appealed to royal administrators, who perhaps supported or even were the source of Sherem's political points of view. Because Zoram had been a servant to a public official in Jerusalem, it is enticing to think that Sherem may have been a Zoramite or may have had Zoramite ties.[6] At least Sherem's pro-legalistic posture conforms with

---

3. Later in the Book of Mormon, the term *brother* is used to imply a relationship of shared faith or suffered hardship (Alma 34:3; 56:2, 45; 58:41).

4. Ringgren, "*ʾāch,*" 188.

5. As Pietro Bovati, *Re-Establishing Justice: Legal Terms, Concepts and Procedures in the Hebrew Bible* (Sheffield, England: JSOT Press, 1994), 30, points out, juridical disputes such as Sherem's claims against Jacob necessarily presuppose a previous juridical bond between the parties: "The *rîb* is a controversy that takes place between two parties on questions of law. For the contest to take place, the individuals in question must have had a previous juridical bond between them (even if not of an explicit nature), that is, it is necessary that they refer to a body of norms that regulates the rights and duties of each."

6. A. Keith Thompson, "Who Was Sherem?" (private communication), has articulated and justified this view. Zoram certainly had connections with the plates of brass and had ties to the royal house in Jerusalem. Interestingly, if Sherem was in fact a Zoramite, then the rift between the

the justifications used by Laman and Lemuel in the Old World when they argued in defense of the people in the land of Jerusalem on the ground that they "were a righteous people; for they kept the statutes and judgments of the Lord, and all his commandments, according to the law of Moses" (1 Nephi 17:22), a view that Zoram may also have readily embraced, given his background. Legalistic arguments such as these, of course, were on a collision course with the prophetic worldview of Jacob, who stood in the tradition of Lehi, Nephi, and the prophets in Jerusalem.[7] An ideological clash similar to the one that had previously pitted certain powerful forces in Jerusalem against the prophets Jeremiah and Lehi, even to the point of involving formal or informal criminal legal charges (Jeremiah 26:8–9; 1 Nephi 1:20),[8] seems to have resurfaced in the New World a generation later in the form of Sherem's accusations against Jacob.

Legally Grounded Religious Issues

Although Sherem's accusations did not result in a legal proceeding as such—no court was ever convened, no elders were assembled to sit in judgment, and no human witnesses were called to testify—his accusations were legally grounded. His allegations arose out of several compelling legal issues that would have confronted any ancient Israelite who did not understand or accept the doctrine of Christ when presented with the specific revelations and prophecies given by Lehi, Nephi, and Jacob concerning Jesus Christ as the coming Messiah. How could a person in the city of Nephi talk of Christ, rejoice in Christ, preach of Christ, and prophesy of Christ (as Nephi boldly declares was done, 2 Nephi 25:24–26) without seeming to commit the crimes of worshipping other gods (Exodus 20:3)? How could a person introduce new revelations without appearing to lead people into other paths (Deuteronomy 13:5) or without running the risk of prophesying falsely under the law of Moses (vv. 20, 22)? Can the Nephite revelations about the coming Messiah be harmonized with the old revelation of the law through Moses? What did Nephi mean when he spoke of "the deadness of the law" (2 Nephi 25:27), and is that an unbecoming and unlawful way to speak of the law of God? Nephi had said,

Zoramites and the Nephites that erupted into warfare in the days of Alma had roots as far back as the contention between Sherem and Jacob.

7. For an extended discussion of this prophetic worldview, see John W. Welch, "Getting through Isaiah with the Help of the Nephite Prophetic View," in *Isaiah in the Book of Mormon*, ed. Donald W. Parry and John W. Welch (Provo, UT: FARMS, 1998), 19–45.

8. John W. Welch, "The Trial of Jeremiah: A Legal Legacy from Lehi's Jerusalem," in *Glimpses of Lehi's Jerusalem*, ed. John W. Welch, David Rolph Seely, and Jo Ann H. Seely (Provo, UT: FARMS, 2004), 337–56.

"Notwithstanding we believe in Christ, we keep the law of Moses" (v. 24); but how should the balance be maintained between believing in Christ and keeping the law of Moses, how does the belief in Christ translate into specific rules or interpretations of the ritual or civil law, and who has the authority to decide how this synthesis will be defined and implemented? These precise problems may have been residual issues from Lehi's day back in Jerusalem, where his life was threatened because of the things that he said he had seen and heard and read in the heavenly book, "manifest[ing] plainly of the coming of a Messiah, and also the redemption of the world" (1 Nephi 1:19). Lehi's teachings actually may have been more compatible with the older religious views that had prevailed during the First Temple period than with the views of the Deuteronomic reformers who transformed Israelite religion during and after the reign of King Josiah during Lehi's lifetime, as Margaret Barker has argued.[9] Although it is difficult to know exactly how the book of Deuteronomy was being interpreted and employed by various religious and political factions in Lehi's Jerusalem, Barker's work shows, at a minimum, that Lehi's and Nephi's teachings would have given rise to lively legal issues and religious controversies in the days of Lehi, Nephi, Jacob, and Sherem.

If we take Sherem's arguments at face value, he essentially resisted the messianic clarifications introduced by the revelations of Lehi and Nephi. He preferred a system of legal rules based on the law of Moses, especially as enforced by certain provisions in the book of Deuteronomy, without any foreshadowing in light of messianic expectation.

Although Sherem's personal motivations remain obscure, he may have contested Jacob's doctrines and interpretations of the law for thoroughly pious reasons. Sherem claimed to believe in "the scriptures" (Jacob 7:10)—namely, in the plates of brass containing the law of Moses. His emphasis on the written word probably indicates that he rejected the oral law and limited his view of authoritative law to provisions found in the written record. Still, he would have believed in the scriptural God of Abraham, Isaac, and Jacob, and he probably rested his opposition to Jacob on such

---

9. For a discussion of the writings of Margaret Barker concerning the Israelite tradition that emphasized, on the one hand, the temple, angels, sacrifice, atonement, divine kingship, covenant, wisdom, heavenly ascent, and revelation, which contrasted with the legalistic reformers who elevated the role of the law to a position of primacy, see Kevin Christensen, "The Temple, the Monarchy, and Wisdom: Lehi's World and the Scholarship of Margaret Barker," and Margaret Barker, "What Did King Josiah Reform?" in Welch, Seely, and Seely, *Glimpses of Lehi's Jerusalem*, 449–542; see also Barker, "Joseph Smith and Preexilic Israelite Religion," in *The Worlds of Joseph Smith: A Bicentennial Conference at the Library of Congress*, ed. John W. Welch (Provo, UT: Brigham Young University Press, 2006), 69–82.

passages as "Thou shalt have no other gods before me" (Exodus 20:3). He resisted religious change that required additions to the written law, arguing strenuously that the law of Moses was "the right way" and that its observance should not be converted "into the worship of a being which . . . shall come many hundred years hence" (Jacob 7:7). He considered the law of Moses sacred, and he viewed Jacob's messianic orientation as divergent and heretical. Sherem may well have cited in his argument such provisions as Deuteronomy 4:2, "Ye shall not add unto the word which I command you, neither shall ye diminish ought from it." While Jacob could have responded by explaining that this limitation was typically included in many ancient laws, treaties, or revelations simply to signify the completeness of the document or speech in which it appears,[10] Sherem could still have invoked the rhetoric of Deuteronomy 4:2, much as it had been used by the Deuteronomic reformers who sought to control the worship of Jehovah exclusively in their strictly centralized legal and religious system.

By taking such a restrictive position regarding Jacob's more expansive teachings, Sherem would have had a legal or moral duty under laws such as Leviticus 5:1 or Deuteronomy 13:6–11 (at least as he could have understood or rationalized the rules behind those provisions) to either take legal action against Jacob or risk falling under the wrath and judgment of God.[11] As Jacob Milgrom explains, Leviticus 5:1 requires any person having knowledge of a crime to step forward in response to a public call for information about the wrongdoing; otherwise "he must bear his punishment," an expression that "implies that the punishment will be meted out by God, not by man."[12] Deuteronomy 13 requires a person who hears

---

10. "Identical warnings are found in wisdom literature concerning the completeness of God's work, . . . and are also attested in treaty literature of the ancient Near East . . . [and] in Mesopotamian literature concerning prophecy." Moshe Weinfeld, *Deuteronomy 1–11* (New York: Doubleday, 1991), 200. For example, the epilogue to the Code of Hammurabi curses any subsequent ruler who might "alter the judgments that I rendered and the verdicts that I gave." Martha T. Roth, *Law Collections from Mesopotamia and Asia Minor*, ed. Piotr Michalowski (Atlanta: Scholars Press, 1995), 135.

11. Sherem likely viewed himself as protecting the social order by bringing accusations against Jacob. Those who initiated juridical actions such as this one "undertake for society the task of prosecuting the evildoer." Bovati, *Re-Establishing Justice*, 69.

12. Jacob Milgrom, *Leviticus 1–16* (New York: Doubleday, 1991), 293–95. See also generally Raymond Westbrook, "Punishments and Crimes," in *The Anchor Bible Dictionary*, ed. David Noel Freedman and others, 6 vols. (New York: Doubleday, 1992), 5:546–56. For a detailed examination of Leviticus 5:1, see Bruce Wells, *The Law of Testimony in the Pentateuchal Codes* (Wiesbaden: Harrasowitz, 2004), 54–82. Although, as Wells rightly argues, this verse refers primarily "to a person who is under obligation to testify but refuses to do so" (p. 55), this requirement is still part of a larger legal system that obligated all members of the community to be vigilant in protecting and promoting the law-abiding status of the society overall. See, for example, Bovati, *Re-Establishing*

anyone enticing people to "go and serve other gods" to be the first to step forward and put that person to death, even if the offender should happen to be a "brother," a son, daughter, wife, friend, or an entire community.[13] Accordingly, Ze'ev Falk has concluded: "In cases of public apostasy it was considered the duty of everyone present to take the law into his own hands, and punish the offender."[14]

Although it would become clear in the end that Sherem was mistaken and "deceived" (Jacob 7:18), these legal provisions and religious obligations in the books of Moses probably ensured that, at the outset, Sherem was taken seriously; he would have been perceived by people in his day as being serious and sincere, as well as religiously and rationally motivated. He is later called a "wicked man" (v. 23) but not an anti-Christ; that label in the Book of Mormon is given only to Korihor.[15] If one categorically lumps Sherem, Korihor, and Nehor together as stereotyped anti-Christs, important distinctions between the actions and motives of the three become so blurred that the actual issues in controversy, the stakes at risk, the

---

Justice: "It is necessary that whoever is aware of the crime should speak out, denouncing the guilty party" (p. 62). "Anyone who becomes aware of a misdeed becomes, by that very fact, a potential accuser of the guilty party. This general principle holds good especially for Israel, which does not distinguish between citizens appointed 'ex officio' to carry out the task of denouncing crimes (public 'officials') and anyone else, who may but is not obliged to do so" (p. 70n15).

13. See Paul E. Dion, "Deuteronomy 13: The Suppression of Alien Religious Propaganda in Israel during the Late Monarchial Era," in *Law and Ideology in Monarchic Israel*, ed. Baruch Halpern and Deborah W. Hobson (Sheffield, England: Sheffield Academic Press, 1991), 147–216, especially 165.

14. Falk, *Hebrew Law in Biblical Times*, 69, citing Exodus 32:27 (where Moses orders the Levites to "slay every man his brother, and every man his companion" who was engaged in the apostasy of worshipping the golden calf) and Numbers 25:7–8 (where Phinehas slays an apostate Israelite and a Midianitish woman). See Westbrook, "Punishments and Crimes," 5:546–56.

15. Significant differences exist between the cases of Sherem, Nehor, and Korihor, as will be discussed further in chapter 10 below, where these three cases are compared. For present purposes, one should note that Sherem was less sophisticated and less extreme than Korihor, and Sherem's assertion that he knew there never would be a Christ contradicts "his own argument that no one could 'tell of things to come.'" Russell M. Frandsen, "Antichrists," in *Encyclopedia of Mormonism*, ed. Daniel H. Ludlow (New York: Macmillan, 1992), 1:45. Moreover, Sherem was deceived only by the "power of the devil" (Jacob 7:18), whereas the devil appeared to Korihor "in the form of an angel" who taught him exactly what to say (Alma 30:53). Of course, Sherem manifested several characteristics of an anti-Christ (denying the need for Christ, using flattery, accusing church leaders of teaching false doctrine, having a narrow view of reality, misreading scriptures, and seeking a sign), as Robert Millet has pointed out in "Sherem the Anti-Christ," in *The Book of Mormon: Jacob through the Words of Mormon: To Learn with Joy*, ed. Monte S. Nyman and Charles D. Tate Jr. (Provo, UT: Religious Studies Center, Brigham Young University, 1990), 175–91; and I do not doubt that Jacob rightly saw Sherem as a "wicked man" (Jacob 7:23), but these similarities are offset by a number of differences. See Duane F. Watson, "False Christs," in *Anchor Bible Dictionary*, 2:761.

various procedures utilized, and the different results obtained in each case either become lost or are rendered inexplicable.

Triggering Open Conflict

It may be that Sherem was brought to the point of confronting Jacob in a legal mode because Jacob had been a publicly outspoken and provocative priest and teacher. Jacob had apparently struggled against the Nephite political rulers who had succeeded Nephi. In public he had spoken sharply against the men of the city of Nephi (Jacob 1:15–2:35), chastising them for becoming "hard in their hearts" (1:15) and decrying their pride and immorality. Jacob had accused them of misunderstanding the scriptures and rationalizing their behavior: "The word of God burdens me because of your grosser *crimes.* For behold, thus saith the Lord: This people begin to wax in iniquity; they understand not the scriptures" (2:23; emphasis added). Jacob had especially condemned those (probably among the leading royalty) who had justified their infidelity by claiming that it was a royal prerogative to act as King Solomon, who had taken many wives (2:23).[16] As with many of Solomon's wives and concubines, some of the women in the city of Nephi may likewise have been foreign women.[17] Jacob's words comprise strong reprimands and accusations against some of the men of the city of Nephi. The strength of his words was elevated especially when he combined them with priestly declarations about ridding his garments of their blood and sins (1:19; 2:2). No doubt these sharp reproofs had made Jacob unpopular in certain powerful circles that had already emerged within this small and newly established community. Perhaps representing the interests of those people who had political reasons to want Jacob's power weakened, Sherem made his move against the now aged Jacob.[18]

---

16. Contrary to the history of the kings in Israel, Deuteronomy 17:17 actually prohibited these rulers from taking too many wives: "Neither shall he multiply wives to himself, that his heart turn not away." The Nephite leaders had evidently violated this rule, for Jacob criticized them for turning their hearts away from their wives and causing many hearts to die, "pierced with deep wounds" (Jacob 2:35; see 3:7).

17. For a discussion of the population and demographics of this community, see John L. Sorenson, "The Composition of Lehi's Family," in *By Study and Also by Faith*, ed. John M. Lundquist and Stephen D. Ricks (Salt Lake City: Deseret Book and FARMS, 1990), 2:174–96; and James E. Smith, "How Many Nephites? The Book of Mormon at the Bar of Demography," in *Book of Mormon Authorship Revisited: The Evidence for Ancient Origins*, ed. Noel B. Reynolds (Provo, UT: FARMS, 1997), 255–94.

18. Jacob was apparently fairly old at the time of this incident. He had already said farewell to his people (Jacob 6:13) and after that had survived "some years" (7:1). Shortly after the death

Sherem's strategy was an attempt to turn the tables on Jacob, by accusing *him* of perverting the scriptures, desecrating the law, and committing a number of other offenses (7:7). Such accusations clearly would have had profound political, religious, and legal ramifications.

Commencement of the Proceeding

Several points indicate that Sherem's complaints against Jacob had direct legal implications. Jacob's statement "and after this manner did Sherem *contend* against me" (Jacob 7:7; emphasis added) offers evidence that the ancient reader or hearer would have understood Sherem's action in a fully legal context, for the English word *contend* is very likely a translation of the Hebrew word *rîb*, "to strive, contend, or raise a controversy." Although this word can refer to any kind of physical conflict or verbal disputation, it is particularly used in introducing or commencing lawsuits in biblical texts: "In most cases *rîb* involves litigation."[19] Its use in connection with an actual lawsuit appears to be indicated in Proverbs 25:8, "Go not forth hastily *to strive*" (emphasis added), that is, to bring a lawsuit. The word *rîb* clearly refers to lawsuits "within thy gates" (Deuteronomy 17:8), appearing regularly in texts establishing rules regarding legal proceedings, witnesses, and judges (e.g., Exodus 23:2–6; Deuteronomy 19:17; 25:1; 2 Chronicles 19:8–10). Indeed, it has been said that "if there were contemporary records extant of ancient Israel's court proceedings or of speech about them, this word [*rîb*] would surely be found" there.[20] The accuser in a *rîb* in the Old Testament typically had personal knowledge of the alleged violation before he commenced his accusation,[21] which compares well with Jacob 7:6, "for I have heard and also know." Verbs of motion in the Hebrew accounts often signify the commencement of a *rîb*.[22] Sig-

---

of Sherem, futile efforts were made to convert the Lamanites (v. 24), and then Jacob "began to be old" (v. 26) and concluded his record.

19. Helmer Ringgen, "*rîb*," in Bottwerweck et al., *Theological Dictionary of the Old Testament*, 13:475. This word often "takes on legal-judicial significance," frequently with God acting as accuser and judge; see Robert D. Culver, "(*rîb*) strive, contend," in *Theological Wordbook of the Old Testament*, ed. Robert Laird Harris, Gleason L. Archer Jr., and Bruce K. Waltke (Chicago: Moody, 1980), 2:2159. The same source states that the Greek counterpart in the Septuagint, *krino*, is likewise a word "with prevalently legal-judicial overtones." For further discussion of the so-called prophetic lawsuit (*rîb*) with God as party and judge, see John W. Welch, "Benjamin's Speech as a Prophetic Lawsuit," in *King Benjamin's Speech: "That Ye May Learn Wisdom,"* ed. Stephen D. Ricks and John W. Welch (Provo, UT: FARMS, 1998), 167–73. See also Bovati, *Re-Establishing Justice*, 31–32, 51.

20. Culver, "(*rîb*) strive, contend," offering Proverbs 25:8 as evidence.

21. Bovati, *Re-Establishing Justice*, 71.

22. Bovati, *Re-Establishing Justice*, 221 (citing Judges 21:22; Proverbs 25:8; Isaiah 66:15–16).

nificantly, Jacob indicates that Sherem "sought much opportunity that he might *come* unto [him]" and was ultimately successful, as he "*came* unto [Jacob]" and began to voice his accusations (vv. 3, 6; emphasis added). Thus it seems that Jacob purposefully used the words *contend against* to describe Sherem's conduct.[23]

Several biblical scholars find it likely that lawsuits in ancient Israel began when one party approached the other and announced something like, "I have a controversy [*rîb*] with you" (compare Hosea 4:1).[24] If these words were spoken at the town gate or at some other public place, a body of city elders would assemble quite spontaneously and proceed to hear and decide the matter. The opponent or accuser would first state his case: "He contends [verb—*rîb*] against [the accused], stating the offence."[25] "Often the plaintiff's case must have sounded very good, for the Hebrew sage observes that he who states his case [*rîb*] first (i.e., the plaintiff) seems right until the other (i.e., the defendant) comes to examine him (Proverbs 18:17)."[26]

However, Sherem's controversy did not materialize into a traditional, judicial lawsuit. No elders or judges are mentioned in Jacob's account because, as this proceeding developed, it never had any need for non-party witnesses to be called or a verdict to be pronounced. Still, Sherem's accusations and supporting evidences were specifically formulated and introduced (Jacob 7:6–7). His words were intended to be very threatening, "to shake [Jacob] from the faith" (v. 5). To dislodge the beliefs of an established priest like Jacob, more than a few rhetorical questions or philosophical inquiries would have been required. Sherem needed to prove that Jacob was wrong, not in a modern rational sense, but in the sense of violating the laws of God. Such proof would shake Jacob, the leading priest in the temple of Nephi, out of his position in the Nephite ritual hierarchy or household of faith since he would be denounced, removed, and punished. To all who heard Sherem's bill of particulars, the case against

---

23. The words *contend* and *contentions* appear 143 times in the Book of Mormon. Like their Hebrew counterpart *rîb*, these words can refer to wars and contentions, physical fighting, political uprisings, and general or legal disputations. All forms of "contentiousness," including lawsuits, are condemned by the Savior (3 Nephi 11:29; 12:25).

24. For an interesting possible reconstruction of a typical legal action in ancient Israel, see Donald A. McKenzie, "Judicial Procedure at the Town Gate," *Vetus Testamentum* 14 (1964): 100–104; the quotation is from p. 102. See also Robert R. Wilson, "Israel's Judicial System in the Preexilic Period," *Jewish Quarterly Review* 74, no. 2 (1983): 229–40; and Ludwig Köhler, *Hebrew Man: Lectures Delivered at the Invitation of the University of Tübingen, December 1–16, 1952*, trans. Peter R. Ackroyd (New York: Abingdon, 1956), appendix entitled "Justice in the Gate," 127–50.

25. McKenzie, "Judicial Procedure at the Town Gate," 102.

26. McKenzie, "Judicial Procedure at the Town Gate," 102.

Jacob probably sounded potent and persuasive until Jacob answered and "confound[ed] him in all his words" (v. 8).

There are reasons to think that Sherem confronted Jacob in a public place like the city gate, temple courtyard, or a gathering place where such controversies were normally heard.[27] If Jacob and Sherem had simply conversed in private, without public witnesses, the pro-Sherem portion of the populace could have suspected foul play when Sherem fell helplessly to the ground, and there would have been less reason for him to make a *public* retraction (Jacob 7:17, 19) of his denial of the Messiah (v. 9) without giving the people more of an explanation of what had happened. Moreover, legal trials usually involved the public. Moses commanded, "All the congregation shall stone him" (Numbers 15:35), the accusation of Naboth occurred "in the presence of the people" (1 Kings 21:13), and the trial of Jeremiah was witnessed by "all the people" gathered against him (Jeremiah 26:9). At a minimum, Sherem's position on these issues must have been known to others in the community, so his confrontation with Jacob carried the weight of more than merely a private conversation or disagreement.

Pietro Bovati has provided readers with the most detailed analysis of controversies reported in the Bible that are of the same type as Sherem's controversy. Bovati calls these actions "juridical" rather than "judicial" because no judge was involved in them.[28] Although these juridical actions were less formal than judicial proceedings,[29] they nevertheless all followed a consistent overall pattern and employed recurring verbal expressions. As Bovati has very informatively and convincingly shown, in broad terms they began with an accusation that demanded justice. That accusation could take the form of declarations or interrogatives. The accuser's purpose was to try to convince the other party of the errors or foolishness of his position and to induce a change. The proceeding often took the form of a dialogue in which the accused responded either by acknowledging his error or by countering with accusations against his accuser. Ultimately, unless a reconciliation was reached, the juridical dispute escalated into a more formal judicial proceeding or, in some cases, the parties resorted to violence or strife. The underlying objective of such a confrontation, therefore, was to attempt to avert hostilities and to restore peace and equanimity between the parties and amidst the affected society as a whole.

---

27. See Köhler, *Hebrew Man*, 127–32.

28. Bovati, *Re-Establishing Justice*, 30–166.

29. Such disputes often took the form of an accusatory, narrative dialogue. Bovati, *Re-Establishing Justice*, 72–74.

For these and further reasons developed below, it is quite clear that Sherem's accusations set in motion the first stage of a classic juridical controversy. With this understanding in mind, the following legal dimensions of this otherwise religious text in Jacob 7 come to light.

Sherem's Accusations

Sherem raised several specific allegations against Jacob.[30] Interestingly, such accusations or allegations in the Hebrew Bible take one of two forms, either "interrogative" or "declarative,"[31] with the declarative form often using the word *behold* (*hinnēh*) to signal "the appearance of the punitive sanction."[32] In Sherem's case, the accusation was declarative: "Behold, I, Sherem declare . . ." (Jacob 7:7). Sherem's accusations involved the three crimes of (1) causing public apostasy, (2) blasphemy, and (3) false prophecy, as follows:

> Ye have *led away much of this people* that they *pervert* the right way of God, and *keep not* the law of Moses which is the right way; and *convert* the law of Moses into the worship of a being which ye say shall come many hundred years hence. And now behold, I, Sherem, declare unto you that this is *blasphemy*; for no man knoweth of such things; for he *cannot tell of things to come.* (Jacob 7:7; emphasis added)

Each of Sherem's accusations can be traced to specific provisions in pre-exilic Israelite legal texts.

Causing public apostasy. It was a serious offense under the law of Moses to lead people or a city into apostasy.[33] While *being* an individual apostate in and of itself was probably not a punishable legal offense under biblical, Nephite, or Jewish law,[34] *leading other people* into apostasy was recognized as a serious infraction under legal rules in the Bible and the

---

30. These points are discussed briefly in my FARMS Update, "Sherem's Accusations against Jacob," *Insights* 11, no. 1 (January 1991): 2. See also Bovati, *Re-Establishing Justice*, 75.

31. Bovati, *Re-Establishing Justice*, 75.

32. Bovati, *Re-Establishing Justice*, 86–87.

33. See Michael D. Guinan, "Mosaic Covenant," in *Anchor Bible Dictionary*, 4:905–9. See also Westbrook, "Punishments and Crimes," 5:546–56.

34. Specific violations of the law, however, were of course punishable. Rules such as "an Israelite, although a sinner, is still an Israelite" (Babylonian Talmud [hereafter TB] *Sanhedrin* 44a) and the fact it was "not within the power of a Jew . . . to renounce his Jewishness" indicate that apostate belief alone was not punishable. Ben-Zion Schereschewsky, "Apostate," in *The Principles of Jewish Law*, ed. Menachem Elon (Jerusalem: Keter, 1975), 377. Compare Alma 1:17–18, "the law could have no power on any man for his belief," but for misconduct the people were "punished."

Talmud.[35] The laws in Deuteronomy 13 condemn to death any person, whether a prophet or brother or son or wife, who says to "the inhabitants of their city, . . . Let us go and serve other gods, which ye have not known" (v. 13; see vv. 2, 6). "Thou shalt not consent unto him, nor hearken unto him; . . . but thou shalt surely kill him" (vv. 8–9).

This was the essence of Sherem's first claim against Jacob, namely, that he had "led away" many of the people into apostasy (Jacob 7:7). Sherem elaborated his accusation further by alleging that Jacob had caused the people to pervert the right *way* of God, not to keep the law, and to convert the law into the worship of an *unknown god*. Sherem could have given no better enumeration of the criteria of apostasy.[36] Indeed, the law of Moses was equally specific. Deuteronomy uses the same word, *way* (*derekh*), in defining this crime as trying to thrust the people "out of *the way* which the Lord thy God commanded thee to walk in" (Deuteronomy 13:5; emphasis added). In Deuteronomic theology and in the Psalms, "the way of God" referred to the Torah, or the commandments and statutes that defined the full state or condition coming from God's covenant with his people, and the highway of salvation that freed Israel from bondage.[37] Turning people away from the right way entailed perversion of the entire law and covenant. Moreover, Sherem's point that Jacob had converted the observance of the law of Moses into the worship of an *unknown* future being seems to have been based precisely on the Deuteronomic prohibition against turning to serve new gods "which ye have *not known*" (vv. 2, 6, 13; emphasis added). Thus it appears that Sherem accused Jacob quite specifically of having illegally led the people into a state of apostasy by turning them away from the law to worship an unknown being. These allegations were not merely vague or ethical criticisms; they were well-formulated accusations, logically derived from specific provisions of the ancient law found on the plates of brass.

Blasphemy. Another capital offense under the law of Moses was blasphemy (Exodus 20:7; Leviticus 24:10–16), a crime that figures prominently and expressly in the cases of Sherem and Korihor and to a limited extent

---

35. "If a beast which does not know any difference between good and evil is stoned because of the mischief it caused, *a fortiori* must a man who caused another to commit a capital offense be taken by God from this world." Sifra, Kedoshim, 10:5, quoted in Haim H. Cohn, "Penal Law," in *Principles of Jewish Law*, 470.

36. An apostate (*mumar* or *meshumed*) has been traditionally defined as one who "denies the Torah and converts to another faith." Schereschewsky, "Apostate," 377. While the word *convert* obviously has a different meaning here than in Jacob 7:7, the underlying problem is the same, namely, denying the law and actively turning away from it in some other direction.

37. K. Koch, "*derekh*," in Botterweck et al., *Theological Dictionary of the Old Testament*, 3:290.

in the trial of Abinadi.[38] Sherem raised this second charge against Jacob when he formally accused him, saying, "I, Sherem, declare unto you that this is blasphemy" (Jacob 7:7). While the precise history of the crime of blasphemy is obscure, there is good evidence that the offense of blasphemy in early biblical times embraced many forms of insolent or seditious speech, whether against God, against the king (1 Kings 21:10), or against another man,[39] and in some cases against holy places or things, including "the word of the Lord" (Numbers 15:31) or the law (a case of blaspheming the law is found in Acts 6:13). Sherem's accusation is the earliest known application of the term *blasphemy* to the specific idea of redirecting the law into the worship of a future messiah, but his complaint fits easily under the ancient legal notion of insolent, contemptuous, or sacrilegious speech, which was broadly understood. Cases based on such a broad-ranging class of misconduct had to be defined and judged on a case-by-case basis, which may explain why Sherem says, "*I* declare unto you" that teaching of the Messiah in this way constitutes blasphemy (Jacob 7:7; emphasis added). An interpretation of the term was apparently needed to make it applicable to Jacob. This would also suggest that Sherem's construction was his own and that he took responsibility for giving an innovative—if not expansive and reaching—meaning to the term *blasphemy*.

False Prophecy. Sherem's words also seem to have advanced a claim of false prophecy. Deuteronomy 18:20 requires that a prophet be put to death if he speaks words in the name of the Lord that God has not commanded him to speak, or if he speaks "*in the name of* other gods" (emphasis added). One can understand how easily Jacob's "preaching . . . the doctrine *of* Christ" (Jacob 7:6; emphasis added) could have been deviously characterized by Sherem as a form of speaking "in the name of" another god.[40] Nephi and Jacob had spoken emphatically about the name of Christ— about magnifying his name; about believing, praying, and baptizing in his name (2 Nephi 9:23–24; 25:13; 31:11; 32:9); and about worshipping the

---

38. See the discussions of blasphemy in the parts of this volume dealing with those cases. See generally Leonard W. Levy, *Treason against God: A History of the Offense of Blasphemy* (New York: Schocken Books, 1981); Haim H. Cohn, "Divine Punishment," in *Principles of Jewish Law*, 523; "Capital Punishment," in *Principles of Jewish Law*, 529; George Horowitz, *The Spirit of Jewish Law* (New York: Bloch, 1953), 183–85; and Westbrook, "Punishments and Crimes," 5:549.

39. See examples given by Shalom M. Paul, "Daniel 3:29—A Case Study of 'Neglected' Blasphemy," *Journal of Near Eastern Studies* 42, no. 4 (1983): 291–94, giving examples from the Middle Assyrian Laws (MAL A2:14–16) and other cuneiform inscriptions. See also J. Weingreen, "The Case of the Blasphemer (Leviticus XXIV 10ff.)," *Vetus Testamentum* 22, no. 1 (1972): 118–23; and Falk, *Hebrew Law in Biblical Times*, 71.

40. The "doctrine *of* Christ" is not only the doctrine *about* Christ but the doctrine *belonging to* Christ, received *from* Christ, and given *in the name of* Christ.

Father in his name (25:16; Jacob 4:5). If Sherem could persuade those who might act as judges to accept his interpretation of Deuteronomy, he could successfully condemn Jacob for speaking in a manner that was forbidden by law. Perhaps to avoid such accusations, the prophets of the Book of Mormon insisted emphatically that God and his Son are "but *one* God" (Alma 11:28–29, 35; emphasis added) and that "the doctrine of Christ" is one with "the only and true doctrine of the Father, and of the Son, and of the Holy Ghost, which is *one* God" (2 Nephi 31:21; emphasis added). Beyond teaching true doctrine, these declarations may have served an important legal function—to affirm that speaking "in the name of" Christ was not to be construed as speaking "in the name of other gods."

Moreover, one test for whether a prophet had spoken truly or falsely in the name of the Lord was to see "if the thing follow not, nor come to pass" (Deuteronomy 18:22). Accordingly, one of Jacob's defenses against the claim that he had committed the crime of false prophecy when he spoke of things far in the future could well have been "wait and see." But it seems that Sherem tried to preclude Jacob from using this defense when he objected that Jacob had spoken of things too far distant in the future, of things to "come many hundred years hence." When Sherem asserted categorically that "*no man* knoweth of *such* things" (Jacob 7:7; emphasis added), he may have been arguing that prophecies of such long-term nature should not easily be tolerated under the law. With shorter-term prophecies, at least one has the chance to verify them or prove their falsity within a reasonable period of time (consider, for example, the five-year prophecy of Samuel the Lamanite in Helaman 14:2).

Jacob's Answer

Following Sherem's accusations, it was Jacob's obligation to answer, as silence would be construed as an admission of guilt or wrongdoing.[41] Indeed, Jacob spoke up boldly, having the Spirit of the Lord, insomuch that he "did confound him in all his words" (Jacob 7:8). Typically, strong language was used by the accused in denying guilt and vindicating himself. Indeed, the "protestation of innocence can be transformed into an accusation against the accuser," turning the tables and now putting him on

---

41. In Micah 3:7, the wicked have no rebuttal: "They shall all cover their lips; for there is no answer of God." According to Falk, *Hebrew Law in Biblical Times*, 59, "omission [i.e., not taking an oath] implied admission of guilt." See the discussion of the legal implications of silence in connection with the trial of Alma and Amulek, discussed below; and compare Bovati, *Re-Establishing Justice*, 72, 93–94, 329–34.

the defensive.[42] Asking two questions (vv. 9–10), Jacob framed the thrust
of his response in the interrogative form, which was a common form of
ancient response or accusation.[43] Modestly, Jacob did not include in the
record further details about what he said to refute Sherem's theories—for
example, casting doubt on Sherem's interpretation of the legal terms he
had used, showing how confused his ideas were, rebutting him with scriptures regarding the coming of the Messiah, withstanding him with contrary testimony and perhaps an oath ("they truly testify of Christ," v. 11),
or causing him to become ashamed and embarrassed. These outcomes are
all possible within the meanings of the possible Hebrew words behind
the English word *confound*, a word often used in the Old Testament to
describe the confusion, reproach, dismay, and shame suffered by people
when their errors are exposed.

Sherem's Demand for a Divine Omen as Dispositive Evidence

Sherem's response to Jacob's rebuttal was ill-fated. He did not retract his
allegations. A retreat would have been hard for him to accomplish without
exposing himself to the serious charge of being a false accuser or false witness under Deuteronomy 19:16–21, for the punishment imposed on those
who falsely initiated lawsuits was "then shall ye do unto him, as he had
thought to have done unto his brother" (v. 19). Instead of withdrawing his
accusations, Sherem challenged Jacob to produce divine evidence to support the testimony and answer that Jacob had given (Jacob 7:13).

Properly or officially consulting the gods through omens, divination,
oaths, and ordeals was indeed a fairly normal practice in ancient Israelite
and ancient Near Eastern trials,[44] though the tactic of appealing to divine
evidence was removed from the judicial process in most cases in later Jewish

---

42. Bovati, *Re-Establishing Justice*, 114. In this connection, Bovati considers this turnaround
to be "part of the very structure of a bilateral encounter," citing the controversy between Laban and Jacob in Genesis 31 and the disputation between Saul and David in 1 Samuel 24 as
examples.

43. Bovati, *Re-Establishing Justice*, 75, 77–78, 114. See Haim H. Cohn, "Pleas," in *Encyclopae-
dia Judaica*, ed. Fred Skolnik and Michael Berenbaum, 2nd ed. (Jerusalem: Keter, 2007), 16:229.
For good examples of questions used in the juridical give-and-take between Laban and Jacob, see
Genesis 31:26, 27, 28, 30, 36, 37.

44. Hans Jochen Boecker, *Law and the Administration of Justice in the Old Testament and Ancient East*, trans. Jeremy Moiser (Minneapolis: Augsburg, 1980), 81–82; Haim H. Cohn, "Perjury"
and "Ordeal," in *Principles of Jewish Law*, 517, 524–25; and Falk, *Hebrew Law in Biblical Times*,
55–56. For example, Section 2 in the Code of Hammurabi calls for an ordeal when a person has
been accused of sorcery but the accuser cannot prove it. See W. McKane, "Poison, Trial by Ordeal
and the Cup of Wrath," *Vetus Testamentum* 30, no. 4 (1980): 474–92.

law.[45] In the Deuteronomic law, however, God was assumed to be in the court (Deuteronomy 19:17), and it was widely held that "God's presence in the court would sufficiently enlighten the minds of the judges to detect the falsehood of [any] testimony in time," as Haim Cohn has explained.[46] The crucial text in this regard is found in Deuteronomy: "If a false witness rise up against any man to testify against him that which is wrong; then both the men, between whom the controversy is, shall stand *before the Lord*" (vv. 16–17; emphasis added). Thus Sherem's conduct requesting Jacob to produce divine evidence was not a casual case of idle sign seeking, but rather followed a significant rule of ancient Israelite jurisprudence.

Divine evidence manifested the will of God in the matter, revealing a powerful dose of divine justice. Such evidence or divine justice was sought in ancient courts, especially when a sole defendant (such as Jacob) insisted upon his innocence but the plaintiff's evidence had come up lacking (as had Sherem's). Saul Berman, with respect to Jewish law generally, explains that in such cases where "the hands of the court are tied because of evidentiary or procedural principles," the court is left little option but to "use the threat of divine retribution as a means of inducing the wrongdoer to remedy the injury of his own free choice."[47] Divine evidence was also used, as was the case here, when no further witnesses could "be produced by either party," in which case "the matter was referred, by Hebrew as well as by other laws, to divine decision."[48]

---

45. "From early rabbinic times, direct divine intervention in the legal process was rejected. Proof was required to satisfy human cognitive capabilities." Bernard S. Jackson, "Susanna and the Singular History of Singular Witnesses," *Acta Juridica* (1977): 39. See M. *Sotah* 9:9; Bernard S. Jackson, "The Concept of Religious Law in Judaism," in *Aufstieg und Niedergang der römischen Welt*, ed. Hildegard Temporini and Wolfgang Haase (Berlin: de Gruyter, 1979), II.19.1:33–52; and Ze'ev W. Falk, *Introduction to Jewish Law of the Second Commonwealth* (Leiden: Brill, 1972), 1:113–14.

46. Cohn, "Perjury," 517.

47. Saul Berman, "Law and Morality," in Elon, *Principles of Jewish Law*, 155. See also generally Westbrook, "Punishments and Crimes," 5:546–56. For further information on evidence, see Joseph M. Baumgarten, "On the Testimony of Women in 1QSa," *Journal of Biblical Literature* 76, no. 4 (1957): 266–69; Haim H. Cohn, "The Proof in Biblical and Talmudical Law," in *La Preuve en Droit*, ed. C. Perelman and P. Foriers (Bruxelles: Bruylant, 1981), 77–98; Warwick Elwin, *Confession and Absolution in the Bible* (London: Hayes, 1883); Ze'ev W. Falk, "Forms of Testimony," *Vetus Testamentum* 11, no. 1 (1961): 88–91; "Oral and Written Testimony," *Iura* 19 (1968): 113–19; Hugh Goitein, *Primitive Ordeal and Modern Law* (London: Allen and Unwin, 1923; Littleton, CO: Rothman, 1980); Irene Merker Rosenberg and Yale L. Rosenberg, "In the Beginning: The Talmudic Rule Against Self-Incrimination," *New York University Law Review* 63, no. 15 (1988): 955–1050; Lawrence H. Schiffman, "The Qumran Law of Testimony (Damascus Document)," *Revue de Qumran* 8, no. 4 (1975): 4603–12; and Hendrik van Vliet, *Did Greek-Roman-Hellenistic Law Know the Exclusion of the Single Witness?* (Franeker, Netherlands: Wever, 1980).

48. Falk, *Hebrew Law in Biblical Times*, 50.

The most common method of drawing divine directions into an ancient legal proceeding was through oaths, curses, and imprecations. As Cohn states, a "widespread method of ascertaining God's judgment was the curse . . . : he who takes the oath before God brings God's curse on himself if he perjures himself (compare 2 Chronicles 6:22–23)."[49] Parties to ancient Near Eastern lawsuits were often required to swear an oath at a temple to confirm the truth of an allegation or to bring a dispute to closure (compare Exodus 22:11).[50] In the same way, oaths were sworn at Israelite temples in connection with legal proceedings. Indeed, the dedicatory prayer for the Temple of Solomon specifically asked God to hear judicial oaths made in that holy place and to judge disputants: "If . . . the oath come before thine altar in this house: then hear thou in heaven, and do, and judge thy servants, condemning the wicked, to bring his way upon his head [in other words, do to him what he wickedly wanted to happen to the person he had accused]; and justifying the righteous, to give him according to his righteousness" (1 Kings 8:31–32; compare 2 Chronicles 6:23). The temple in the city of Nephi may well have served similar functions, for it was expressly modeled "after the manner of the temple of Solomon" (2 Nephi 5:16).[51] Thus Jacob, as the priest of that temple, could have expected Sherem's demand that the case be submitted to divine judgment by seeking some manifestation of the will of God concerning the matter.[52]

When oracular or divine evidence was forthcoming, it was typically viewed as conclusive and irrefutable. Thus there is evidence in Jewish law that when a case was in doubt, one of the parties would be urged to assume divine judgment upon himself "if he wish[ed] to fulfill his duty in the sight of heaven."[53] Indeed, Falk concluded that, "in the absence of proof, the accused had to take an oath or undergo another form of ordeal, and omission to do so implied admission of guilt."[54] Thus for several reasons,

49. Cohn, "Ordeal," 524. Falk, *Hebrew Law in Biblical Times*, 50–51: "Such rulings were obtained after trial by ordeal, by taking the risk that a curse would fall upon the guilty party, by taking an oath or by lot." See Douglas Stuart, "Curse," in *Anchor Bible Dictionary*, 1:1218–19.

50. See the discussion in Boecker, *Law and the Administration of Justice*, where one lawsuit begins, "On oath to the king!" (p. 23). Boecker notes that "the oath was the decisive form of proof in the legal assembly" (p. 26) and that in biblical law the oath was taken only by the accused (p. 35–36); see also pp. 108, 129–30, 168–69.

51. For more information on temples, see William A. Ward, "Temples and Sanctuaries: Egypt," in *Anchor Bible Dictionary*, 6:369–72.

52. "Because, as Creator of the world, God is universal, it is he who judges the nations with justice, requiting every person justly (Gen 15:14; 1 Sam 2:10; Ps 76:89; 110:6)." Temba L. J. Mafico, "Judge, Judging," in *Anchor Bible Dictionary*, 3:1106.

53. Berman, "Law and Morality," 155, citing BM 37a.

54. Falk, *Hebrew Law in Biblical Times*, 59.

Sherem's case was the very kind of case that would have demanded that the parties produce some form of divine evidence, and the issues raised by Sherem would have been conclusively established if the Lord had indicated his approval of Sherem's assertions.

The best-known instance of divine judgment in the law of Moses is found in Numbers 5:11–31, outlining a procedure whereby a husband who jealously suspected his wife of committing adultery but had no witnesses to prove it could bring her to the temple and have her undergo what most scholars view as a type of ordeal in which God became the judge.[55] The priest would write the words of a curse on a scroll and blot the words with bitter water and then give her that bitter water to drink. If she was innocent, the water would have no effect, and the husband was not guilty of raising a false accusation. If she was guilty, this procedure brought a curse upon her and "the Lord doth make [her] thigh to rot, and [her] belly to swell"; she was thereby condemned. A historical precedent for the use of another ordeal in Israelite law can be found when Moses burned and ground up the golden calf, sprinkled the powder on water, and commanded all who worshipped the calf to drink it (Exodus 32:20).

These texts show that seeking oracular signs would have been a likely, if not the only, legal strategy open to Sherem since his suit had quickly arrived at a standoff with his accusations on the one hand and Jacob's denial and rebuttal on the other. With no other witnesses that could be called to testify on the matter, Sherem did perhaps the only thing he could do by moving that the case be submitted to God's judgment when he asked, "Show me a sign" (Jacob 7:13).

Jacob's Compliance

Perhaps reluctantly, Jacob obliged Sherem because he had pressed the issue. As the leading priest and prophet in the city of Nephi, Jacob fashioned and administered the ordeal.[56] He was careful to declare his own neutrality in the procedure, so that God's judgment (rather than Jacob's) could be manifested, and to call upon God to show specifically that "he has power, both in heaven and in earth; and also, that Christ shall come" (Jacob 7:14). By asking God to show that Christ would come, Jacob made it clear that the explicit aim of the sign was to refute Sherem's third charge, that of false prophecy; at the same time, he also turned his defense into

---

55. Tikva Frymer-Kensky, "The Strange Case of the Suspected Sotah (Numbers V 11–31)," *Vetus Testamentum* 34, no. 1 (1984): 11–26; and Mafico, "Judge, Judging," 3:1106.

56. For more information on ordeals in general, see Merlin D. Rehm, "Levites and Priests," in *Anchor Bible Dictionary*, 4:304.

an accusation and called on God to settle the controversy, a well-attested juridical strategy in the ancient sources.[57]

It is not common, of course, for a prophet to comply with a request for a sign, and Deuteronomy 13:1–5 precluded prophets themselves from using signs to establish their own truthfulness: "If there arise among you a prophet . . . and giveth thee a sign or wonder, and the sign or wonder come to pass, whereof he spake unto thee, saying, Let us go after other gods, . . . thou shalt not hearken unto the words of that prophet." Signs such as those given by the priests of Pharaoh were still inadequate to prove that people should follow "other gods," and witchcraft was sternly prohibited: "Thou shalt not suffer a witch to live" (Exodus 22:18). Indeed, Jacob showed his reluctance about invoking any sign-seeking procedure when he expressed concern that he himself might thereby be criticized for tempting or trying God (Jacob 7:14).[58] It is reasonable to ask, therefore, why Jacob would have continued to pursue a sign under such circumstances. There may be several reasons:

1. Sherem's request was not a casual one. It was made in the context of a serious accusation, placing Jacob's official standing and mortal life in jeopardy. Jacob's defenses had been rejected by Sherem. Although Jacob was able to confound Sherem at first, Sherem responded by testifying that he knew there was no Christ: "I know that there is no Christ, neither has been, nor ever will be" (Jacob 7:9), therefore effectively implying that Jacob was a liar or had borne false witness. Jacob's character, office, and testimony had been directly attacked. Turning to God in such a case was not a trivial or trifling matter.[59]

2. Jacob was not the one who called for the sign. The rules prohibiting a prophet from coming forward and showing a sign in an effort to lead the children of Israel into apostasy or idolatry assume that the false prophet was the instigator of the oracular demonstration. Divination through the use of magic or oracles was commonly practiced in the ancient world, and thus the law of Moses was wise in warning the Israelites against anyone who came in the name of some other god, offering signs to lead them astray. Jacob, however, could not be accused of such an abuse, for he had not come offering any sign or wonder on his own behalf.

---

57. Bovati, *Re-Establishing Justice*, 58–59.

58. See Köhler, *Hebrew Man*, 139–40, discussing the infrequent role of priests in Hebrew trials and surmising that allowing an oracle to decide the outcome of a case was viewed as "the last resort."

59. Referring to the story of Achan in Joshua 7, Wilson writes, "This method of determining guilt by oracle is a dangerous one to use in any lineage trial and is usually avoided whenever possible." Robert R. Wilson, "Israel's Judicial System in the Preexilic Period," *Jewish Quarterly Review* 74, no. 2 (1983): 237.

3. Jacob had legal and spiritual support for his compliance. When Jacob reasserted himself as a witness as well as a party, he marshaled the scriptures as evidence in his behalf (Jacob 7:10–11) and cited his personal experiences with the Holy Ghost as further testimony on his side of the case: "It has also been made manifest unto me by the power of the Holy Ghost" (v. 12).

4. Jacob had introduced the factor of divine manifestation. By testifying of that manifestation, Jacob effectively opened a way for Sherem to demand some corroboration of "this power of the Holy Ghost, in the which [Jacob claimed to] know so much" (Jacob 7:13). Having himself introduced the evidence of the Holy Ghost into the contest, Jacob could scarcely object to Sherem's motion that Jacob now somehow support his introduction of such divine evidence by providing the sign requested by Sherem.

5. Both parties thus found themselves in a bind, each needing support for their accusations against each other. The entire process was at a logical impasse. By accusing Jacob on several counts, particularly of apostasy, Sherem forced Jacob's hand too. The charges of apostasy and blasphemy placed the very status and reliability of Jacob's testimony in legal doubt. "Jewish law holds the testimony of an apostate to be unreliable, since he disavows the whole of the Torah and is therefore liable to be untruthful."[60] Thus, ascertaining God's will may have been the only logically consistent way to obtain competent evidence on the issue, for if Sherem assumed that his accusation of apostasy was true, then he had no choice but to object to the admissibility of everything Jacob, as an apostate, would say.

6. Resorting to divine judgment in this situation was not only logical but also natural and suitable. Under ancient Israelite law, divine punishment applied specifically to cases of reproaching the Lord or despising the word of the Lord (Numbers 15:30–31), which would include "public blasphemy" and "offenses [that] are mostly of a religious or sacerdotal

---

60. Schereschewsky, "Apostate," 378. For more information on testimony, see James A. Friend, "Do Not Testify according to the Majority" (in Hebrew), *Bibliotechka Mezhdunarodnika* 26 (1981): 129–36; Chiam Milikowsky, "Law at Qumran—A Critical Reaction to Lawrence H. Schiffman, *Sectarian Law in the Dead Sea Scrolls: Courts, Testimony, and the Penal Code*," *Revue de Qumran* 12, no. 2 (1986): 237–49; Jacob Neusner, "By the Testimony of Two Witnesses in the Damascus Document IX, 17–22 and in Pharisaic-Rabbinic Law," *Revue de Qumran* 8, no. 2 (1973): 197–217; Lawrence H. Schiffman, *Sectarian Law in the Dead Sea Scrolls: Courts, Testimony, and the Penal Code* (Leiden: E. J. Brill, 1975); Hendrick van Vliet, *No Single Testimony: A Study on the Adoption of the Law of Deut. 19:15 par. into the New Testament* (Utrecht, Netherlands: Kemink and Zoon, 1958); and Ben Zion Wacholder, "Rules of Testimony in Qumranic Jurisprudence: CD 9 and 11Q Torah 64," *Journal of Jewish Studies* 40, no. 2 (1989): 163–74.

[priestly] character."[61] Accordingly, Jacob expressly named heaven and earth as the ultimate domain of this stage of their trial by ordeal: "If God shall smite thee, let that be a sign unto thee that he has power, both in heaven and in earth; and also, that Christ shall come" (Jacob 7:14).[62]

In sum, Sherem's accusations were all of a religious or sacral nature, one of them being a charge of public blasphemy. Thus he could have expected, in addition to any judicial punishment meted out by a court against Jacob, that God himself would additionally and independently take action against Jacob for such transgressions and offenses against God.[63] By the same token, Jacob could have been seen as obstructing justice if he had refused to seek God's will in the matter. As the case unfolded, of course, the requested sign was given; God smote Sherem (Jacob 7:15).

Manifestation of Divine Punishment

As Jacob asked that the will of the Lord be done, "the power of the Lord came upon [Sherem], insomuch that he fell to the earth" (Jacob 7:15). The record does not say exactly what had happened to him. Sherem was not struck dumb; unlike Korihor[64] he continued to speak. He may have been

---

61. Cohn, "Divine Punishment," 523. Numerous provisions under the law of Moses were not enforced by human courts but were left to God, who would "cut off" the offender. Many of these crimes deal with acts committed in private, making their detection, conviction, or punishment quite unfeasible. See, for example, Leviticus 7:25–27; 17:10–14; 23:29–30; 26:14–43; Deuteronomy 27:14–26; 28:15–68. For more information, see George Wesley Buchanan, "The Courts of the Lord," *Vetus Testamentum* 16, no. 2 (1965): 231–32; Catherine Chin, "Job and the Injustice of God: Implicit Arguments in Job 13.17–14.12," *Journal for the Study of the Old Testament* 64 (1994): 91–101; P. Dacquino, "La formula 'Giustizia di Dio' nei libro dell' Antico Testamento," *Rivista Biblica* (Italiana) 17 (1969): 103–19, 365–82; Tikva S. Frymer-Kensky, "The Judicial Ordeal in the Ancient Near East," 2 vols. (PhD diss., Yale University, 1977); Baruch Halpern, "Yahweh's Summary Justice in Job XIV 20," *Vetus Testamentum* 28, no. 4 (1978): 472–74; J. Ruwet, "Misericordia et Iustitia Dei in Vetere Testamento," *Verbum Domini* 25 (1947): 35–42, 89–98; Peretz Segal, "The Divine Verdict of Leviticus X 3," *Vetus Testamentum* 39, no. 1 (1989): 91–95; Konrad Stock, "Gott der Richter: Der Gerichtsgedanke als Horizont der Rechtfertigungslehre," *Evangelische Theologie* 40, no. 3 (1980): 240–56; Gerhard von Rad, *Old Testament Theology*, trans. D. M. G. Stalker, 2 vols. (New York: Harper and Row, 1962–65); and Timothy M. Willis, "Yahweh's Elders (Isa 24,23): Senior Officials of the Divine Court," *Zeitschrift für die alttestamentliche Wissenschaft* 103, no. 3 (1991): 375–85.

62. The heavens and the earth were typically called upon by the Hebrew prophets to stand as witnesses against the wicked. See Isaiah 1:2 and Hosea 2:21. The calling of witnesses in "prophetic lawsuits" is discussed in John W. Welch, "Benjamin's Speech as a Prophetic Lawsuit," 225–32. In Jacob 7:14, Jacob did not call upon the heavens and the earth as witnesses against Sherem, but he still named these two spheres of being as the venues for the sign to be given to Sherem.

63. Cohn, "Divine Punishment," 523.

64. For a discussion of the sign seeking and curse of Korihor, together with the use of curses in the ancient Mediterranean to debilitate opponents, especially in a litigation setting, see chapter 9 below on the trial of Korihor.

paralyzed by God to prevent him from going about among the people, or he may have been hit with such divinely inspired astonishment that when he fell he was seriously injured. All we know is that after falling to the ground, Sherem had to be nourished for "many days" (v. 15) but never recovered.

The fact that Sherem survived for several days would have tended to exculpate Jacob from any legal liability for his death and exclude him as the legal cause of Sherem's demise, for biblical law held that a tort was not the proximate or culpable cause of death if the injured party survived for a day or two after the injury.[65] For Sherem's death, God alone was responsible.

Surely, the people in the city of Nephi interpreted the outcome of this case solely as a manifestation of God's judgment. Sherem himself spoke to the people in terms of the "eternal [i.e., divine] punishment" he would suffer, and he feared that he would have to bear his awful sin forever (Jacob 7:18–19). His concerns and phraseology may have arisen from the words most frequently used in the Torah to describe God's punishment, unequivocally stating that the victim of divine judgment must "bear his guilt" or "bear his iniquity" (e.g., Leviticus 5:1; 7:18; 17:16; 20:19; 24:15; Numbers 5:31), sometimes coupled with the expression "lest ye die" (Exodus 28:43; Numbers 18:32). Thus Sherem's fate was directly and solely the result of his unsuccessful submission to a divine ordeal. The judgment of God came in a way that was direct, immediate, and out of the hands of society.[66]

Sherem's Confession

Shortly before his death, Sherem requested that a public assembly be convened so that he could speak to the people. The people were given one day's notice ("gather together on the morrow," Jacob 7:16), and apparently a formal public announcement was sent out to the entire populace. The assembly met so that Sherem could publicly confess his error and retract his previous teachings. Confession marked the end of a *rîb*.[67] As Sherem

---

65. Compare Exodus 21:20–21 regarding the survival of a slave for a day or two after a beating; all the more would this be the case with the survival of a free citizen. Consider also the concept of causation in Jewish law generally. See David Daube, "Direct and Indirect Causation in Biblical Law," *Vetus Testamentum* 11, no. 3 (1961): 246–69.

66. "Judicial ordeals are distinguished by two important and interrelated aspects: the god's decision is manifested immediately, and the result of the trial is not in itself the penalty for the offense. . . . Not only does God decide whether [the party] is guilty, but even the right of punishment is removed from society and placed in the hands of God. . . . The individual . . . puts himself under divine jurisdiction, expecting to be punished by God if the oath-taker is guilty." Frymer-Kensky, "The Strange Case of the Suspected Sotah," 24. This represented an acknowledgment of God's ultimate sovereignty, as the parties (literally) "prayed" for relief; see *Encyclopaedia Judaica*, 3:751; 5:708.

67. Bovati, *Re-Establishing Justice*, 94.

was known for his skillful use of words (v. 4), it should not go unnoticed that his statement is elegantly chiastic[68] and therefore could have been carefully prepared in advance:

> He spake plainly unto them and denied the things which he had taught them, and confessed the Christ, and the power of the Holy Ghost, and the ministering of angels. And he spake plainly unto them, that he had been deceived by the power of the devil. And he spake of hell, and of eternity, and of eternal punishment. And he said,
>
> I *fear* lest I have committed the unpardonable sin,
>> for I have *lied unto God*;
>>> for I denied *the Christ*,
>>>> and said that I believed *the scriptures*;
>>>> and *they* truly
>>> testify of *him*.
>> And because I have thus *lied unto God*
> I greatly *fear* lest my case shall be awful; but I confess unto God.
> (Jacob 7:17–19)

In this confession, Sherem spoke plainly, clearly retracted his past erroneous assertions, and made an affirmative declaration embracing Jacob's theology. This fits the prototypical form of the ancient confession; the typical options open to an accused in a juridical proceeding who wished to confess his guilt were (1) to make an outright confession; (2) to say, "I have sinned"; or (3) to declare, "You are (in the) right."[69] Interestingly, Sherem's confession reflects all three of these conventions: He made an explicit confession, saying "I confess unto God" (Jacob 7:19); he openly "denied the things which he had taught" and admitted that he had "lied" and sinned (vv. 17–19); and he "confessed," even echoing Jacob's oath-bound word *truly* (v. 11) in affirming that the scriptures *truly* testify of Christ (v. 19).

---

68. For an introduction to the main principles of chiasmus in ancient literatures, see John W. Welch, ed., *Chiasmus in Antiquity: Structure, Analyses, Exegesis* (Hildesheim: Gerstenberg, 1981; Provo, UT: Research Press, 1999), 9–15. Inverted, chiastic structures (which follow a pattern that introduces a set of words in one order and then repeats them in the opposite order) can be particularly effective in legal settings: "Justice [chiastically] demands, 'as thou hast done, it shall be done unto thee: thy reward shall return upon thine own head' (Obadiah 1:15; see also Jeremiah 17:10). . . . No literary device could better convey the 'measure for measure' balancing concept of talionic justice than does the literary equilibrium of chiasmus." John W. Welch, "Chiasmus in Biblical Law: An Approach to the Structure of Legal Texts in the Bible," in *Jewish Law Association Studies IV: The Boston Conference Volume*, ed. Bernard S. Jackson (Atlanta: Scholars Press, 1990), 10.

69. Bovati, *Re-Establishing Justice*, 94; see generally pp. 94, 103–5.

Although Sherem's confession follows these standard conventions to the hilt, his words seem to have been voluntary and sincere. Unlike Nehor's and Korihor's confessions (Alma 1:15; 30:51–53), Sherem's confession appears to have been entirely self-scripted. Sherem attributed his error to the devil and expressed his deep concerns about the eternal welfare of his soul because he had lied to the God who had already manifested his judgment upon him in the flesh and who would soon judge his "case" after his death.

Besides seeing in this admission of anxiety and guilt a sincere expression of regret, Jacob and the people probably saw Sherem's confession as fulfilling several legal functions. Obtaining a confession was a desired, if not a required, part of ancient Israelite criminal trials.[70] As early as the case of Achan, Joshua entreated the already-identified culprit to "give glory to the Lord God of Israel, and make confession unto him" (Joshua 7:19). Citing this ancient case as its source, the Babylonian Talmud devotes an entire section[71] to the requirement that all convicts be asked to confess before they are executed (although by this time the element of glorifying God had been dropped): "When he is about ten cubits away from the place of stoning, they say to him, 'Confess,' for such is the practice of all who are executed."[72] It was considered so necessary to obtain a confession that if the person being executed did not know what or how to confess, the people involved in carrying out the execution had to "instruct him [to say], 'may my death be an expiation for all my sins.'"[73]

The purpose for such postverdict confessions was not to reverse the conviction. Pardon is not always possible or appropriate.[74] Sherem's case had already gone to divine judgment before any thought had been given to confession, and thus the procedure was legally, let alone physically, beyond the reach of clemency. Similarly, Achan was still executed, despite his full and honest confession detailing precisely what he had done (Joshua 7:20–21). However, the rabbis understood Achan's confession to have

---

70. Bovati, *Re-Establishing Justice*, 98–99.

71. TB *Sanhedrin* 6:3, 43b.

72. TB *Sanhedrin* 6:3, 43b.

73. TB *Sanhedrin* 6:3, 43b. For the biblical period, see Falk, *Hebrew Law in Biblical Times*, 52–55. In later Judaism, this confession came to be used as a deathbed prayer of confession, since all mankind are sinners. See Solomon Bennett Freehoff, *The Jewish Prayerbook* (Cincinnati: Commission on Information about Judaism, 1945); and Adolf Büchler, *Studies in Sin and Atonement in the Rabbinic Literature of the First Century* (London: Oxford University Press, 1928). See also *Encyclopaedia Judaica* 1:411 ("A dying man is presumed not to be frivolous on his deathbed, and his admissions are irrevocable").

74. Bovati, *Re-Establishing Justice*, 159.

improved his postmortal condition: "He who confesses has a portion in the world to come."[75] By confessing, even a convicted murderer hoped that his standing might be better before God. Surely Sherem hoped that his death would constitute an expiation of his sins before God, although he still knew he would die and he still feared the worst, for his sin was not only against man but also against God (Jacob 7:19).

Comporting with the ancient procedure, Sherem's confession both acknowledged his transgressions and extolled the powers of God. To glorify and acknowledge God, Sherem "confessed the Christ and the power of the Holy Ghost, and the ministering of angels" (Jacob 7:17). To admit his transgressions, Sherem "denied the things which he had taught," stated plainly "that he had been deceived by the power of the devil," and spoke of hell and eternal punishment (vv. 17–18).

The latter words in his confession, however, clearly indicate that Sherem feared that he still would have no part in the world to come.[76] This was because he had "lied unto God," presumably by swearing an oath, invoking the name of God, and averring that he believed the scriptures while at the same time denying the Messiah (Jacob 7:19). Having borne false witness against Jacob, Sherem deserved to die (Deuteronomy 19:16–19);[77] but having offended God, he knew his eternal case would be just as bad as his earthly situation, if not worse. As Eli commented regarding his sons who had caused the Lord's people to transgress, "If one man sin against another, the judge shall judge him: but if a man sin against the Lord, who shall intreat for him?" (1 Samuel 2:25). Being pardoned for sinning against God, sins that typically involved teaching religious falsehoods or serving false gods (Deuteronomy 20:18; Exodus 23:33), was difficult for the guilty party to count on,[78] as Sherem greatly feared.

A public confession was especially necessary in Sherem's case because he had proved himself to be a false accuser and, in effect, a false witness. Having initiated a false complaint against Jacob and having testified that he believed in the scriptures while denying the Messiah, Sherem became subject to the provisions of Deuteronomy 19:16–21, which require the

---

75. TB *Sanhedrin* 6:3, 43b. See Wilson, "Israel's Judicial System," 237–39, for a discussion of Achan's case.

76. The Talmud discusses the cases of several people who were said not to have a share in the world to come because of their wickedness, idolatry, and crimes against God. For example, see TB *Sanhedrin* 89a, 90a, 107b–108a, 111b.

77. While the commandment against bearing false witness (Exodus 20:16) prohibits lying in general, it condemns more specifically those who are false accusers or perjurers in formal legal proceedings (Exodus 23:1–2, 6–7).

78. Bovati, *Re-Establishing Justice*, 130.

unflinching punishment of all who "rise up against any man to testify against him that which is wrong" (v. 16).

Under this provision in the law of Moses, whose stringent enforcement Sherem himself had advocated, it was necessary for the people in a city to "put the evil away" from their midst (Deuteronomy 19:19). To do this, all the men in the community were commanded by law to "hear, and fear, and . . . henceforth commit no more any such evil" (v. 20). Specific examples of this practice are found in several situations involving public offenses. This ancient rule was interpreted in rabbinic times as requiring that "all convictions of perjury must be given wide publicity,"[79] preferably at a festival assembly,[80] so that all would know to disregard the words of the false witness. Also, according to later Jewish jurisprudence, "the punishment suffered by the criminal serves both as an expiation for the community at large and as an atonement for the murderer, provided, however, that he repents and makes full confession of his crime."[81]

Sherem's public confession fulfilled these requirements, manifesting that a similar understanding of the Deuteronomic law of false accusation and its accompanying oral traditions existed among the Nephites. All people in the land of Nephi were commanded to assemble, and there the multitude heard and "witnessed" (Jacob 7:21) what Sherem said. His case was given wide publicity. All the people feared, becoming "astonished exceedingly, insomuch that the power of God came down upon them, and they were overcome that they fell to the earth" (v. 21).

It is not clear, however, whether Sherem's confession was given at a special assembly or at a regular, calendared festival convocation. The original intent of Deuteronomy 19:20 seems to have called for a special assembly, and indeed it appears that Sherem's assembly was convened for the sole purpose of hearing his confession. It was called at his instigation, and with great urgency, as Sherem perceived the nearness of his own death (Jacob 7:16). On the other hand, taking into account that Jacob and his people waited many days before taking this public action (v. 15), and

---

79. Cohn, "Perjury," 517. "Public announcements must be made for four [malefactors]: a *mesith*, a 'stubborn and rebellious' son, a rebellious elder, and witnesses who are proved *zomemim* [conspiring witnesses]; . . . it is written, And those which remain [shall hear and fear]" (TB *Sanhedrin* 89a); see Maimonides, Yad, *Edut* 18:7.

80. The earliest practice reflected in TB *Sanhedrin* 10:6, 89a, was both to execute the false accuser and to proclaim his guilt on the next festival day following his conviction. On such a day the people of Israel would be gathered together where they could "hear and fear."

81. Hyman E. Goldin, *Hebrew Criminal Law and Procedure* (New York: Twayne, 1952), 23, citing Maimonides, *Hilkot Teshubah* 1:1. See also Westbrook, "Punishments and Crimes," 5:546–56.

that Sherem's assembly was called in the same manner in which Benjamin convened the festival-like assembly for the coronation of his son Mosiah (compare v. 16 and Mosiah 1:10), and further considering the ritual way in which the people of Jacob seem to have responded to the manifestation of God's power among them (Jacob 7:21; compare Mosiah 4:1–2), Sherem's public assembly appears to be at least similar in some respects to a regular festival appearance of the people before the Lord, as was required three times a year under the Code of the Covenant (Exodus 23:14–17).

In either event, whether it was given at a regular or special convocation, the net effect of Sherem's confession was collective—to reconcile the people with their God: "Peace . . . was restored again among the people" (Jacob 7:23). Indeed, as Bovati has argued,[82] the overriding purpose of all legal proceedings in ancient Israel was to restore the peace, to reestablish righteousness, "to restore justice."[83] Because "justice consists of a relationship between individuals," if a person has upset the peace of such human relationships, "then the inherent aim of a trial" is to "silence a person for good" in order to reestablish "justice itself."[84]

In addition, more was involved in biblical jurisprudence than just *human* interrelations, and thus it is significant that Jacob 7:23 also declares that "the love of God was restored again among the people." By concluding his account with this important declaration, Jacob left with one final indication that the law of Deuteronomy 13 was indeed integral to Sherem's case. The reason given in Deuteronomy for the detection and punishment of false prophets, evil dreamers, and sign givers is this: by such exercises "the Lord your God proveth you, to know whether ye *love the Lord your God* with all your heart and with all your soul" (Deuteronomy 13:3; emphasis added). Having successfully passed through just such a serious test regarding the Nephites' understanding of the requirements of Deuteronomy 13 concerning their duty to go after no other gods, Jacob ends his record quite deliberately by confirming that the people of the city of Nephi were fully reestablished in the love and the blessing of the Lord.

Sherem's Death

In the end, Sherem died. The plain meaning of the English text is that he died without human intervention: "When he had said these words he

---

82. For the importance of reconciliation as a desired outcome of legal conflict, see Bovati, *Re-Establishing Justice*, 119–66.

83. Bovati, *Re-Establishing Justice*, 342–43.

84. Bovati, *Re-Establishing Justice*, 342–43.

could say no more, and he gave up the ghost" (Jacob 7:20).[85] While this result may seem extremely harsh to modern readers, it was within normal expectations under ancient legal and religious precepts.[86] One man who had blasphemed, even though aggravated during an altercation, was publicly executed (Leviticus 24:23);[87] and another man who had been found gathering sticks on the Sabbath, perhaps to light a fire in worship of a false god, was stoned (Numbers 15:32–36).[88] Equally, divine judgment had once eradicated the wicked from the host of Israel when the earth opened up and consumed Dathan and Abiram and all their households (Deuteronomy 11:6). Often, "divine punishment is expressed in terms of simple death (e.g., Numbers 18:7) as well as of 'bearing one's iniquity.'"[89] And thus it was in the case of Sherem, who in the end was called a "wicked man" (Jacob 7:23), a flagrant false accuser who bore the punishment for his wrongdoing.

The modern reader should not overlook the close linguistic connection in Hebrew between the proper noun *Satan* (found as a title for the devil in the Hebrew Bible as early as 1 Chronicles 21:1, with many additional occurrences in the Book of Moses) and the general word *satan*, meaning "adversary," "opponent," "accuser," or "plaintiff" (as in Job 1:6; 2:1). The proper name *Satan* is "commonly derived from the root *satan*, which means 'to oppose, to plot against.' The word thus basically connotes an adversary."[90] So when Sherem is described by Jacob as having "much power of speech, according to the power of the *devil*" (Jacob 7:4; emphasis added), one may conjecture that Jacob was commenting on or alluding to the power of Sherem's formidable skills *as a plaintiff* (a *satan*), as well as remarking about the source of those powers (Satan). Likewise, when Sherem was "deceived by the power of the devil" (v. 18), he was also partly deceived by his overconfidence in the adversarial process. On the other side of the same coin, Sherem was patently wicked (v. 23). Along with his other faults, he had been shown to be a false or malicious accuser (ʿed hamas) under Deuteronomy 19:21.

---

85. The possibility need not be entirely precluded, however, that this is a euphemism, meaning that Sherem completed his confession and then was executed.

86. For an even more drastic case, see the account of the sudden deaths of Ananias and Sapphira in Acts 5:1–11, who had lied not only to man but also to God.

87. Weingreen, "The Case of the Blasphemer," 118–23.

88. J. Weingreen, "The Case of the Woodgatherer (Numbers XV 32–36)," *Vetus Testamentum* 16, no. 3 (1966): 361–64.

89. Cohn, "Divine Punishment," 523.

90. Arvind Sharma, "Satan," in *The Encyclopedia of Religion*, ed. Mircea Eliade et al. (New York: Macmillan, 1987), 13:81.

One also assumes that a Nephite listener might have mused at the resemblance between Sherem's name and the Hebrew word *ḥerem*. When a criminal was convicted of a capital offense, he was placed under a ban, a *ḥerem*, meaning "the proscription of a man or thing for immediate or ultimate destruction, whether by way of punishment, . . . to please God, . . . or to prevent mischief."[91] More than being seen as a mere loser or wrongdoer in the modern sense, Sherem had polluted his entire character with his litigious error: As Falk asserts, Israelite thought "did not conceive of crime as a singular phenomenon, but rather as a blemish upon the criminal's character that could be wiped out only by the appropriate sanction."[92]

Even if Sherem somehow originally thought that his action was well motivated or that he was justified in his conduct, he had miscalculated and misjudged. The ancient Israelite mind included within its concept of sin and defilement many forms of error and misconduct. Thus, mistakenly touching the ark of the covenant was punishable at the hands of heaven, even if the culprit may have had good intentions (1 Samuel 6:6–8; 1 Chronicles 13:9–10). Sherem's offenses were not trifling ones. In modern law, perjury is hardly ever prosecuted, and bringing a frivolous or malicious lawsuit is rarely punished in any way because convictions in such cases are extremely hard to win; but this was not the case under the law of Moses or the laws of the ancient Babylonians. Under the laws of the ancient Near East, the crimes of perjury—namely, the bearing of false witness under oath or the failure to prove one's sworn accusation against another—were apparently vigorously prosecuted, and offenders were seriously punished.[93] Section 17 of the laws of Lipit Ishtar provided that "if a man, without grounds (?), accuses another man of a matter of which he has no knowledge, and that man does not prove it, he shall bear the penalty of the matter for which he made the accusation."[94] Section 3 of the laws of Hammurabi required: "If a man comes forward to give false testimony in a case but cannot bring evidence for his accusation, if that

---

91. Haim H. Cohn, "*ḥerem*," in Elon, *Principles of Jewish Law*, 539–40. Proscribed men or things, like Sherem, were wicked, polluted, and taboo.

92. Falk, *Hebrew Law in Biblical Times*, 68.

93. For more information on perjury, see David Daube, *Witnesses in Bible and Talmud* (Oxford: Oxford Centre for Postgraduate Hebrew Studies, 1986); Joseph Plescia, *The Oath and Perjury in Ancient Greece* (Tallahassee: Florida State University Press, 1976); and Richard H. Underwood, "False Witness: A Lawyer's History of the Law of Perjury," *Arizona Journal of International and Comparative Law* 10, no. 2 (1993): 215–52.

94. Roth, *Law Collections*, 29.

case involves a capital offense, that man shall be killed."[95] The same type of punishment was required by biblical law and elsewhere in ancient Near Eastern law: "Then shall ye do unto him [the false accuser], as he had thought to have done unto his brother" (Deuteronomy 19:19).[96] Apparently much the same rule applied to false witnesses as it did to false accusers, so much so that it is sometimes difficult to distinguish between these two closely related offenses. Boecker went so far as to claim that in ancient Near Eastern law "unproven accusations and unproven testimony are . . . regarded as equivalent to false accusations and false witness."[97]

Cases of false accusation were among the few instances under the law of Moses where talionic justice (measure for measure, "life shall go for life, eye for eye, tooth for tooth, hand for hand, foot for foot") was mandated and clemency was not to be given: "Thine eye shall not pity" (Deuteronomy 19:21).[98] In Sherem's case, he had contravened many important rules: he had accused Jacob of several capital offenses and had failed to prove any of them, he had lied and thus had borne false witness, and he had attempted to lead the people astray under evil influences and false pretenses (Jacob 7:3, 18). Sherem's death, therefore, suited his crimes and conditions. His is a classic case where talionic justice and divine retribution were appropriately applied under ancient Israelite law.[99]

The Legacy of Sherem's Case

The outcome of Sherem's case provided a landmark in Nephite history. It effectively decided that the priests (and not the rulers in the palace

---

95. Roth, *Law Collections*, 81; for more on capital punishment, see Edwin M. Good, "Capital Punishment and Its Alternatives in Ancient Near Eastern Law," *Stanford Law Review* 19 (1967): 947–77.

96. Boaz Cohen, "Evidence in Jewish Law," *Recueils de la Société Jean Bodin* 16 (1965): 108; Cohn, "Perjury," 516–17; and Falk, *Hebrew Law in Biblical Times*, 73. In Neo-Babylonian law, in Lehi's day, "the penalty that the false accuser was trying to inflict on the defendant was imposed on the false accuser." Joachim Oelsner, Bruce Wells, and Cornelia Wunsch, "Neo-Babylonian Period," in *A History of Ancient Near Eastern Law*, ed. Raymond Westbrook (Leiden: Brill, 2003), 2:965. In later Jewish law, the effect of the biblical law was limited by tendentiously holding that the word *witness* in Deuteronomy 19:16 was a collective term, so that the drastic injunction of Deuteronomy 19:19 was applied "not to one witness but to a group of two or more witnesses" only; see Goldin, *Hebrew Criminal Law*, 220.

97. Boecker, *Law and the Administration of Justice*, 81.

98. Under rabbinic law some sages softened this result, however, by arguing that the death penalty applied only when the perjurer was detected in the narrow window of time between when "a man had been sentenced on the strength of false testimony, but before he was executed" (Cohn, "Perjury," 517), and by abolishing most forms of identical talionic penalties (Cohn, "Talion," in Elon, *Principles of Jewish Law*, 525).

99. See generally H. B. Huffmon, "Lex Talionis," in *Anchor Bible Dictionary*, 4:321–22; also Westbrook, "Punishments and Crimes," 5:546–56.

or men in the general population) would have power in the city of Nephi to interpret the law; Jacob's prophetic interpretation of the law of Moses prevailed when God rejected Sherem and his legal and religious views. Coming during the crucial early years of the establishment of the Nephite monarchy and religious observances, this case validated the messianic teachings of Lehi, Nephi, and Jacob, and it strengthened the role of the prophets, temple priests, and consecrated teachers in construing the law. The outcome of Sherem's case validated the authority of the prophetic office and tradition, which had in fact come under attack and had been rejected already by some Nephites during Jacob's lifetime (Jacob 6:8).

Furthermore, from a strictly legal point of view, if they had been successful, Sherem's accusations would have had severe consequences and repercussions; his interpretations would have been taken very seriously by all people in the city of Nephi. This case not only reinforced the fact that the crime of falsely accusing any person of a capital offense under the law of Moses exposed oneself to punishment by death (Deuteronomy 19:18–21), but it also opened the way for faithful Nephite leaders to proclaim the gospel of Jesus Christ without the threat of legal complications or contentions.

No wonder Jacob chose to conclude his book with the case of Sherem. This account not only places a seal of divine ratification on Jacob's entire life and ministry but it also introduces the period that follows in Nephite civilization. During the next generation, Enos was able to "declare the word according to the truth which is in Christ . . . in all [his] days" (Enos 1:26), and "there were exceeding many prophets" among them who preached harshly, especially about "the duration of eternity, and the judgments and the power of God, and all these things—stirring them up continually to keep them in the fear of the Lord" (vv. 22–23). Then Jarom, with great continuing patience, was able to be "exceedingly strict" in observing the law of Moses and not blaspheming (Jarom 1:5), and also was able to teach "the law of Moses, and the intent for which it was given, persuading [the people] to look forward unto the Messiah, and believe in him to come" (v. 11). It was the case of Sherem, perhaps more than any other key event in early Nephite law, religion, or society, that had made it clear that the law was to be taken very seriously and, at the same time, had cleared the way for this entrenchment and ascendancy of the revelations, interpretations, and teachings of Lehi, Nephi, and Jacob among the Nephites.

The case of Sherem set the tone of righteous judgment underlying all that follows in the Book of Mormon. Sherem's wrongful accusations set the pattern of unrighteous judgment and abuse of process. On the one hand, the essence of judging unrighteously is to be found in contentiousness, overconfidence, and showing disrespect for the Lord's anointed high priest. On the other hand, Jacob's success in faithfully and patiently withstanding Sherem's affront would become the model of righteous judgment, allowing justice to be manifest in the overt judgments and revelations of God.

CHAPTER SIX

The Trial of Abinadi

The second major legal proceeding in the Book of Mormon is the trial of a prophet named Abinadi, found in Mosiah 12–17. This is one of the most thoroughly reported legal incidents in the Book of Mormon, and it is considerably more complicated than Sherem's encounter with Jacob. Abinadi's potent condemnations of the unsavory King Noah and the unrepentant people in the city of Nephi gave rise to at least four separate accusations stated as legal causes of action (lying, prophesying falsely, blaspheming, and reviling). These accusations were leveled against Abinadi by three distinct parties, namely, the people at large, the priests of Noah, and Noah himself. Abinadi was ultimately executed, becoming the first reported martyr in the Book of Mormon.[1]

Abinadi's expositions and prophecies are thoroughly embedded in the judicial setting of his trial. The account of the trial and the surrounding narrative are replete with legal terms and forensic strategies that lend themselves readily to detailed analysis. Many legal elements in this record can be compared closely with ancient Israelite and subsequent Jewish judicial practices; in certain respects, however, Noah's court diverged from the traditional ancient precedents. An awareness of all these factors aids our understanding of Abinadi's courage in the face of these inequities. The trial of Abinadi raises many questions worthy of consideration in this analysis, from authorship of the account to the jurisprudential import of its many legal details.

---

1. The main ideas in this chapter were first circulated in two of my FARMS Preliminary Reports, "Judicial Process in the Trial of Abinadi" (Provo, UT: FARMS, 1983) and "Ancient Near Eastern Law and the Book of Mormon" (Provo, UT: FARMS, 1981), parts of which were presented at the regional meeting of the Society of Biblical Literature and American Association of Religions in Denver on April 16, 1982, and also formed the basis of Lew W. Cramer, "Abinadi," in *The Encyclopedia of Mormonism*, ed. Daniel H. Ludlow (New York: Macmillan, 1992), 1:5–7.

Who Wrote Mosiah 11–17?

The Book of Mormon account of Abinadi's trial and execution is re-markably lengthy and quite precise. It is one of the longest trial accounts to have survived from antiquity anywhere. It rewards close scrutiny. But before these chapters can be analyzed from a legal perspective, one must consider how this text originated. This text has a complex history. It is not entirely certain who spoke, reported, wrote, compiled, edited, or abridged the materials in Mosiah 11–17 as we now have them, or why these original reports or records were created. Yet it makes a difference who wrote this account and why. Obviously, the story would certainly have been told differently if it had been written by King Noah or one of his scribes as part of an opinion of the court.

The case of Abinadi began with the words that he spoke in public. Those words were then reported to King Noah by the people who had arrested Abinadi and handed him over to the royal court. Words were then spoken in court by Abinadi, the king, and his priests.

A primary or preliminary written record of the trial of Abinadi was then generated by a second voice, that of Alma the Elder (Mosiah 17:4), who personally witnessed most of these legal proceedings as a member of the court. Alma was a knowledgeable, dynamic, and dedicated person who sat as a young priest judging this case until he spoke in Abinadi's defense and was expelled by Noah from his seat of judgment (vv. 2–3). As a pro-Abinadi reporter, Alma focused mainly on the words of Abinadi and not on the arguments or concerns of the government. Even with the very best of motivations, it would have been difficult for Alma to overcome his animus against Noah and to temper his avid sympathies for Abinadi in order to write an unbiased report of what transpired in that courtroom.

Although Alma created and used this record primarily to serve his immediate religious needs and purposes in "teach[ing] the words of Abinadi" to his recent converts (Mosiah 18:1), this report also served many other lasting purposes, both legal and religious. Alma's text purposefully vindicated Abinadi, thus protecting Alma himself from any possible attempts that Noah and his cohorts might make to characterize Abinadi as a criminal who had been justifiably convicted and executed or to pursue Alma and punish him as a fugitive from justice and a political dissident. Alma's report placed the weight of responsibility for Abinadi's death on King Noah, paving the way, in a sense of poetic justice, for the reciprocal demise of the king consonant with the legal principle of talionic justice. Beyond serving these immediate needs, Abinadi's commentaries on the meaning of the law of Moses, his use of the Ten Commandments, and his success in withstanding the first three charges brought against him provided authoritative interpretations concerning several provisions in Nephite law and religion for many years to come.

In his place of hiding, Alma took "many days" to write "all the words which Abinadi had spoken" (Mosiah 17:4). We can assume that Alma wrote from memory since it is unlikely that he could have taken or retained any written notes of the proceeding. It is unclear what he eventually wrote on or how he managed to keep that memoir safe and secure, especially after he and his people were taken and held in bondage for several years in the land of Helam (Mosiah 23–24). Many, but perhaps not all, of Abinadi's words survived and were eventually included in the final record. The immediacy of Alma's writing, however, gives to the Book of Mormon account of Abinadi's case high documentary credentials. Nevertheless, because of the inclusion of details that Alma would not have been able to witness firsthand (such as what occurred after he was dismissed), it remains uncertain whether all the words in Mosiah 11–17 came from Alma or in part from others. Some of the narrative setting for the trial in Mosiah 12, some of the words attributed to Abinadi or Noah, and information about the conclusion of this case may have been contributed by others. Indeed, there are several likely candidates for such contributors.

Some of Alma's converts may have informed him about the case. After all, Alma may not have been present at the arrest of Abinadi, and he certainly was not present for the execution, so information about these events must have come from someone else. Alma's followers may have heard Abinadi deliver his message and may have been converted by the spirit with which he spoke. They may well have witnessed the arrest or the execution of Abinadi, and they may have been a first- or secondhand source for information reported in Mosiah 12 and 17.

In addition, Limhi's royal record probably included a report of the trial of Abinadi. Limhi was the son of King Noah and grandson of King Zeniff. One can be virtually certain that Limhi would have been present and would have known a great deal about Abinadi's case. Because Alma would not have personally known, for example, what transpired during the deliberations of the priests after he was expelled from the court, the record of Limhi becomes the prime candidate for the primary source material for that portion of the trial and perhaps also for a number of the procedural comments and official steps that led up to the execution of Abinadi. It is likely that an account of the trial of Abinadi and the demise of King Noah was included on the plates that contained the record of the people of Zeniff and that were "brought before Ammon" (Mosiah 8:5), since Limhi recounted these events in the public gathering when records were exchanged with Ammon (7:26–28). That record eventually ended up in the royal archive in Zarahemla either upon Ammon's return or after the Limhite reunion with the Nephites in the land of Zarahemla shortly after the time of Ammon's scouting expedition to the land of Nephi.

Moreover, Limhi could have told the story himself to Alma the Elder when they met in the north after both the people of Alma and the people of Limhi had escaped to Zarahemla from the land of Nephi. It is also possible that the explorer Ammon kept a record and reported back to Zarahemla what he had learned about the history of Zeniff's colony—including the extraordinary trial and fateful execution of Abinadi—since the prophecies and execution of Abinadi were clearly seen as key factors in explaining why Ammon found the people of Limhi in awful bondage (Mosiah 7:26–27).

Eventually, someone composed the book of Mosiah, in which the trial of Abinadi figures as the centerpiece.[2] King Mosiah may have shaped the writing of the book that bears his name, for the book of Mosiah begins with the exemplary life and farewell speech of his father, King Benjamin (Mosiah 1–6); but the book of Mosiah ends with the resignation speech of Mosiah, who abdicated the throne and inaugurated the reign of the judges in the land of Zarahemla, with Alma the Younger becoming the first chief judge (Mosiah 29). Significantly, one of the main purposes of the book of Mosiah is to justify this major political change. Indeed, the book of Mosiah uses the "wickedness and abominations" of King Noah, including his willingness to destroy anyone who would not obey his laws, as its prime illustration of the evils of kingship, thus establishing the need to eliminate this institution (vv. 18, 22–23). That being the case, Alma the Younger seems to be the candidate who would have been most interested in constructing the book of Mosiah.

Alma the Younger would have had powerful motivations for preserving and retelling the story of the trial of Abinadi. He would have had strong interests in documenting and elevating his father's important conversion during the trial of Abinadi, while at the same time solidifying his own position as the first chief judge against the challenges that indeed would soon arise in some quarters of Zarahemla by those who preferred kingship and wanted "Amlici to be a king over the people" (Alma 2:2). He also would have had access to the written and oral reports of his father, which he could have combined with the record of Limhi and with information

---

2. The chiastic structure of the book of Mosiah, with the trial of Abinadi standing at the center, is displayed in John W. Welch, "Chiasmus in the Book of Mormon," *BYU Studies* 10, no. 1 (1969): 82.

he could have readily gathered from his father's initial converts, some of whom he would have known and may have interviewed. Alma was the son and namesake of his father, and because the conversion of Alma the Elder occurred during the trial of Abinadi, Alma the Younger must have heard his father speak of this pivotal event many times.

By profession, Alma the Younger was a judge (Mosiah 29:44). He would have had great professional interest in an important case of this nature. He would have had the technical legal skills necessary to understand legal nuances and to document the story as fully as possible.

Moreover, Alma the Younger became the high priest in the city of Zarahemla and would have had great interest in criticizing the role of the wicked and apostate priests of Noah, some of whom would soon affiliate with the Nehorites, Alma's archenemies in the city of Ammonihah. These Nehorites were the followers of Nehor, whom Alma executed in the first year of his judgeship. Associating the priests of Nehor with the wicked priests of Noah would certainly have cast them in a bad light, to Alma's advantage. Showing that the priests of Noah were in fact the ultimate agitators who pressed for the execution of Abinadi might have given Alma further assurances that he had done the right thing in executing Nehor.

Beyond that, as the first chief judge, Alma needed to convince all of the people in the land of Zarahemla that abandoning kingship was politically prudent. When King Mosiah eventually abdicated and the voice of the people selected Alma as the chief judge, Mosiah used the case of Noah as his star evidence in arguing that kingship was not a good idea in general (Mosiah 29:18). Alma would have had a vested interest in being sure that all of the people in the city of Zarahemla knew and understood exactly how bad a king like Noah could be. In any event, it is clear that Alma the Younger stood in a prime position to preserve, structure, and promote the story of Abinadi as it has come down to us today.

By shaping the account of the trial of Abinadi in such great detail, Alma would also have appealed to the people of Limhi, letting them know that he did not blame the people of Limhi for the bondage under which they had suffered. King Noah and his wicked priests were to blame for their agony and suffering, and it was precisely for this reason—placing all people on an equal ground and giving them equal burden for their wrongdoing rather than bringing people under the burdens of wickedness and mismanagement by a ruling monarch—that King Mosiah justified his abdication in Mosiah 29.

It should also be remembered that Alma the Younger possessed the plates of brass. He was, for a time, the official Nephite record keeper

(Mosiah 28:20). Some readers may wonder whether Abinadi was able to quote Isaiah 53 and Exodus 20 as precisely as the record reports, and how Alma was then able to go out into the wilderness and remember precisely what Abinadi had said. It seems at least possible that, however accurately Abinadi quoted or paraphrased those two sources, it would have fallen upon Alma the Younger, as holder of the plates of brass, to have at least checked Abinadi's words against the texts in his custody, which may explain the precise quotation of these lengthy texts in the final version of this account.

If Alma the Younger was not responsible for the overall architecture of the book of Mosiah, it seems highly likely that he was at least the writer who constructed major parts of the book of Mosiah, the book that bears the name of Alma the Younger's immediate predecessor in power. The book of Mosiah gives center stage to the account of the conversion of Alma's father, his immediate predecessor in the office of high priest. The book of Mosiah also serves a major political purpose: it celebrates the unity of various peoples in the land of Zarahemla. As a public record, it emphasizes at its beginning the unity that was achieved among the Nephites and the Mulekites under the reign of King Benjamin; it chronicles the reunion of the Limhites and the people of Alma with their kinsmen in Zarahemla; it explains how Mosiah became king and how Alma the Elder became the high priest, and then how those offices were united in the person of Alma the Younger. Thus, the book of Mosiah functions largely as a prologue and rationalization for the ascendancy of Alma the Younger as the premier leader in the united land of Zarahemla.[3]

Finally, Mormon, the abridger of the work as a whole, may have shortened or paraphrased portions of the text of Abinadi's trial, although there seems to be little reason for him to have changed the underlying record very much. The records at his disposal may have included the record of Limhi, the complete abdication speech of King Mosiah, and other items pertinent to the trial of Abinadi. We know that Mormon was very interested in the prophecies of Abinadi, for he found in them authoritative predictions of the burdens and destruction that eventually came upon his own people (Mormon 1:19). Mormon was also highly critical of the worship of idols in the decadent world around him (4:14, 21; 5:15), and thus he would have taken special note of the fact that Noah and his priests were criticized most explicitly because of their idolatry (Mosiah 9:12; 11:6).

---

3. While it is possible that King Mosiah had something to do with the writing of the book that bears his name, I find little evidence that he did so. Mosiah's sons are given little attention in the book of Mosiah, and his father, Benjamin, overshadows Mosiah himself.

Mormon's comments in Helaman 12 about the destructive effects of pride show that he would have been thoroughly disgusted by Noah's prideful excesses (11:2–15). Mormon may well have selected, abridged, edited, added to, or shaped parts of this section of the book of Mosiah as he compiled his set of plates, but it would not have served Mormon's purposes to create such a lengthy and detailed account of the trial itself. Only a lawyer, not a general, would care to give us all the legal information that we find in these chapters; and only a high priest still interested in the law of Moses would care to quote all of the Ten Commandments, let alone include the extensive midrashic exegesis of Isaiah 52 channeled through Isaiah 53 that is found in Mosiah 12–16.

It is true that Mormon and other Nephites must have been delighted to find such strong and early predictions and understanding of the role of the true Messiah in ancient Israel, and for that reason Mormon was likely eager to include so much of this material in the history of his people; but the underlying text itself must have been something he found on the large plates of Nephi and then incorporated without much change into the plates of Mormon. The account does not appear to be a retrospective tale told by Mormon five hundred years after the fact. A document with such contemporaneous validity can be scrutinized carefully for legal and technical details in order to extract as much judicial information as possible. This information can be attributed with confidence to the legal system that operated during the mid-second century BC in the land of Nephi.

King Noah's Excesses

The trial of Abinadi took place around 150 BC, near the end of the reign of King Noah over the city of Nephi.[4] The prophet's rebukes and curses came in response to the king's excesses. Noah had ruled for several years over a small group[5] of reactionary, stiff-necked Nephites who had

---

4. See chart 17 in John W. Welch and J. Gregory Welch, *Charting the Book of Mormon: Visual Aids for Personal Study and Teaching* (Provo, UT: FARMS, 1999). This date is only approximate; the trial may have been as much as ten years earlier or fifteen years later.

5. Zeniff began with a "large number" of people (Omni 1:27) about 200 BC, but only fifty in the initial party survived (Omni 1:28), so the number of settlers was very small. A dozen years later (Mosiah 9:11), 279 men in the colony were killed, which must have been a large percentage of the Nephites then in that land. Twenty-two years passed (Mosiah 10:3), Zeniff grew old (Mosiah 10:22), and Noah became king. Thus, when the trial of Abinadi took place near the end of Noah's reign, the population in the city of Nephi still must have been quite small. When Alma converted some 450 souls and fled with them into the wilderness (Mosiah 18:16, 34–35), he would have made a sizable dent in Noah's population base. Understandably, Noah and his soldiers came after Alma, among other reasons, to return these people to their fields and posts in what must have been a fragile economy and vulnerable society. No small part of this motivation, too,

returned a generation earlier under Noah's father, Zeniff, to the land of Nephi to reclaim their legal inheritance. By worldly standards Noah had been a successful king, but he had grown arrogant and oppressive. He had constructed large public buildings for his own aggrandizement, collected a tax of 20 percent (in effect a double tithe) on "all they possessed" (Mosiah 11:3),[6] appointed his own sympathizers as priests, and lived extravagantly and excessively, at least by the standards possible in this relatively modest and primitive society.

Although he had become lax in his commitment to follow the law of Moses as the law was understood by Abinadi, as it had been taught by the prophets Nephi and Jacob, and as dictated by any sensible understanding, Noah and his priests still purported to teach and presumably abide by the law of Moses (Mosiah 12:28), at least as they understood it. One must wonder, at the outset, how much of the Torah Noah and his priests had in written form. Perhaps they learned it only by memory through oral transmission, which was the preferred mode of instruction and learning in the ancient world, particularly among some Jewish sects, such as the Pharisees, who even valued oral traditions in preference to (in other ways incomplete and untrustworthy) written records.[7] If Zeniff's colony possessed a copy of the law, perhaps Noah read the law "all the days of his life" as required of kings by Deuteronomy 17:19. In whatever forms and from whatever sources they knew the law, Abinadi and Noah obviously disagreed about how the law should be understood and applied, but at

---

would have stemmed from the people's support of the extravagant lifestyles of King Noah and his ruling class (Mosiah 11:3–4).

6. In ancient Israel, the tithe "in its original form was a tax associated with palace and Temple." Moshe Winfeld, "Tithe," in *Encyclopaedia Judaica*, ed. Cecil Roth et al. (Jerusalem: Keter, 1972), 19:738. The Levites and priests were variously entitled to a 10 percent tithing (Leviticus 27:30–33; Numbers 18:21–32; Deuteronomy 14:22–29); additionally, the king could collect another 10 percent (1 Samuel 8:15–17). Together this would amount to a 20 percent flat tax. By modern standards, that would not seem excessive, but in light of the benefit returned by Noah to his people it was probably well beyond. See Daniel C. Snell, "Taxes and Taxation," in *The Anchor Bible Dictionary*, ed. David Noel Freedman et al. (New York: Doubleday, 1992), 6:338–40.

7. For a thorough treatment of the oral dimension of biblical law, see James W. Watts, *Reading Law: The Rhetorical Shaping of the Pentateuch* (Sheffield, England: Sheffield Academic Press, 1999). For very insightful explorations of orality in Jewish education, see Birger Gerhardsson, *Memory and Manuscript: Oral Tradition and Written Transmission in Rabbinic Judaism and Early Christianity* (Grand Rapids, MI: Eerdmans, 1998). On the "Oral Torah," see Daniela Piattelli and Bernard S. Jackson, "Jewish Law during the Second Temple Period," in *An Introduction to the History and Sources of Jewish Law*, ed. Neil S. Hecht et al. (Oxford: Oxford University Press, 1996), 22–24; Alan J. Avery-Peck, "Oral Tradition: Early Judaism," in *Anchor Bible Dictionary*, 5:34–37; and Abraham Cohen, *Everyman's Talmud* (1949; repr., New York: Schocken Books, 1975), 146–49.

least they shared a common legal groundwork of commitment to the law of Moses out of which a legal controversy could ensue.[8]

From the legalistic approach of their treatment of Abinadi, it would appear that Noah and his priests spent a fair amount of time discussing the law, if for no other purpose than to justify their conduct and to get as close to the edge of legality as they possibly could. Indeed, Noah may have rationalized his conduct in all instances. Many of the things Noah did were morally and spiritually derelict, especially because he did them to the point of excess, such as drinking heavily (Mosiah 11:15; compare Proverbs 31:4–7, which admonishes leaders not to drink wine or strong drink, "lest they . . . forget the law, and pervert the judgment of any of the afflicted"), having many wives and concubines (Mosiah 11:2, 4; the king was prohibited from this too, according to Deuteronomy 17:17, but only if taken to excess),[9] adorning the temple with special seats for the privileged priests (the ancient Israelite sense of social justice strongly favored a classless society), and being lazy and "riotous" (Mosiah 11:14). But he may have argued that these infractions of the moral code did not comprise legally actionable transgressions under ancient Israelite law. Polygamy and concubinage, for example, were not against the traditional law of Moses (although Lehi had restricted his sons in this regard, Jacob 3:5). Noah was greedy and vain (Mosiah 11:1–9), but were there "laws" against such traits? Without much difficulty, Abinadi could see through such self-serving sophistry.

The record accuses Noah of serious infractions. In general, we are told that "he did not walk in the ways of his father. For behold, he did not keep the commandments of God, but he did walk after the desires of his

---

8. Pietro Bovati, *Re-Establishing Justice: Legal Terms, Concepts and Procedures in the Hebrew Bible* (Sheffield, England: JSOT Press, 1994), 30, explains: "The *rîb* is a controversy that takes place between two parties on questions of law. For the contest to take place, the individuals in question must have had a previous judicial bond between them (even if not of an explicit nature), that is, it is necessary that they refer to a body of norms that regulates the rights and duties of each. This underlying relationship between the individuals affects not just the origin but also the progress of a dispute that is substantiated by juridical arguments and requires a solution in conformity with the law."

9. For further information, see David Daube, "'One from among Your Brethren Shall You Set King over You,'" *Journal of Biblical Literature* 90, no. 4 (1971): 480–81; Moshe Greenberg, "Biblical Attitudes toward Power: Ideal and Reality in Law and Prophets," in *Religion and Law: Biblical-Judaic and Islamic Perspectives*, ed. Edwin B. Firmage, Bernard G. Weiss, and John W. Welch (Winona Lake, IN: Eisenbrauns, 1990), 101–12; Helen Ann Kenik, "Code of Conduct for a King: Psalm 101," *Journal of Biblical Literature* 95, no. 3 (1976): 391–403; and Georg C. Macholz, "Die Stellung des Königs in der israelitischen Gerichtsverfassung," *Zeitschrift für die alttestamentliche Wissenschaft* 84, no. 2 (1972): 157–82.

own heart" (Mosiah 11:1–2). Not walking after the ways of one's father was presumptively illegal and iniquitous. The essence of a wicked king is found in the fact that "he teareth up the laws of those who have reigned in righteousness before him" (29:22). In the prologues and epilogues to ancient Near Eastern law codes, searing curses are placed upon successor kings who change the laws.[10] But it was still the prerogative of new kings to issue their own laws, and so Noah may have argued that he was still within his royal rights to legislate as he did.

But in what ways did he "not keep the commandments of God"? The most serious of legal violations that Noah is explicitly accused of committing were (1) idolatry (Mosiah 11:6) and (2) disregarding the law that prohibited the king from economic excesses and pride (Deuteronomy 17:16–20). Regarding idolatry, it goes without saying that making and worshiping graven images was forbidden under Exodus 20:2–6, standing significantly and "[without] parallel in the history of religion" at the very head of the law of Moses;[11] but perhaps Noah stopped short of actually making images of other gods and simply made reliefs of himself, of his priests, or of birds (perhaps quetzals?) or animals (perhaps jaguars?), such as are found in the archaeology of highland Guatemala from this time period. How far an observant person can go in making statues or depictions of people or animals has long been a hotly debated topic between various Jewish sects. The contours of the law regarding idolatry, even in biblical times, are notoriously imprecise.[12] Biblical authors usually do not "distinguish between worshipping other gods (with or without images), the worship of images, and the worship of Yahweh using images,"[13] although these

---

10. See, for example, the curses in the epilogue to the Code of Hammurabi.

11. Hans Jochen Boecker, *Law and the Administration of Justice in the Old Testament and Ancient East*, trans. Jeremy Moiser (Minneapolis: Augsburg, 1980), 145.

12. For a very helpful discussion of the law against idols and idolatry beginning in the biblical period, see Joseph Gutmann, "The 'Second Commandment' and the Image in Judaism," *Hebrew Union College Annual* 32 (1968): 161–68. See further Herman Chanan Brichto, "The Worship of the Golden Calf: A Literary Analysis of a Fable on Idolatry," *Hebrew Union College Annual* 54 (1983): 1–44; Boaz Cohen, "Art in Jewish Law," *Judaism* 3, no. 2 (1954): 165–76; Christoph Dohmen, *Das Bilderverbot: Seine Entstehung und seine Entwicklung im Alten Testament*, Bonner Biblische Beiträge 62 (Frankfurt: Athenäum, 1987); Christopher R. North, *The Essence of Idolatry*, Beiheft zur Zeitschrift für die alttestamentliche Wissenschaft 77 (Berlin: de Gruyter, 1958), 151–60; Silvia Schroer, *In Israel gab es Bilder: Nachrichten von darstellender Kunst im Alten Testament*, Orbis Biblicus et Orientalis 74 (Frieburg, Switzerland: Veandenhoeck and Ruprecht, 1987); Mark S. Smith, *The Origins of Biblical Monotheism: Israel's Polytheistic Background and the Ugaritic Texts* (Oxford: Oxford University Press, 2001), 182–94; and Matitiahu Tsevat, "The Prohibition of Divine Images according to the Old Testament," in *Wünschet Jerusalem Frieden*, ed. Matthias Augustin and Klaus-Dietrich Schunck (Frankfurt am Main: Peter Lang, 1988), 211–20.

13. Edward M. Curtis, "Idol, Idolatry," in *Anchor Bible Dictionary*, 3:379.

practices may well have been enforced differently. For example, "were the Second Commandment in its entirety to be taken literally, the construction of Solomon's Temple, with its graven images, such as the cherubim and the twelve oxen which supported the molten sea, would obviously have been a direct violation and transgression. Yet no censure was invoked by the biblical writers."[14] The fact that the prophets regularly accused many people in Israel of committing idolatry and yet most of them evidently went unpunished indicates that people did not fundamentally agree on strict definitions or required punishments for this offense. The situation was apparently similar in the New World. As in pre-exilic Israel, idols and idolatry are mentioned as problems in all eras of Nephite history, especially in the land of Nephi, where it seems to have been a prevalent practice from the days of Jacob and Enos down to the times of King Noah and the sons of Mosiah.[15] So one can be confident that Noah, operating in the historical capital of the land of Nephi, had his own definition of idolatry—however flimsy his legal logic may have been—that his own practices conveniently did not contravene. Noah and his priests had evidently gone too far with the local practice in this regard, much to Abinadi's horror. As was Abinadi, the prophets Hosea and Amos were especially outspoken against

---

14. Gutmann, "The 'Second Commandment,'" 163.

15. In addition to the ample references to idolatry found in the Isaiah chapters quoted in the Book of Mormon, Jacob in the city of Nephi placed a curse on the Nephites if they were to "worship idols, for the devil of all devils delighteth in [idols]" (2 Nephi 9:37). Soon the Lamanites living around the land of Nephi became "full of idolatry" (Enos 1:20), and this condition continued in that land down to the time of Noah (Mosiah 9:12) and beyond, as Ammon found (Alma 17:15) and as Mormon experienced (Mormon 4:14, 21). Alma the Younger, in the years when he rebelled against his father's ways, "became a very wicked and an idolatrous man" (Mosiah 27:8). What stronger way would there have been for him to express his rejection of his father's covenant practices than for him to have adopted the practices of Noah and his priests that stood as the polar opposite of his father's religion and teachings? Idol worship was also present in the land of Zarahemla in Alma's day. After he became the chief judge and high priest, Alma the Younger made a special point of listing idolatry and the closely related crime of sorceries as the first two evils that were not to be practiced by his people but were observed by those who did not belong to Alma's covenant community (Alma 1:32). When he spoke to the people in Gideon, who had recently escaped from the idolatrous land of Nephi, Alma expressed confidence in them that they would not revert to the practices that had led to their suffering and downfall in the city of Nephi: "I trust that ye are not lifted up in the pride of your hearts; yea, I trust that ye have not set your hearts upon riches and the vain things of the world; yea, I trust that you do not worship idols" (Alma 7:6). The Zoramite apostates and the followers of Gadianton were, first and foremost, characterized by their idolatry: "Zoram, who was their leader, was leading the hearts of the people to bow down to dumb idols" (Alma 31:1); the Gadianton oaths were evidently made before idols: "and did build up unto themselves idols of their gold and their silver" (Helaman 6:31). Mormon clearly saw idol worship as one of the seven sins "which brought upon [the Nephites] their wars and their destructions," as he lists in Alma 50:21.

idolatry (Hosea 8:4; 13:2; Amos 3:15; 6:4), and the Deuteronomic reforms of King Josiah involved severe "iconoclastic strictures,"[16] but Noah could cite opposing precedents, such as the cherubim in the temple, in arguing for a somewhat looser legal definition of the crime of idol making or idol worshipping.

Similarly, there are laws prohibiting pride and economic excess in Deuteronomy 17, but quantifiable limits would be imprecise and difficult to pin down under the best of circumstances. Pride, riches, spacious buildings, and idol worship are often linked together in the Book of Mormon (e.g., 1 Nephi 11:36; Alma 1:32; 7:6; 31:27–28), but nowhere more graphically than in the case of Noah. Still, Noah could well have argued that it was his right as a king to tax, to build, to encourage economic growth, and to provide for the common defense. Just how far he could go in these efforts would have been open to dispute.

Interestingly, Noah is also accused in the record of acting in such a way that he "did cause his people to commit sin," causing them "to do that which was abominable in the sight of the Lord" (Mosiah 11:2). What is meant by this is unclear, but several possibilities present themselves. Did he cause them, for example, to break the Sabbath by requiring them to work on that day? Did he cause the society to languish in impurity by not following the laws of ritual or sexual purity, perhaps regarding laws of menstruation or cleansing after childbirth (sexual sins are described as abominations in Leviticus 18 and 20, but many other sins are similarly described, Proverbs 6:16–19)? Or did Noah cause his people to commit sin simply by not seeing that they were taught appropriately (as was the duty of the priests to do under Deuteronomy 31:11; see the accusation to this effect in Mosiah 12:26), or by failing to enforce the law against violators (perhaps because he needed people in his small and beleaguered community and would not have wanted to put any able-bodied men to death)? Again, the record is unclear, which is understandable since it is Abinadi, not Noah, who was on trial.

Nevertheless, that Noah was wicked is abundantly clear, certainly from Alma's perspective (assuming that Alma was the one who most influenced the writing of the narrative prologue for the trial of Abinadi, which contrasts so exquisitely with the puffing prologues that ancient kings, such as Hammurabi or Eshnunna, typically wrote for themselves to extol their grand and benevolent accomplishments). Thus, carrying out the traditional role of the Israelite prophets, who were often called by

---

16. Gutmann, "The 'Second Commandment,'" 168. See Roland de Vaux, *Ancient Israel: Its Life and Institutions* (New York: McGraw-Hill, 1965), 2:290, 307–8, 333–34.

God to preach repentance to errant royalty and wayward populations,[17] Abinadi was justified in speaking out sharply against King Noah and his people. Having made his pronouncement in the form of a classic "prophetic lawsuit,"[18] in which the prophet speaks legalistically in the name of the Lord, Abinadi exposed himself willingly to the legal system in the city of Nephi. The final outcome of this prophetic castigation soon hung on the inner workings of legal processes under Noah's administration.

Abinadi's Words and His Arrest by the People

The trial of Abinadi arose out of words he spoke to the townspeople within the city of Nephi (Mosiah 12:1–17). The older people in that audience could have been among the original group that had returned to the land of Nephi with Zeniff about forty years earlier (Omni 1:27–29), while the younger men in the crowd would have been born members of this small enclave of reactionary Nephites. These people had endured considerable hardships in repossessing the land and temple of Nephi, the traditional hallmarks of the people of Nephi. Apparently they strongly preferred to live in that place (in spite of the disadvantages of isolation and subjugation they suffered there) rather than in the foreign land of Zarahemla as a minority but privileged party among the people of Zarahemla (the Mulekites). Thus the people in the city of Nephi may well be seen as self-righteous zealots[19] who had struggled to repossess this sacred land and who considered themselves blessed and prospered by the Lord for their sacrifice (Mosiah 10:19–22). They must have taken pride in their independence and separatism, for they had negotiated with King Laman to obtain the land, had fought the Lamanites, and had paid tribute to them in order to maintain their place in the land of Nephi. They would have thought of themselves as having reestablished and preserved the correct and legitimate ancient Nephite capital and original temple city. Given their success under such difficult circumstances, this audience probably

---

17. For an excellent discussion of the literary complexity of Mosiah 11–17 and its abundant allusions to the Deuteronomic narratives involving prophetic confrontations against the wicked kings Jeroboam (1 Kings 14) and Ahab (1 Kings 20), see Alan Goff, "Uncritical Theory and Thin Description: The Resistance to History," *Review of Books on the Book of Mormon* 7, no. 1 (1995): 170–207, esp. 192–206. For more on the role of prophets, see John J. Schmitt, "Prophecy: Preexilic Hebrew Prophecy," in *Anchor Bible Dictionary*, 5:482–89.

18. See the discussion of prophetic lawsuits in John W. Welch, "Benjamin's Speech as a Prophetic Lawsuit," in *King Benjamin's Speech: "That Ye May Learn Wisdom,"* ed. John W. Welch and Stephen D. Ricks (Provo, UT: FARMS, 1998), 225–32.

19. Zeniff describes himself as being "over-zealous to inherit the land of [his] fathers" (Mosiah 9:3).

would have been particularly predisposed to reject any condemnation of their lives and practices.

This was at least the second time that Abinadi had spoken publicly in the city of Nephi. Two years earlier, Abinadi had prophesied that the Lord would visit this people in his anger, that they would be delivered into the hands of their enemies, that their enemies would bring them into bondage and afflict them, and that none would deliver them—not even God himself would hear their cries for relief (Mosiah 11:20–26).[20] For saying such things on that earlier occasion, Abinadi had been condemned to die (v. 28), but he had managed to escape with his life. Now Abinadi had returned.

As before, he again accused the entire population of wickedness and abominations (Mosiah 12:2). But this time he expanded his prophecy, making not only the people generally but King Noah specifically a target of the Lord's censure. On this occasion, Abinadi's words against the people took the form of an Israelite woe oracle[21] or prophetic lawsuit.[22] Abinadi reiterated his pronouncements of woe against the people even more graphically than before, proclaiming that the Lord had a grievance against the people and would visit them in his anger "because of their iniquities and abominations"; that they would be "brought into bondage," "smitten on the cheek," "driven by men," and "slain"; and that "vultures of the air, and the dogs, yea, and the wild beasts" would "devour their flesh" (v. 2). Abinadi also heaped upon the people various curses and divine punishments of sore afflictions, famine, pestilence, insects, hail, wind, burdens, and utter destruction, "that they shall howl all the day long" (v. 4).

In addition, he leveled accusations against King Noah. Abinadi prophesied that "the life of King Noah shall be valued even as a garment in a hot furnace" (Mosiah 12:3) and that Noah would be "as a dry stalk of the field, which is run over by beasts and trodden under foot" and "as

---

20. See Bovati, *Re-Establishing Justice*, 62, 68–70.

21. See Steven Horine, "A Study of the Literary Genre of the Woe Oracle," *Calvary Baptist Theological Journal* 5, no. 2 (1989): 74–97.

22. See note 18 above. On prophetic lawsuits, see generally Berend Gemser, "The '*rib*' or Controversy-Pattern in Hebrew Mentality," in *Wisdom in Israel and in the Ancient Near East*, ed. M. Noth and D. Winton Thomas, Supplements to Vetus Testamentum, vol. 3 (Leiden: Brill, 1955): 120–37; Hans J. Boecker, *Redeformen des Rechtslebens im Alten Testament* (Neukirchen: Neukirchener, 1964; rev. ed. 1970); J. Carl Laney, "The Role of the Prophets in God's Case against Israel," *Bibliotheca Sacra* 138, no. 552 (October 1981): 313–25; Eberhard von Waldow, *Der traditionsgeschichtliche Hintergrund der prophetischen Gerichtsreden*, Beiheft zur Zeitschrift für die alttestamentliche Wissenschaft 85 (Berlin: Töpelmann, 1963); Kirsten Nielsen, *Yahweh as Prosecutor and Judge: An Investigation of the Prophetic Lawsuit* (Sheffield, England: JSOT, 1978); and Bovati, *Re-Establishing Justice*, 108.

the blossoms of a thistle, which, when it is fully ripe, if the wind bloweth, [are] driven forth upon the face of the land," except he repent (vv. 11–12). These words against Noah are in the classic form of an ancient Near Eastern simile curse.[23] Curses, which were special forms of malediction in the ancient world,[24] sometimes took the form of a simile. For example, an Aramaic treaty from about 750 BC contains the incantation "Just as this wax is burned by fire, so may Matî'el be burned by fire."[25] Perhaps the Nephites would have heard in Abinadi's curses an echo of the simile curse that Jeremiah pronounced against the temple in Jerusalem: "I will make this house like Shiloh" (Jeremiah 26:6), an allusion to the destruction of the shrine at Shiloh that resulted in the loss of the ark of the covenant. The point of Jeremiah's curse was that even the tabernacle and the ark had not protected the Israelites at Shiloh, and similarly the temple at Jerusalem would not protect the kingdom of Judah, except its people repent and remain righteous.[26] Abinadi's curse also carried the warning that the temple in the city of Nephi would not shelter the people as long as they retained

---

23. See Deuteronomy 27:14–26 for examples of such oaths spoken in the form of curses directed against the entire populace. See also Haim H. Cohn, "Oath," in *The Principles of Jewish Law*, ed. Menachem Elon (Jerusalem: Keter, 1975), 615.

24. F. Charles Fensham, "Malediction and Benediction in Ancient Near Eastern Vassal-Treaties and the Old Testament," *Zeitschrift für die alttestamentliche Wissenschaft* 74 (1962): 1–9. See also Douglas Stuart, "Curse," in *Anchor Bible Dictionary*, 1:1218–19; Jeff S. Anderson, "The Social Function of Curses in the Hebrew Bible," *Zeitschrift für die alttestamentliche Wissenschaft* 110, no. 2 (1998): 223–37; Herbert C. Brichto, *The Problem of the 'Curse' in the Hebrew Bible*, Journal of Biblical Literature Monograph Series, no. 13 (Philadelphia: Society of Biblical Literature, 1963); Stanley Gevirtz, "West-Semitic Curses and the Problem of the Origins of Hebrew Law," *Vetus Testamentum* 11, no. 2 (1961): 137–58; Johannes Hempel, *Die israelitische Anschauungen von Segen und Fluch im Lichte altorientalischer Parallelen*, Beiheft zur Zeitschrift für die alttestamentliche Wissenschaft 81 (Berlin: de Gruyter, 1961), 30–113; Horine, "A Study of the Literary Genre of the Woe Oracle," 74–97; Paul Keim, "'Cursed Be . . .': Mundane Malediction and Sacral Sanction in Biblical Law," *Society of Biblical Literature Biblical Law Group* 20 (November 1994); and Willy Schottroff, *Der Altisraelitische Fluchspruch* (Neukirchen-Vluyn: Neukirchener, 1969).

25. Sefire I Treaty A37, in Joseph A. Fitzmyer, *The Aramaic Inscriptions of Sefire* (Rome: Pontifical Biblical Institute, 1967), 14–15; and Delbert R. Hillers, *Treaty-Curses and the Old Testament Prophets* (Rome: Pontifical Biblical Institute, 1964), 18. Compare 1 Kings 14:10–11. Simile curses in the Book of Mormon are discussed further in a paper by my law student Mark J. Morisse titled "Simile Curses in the Ancient Near East, Old Testament and Book of Mormon," distributed originally as a FARMS Preliminary Report in 1986 and published under the same title in *Journal of Book of Mormon Studies* 2, no. 1 (1993): 124–38. See also Donald W. Parry, "Hebraisms and Other Ancient Peculiarities in the Book of Mormon," in *Echoes and Evidences of the Book of Mormon*, ed. Donald W. Parry, Daniel C. Peterson, and John W. Welch (Provo, UT: FARMS, 2002), 156–59.

26. Discussed further in John W. Welch, "The Trial of Jeremiah: A Legal Legacy from Lehi's Jerusalem," in *Glimpses of Lehi's Jerusalem*, ed. John W. Welch, David Rolph Seely, and Jo Ann H. Seely (Provo, UT: FARMS, 2004), 341–43; quotation on p. 342.

their wicked ways. Just as Jeremiah's words immediately entangled him in litigation, Abinadi's words also precipitated direct legal accusations.

Moreover, it was an official duty of the ancient Israelite priests to remind all Israel of the curses that fall upon the wicked and to impose these curses ritually: "And the Levites shall speak and say unto all the men of Israel with a loud voice, Cursed be the man . . ." (Deuteronomy 27:14–15; vv. 15–26 give twelve specific curses). The people of Israel were supposed to echo the priest ceremoniously: "And all the people shall answer and say, Amen" (v. 15). In a sense, the utterance of curses by the prophet Abinadi fulfilled this priestly function that undoubtedly had been neglected by the self-serving and derelict priests of Noah. But people in his audience may well have wondered, "By what authority does this man usurp the rights and duties of the temple priests?" Even more particularly, Abinadi's words were more than mere warnings against wickedness in general. They were aimed personally at certain individuals, and thus his words would have been extremely provocative, carrying the weight of injurious indictments and ominous forebodings of impending harm.

Indeed, Abinadi's words against Noah's life were extremely demeaning and dreadful. Burning in a furnace, kiln, or oven was a debasing form of punishment in the ancient world and would be a grim execution under any circumstances. Two slaves at the time of Hammurabi, for example, were burned to death in a furnace, apparently pursuant to a royal decree.[27] Threats, curses, and verbal assaults were thought by ancient peoples to cause actual injury. Modern people shrug off such verbal attacks, thinking that sticks and stones can break bones but words alone are not to be feared. Ancient people, however, were extremely wary of a curse hanging over them, especially if the curse invoked the wrath of a god upon the targeted person. For example, Hittite law provided, "If a free man kills a snake, and speaks another's name, he shall pay one mina . . . of silver. If [the offender] is a slave, he himself shall be put to death."[28] Harry Hoffner observes that doubtless "analogic magic" is involved here; "he who kills the snake probably said something like, 'As this snake dies, so may so-and-so (i.e., his enemy) also die.'"[29]

---

27. The letter of Rim-Sin, king of Larsa, pertaining to this case is discussed by John B. Alexander, "New Light on the Fiery Furnace," *Journal of Biblical Literature* 69, no. 4 (1950): 375–76. Compare Daniel 3; 3 Nephi 28:21; 4 Nephi 1:32. Burning was an unusual form of punishment, usually reserved in Israel for the foulest and most defiling offenders. See further the discussion of Abinadi's execution below.

28. Harry A. Hoffner Jr., *The Laws of the Hittites: A Critical Edition* (Leiden: Brill, 1997), 136.

29. Hoffner, *Laws of the Hittites*, 217, giving further scholarly sources on the use of such simile curses among the Hittites.

Under biblical law, people were required to call their neighbors to repentance (Leviticus 5:1), but they were granted legal immunity from liability under the law of slander in doing so, provided they did not go overboard. "Thou shalt not hate thy brother in thy heart"; "thou shalt surely rebuke thy neighbor, and not bear sin because of him" (19:17).[30] Jacob Milgrom emphasizes the importance in this statement of ethical duty in making one's rebuke public, even in a forensic sense, in a judicial procedure, rather than holding bad feelings against a brother inwardly: You shall not hate your brother (Israelite) in your heart. "Reprove your fellow openly . . . so that you will not bear punishment because of him."[31] At Qumran, the duty to "make reproof," as Abinadi does, would become "a cardinal requirement for its members,"[32] and so Abinadi may have felt not only duty bound by the calling of the Lord but also legally justified by this requirement of the Levitical Holiness Code to rebuke those who had wandered into wicked and forbidden paths.

The law of reproof, however, was also coupled immediately with the tempering requirement to "love thy neighbor as thyself" (Leviticus 19:18). The sectarians at Qumran required any reproof to be issued "in truth, humility, and lovingkindness."[33] Talmudic jurists further understood Leviticus 19:17 to mean that "you may reprove your neighbor so long as you do not insult him."[34] Perhaps people in Abinadi's audience felt that he had not shown forth adequate kindness following his rebuke; possibly they gave him little chance to do so.

Curses in the Psalms express strong feelings against those who have broken the law, and while they may seem vindictive or angry to the wicked, to the righteous these curses depict Jehovah as a protective warrior violently opposing sin and purifying the community.[35] Curses were believed to affect the target, the speaker, and the community in many psychological, social, religious, and legal ways;[36] and so for reasons such as these, the

30. Translation from Haim H. Cohn, "Slander," in Elon, *Principles of Jewish Law*, 513.

31. Jacob Milgrom, *Leviticus 17–22* (New York: Doubleday, 2000), 1647–48.

32. Milgrom, *Leviticus 17–22*, 1648, citing the *Damascus Document* 9:17–19.

33. 1QS 5:25–6:1, quoted in Milgrom, *Leviticus 17–22*, 1650.

34. Cohn, "Slander," 513.

35. Robert Althann, "The Psalms of Vengeance against Their Ancient Near Eastern Background," *Journal of Northwest Semitic Languages* 18 (1992): 1–11.

36. Keim, "'Cursed Be . . .'" 26. See Lyn M. Bechtel, "Shame as a Sanction of Social Control in Biblical Israel: Judicial, Political, and Social Shaming," *Journal for the Study of the Old Testament* 16, no. 49 (1991): 47–76. For more information on curses, see Walter Farber, "Wehe, wenn . . . !" *Zeitschrift für Assyriologie* 64, no. 2 (1975): 177–79; M. Filipiak, "Spoleczno-prawne znaczenie zorzeczen u Pismie swietym" (in Polish), *Ruch Biblijny i Luturgiczny* 21 (1968): 32–39; M. Filipiak, "Znaczenie Przeklenstwau Kodeksach Prawnych Piecicksiegu (Le sens des maledictions dans les

people in the city of Nephi would not have taken Abinadi's strident, if not insulting, curses lightly.

Moreover, beyond having social or legal impact, Abinadi's curses impugned the worthiness of Noah to act in a priesthood capacity before God. Noah's garment could easily have represented his authority before God, just as Elijah's mantle given to Elisha had symbolized his rights in the priesthood.[37] When Moses tried to prepare the children of Israel to see God on Mount Sinai, he told them to "wash their clothes, and be ready against the third day" (Exodus 19:10–11). Seeing the lightning, fire, and smoke that "ascended as the smoke of a furnace" (v. 18), however, the people stayed below "lest [the Lord] break forth upon them" and consume them with fire (v. 24). When Abinadi cursed Noah "as a garment in a hot furnace," he implied that Noah had broken into a sacred area, had defiled it, and would be punished by God. Other scriptures gathered by John Tvedtnes further demonstrate that "a garment visibly tainted by the plague is to be burned" (see Leviticus 13:52, 57), that "a ceremonial burning of worn-out priestly clothing took place in the Jerusalem temple of Christ's time," and that burning by fire was generally indicative of God's eradication of serious sin.[38]

In light of these powerful applications, Abinadi must have known that his curses would be highly inflammatory, for he entered the city covertly, in disguise.[39] He probably knew that his disguise would not shield him for very long, but this ploy gave him enough time to attract a curious crowd to

codes juridiques du Pentateque)," *Annales Theologico-Canonici* 15 (1968): 47–59; Lewis S. Ford, "The Divine Curse Understood in Terms of Persuasion," *Semeia: An Experimental Journal for Biblical Criticism* 24 (1982): 81–87; Johannes Hempel, *Die israelitische Anschauungen von Segen und Fluch im Lichte altorientalischer Parallelen,* Beiheft zur Zeitschrift für die alttestamentliche Wissenschaft 81 (1961): 30–113; Immanuel Lewy, "The Puzzle of DT. XXVII: Blessings Announced, but Curses Noted," *Vetus Testamentum* 12, no. 2 (1962): 207–11; and Schottroff, *Der Altisraelitische Fluchspruch.*

37. Fred E. Woods, "Elisha and the Children: The Question of Accepting Prophetic Succession," *BYU Studies* 32 (1992): 47–58.

38. John A. Tvedtnes, "'As a Garment in a Hot Furnace,'" *Journal of Book of Mormon Studies* 6, no. 1 (1997): 76–79.

39. Alan Goff, "Abinadi's Disguise and the Fate of King Noah," FARMS Update, *Insights* 20, no. 12 (December 2000): 2, discusses the typological meaning of prophets gaining an audience with the king by means of a disguise, as developed by Richard Coggins, "On Kings and Disguises," *Journal for the Study of the Old Testament* 50 (1991): 55–62. Abinadi's behavior fits broadly within the biblical imagery that nothing is hidden from God and that kings are unable to see the truth until the prophet reveals himself from behind his disguise. See, for example, the prophet who put ashes on his face to hide his identity from King Ahab (1 Kings 20:38). But in Abinadi's case, it does not appear that he was trying to hide his identity from King Noah, for Abinadi revealed himself as soon as he was within the city.

whom he delivered his final public statement (Mosiah 12:1–8). Since Abinadi had been in trouble with King Noah's legal system in the city of Nephi two years earlier (11:26–28), he would have been fully aware that the city's judicial system would allow the people to apprehend him as soon as he was detected. Moreover, Abinadi's case was much weaker the second time around, for his previous prophecies had not yet been fulfilled even though two full years had elapsed. This non-eventuality exposed him quite clearly to a charge of false prophecy under Deuteronomy 18:22, "When a prophet speaketh in the name of the Lord, if the thing follow not, nor come to pass, that is the thing which the Lord hath not spoken, but the prophet hath spoken it presumptuously: thou shalt not be afraid of him."

Under ancient biblical law, the general population in the city of Nephi was obligated to enforce the law (Leviticus 5:1). The biblical system used no police, sheriffs, marshals, or public prosecutors. Indeed, it appears that the king had little or no authority in antiquity to initiate a lawsuit. No known legal case from antiquity was initiated by a king as a plaintiff or prosecutor. King Jehoshaphat instructed his rulers to judge "what cause soever *shall come to you* of your brethren" (2 Chronicles 19:10; emphasis added). Even wicked Queen Jezebel and King Ahab did not (and perhaps could not) bring their action against Naboth personally, but they arranged for two false witnesses to testify against Naboth "in the presence of the people" in their scheme of using the judicial system to confiscate Naboth's vineyard (1 Kings 21:10–13).

Any adult male could convene a court of city elders in a relatively spontaneous fashion to judge the accused.[40] In such cases, the town elders would act simultaneously as judges, prosecutors, defenders, and witnesses.[41] Israelite elders generally took this legal responsibility seriously, applying the law as accurately and as mercifully as possible. Thus the trial of Abinadi began in a normal fashion with the men of the city acting spontaneously (Mosiah 12:9). Abinadi's arrest by the people and their

---

40. Under the law of Moses, justice at the "city gates" was administered by the local elders, leading citizens, and heads of families in the individual towns. Biblical examples of the spontaneity and the seriousness with which these popular courts dispensed justice are found in Deuteronomy 22:13–21; Ruth 4:1–91; and 1 Kings 21:11–13. A group of ten elders was sufficient to constitute a court in Ruth 4. See the discussions of Donald A. McKenzie, "Judicial Procedure at the Town Gate," *Vetus Testamentum* 14, no. 1 (1964): 100–104; John L. McKenzie, "The Elders in the Old Testament," *Biblica* 40 (1959): 522–40; de Vaux, *Ancient Israel*, 1:152; and Ze'ev W. Falk, *Hebrew Law in Biblical Times: An Introduction*, 2nd ed. (Winona Lake, IN: Eisenbrauns; Provo, UT: Brigham Young University Press, 2001), 36–37. See further Deuteronomy 21:19; 25:7; Amos 5:10, 12, 15; Zechariah 8:16.

41. Boecker, *Law and the Administration of Justice*, 34–35. See Temba L. J. Mafico, "Judge, Judging," in *Anchor Bible Dictionary*, 3:1106.

ensuing preliminary deliberations comprised a legitimate procedure, not mobocracy. But if the people normally had plenary jurisdiction to handle a case such as this if they chose to, why did they turn Abinadi over to the king? Would they not have won favor in the eyes of Noah by proceeding immediately to rid the kingdom of this pesky fellow?

Facts Found and Charges Formulated by the People

Although the people took initial jurisdiction over Abinadi, they did not dispose of the case themselves. They "were angry with him" and held him only long enough to formulate two specific charges against him, to find to their own satisfaction that misconduct had occurred, and to decide to deliver him to the king (Mosiah 12:9). Before the king's very person, they repeated Abinadi's precise words as evidence against the accused, countered Abinadi's charges by loyally affirming the innocence of the king, and asserted their own strength and alleged worthiness in order to enhance their standing in the action (vv. 9–16). An assertion of innocence such as this is a typical element of an ancient legal controversy.[42] The people pled their innocence before King Noah, saying, "And now, O king, behold, we are guiltless, and thou, O king, hast not sinned," and accused Abinadi of bearing false witness and of prophesying falsely (v. 14).

Several factors explain why the people were correct in deciding not to retain jurisdiction over this particular case. Two charges were to be leveled against Abinadi by the people: (1) that he had lied concerning the king and (2) that he had falsely prophesied evil about the people—as they alleged, "This man has lied concerning you, and he has prophesied in vain" (Mosiah 12:14). As seen above in the case of Sherem, lying, bearing false witness, or making an unwarranted accusation were serious offenses (Exodus 20:16), typically punishable under the rubric that "then shall ye do unto him, as he had thought to have done unto his brother" (Deuteronomy 19:19). The crime of false prophecy was also a very serious offense: "Even that prophet shall die" (18:20).[43] It is not clear, however, that the

---

42. "In civil cases the plaintiff would take hold of the defendant and bring him before the court (Deuteronomy 21:19) or summon him to appear at a hearing (Job 9:19). On the other hand, in criminal cases the accused was put to trial upon the information of witnesses and taken into custody until judgment was pronounced (Leviticus 24:12; Numbers 15:34; 1 Kings 22:27; Jeremiah 37:15). Both parties then submitted their pleadings, accusing their opponents and asserting their own innocence." Falk, *Hebrew Law in Biblical Times*, 58–59. Compare the biblical case of Zelophehad's daughters, who pled their dead father's innocence before the king, asking him to grant them inheritance from his estate (Numbers 27:1–11).

43. See Deuteronomy 13:5; and Hyman E. Goldin, *Hebrew Criminal Law and Procedure* (New York: Twayne, 1952), 37, 207, 215. For more information on lying, see Norman Frimer,

people at large had either the legal authority or a compelling case to justify them in proceeding against Abinadi on these two particular charges. Moreover, by previous decree, Noah had asserted jurisdiction over Abinadi as a wanted offender (Mosiah 11:27–28).

Jurisdiction over the Charge of Lying about the King

While lying was considered seriously unholy and immoral (e.g., Leviticus 19:11; Hosea 4:2), biblical law probably considered bearing false witness to be the equivalent of a public crime, one enforceable by the local courts, only if a person lied as an accuser or witness in a legal setting.[44] "The words translated 'false witness' [Exodus 20:16] are technical terms designating a person who offers false or deceptive testimony in a trial."[45] Accordingly, because Abinadi's words were not spoken in a legal setting, they would not have given rise to the type of matter over which the town elders would normally have had jurisdiction. Likewise, it is not likely that ancient Israelite law recognized slander as a general crime or tort.[46]

Thus it is significant that Abinadi was not accused of lying or slander in general, but specifically of lying *about the king*. This seems akin to reviling the king or the clan's leader, which was indeed an express and heinous crime closely related to blasphemy against deity: "Thou shalt not revile the gods [*elohim*], nor curse the ruler of thy people" (Exodus 22:28).[47] Cursing and reviling are presented in this legal provision as parallel, if not synonymous, terms.[48] Certainly, Abinadi has openly "curse[d] the ruler" of this people. Moreover, the sense of this passage need not require any specific verbal conduct, for this verse also embraces the ideas of disregarding the ruler, holding him in contempt, or doing "anything which is an assault" on his civil or moral authority.[49] Abinadi, again, readily qualifies.

"A Midrash on Morality or When Is a Lie Permissible," *Tradition: A Journal of Orthodox Jewish Thought* 13–14 (Spring–Summer 1973): 23–34.

44. Haim H. Cohn, "Perjury," in Elon, *Principles of Jewish Law*, 516–17.

45. Dale Patrick, *Old Testament Law* (Atlanta: John Knox, 1985), 56.

46. Cohn, "Slander," 513–14, citing Maimonides: "Mere talk does not amount to an overt act, and only such acts are punishable (Yad, *Sanhedrin* 18:2)." Leviticus 19:17 was interpreted to mean that one could reprove a neighbor so long as it was not done insultingly. The rabbis, however, considered a public slanderer to be a grave sinner who would be punished by God, having "no share in the world to come." Babylonian Talmud (hereafter TB) *Avot* 3:11, quoted in Cohn, "Slander," 513.

47. Falk, *Hebrew Law in Biblical Times*, 71; and Joe M. Sprinkle, *'The Book of the Covenant': A Literary Approach* (Sheffield, England: JSOT Press, 1994), 167. The word *elohim* might better be translated as a name of the supreme God.

48. Eric E. Vernon, "Illegal Speech: Blasphemy and Reviling," *Studia Antiqua: The Journal of the Student Society for Ancient Studies* (Summer 2003): 117–24.

49. Sprinkle, *'The Book of the Covenant,'* 168.

Anyone committing this particular crime or accused of such misconduct was probably handed over to the king himself for reprimand or punishment, as would seem to be the natural thing to do. Maimonides, in the Middle Ages, held that it was "the prerogative of the king to kill any person disobeying or slandering him,"[50] but whether such a royal prerogative was absolute in ancient Israel is open to doubt. Something of this practice, however, can be traced back into the times of David and Solomon, after whom King Noah seems to have patterned much of his life: "The principle that the king could take direct legal action in the event of crimes against the crown was further developed by David and Solomon, both of whom used this notion to eliminate political troublemakers and possible rivals (2 Samuel 1:1–16; 4:1–12; 19:16–43; 21:1–14; 1 Kings 2:19–46)."[51] Accordingly, Abinadi's resounding public curses against Noah would probably have been of direct legal concern only to the throne, and so it was appropriate for them to turn this matter over to the king himself, to "do with him as seemeth [him] good" (Mosiah 12:16).

Evidently the phrase "to do as seems good" reflects some kind of formality in ancient law,[52] for otherwise it would be an odd thing for the people to say to their king. One would think that in most cases a king would not need permission of his subjects to do what he wanted. But whenever a lawsuit begins in the hands of one group of people, it would be legally important for those people to relinquish their jurisdictional interest in the case as they formally turn the matter over to someone else. Thus the transfer of power and discretion to the ruling authorities to do as they wished is similarly reflected in Jeremiah's words to the king's princes who tried Jeremiah for prophesying against Jerusalem. After being arrested by the people, Jeremiah willingly submitted himself to the jurisdiction of the rulers: "I am in your hand: do with me as seemeth good and meet unto you" (Jeremiah 26:14). In Jeremiah's case, he was about to be killed by the people, so his chances were certainly better before the princes and rulers.

Two years earlier, when Abinadi had warned the people and called them to repentance (Mosiah 11:20–25), Noah had taken an express interest in Abinadi's case. Noah had said, "Who is Abinadi, that I and my

---

50. Haim H. Cohn, "Extraordinary Remedies," in Elon, *Principles of Jewish Law*, 551, citing Maimonides, Yad, *Melakhim* 3:8.

51. Robert R. Wilson, "Israel's Judicial System in the Preexilic Period," *Jewish Quarterly Review* 74, no. 2 (1983): 242.

52. A similar phrase, "Let my lord do what pleases him," appears in two texts from Mari regarding the king's discretion to handle the words of prophets as he wished. See William L. Moran, "New Evidence from Mari on the History of Prophecy," *Biblica* 50, no. 1 (1969): 21n2. I thank Paul Y. Hoskisson for drawing this article to my attention.

people should be judged of him, or who is the Lord, that shall bring upon my people such great affliction? I command you to bring Abinadi hither, that I may slay him" (vv. 27–28). Thus the people may have readily concluded that exclusive jurisdiction over any case involving Abinadi had already been taken by King Noah. Especially in a case such as Abinadi's that potentially involved a capital offense, Nephite jurisprudence seems to have reserved jurisdiction only to the highest governmental authority. At least in the land of Zarahemla under the later reign of the judges, no man could be put to death according to the laws of the land "except they had power from the governor of the land" (3 Nephi 6:24). For purposes of comparison, similar provisions are found in Hittite Law 44b, which places all cases involving the magical misuse of impurities under the exclusive jurisdiction of the king, and in the Law of Eshnunna 48, which requires that a capital charge "(belongs) to the king himself."[53] Thus, for several reasons the people in the city of Nephi rightly determined that jurisdiction had been taken out of their hands and they should turn Abinadi over to Noah without delay.

Jurisdiction over the Charge of False Prophecy

While it was a crime under ancient Israelite law to prophesy falsely, little is known about actual trials of false prophets in the ancient Israelite period, and even less is said about such cases in rabbinic literature.[54] Nevertheless, the legal right to try a person for this capital offense also appears to have been out of the hands of the population at large. During the time of Jeremiah, two known cases of false prophecy, one against Jeremiah and the other against Urijah, were pursued by the king or his princes (Jeremiah 26:10, 21); and during the rabbinic period, such actions were heard only by the Sanhedrin.[55] Although it is unclear whether the

---

53. See, for example, Hoffner, *The Laws of the Hittites*, 189; and Reuven Yaron, *The Laws of Eshnunna*, 2nd rev. ed. (Jerusalem: Magnes, 1988), 119–20.

54. Although they are not tried in a formal court, false prophets are reported to have suffered ill-fated deaths; for example, the slaughter of the priests of Baal after their trial by ordeal with Elijah (1 Kings 18:40; 19:1) and the death of Hananiah (Jeremiah 28:15–17). See also the threats against false prophets in Jeremiah 5:12–13; 14:14–16; 29:21; and Zechariah 13:2. The prophet Urijah was tried and executed (Jeremiah 26:21–23). Regarding the deaths of righteous prophets, see 2 Chronicles 36:15–16 and Matthew 23:37.

55. Goldin, *Hebrew Criminal Law*, 76; and Joseph M. Baumgarten, "The Duodecimal Courts of Qumran, Revelation, and the Sanhedrin," *Journal of Biblical Literature* 95, no. 1 (1976): 73. The Great Sanhedrin, as distinguished from the small sanhedrins, had jurisdiction over alleged false prophets. Haim H. Cohn, "Bet Din," in Elon, *Principles of Jewish Law*, 562; TB *Sanhedrin* 1:1, 16a. It appears, however, that the small sanhedrins carried out the functions of the great court in capital cases, which would include the trying of false prophets if the larger court was inaccessible.

Nephites would have known specifically of these jurisdictional technicalities, the conduct of the people in turning Abinadi over to King Noah was consistent with these precedents and with Noah's prior order, and thus they acted correctly in deciding to deliver Abinadi to the king and his priests to be judged.

Taken, Bound, and Carried

After the people had determined that Abinadi was in the wrong (Mosiah 12:9, 14), they delivered him to King Noah. Following a practice routinely repeated in the legal cases in the Book of Mormon, the populace "took him and carried him bound before the king" (v. 9). This same language appears in the arrests of Korihor; the Ammonites in the city of Jershon "took him, and bound him, and carried him before Ammon" (Alma 30:20), just as in the city of Gideon he was "taken and bound and carried before the high priest" (v. 21). That this threefold formulaic expression reflects a widespread customary practice among the Nephites and Lamanites is confirmed by other reports. The people of Ammonihah "took . . . and bound . . . and took [Alma and Amulek] before the chief judge" (14:4). When Ammon entered the land of Ishmael, the Lamanites "took him and bound him, as was their custom . . . and carr[ied him] before the king" (17:20; see Mosiah 7:7). Later, Nephi, the son of Helaman, was "taken and bound and brought before the multitude" for interrogation (Helaman 9:19). This Book of Mormon practice may have derived from the biblical instruction that a complainant should "take hold of the defendant and bring him before the court."[56] Why or how they bound Abinadi, or how long he remained bound, is not clear. If they bound his feet, perhaps readers should understand that the people literally carried these defendants into court.

The Judicial Roles of the King and Priests

One of the most interesting aspects of the trial of Abinadi is the interaction between King Noah and his priests. At some times in the trial, Noah appears to have been in control, while his priests served in an advisory capacity; in other respects, the priests seem to have been in charge, formulating the precise allegations and determining the ultimate outcome. These concurrent roles may reflect the fact that two charges had been brought against Abinadi, and each called for different judicial treatment.

Pursuant to an important legal directive attributed to King Jehoshaphat in 2 Chronicles 19:11, one may surmise that the king in ancient

---

56. Falk, *Hebrew Law in Biblical Times*, 58, following Deuteronomy 21:19.

Israel had power over "all the king's matters," while the priests had jurisdiction in "all matters of the Lord," or religious concerns.[57] It appears that a similar division of legal responsibilities also existed among the Nephites, based either on something like Jehoshaphat's precedent or on Nephi's conferral of royal authority on some (Jacob 1:9) and priestly authority on others (2 Nephi 5:26). Thus one may infer that Noah had power over Abinadi's first alleged offense of lying about the king, while the priests would have had responsibility to resolve the charge that he had prophesied falsely. Moreover, where Noah was the injured party and was also "a hierarchical superior," he had the natural ability to "act as both plaintiff and judge, bringing the defendant before his own court, as Saul had done with Ahimelech" (1 Samuel 22:11–16).[58]

Under such a traditional division of legal duties, Noah essentially had administrative control. He had authority to convene the court: "He commanded that the priests should gather themselves together," and his purpose was to "hold a council with them what *he* should do" (Mosiah 12:17; emphasis added), which Noah understood broadly. Noah also had the power to command his priests to follow his orders. When Noah became incensed at Abinadi's unequivocal accusation that he and his priests were idolaters (vv. 33–37), Noah commanded his priests to seize Abinadi and take him away and kill him (13:1). Likewise, Noah "caused" his servants and guards to pursue Alma when he was expelled and fled from the court; and he "caused"

---

57. See Welch, "The Trial of Jeremiah," 346–47. Falk, *Hebrew Law in Biblical Times*, 47, notes: "Originally the priests were perhaps satisfied with the jurisdiction in religious matters." See Elliot N. Dorff and Arthur Rosett, *A Living Tree: The Roots and Growth of Jewish Law* (Albany: State University Press, 1988), 62–64; and Keith W. Whitelam, *The Just King: Monarchial Judicial Authority in Ancient Israel* (Sheffield, England: JSOT Press, 1979), 202–3. Keith W. Whitelam, "King and Kingship," in *Anchor Bible Dictionary*, 4:44, says, "The king was the central symbol of the social system. His prime function was the establishment and maintenance of order throughout the kingdom. The king's functions as warrior (1 Sam 8:20), judge (1 Sam 8:5; 2 Sam 12:1–15; 14:1–24; 15:1–6; 1 Kgs 3; 21:1–20; 2 Chr 19:4–11), and priest (1 Sam 13:9–10; 14:33–35; 2 Sam 6:13, 17; 24:25; 1 Kgs 3:4, 15; 8:62; 9:25; 12:32; 13:1; etc.) are all interrelated elements of this fundamental task. They were all essential to the maintenance of a divinely ordained order which was conceived of in cosmic terms and covered all aspects of a society's and individual's existence." See further William F. Albright, "The Judicial Reform of Jehoshaphat," in *Alexander Marx Jubilee Volume* (New York: Jewish Theological Seminary of America, 1950), 61–82; M. Lahav, "Jehoshaphat's Judicial Reform," in *Yaacov Gil Jubilee Volume*, ed. Y. Hocherman, M. Lahav, and Z. Zemarion (Jerusalem: Rubin Mass, 1979), 141–48; Gosta W. Ahlström, *Royal Administration and National Religion in Ancient Palestine* (Leiden: Brill, 1982), 54; and Wilson, "Israel's Judicial System," 243–48 (arguing that "there is no compelling reason to question the general accuracy of the account" in 2 Chronicles 19 as a description of the legal system during the monarchical period, 245).

58. Raymond Westbrook, "Biblical Law," in *An Introduction to the History and Sources of Jewish Law*, ed. N. S. Hecht et al. (Oxford: Oxford University Press, 1996), 10; see Bovati, *Re-Establishing Justice*, 34, 176.

them to hold Abinadi for three days in prison (17:3–6). At the end of the hearing, the king again "counseled with his priests" (17:6). The fact that Noah counseled with his priests, even regarding the crime of cursing his person or lying about him, may indicate that he was not regularly involved in judicial affairs. He did not act patiently with the judicial process, for he behaved impetuously throughout the entire case (e.g., 13:1).

While Noah appears to be in charge of the court, functioning as its sole voice and ultimate decision maker, in the end he was deeply influenced by the opinions of the priests (Mosiah 17:11–12). The role of these priests was not merely advisory. They were actively involved in the trial, conducting the direct examination of the accused (12:19–20) and seeking a basis whereby "*they* might have wherewith to accuse him" (v. 19; emphasis added). Given their line of interrogation against Abinadi, it appears that they were seeking evidence to support a conviction on the grounds of false prophecy, an offense over which priests normally would have had jurisdiction.[59] Similarly, it was the priests who eventually formulated the religiously based charge of blasphemy that Noah announced as the verdict of the priests' formal deliberations: "Having counseled with his priests, . . . he said unto him: Abinadi, *we* have found an accusation against thee" (17:6–7; emphasis added). After Abinadi rebuffed that charge, Noah himself was "about to release" Abinadi, but it was the priests who "lifted up their voices against [Abinadi] and began to accuse him" with yet another charge (vv. 11–12). Thus the priests had great power in this proceeding to conduct the examination of the accused, to advise the king, to raise accusations on their own initiative based on words Abinadi had spoken in their presence, and even to contravene the decision that Noah was leaning strongly toward making. Ultimately, it was the priests themselves who fashioned and conducted the execution of Abinadi: "And it came to pass that *they* took him and bound him, and scourged his skin with faggots, yea, even unto death" (v. 13; emphasis added). In the end, therefore, it was "the priests who caused that he should suffer death by fire" (Alma 25:9). They were the more blameworthy (Mosiah 7:28) after Noah released Abinadi and "delivered him up [to the priests] that he might be slain" (17:12).

This confluence of royal and priestly jurisdiction accurately reflects what is known about the judicial roles of the king and the Israelite priests in ancient Israel.[60] The Levites are mentioned as officers and judges during the reign of King Solomon (1 Chronicles 23:4), although their precise

---

59. Cohn, "Bet Din," 562–63.

60. Wilson, "Israel's Judicial System," 241–48.

legal functions are not stated. Regarding the judicial roles of the king, it is generally believed among biblical scholars that while the king in Israel did not function as a judge in day-to-day civil or criminal matters,[61] one of his ideal duties was "to guarantee the true administration of justice throughout the land."[62] By the time of the Mishnah, the king held no judicial power whatever, except in military affairs or in the extraordinary case of someone disobeying or slandering him: "A king can neither judge nor be judged, he may not bear witness nor be witnessed against."[63] Thus one would not expect King Noah to have been involved regularly in normal judicial proceedings—especially when those cases involved priestly affairs. The statement of King Zedekiah regarding the trial of Jeremiah, who was accused of false prophecy, corroborates this view: "For the king is not he that can do any thing against you" (Jeremiah 38:5).

Falk and de Vaux point out, however, that the king, especially in the early monarchy of Israel, was capable of functioning as if he were a plenary tribal judge in all kinds of cases.[64] Thus it would not have been unprecedented for Noah, especially in Zeniff's small city-state in the land of Nephi, to assume the role of judge as he saw fit; but based on Noah's impatience and awkwardness with the process, this role seems to have been an unusual one for him. Kings in early Israel could take jurisdiction or refuse it on a case-by-case basis; one assumes that King Solomon could easily have sent the two women arguing over one baby back to their village so that the town elders could resolve the dispute. Thus when the people turned Abinadi over to Noah, they acknowledged and expected that the king would "do with him as seemeth [him] good" (Mosiah 12:16).[65] It would be consistent with Noah's selective observance of the law of Moses generally (v. 28) for him to take a case or ignore the matter based largely on expedience. Evidence indicates that kings like Noah, however, typically and understandably took jurisdiction over cases involving military matters, suits involving the crown or the royal family, and affairs in the capital

---

61. For a good discussion of the role of the king in this judicial system, see Boecker, *Law and the Administration of Justice*, 40–49. Boecker concludes that the judicial powers of the king in ancient Israel were always limited and perhaps eliminated during the Deuteronomic reforms in the seventh century BC (Deuteronomy 16:18; 17:8–12).

62. Whitelam, *Just King*, 37. See Wilson, "Israel's Judicial System," 242: "The king is directly responsible for maintaining justice in the land and assuring all citizens equal access to the courts." See further Mafico, "Judge, Judging," 3:1106.

63. TB *Sanhedrin* 2:1, 18a.

64. 1 Samuel 8:5; 2 Samuel 8:15; 12:1; 14:4; 1 Kings 3:9, 16; Psalm 72:1–4; Jeremiah 22:15–16. Falk, *Hebrew Law in Biblical Times*, 50; and de Vaux, *Ancient Israel*, 1:151.

65. Compare the conduct of the Greek soldiers who turned Helen over to Menelaus and gave him authority to do with her however he saw fit. Euripides *Trojan Women* 872–75.

city.[66] In no known historical instance, however, did the king in Israel act as a judge on his own motion.[67] Even the royal courts in Jerusalem appear to have acted only as a resource for local town courts in cases where the elders felt unsure about their action.[68] Thus while King Noah may well not have been involved in the routine judicial system of his land, when Abinadi's case arose in the capital city and involved the royal house itself, it was the kind of case that King Noah would almost have been forced to take part in once it had been brought to him.

Imprisonment Pending Trial or Judgment in Difficult Cases

Noah put Abinadi in prison pending trial (Mosiah 12:17). Prisons had limited use in the administration of justice in ancient Israel and in the ancient Near East, although prisons were more extensively used in Egypt.[69] Their main function in Israel seems to have been the holding of accused persons pending trial or judgment, particularly when the laws or procedural rules were uncertain. Examples of the use of prisons to detain accused but untried individuals in the face of legal uncertainties are found in the case of the son of an Egyptian man and an Israelite woman who blasphemed during an altercation ("And they put him in ward, that the mind of the Lord might be shewed them," Leviticus 24:12) and in the obscure case of the man who was found gathering sticks on the Sabbath ("And they put him in ward, because it was not declared what should be done to him," Numbers 15:34). King Benjamin banned the use of dungeons in the land of Zarahemla (Mosiah 2:13), but prolonged imprisonment was common among the Jaredites and apparently also to a lesser extent among the Lamanites (Alma 23:2; Helaman 5:21) and the wicked people of Ammonihah (Alma 14:22–23).

Preliminary Council

While Abinadi was being held, Noah met with his priests to discuss what should be done (Mosiah 12:17–18).[70] In light of the fact that Alma

---

66. Boecker, *Law and the Administration of Justice*, 42–45; and Wilson, "Israel's Judicial System," 242.

67. See generally Goldin, *Hebrew Criminal Law*, 83n11, citing Maimonides, *Hilkot Sanhedrin* 2:5.

68. Deuteronomy 17:8–12; and Boecker, *Law and the Administration of Justice*, 48–49. See also Raymond Westbrook, "Punishments and Crimes," in *Anchor Bible Dictionary*, 5:546–56.

69. On prisons generally, see Menachem Elon, "Imprisonment," in Elon, *Principles of Jewish Law*, 535–39; Haim H. Cohn, "Practice and Procedure," in Elon, *Principles of Jewish Law*, 581; Falk, *Hebrew Law in Biblical Times*, 59; Goldin, *Hebrew Criminal Law*, 38; Karel van der Toorn, "Prison," in *Anchor Bible Dictionary*, 5:468–69; David L. Blumenfeld, "The Terminology of Imprisonment and Forced Detention in the Bible" (PhD diss., New York University, 1977); and Olivia Robinson, "Private Prisons," *Revue Internationale des Droits de l'Antiquité* 15 (1968): 389–98.

70. Compare Bovati, *Re-Establishing Justice*, 240–41.

was soon able to attract a sizable group of converts to follow him and the teachings of Abinadi, Noah and his priests must have had reason to worry about the threat of Abinadi's growing popularity. Therefore, although they could have taken Abinadi and executed him immediately on the strength of the prior decree of Noah from two years earlier, they must have thought it would be more effective to find some way to embarrass Abinadi or to get him to disgrace himself. They may have begun their deliberations by conferring about what legal or political result they hoped to achieve in the case and specifically what kind of punishment they should seek to impose. Few alternatives existed under ancient Israelite law in this regard. Long-term imprisonment was probably not an option.[71] Monetary fines or payment to compensate for the wrong (*kofer*) would have been improper under the law of Moses.[72] Banishment (*ḥerem*) was a possibility, but it appears to have been rarely invoked,[73] and it would not have prevented Abinadi from sneaking back into the city yet again in another disguise and creating further disturbances or infractions. Beating or flogging were distinct possibilities (Deuteronomy 25:1–3), but this punishment was normally used for disobedience.[74] Likewise, penal slavery would have been inappropriate under biblical law.[75] Only two obvious options remained open: either to let Abinadi go free[76] and leave his fate to the divine judgment of God or to impose the death penalty. The death penalty was the most common

---

71. Punishments available under Hebrew criminal law are discussed elsewhere. In contrast to the laws of ancient Israel's ancient neighbors, biblical law seems to have allowed fewer long-term options to courts and judges. The basic possibilities were death (by stoning, hanging, burning, or slaying with the sword), flogging, or banishment. Torture, mutilation, and prolonged incarceration are virtually absent from the biblical law codes and historical accounts.

72. Ancient Israelite law did provide for the satisfaction of certain offenses through the payment of monetary fines, but these were all offenses against property, such as theft. See, for example, Exodus 22:1, 4; and Goldin, *Hebrew Criminal Law*, 61. Talmudic law also allowed monetary compensation for shaming a person (*boshet*), and rabbis at various times determined fixed amounts to pay in compensation for such acts. See Mishna *Bava Kamma* 8:6; and Shalom Albeck, "Damages," in Elon, *Principles of Jewish Law*, 332.

73. Excision (*karet*), being "cut off from the people," is mentioned often in the Bible, for example, Leviticus 20:18. Goldin, *Hebrew Criminal Law*, 41nn22–26, notes, "In the Scripture, there are twenty-one offenses which merit the punishment of *karet*." The offenses of which Abinadi was accused were usually not punished in this way.

74. The punishment of flagellation, mentioned in Deuteronomy 25:1–3, was typically given only upon the transgression of Mosaic prohibitory law. See Goldin, *Hebrew Criminal Law*, 49–53; and Westbrook, "Punishments and Crimes," 5:546–56.

75. Penal slavery applied only to those guilty of theft or other destruction of property. See Goldin, *Hebrew Criminal Law*, 57–58; and Muhammad A. Dandamayev, "Slavery," in *Anchor Bible Dictionary*, 6:58–65.

76. Hezekiah did not punish Micah even though he had prophesied evil against Jerusalem (Jeremiah 26:18–20).

punishment prescribed for serious offenses against God or one's superiors under the law of Moses.[77]

Noah and his priests probably also discussed the charges and how to conduct the trial. They would have needed to decide which of the two charges to address first. They decided to begin with false prophecy. They had a better chance of success in arguing with Abinadi about interpretive prophetic issues, especially since his prophecies made two years ago had not come to pass, than in trying to prove that Abinadi was mistaken in his condemnation of Noah, whose conduct would not have been legally easy to defend or politically wise to expose. Indeed, the facts were not on Noah's side.

Another concern would have been the need for witnesses. No Israelite could be convicted of a capital crime without two witnesses (Numbers 35:30; Deuteronomy 17:6), and this rule would have been known to the priests of Noah since they purported to observe the law of Moses. Some priests may have argued that this requirement had already been satisfied since the people had witnessed against Abinadi and had simply turned him over to the king for sentencing. But others must have concluded that further evidence was needed against Abinadi, for they sought in their interrogation to obtain "wherewith to accuse him" (Mosiah 12:19). No further witnesses were ever called against Abinadi on the charge of false prophecy because this accusation was soon dropped, and with respect to the later charges of blasphemy (17:7–8) and reviling (v. 12) arising out of Abinadi's unambiguous statements during the trial, the priests themselves could serve as firsthand witnesses.

Noah and the priests may also have discussed whether they should try to extract a confession from Abinadi before they executed him and, if so, what form the confession should take.[78] As seen above in the discussion of Sherem's case, Israelite law preferred that a person not be put to death until an acknowledgment of guilt had been extracted.[79] Consequently, Noah and his priests may have conferred about what might be said or done to convince the determined Abinadi to admit that he was wrong.

Israelite law did not give the accused the right to remain silent.[80] In assessing statements by the accused, the typical court found it necessary

---

77. Haim H. Cohn, "Capital Punishment," in Elon, *Principles of Jewish Law*, 526; and Westbrook, "Punishments and Crimes," 5:546–56.

78. See Bovati, *Re-Establishing Justice*, 94–109, for an exploration of the different forms of confessions.

79. See citations above regarding Sherem's confession. Goldin, *Hebrew Criminal Law*, 133.

80. "The rule against self-incrimination dates only from talmudic times." Haim H. Cohn, "Confession," in Elon, *Principles of Jewish Law*, 614. See Aaron Kirschenbaum, *Self-Incrimination in Jewish Law* (New York: Burning Bush Press, 1970), 25–33.

to consider the accused's demeanor[81] and his declaration of innocence, especially when made under oath. Perhaps hoping that Abinadi would recognize the error of his ways and confess, or alternatively seeking further evidence against him, Noah's priests planned to ask Abinadi at least one question (Mosiah 12:20–24) that they hoped would lead him to acknowledge his guilt and error. Mosiah 12:19 explains that Noah and his priests "began to question him, that they might cross him." Apparently they planned thereby to expose a contradiction in Abinadi's teachings and thus convince him—and the people—of the error of his ways.[82]

Confrontation by the Priests

Abinadi was then brought before the court to answer questions raised by the priests. Little is known about the priests of Noah or how they normally functioned. They probably had religious as well as judicial powers, particularly in ascertaining the veracity of witnesses and administering evidentiary procedures (Numbers 5:15–27; Deuteronomy 17:9; 19:17–18; 21:5). In addition, they served, as did all Nephite priests, as teachers of the people (Mosiah 12:25, 28). Reading and teaching the law to the people was indeed one of the duties of the priests and the king of Israel (Deuteronomy 31:9–13).

King Noah consecrated his own priests after dismissing the priests who had been ordained by his father, Zeniff (Mosiah 11:5). In the record, the priests facing Abinadi are often called "the priests of Noah" or "his priests" (vv. 4, 14; 13:1; 17:6), indicating that the body was closely affiliated with the royal palace and its temple precinct. In Zeniff's reign, such priests in the land of Nephi may have enjoyed greater independence from the king than under Noah's regime, for the text implies that in putting "his priests" into power, Noah significantly changed the affairs of the kingdom (11:4), though it was customary for new priests to be installed and personnel to be reconstituted as a part of each new king's coronation (6:3; compare 2 Chronicles 19:5–6). Noah's priests were supported by taxes (Mosiah 11:3–6). They spoke "flattering things" to the public (v. 7),

---

81. Rashi, *ad Gemara* 36b–37a, explains that the judges sat in a semicircle "to be afforded an opportunity to closely observe [the witnesses'] faces." Goldin, *Hebrew Criminal Law*, 112n16. See TB *Sanhedrin* 4:2, 36b.

82. It was the duty of the court to examine thoroughly a witness or accuser, especially to expose any contradictions in his testimony (similar is the priests' attempt to "cross" Abinadi in Mosiah 12:19). Maimonides says the judges must "probe into their accuracy and refer them back to previous questions so as to make them desist from or change their testimony if it was in any way faulty." Haim H. Cohn, "Witness," in Elon, *Principles of Jewish Law*, 610. This was standard practice not only here but also in the searching examination of Korihor, of Alma and Amulek (esp. Alma 11:35, where a conflict in the testimony is purportedly exposed), and of Nephi (Helaman 9:19).

although no indication is given of what they said. The fact that Abinadi accused them of leading the people into idolatry indicates they had control over the temple in the city of Nephi. They had special seats set above the rest and behind a public pulpit, apparently located in the temple precincts (vv. 10–12).

The intriguing question regarding the number of Noah's priests can only be answered tentatively, but there are some clues, both in ancient practice and in the text itself. In the biblical period, "priests in general . . . were mentioned in the plural," which accorded with typical ancient Near Eastern practice.[83] The text never says how many priests served in Noah's temple or court, but the fact that the warrior Gideon instantly associated the priests of Noah with the abduction of twenty-four of the Lamanite daughters as soon as he learned how many young women had been taken, causing the Lamanites to come back on the attack against the city of Nephi, certainly suggests that there were about twenty-four priests on Noah's court (Mosiah 20:5, 17–18). Noah, of course, is not to be counted among those who carried off the young Lamanite women, since he had already been put to death by his own priests (19:20); but the vacancy created when Alma was expelled from the court (17:3–4) would probably have been filled with a replacement either during or shortly after the trial.

Evidence from several periods of history indicates that the numbers twelve or twenty-four (two times twelve) were often associated with judicial bodies or functions in ancient Israel.[84] In the biblical period, courts were established in each of the twelve tribes (Deuteronomy 16:18). Later literature in the *Manual of Discipline* from Qumran asserted that when Jehoshaphat appointed "Levites, priests and elders" as judges (2 Chronicles 19:8), he appointed twelve in each group.[85] The Davidic tabernacle and Solomonic temple services were in continuous operation with twenty-four courses of priests (1 Chronicles 24:3–18), and when David appointed his prophetic cantors, he established twenty-four orders, each with twelve members (25:1–31). Twenty-four priests are shown as a group in one depiction of Ramses's court in Egypt,[86] and David and Solomon may have patterned their own priestly organizations after this numerical feature.

---

83. Falk, *Hebrew Law in Biblical Times*, 48.

84. This subject is briefly discussed in John W. Welch, "Number 24," in *Reexploring the Book of Mormon*, ed. John W. Welch (Salt Lake City: Deseret Book and FARMS, 1992), 272–74. Recall also the twenty-four commandments in Exodus 22–23, discussed above in chapter 3.

85. 1QS 2:1–3, in *Texts Concerned with Religious Law*, part 1 of *The Dead Sea Scrolls Reader*, ed. Donald W. Parry and Emanuel Tov (Leiden: Brill, 2004), 211.

86. The Ramses exhibit at Brigham Young University (1985–86) contained an item showing a group of twenty-four priests. In addition, in Egypt the land "was divided into Nomes, each with

Thus, although direct evidence of duodecimal courts in pre-exilic Israel is lacking, indirect and culturally related evidence gives the number twenty-four presumptive judicial significance in Lehi's day and before.

In the Dead Sea Scrolls from Qumran, the evidence for courts of this number becomes much clearer. In that legal system, judicial disputes were brought before a court called "the council of the community."[87] This deliberative body was composed of two panels of twelve—twelve priests and twelve laymen—for a total of twenty-four judges. The commentary, or pesher, on Isaiah 54:11–12 found at Qumran states that these twenty-four judges were to "give light by the judgment of the Urim and Thummim."[88]

Further judicial significance for the number twenty-four appears in the New Testament Apocalypse, where it is prophesied that twenty-four elders will judge the world. In that book, these twenty-four elders are mentioned twelve times (Revelation 4:4, 10; 5:5, 6, 8, 11, 14; 7:11, 13; 11:16; 14:3; 19:4; compare *2 Enoch* 4:1). Similarly, in ancient Babylon, twenty-four star-gods were said to judge the world.[89]

Of more direct relevance to legal practices and thus to Noah's court in the New World is the fact that early explorers in Central America reported that the indigenous king in highland Guatemala relied heavily on a council of twenty-four officials as he administered the affairs of state: "The supreme council of the monarch of Quiche was composed of 24 grandees, with whom the king deliberated on all political and military affairs. These counsellors were invested with great distinctions and many privileges. . . . The administration of justice, and the collection of the royal revenues, were under their charge."[90]

The possible connection between the priests of Noah and the number twenty-four (Mosiah 20:5, 17–18) is further corroborated by the fact that this number is significant throughout the Book of Mormon in judicial and testimonial contexts. The number of the gold plates of Ether was twenty-four, a fact that is repeatedly mentioned (8:9; Alma 37:21; Ether 1:2). These plates were seen as a "testimony" (Mosiah 8:9) of the "judgments of God" upon those people (Alma 37:30), and their contents were brought "to light" (*urim*) by the use of "interpreters" (Mosiah 28:13–16;

---

a ruler or judge over it, and these judges in later times amounted to seventy-two," or three times twenty-four. J. Garnier, *The Worship of the Dead* (London: Chapman and Hall, 1904), 258.

87. 1QS 8:1, in *Texts Concerned with Religious Law*, 31.

88. Baumgarten, "The Duodecimal Courts," 59–78.

89. Diodorus Siculus, *Bibliotheca Historica* 2:31.2.

90. Domingo Juarros, *A Statistical and Commercial History of the Kingdom of Guatemala in Spanish America*, trans. John Baily (London: John Hearne, 1823), 189. I thank John L. Sorenson for drawing this source to my attention.

Alma 37:21–25).[91] Twenty-four survivors remained at the end of the final destruction of the Nephites to serve, in effect, as witnesses of the judgment of God upon their people (Mormon 6:11, 15). There were other survivors (v. 15), so perhaps these twenty-four somehow stood as a body of special witnesses. Together with the twelve apostles, the twelve Nephite disciples will act as final judges of the world (3 Nephi 27:27), for a total of twenty-four. The number twelve is likewise involved in the Book of Mormon in matters of judgment: God's heavenly court, which passed judgment on Jerusalem in Lehi's opening vision (1 Nephi 1:13), consisted of twelve members (v. 10).

Worth mentioning also is the number twenty-three, which was important in later Jewish courts. In rabbinic times, official courts consisted of three, twenty-three, or seventy or seventy-one judges,[92] which may offer some additional, although later, parallels to the priests of Noah. The number twenty-four, which was found frequently in biblical times, was reduced by one in Pharisaical Judaism, perhaps to avoid the possibility of a tie vote; thereafter, the number twenty-three became a common element in judicial bodies under Jewish law.[93] In the Second Temple period, the largest Jewish court was the Great Sanhedrin, whose number was associated with the seventy elders who went up onto Mount Sinai with Moses (Exodus 24:1, 9; Numbers 11:16–17).[94] Members of the large Sanhedrin sat in three rows (two of twenty-three and one of twenty-four). Although only one Great Sanhedrin was ever authorized in Judaism[95]—particularly to hear cases of religious crimes, to interpret scripture, and to regulate ritual[96]—smaller local sanhedrins functioned if the large court was inaccessible. Any city with a population of 120 families (or 230 people) could

---

91. Compare the pesher on Isaiah 54:11–12 mentioned above. Juarros, *Statistical and Commercial History*, 384, also refers to the use of a similar oracle by the indigenous people of Guatemala: "The judges quitted their seats, and proceeded to a deep ravine, where there was a place of worship, wherein was placed a black transparent stone, of a substance much more valuable than the *chay* [obsidian]; on the surface of this tablet the Deity was supposed to give a representation of the fate that awaited the criminal. . . . This oracle was also consulted in the affairs of war."

92. Cohn, "Bet Din," 561–62.

93. See Mishnah *Sanhedrin* 4:1 and the talmudic discussion in TB *Sanhedrin*, 17a.

94. See generally Anthony J. Saldarini, "Sanhedrin," in *Anchor Bible Dictionary*, 5:975–80.

95. Sidney B. Hoenig, *The Great Sanhedrin* (Philadelphia: Dropsie College, 1953), 62; TB *Sanhedrin* 1:1, 2a. The Sanhedrin initially functioned in Jerusalem; see James E. Priest, *Governmental and Judicial Ethics in the Bible and Rabbinic Literature* (New York: KTAV, 1980), 92. After the Romans destroyed Jerusalem in AD 70, the Great Sanhedrin moved to various locations and continued to act as the Jewish Supreme Court. Hoenig, *Great Sanhedrin*, xiii; and Priest, *Governmental and Judicial Ethics*, 92.

96. See Hoenig, *Great Sanhedrin*, 86–89.

organize a "small sanhedrin" of twenty-three members,[97] representing one of the three panels that comprised the Great Sanhedrin. Noah's court may have reflected similar backgrounds or influences in its configuration.

Thus Noah's court likely consisted of twenty-four priests who would have taken particular interest in hearing cases involving religious offenses or rebellious elders. Although the origin of the Great Sanhedrin in Jerusalem and the related rise of small sanhedrins in outlying towns in Palestine is obscure and is not specifically evidenced as far back as Lehi, several interesting parallels between the functions of those small sanhedrins and Noah's court of apparently similar size seem noteworthy. The similarities may have developed independently among the Jews and Nephites, or they may have sprung from common roots associated with the older courts or concourses of twenty-four. In particular, the Jewish courts of twenty-three had authority over capital cases, and possibly over the imposition of flogging.[98] They had the power to execute rebellious elders,[99] something like the kind of case presented to the court in the trial of Abinadi.

The Roles of the Parties and Participants

In the trial of Abinadi, nothing indicates that any lawyers were present, either as prosecutors or as advocates for the accused. This is consistent with ancient legal practice. All people in ancient Israel were expected to know the law (Deuteronomy 31:12), to do justice, and, especially for the adult men, to be involved in the judicial process. Because "biblical law requires that 'the two parties to the dispute shall appear before the Lord, before the priests or magistrates' (19:17), i.e., in person and not by proxy,"[100] private lawyers were not employed in this legal system to represent the

---

97. TB *Sanhedrin* 17b; Baumgarten, "The Duodecimal Courts," 73; and Priest, *Governmental and Judicial Ethics*, 91. Baumgarten explains that the figure 120 stands for twelve panels of ten, each panel representing one of the twelve tribes. See TB *Sanhedrin* 1:1, 2a, for alternative minimum populations that could support a small sanhedrin and the methods used to arrive at those figures. The number 230 is derived from twenty-three minyans of ten. The number twenty-three may have been used because there were this many judges seated on each of the three semicircular rows when the Great Sanhedrin convened.

98. Cohn, "Bet Din," 562; Baumgarten, "The Duodecimal Courts," 73; and Priest, *Governmental and Judicial Ethics*, 91. On flogging or scourging, see note 166 below.

99. See Hoenig, *Great Sanhedrin*, 98–99. This crime was in later times defined as advocating schismatic opinions with an intent to act contrary to the majority. Normally, however, mere statements were not enough to prove an intent to act contrary to the community majority. Although Abinadi's opinions were clearly critical, schismatic, and provocative, there is no reason to believe that he advocated overthrowing the king or any other action. Thus the crime of being a rebellious elder never figures expressly in the trial of Abinadi.

100. Haim H. Cohn, "Attorney," in Elon, *Principles of Jewish Law*, 573.

defendant or to advocate a certain result.[101] This practice was apparently followed in all matters, whether we would consider them to be criminal or civil in nature.[102] Accordingly, Abinadi appeared and spoke in person.

In proceedings before these ancient bodies, no official functionary served in the modern role of prosecuting attorney. For example, under Jewish law, in a case tried by a small or large sanhedrin, one of the judges was designated to record all of the arguments for acquittal, while another recorded those for conviction.[103] As such, the members of the court did not necessarily act during the hearing or investigation as impartial, detached judges. This practice appears to stem from the early biblical period. Judges and witnesses were not viewed as neutral, detached testifiers, as McKenzie argues: "These witnesses are not in any sense merely objective informants. Their role is similar to that played in a modern lawsuit by the advocate for the defence and the counsel for the prosecution."[104] In a similar fashion, the priests of Noah took an aggressive role in the trial of Abinadi, with some of them leading out as accusers.

In cases involving offenses against the public, such as the prosecution of the false prophecy charge against Abinadi, ancient Israelite or Jewish courts typically "initiated the proceedings and dispensed with prosecutors" after being prompted to action by witnesses.[105] Likewise, witnesses were called, as necessary, by the sanhedrins. In later Jewish practice, any person desiring to speak in defense of the accused was, in theory, "allowed and even encouraged to do so";[106] but there is no evidence of this practice in biblical times. Obviously, no witnesses in Abinadi's defense volunteered or were summoned by Noah's court.

In terms of physical positioning, it appears that Abinadi remained standing throughout his trial.[107] The priests, however, were seated (see

---

101. Dov I. Frimer, "The Role of the Lawyer in Jewish Law," *Journal of Law and Religion* 1, no. 2 (1983): 297–305. Falk, *Hebrew Law in Biblical Times*, 59, however, assumes that an accused could be accompanied on certain occasions by counsel standing on his right hand, citing Psalm 109:31, but it is unclear whether the Lord is viewed in this verse as legal counsel, as an accuser of those who have wronged the poor, or as a judge.

102. "The rule is that parties must litigate in person and may not be represented." Cohn, "Practice and Procedure," 575 (see p. 577), and "Attorney," 573. This rule applied unless representation was necessary to avoid injustice.

103. TB *Sanhedrin* 36b–37a.

104. McKenzie, "Judicial Procedure at the Town Gate," 102.

105. Cohn, "Practice and Procedure," 581.

106. Cohn, "Practice and Procedure," 581. The expulsion of Alma from the court is therefore all the more egregious.

107. The image of standing before the judgment bar of God and standing as a witness would appear to reflect the normal practice in the city of Nephi (Mosiah 16:10; 17:10).

Proverbs 20:8; Job 29:7; Ruth 4:2) and had to "stand forth" when they attempted to lay their hands on him (Mosiah 13:2).[108] Seats for judges were prominent in the gates of ancient Israelite cities, and no physical feature of the Nephite justice system is more prominent than is the governmental judgment seat, which is mentioned forty-seven times in the Book of Mormon.[109] Because the seats that Noah had built for himself in his palace and for his high priests and priests in his temple (11:9–11) are mentioned conspicuously in the narrative prologue to the trial of Abinadi, one would surmise that this proceeding took place in one or both of those venues.[110] King Noah was actively involved in the trial of Abinadi, which likely comports with biblical law practice. While the king did not have a place on the Great Sanhedrin (although the high priest did) during rabbinic times,[111] a reasonable speculation is that before 47 bc the law did not forbid kings from taking a place as leader of the Sanhedrin.[112]

The Direct Examination of Abinadi

When Noah's court convened and brought Abinadi before them, he was examined by the priests who sought to "cross him, that thereby they might have wherewith to accuse him" (Mosiah 12:19). As mentioned above, it was normal in biblical and rabbinic courts for some of the witnesses or members of the small sanhedrin to act as prosecutors. Thus it is not surprising to see some of the priests of Noah diligently and aggressively inquiring in order to root out any evidence of wrongdoing. It seems excessively harsh, however, for them to have started with arguments on the side of the prosecution. The rabbinic courts, for example, began with arguments for acquittal.[113] The priests of Noah may have been ignorant or malicious in proceeding as they did. On the other hand, speaking last, as Abinadi did, is usually a forensic advantage. In any event, the priests may have begun the proceeding by interrogating Abinadi because the people had already in effect declared him guilty, thereby removing any potential presumption of his innocence.

---

108.   See also Bovati, *Re-Establishing Justice*, 231–33.

109.   Welch, "The Trial of Jeremiah," 348–49.

110.   Later, in Jerusalem, members of the Great Sanhedrin had particular seats (which is, again, similar to the use of the ornate seats by Noah's priests). Members of the Jewish court sat in three semicircles in descending order of age, with the leader at the center and the members alternating closest to him on both sides from the oldest down to the youngest. Hoenig, *Great Sanhedrin*, 56; TB *Sanhedrin* 4:2, 36b; and Goldin, *Hebrew Criminal Law*, 112n16, citing Rashi, *ad Gemara*, 36b.

111.   Hoenig, *Great Sanhedrin*, 54; and TB *Sanhedrin* 2:1, 18a.

112.   See Hoenig, *Great Sanhedrin*, 186; and de Vaux, *Ancient Israel*, 1:378, stating that after the exile, the high priest took the place of the king.

113.   Goldin, *Hebrew Criminal Law*, 107; and Cohn, "Practice and Procedure," 582.

It appears that the priests intended, by their direct examination, to catch Abinadi in conflict with scripture.[114] In essence, they quoted to him from Isaiah 52 and selectively asked him why he bore tidings of doom and destruction when Isaiah had declared that the beautiful and true prophet brings good tidings and publishes peace: "How beautiful upon the mountains are the feet of him that bringeth *good* tidings" (Mosiah 12:20–22; emphasis added). The priests' further quoting of Isaiah affirmed that redeeming Jerusalem was a cause for great joy: "They shall see eye to eye when the Lord shall bring again Zion; break forth into joy" (vv. 22–24). Moreover, whereas Isaiah had invited Zion to "put on thy beautiful garments" (Isaiah 52:1), Abinadi had valued Noah's life as a garment in a furnace (Mosiah 12:3, 10). Whereas Isaiah had spoken in glowing terms of the people, that no more would "come into thee the uncircumcised and the unclean" (Isaiah 52:1), Abinadi had condemned the people as wicked and worthy of destruction (Mosiah 12:8–9). And while Isaiah had assured Jerusalem of loosing herself "from the bands of thy neck" (Isaiah 52:2), Abinadi prophesied that the people "shall be brought into bondage" (Mosiah 12:2). This passage of scripture quoted to Abinadi by the priests could very well have been one of the theme texts that had been used often by Zeniff's colony as they rejoiced over their redemption of the land of their inheritance and temple like Solomon's (the temple in the city of Nephi was patterned after the temple of Solomon, which stood adjacent to Mount Zion). In the face of Isaiah's prophecy and its apparent glorious fulfillment by Zeniff's people, how did Abinadi dare to accuse both the king and his people of falling under God's worst judgments?[115]

The priests of Noah may have tried to prove that Abinadi's prophecies contradicted the word of God as spoken by Isaiah for two related reasons: they wanted to prove him wrong or show that he did not understand Isaiah correctly, and they probably wanted to prove that he was not speaking the word of the Lord and was therefore a false prophet. The definition of false prophecy in Deuteronomy 18 made it a capital offense to prophesy things in the name of the Lord "which I have not commanded him to speak" (Deuteronomy 18:20). Abinadi had clearly invoked the name of Jehovah as the source of his prophecy: "Thus has the Lord commanded me,"

114. Dana M. Pike takes this argument and places the logic and strategy of the priests of Noah in its larger context within Isaiah 52 in his essay "'How Beautiful upon the Mountains': The Imagery of Isaiah 52:7–10 and Its Occurrences in the Book of Mormon," in *Isaiah in the Book of Mormon*, ed. Donald W. Parry and John W. Welch (Provo, UT: FARMS, 1998), 249–91, esp. 261–65.

115. For an explanation of the connections between Isaiah 52 and Isaiah 53 manifested in Abinadi's extremely insightful response to his accusers, see John W. Welch, "Isaiah 53, Mosiah 14, and the Book of Mormon," in Parry and Welch, *Isaiah in the Book of Mormon*, 293–312, esp. 294–97.

and "the Lord said unto me" (Mosiah 12:1, 2). In order to know "the word which the Lord hath not spoken," the judges were to apply the following test: "If the thing follow not [literally 'is not'], nor come to pass, that is the thing which the Lord hath not spoken" (Deuteronomy 18:22). One option, of course, was to wait and see if the prophecy came to pass. Another approach apparently was to test the prophecy against other texts known to be valid to see if the new prophecies "follow not" or "are not" in the sense that they are inconsistent with the established word of the Lord.[116]

Abinadi's Defense and Counterclaims

Abinadi's rebuttal was an extensive and brilliant explanation of the true essence of redemption and how it brings good tidings to those who accept Christ (Mosiah 12:29–37; 13–16). His words comprise an intricate and elaborate commentary, or midrash, on the text from Isaiah 52 that the priests quoted. His position was based on solid ground, for Isaiah had also clearly stated that "they that rule over them make them to howl" (Isaiah 52:5); and, accordingly, Abinadi predicted that the people of Noah "shall howl all the day long" due to the influence of their wicked priests and leaders on them (Mosiah 12:4).

Casual readers might wonder if Abinadi's speech was responsive to the specific question posed to him by the priests, but on close examination it is clear that his answer is constructed around specific words and phrases in Isaiah 52. For example, Isaiah 52:3 reads, "Ye shall be *redeemed* without money" (emphasis added), and Abinadi spoke frequently of God's redeeming power (Mosiah 13:32; 15:9, 12, 23; 16:3–6, 15). After asking, "Who shall declare his [Christ's] generation?" (from Isaiah 53:8), Abinadi explained that "when his [Christ's] soul has been made an offering for sin he [Christ] shall see his seed" (Mosiah 15:10), for his seed are all the prophets and the righteous, and they shall be seen by Christ as "heirs of the kingdom of God" (vv. 11–13). Further, the prophets are they who have published peace, good tidings, and salvation, mentioned in Isaiah 52:7 (Mosiah 15:13–14). Thus Abinadi took Isaiah's declaration "Thy God reigneth!" (Isaiah 52:7) and shifted it to read "*the Son* reigneth" (Mosiah 15:20; emphasis added), meaning that the Son had power over death. This brought Abinadi to testify not only that the righteous will be resurrected to

---

116. See Moses Buttenwieser, *The Prophets of Israel from the Eighth to the Fifth Century: Their Faith and Their Message* (New York: Macmillan, 1914), 31–32. This line of reasoning was first applied to Abinadi by David Warby; see David Warby and Lisa B. Hawkins, "The Crime of False Prophecy under Ancient Israelite Law," FARMS Preliminary Report (Provo, UT: FARMS, 1983), recently revised and published as David W. Warby, "The Book of Mormon Sheds Valuable Light on the Ancient Israelite Law of False Prophecy," *Studia Antiqua* (Summer 2003): 107–16.

stand before God (15:20–25) but also that *all* people will come forth to be judged (15:26–16:2), for the Lord's salvation will be declared to all (15:28). Hence, the Lord's "watchmen shall lift up their voice" (15:29), heralding the time when, as Isaiah said, "the Lord hath made bare his holy arm in the eyes of *all* the nations; and *all the ends of the earth* shall see the salvation of our God" (Isaiah 52:10; emphasis added), and so "every nation, kindred, tongue, people . . . shall confess before God that his judgments are just" (Mosiah 16:1). Indeed, Abinadi's speech responded precisely and thoroughly to the priests' interrogatory. His remarks were completely relevant to the strategy employed against him at this stage in his trial.

Abinadi also raised affirmative counterclaims, accusing the priests themselves of pretending to teach the people, of misunderstanding the spirit of prophecy, and of perverting the ways of the Lord (Mosiah 12:25–26). In effect, Abinadi accused the priests of lying about their own behavior, of denying true prophecy, and of leading people into apostasy, countering their claims but at the same time adding to the very charges brought against himself.

Interestingly, Abinadi never specifically charged Noah and the priests of the egregious offense of idolatry, even though this was clearly one of their sins (Mosiah 11:6). To make this point, Abinadi did not need to do any more than quote Exodus 20:3–4 (or Deuteronomy 5:7–8) to them: "Thou shalt have no other God before me. Thou shalt not make unto thee any graven image" (Mosiah 12:35–36). After Noah interrupted him on this very point, Abinadi withstood his accusers with the power of God. Abinadi then began again by repeating the prohibition against idolatry (13:12) and then completing his recitation of the Ten Commandments by way of further indictment.[117]

Abinadi also elaborately critiqued the narrow, strictly literal understanding of the law of Moses that apparently thrived in the colony of Zeniff. Noah's priests appear to have observed the law of Moses, at most, only so far as the letter of the law was concerned. They unqualifiedly purported to "teach the law of Moses" (Mosiah 12:28), which would mean that they must have spent a fair amount of time constructing rationalizations to show that their extravagances and excesses were not literally against that law. But Abinadi showed that more was required in order to teach and live the law of God than merely meeting the letter of the law. From the teachings of Nephi and Jacob (2 Nephi 25:12–19; Jacob 4), the priests of

---

117. For a close examination of the Decalogue and its use by Abinadi, see David Rolph Seely, "The Ten Commandments in the Book of Mormon," in *Doctrines of the Book of Mormon*, ed. Bruce A. Van Orden and Brent L. Top (Salt Lake City: Deseret Book, 1992), 166–81.

Noah should have understood the same point already. Abinadi's direct question and assertion was a stinging condemnation: "Have ye done all this? I say unto you, Nay, ye have not. And have ye taught this people that they should do all these things? I say unto you, Nay, ye have not" (Mosiah 12:37). These words provoked a swift retort.

Noah Calls Abinadi "Mad"

Noah interrupted Abinadi's testimony at this point and ordered that Abinadi be removed and killed, "for he is mad" (Mosiah 13:1). Abinadi withstood the people who attempted to carry out this order by speaking "with power and authority from God" as his face shone like Moses's "while in the mount of Sinai" (vv. 2–6).

No insanity defense existed under biblical law. Even a "mad" person could be punished if he had broken the law.[118] By calling Abinadi mad, Noah was clearly not conceding that Abinadi was insane and therefore unfit to stand trial. More specifically, being "mad" (*shāgᶜ*) was a derogatory label often used to describe the ravings of false prophets in the Old Testament; for example, Hosea 9:7 reads, "The prophet is a fool, the spiritual man is mad."[119] In the ancient world, madness in the sense of mental illness was usually explained as the result of evil spirits (e.g., Mark 3:22); if a man were to speak by the power of some spirit other than the spirit of God, then it stood to reason that he was speaking through the power of the evil one and thus would necessarily be a false prophet (see Jeremiah 29:26). Assuming that Noah knew something of this language or logic and that he had such ideas in mind as he spoke, he was using the word *mad* to strengthen the false-prophecy charge and was urging the court to move quickly to convict and execute Abinadi for being dangerous and bewitched: "Slay him; for what have we to do with him, for he is mad" (Mosiah 13:1).

Noah's reaction was predictable, for he had made up his mind in this regard two years earlier. The fact that Abinadi's legal chances were poor no matter what he said in his defense contributed to a lack of decorum on both sides at trial. Besides Noah's outburst, Abinadi's conduct cannot be considered very orderly either. He launched immediately, after only one question, into a lengthy statement, never giving the judges a chance to develop the issues or ask another question. To have held the floor, Abinadi must have

---

118. Falk, *Hebrew Law in Biblical Times*, 69.

119. Victor P. Hamilton, "*shāgᶜ*, be mad," in *Theological Wordbook of the Old Testament*, ed. R. Laird Harris, Gleason L. Archer Jr., and Bruce K. Waltke (Chicago: Moody, 1980), 2:2328. See also 2 Kings 9:11.

been extremely animated as he, filled with the Spirit of God, recited the law and heaped contemptuous accusations upon the priests and Noah.

Abinadi's Appeal to God as His Witness

It was typical for defendants in antiquity to appeal to God to verify their innocence.[120] This appeal often took the form of an oath: "The oath existed in Hebrew law only on the part of the accused. . . . An accused person could exculpate himself with an oath. . . . The oath brought the divinity into the process of legal investigation."[121] Similarly, in Noah's proceeding Abinadi appealed to God to verify his innocence and truthfulness in several ways. Abinadi vowed that God would smite his accusers if they dared to lay their hands on him (Mosiah 13:3). He further testified that the Lord had sent him to prophesy against the people (v. 26), and he appealed to the priests themselves to acknowledge that he had spoken the truth: "Yea, ye know that I speak the truth" (12:30).

Noah and his priests, however, were intransigently committed to their royal prerogatives and rationalizations. Their political views may have drawn support from the administrations of the kings of Israel, especially that of Solomon, with his powers, priests, wives, temple, and grand public works. Abinadi countered that incorrect model of kingship by arguing that the true type of all things mentioned in the law was the eternal king (Mosiah 13:31, 33). He also testified "concerning the coming of the Messiah, . . . that God himself should come down among the children of men" (vv. 33–34).

Next, as I have discussed in greater detail elsewhere,[122] Abinadi quoted Isaiah 53, which immediately follows the passage that the priests had challenged Abinadi to explain. After explaining how that text speaks of the ultimate redemption (Mosiah 15:8–9), he explained the phrases of Isaiah 52:7–10 in that light. "[H]is generation," or God's seed, are "whosoever has heard the words of the prophets" and "all those who have hearkened unto their words, and believed that the Lord will redeem his people" (Mosiah 15:10–11); the prophets are they "who have published peace, who

---

120. After an accused had been convicted and even sentenced to death, he could procure a rehearing of sorts merely by proclaiming, "I have somewhat to argue in favor of my acquittal." TB *Sanhedrin* 6:1, 42b. If he swore by God of his innocence, so much greater his claim of innocence.

121. Boecker, *Law and the Administration of Justice*, 35. For more information on vows, see George W. Buchanan, "Some Vow and Oath Formulas in the New Testament," *Harvard Theological Review* 58, no. 3 (1965): 319–26; Ze'ev W. Falk, "Notes and Observations on Talmudic Vows," *Harvard Theological Review* 59, no. 3 (1966): 309–12; Samuel Rosenblatt, "The Relations between Jewish and Muslim Laws concerning Oaths and Vows," *American Academy for Jewish Research* (1936): 229–44; and Lawrence H. Schiffman, "The Law of Vows and Oaths (Num. 30, 3–16) in the *Zadokite Fragments* and the *Temple Scroll*," *Revue de Qumran* 15, nos. 1–2 (1991): 199–214.

122. Welch, "Isaiah 53, Mosiah 14, and the Book of Mormon," 294–301.

have brought good tidings" (v. 14); "how beautiful are the feet of those that are still publishing peace" and of "the founder of peace, yea, even the Lord" (vv. 16, 18). The watchmen on the towers are those who will lift up their voices at the time when the salvation of the Lord "shall be declared to every nation" (vv. 28–29). Finally, Abinadi asserted that "all shall see the salvation of the Lord," that all "shall confess before God that his judgments are just," and that God's judgments shall stand against all those—such as the wicked priests—who remain in carnal and sensual sin and in rebellion against God (16:1–5), having been "warned of their iniquities" and yet refusing to repent (v. 12). It is hard to imagine a more sophisticated and insightful analysis of the complexities of Isaiah 52 and 53.

Strong statements such as these would have made the typical Israelite judge extremely wary of passing judgment incorrectly or unrighteously for fear of offending God. As discussed in chapter 3 above, the duty to "judge righteously" was incumbent upon all who served as judges in Israel.[123] Jehoshaphat admonished his judges: "Deal courageously, and the Lord shall be with the good" (2 Chronicles 19:11). Strong provisions in the code of judicial responsibility required judges under the law of Moses to "keep . . . far from a false matter; and the innocent and righteous slay thou not: for I will not justify the wicked" (Exodus 23:7). The Psalms are full of strong pronouncements praising those who judge righteously and condemning those who do not (e.g., Psalm 33:5; 67:4; 71:4; 99:4). Thus it is understandable that Abinadi's words had a sobering effect at least on some of the people. Abinadi's quotation of the Ten Commandments, his power through God to resist the priests when they tried to restrain him, and his explication of Isaiah 53 constituted a brilliant forensic performance, a *tour de force*, a remarkable discourse under any circumstance. But it was all the more astounding and meaningful coming from a man who was on trial for his life and who needed to respond articulately and persuasively, on the spot, to the specific question put to him by his adversaries, the priests. They became hesitant to interfere (Mosiah 13:5), and they remained silent until Abinadi concluded his message.

Noah's Command

When Abinadi completed his lengthy testimony, Noah again commanded the priests to take Abinadi and kill him: "The king commanded

---

123. For more information on judgment, see Ze'ev W. Falk, "'Words of God' and 'Judgments,'" *Estratto da Studi in onore di E. Volterra* 6 (1969): 155–59; Eberhard Klingenberg, "Judgment and Settlement in Court in Jewish and Comparative Legal History," *Jewish Law Annual* 8 (1989): 135–45; and Leon Morris, "Judgement and Custom," *Australian Biblical Review* 7 (1959): 72–74.

that the priests should take him and cause that he should be put to death"
(Mosiah 17:1). If Noah was expressing here a verdict regarding the false
prophecy charge, he was probably acting out of order in voicing his opinion
so quickly. Since King Noah was the senior authority in the court and was
bound to act under the rule of law (Deuteronomy 17:19), his vote should
probably have been heard last, especially if he was seriously interested in
taking counsel from his priests.[124] The explanation given for this conventional rule was that the younger judges should speak first because otherwise they might be unduly influenced to follow the opinions of their older
colleagues if the senior members of the court spoke preemptively.[125]

It seems more likely, however, that Noah's order shifted the focus of
the trial away from the false-prophecy charge and over to the second cause
of action against Abinadi: that he had lied about the king and his lifestyle
filled with debauchery. While Noah could see that the priests had made no
headway on the false-prophecy charge (which is never mentioned again
in the account after this point, apparently having been dropped from
the trial), Noah could still assert uncontested jurisdiction over the other
charge, namely, that Abinadi had lied about the king. Noah alone could
issue a verdict without further deliberation on that matter because it was
jurisdictionally one of "the king's matters" (2 Chronicles 19:11).

The idea that Noah shifted the focus of the trial in precisely this manner is supported by the thrust of Alma's defense, which was based on his
personal knowledge "concerning the iniquity which Abinadi had testified
against them" (Mosiah 17:2). In other words, Alma knew that Abinadi had
not lied about the iniquity of the king and his priests. Therefore, it is likely
that Noah's order calling for Abinadi's execution would have stood, except
for Alma's daring intervention.

As it happened, Noah's order was not carried out. But what kind of
verdict was this that could be rebutted and ignored by the court or the
priests? Perhaps it was not intended to be a final order. Indeed, the concept of a "final judgment" probably did not exist in the ancient world. If
a person was willing to go to a temple or to the gate and swear an oath
of innocence, for example, charges could be dropped,[126] and presumably

---

124. At least in rabbinic times the leader of the Sanhedrin and the eldest members voted last.
Cohn, "Practice and Procedure," 582.

125. Cohn, "Practice and Procedure," 582.

126. For example, Pir'i-ilishu, an Amorite soldier, was given the opportunity to go to a public place and take an oath in order to avoid a penalty. Henry Frederick Lutz, *The Verdict of a
Trial Judge in a Case of Assault and Battery* (Berkeley: University of California, 1930), plate 4,
pp. 379–81, cited in Martha T. Roth, "Mesopotamian Legal Traditions and the Laws of Hammurabi," *Chicago-Kent Law Review* 71, no. 1 (1995): 31.

other forms of reconciliation or settlement could intervene after the court had reached its decision and before a sentence had been carried out. Under later Jewish law, court verdicts did not become "final" until they were actually being carried out: "As long as the sentence has not been carried out, the judgment is subject to revision."[127] Thus it is not exceptional or irregular that the debate about Abinadi's fate continued even after Noah had said that he should be put to death.[128] The court continued by allowing Alma to speak, by expelling Alma and putting Abinadi in prison, and by declaring a three-day recess (Mosiah 17:2–8).

Alma's Defense of Abinadi

As mentioned above, it was usual in Jewish law for some members of the court to speak on behalf of the accused. "The deliberations [of the judges] must always start with a view propounded in favor of the accused,"[129] although this was interpreted in the Talmud to mean that the court only had to ask the accused "whether he could adduce any evidence in rebuttal, or [to] reassur[e] the accused that if he was innocent he had nothing to fear."[130] While it is unknown what procedures or protocols may have normally been used in this regard in Nephite or ancient Old World courts, a similar role of viewing the case favorably toward the accused may have been actually assigned by the court to Alma (although, given the prevailing attitude of these judges, perhaps this assignment was made with the expectation that Alma would not take his assignment quite so seriously). Or perhaps, as would seem more likely, Alma took this role upon himself, sensing that justice demanded that someone should speak in defense of Abinadi. In either event, Alma was obligated as a judge under the law of Moses to view the charges honestly and thus in a light favorable to the accused. As noted above, the instructions given by King Jehoshaphat set the general standard for judicial responsibility in ancient Israel: "Thus shall ye do in the fear of the Lord, faithfully, and with a perfect heart. . . . Deal courageously, and the Lord shall be with the good" (2 Chronicles 19:9, 11). Jehovah's code of judicial conduct found in Exodus 23:1–3 and 6–8 similarly prohibited judges from perverting justice: "Thou shalt not follow a multitude to do evil; . . . the innocent and righteous slay thou

---

127. Cohn, "Practice and Procedure," 583.

128. See Wilson, "Israel's Judicial System," 242, to compare King Noah's influence with that of Saul in 1 Samuel 22.

129. Cohn, "Practice and Procedure," 582; and TB *Sanhedrin* 4:1, 32a.

130. Cohn, "Practice and Procedure," 582; TB *Sanhedrin* 4:1, 32b; TJ *Sanhedrin* 4:1, 22a; and Yad, *Sanhedrin* 10:7.

not" (vv. 2, 7).[131] Alma acted in accordance with these venerable codes of judicial conduct as he rose courageously to speak, acting faithfully out of personal conviction of the truthfulness of Abinadi's case. He "believed the words which Abinadi had spoken . . . ; therefore he began to plead with the king" (Mosiah 17:2).

The need for the presentation of arguments in favor of the defense was strongly felt under Jewish law. During the rabbinic period, if a guilty verdict in a capital case before the Great Sanhedrin was unanimous, that was ground for a mistrial since talmudic law required the judges to reach a "clear majority," which implied that there must be a minority: "If no such majority has emerged, the case is adjourned to the next day. . . . Where the whole court is unanimous that the accused be convicted, proceedings are adjourned and deliberations continued until at least one judge changes his view and votes for an acquittal."[132] This rule, however, probably would not have applied in the smaller Jewish courts, where eventually it was held that achieving "unanimity was as good as, or even better than, a majority."[133] Alma's unwillingness to concur in the conviction of Abinadi destroyed the possibility of the court achieving a unanimous consensus, and his fervor would have been very unsettling to Noah and the other priests. They may have remembered the gruesome divine punishment of King Ahab under similar circumstances for his miscarriage of justice against the innocent Naboth (1 Kings 21–22).

The most potent legal aspect of Alma's defense of Abinadi was that it forced King Noah to drop the charge that Abinadi had lied about the king. Although the text is silent on this point, it appears that Alma spoke out boldly and irrefutably concerning the iniquities of Noah and his priests (who otherwise would not have sought to kill Alma). If so, Alma's argument probably stressed the truthfulness of what Abinadi had said about the king and his government, for Alma "knew concerning the iniquity which Abinadi had testified against them" (Mosiah 17:2). By emphatically corroborating the truth of Abinadi's words, Alma effectively negated and refuted the charge that Abinadi had lied.

As a further consequence of his bold statement, Alma's defense of Abinadi effectively took the matter out of the king's jurisdiction and left standing only the false-prophecy charge, over which the priests had primary responsibility. But on that claim, the priests had made no headway

---

131. See further J. W. McKay, "Exodus XXIII 1–3, 6–8: A Decalogue for the Administration of Justice in the City Gate," *Vetus Testamentum* 21, no. 3 (1971): 311–25.

132. Cohn, "Practice and Procedure," 583.

133. Cohn, "Practice and Procedure," 583.

in their feeble attempt to cross Abinadi in his words. On this charge, it would seem that they lacked sufficient votes to convict, and so they abandoned the charge of false prophecy completely.

A Young Man

Moreover, Alma was the first of the priests to indicate his opinion in the case. He voted "not guilty" and urged that Abinadi be acquitted and released absolutely without any punishment whatsoever: Let him "depart in peace" (Mosiah 17:2). The text mentions at this point that Alma was "a young man." This appears to be significant, for the youngest members of the Sanhedrin were required to vote first in capital cases decided by that body.[134] As mentioned above, this was to protect the younger members from being unduly influenced by the senior members of the court.[135] Perhaps a similar practice was followed in Noah's court, which would help explain why Alma was able to get the floor and keep it long enough to make clear his open opposition to the obvious preferences of the king.

Alma's Expulsion from the Court

Alma's impassioned plea enraged Noah. Perhaps this was especially because two witnesses (Abinadi and Alma) now adamantly testified against Noah and his practices, sufficient to raise a serious indictment against the king himself: "At the mouth of two witnesses . . . shall the matter be established" (Deuteronomy 19:15). Moreover, there was little hope of having Alma change his opinion, for Exodus 23:2, consistent with ancient Near Eastern practice (Code of Hammurabi, section 5), sternly warns judges against changing their opinions: "Neither shalt thou speak in a cause to decline after many to wrest judgment"; that is, a judge should not be swayed or coerced by the majority.[136] Either Abinadi was wrong and therefore culpable, or else he and Alma were right and Noah was guilty. Assuming that the body of the priests was, to some extent, independent from the king (kings were not immune from judicial process under ancient Israelite law, Deuteronomy 17:19),[137] concerns for his

---

134. TB *Sanhedrin* 4:1, 36a. Incidentally, the name *Alma* may mean "young man" in Hebrew, so there may be a play on words in Mosiah 17:2.

135. Cohn, "Practice and Procedure," 582.

136. See Falk, *Hebrew Law in Biblical Times*, 60; compare Code of Hammurabi, section 5, which imposes a twelvefold penalty and disqualification as a judge in future cases in the event that a judge alters his decision in a case after it has been rendered and deposited in a sealed document.

137. The Mishnah states unequivocally, "The King can neither judge nor be judged, he may not bear witness nor be witnessed against." TB *Sanhedrin* 2:1, 18a. However, the Tosefta *Sanhedrin* 4:2 claims: "If he have transgressed a positive or negative command he is treated as an

own political well-being could well have triggered Noah's violent response against Alma's apparent insubordination. Also, Alma may have had a prior reputation for sympathizing with Abinadi and his previous prophecies (it seems unlikely that Alma would have been unaware of Abinadi's prophecies delivered two years earlier); the fact that Alma was able to attract a following so quickly after Abinadi's death would strongly indicate that a segment of the population in the city of Nephi, perhaps led informally by Alma, was already inclined to agree with Abinadi. Based on such concerns and likely circumstances, Noah caused Alma to be expelled from the court and sent his personal servants (apparently not officers of the court) with instructions to kill Alma.[138] Alma managed, however, to escape.

Members of the Sanhedrin and presumably judges in other ancient courts could be removed in certain cases, but nothing in Alma's account would give Noah grounds for Alma's removal in this case, let alone for attempting to execute him. Much as we today impanel alternate jurors who can replace jurors unable to continue serving on the panel, sanhedrins regularly had additional elders who could step in and sit on the court should the need arise.[139] Therefore, expelling Alma from the court would not necessarily have reduced the number of judges who passed judgment on Abinadi, nor would it have been grounds for a mistrial or a delay. But Noah's seeking to slay Alma—if this order was based only on Alma's expression of a dissenting judicial opinion—was certainly extralegal and extraordinary.

Three Days in Prison

Abinadi was next bound and cast into prison for three days while the priests and Noah deliberated further over the case (Mosiah 17:5–6). It was typical "according to ancient Jerusalem custom" for the conference of the judges to be conducted in private.[140] But why was the trial of Abinadi interrupted for so long and precisely for this length of time?

---

ordinary commoner in every respect." Goldin takes a middle ground, explaining that only a king belonging to the house of David may act in a judicial capacity or be put on trial. The rationale is that the king "would not submit to the decision of the court." Goldin, *Hebrew Criminal Law*, 83–84n11, citing Maimonides, *Hilkot Sanhedrin* 2:5, for support that this was the prevailing law.

138. The text refers to Noah's servants. Either Noah had completely corrupted the judicial system, or the "servants" sent to slay Alma were personal servants sent to seek personal, and not official, vengeance.

139. Hoenig explains that a judge who wished to leave the court first had to ascertain whether a quorum of twenty-three would remain in his absence. Hoenig, *Great Sanhedrin*, 105.

140. Cohn, "Practice and Procedure," 578.

Three legal reasons might explain this delay in Abinadi's trial. First, Abinadi may well have entered the city of Nephi on or around Pentecost.[141] First, if the three days after Abinadi's speech were holy festival (and therefore Sabbath) days, the court would have been precluded from reconvening sooner.[142] Indeed, Pentecost appears to have been a three-day event in the late spring or early summer each year on the ancient Israelite calendar, for that festival commemorated the three days when the people of Israel sanctified themselves for the appearance of the Lord to Moses on Mount Sinai when the Ten Commandments were issued. The Lord summoned the people with the promise that on "the third day the Lord will come down in the sight of all the people upon mount Sinai" (Exodus 19:11); "and it came to pass on the third day" that God answered Moses (vv. 16–19).

Second, it was considered improper, at least under rabbinic jurisprudence, for courts to try a person on any given day for more than one capital offense.[143] It is possible that a similar tradition had developed and was observed in Nephite law, although there is no direct evidence of any such legal requirement in early biblical times. Having failed to catch Abinadi in any conflict with the scriptures, and having been thwarted by Alma's unexpected defense from pressing further their accusation of prevarication, Abinadi's accusers would have been compelled to abandon both charges. They may have felt bound by some procedural sense of justice to delay the trial, or they may have simply sensed the pragmatic need to regroup and to wait for another day to try again on another claim.

Third, Jewish law also prohibited a court from entering a guilty verdict on the same day on which the testimony was heard.[144] It is possible that the Nephites observed a similar practice, but the evidence is not decisive. Nehor's execution may have occurred a day or two after his trial, for his death is reported in a verse that begins "and it came to pass" (Alma 1:15), possibly indicating a passage of time. Similarly, enough time elapsed between Paanchi's conviction and his execution that his followers could meet during the interval and send a delegate to assassinate Pahoran

---

141. See my discussion of Abinadi and Pentecost in Welch, *Reexploring the Book of Mormon*, 135–38, and in the excursus that follows this subsection.

142. Because it would be improper to reconvene on the Sabbath or a festival day—even to announce the verdict—the Sanhedrin never met on the eve of such days. TB *Sanhedrin* 4:1, 32a; Hoenig, *Great Sanhedrin*, 106n7; and Cohn, "Practice and Procedure," 580. This rule has a basis in the most ancient laws of the Sabbath. See generally Gerhard F. Hasel, "Sabbath," in *Anchor Bible Dictionary*, 5:849–56.

143. Cohn, "Practice and Procedure," 581.

144. Hoenig, *Great Sanhedrin*, 106; and Cohn, "Practice and Procedure," 580.

(Helaman 1:9). Interestingly, under Islamic law, the punishment for apostasy is death, but some Muslim jurists argue that "the apostate must be given a period of time in which to recant and return. . . . The Hedaya recommends three days of imprisonment before execution."[145]

Possibilities such as these suggest that the three-day hiatus in the trial of Abinadi may not have been merely strategic or malicious on the part of Noah and his priests, but may reflect an observance by the court of procedural formalities or religious requirements.

Did Abinadi Appear in the City of Nephi on Pentecost?

An important part of the law of Moses, and one that ties in closely with Abinadi's quotation of the Ten Commandments, required the observance of certain holy days each year (e.g., Exodus 23:14–19).[146] Fifty days after Passover on the ancient Israelite calendar was the festival of Pentecost, or Shavuot (Weeks), which commemorated Moses's receiving the Ten Commandments at Sinai. For several reasons, it appears that Abinadi entered the city of Nephi around the time of Pentecost. Not only does he quote the Ten Commandments to Noah and his priests, but he also draws on many religious themes that were distinctively associated with the Pentecost season in ancient Israel. Understanding this likely festival background to Abinadi's words adds yet another dimension to the legal backgrounds of the trial of Abinadi, as the following excursus briefly explains.

Shavuot marked the concluding phase of Passover.[147] It was also an agricultural holiday sometimes called the Day of the Firstfruits (Numbers 28:26). It was a pilgrimage festival, with a "holy convocation" (Leviticus 23:21) rejoicing in the bounty of the spring, especially the new wheat (Deuteronomy 16:9–12; 26:5–11). Just as Passover marked a time of poverty and bondage for Israel, Pentecost exulted in a time of bounty, with offerings of leavened bread baked from the new crop of wheat (Leviticus 23:17) and of the choicest firstfruits. At this same time of the year, Moses received the Ten Commandments on Mount Sinai (Exodus 19:1). Thus,

145. I am grateful to David F. Forte for drawing this point to my attention. See his "Apostasy and Blasphemy in Pakistan," *Connecticut Journal of International Law* 10 (1994): 47, pointing out also that the Maliki school allows up to ten days for recantation.

146. For further discussion about the role of ancient Israelite festivals under the law of Moses and in the Book of Mormon, along with caveats and methodological comments applicable not only to King Benjamin's speech but also to the narrative setting of the trial of Abinadi, see Terrence L. Szink and John W. Welch, "King Benjamin's Speech in the Context of Ancient Israelite Festivals," in Welch and Ricks, *King Benjamin's Speech*, 149–58.

147. Abraham P. Bloch, *The Biblical and Historical Background of the Jewish Holy Days* (New York: KTAV, 1978), 179.

in antiquity, Pentecost probably also celebrated God's giving of the law to Moses. The connection between Pentecost and the giving of the law is well documented from the time of the Talmud,[148] but exactly when this connection was first established in ancient Israelite practice is a matter of historical debate. Moshe Weinfeld, however, argues convincingly that this connection was made very early in Israelite history, as evidenced by Psalms 50 and 81, which he concludes were the words of hymns sung at Pentecost.[149]

In this setting, several arguments can be marshaled to support the idea that the trial of Abinadi took place on or around Pentecost. In general, timing would have been important to Abinadi. He had already been expelled once from the city (Mosiah 11:26–29). Reentry on or near a festival day would have given him a ready audience, as virtually all of Abinadi's words deal with themes that would have been especially pertinent at the time of Pentecost. The following points suggest possible thematic connections between the account of Abinadi and Pentecost:

- When a bounteous grain season was at hand, Abinadi cursed the crops: he prophesied that the Lord would send destructive hail and dry winds upon the people and that insects too would "pester their land . . . and devour their grain" (Mosiah 12:6).
- While Israel's deliverance from bondage was being celebrated, Abinadi called upon Exodus terminology to proclaim that bondage will return: "They shall be brought into bondage; and none shall deliver them" (Mosiah 11:23), "and I will cause that they shall have burdens lashed upon their backs" (12:2, 5; compare Exodus 1:11).
- At precisely the time when Noah's priests would have been hypocritically pledging allegiance to the Ten Commandments and celebrating the giving of the law, Abinadi rehearsed to them those very commandments (Mosiah 12:33–36; 13:12–24). On any other day, this might have seemed a strange defense for a man on trial for his life, but not on Pentecost.
- Indeed, the connection with Pentecost could hardly have been made more graphically than when Abinadi's "face shone with exceeding luster, even as Moses' did while in the mount of Sinai, while speaking with the Lord" (Mosiah 13:5; Exodus 34:29–30).

---

148. Bloch, *Biblical and Historical Background of the Jewish Holy Days*, 186–88; and TB *Shabbat* 86b. See also Raymond F. Collins, "Ten Commandments," in *Anchor Bible Dictionary*, 6:383–87.

149. Moshe Weinfeld, "The Decalogue: Its Significance, Uniqueness, and Place in Israel's Tradition," in *Religion and Law: Biblical-Judaic and Islamic Perspectives*, 26–32.

This is an obvious reference to the time when Moses received the law, probably the main event celebrated on Shavuot.

- A number of connections between Abinadi and Exodus 19 further involve him with Pentecost. For example, cursing Noah to be like a "garment in a hot furnace" recalls the fact that Mount Sinai became a furnace (Exodus 19:18) and that people whose garments were unclean were not "ready" for the coming of the Lord (vv. 10–15).

- The ancient festival appears to have been a three-day event (Exodus 19:11), which could explain why Abinadi's trial was postponed for "three days" (Mosiah 17:6), as discussed above.

- At Sinai, the people had looked forward to an appearance of the Lord: on "the third day the Lord will come down in the sight of all the people" (Exodus 19:11). Abinadi's testimony was that the Lord would come down again (Mosiah 15:1), an idea that King Noah and his priests found to be blasphemous (perhaps because they thought Abinadi was implying that this earlier time when the Lord came down was not enough).

- In addition, intriguing parallels exist between Psalm 50 and Abinadi's piercing rebukes of the priests. If this psalm was known and used as a Pentecost hymn in Abinadi's world as Weinfeld avers it was in ancient Israel, several of its lines would have found a haunting echo in Abinadi's stinging prophetic words.

  » For example, Psalm 50:2 begins, "Out of Zion, the perfection of beauty, God hath shined." The irony would have been insufferable when "the Spirit of the Lord was upon [not Noah's colony but upon Abinadi], and his face shone with exceeding luster" (Mosiah 13:5).

  » Psalm 50:3 reads: "Our God shall come, and shall not keep silence." Abinadi boldly affirmed the same, "that God himself shall come down" (Mosiah 15:1; see 17:8).

  » In Psalm 50:4–7, God brings a metaphorical lawsuit to "judge his people" (v. 4; compare 82:1). Likewise, Abinadi's words take this very form, that of a prophetic lawsuit.[150] The psalmist intones, "I will testify against thee" (50:7). Abinadi does precisely that.

  » Psalm 50:8–14 makes it clear that the Lord prefers thanksgiving and devotion rather than sacrifices. To the same effect, Abinadi requires the commandments of God to be "written in your

---

150. See notes 18 and 22 above.

Did Abinadi Prophesy against King Noah on Pentecost?

Israelite Pentecost	Abinadi
Celebrating the first grain harvest	Cursed their grain (Mosiah 12:6)
Rejoicing in bounty	Sent hail, winds, insects (12:6)
Remembering deliverance from bondage in Egypt	Prophesied that the people would be brought back into bondage (11:21)
"Taskmasters to afflict them with their burdens" (Exodus 1:11)	"I will cause that they shall have burdens lashed upon their backs" (12:5)
Celebrating the giving of the Ten Commandments to Moses (Exodus 20)	Sternly recited the Ten Commandments given to Moses (12:34–36; 13:15–24)
Moses's face shone (Exodus 34:29)	Abinadi's face shone (13:5)
Mount Sinai became like a furnace (Exodus 19:18)	Prophesied that Noah's life would be like a garment in a furnace (12:3)
Stern condemnation of abominations	Stern condemnation of iniquity (12:2, 37)
A three-day festival (Exodus 19:11)	Cast into prison three days (17:6)
"The Lord will come down in the sight of all the people" (Exodus 19:11)	The Lord will come among the children of men (15:1)
Liturgical use of Psalms 50 and 82	Use of elements from Psalms 50 and 82
"Our God shall come" (Psalm 50:3)	"God . . . shall come down" (15:1)
"What hast thou to do to declare my statutes?" (Psalm 50:16)	"What teach ye this people?" (12:27)
"[Thou] hast been partaker with adulterers" (Psalm 50:18)	"Why do ye commit whoredoms?" (12:29)
"I will testify against thee" (Psalm 50:7)	Abinadi testified against them (17:10)
Thanksgiving and devotion are better than sacrifice (Psalm 50:8–14)	Having the commandments "written in your hearts" is better than sacrifices (13:11, 30)
Sacrifices are not for nourishment (Psalm 50:12)	Sacrifices are to signify "types of things to come" (13:31)
In day of trouble, if righteous call upon him, he will deliver them (Psalm 50:15)	God will not hear the prayers of the wicked (11:25)
Qualifications required to "declare my statutes" (Psalm 50:16)	"If ye teach the law of Moses why do ye not keep it?" (12:29)
Condemn those who wrongfully become rich and commit whoredoms (Psalm 50:18)	Condemn those who wrongfully become rich and commit whoredoms (12:29)

Israelite Pentecost	Abinadi
"Tear you in pieces, and there be none to deliver" (Psalm 50:22)	"Shall devour their flesh" and "none shall deliver them" (Mosiah 12:2; 11:23)
"Shew the salvation of God" (Psalm 50:23)	Showing "salvation" of God (12:21, 24, 31, 32; 13:27, 28; 15:14, 18, 24–31; 16:1)
"Children of the most High" (Psalm 82:6)	"His seed" (15:10)
Death (Psalm 82:7)	Death (15:19–20)
Judged by God (Psalm 82:8)	Judgment by God (15:21–16:12)

hearts" (Mosiah 13:11). If God "were hungry," he had no need for man to give him bullocks or goats, for all the world is already his (Psalm 50:12); therefore the purpose of sacrifice must be something else. As Abinadi explains, the laws of sacrifice were given as spiritual "types of things to come" (Mosiah 13:31).

» Psalm 50:15 promises that, "in the day of trouble" if the righteous will call upon him, he "will deliver" them. Abinadi makes it clear that if the wicked people of Noah call upon God, "[he] will not hear their prayers, neither will [he] deliver them" (Mosiah 11:25).

» Psalm 50:16–21 shows that Pentecost also became a day of stern admonition. People were chastised who rejected instruction and collaborated with lawbreakers: "What hast thou to do to declare my statutes, . . . seeing thou hatest instruction? . . . When thou sawest a thief, then thou consentedst with him, and hast been partaker with adulterers" (vv. 16–18). Transgressors were reprimanded publicly: "But I will reprove thee, and set them in order before thine eyes" (v. 21). Surely Abinadi reproved and then set the teachings of the Lord in perfect order openly, before the very eyes of Noah and his priests.

» A warning like Abinadi's must have been especially potent on a day when the people were venerating the law. Psalm 50:16 asks what a person must do in order to teach the law, "to declare my statutes." The implicit answer is that one must keep the law. This is exactly Abinadi's point: "And again he said unto them: If ye teach the law of Moses, why do ye not keep it?" (Mosiah 12:29). Both Psalm 50 and Abinadi particularly condemn those who wrongfully become rich and those who commit whoredoms (Psalm 50:18; Mosiah 12:29).

» Otherwise, God will "tear you in pieces, and there be none to deliver" (Psalm 50:22). This compares with Abinadi's words, "and the vultures of the air, and the dogs, yea, and the wild beasts, shall devour their flesh" (Mosiah 12:2), and "none shall deliver them" (11:23).

» Moreover, Psalm 50 ends with the assurance "to him that ordereth his conversation aright will I shew the salvation of God" (v. 23). Showing the "salvation" of God (Mosiah 12:21, 24, 31, 32; 13:27, 28; 15:14, 18, 24, 27, 28, 31) was exactly what Abinadi explicitly and comprehensively did. His closing statement even began with the headline "The time shall come when all shall see the salvation of the Lord" (16:1).

- Psalm 82, the other Pentecost psalm identified by Weinfeld, sings of the time when that salvation will be seen. Recognizing that "ye are gods, and all of you are children of the most High" (v. 6), the psalmist still reminds Israel that all people must "die like men" (v. 7). Nevertheless, all the earth will yet be judged (v. 8). Abinadi also expounds on the theme of "who shall be his seed?" (Mosiah 15:10)—namely, "all those who have hearkened unto [the prophets'] words, and believed that the Lord would redeem his people, and have looked forward to that day for a remission of their sins" (v. 11). He then speaks soberly about death and dying (vv. 19–20) and being raised to stand before God to be judged (15:21–16:12).

Taken together, these details all point to one conclusion: No other day on the ancient Israelite calendar fits the message, words, and experience of the prophet Abinadi more precisely or more appropriately than does the ancient Israelite festival of Pentecost. It is thus ironic that, at the very time when Noah and his people would have been celebrating the law, the most unfortunate judicial result in Nephite history should have taken place.

Noah Lodges the Further Accusation of Blasphemy

When Abinadi was finally brought again before the king and the priests after the three-day recess, a new charge was raised. Abinadi was charged with blasphemy on the grounds that he had testified (Mosiah 13:34) that God would himself come down among the children of men (17:8). Noah also stipulated the punishment to be inflicted:[151] "Thou hast

---

151. McKenzie, "Judicial Procedure at the Town Gate," 102, states that in lodging his formal complaint the accuser should state "perhaps also the punishment which [the accused] should suffer," citing Jeremiah 26:11.

said that God himself should come down among the children of men; and now, for this cause thou shalt be put to death unless thou wilt recall all the words which thou hast spoken evil concerning me and my people" (v. 8).

In ancient Israelite law, blasphemy was indeed a capital offense: "He that blasphemeth the name of the Lord, he shall surely be put to death" (Leviticus 24:16). In stating the charge of blasphemy against Abinadi, King Noah said, "We have found an accusation against thee, and thou art *worthy of death*" (Mosiah 17:7; emphasis added). Jeremiah was arraigned with the similar phrase "Thou shalt surely die" (Jeremiah 26:8), or "For this you must die." The Hebrew expression used in Jeremiah's case was *mot tamut*, literally "die a death," and is related to the legal formula *mot yumat*, which is often used in legal contexts (e.g., throughout the Code of the Covenant in Exodus 21–23) to describe offenses for which a person is subject to the death penalty or is "worthy of death."[152] Apparently this same formulation was used by King Noah as he stated this new charge against Abinadi.

Speaking disrespectfully or insolently about God (as the priests thought Abinadi had done) could easily have been taken as blasphemy under the law of Moses.[153] In the Old Testament, blasphemy is often associated with scornful, reproaching speech (Isaiah 37:6; Psalm 74:18) and improper, iniquitous forms of worship (Isaiah 65:7; Ezekiel 20:27). Thus the concept of blasphemy was broad enough to encompass any speech that was perceived as demeaning or defaming of God. To a priest who does not understand or accept the doctrine of the condescension of God (as taught in 1 Nephi 11:16–21), the idea of Deity coming down to earth and becoming mortal in order to suffer wounds, afflictions, chastisements, judgments, punishments, and death at the hands of insolent humans could easily appear to qualify as legally actionable blasphemous speech. The seriousness of the offense of blasphemy under Nephite law is seen on several occasions in the Book of Mormon, such as in the accusation raised by Sherem against Jacob (Jacob 7:7) and in the offense finally committed by Korihor (Alma 30:30).

---

152. See discussion and references in Welch, "Trial of Jeremiah," 344–45.

153. On the crime of blasphemy, see further Karin Finsterbusch, "Christologie als Blasphemie: Das Hauptthema der Stephanusperikope in lukanischer Perspektive," *Biblische Notizen* 92 (1998): 38–54; Rodney R. Hutton, "The Case of the Blasphemer Revisited, Lev. XXIV 10–23," *Vetus Testamentum* 49, no. 4 (1999): 532–41; Hutton, "Narrative in Leviticus: The Case of the Blaspheming Son, Leviticus 24:10–23," *Zeitschrift für Altorientalische und Biblische Rechtsgeschichte* 3 (1997): 145–63; Dennis H. Livingston, "The Crime of Leviticus XXIV 11," *Vetus Testamentum* 36, no. 3 (1986): 352–54; H. Mittwoch, "The Story of the Blasphemer Seen in a Wider Context," *Vetus Testamentum* 15, no. 3 (1965): 386–89; and Shalom M. Paul, "Daniel 3:29—A Case Study of 'Neglected' Blasphemy," *Journal of Near Eastern Studies* 42, no. 4 (1983): 291–94.

Noticeably, unlike Jacob, Abinadi was not accused of speaking blasphemously against the law, even though he had said that "the time shall come when it shall no more be expedient to keep the law of Moses" (Mosiah 13:27). Apparently, Abinadi was careful enough to reaffirm his commitment to observing the law, telling the priests that "it is expedient that ye should keep the law of Moses as yet" (v. 27), and thus he did not leave himself open to a charge that he had perverted or abrogated the law of Moses as Jacob found himself so accused. Abinadi was only accused of speaking improperly or in a demeaning manner about God by declaring that the Messiah would be God (v. 33; see 7:27) and that Christ the Lord was "the very Eternal Father" (16:15) and, most of all, by saying "that God himself should come down among the children of men and take upon him the form of man" (13:34). These kinds of statements could well raise the issue of blasphemy in ancient times.[154]

Abinadi's Final Opportunity to Recant

This time Noah's verdict and sentence were conditional. If Abinadi would recall all the evil he had spoken about Noah and the people, the charge of blasphemy would be dropped: "and now, for this cause thou shalt be put to death unless thou wilt recall all the words which thou hast spoken evil concerning me and my people" (Mosiah 17:8). This is a curious plea bargain for Noah to offer. Why should the crime of offending God be dropped if the offender withdraws his words not against God but against the king and his people? Noah's deal may have rested on the idea that "certain sins against God could be wiped out by making amends to the priests."[155] In any case, Noah and his priests had much to gain by getting Abinadi to recant. Since in antiquity maledictions like Abinadi's were thought to inflict great palpable harm, Noah and his priests were probably willing if not anxious to compromise on their claim that Abinadi had offended God if they could get Abinadi to retract the threatening and ominous woes he had pronounced upon them and the people. Indeed, the legitimate functions of ancient Israelite courts included protecting the holiness and well-being of the community and preserving the purity of the religion. Therefore, if Abinadi were willing to lift the ominous cloud that still hung over these people, one of the main functions of the court,

---

154. The issues and the literature concerning the crime of blasphemy are covered well in Darrell L. Bock, *Blasphemy and Exaltation in Judaism: The Charge against Jesus in Mark 14:53–65* (Grand Rapids, MI: Baker Books, 2000). For further information, see the discussion of blasphemy in the case of Sherem in chapter 6 of the present volume.

155. Falk, *Hebrew Law in Biblical Times*, 74.

from Noah's point of view, would be satisfied. Nevertheless, Noah's conduct here is despicable and wholly self-interested. His willingness to forget the charge that Abinadi had blasphemously offended God if Abinadi would simply withdraw his words is blatantly driven by selfish, unrepentant concerns.

It would seem that Noah's willingness to compromise himself put Abinadi in a strong bargaining position. Abinadi could have offered to recall all the evil he had spoken about Noah and his people, provided they would agree to change their ways. Perhaps Noah and his priests would have been sufficiently motivated to agree on some kind of settlement. It is doubtful, however, that the idea of negotiating such a compromise would have occurred to any of these parties at this moment. Abinadi felt that his message was set in stone by the will of the Lord, and he had no right as the Lord's messenger to change that message in the least respect,[156] especially for the selfish purpose of obtaining his own release. Noah, on the other hand, was equally unyielding and wanted unconditional vindication. He would not be inclined to modify his offer very much under any circumstance. The enforcement of justice in ancient Israel was usually severe (e.g., the trial of the blasphemer in Leviticus 24, the trial of the wood gatherer in Numbers 15, the execution of Achan in Joshua 7, and the trial of Naboth in 1 Kings 21 all ended in the death of the accused). There may have been some room for mercy and leniency, but typically not very much (2 Chronicles 19:6, 9), at least, it seems, until the rabbinic period.[157] To preserve the appearance of justice and mercy, Noah would need to give Abinadi a chance to recant and would want to

---

156. On the duty of ancient messengers to deliver their master's message word for word, see John W. Welch, "The Calling of Lehi as a Prophet in the World of Jerusalem," in Welch, Seely, and Seely, *Glimpses of Lehi's Jerusalem*, 428.

157. For example, Goldin, *Hebrew Criminal Law*, 120n7. Rabbinic courts frequently pleaded with the accused hoping that a change of heart would make it unnecessary for them to carry out the execution. The overriding desire for mercy and leniency is explained by Danby: "One of the rabbinic canons was that their code must show 'mercy in judgement' in the highest degree. Their judicial body was regarded as best fulfilling its functions when it sought to act as 'counsel for the defence'; if there seemed to be no extenuating circumstances in the prisoner's favour, the judges were to do their utmost to find some. . . . The prisoner must be robbed of no chance which might in any way tell in his favour. This particular standpoint receives its strongest expression in *Makkoth* I.10 [7a]: 'The Sanhedrin which condemns to death one man in seven years is accounted murderous. According to R. Eleazar Azaria, it would be a murderous court even if it condemned one man in seventy years. R. Tarphon and R. Akiba assert that if they had been in the Sanhedrin [i.e., when it possessed capital powers] no man would ever have been condemned to death by it.'" Herbert Danby, *Tractate Sanhedrin: Mishnah and Tosefta: The Judicial Procedure of the Jews as Codified towards the End of the Second Century A.D.* (New York: Macmillan, 1919), xiv–xv.

go far enough to appear that he had been merciful. He did not, however, go beyond the barest minimum in offering leniency to Abinadi.

Abinadi Offers to Undergo Trial by Ordeal

Abinadi firmly refused to recall any of his words, even on pain of death: "I will not recall the words which I have spoken . . . for they are true. . . . Yea, and I will suffer even until death, and I will not recall my words, and they shall stand as a testimony against you. And if ye slay me ye will shed innocent blood,[158] and this shall also stand as a testimony against you at the last day" (Mosiah 17:9–10). In the trial of Jeremiah, the prophet did not retract his warning but informed the people that the Lord would spare them if they would "amend [their] ways and [their] doings, and obey the voice of the Lord" (Jeremiah 26:13).[159] At an earlier point, Abinadi's curses could have been avoided through repentance (Mosiah 12:8), but at this point in his trial Abinadi seems to have offered Noah no such relief. The prophets Abinadi and Jeremiah both stood adamantly by their words, and Jeremiah likewise had exclaimed, "If ye put me to death, ye shall surely bring innocent blood upon yourselves and upon this city, and upon the inhabitants thereof" (Jeremiah 26:12–15).

Although ordeals are not mentioned as often in ancient Israelite law as they are in ancient Near Eastern law, they were normal parts of biblical jurisprudence, where they often served to validate the innocence of the accused.[160] Submitting to an ordeal was often an accused's last hope of establishing his innocence or vindicating his testimony. In Abinadi's

---

158. Blood unlawfully shed is "innocent blood" (Deuteronomy 19:10, 13; 27:25; 1 Samuel 19:5). The concept of innocent blood appears in the Book of Mormon in Alma 1:13; 14:11. Under the law of Moses, the ruling authorities had the duty "to prevent the shedding of innocent blood." Goldin, *Hebrew Criminal Law*, 22. For more information on trial by ordeal, see Godfrey R. Driver and John C. Miles, "Ordeal by Oath at Nuzi," *Iraq* 7 (1940): 132–38; F. Charles Fensham, "The Battle between the Men of Joab and Abner as a Possible Ordeal by Battle?" *Vetus Testamentum* 20, no. 3 (1970): 356–57; Meredith G. Kline, "Oath and Ordeal Signs," *Westminster Theological Journal* 27 (1964–65): 115–39; P. Kyle McCarter, "The River Ordeal in Israelite Literature," *Harvard Theological Review* 66, no. 4 (1973): 403–12; William McKane, "Poison, Trial by Ordeal and the Cup of Wrath," *Vetus Testamentum* 30, no. 4 (1980): 474–92; Julian Morgenstern, "Trial by Ordeal among the Semites and in Ancient Israel," in *Hebrew Union College Jubilee Volume (1875–1925)*, ed. David Philipson et al. (Cincinnati: n. p., 1925), 113–43; and Karel van der Toorn, "Ordeal Procedures in the Psalms and the Passover Meal," *Vetus Testamentum* 38, no. 4 (1988): 427–45.

159. The relevant part of the trial of Jeremiah is discussed in Welch, "The Trial of Jeremiah," 349–51.

160. Notably in the quasi-ordeal in Numbers 5 of the drinking of the bitter waters by the woman suspected of adultery. See the discussion above, in connection with Sherem. In the cases of Sherem and Korihor, the ordeal was used for a different purpose, namely, to substantiate witness testimony. See Bovati, *Re-Establishing Justice*, 335.

case, he offered to suffer whatever pain Noah desired to inflict upon him: "I will suffer even until death" (Mosiah 17:10). Abinadi also asserted that if he were to die in the ordeal, two witnesses would then remain against Noah: first, Abinadi's words "[would] stand as a testimony," and second, Abinadi's innocent blood would "also stand as a testimony" (v. 10).[161]

Noah would have understood well the force of having these two witnesses stand against him.[162] Adding Alma's testimony would make a total of three witnesses—enough to satisfy even the extra three-witness rule of Deuteronomy 19:15. Noah would also have comprehended the legal risk involved in allowing Abinadi to subject himself to a divine ordeal should he come out victorious: if Abinadi were vindicated by the suffering inflicted upon him, Noah would have to set him free, which would undoubtedly trigger civil unrest in the city of Nephi and bring an end to his political and religious regime. Noah was foiled and frustrated. His effort to rid himself and his city of Abinadi's ominous prophecies had failed. The legal effect of Abinadi's offer to endure whatever the king chose to inflict upon him was to assert again his total innocence and to require Noah to make the next move in the trial.[163] He chose not to submit the matter to some kind of divine determination or inquisition by ordeal.

Noah Almost Withdraws the Accusation

Upon Abinadi's refusal to recall any of his words, Noah's accusation of blasphemy and his death sentence (Mosiah 17:7–8) became unconditional. Presumably Noah and the priests had agreed to accept that outcome before they brought Abinadi back into the court. Noah, however, fearing the seriousness of having Abinadi's testimony confirmed by ordeal or by his innocent blood, virtually reversed the verdict and "was about to release" Abinadi, "for he feared his word; for he feared that the judgments of God would come upon him" (v. 11). Indeed, as seen above, a guilty verdict in a capital case before a Jewish court could always be reversed before the execution if further information came before the court and justified a reversal. Abinadi's offer to endure an ordeal could well have been viewed by a court as constituting such additional information.

---

161. Jeremiah also threatened the judges in his case with the prospect of shedding innocent blood (Jeremiah 26:15).

162. Rabbinic authority held that the testimony of two witnesses, properly established, could stand as an alibi against even one hundred witnesses. See Goldin, *Hebrew Criminal Law*, 234–35n16, citing Makkot 1:7, 5b.

163. Merely by saying, "I have somewhat to argue in favor of my acquittal," even if that claim were mere subterfuge, a convicted party could return to the court several times before he could be legally executed under rabbinic procedure. See Goldin, *Hebrew Criminal Law*, 132n5.

The Charge of Reviling the King

Asserting a legal role separate from that of the king, the priests at this point resisted Noah's decision and would not allow the case to be dismissed: "But the priests lifted up their voices against [Abinadi], and began to accuse him" (Mosiah 17:12). Acting now in the role of accusers rather than judges,[164] they themselves introduced yet a further accusation into the trial, namely, that Abinadi had "reviled the king" (v. 12), the fourth legal charge brought against Abinadi.

Reviling the leader of one's people was doubtlessly considered to be impolitic, insolent, and in violation of the principles of the law of Moses: "Thou shalt not revile the gods, nor curse the ruler of thy people" (Exodus 22:28). Cursing one's ruler was closely associated with the crime of cursing God, or blasphemy (v. 28; 1 Kings 21:10, 13), the third accusation that had been brought against Abinadi. Abinadi had reviled the king when he cursed him in the public gathering (Mosiah 12:3) and when he asserted that his own words would be authenticated by ordeal and would stand as a testimony against Noah's iniquity (17:10). Abinadi thereby accused Noah of such wickedness that he would be consumed in the furnace, just as the unholy and impure members of the house of Israel were told that they would die if they broke through into the sacred space on Mount Sinai, which "was altogether on a smoke, . . . and the smoke thereof ascended as the smoke of a furnace" (Exodus 19:18). In other words, Abinadi's curse implied that Noah and the priests under him were unworthy to stand in the presence of God, which effectively nullified their right to officiate in God's temple that had been built by Nephi in the city of Nephi. Moreover, Abinadi reviled the king when he said that if the king were to kill him he would illegally shed innocent blood (Mosiah 17:10), for this denied the legitimacy of the king's official or legal actions. Abinadi's claims were offensive reproaches, if not approaching sedition or treason.

Most importantly in terms of bringing the trial of Abinadi to an end, to successfully convict Abinadi of reviling did not require the court to prove that he was lying. Only disloyalty and disrespect, not truth or falsehood, were now at issue. Truth would not appear to be a defense to this crime. It is not likely that Abinadi could have defended himself by claiming that he had had nothing but the king's best interests in mind. True as that might have been, his words still "curse[d] the ruler of [this] people."

---

164. See Bovati, *Re-Establishing Justice*, 287–305, for a discussion of witnesses and accusers in a debate between accused and judge.

Legal Charges Brought against Abinadi

Charge	Evidence	Mosaic Law in Question
1. Lying (Mosiah 12:14)	Abinadi had said that the people had hardened their hearts and had committed evil abominations (Mosiah 12:1)	"Thou shalt not bear false witness" (Exodus 20:16) "Thou shalt not raise a false report" (Exodus 23:1) "Ye shall not . . . lie" (Leviticus 19:11)
2. False prophecy (Mosiah 12:14)	"He pretendeth the Lord hath spoken it" (Mosiah 12:12)	"The prophet [who] shall presume to speak a word in my name, which I have not commanded him to speak, . . . shall die" (Deuteronomy 18:20)
3. Blasphemy (Mosiah 17:7–8)	Abinadi had said that God himself would come down (Mosiah 7:26–28; 15:1–8)	"He that blasphemeth the name of the Lord, he shall surely be put to death" (Leviticus 24:16)
4. Reviling against the king (Mosiah 17:12)	With a simile curse, Abinadi said that Noah's life would be as a garment in a hot furnace (Mosiah 12:3, 10–12)	"Thou shalt not revile the gods, nor curse the ruler of thy people" (Exodus 22:28)

In the end, it was for the offense of reviling that Abinadi was executed. Nevertheless, this charge was probably only a makeweight. When Limhi described the execution of Abinadi about twenty-five years after the fact, he told Ammon unequivocally that Abinadi was executed for allegations of blasphemy, not reviling:

> And because he said unto them that Christ was the God, the Father of all things, and said that he should take upon him the image of man, and it should be the image after which man was created in the beginning; or in other words, he said that man was created after the image of God, and that God should come down among the children of men, and take upon him flesh and blood, and go forth upon the face of the earth—and now, because he said this, they did put him to death. (Mosiah 7:27–28)

Limhi's disclosure would seem to indicate that the charge of reviling the king, which was closely related to blasphemy in any event, either was introduced by the priests of Noah as a pretext or at least came to be understood as akin to blasphemy among Limhi's people.

In raising the final accusation of reviling, the priests cried out against Abinadi. Whether this was an orderly procedure or unruly action is not clear. They "lifted up their voices against him" (Mosiah 17:12). This wording could refer to orderly voting, to further argumentation, or to unorganized shouting. That they "began to accuse him" (v. 12) suggests the semblance of an orderly process.

Abinadi's Conviction by the King

The words of the priests angered Noah once again: "Therefore the king was stirred up in anger against him" (Mosiah 17:12). The priests' charge that Abinadi had reviled the king and Abinadi's threat that innocent blood would stand against Noah appear to have been "matters of the king" over which Noah had the final word. Indeed, Noah alone entered the judgment against Abinadi and turned him over for execution: "*He* [Noah] delivered him up that he might be slain" (v. 12).[165]

Execution

Abinadi was taken and bound, and his skin was "scourged . . . with faggots" (Mosiah 17:13)[166] until he "fell, having suffered death by fire"

---

165. See Bovati, *Re-Establishing Justice*, 344–63, in which he discusses the sentencing and execution stages of a trial.

166. Some discussion has arisen over the word *scourged* and whether it should be read as *scorched*. If *scourging* in this context means "whipping" and if by *faggots* we are to understand burning bundles of wood (or even bundles of wood to be burned), it is hard to imagine the process of Abinadi's execution. Was his skin whipped with these incendiary bundles? Robert Matthews suggests that "Abinadi's tormentors took burning torches and poked him with these, burning his skin until he died." See his "Abinadi: The Prophet and Martyr," in *The Book of Mormon: Mosiah, Salvation Only through Christ*, ed. Monte S. Nyman and Charles D. Tate Jr. (Provo, UT: Religious Studies Center, Brigham Young University, 1991), 102. This would be an odd procedure, yet Abinadi's death was novel: he was "the first that suffered death by fire because of his belief in God" (Alma 25:11).

Royal Skousen carefully marshals textual, semantic, and visual (or auditory) evidence to argue that the most reasonable reading of this text is "scorched his skin with faggots." Royal Skousen, "'Scourged' vs. 'Scorched' in Mosiah 17:13," FARMS Update, *Insights* 22, no. 3 (2002): 2–3; and his *Analysis of Textual Variants of the Book of Mormon: Part Three, Mosiah 17–Alma 20* (Provo, UT: FARMS, 2006), 1362–64. Indeed, the word *scorched* appears in verse 14, and so *scourged* could have been written in error in verse 13.

Hugh Nibley argued that the words *scourged* and *scorched* are etymologically identical (*Teachings of the Book of Mormon, Semester 2* [Provo, UT: FARMS, 1993], 109, 117), which dodges the textual issue but still leaves readers wondering if Abinadi was scourged (beaten, tormented), scorched (singed, burned), or both.

Robert F. Smith, in correspondence on March 30, 2002, adds that the *Oxford English Dictionary* (Oxford: Oxford University Press, 1933), 9:238–39, offers various spellings for *scorch*, including *scorge*, leading to the possibility that "we may even have a confluence in spellings and

(v. 20). The ultimate form of Abinadi's punishment is significant: he was burned, just as he had prophesied that Noah's life would "be valued even as a garment in a hot furnace" (12:3).[167] This customized form of punishment was evidently designed, fashioned, and introduced specifically by the priests, "who caused that he should suffer death by fire" (Alma 25:9). Moreover, faggots, or bundles of sticks used for fuel, were involved, perhaps because Abinadi had prophesied that the people would "have burdens [bundles of sticks?] lashed upon their backs" (Mosiah 12:5). Although a few recorded cases of actual burnings at the stake exist in late antiquity,[168] nothing in the Book of Mormon record indicates that Abinadi was burned while tied to a stake. Instead, it appears that Noah's priests tailored an unprecedented mode of execution for Abinadi alone that mirrored the evil that Abinadi had said would befall, and did indeed befall, King Noah. This unique and extraordinary punishment conformed with the talionic concepts of justice in ancient Israel and in the ancient Near East, where the punishments were individually designed in unusual cases to suit the crime.[169]

---

meanings" here, namely, that Abinadi was both scorched and flogged "simultaneously or progressively." Webster's *American Dictionary of the English Language* (1828) allows that the meanings of *scourge* include to "punish with severity, to chastise," and to "torment or injure," and all of these meanings are possible.

Brant Gardner reported on an Aztec drawing with a caption that shows "a youthful miscreant being scourged with what are described as 'burning firebrands'" ("Scourging with Faggots," FARMS Update, *Insights* 21, no. 7 [2001]: 2–3), but the Book of Mormon gives the definite impression that Abinadi was not executed in some normal fashion, and so the relation between his execution and these Aztec punishments remains uncertain.

Lucy Mack Smith once said that she would stand by her conviction of her son's testimony even "if you should stick my flesh full of faggots, and even burn me at the stake." Richard L. Bushman, *Joseph Smith and the Beginnings of Mormonism* (Urbana: University of Illinois Press, 1984), 109. *Foxe's Book of Martyrs* reprints an original woodcut showing a righteous man being beaten with bundles of willow branches, but they are not burning. John Foxe, *Foxe's Book of Martyrs*, ed. G. A. Williamson (Boston: Little and Brown, 1965), 419. So what actually happened to Abinadi remains obscure except for the outcome, that he "suffered death by fire" (Mosiah 17:20), which was what he had prophesied (vv. 15, 18) and how his execution was later described (Alma 25:9, 11).

167. The book of Leviticus requires any "garment" that carries any of the plague of leprosy to be "burnt in the fire" (Leviticus 13:52, 57). Fire, in this case, was a means of removing impurity. In addition, "the daughter of any priest, if she profane herself by playing the whore, she profaneth her father: she shall be burnt with fire" (21:9). Just as a priest would burn the offerings, a daughter who profaned her priestly father would be burned.

168. See, for example, TB *Sanhedrin* 7:2, 52a; and Tosefta *Sanhedrin* 9:11a. This early practice was apparently changed by the talmudic authorities, who preferred mitigating the severity of the punishment and shunned any punishment that would mutilate the body. Goldin, *Hebrew Criminal Law*, 35.

169. See, for example, Goldin, *Hebrew Criminal Law*, 21; also H. B. Huffmon, "Lex Talionis," in *Anchor Bible Dictionary*, 4:321–22.

In early Israelite and later Jewish courts, executions were normally carried out immediately following the issuance of the final verdict,[170] as was the case here. Moreover, the accusers were required to carry out the execution: "The hands of the witnesses shall be first upon him to put him to death, and afterward the hands of all the people" (Deuteronomy 17:7). The accusers were given this task because "it is they who claim to have personal knowledge of his guilt, while others merely rely upon their statement."[171] Floggings were further required to take place in the presence of the convicting judge (25:2).[172] In Abinadi's case, his accusers, in the end, were the priests. They were the ones who brought up the charge and accused him of reviling the king (Mosiah 17:12). Thus it became the duty of the priests to carry out the execution, which they did: "And it came to pass that *they* took him and bound him, and scourged his skin with [burning] faggots, yea, even unto death" (v. 13). That the priests were the instigators and primary leaders in carrying out the execution of Abinadi, of course, does not rule out the participation of the general populace as well. They, too, were accusers of Abinadi (12:9–14) and thus were also interested participants. In the end, the people as a whole were collectively responsible before God for the death of this prophet, as King Limhi will later acknowledge (7:25–26, 28).

The place of execution was normally outside the city walls.[173] Thus when Abinadi was "taken" prior to his execution, he was probably taken outside the city of Nephi, as occurred more explicitly in the execution of Nehor (Alma 1:1–15, on the top of a hill) and apparently in the execution of Zemnarihah (3 Nephi 4:28, on the top of a tree).

Scourging or beating was the normal form of punishment for disobedience in biblical law (Deuteronomy 25:2). Reviling the king may have been viewed as a form of royal disobedience, thus calling for some form of beating. Hence, we may suspect that Abinadi was not only burned but also scourged or beaten. When being flogged, the culprit was normally bound and required to lie on the ground. It is possible that the binding mentioned in Mosiah 17:13 reflects this standard Israelite practice. If this

---

170. TB *Sanhedrin* 6:1, 42b. The verdict and the execution were pronounced on the same day; testimony evidence was heard on the day or days before. See also Bovati, *Re-Establishing Justice*, 371–76.

171. Goldin, *Hebrew Criminal Law*, 136n17. See also McKenzie, "Judicial Procedure at the Town Gate," 103; Falk, *Hebrew Law in Biblical Times*, 61; and Bovati, *Re-Establishing Justice*, 381–82.

172. De Vaux, *Ancient Israel*, 1:153.

173. Goldin, *Hebrew Criminal Law*, 30–31. See, for example, Leviticus 24:14, 23; Numbers 15:35–36; 1 Kings 21:13.

is so, it shows graphically that the priests of Noah were doubly severe on Abinadi, inflicting two forms of punishment at the same time. Beating was normally not to be excessive (Deuteronomy 25:3), and according to later law it was not to be administered in connection with capital punishment.[174] The scourging of Abinadi would therefore reflect an extreme punishment and probably a serious corruption of and departure from the normal principles of biblical and Jewish law.[175]

As the flames began to scorch him, Abinadi uttered his final curse upon Noah and his priests: "Behold, even as ye have done unto me, so shall it come to pass that thy seed shall cause that many shall suffer the pains that I do suffer. . . . And it will come to pass that ye shall be afflicted with all manner of diseases. . . . Yea, and ye shall be smitten on every hand, . . . and then ye shall suffer, as I suffer, the pains of death by fire" (Mosiah 17:15–18). Because Abinadi eventually "fell" (v. 20), he very well could have been standing when he issued his final testimony and curses. This is not an idle point. Had Abinadi struggled to rise up, after being beaten lying down, or had he remained standing during that torture? Either way, by standing Abinadi symbolically connoted his innocence. In Akkadian the phrase "to stand up" signifies "in a juridical context . . . the prevailing over an adversary in a lawsuit."[176] By standing, he also gave greater testimonial and judgmental impact to his words.[177] It was typically said that judges in ancient Israel stood to read their verdicts.[178] To the very end, Abinadi carried out his divinely appointed mission of delivering the judgments of God upon Noah and his wicked followers.

---

174. See Goldin, *Hebrew Criminal Law*, 50n66, citing Rabbi Akiba in Makkot 3:1 (13b) and Maimonides, *Hilkot Sanhedrin* 18:1, for this view of Rabbi Akiba. Flogging or beating was a disciplinary punishment only, and not a form of capital punishment; Haim H. Cohn, "Flogging," in Elon, *Principles of Jewish Law*, 532–33.

175. See, however, TB *Berakhot* 58a (9:1), as discussed by Jonah Fraenkel, "Ma'aseh be-R. Shila," *Tarbits* 40 (October 1970): 33–35, 38–39.

176. Shalom M. Paul, "Unrecognized Biblical Legal Idioms in the Light of Comparative Akkadian Expressions," *Revue Biblique* 86, no. 2 (1979): 237.

177. The Tosefta *Sanhedrin* 6:2 requires that "men must stand when they pronounce sentence, or bear witness, or ask for absolution from vows, or when they remove anyone from the status of priesthood or of Israelitish citizenship." Many sources note the significance of judges standing. For example, it has been suggested that, in Acts 7:56, the standing Son of Man should be understood as judging those who stoned Stephen. Rudolf Pesch, *Die Vision des Stephanus* (Stuttgart: Katholisches Bibelwerk, 1966), 19–20. See Bovati, *Re-Establishing Justice*, 233–38, 376–80 (dealing with retribution).

178. McKenzie, "Judicial Procedure at the Town Gate," 103: "When common agreement has been reached, they [the judges] rise (Psalm 3:8; 35:2) to give the verdict (Joel 3:14; 1 Kings 20:40)."

It is notable that Abinadi prophesied that the seed of the priests would "cause that many shall suffer the pains that I do suffer, even the pains of death by fire" (Mosiah 17:15), and that he condemned the priests to suffer the same fate as he: "Ye shall suffer, as I suffer, the pains of death by fire" (v. 18). As was seen in connection with the case of Sherem, the Israelite concept of justice called for false accusers to suffer the same punishment that they might wrongly inflict upon the accused (see Deuteronomy 19:16–21). Having wrongly executed Abinadi, Noah and his priests should suffer just as he had suffered according to the ancient concept of reciprocal justice. It was also common for ancient peoples to expect God to visit the sins of the fathers in some way upon their posterity,[179] and in this vein Abinadi predicts that the children of priests would use the same illegal punishment on others (Alma 25:5), implicitly prophesying that they will incur the same measure of God's wrath as will the priests themselves and perhaps presaging the destruction by fire that came upon the wicked in 3 Nephi 9:11, especially on those who had killed the prophets.

Death by fire was rare under Israelite law, administered rarely in the cases of adultery involving a priest's daughter (Leviticus 21:9) and as punishment for specific types of incest or whoredom.[180] In Babylonia, a looter who went into a burning house to put out the fire but instead stole property from that place would have been "thrown into that same fire."[181] Thus the Book of Mormon accurately points out that the burning of Abinadi was introduced for the first time in Nephite law by the priests of Noah as a punishment for a religious offense and perhaps for any offense: "Abinadi was the first that suffered death by fire because of his belief in God" (Alma 25:11). This explicit reminder in the record purposefully points out the irregularity of this illicit mode of punishment.

In the end, Abinadi suffered a martyr's death "because he would not deny the commandments of God, having sealed the truth of his words by his death" (Mosiah 17:20). Due to his piety and devotion to the Lord, he preferred death over disobedience, knowing that his blood would stand again as a testimony against his accusers at the last day.[182]

---

179. Exodus 20:5; Numbers 14:18; Deuteronomy 23:2; see also the epilogue to the Code of Hammurabi.

180. Judah ordered that Tamar be burned for her whoredom (Genesis 38:24), perhaps reflecting pre-Mosaic practices in Israel. Under the Code of Hammurabi, section 110, a nun guilty of misconduct was put to death by burning, and under section 157, incest by a man with his mother after the death of his father was punishable by burning both the man and his mother.

181. Code of Hammurabi, section 25.

182. For more on martyrdom and witnessing, see chapter 8 on Alma and Amulek below.

The Legacy of the Trial of Abinadi

Without any doubt, the trial of Abinadi illustrates by negative example many principles of judging righteously. Noah and his priests put their hands together as wicked accusers; he and his leading priests had exerted pressure on younger judges to "follow a multitude to do evil," had wrested judgment, and had slain "the innocent and righteous" (Exodus 23:1, 2, 6, 7). In contrast, judging righteously calls for humility, admitting error, avoiding excess, and not placing oneself above the law. Observing the letter of the law is not enough.

Interestingly, in many respects, the trial of Abinadi reflects quite extensively many procedural and substantive aspects of ancient Israelite law. Of all the trials in the Book of Mormon, this trial conforms the most closely to pre-exilic biblical law, as one would expect largely because the later legal trials recorded in the books of Alma and Helaman arose during the reign of the judges in the Nephite republic after the law reforms of King Mosiah. Living before any such reforms, Noah and his priests seem to have understood quite thoroughly the technical ancient legal distinctions between offenses such as slanderous speech, false prophesy, blasphemy, and reviling the leader of the people; and they evidently respected the jurisdictional rights of the variously aggrieved parties to press charges and seek justice concerning the alleged political, religious, or personal violations that may have affected them each respectively. Nothing in the trial of Abinadi is out of legal character with biblical law traditions in the late monarchical period.

While it is true that Noah and his priests acted in a coldhearted and self-indulgent manner and undoubtedly violated the spirit of many teachings and requirements of the law of Moses, it also seems that they expended great efforts in attempting to rationalize their conduct in order to preserve the appearances of living the law of Moses. Although certain irregularities are evident in this proceeding, it should be noted that the court of Noah seems to have tried to respect at least the outward appearances of law and order. They did not simply take Abinadi out and stone him or shoot arrows at him, as happened to certain other prophets such as Samuel the Lamanite; they at least tried to frame their arguments in a scriptural context. Though they observed a form of justice with a semblance of legality, they corruptly subverted the spirit and purpose of the law. For that very error, Abinadi had criticized Noah and his judges (Mosiah 12:29); and because of that deep-rooted perversion of justice, Abinadi was scandalously executed.

Abinadi's testimony and martyrdom left an enduring theological message and legal legacy on several counts.[183] His recitation of the Ten Commandments, with his face shining like the face of Moses at Sinai, affirmed that righteous people must live the laws of God strictly and with proper understanding and with the proper spirit. The key to understanding the performances and ordinances of the law of Moses was in seeing "that all these things were types of things to come" (Mosiah 13:31). In his own death, Abinadi bore afflictions similar to those foretold of the suffering servant in Isaiah 53, and the treatment Abinadi received foreshadowed the trials, suffering, and death of the Holy One of Israel himself. All of this reinforced the point that salvation does not come through the law as such and that the spirit of the law is in the Lord God who himself would come down in flesh and in power, eventually to bring a righteous judgment on all the people of the earth.[184] Thus the case of Abinadi put to rest the last vestiges among the Nephites of claims such as Sherem's that the law of Moses alone "is the right way" (Jacob 7:7) and that preaching one's belief in Christ was somehow blasphemous. Certain people in the Book of Mormon after Abinadi would continue to reject the idea that the atonement of Christ was necessary (Nehor), or that the divinity of Christ was logically possible (Zeezrom), or that the coming of Christ was knowable (Korihor)—but no longer would these dissenters argue that the doctrine of Christ was inconsistent with the law of Moses.

Abinadi's stature as a prophet of Christ was securely enhanced by the prompt and literal fulfillment of his prophecies about the fate of Noah and his priests. Abinadi prophesied that the people of Limhi would be hunted and driven, which soon came to pass (Mosiah 20:21). Abinadi prophesied that Noah and his priests would suffer death in a manner similar to the death they inflicted upon Abinadi; and before long Noah was burned to death by his men, who ultimately refused to follow him into cowardly escape (19:20), and almost all of the seed of Amulon and his fellow priests were killed by the Nephites in battle (Alma 25:4). The remainder asserted power over the Lamanites and "caused that many of the Lamanites should perish by fire because of their belief" (v. 5). Moreover, the Amulonites soon became closely allied with the Amalekites (perhaps the same group elsewhere called Amlicites?),[185] who were of the order of Nehor (21:4;

---

183. For a general review of Abinadi's teachings and influence, see Robert J. Matthews, "Abinadi: Prophet and Martyr," *Ensign,* April 1992, 25–30; and "Abinadi: The Prophet and Martyr," 91–111.

184. Compare Mafico, "Judge, Judging," 3:1106.

185. John L. Sorenson, "Book of Mormon Peoples," in *Encyclopedia of Mormonism,* 1:194.

24:29), and took up arms against the Ammonite converts (24:2). Thus the seed of Amulon may stand behind the burning of the faithful women and children and sacred books in Ammonihah (14:8), which may have provoked the Lamanites to invade and destroy that city (25:2). In any event, Abinadi's prophecy that his executioners would cause others to die by fire and likewise suffer death by fire followed the seed of the priests of Noah into the next two or three generations.

Likewise, the Pyrrhic legal victory of Noah's priests in persuading him to put Abinadi to death for reviling the king seems to have set a precedent that especially encouraged the followers of Nehor to raise that same charge in later cases against other prophets who came with strong words of divine judgment against wicked rulers and administrators (Alma 12:4; 14:2, 5, 7). Although the crime of reviling the king would become inapplicable among the Nephites once they abandoned their use of kingship, the crime of reviling was modified and raised by the Nehorites in Ammonihah against Alma and Amulek, who were accused of reviling the laws and legal officers of the city (10:24; see chapter 8 below). Perhaps realizing the fate that eventually befell both the priests of Noah and the Nehorites in Ammonihah for wrongly using this legal strategy, the followers of Gadianton later were smart enough only (but still unsuccessfully) to attempt to get others to accuse the prophet Nephi of reviling the people and the law (Helaman 8:2; see chapter 12 below).

Abinadi's prophecies of doom and destruction also became archetypal and influential. Just as his prophecy that the unrepentant people of Noah and Limhi would have burdens lashed on their backs and would suffer pestilence and destruction was literally fulfilled, so Mormon remembered Abinadi as a true prophet of destruction.[186] While Mormon's account of the final destruction of the Nephites details the fulfillment of many prophecies of their doom, demonstrating that the power of the evil one was "wrought upon all the face of the land," Mormon states specifically that this lamentable condition particularly fulfilled "all the words of Abinadi, and also Samuel the Lamanite" (Mormon 1:19).

In terms of the ensuing religious and political history of the Nephites in the years that immediately followed Abinadi, the trial of Abinadi became a powerfully influential event in Nephite politics and government. Alma the Elder, whose conversion was based on the testimony of Abinadi, soon would establish a church organization in the land of Zarahemla based on covenants to God and not to the king. Alma the Younger and the four sons

---

186. See Bovati, *Re-Establishing Justice*, 122, for a discussion of how war "expresses and resolves a legal controversy."

of Mosiah were extolled as missionaries who "did publish peace" (Mosiah 27:37), echoing Abinadi's interpretation of Isaiah 52:7 in declaring that the Lord reigns. Alma's experience in the court of Noah was the source of the fundamental distrust of kingship that finally led, about sixty years later, to the abandonment of kingship among the Nephites. The wickedness, abominations, iniquities, calamities, contentions, bloodshed, lawlessness, and perversions of King Noah are specifically cited by King Mosiah as the main evidence in persuading the people to choose by popular voice that "it is not expedient that ye should have a king or kings to rule over you" (Mosiah 29:16; see 29:17–23),[187] ushering in the reign of judges and a new chapter in the judicial history of the Nephites.

---

187. For further evidence that the Book of Mormon recognizes Noah as a wicked king who suffered the judgment of God, see Goff, "Uncritical Theory," 201–2, in which he compares the reigns of King Jeroboam, King Ahab, and King Noah. For example, a major character appears to all three kings in disguise (1 Kings 14; 20; 22; Mosiah 12:1); further, all three kings are idolatrous, walk in the way of wickedness, cause the people to sin, and put the prophet to death, and either the people or the wicked king is eaten by dogs and/or fowls. The fact that the same elements are recorded in each of these accounts perhaps is evidence of a Book of Mormon author consciously reflecting the typical qualities of a wicked king.

CHAPTER SEVEN

THE TRIAL OF NEHOR

About sixty years after the trial of Abinadi in the city of Nephi, several major political changes and legal reforms occurred in the land of Zarahemla. During that sixty-year interim, Alma the Elder, the righteous judge who had voiced his opinion that the charges against Abinadi should be dropped, had gathered a group of 450 followers and had led them northward from the land of Nephi to the capital city of Zarahemla, where Alma soon earned the trust and cooperation of Mosiah, the king of Zarahemla. Soon afterward, a man named Nehor had become popular in Zarahemla as a countercultural figure. When none of the four sons of King Mosiah were willing to be groomed as his successor, Mosiah (with the concurrence of the populace) replaced the kingship with "the reign of the judges"; and Alma's son, Alma the Younger, was installed as the first chief judge in about 92 BC. Within a year, King Mosiah (at the age of sixty-three) and Alma the Elder (aged eighty-two) both died.

Against the backdrop of these complicated and significant developments, the trial of Nehor occurred in the very first year of the new regime in Zarahemla with Alma, the new head of state, sitting as a sole judge. The trial of Nehor is a classic case of a newly installed judge having to make a decision that, either way, was certain to offend and be unpopular with one group or another within his community. Courageously, Alma issued a verdict that took a strong stand against any personal use of violence in trying to engineer social change or resolve intersectional differences within the Nephite capital.

Political and Religious Pluralism in Zarahemla

The trial of Nehor must be understood against its historical and social contexts. At this time, the land of Zarahemla had become a very diverse place because of several major demographic changes. This development presented the Nephite leaders with a number of political and religious challenges. King Mosiah's reign, from about 124 to 91 BC, was marked by an influx of several groups of people into his territories in the land of Zarahemla. These new arrivals of political and religious refugees, most of whom were not assimilated or did not blend easily into the established community, resulted in increased cultural pluralism and heightened political instability in Zarahemla. The Nephites, although they were the rulers, had always been and would continue to be in the minority. There were "not so many . . . who were descendants of Nephi, as there were of the people of Zarahemla, who was a descendant of Mulek, and those who came with him" (Mosiah 25:2). Furthermore, the fact that the Nephites kept track of their lineages and tribal group identities (as Nephites, Jacobites, Josephites, and Zoramites,[1] as well as descendants of Nephi and Zarahemla) indicates that the Nephites and the Mulekites had not merged completely into one undifferentiated society. For three generations under Kings Mosiah the first, Benjamin, and Mosiah the second, most of the descendants of Zarahemla (generally called Mulekites by modern readers) had been willing hosts to the Nephites; evidently, the superior Nephite language skills, impressive law codes, altruistic ideals, and long-standing spiritual traditions made them attractive and effective rulers.

Some of the Mulekites, however, must have soon come to the realization that their own ancestors had come not only from the tribe of Judah but also from the royal line of David, through Zedekiah, the king of Jerusalem. One may suspect that, before too long, some of those Mulekites began asserting their inherited rights of kingship, if only in private. People of this persuasion may eventually have associated with those who wanted to install Amlici as king (Alma 2:2) and who, under him, would take up arms in civil revolt against Alma in the fifth year of the reign of the judges in Zarahemla, soon after the abandonment of the kingship by Mosiah. These Mulekitish people may also have surfaced again, a few years later, in the form of the persistent royalist undercurrent of the so-called king-men (51:5). Interestingly, the root letters *m-l-k* in the Hebrew word for king, *melek*, may linguistically or at least phonetically have linked together these three groups (Mulekites, Amlicites, and king-men, and probably others)[2]

---

1. Lehi divided his clan into seven groups or tribes. "Seven Tribes: An Aspect of Lehi's Legacy," in *Reexploring the Book of Mormon*, ed. John W. Welch (Salt Lake City: Deseret Book, 1990), 93–95. This tribal organization persisted in Nephite society from the time of Lehi and his son Jacob in the sixth century BC even until the final generation of Mormon in the fourth century after Christ (2 Nephi 1:28–2:1; 3:1; Jacob 1:13; 4 Nephi 1:36; Mormon 1:8).

2. The Amalekites—also variously spelled as *Amelicites* (Alma 24:1), *Amaleckites* (43:6), *Amelekites* (43:6), *Amalickites* (43:13), and *Amelickites* (43:20) in the original manuscript of the Book of Mormon—and Amalickiah may also be associated with one or more of these groups. See

socially and politically. The strength of the Mulekite undercurrent is openly evident two generations later when a Mulekite named Coriantumr, who was of royal blood, being "a descendant of [King] Zarahemla" (Helaman 1:15), opportunistically seized a moment of great weakness in the land of Zarahemla upon the execution of the conspirator Paanchi[3] and the ensuing assassination of the ruling Nephite chief judge Pahoran. Coriantumr, the would-be heir, marched straight into the heart of the land of Zarahemla with a numerous host, took over the city, and smashed the new Nephite chief judge Pacumeni "against the wall," killing him (vv. 17–21).

Unlike the Mulekites, who descended from the royal house of David, the Nephites came from the tribe of Manasseh (Alma 10:3) and had no obvious precedents to reinforce any claim to the throne they may have wanted to assert. Their strongest claim to the kingship devolved through their patriarchal ancestor Nephi (1 Nephi 2:22; Jacob 1:9–11), and yet he himself had become a king reluctantly, opposing the ideology of kingship (2 Nephi 5:18–19); and his traditional royal lands had been abandoned by his successors and retaken by Kings Zeniff, Noah, and Limhi. Nevertheless, the Nephites in Zarahemla continued to assert that "the kingdom had been conferred upon none but those who were descendants of Nephi" (Mosiah 25:13).

Adding to the demographic complexity, the people of Limhi had made a dramatic escape from the city of Nephi and arrived in the land of Zarahemla shortly after Mosiah began his reign as king (Mosiah 22:13). The Limhites became Mosiah's subjects, but these righteous, quiet people seem to have settled and remained separate from the city of Zarahemla. They lived in the valley of Gideon, mentioned in Alma 6:7, which appears to have been named after the Limhite warrior named Gideon. If normal social conditions prevailed among the diverse populations in the land of Zarahemla, it is unlikely that many of these newcomers or refugees were fully assimilated as equal citizens into the upper levels of Nephite society. Although Limhi had earlier been named king by his people (Mosiah 19:26), he and his family and followers apparently voluntarily surrendered

---

J. Christopher Conkling, "Alma's Enemies: The Case of the Lamanites, Amlicites, and Mysterious Amalekites," *Journal of Book of Mormon Studies* 14, no. 1 (2005): 108–17. The textual history of the variant spellings of *Amalekites*, which Royal Skousen argues is a misspelling of *Amlicites*, is found in his *The Original Manuscript of the Book of Mormon* (Provo, UT: FARMS, 2001) under the passages cited and in his *Analysis of Variants of the Book of Mormon, Part Three: Mosiah 17–Alma 20* (Provo, UT: FARMS, 2006) under Alma 2:11–12, pp. 1606–9. Just as the name *Gadianton* was used to refer to several similar robber groups under different leaders, the name *Amlicites* seems to have been used to identify several dissident king groups.

   3. The case of Paanchi is discussed in chapter 11 below.

their claim to kingship; after all, they knew from their own firsthand experiences the kinds of problems that had been foisted upon them by the manipulative and overreaching administration of King Noah (Mosiah 11:3–4). Accordingly, they would not likely have been among those who were agitating for the reinstitution of the kingship after the law reforms of Mosiah.

To compound matters further, the arrival of another group of people led by Alma the Elder added to the growing political diversity in Zarahemla, and their piety introduced new religious dimensions into the situation. The covenantal people of Alma had been miraculously delivered from bondage and were readily accepted in Zarahemla by the Nephites (Mosiah 24:25). Almost immediately, the young King Mosiah invited Alma to go "from one body to another" preaching and baptizing (25:15). Many converts entered into Alma's order, and soon Mosiah granted Alma the extraordinary privilege of "establish[ing] churches throughout all the land of Zarahemla . . . and gave him power to ordain priests and teachers over every church" (v. 19), though little is known about the relationship between these church units and the larger organization of the kingdom ruled by Mosiah. While Mosiah righteously desired to encourage Alma's old and new converts to keep the covenant or vow they had made with God,[4] the king created several political problems by permitting them this exceptional status. Since the temple of Zarahemla was still functioning, Mosiah weakened his own interests and those of his temple priests by allowing Alma to ordain other priests, especially when they taught that priests should not be supported by the people but "should labor with their own hands for their support" (18:24). Economically, Mosiah encouraged social fragmentation by permitting Alma to create separate enclaves of religious covenanters, especially when they shared their property principally among themselves according to their respective needs and abilities (v. 29), which practice differed in several ways from the requirement imposed by King Benjamin that all people under his jurisdiction should share of their substance with the beggar in dire need who petitions for help (4:16). King Mosiah's privileging of Alma's enclave must have set a powerful and somewhat awkward precedent when less desirable religious,

---

4. On the importance of religious vows among ancient Israelites, see Numbers 30:1–15. The law required that "if a man vow a vow unto the Lord, or swear an oath to bind his soul with a bond; he shall not break his word, he shall do according to all that proceedeth out of his mouth" (v. 2). The potency of oaths, vows, or covenants among the Nephites is well evidenced in the Book of Mormon in the oath of Nephi to Zoram (1 Nephi 4:33), in the covenant of the Ammonites (Alma 24:18–22), in the exchange between Moroni and Zerahemnah (Alma 44:8–15), and elsewhere.

hereditary, or political groups, such as Nehor's followers, began to seek or assert the right to equal privileges and circumstances.

During the next twenty years, from about 115 to 95 BC, strong social undercurrents began to divide the people in Zarahemla very deeply. Already, powerful political factions were forming. For a time, the four sons of Mosiah and Alma the Younger joined forces with those who sought to destroy Alma the Elder's church (Mosiah 27:8). This group of dissenters rejected the Nephite traditions, did not believe in the resurrection, denied the coming of Christ, refused to be baptized by Alma, and would not pray (26:1–4). It seems likely that Nehor would have been a rising leader among the agitators who militated against the church founded by Alma, the members of which had become "a separate people as to their faith, and remained so ever after" (v. 4). This was a precarious time for the Nephite rulers and for Alma the Elder. Their political, social, and religious positions must have hung in the balance literally from day to day.

From Kingship to Judgeship

When none of his four sons were willing to step into his shoes, King Mosiah responded to the political problems at hand by abandoning the formal designation of kingship and by convincing the people to adopt a new style of government led by a chief judge who was confirmed by the voice of the people (Mosiah 29). Mosiah's solution was the most sweeping judicial reform in Nephite history.[5] His new system for the administration of justice contained features that would have made it appealing to every interest group in the land of Zarahemla.

For one thing, dropping the title of king would have appealed readily to Limhi's group and to Alma's followers, who remembered vividly the consequences of the perversions and excesses of kingship under Noah. Even if this change would prove to be more nominal and cosmetic than substantive, it would have immediately neutralized any arguments between Nephites and Mulekites over kingship claims.

Significant innovations at the lower court level would have appealed to those who favored dramatic change, while those who were happy with the status quo would have recognized that the chief judgeship was truly not much different than the kingship had been. The chief judge continued to serve as the governing administrator, as the commander in chief of the army, and as the high priest; accordingly, Alma retained the royal insignia of the ball, the sword, and the sacred books, as the Nephite kings had done since the time they began to rule in Zarahemla a century earlier (Mosiah 1:16).

---

5. See generally "The Law of Mosiah," in Welch, *Reexploring the Book of Mormon*, 158–61.

The reforms of Mosiah changed the administration of justice procedurally and organizationally but not substantively, for the judges under
the new system were required to continue to judge "according to the law
which has been given" (Mosiah 29:28), presumably meaning "the laws
which have been given you by our fathers, which are correct, and which
were given them by the hand of the Lord" (v. 25). This differentiation
would have appealed to the people in the land who considered themselves
substantively bound by their former oaths and vows, such as the covenants
made by the people thirty-three years earlier under King Benjamin (5:6;
6:3; 26:1; 29:46) or by the followers of Alma the Elder.

Moreover, Mosiah's proposal appeared to have adequate checks to
ensure that the lower judges would judge according to the traditional
law. The lower judges could be sanctioned by a higher judge for judicial
misconduct (e.g., violating any of the judicial requirements articulated in
Exodus 23:1–9), and the higher judges could be subjected to judgment by
some of the lower judges at the behest of the people (Mosiah 29:28–29).
This feature would have been attractive to all groups, each of whom would
have had concerns about appearing before judges who were not accountable to higher authority in one way or another to judge righteously. Nothing in Nephite history indicates, however, that the higher judges had the
authority to overrule a decision of a lower judge on substantive grounds
through a process of appellate review, although it would seem likely that
an aberrant ruling would be vacated if the judge involved was unseated for
judicial irregularities or unethical behavior.

The law of Mosiah also involved the people to some extent in the instal-
lation of these judges (Mosiah 29:25). Although it is not clear who was entitled to vote (probably only adult males, as was universally the case in ancient
and premodern societies), the voice of the people was somehow heard. It is
also unclear whether the judges were elected and empowered to serve only
by and in local neighborhoods or if they held citywide or landwide offices,
for the record is silent about the procedures followed in any actual elections
and installations of these judges. In the case of the chief judge, it appears
that he was named or nominated with some kind of presumptive claim of
power and then was given power by the high priest or outgoing chief judge
after having been acknowledged by the voice of the people. For example, in
the case of Nephihah, who became the second chief judge, Alma selected
him as "a wise man who was among the elders of the church, and gave him
power according to the voice of the people" (Alma 4:16).

Nevertheless, to those in Zarahemla who favored the idea of democra-
tization, Mosiah's reform not only offered continuity with the theological

values and covenant laid down by King Benjamin, but it also took strong practical steps in the direction of popular reform. In many ways, Benjamin's speech had paved the way theologically, a generation earlier, for Mosiah's democratizing reform, as Benjamin had created within the land of Zarahemla a profound sense of equality among all his people, a universal humiliation of all of them before God, an opportunity for all to participate in the royal covenant with God, and a popular sharing of blessings and responsibilities that were usually reserved only to the king.[6]

Additionally, Mosiah's system appeared to be fair by making every person individually (not tribally or collectively) accountable for his actions (Mosiah 29:31), and every man was given "an equal chance throughout all the land; yea, and every man expressed a willingness to answer for his own sins" (v. 38), whatever that entailed.

His program also appeared to be practicable in the sense that it provided for judges and legal assistants to receive payment for their services (Alma 11:1), even though this compensatory system would quickly be abused in the city of Ammonihah (v. 20).

Finally, and most significantly, establishing a free sphere for beliefs (Alma 1:17; 30:7) would have appealed to parties across the spectrum. The rule that "the law could have no power on any man for his belief" (1:17) would have appealed just as much to Alma the Elder and his observant followers as to Nehor and the dissidents who followed him. For all of these reasons, Mosiah's reform was embraced readily by a strong majority of the people in his land.

Before the approval of Mosiah's reforms by the voice of the people, however, the political situation in Zarahemla must have been very tense. The four sons of Mosiah had each chosen to leave the land of Zarahemla (for fourteen years, as it turned out) rather than stay and become king. Besides sincerely desiring to preach the gospel to the Lamanites, these four apparent heirs to the throne may have wanted to put distance between themselves and any political factions that might have tried to pressure them to become king. They also may have wanted to get themselves out of harm's way, for they did not go out as royal ambassadors but preferred to remain anonymous, in Ammon's case even assuming the role of servant in the household of a Lamanite king (Alma 17:25). The undercurrents of political unrest in Zarahemla abated for a short time after the reforms of

---

6. John W. Welch, "Democratizing Forces in King Benjamin's Speech," in *Pressing Forward with the Book of Mormon*, ed. John W. Welch and Melvin J. Thorne (Provo, UT: FARMS, 1999), 110–26; and "Benjamin's Speech: A Masterful Oration," in *King Benjamin's Speech: "That Ye May Learn Wisdom,"* ed. John W. Welch and Stephen D. Ricks (Provo, UT: FARMS, 1998), 58–59.

Mosiah, but by the beginning of only the fifth year of the new regime, a full-scale civil war had erupted (2:1); such a massive revolution probably could not have broken out so suddenly had troubles not been brewing for several years.

In the face of these tensions and potentials for discord, Alma the Younger was confirmed or approved by the voice of the people as "the first and chief judge" (Mosiah 29:44; see the ancient heading at the beginning of the book of Alma). Alma the Younger was undoubtedly well qualified for the job, but he was also what we might call an ideal compromise candidate. When he became a member of his father's group, he effectively positioned himself outside of any disputes over vested interests that may have existed between the main body of Nephites and the majority Mulekite population; his father's service as a priest in the city of Nephi gave him religious and political ties to the Limhites; and Alma the Younger's prior efforts to destroy the churches established by his father may have given the Nehorites hope that Alma would still be subtly influenced by, or at least compromised by, his youthful predilections.

Very shortly after Alma the Younger was appointed, Alma the Elder died (Mosiah 29:45). His death at age eighty-two was probably not unexpected, but the timing would certainly have been unsettling. King Mosiah, the son of Benjamin, also died in that same year, at the age of sixty-three (v. 46), further weakening the nascent regime. Suddenly, the freshman chief judge, himself still a relatively young man (probably in his mid-thirties), found himself without the authoritative support of his father; without the experienced advice of Mosiah, his former regent; and without the active association of his four closest and most influential friends, the four sons of Mosiah.

The Rise of Nehor

Sensing an opportunity under the equality promised by the new legal regime, and perhaps also seizing a moment of political shakiness as the reign of the judges was in its infancy, Nehor took advantage of the situation. This provocative leader of a rapidly growing countercultural movement "began to establish" a new religious group (Alma 1:6), one openly opposed to the covenantal communities organized by Alma. Rooted and standing principally in opposition to Alma's ecclesiastical program, the Nehorite movement apparently began by drawing together those who wanted to separate themselves forever as a distinct people, who refused to pray, and who rejected the practice of baptism for the cleansing of sins and the adoption of a personal covenant of righteous living (Mosiah 26:4).

It should be noted, however, that unlike Korihor (Alma 30),[7] Nehor was neither an agnostic nor an atheist; and unlike Sherem,[8] he was not a proponent of the law of Moses. Nehor accepted the existence of God: he believed that God had created the world, and he termed his teachings "the word of God" (1:3), to be used for the worship of God (11:24; 21:6).

Working openly and publicly, Nehor came out in direct opposition to some of Alma's teachings, especially by arguing that priests "ought not to labor with their hands" (Alma 1:3; compare 30:53), possibly citing the Israelite practice of supporting the Levites in defense of his position (Numbers 35:2–8). It seems logical to assume that he also argued that the reforms of Mosiah, which provided wages for judges, had not gone far enough in compensating judicial officers but should also have provided support for religious leaders, much as the system under the kingship would have financed the operation of the temple by priests in the city. One can only wonder what happened to the "holy prophets" and temple officials, who assisted King Benjamin and were perhaps even supported by him only a generation earlier (Words of Mormon 1:16), once the king was eliminated from the political and religious landscape. But the fact that Nehor adamantly rejected Alma's high priesthood after the holy order of the Son of God seems clear from Alma's otherwise odd, last-ditch effort to expound the doctrine of the priesthood to his Nehorite accusers in the city of Ammonihah a few years later (Alma 12–13).

Other Nehorite doctrines can be culled from the book of Alma, sometimes from the text and other times by reading between the lines. Nehorite threads run through the stated and unstated assumptions of Alma's opponents in Ammonihah (Alma 9–16); in several of the teachings of Korihor (Alma 30); and in the false ideas that Alma's wayward son, Corianton, had for a time adopted (Alma 39). In particular, Alma 1:4 states that Nehor (or those who appear to have been influenced by him) taught that all mankind would be saved, that God had "redeemed all men," and that people should not fear and tremble but should lift up their heads and rejoice, for "all men should have eternal life." Nehor and his followers denied the existence of sin and punishment (1:4; 11:43–45; 39:4), rejected prophecy and the Nephite traditions (8:11; 21:8; 30:13, 24; 39:17), and disavowed the resurrection and final judgment (11:41–43; 21:9; 30:18; 40:1), arguing that God had created all people and would therefore equally restore them all through his redemption (1:4; 30:25; 41:1).

---

7. See the discussion in chapter 9 below.
8. Discussed in chapter 5 above.

Legal Issues Raised by the Slaying of Gideon

One day, still in the inaugural year of the reign of judges, while Nehor was going to preach to his followers, he encountered the elderly Limhite warrior named Gideon, who had become one of the officers (a teacher) in Alma's church (Alma 1:7) in addition to being a respected former military leader who had personally fought against the wicked King Noah. A dispute arose between Gideon and Nehor concerning the teachings of Nehor, a fight ensued, and the aged Gideon was killed. Nehor "began to contend with him sharply, that he might lead away the people of the church; but [Gideon] withstood him, admonishing him with the words of God. . . . [Nehor] was wroth with Gideon, and drew his sword and began to smite him. Now Gideon being stricken with many years, therefore he was not able to withstand his blows, therefore he was slain by the sword" (vv. 7, 9).

When Nehor was brought before Alma to be judged, his trial was a major test of Alma's political and judicial power in the fledgling reign of the judges. How would the new system of judges work? What would the power of the chief judge be? Would Alma be able to enforce his verdicts? Did the lower judges or the voice of the people (Mosiah 29:28–29) have jurisdiction over a landmark case such as this, or did the chief judge have authority to hear this case entirely on his own? How would the recently enunciated principle of equality (v. 38) and the rubric that a person could not be punished for his beliefs (Alma 1:17) be interpreted and applied in actual practice? Did members of one church in the land of Zarahemla still have the duty (as Israelites had under the law of Moses; Leviticus 5:1) to prevent other people in the land from trespassing the laws of God or of the state, or had the reforms of Mosiah relieved them of this duty in the interests of allowing each person to be accountable only to God for his iniquities or sins? All these were open questions that would be tested and settled, intentionally or unintentionally, by the precedent-setting trial of Nehor. Thus this important trial, which arose in the first year of the reign of judges, stands prominently at the head of the book of Alma, which book we may well call "the book of the reign of the righteous judges." This crucial proceeding and decision, like *Marbury v. Madison*,[9] defined and established the scope of the judicial powers of the Nephite chief judgeship.

---

9. United States Supreme Court, 1 Cranch 137 (1803); this was the first case to hold an act of Congress invalid, thereby establishing the power of the Supreme Court to declare unconstitutional any action of government that exceeded the limits established by the Constitution. Few cases ever decided by the United States Supreme Court have had greater impact than this landmark case, for it defined the powers of the respective branches of the federal government itself.

Gideon's Admonition of Nehor

The fray began when Gideon "admonish[ed Nehor] with the words of God" (Alma 1:7). Gideon's words may or may not have had any legal significance at the time they were spoken. On the one hand, the sharp words between Nehor and Gideon may have simply been a heated theological debate. On the other hand, these words may have served a legal function. The law of Jehoshaphat, for example, required "judges in all the land" to warn "your brethren that dwell in their cities . . . that they trespass not against the Lord" (2 Chronicles 19:5, 10).[10] This principle, that potential offenders should be warned, remained a powerful element in Jewish law down through the ages, and it certainly could have found its way into Nephite law as well. The warning requirement survived and developed to such an extent under Jewish law that no person could be convicted of a crime unless the witnesses could testify that they had warned the offender that he was breaking the law and had put him on notice of what the punishment would be.[11] Thus Gideon's admonition may have constituted a formal legal warning or a threat to commence litigation, calling upon God to manifest his displeasure with Nehor. In addition, it is possible that Gideon warned Nehor against leading people into the worship of false gods (Deuteronomy 13:6) or accused him of violating some other traditional religious law. In any event, something about Gideon's words was upsetting enough to Nehor that Nehor resorted to violence.

If Gideon's words were in fact some kind of legal warning coming from an officer of Alma's church, this would explain why Nehor found those words to be so offensive. Perhaps he saw Gideon's bold declarations as a threat to the "equal chance" that had been promised to all people in the land by the reform of Mosiah (Mosiah 29:38). Even if Gideon did not intend his words to be a formal legal warning, Alma had good reason to mention this detail in his account of the trial of Nehor, for this factor shows that Nehor was legally warned and adequately admonished before he grew angry. Therefore, Nehor could have been legally expected to control himself more than he did.

---

10. For more information on warnings, see Elias J. Bickerman, "The Warning Inscriptions of Herod's Temple," *Jewish Quarterly Review* 37, no. 4 (1947): 387–405; and Peretz Segal, "The Penalty of the Warning Inscription from the Temple of Jerusalem," *Israel Exploration Journal* 39, nos. 1–2 (1989): 79–84.

11. Haim H. Cohn, "Penal Law," in *The Principles of Jewish Law*, ed. Menachem Elon (Jerusalem: Keter, 1975), 473–74. Babylonian Talmud (hereafter TB) *Sanhedrin* 8b.

Arrest by the People of the Church

The text does not say how or where, but sometime soon after the slaying of Gideon, Nehor was apprehended "by the people of the church" (Alma 1:10), who were carrying out a normal civilian right and duty.[12] Had the captors been present when Gideon spoke out against Nehor? There seem to have been plenty of witnesses to the killing. If several men were already present at that time, then it would seem that Gideon's verbal confrontation with Nehor was planned. Gideon's delegation may have been formally sent by someone to oppose or moderate Nehor as he went about preaching. Or it may have been an accidental private encounter.

Apparently Nehor did not resist the arrest, for Alma does not say that Nehor was "bound" according to the normal practice seen in other cases (e.g., the apprehending of Ammon and his embassy in Mosiah 7:7 and the arrests of Alma and Amulek in Alma 14:4, of Ammon in Alma 17:20, and of Nephi in Helaman 9:19). Nor does it seem that Nehor's followers objected to the arrest. Apparently, Nehor was fairly confident in his legal and influential position, and thus he submitted to the trial without resistance.

Of course, Nehor would have to defend himself in this trial. Indeed, Alma's account states that Nehor "pleaded for himself" (Alma 1:11). As was the case in most ancient criminal trials, defendants had to appear on their own behalf and had no attorneys to represent them.[13]

Nehor's Defenses

The most important information for understanding the substantive issues and legal dynamics of this trial was, unfortunately, either unreported by Alma in his personal records or omitted by the compiler or abridger of the book of Alma. While the record states that Nehor's arguments were presented "with much boldness" (Alma 1:11), it tells nothing about the content of his forceful arguments. One is left to wonder what sorts of defenses he could have raised. Here was a public figure who had killed an old man with a sword, yet he mounted a courageous and vigorous defense for himself. What could he have said? Several viable possibilities present themselves:

1. Nehor may have raised a jurisdictional issue, arguing that he had been taken to the wrong court. The law of Mosiah provided specifically

---

12. See above on the arrest of Abinadi. See also Pietro Bovati, *Re-Establishing Justice: Legal Terms, Concepts and Procedures in the Hebrew Bible* (Sheffield, England: JSOT Press, 1994), 217–22.

13. See sources cited above in connection with the trial of Abinadi. As discussed below, the role of the lawyers and officials in the city of Ammonihah is somewhat unclear; in any event, their corrupt conduct was not contemplated, let alone authorized, by the law of Mosiah.

that there should be *lower* judges and that *they* would judge the people (Mosiah 29:25, 28). The only stated role of the higher judges was to see that the lower judges judged "according to the law" (v. 28). Accordingly, Nehor may have taken the position that he should have been tried by lower judges, possibly in a district friendly to him, especially if he had been "taken" some distance to appear before Alma (Alma 1:10). Such novel jurisdictional and procedural questions, however, were probably still open to interpretation as a case of first impression under the new legal system established by Mosiah, for the text goes out of its way to point out that this was "the first time" that such a case had arisen (v. 12). Thus it set an important precedent when Alma, the chief judge, took original jurisdiction over Nehor. This action claimed or expanded the power of the highest judge beyond anything stated explicitly in the reforms of Mosiah 29. His verdict stood as a ruling of the chief judge, without the involvement of any other judges and without any appeal to the voice of the people at large. Under such circumstances, certainly Nehor could have questioned the fairness or "equity" (Alma 10:21; Helaman 3:20; 3:37; 3 Nephi 6:4) of this treatment, especially since his accusers were "members of the church" who had selected their own leader to be Nehor's judge.

2. Similarly, Nehor may have argued that he was at least entitled to be tried by more than one judge. Jethro cautioned Moses strongly against serving as a sole judge and advised him to delegate judicial duties to many others: "Thou shalt provide out of all the people able men . . . and let them judge the people at all seasons" (Exodus 18:21–22). Multiple judges, therefore, became normally expected, if not required, under Israelite and Jewish law (three, twenty-three, seventy-one) to hear, debate, and decide cases—as with the elders at the gate in the action of Boaz purchasing the estate of Elimelech before "the elders" (Ruth 4:9), as in the trial of Naboth before "the elders and the nobles" at Megiddo (1 Kings 21:11), or in the trial of Jeremiah before the "princes . . . and priests" at Jerusalem (Jeremiah 26:16).[14] In the Book of Mormon, a council of priests had earlier served as judges in the trial of Abinadi (Mosiah 12:17), but as far as we know, the fledgling law of Mosiah had spoken only of *judges* who would judge (29:25, 28). Initially, nothing in the law of Mosiah seems to have expressly addressed the question of whether the chief judge could decide a case sitting as a sole justice. Thus when Alma proceeded to rule in Nehor's

---

14. Local courts may "have consisted of a single judge, sitting perhaps together with the elders," but "the court at the central sanctuary" utilized "a number of judges." Ze'ev W. Falk, *Hebrew Law in Biblical Times*, 2nd ed. (Provo, UT: Brigham Young University Press; Winona Lake, IN: Eisenbrauns, 2001), 49.

case by himself, he set a powerful precedent regarding the supreme office of the chief judge—a precedent that was apparently followed throughout the reign of the judges.[15] Indeed, Alma had the precedents of Numbers 25:1–5 and Deuteronomy 25:1–3 on his side: in those criminal cases, the judge acted alone.[16] Perhaps ironically, Alma and Amulek would later be brought to stand "before the [single] chief judge of the [Nehorite] land" of Ammonihah (Alma 14:4).

3. Although self-defense was an excuse for killing an attacker,[17] it is unlikely that Nehor argued that he killed the elderly Gideon in self-defense, even though Gideon may have been armed[18] and was certainly well known as a strong and aggressive warrior (Mosiah 19:5, 18, 22). Alma's statement of the facts in this case leaves no doubt that Nehor was the aggressor and that the aged Gideon posed no serious physical threat to Nehor, who was "large, and was noted for his much strength" (Alma 1:2, 9).

Perhaps, however, Nehor attempted to assert other mitigating circumstances. He had become very angry (Alma 1:9). Could he have argued that his action was "unintentional," in the heat of passion? Probably not. While Jewish law recognized a broad range of exemptions from criminal responsibility, "much wider in Jewish than in other systems of law,"[19] little support can be found in Israelite law for the idea that anger ever constituted duress, excusing conduct that is otherwise criminal. Indeed, Numbers 35:20–22 mentions "hatred" and "enmity" as culpable states of mind in cases of capital homicide, but anger is never contemplated under the rubric of killing any person "at unawares" (v. 11). That in Nephite culture anger was presumptively reprehensible and punishable is reflected in Ammon's admonition to Lamoni's father: "If thou shouldst fall at this time, in thine anger, thy soul could not be saved" (Alma 20:17).

---

15. See the appearance of Korihor before a single chief judge in the cities of Jershon, Gideon, and Zarahemla, although in those cities these chief judges were sometimes assisted by a high priest.

16. Falk, *Hebrew Law in Biblical Times*, 49.

17. Cohn, "Penal Law," 474.

18. It seems that he was armed or at least was wearing some kind of protective armor, since he withstood several blows before he was killed (Alma 1:9). His disadvantage was likely due to his advanced age, which would explain why his age is mentioned. However, Gideon's armor or weapons, assuming he had some, goes unnoted, and the absence of any mention of his being armed strengthens the case that Gideon was seen by Alma as having been completely innocent.

19. Cohn, "Penal Law," 471. For further information on intent, see Gary A. Anderson, "Intentional and Unintentional Sin in the Dead Sea Scrolls," in *Pomegranates and Golden Bells*, ed. David P. Wright, David Noel Freedman, and Avi Hurvitz (Winona Lake, IN: Eisenbrauns, 1995), 49–64; and David Daube, *Sin, Ignorance and Forgiveness in the Bible* (London: Liberal Jewish Synagogue, 1960).

4. More persuasively, Nehor may have argued before Alma's court that he had not committed the crime of intentional homicide. Paradigmatically speaking, the crime of murder under the law of Moses required a high degree of intent.[20] Preplanning or some form of "lying in wait" (Exodus 21:13; Numbers 35:20) or "hatred" against an enemy (Numbers 35:20–22) was a typical element of this crime (note the word *deliberately*, i.e., "with deliberation," in 2 Nephi 9:35). These legal elements, set forth especially in Numbers 35:22–25, would at least have given Nehor something powerful to argue about. Specifically concerning a case like Nehor's, who had smitten another "with an instrument of iron" (Numbers 35:16), the text in Numbers 35:22–25 reads: "But if he thrust him suddenly without enmity, or have cast upon him any thing without laying of wait, . . . the congregation shall deliver the slayer . . . to the city of his refuge." It seems that Nehor could have argued forcefully that he had not harbored the requisite hatred or preplanned desire to do Gideon harm.[21] Certainly Nehor did not plan or preconceive the confrontation (Alma 1:7). Moreover, biblical law seems to have recognized the element of fighting as a mitigating factor in settling the liabilities of men who had been parties to a brawl. For example, the case of the blasphemer in Leviticus 24 may well have been made a hard case because the name of God had been uttered as two men "strove together in the camp" (Leviticus 24:10); and if "men str[o]ve and hurt a woman with child," the act of causing a miscarriage was not considered a capital offense (Exodus 21:22). Presumably, some leniency was normally shown in cases where people acted improperly but under the heat of an altercation, or if injury was caused inadvertently as a consequence of a scuffle.[22] Nehor may have argued for clemency along these lines. Indeed, it is significant that Nehor was not convicted of murder per se (Alma 1:12), indicating that his argument, if made in this regard, may have been partially successful, even if it was ultimately inconsequential.

---

20. See sources cited in John W. Welch, "Legal Perspectives on the Slaying of Laban," *Journal of Book of Mormon Studies* 1 (1992): 119–41. See also Bernard S. Jackson, *Wisdom-Laws: A Study of the Mishpatim of Exodus 21:1–22:16* (Oxford: Oxford University Press, 2006), 122–30; Peter Haas, "'Die He Shall Surely Die': The Structure of Homicide in Biblical Law," in *Thinking Biblical Law*, ed. Dale Patrick (Atlanta: Scholars Press, 1989), 122–30; and Hermann Schulz, *Das Todesrecht im Alten Testament: Studien zur Rechtsform der Mot-Jumat-Sätze*, Beiheft zur Zeitschrift für die alttestamentliche Wissenschaft 114 (Berlin: Töpelmann, 1969).

21. Thus Nehor could have overcome the presumption of intent that normally arises when the use of a sword is involved; Haim H. Cohn, "Homicide," in Elon, *Principles of Jewish Law*, 475–76.

22. See Jackson, *Wisdom-Laws*, 172, 175, 179–81; Jonathan R. Ziskind, "When Two Men Fight: Legal Implication of Brawling in the Ancient Near East," *Revue Internationale des Droites de l'Antiquité* 44 (1997): 13–42.

5. Since this case arose in the context of commotion over religious freedom, the issue of equality may also have figured in Nehor's defense. The law of Mosiah provided that "every man should have an equal chance" (Mosiah 29:38) and that "the law could have no power on any man for his belief" (Alma 1:17). It seems clear that Nehor was trying to "lead away the people of the church" when Gideon began remonstrating against him (v. 7), and thus Nehor's right to say what he wanted and to go where he wanted may have been one of the issues at stake. Nehor may have become enraged because he thought his rights or privileges were being abridged, and he may have argued that he was entitled to use force to assert his rights against Gideon's encroachments.

While we do not know what arguments Nehor may or may not have raised in his own defense, we can well imagine that the record is correct when it states that he pleaded for himself "with much boldness" (Alma 1:11). Nehor made arguments of some kind, and it appears that they had some substance behind them, as the foregoing possibilities suggest. With these types of legal arguments in mind, we can easily appreciate the challenge that Alma was up against in judging this formidable case.

Nehor Held Guilty of Enforcing Priestcraft

In spite of his bold defense, Nehor was convicted. Alma's verdict began by stating, "Behold, this is the first time that priestcraft has been introduced among this people. And behold, thou art . . . guilty of priestcraft" (Alma 1:12). Priestcraft was specifically defined in Nephite writings as preaching for self-aggrandizement and to get gain (2 Nephi 26:29), something Nehor had clearly done (Alma 1:3). Priestcraft, however, was not against the law, strictly speaking; it was tolerated openly during the reign of judges (e.g., v. 16), although it was condemned as immoral and evil. Since God was the one who had forbidden priestcraft in a prophetic text that made no mention of any human penalty (2 Nephi 26:29–30), and since the public law of Mosiah guaranteed freedom of belief and an "equal chance," it seems clear enough that divine justice was all that could touch a person who was guilty of priestcraft alone.

But Nehor was found guilty of more than simple priestcraft. In the final analysis, Nehor was executed not for murder, and not for priestcraft, but for a composite offense of endeavoring to enforce priestcraft by the sword (Alma 1:12). Alma's judicial brilliance is evident in the way he fashioned this ruling. As suggested above, a simple charge of murder was problematic (if not precluded) under Numbers 35, and as far as we know, no human punishment was prescribed for priestcraft alone in any specific text.

By innovatively combining these two offenses, however, Alma was able to convict Nehor of killing for the culpable purpose of enforcing priestcraft. Whereas proof of a culpable homicide under ancient Israelite law required the showing of an evil motive of hatred or premeditation (the presumption of which was provided if the slaying occurred with a weapon "of iron," Numbers 35:16), Alma found evidence of a conscious and presumptuous motive in Nehor's use of a sword to enforce his economic interests as a religious leader, which intended outcome Alma subsumed under the evil of priestcraft. In other words, I would see Mosiah's law against murder as supplying the element of the *actus reus*[23] necessary for Nehor's conviction, while the moral and religious turpitude of priestcraft can be seen as providing the required *mens rea*[24] sufficient to support a verdict requiring capital punishment.

That Alma's decision was innovative is borne out by the fact that he gave a rationale for his verdict. He said, "Were priestcraft to be enforced among this people it would prove their entire destruction" (Alma 1:12). Normally, a verdict in a criminal case under ancient or Jewish law would not be given a rationale; indeed, in Jewish legal practice generally "the sentence pronounces the accused guilty and specifies the punishment to be inflicted on him; it is not reasoned."[25] The fact that the accused had been found in violation of the normal law was sufficient justification for the judgment. It would appear, however, that Alma gave a reason for his ruling, since (as he says) this fact presented an exceptional case of first impression not only involving a new situation (v. 12) but also interpreting the new application of the law of Mosiah.

In stating his rationale, Alma followed the rubric of ancient Israelite law that is embodied in the principle that it is better for one to perish than for the entire people to be destroyed.[26] Alma offered a type of "slippery slope" argument in support of his verdict: if Nehor were acquitted and his conduct condoned, such a result would lead to national disaster. In fact, it "would prove their entire destruction" (Alma 1:12). As evidenced not only

---

23. "Guilty action." Alma 1:17–18 makes it clear that a person under Nephite law could not be convicted of a crime under the law of Mosiah without committing some overt guilty action.

24. "Guilty mind." Exodus 21:13–14 and Numbers 35:20–21 show that an evil motive or state of mind was required.

25. Haim H. Cohn, "Practice and Procedure," in Elon, *Principles of Jewish Law*, 583. Cohn explains that no reasons were given in criminal cases because the defendant had been present throughout the deliberations. See also Falk, *Hebrew Law in Biblical Times*, 60–61: "Judges . . . were not bound to give reasons for their decisions."

26. John W. Welch and Heidi Harkness Parker, "Better That One Man Perish," in *Pressing Forward with the Book of Mormon*, 17–19. Compare 1 Nephi 4:13.

here, but also by the angel's justification for Nephi's slaying of Laban (1 Nephi 4:13) and in Alma's self-exoneration in smiting Korihor (Alma 30:47), Nephite jurisprudence in hard cases favored the collective well-being of the righteous community over the unrestrained rights of individuals who actively impeded goodness or promoted wickedness.[27] The same was true under the law of Deuteronomy 13:1–11, where preserving the faithfulness of Israel to God outweighed the right to life of any person—even when the offender was one's wife, "which is thine own soul," who tried to entice or deceive others into worshipping other gods.[28] Thus in several ways Alma's reasoning is at home in the world of ancient Israelite law where "legal and moral norms are not distinguished by any definitional criteria"[29] and where righteous judgments are issued "courageously" and "in the fear of the Lord, faithfully, and with a perfect heart" (2 Chronicles 19:9, 11). Alma's logic, justified by the fact that he not only sat as chief judge but also served concurrently as high priest, is further paralleled in later Jewish law that used morality to "expand the scope of enforcement" under the rubric of doing so "for the benefit of society."[30]

Nehor Sentenced to Die

Having held Nehor guilty of a culpable slaying, Alma was compelled by several forces to impose the death penalty. One was his concern about the blood guilt that he and his people would suffer if the blood of Gideon was not avenged by the death of Nehor. "Were we to spare thee, his blood would come upon us for vengeance" (Alma 1:13), Alma explained. The practice requiring a next of kin to act as the "avenger of blood" (Deuteronomy 19:12) dates from the earliest periods of biblical law (Genesis 9:5–6),[31]

---

27. The legal principles and problems behind the concept that it is better for one man to die than for an entire community to perish is discussed by R. David Aus, "The Death of One for All in John 11:45–54 in Light of Judaic Traditions," in *Barabbas and Esther and Other Studies in the Judaic Illumination of Earliest Christianity*, ed. Jacob Neusner et al. (Atlanta: Scholars Press, 1992); and Nahum Rakover, "The One vs. the Many in Life and Death Situations," in *Jewish Law Association Studies VIII: The Jerusalem 1994 Conference Volume*, ed. E. A. Goldman (Atlanta: Scholars Press, 1996), 129–53. I will discuss this concept further in a forthcoming publication about Nephi's slaying of Laban (1 Nephi 4:13).

28. Haim H. Cohn, "Rebellious Son," in Elon, *Principles of Jewish Law*, 492, explaining that the rebellious son, according to the Talmud, was to be killed before he committed a serious crime, since "God considered it better for him to die innocent than to die guilty." See TB *Sanhedrin* 8:5, 71b–72a.

29. Saul Berman, "Law and Morality," in Elon, *Principles of Jewish Law*, 153.

30. "*mi-penei tikkun ha-olam.*" Berman, "Law and Morality," 154, explains that the Jewish law was expanded, mostly in societal laws, "to encompass as broad as possible a range of morally desirable behavior."

31. James L. Rasmussen, "Blood Vengeance in the Old Testament and Book of Mormon" (FARMS Preliminary Report, 1981). See also Wayne T. Pitard, "Vengeance," in *The Anchor Bible*

but the need for one of Gideon's next of kin to avenge his death had long been superseded by such rules as Exodus 21:12–14, Numbers 35:1–34, and Deuteronomy 21:1–9, which took the matter out of the hands of individuals and made it a mandatory duty of the "congregation" or the "elders" to slay the killer: "*Ye* shall take no satisfaction [i.e., money] for the life of a murderer, which is guilty of death: but he shall be surely put to death" (Numbers 35:31; emphasis added). If the judges did not prevent or punish the shedding of "innocent blood," the guilt of blood attached to all their people.[32] Alma reflected his awareness of this public duty in his concern that Gideon's blood would come upon himself and all his people if Nehor were not executed: "His blood would come upon us" (Alma 1:13).

Another factor at work here was the newly promulgated law of Mosiah. In homicide cases after Mosiah's reign, Nephite law clearly continued to require "the life of him who hath murdered" (Alma 34:12; see 1:18; 30:10). Convicted of a culpable slaying, Nehor was thus "condemned to die, according to the law which has been given us by Mosiah, our last king" (1:14).

Alma went on, however, to state that the newly adopted law of Mosiah "has been acknowledged by this people; therefore this people must abide by the law" (Alma 1:14). One may wonder why Alma appended this additional justification for the sentence he imposed. Alma's reminder may have been designed to quell the protests from Nehor's followers that surely were to follow. Alma's resort to popular authority may also have served to reinforce the power of the newly arranged system of judges to impose the death penalty. The power to judge that had been expressly granted to these judges (Mosiah 29:11) would seem to include the implied power to sentence and carry out punishments, but such a conclusion was not necessarily a given. Toward the end of the era of the Nephite judges, for example, it was technically the case that all death sentences had to be approved by the governor of the land (3 Nephi 6:22–23), demonstrating that the power to execute death sentences was a subject of tight control in Nephite society. It seems that Alma was the first to claim for the new judges under the law of Mosiah the power not only to judge but also to execute; he justified doing so on the ground that since the people themselves had no

---

Dictionary, ed. David Noel Freedman et al., 6 vols. (New York: Doubleday, 1992), 6:786–87; M. Athidiyah, "Scapegoat" (in Hebrew), *Beit Mikra* 6 (1961): 80; and Klaus Koch, "Der Spruch 'Sein Blut bleibe auf seinem Haupt' und die israelitische Auffassung vom vergossenen Blut," *Vetus Testamentum* 12, no. 4 (1962): 346–416.

32. Cohn, "Homicide," 475–76; Hyman E. Goldin, *Hebrew Criminal Law and Procedure* (New York: Twayne, 1952), 22; and Falk, *Hebrew Law in Biblical Times,* 73. See Numbers 35:33; Deuteronomy 19:10; 21:8.

option open to them but to execute the murderer (Alma 1:18; 30:10), the judge, empowered by the voice of the people, could and should carry out or supervise the execution of that eventuality himself. Here again, Alma's conduct conforms with biblical law: "The judge's duty also included the execution of the punishment."[33]

Nehor's Confession

As was typically required,[34] "it came to pass that" Nehor was taken to a place of execution, where "he was caused, or rather did acknowledge, between the heavens and the earth, that what he had taught to the people was contrary to the word of God" (Alma 1:15). Ancient executions happened without delay (Leviticus 24:23; Numbers 15:36; 1 Kings 21:13). Notably, the Mishnah would later require specifically that the confession take place near the place of execution—only ten cubits away.[35] Similarly, Alma's record concisely states that "they carried him upon the top of the hill Manti, and *there* he was caused" to confess (Alma 1:15; emphasis added).

From the fact that Nehor "was caused" to confess (or at least was given occasion under pressures beyond his control to confess), one is tempted to conclude that Nehor did not offer his confession completely willingly. He would, of course, have been given the opportunity to confess that he had shed innocent blood by enforcing priestcraft with the sword. That would have been the normal confession, since that was the crime for which he was being executed. But the personal incentive for making such a confession was presumably to improve one's lot in the world to come before the judgment bar of God, and Nehor could not make any such confession without repudiating his own teaching that "all men should have eternal life," for he believed that God had unilaterally "redeemed all men" (Alma 1:4). Thus it seems that a confession more acceptable to Nehor had to be formulated, namely an admission that "what he had taught to the people was contrary to the word of God" (v. 15), which is all he ultimately confessed. In other words, we can see that Nehor confessed the minimum amount possible. Indeed, Nehor had "termed" his teachings "the word of God" (v. 3); in doing so, he must have known that his teachings were patently contrary to "the word of God" as Alma understood and used that term. Accordingly, Nehor could confess voluntarily that he had taught the people "contrary to [Alma's] word of God," even if making this confession

---

33. Falk, *Hebrew Law in Biblical Times*, 61.

34. See the analysis of Sherem's confession, discussed in chapter 5 above. See also Bovati, *Re-Establishing Justice*, 95–96.

35. TB *Sanhedrin* 6:3, 43b.

was not formulated from his point of view or stated entirely of his own volition. That his confession was obtained under duress seems confirmed by the fact that Nehor's followers did not abandon his doctrine as a consequence of his confession.

An Ignominious Death

Finally, Nehor was "carried . . . upon the top of the hill Manti" (Alma 1:15). Apparently he did not go willingly, for he had to be "carried" to the place where he was executed. That place was evidently outside of town, where places of execution were typically located.[36] The top of the hill Manti could have been selected as the place of execution for several reasons. First, Nehor made his confession "between the heavens and the earth" (v. 15); the top of a hill or mountain served as a meeting ground between heaven and earth, between God and man. There Nehor's confession could be made binding both in heaven and on earth, both for his own eternal benefit and for the sake of the city of Zarahemla. In a sense, the hilltop, representing a cosmic mountaintop, was also a no-man's-land, between sky and earth, where neither the heaven above nor the earth below needs to receive the vile offender.[37] The place between heaven and earth was also seen in the Hebrew Bible as a place of divine judgment: "And David lifted up his eyes, and saw the angel of the Lord stand between the earth and the heaven, having a drawn sword in his hand" (1 Chronicles 21:16). Thus, in this symbolic view of the universe, the location selected for Nehor's confession was a potent place for the final confirmation and execution of Alma's judgment.

Second, a hilltop would have been a likely place for a stoning, and Nehor was probably stoned, since that was the prescribed form of ordinary execution for a punishable homicide (e.g., Leviticus 24:23; Numbers 15:36; 1 Kings 21:13; 2 Chronicles 24:21).[38] According to rabbinic law, the person being stoned was usually pushed off a high place into a pit so that the impact of the fall would knock him unconscious or seriously injure him and so that the witnesses and the people standing above him could then cast their stones down on him more effectively;[39] perhaps for similar reasons, Nehor was taken to a high place for his execution. Still,

---

36. See the discussion of Abinadi's execution in chapter 6 above. See also 1 Kings 21:13; Deuteronomy 17:5; 21:19–21; and Goldin, *Hebrew Criminal Law*, 131n2.

37. Hugh W. Nibley, *The Prophetic Book of Mormon*, ed. John W. Welch (Salt Lake City: Deseret Book and FARMS, 1989), 250.

38. Haim H. Cohn, "Capital Punishment," in Elon, *Principles of Jewish Law*, 526.

39. TB *Sanhedrin* 6:5, 45a; and Haim H. Cohn, "Capital Punishment," in Elon, *Principles of Jewish Law*, 527.

the possibility that Nehor was executed by the sword cannot be ruled out since that mode of execution was reserved for apostates (Deuteronomy 13:15). Moreover, an execution in this manner would have followed the talionic principle of fashioning the punishment to mirror the crime, and Nehor had attempted to enforce priestcraft by the sword. It seems likely, however, that if he had been executed in this more remarkably symbolic manner, something would have been said to that effect.

Third, after the person was executed, his body was hung upon a tree to be conspicuously displayed: "If a man have committed a sin worthy of death, and he be to be put to death, and thou hang him on a tree: His body shall not remain all night upon the tree" (Deuteronomy 21:22–23).[40] The person so hung was "accursed of God" (v. 23), and thus his death was shameful and "ignominious" (Alma 1:15).[41]

Further insult and infamy could have been added if Nehor's body was denied a burial or if his body, like the prophet Urijah's, was cast into a common grave (Jeremiah 26:23). In Isaiah's poetic prophecy of the fall of a tyrant, the king suffers the disgrace of not being buried: "Thou shalt not be joined with them in burial, because thou hast destroyed thy land, and slain thy people" (Isaiah 14:20). Thus, denying Nehor the dignity of a burial, which would have infuriated his followers, may also have been part of the ignominy of Nehor's death, carried out so that the "land not be defiled" (Deuteronomy 21:23).

Aftermath

The trial of Nehor rightly stands at the beginning of the book of Alma. Undoubtedly, many other important events occurred in the first year of the reign of judges, but none was so noteworthy as the trial of Nehor, the main event reported for that year. This proceeding was a monumental case in the political and religious history of the Nephites. It was also a crucial test case and a defining moment in the life of Alma the Younger, whose professional involvement and theological interest in legal matters remained a strong thread throughout his life.

Alma himself probably recorded the details of this case in his own initial writings. As one would expect from a man who was a jurist by profession, legal cases or concepts are witnessed in many of Alma's writings.

---

40. "Persons put to death for public crimes were mostly stoned and then hanged." Falk, *Hebrew Law in Biblical Times*, 73. See Raymond Westbrook, "Punishments and Crimes," in *Anchor Bible Dictionary*, 5:546–56.

41. Webster's *American Dictionary of the English Language* (1828) refers to hanging, whipping, cropping, and branding as ignominious punishments; s.v. "ignominious."

Legal principles pervade Alma's detailed account of his encounters at Ammonihah (Alma 9–16),[42] and the same is true for the account of his involvement in the trial of Korihor (Alma 30)[43] and his elaborate explanation of the operation of justice and mercy to his son Corianton (Alma 42). As prologue to the book of Alma, the case of Nehor rightly stands as a guiding example of Alma's concept of judging righteously, by showing how Alma creatively fashioned a punishment that was suitable to the facts and requirements of the particular case, by demonstrating Alma's concern for avenging the innocent blood of the slain Gideon, and by protecting society by condemning and deterring acts of violence.

Moreover, the political and legal ramifications of the trial of Nehor established how the new system of judges would work. With this case as an unforgettable precedent, not only could the chief judge correct and censure the lower judges, but he could also take original jurisdiction over certain cases brought to him, and he would be able to enforce his verdicts. While this case enlarged the defined authority of the chief judge, it also effectively shifted the balance of political power somewhat away from the voice of the people and the lower, more popular judges. The provisions in Mosiah's reforms that guaranteed equality (Mosiah 29:38) and freedom of belief (Alma 1:17) had the potential of being interpreted very broadly to expand the powers of the diffuse democratic factions in the land of Zarahemla. Any such tendency to expand those provisions excessively, however, was deterred by the holding in Nehor's case. More than simply prohibiting people from enforcing their beliefs by physical compulsion, the trial of Nehor tended to disable Nehor's followers and to alienate them from the new reign of judges. Furthermore, the fact that Alma went out of his way to exculpate and exonerate Gideon from any wrongdoing in this case must have emboldened the members of the church to perform their duty to prevent people in other religious groups from trespassing the laws of God or of the state.

Nevertheless, it seems likely that these legal developments and attitudes contributed to the polarization of segments of Nephite society that quickly ensued. The followers of Nehor had to be careful to preach only those doctrines that they sincerely believed, for otherwise they now could be punished for lying (Alma 1:17). People outside Alma's church began

---

42. See the discussion of the trial of Alma and Amulek in chapter 8 below. The compiler or abridger introduced the account of those events in the Nehorite city of Ammonihah with the caption "the words of Alma," proving that the accounts of these legal events can be attributed to Alma himself.

43. See chapter 9 below.

a verbal persecution of those in the church; and while members of the church were strictly prohibited from persecuting any people who did not belong to the church (v. 21), many church members "began to contend warmly with their adversaries, even unto blows" (v. 22). Significantly, they hit each other only with their fists because the case of Nehor had made it clear that it was illegal to enforce one's religious beliefs with a weapon, but the holding said nothing about other kinds of striking.

Almost certainly as a result of this verdict and execution, the rift between the people of Christ and members of other groups within the community deepened in the second year of the reign of judges. Recalcitrant and bellicose members of the church were excommunicated (Alma 1:24), undoubtedly becoming bitter enemies to Alma and the church. In the fifth year of the judges, violent hostilities erupted. Amlici, "being after the order of the man that slew Gideon by the sword, who was executed according to the law" (2:1), had drawn away many people after him and had become "very powerful" (v. 2). It makes sense to see Amlici as Nehor's successor or at least as his champion. Amlici not only opposed the reforms of Mosiah, but he probably argued that the execution of his mentor was a flagrant miscarriage of justice. He sought to scrap the government formed by Mosiah; Amlici and his people wanted to return the form of government in Zarahemla to a kingship and "to establish Amlici to be king over the people" (v. 2).

Amlici's reaction constituted a rejection of everything that Alma and the reforms of Mosiah stood for. Political support for this opposition movement must have gathered momentum from several sectors in Zarahemla: more than ever, the Mulekites (who descended from Mulek, the son of Zedekiah, the last king of Judah before the exile) would likely have wanted to see the return of the kingship; the aristocratic Nephites or priests (who had been displaced or left unemployed as a result of the reforms of Mosiah and Alma), the followers of Nehor, and the excommunicated church members whose names were "blotted out" (Alma 1:24) would also have felt increasingly alienated from the Nephite leaders. In less than five years after the trial of Nehor, Alma thus found himself engaged in a life-and-death struggle against Amlici's group in an effort to maintain the Nephite reign of the judges.

Alma was deeply involved in this problem. He personally fought a bloody civil war against the insurgent Amlici. Despite his victory over Amlici, Alma grew uncomfortable with the situation. War takes a devastating toll on its participants, and Alma now shouldered the responsibility for not only the judicial execution of Nehor and his own hand-to-hand killing of Amlici in battle but also the terrors of a civil war in the land of Zarahemla that ended in the death of many friends and brothers on both sides of the dispute. Did he feel sorry about the consequences of the trial of Nehor? Did he grow uncomfortable bearing the burdens of being a judge and having to make hard decisions that triggered explosive repercussions?

Averting any accusation that he himself had enforced his beliefs by the sword, Alma eventually—after eight rigorous years of service as the chief judge—relinquished all of his military, judicial, and political responsibilities (Alma 4:16–20). He did this in order to go forth preaching "the word of God" (to reclaim the phrase that Nehor had co-opted), pulling down "all the pride and craftiness and all the contentions which were among his people" and "bearing down in pure testimony" against the people in an effort to establish righteousness and justice "according to the spirit of revelation and prophecy" (vv. 19–20).

But even Alma's victory over Amlici and his impassioned spiritual ministry did not stem the tide of fragmentation or put an end to Nehorism. For a time, the Zoramites remained loyal to the Nephites, but not for long. In the next few years, the Zoramites would leave Zarahemla, moving northward, to claim and settle the land of Antionum and to build a city of their own where their ruling class would exploit the poor and fundamentally oppose the Nephite ideals of social justice and economic equality. At the same time, Nehorism would gather strength to the south of Zarahemla in the city of Ammonihah, which would become the seat of legal corruption and injustice against Alma himself. Ammonihah would remain a hotbed and stronghold of the Nehorites until it was reduced to a "heap," going down in infamy as the "Desolation of Nehors" (Alma 16:11), as the next legal case in the Book of Mormon will show.

CHAPTER EIGHT

The Trial of Alma and Amulek

Nine years after the execution of Nehor and four years after Alma's military victory over Amlici, who was an ardent follower of Nehor (Alma 2:1), Alma relinquished the judgment seat to Nephihah (4:15–18) and set out on a religious mission to preach the word of God, to recommit the righteous (5:26), and to excommunicate the unrepentant (6:3). After considerable success in the cities of Zarahemla, Gideon, and Melek, Alma met the greatest challenge of his tenure as high priest upon arriving at the city of Ammonihah. While Alma's prayers that he might win a few converts in Ammonihah were answered by the conversion of a few local residents who believed and repented (8:10; 10:10; 15:1–3), he and his main convert, Amulek, were arrested, accused, and held by these Nehorites for more than a month in prison.

Nehorism had taken so firm a hold in Ammonihah that one wonders if it might not have once been Nehor's home or primary region. Not only was the chief judge in that city a leader "after the order and faith of Nehor" (Alma 14:16), but the general population there subscribed to Nehorism and refused to acknowledge Alma's priesthood, all of which is evident from their words and deeds, the popularity of Zeezrom's arguments, and the fierce hostility harbored by the people against Alma (8:12–13). Moreover, when Ammonihah was destroyed, it was called the "Desolation of Nehors" (16:11).

Alma 8–14 gives a jarring account of Ammonihah's perversion of justice. In this case, Alma and Amulek were wickedly imprisoned, and the women and children of their followers were viciously executed. These manifold miscarriages of justice and administrative abuses, coupled with the conclusive denomination of the city of Ammonihah as an apostate city, provided irrefutable evidence that divine justice was properly served when that city was reduced to a putrid heap shortly afterward by an invading Lamanite army.

Alma and Amulek's experiences in Ammonihah also reveal much of the Hebraic legal traditions inherited by the Nephites. While only a few elements of these proceedings are mentioned expressly in Alma 9–16, they provide interesting insights about the legal system in Ammonihah during the early years of the Nephite reign of judges.

The account recorded in these eight chapters bears the definite fingerprints of Alma as a firsthand participant in the events that transpired during these unforgettably searing months. The account is lengthy and detailed. Speeches and statements by accusers and interrogators are presented in the kind of insightful depth and legal precision that would be worthy of a person, such as Alma, who had extensive experience in the administration of justice. Moreover, the closing of this case in Ammonihah tied up the last remaining loose end in Alma's legal, political, military, and religious campaigns against Nehorism. The destruction of Ammonihah vindicated Alma's determined civic stance. With the eradication of this nest of unrighteousness, Alma's priestly duties were also fulfilled, ridding the land of Zarahemla of this source of abominations. The case also had great personal significance for Alma. Several years later, he would poignantly remember being delivered "from prison, and from bonds, and from death" (Alma 36:27), almost certainly referring to his imprisonment here in Ammonihah. In addition, the conversion of the very shrewd lawyer Zeezrom, whom the record goes out of its way to present as a formidable forensic opponent, must have been especially gratifying to Alma, the former judge. By giving such a full account of Amulek's faithfulness, Alma certainly went a long way toward validating Amulek in the eyes of his associates in Zarahemla. When he returned to Zarahemla with Amulek, he took him into his confidence as a prominent companion in church affairs (Alma 31:6). While Mormon for various reasons would have found this episode worthy of occupying so much space in his final abridgment of the Nephite records,[1] many factors in this account point strongly and reliably toward Alma as its primary author.

"Thou Hast No Power over Us"

Alma went to Ammonihah "to preach the word of God unto them" (Alma 8:8). He exercised faith and prayed, pleading with the Lord to pour out

---

1. Mormon took particular interest in bringing people to repentance and to walk in wisdom's paths (Helaman 12:5, 22), warning people that they will be destroyed if they reject the prophets (Mormon 1:19) and preparing people to "stand before the judgment-seat of Christ, to be judged according to [their] works" (Mormon 6:21). All of these themes are strongly manifested in the words of Alma and the events that ensued upon their rejection.

his Spirit upon the people, but "Satan had gotten great hold upon the hearts of the people" (v. 9), and they would not listen. Raising a serious jurisdictional objection both as text and pretext, the people of Ammonihah argued that "because we are not of thy church we know that thou hast no power over us" (v. 12). They resisted Alma's words and treated him rudely and disrespectfully: they reviled him, spat on him, and cast him out of the city (v. 13).

While it was a crime to curse a political ruler under the law of Moses (Exodus 22:28)—to which the Nephite people adhered (2 Nephi 25:24)—Alma was no longer the chief judge over the land; he was now only the high priest (Alma 8:11). Apparently the people of Ammonihah depended heavily on this jurisdictional argument in justifying their position and in rationalizing their behavior. Perhaps they based their reasoning on the fact that an extraordinary grant of authority from King Mosiah to Alma the Elder had been required to give Alma the Elder authority to judge others in religious matters (Mosiah 26:8, 12), and now that Alma the Younger was no longer the chief judge he lacked any such authority with respect to the city or people of Ammonihah. Even more to the point, perhaps they recalled that Alma himself had taken jurisdiction over the trial of their leader Nehor—a judicial assertion of power to which the people of Ammonihah no doubt objected and took exception. For that reason, perhaps, they intentionally turned the tables on Alma and taunted him because he no longer held political jurisdiction over their city.

At this time in Nephite history, "the law could have no power on any man for his belief" (Alma 1:17; see 30:7). Therefore, even though Alma was the high priest over the land of Zarahemla, people in that land were free to distance themselves from any particular religious organization. Thus, religious iniquity or sinfulness in Ammonihah was protected under the law of Mosiah from legal prosecution, unless it resulted in prohibited overt conduct. Being wicked or apostate were religious offenses for which the people of Ammonihah could not be officially punished, either under the laws of the land or by the church over which Alma had authority (8:12).

After being rejected on the basis that he had no authority over the people, Alma left Ammonihah but was soon commanded by God to return and condemn the city: "Say unto them, except they repent the Lord God will destroy them," for they had begun to "study" ways in which they might "destroy the liberty of thy people" (Alma 8:16–17). Because they sought to destroy the liberty of the people in the land of Zarahemla, the warning decree set forth nothing less than their own destruction.[2]

---

2. Indeed, destruction becomes a dominant leitmotif in chapters 9–16: the words *destroy*, *destroyed*, and *destruction* are found a total of thirty-five times throughout this narrative.

Alma Received by Amulek

Alma returned to Ammonihah and was received by Amulek, a promi-nent local resident of the city. Amulek was proud of his distinguished Nephite ancestry (Alma 10:2–4), but it probably alienated him from the anti-Nephite crowd in Ammonihah. Amulek's family was probably used to distinction, as shown by Amulek's awareness (and apparently his audi-ence's as well) of his ancestor who interpreted miraculous writing on the temple wall (v. 2). Amulek himself soon received guidance from an angel of the Lord. On the fourth day of the seventh month, Amulek left home to visit close kindred (vv. 6–7). Perhaps he and his family were on their way to celebrate a traditional Israelite feast with extended family, for the seventh month was a prime festival time on the annual calendar under the law of Moses. Indeed, if the Nephite calendar began the year in the fall, then their seventh month fell in the spring and was the month of Passover; otherwise, if their calendar began in the spring, the seventh month was in the fall, the time of Rosh Hashanah, the Feast of Tabernacles, and Yom Kippur.[3] Assuming that Amulek was traveling to be with his close family relatives during the Passover season, perhaps he anticipated that Elijah was coming when the angel told him to return home to "feed a prophet of the Lord" (v. 7).[4] Although the visitor turned out not to be Elijah com-ing before "the great and dreadful day of the Lord" (Malachi 4:5), Alma did come to announce the day of destruction in the city of Ammonihah. Indeed, in that very year, the destroying angel passed over only the few in that land who were willing to receive Alma's message.

Alma stayed as a guest in Amulek's household. In ancient society, an out-of-town traveler typically needed to have a local patron in order to re-

---

3. For a discussion of the ancient Israelite calendar and the festivals of the first and seventh months, see Terrence L. Szink and John W. Welch, "King Benjamin's Speech in the Context of Ancient Israelite Festivals," in *King Benjamin's Speech: "That Ye May Learn Wisdom,"* ed. John W. Welch and Stephen D. Ricks (Provo, UT: FARMS, 1998), 147–223, esp. 149–58.

4. Elijah called himself "a prophet of the Lord" in his famous confrontation against the priests of Baal: "I, even I only, remain a prophet of the Lord" (1 Kings 18:22). Although this title appears on a few other occasions in texts about the time of the First Temple (1 Samuel 3:20; 1 Kings 22:7; 2 Kings 3:11; 2 Chronicles 28:9), Elijah's declaration to the people that he alone re-mained as "a prophet of the Lord" could well have associated him with this distinctive title, which is the precise phrase used by the angel who spoke to Amulek. The return of Elijah, who was taken up into heaven (2 Kings 2:11) was prophesied as early as Malachi 4:5, a little after the time of Lehi. Although the traditions about the cup of Elijah at Passover and his role at the judgment of the world cannot be documented into pre-exilic times (Abraham P. Bloch, *The Biblical and Historical Background of Jewish Customs and Ceremonies* [New York: KTAV, 1980], 237–39), Elijah loomed large enough in pre-exilic Israel that expectations of his return may have originated in that era.

main legally or comfortably within a city.[5] Amulek's hospitality may have rankled his fellow citizens, for Alma had already been expelled from town (Alma 8:13). Although Alma prudently waited awhile before he began preaching to the townspeople, it seems unlikely that he, a person of public stature, could have remained at Amulek's home for some time ("many days," according to v. 27) without his presence there becoming somewhat known in the community. Hosting Alma must have sooner or later ostracized both Amulek and his family socially since Amulek's actions were, in effect, acts in defiance of the prior determination of the town elders who had expelled Alma.

After "many days" as a house guest instructing Amulek, Alma spent a few days preaching and converting a group of loyal followers (Alma 14:7) before he and Amulek were cast into prison, where they likewise spent "many days" (v. 22). They were liberated on the twelfth day of the tenth month when the walls of the prison were brought down on their accusers (vv. 23–27). There was a total of three months and eight days (about one hundred days) between Alma's return to Ammonihah and this deliverance from prison. If this total time was divided about equally between two periods of "many days," Alma and Amulek first spent about fifty days together before their imprisonment and then suffered about fifty days in prison. However, if Alma and Amulek delivered their public message during or at the end of that same "seventh month" (as might be indicated in Amulek's speech when he said, "I went on rebelling against God, in the wickedness of my heart, even until the fourth day of *this* seventh month," 10:6), then Alma spent about twenty-five days instructing Amulek and his group of converts, and he and Amulek spent the eighth, ninth, and part of the tenth month, or about seventy-five days, in prison.

After those days of instruction and private association with Alma, Amulek was converted and called to "go forth and prophesy" that if the people would not repent, the Lord would not turn away his "fierce anger" (Alma 8:29). Amulek accepted the call, and together he and Alma commenced their public mission (9:1). The exact text and precise date of their judgment speech is not known, but fifty days after Passover would place their public declaration, like Abinadi's, very close to the time of the Feast

---

5. "Travellers often had no alternative to using private hospitality. And private hospitality continued to play a significant role long after the increased pace of movement had planted inns all over the land. Traders counted on being lodged with business associates, the noble or wealthy with their influential friends, and the humble with whoever would take them in. Families in different cities united by ties of friendship extended hospitality to each other from generation to generation." Lionel Casson, *Travel in the Ancient World* (London: George Allen & Unwin, 1974), 87.

of Pentecost, a time traditionally associated with remembering the law and calling the nation to repentance.[6]

Evidently, Alma prophesied that the earth would pass away (Alma 9:2) and that the city of Ammonihah would be destroyed "in one day" (v. 4). The people of Ammonihah found these two ideas preposterous, but Alma's prophecy about the single-day destruction was eventually fulfilled and duly recorded (16:10).

The Need for Two Witnesses

The people of Ammonihah rejected Alma's testimony out of arrogance and incredulity, to be sure, but their rejection also had legal grounds. Their penchant for legal detail manifests itself when they reject Alma's testimony on the technicality that he appeared to be a sole witness or testifier.[7] Rather than addressing the truthfulness of Alma's claims by accusing him of being a false witness or a false prophet (as had been the failed strategy of King Noah and his priests against Abinadi), these people argued that if God were to condemn this city as an apostate city, he would need more than one witness to stand against it in such a weighty matter: "Who art thou? Suppose ye that we shall believe the testimony of one man, although he should preach unto us that the earth should pass away? . . . Who is God, that sendeth no more authority than one man among this people?" (Alma 9:2, 6). An accusation such as this one for apostasy, they correctly and forcefully argued, needed to be supported by two witnesses: "If there be found among you, within any of thy gates . . . transgressing his covenant, and hath gone and served other gods, . . . at the mouth of two witnesses, or three witnesses, shall he that is worthy of death be put to death; but at the mouth of one witness he shall not be put to death" (Deuteronomy 17:2–6). In general, pentateuchal law required that "one witness shall not rise up against a man for any iniquity, or for any sin, in any sin that he sinneth: at the mouth of two witnesses, or at the mouth of three witnesses, shall the matter be established" (19:15; see 17:6; Numbers 35:30; 1 Kings 21:10).[8]

---

6. See the discussion of Pentecost in connection with the trial of Abinadi, in chapter 6 above.

7. On the problem of single witnesses, see Bernard S. Jackson, "'Two or Three Witnesses'" and "*Testes Singulares* in Early Jewish Law and the New Testament," in *Essays in Jewish and Comparative Legal History*, ed. Bernard S. Jackson (Leiden: Brill, 1975), 153–71, 172–201.

8. On the strong need for two or three witnesses in order to constitute sufficient testimony, especially in the absence of any other documentary or physical evidence (as was the case in Ammonihah), see Bruce Wells, *The Law of Testimony in the Pentateuchal Codes* (Wiesbaden: Harrassowitz, 2004), 84–108. See generally Haim H. Cohn, "Evidence," in *The Principles of Jewish Law*, ed. Menachem Elon (Jerusalem: Keter, 1975), 599; Cohn, "Witness," in Elon, *Principles of Jewish Law*, 605–6; Ze'ev W. Falk, *Hebrew Law in Biblical Times: An Introduction*, ed. John W. Welch, 2nd ed. (Provo, UT Brigham Young University Press; Winona Lake, IN: Eisenbrauns, 2001), 59;

This rule was especially well established and observed about the time of Lehi and during the Neo-Babylonian period.[9]

However, Abinadi had testified alone in the city of Nephi (Mosiah 11:20), and Alma had worked alone in the cities of Zarahemla, Gideon, and Melek (Alma 5:1–2; 6:7–8; 8:4). Prophets delivering judgment speeches or messages of destruction in the Old Testament usually stood and spoke alone, sometimes calling on heaven and earth or prior prophets as their corroborating witnesses. Further, a prophetic warning, accusation, or call to repentance was not precisely equal to a legal indictment.[10] In Ammonihah, however, given the hardness of these people's hearts, a single witness (especially Alma's testimony) would not suffice. Perhaps the people sensed the imminent legal implications that attended Alma's denouncing them as an apostate city, and thus they demanded stronger testimony. In any event, by demanding a second witness, the people of Ammonihah moved Alma's encounter from the sphere of religious exhortation to the domain of the law and unwittingly laid the groundwork for the entrance of Amulek as the required second witness only a short time later.

Moreover, because they invoked the two-witness rule, it seems that the Nehorites accepted the validity of the law of Moses, at least with respect to such points of civil procedure. Similarly, because they believed that God had created all men and had redeemed all men (Alma 1:2–4), it appears that they did not object in principle to the concept of redemption, an important element of the law of Moses; they simply believed that all people had been redeemed. They were not, however, nihilists, anarchists, or antinomians; they clearly took cover behind certain technicalities of the law, and they alleged that Alma had crossed over a legal line by testifying against them. Accordingly, when Alma had made his point, the people tried to lay their hands on him (9:7). Perhaps they thought they could punish him as a single, and therefore false, accuser or on some other legal ground.

Alma's Testimony concerning Accountability

Alma answered the Nehorites' tactic with another bold testimony and interesting response (Alma 9:8–30). His line of reasoning focused on their

---

Hyman E. Goldin, *Hebrew Criminal Law and Procedure* (New York: Twayne, 1952), 234–36; and James E. Priest, *Governmental and Judicial Ethics in the Bible and Rabbinic Literature* (New York: KTAV, 1980), 262.

9. F. Rachel Magdalene, "On the Scales of Righteousness: Law and Story in the Book of Job" (PhD diss., University of Denver and Iliff School of Theology, 2003), 83nn136–38; and Wells, *Law of Testimony in the Pentateuchal Codes*, 108–26.

10. See further the discussion of the prophetic lawsuit in John W. Welch, "Benjamin's Speech as a Prophetic Lawsuit," in *King Benjamin's Speech*, 225–32.

degree of accountability: the higher their level of knowledge, the greater their accountability. His words to the people were firm, reminding them first of their past and asking how it was possible that they could have forgotten the experiences of their fathers and the commandments and blessings of God (vv. 8–10). He cited the Lamanites as a case in point of those who did not keep the commandments and were "cut off from the presence of the Lord" (9:13). Nevertheless, he argued, the Lamanites will fare better "in their state of ignorance" (v. 16) than the people of Ammonihah who transgress "after having had so much light and so much knowledge given unto them" (v. 19); for the Lamanites sin in ignorance, but the people of Ammonihah act in rebellion (vv. 16, 24).

As a principle of law, as well as doctrine, greater understanding implies a higher level of culpability. For example, according to Exodus 21:29, if a man knows that his ox is prone to gore people and the ox kills someone by goring, the owner, as well as the ox, is put to death. Under Jewish law, ignorance of the law was not an excuse that completely exculpated the transgressor;[11] but one's degree of knowledge affected the availability of atonement and forgiveness. Atonement was possible and necessary under the law of Moses for sins committed in ignorance (Numbers 15:27–28). Open rebellion, however, was much more difficult to deal with—if not unforgivable (Numbers 15:30–31; Mosiah 2:33–38). Accordingly, Alma's argument agrees with ancient jurisprudence as well as with sound doctrine: mercy would be far more readily available to the Lamanites than to the Ammonihahites.

Because their hearts were grossly hardened, the people of Ammonihah were condemned several times by Alma to "utter destruction" (Alma 9:12, 18, 24; 10:18, 22). Alma specifically prophesied that "the Lamanites shall be sent" to bring about that utter destruction (Alma 9:18). The words "utter destruction," "utterly destroy," and similar phrases appear almost exclusively in scripture in the Old Testament and in the Book of Mormon. This expression may have had legal connotations. Its main occurrences in the Pentateuch refer to the prescribed annihilation of the Canaanite cities during the Israelite conquest (Numbers 21:2; Deuteronomy 7:2; 12:2; 20:17), and in the historical and prophetic books it is often associated with destroying idolaters, notably the heinous Amalekites (1 Samuel 15; Isaiah 2:18). Thus, in addition to being extremely provocative, this rather distinctive expression appears to have been reserved for use in terminally

---

11. Haim H. Cohn, "Penal Law," in Elon, *Principles of Jewish Law*, 473–74, ties the excuse of ignorance to the talmudic insistence on prior warning. Falk, *Hebrew Law in Biblical Times*, 69, points out that "ignorance of the law" was recognized as an excuse, but "atoning for his misdeed" was still required.

idolatrous cases. Alma's repeated pronouncement of this ultimatum categorized the city of Ammonihah with the worst of the wicked cities ever placed under the divine judgment of obliteration and threatened the city with total eradication and disappearance.

In response, the people immediately sought to imprison Alma (Alma 9:31–32). Even though their Nehorite doctrine, in theory, avowed belief in a God who would redeem all people, Alma's words in Alma 9 were extreme and could not be ignored. The people of Ammonihah lost their composure and became "angry" with Alma, specifically when he accused them of being "a lost and a fallen people" (vv. 30, 32). To these legally minded people, the offensive connotations of being consigned to "utter destruction" escalated to a nearly criminal accusation in the threatening implications of Alma's words when he called them "a lost and a fallen people." Alma thereby effectively identified them as an apostate people under Deuteronomy 13, making them subject to the mandate of annihilation.[12]

The Law of Apostate Cities

As I have shown in more detail elsewhere, it appears highly likely that Alma had Deuteronomy 13:12–17 specifically in mind in his accusation of the wicked people in the city of Ammonihah.[13] That legal text provided that an apostate city should be destroyed and anathematized in a particular way, involving a thorough investigation that produced clear evidence that the inhabitants of the city had withdrawn to serve other gods and had become "children of Belial" (or of Satan, Alma 8:9), followed by execution by the sword, leaving the city as "an heap for ever" (Deuteronomy 13:16). Of course, Alma no longer commanded the armies of the Nephites, and thus he did not have the military power at his disposal to carry out the destruction of an apostate city by his own physical means, but in due time God brought the scourge of war upon the city of Ammonihah at the hands of an invading Lamanite army that would "slay the people and destroy the city" utterly, killing "every living soul" (Alma 16:2, 9).

Amulek's Testimony of Alma's Truthfulness

As Alma was about to be taken to prison, Amulek stepped forward to stand as a second witness in support of Alma's testimony. It must have

---

12. See generally Raymond Westbrook, "Punishments and Crimes," in *The Anchor Bible Dictionary*, ed. David Noel Freedman et al., 6 vols. (New York: Doubleday, 1992), 5:546–56.

13. John W. Welch, "The Destruction of Ammonihah and the Law of Apostate Cities," in *Reexploring the Book of Mormon*, ed. John W. Welch (Salt Lake City: Deseret Book and FARMS, 1992), 176–79; and "Law and War in the Book of Mormon," in *Warfare in the Book of Mormon*, ed. Stephen D. Ricks and William J. Hamblin (Salt Lake City: Deseret Book and FARMS, 1990), 91–95.

taken extraordinary courage for Amulek to rise to this occasion. Up to this point, nothing of a public nature had indicated that anyone could or would be available to serve as a second witness, or more technically as a second accuser, in support of Alma.[14] Amulek proved faithful and potent on this occasion. Later he would similarly serve at Alma's side as a second witness in the wicked Zoramite city of Antionum (Alma 31–35), once again satisfying the demands of the two-witness rule.

Amulek first established and qualified himself as a credible witness by stating his genealogy and his economic status in the community (Alma 10:2–4). One wonders why Amulek introduced himself this way: perhaps he was somewhat unknown to some groups of people in the city, or perhaps it was simply natural and typical for Nephite witnesses to state their credentials at the beginning of their testimony.

Amulek next testified that an angel had told him that Alma was a holy man, and he swore with a solemn oath—"as the Lord liveth"—that Alma spoke the truth (Alma 10:9–10). The swearing of such an oath not only enhanced the seriousness of a witness's demeanor but also exposed him to divine punishment should the testimony be untrue. The commandment "Thou shalt not take the name of the Lord thy God in vain" (Exodus 20:7) has been interpreted to have applied originally to judicial settings and to have prohibited witnesses from implicating God in their act of perjury or false swearing.[15] Moreover, "typically, ancient Near Eastern courts did not impose penalties for false accusation when [the accusers] utilized the oath. Instead, they transferred the responsibility for the execution of justice and the imposition of punishment to the divine realm."[16] Thus, by swearing a divine oath, Amulek may well have shielded himself from human remonstration but exposed himself to divine retribution.

The initial reaction of the people to Amulek's legal maneuver was astonishment (Alma 10:12). The details of Amulek's testimony must have taken them quite by surprise. Some of the people wanted to question Alma and Amulek further, scheming to "catch them in their words, that they might find witness against them," and seeking one of two possible punishments for Alma and Amulek: death or imprisonment (v. 13). But

---

14. For more on witnesses, see Pietro Bovati, *Re-Establishing Justice: Legal Terms, Concepts and Procedures in the Hebrew Bible* (Sheffield, England: JSOT Press, 1994), 236, 263.

15. See Exodus 20:7; Deuteronomy 5:11; Leviticus 19:12; Psalm 24:3–4; Ecclesiastes 9:2; Jeremiah 5:2; Zechariah 8:15–17; Matthew 5:33–39. "He who takes the oath before God (cf. Ex. 22:7–8, 10) brings God's curse on himself if he perjures himself." Haim H. Cohn, "Ordeal," in Elon, *Principles of Jewish Law*, 524. "False or useless swearing by God is one of the grave sins prescribed in the Decalogue." Cohn, "Oath," in Elon, *Principles of Jewish Law*, 616.

16. Wells, *Law of Testimony in the Pentateuchal Codes*, 146.

Amulek, perceiving the plot of the lawyers "as they began to question him" (v. 17), seized the opportunity and took the offensive.

Amulek's Defense and Statement on Collective Responsibility

Amulek did not wait to be questioned. He proceeded immediately to defend himself, accusing the people of "laying traps and snares to catch the holy ones of God" and calling the people "wicked and perverse" (Alma 10:17). Amulek's words may well have recalled Isaiah's curse on those who "lay a snare for him that reproveth in the gate" (Isaiah 29:21), in other words, a curse on those who try to trip up plaintiffs who bring valid actions against the wicked at the town gate or in a public proceeding. To the ancient mind, Amulek's accusation that the people were laying "traps and snares" would have been especially effective since such conduct was unquestionably premeditated. Lying in wait to catch and slay another person, for example, was expressly condemned as reprehensible and despicable conduct (Exodus 21:13–14).

Amulek next made a strong statement about the collective responsibility of people for their ultimate preservation or destruction (Alma 10:22–23). Comparing the situation in Ammonihah to the wickedness of the world "in the days of Noah," Amulek declared that "if it were not for the prayers of the righteous, who are now in the land, that ye would even now be visited with utter destruction" (v. 22). Only by such intercessory prayers were the people collectively spared, and accordingly, "if ye will cast out the righteous from among you then will not the Lord stay his hand; but in his fierce anger he will come out against you" (v. 23). Either through repentance or through rejection of the righteous few, those residing in Ammonihah would choose to rise or fall together.

This concept of collective or corporate responsibility was an important element in ancient Israelite jurisprudence that surfaces at several stages of this case. Under this basic sociolegal concept, each person in a group was held responsible for the collective conduct of "the whole." Thus the blessing or cursing of an entire land or town or family turned on the behavior of any and all of its members. Nuances in the degree of one's culpability or responsibility were overridden by this dominant sense of collective well-being.

The notion of collective responsibility manifests itself on several occasions in the Bible, but nowhere is it more pronounced than in Joshua 7. After divine influence had detected that an Israelite soldier named Achan had violated orders by hiding under his tent floor the booty he had taken in battle, he and his sons and daughters (presumably unaware of what Achan had done), along with all of his animals and property, were stoned to death and burned (vv. 24–25). Other soldiers and all Israel seemed to be suffering innocently because of Achan's wrongdoing. Likewise, in 2 Samuel 21:1–14, one encounters the idea that the bloodguilt of Saul was visited upon him and upon his entire house collectively. Several other biblical texts assume that the nation can be punished for the wrongs of the king.[17]

While modern Western minds might think it unfair for God or society to hold all people in a family or city equally culpable for the wrongs of a few, as a very practical matter the fortunes of ancient communities rose or fell in several immediate senses on the conduct of each and every member. Economically, socially, politically, militarily, and in many other ways, the daily survival of most ancient peoples depended directly on the success and cooperation of the entire group. The fates of entire armies were determined by the success or failure of their heroes, such as David and Goliath, Achilles and Hector, or perhaps to some extent in the face-off between Alma and Amlici (Alma 2:29–33). Thus the idea of collective justice was a significant principle of ancient law, often given precedence over the ideas of individual merit or responsibility, as is widely discussed by biblical law scholars and in classical literature.[18] The concept of collective responsibility also surfaces many times in the Book of Mormon.[19]

Joel S. Kaminsky has written the most recent major treatise on the ancient Israelite concept of collective justice.[20] Among other things, he shows that this concept is best understood as a composite of several theological and human elements. Theologically, it draws conceptual energy from the ideas of divine justice and divine anger; it grounds its legitimacy in the idea of covenant, and it seems fair and plausible in light of the

17. Joel S. Kaminsky, *Corporate Responsibility in the Hebrew Bible* (Sheffield, England: Sheffield Academic Press, 1995). On pages 67–95, Kaminsky provides a thorough analysis of Joshua 7, and on pages 96–113 he discusses 2 Samuel 21. For further discussion by law student Andrew G. Cannon, see "We're All in the Same Boat: Old Testament and Book of Mormon Concepts of Corporate Responsibility as a Complement to Individual Responsibility for Describing Our World" (2006, paper in the Howard W. Hunter Law Library, Brigham Young University).

18. For example, Falk, *Hebrew Law in Biblical Times*, 67–70.

19. Solid papers that have been written over the years on this topic by students in my law school course on ancient laws in the Bible and Book of Mormon include Geoffrey Potts, "Communal Liability and Joint and Several Liability" (1989, paper in the Howard W. Hunter Library, Brigham Young University); and Jeffrey B. Teichert, "The Principle of Collective Salvation in Ancient Israelite Law" (1994, paper in the Howard W. Hunter Law Library, Brigham Young University).

20. Kaminsky, *Corporate Responsibility in the Hebrew Bible*. For further thoughts about the limited circumstances under which group responsibility applies both in ancient and in modern times, see Saul Levmore, "Rethinking Group Responsibility and Strategic Threats in Biblical Texts and Modern Law," *Chicago-Kent Law Review* 71, no. 1 (1995): 85–121.

willing acceptance by people of collective benefits and religious blessings. On the human side, collective responsibility emerges from the general consequences that are naturally thought to arise from human error, sin, and culpability. Bloodguilt also plays a role, making all people subject to the taint. Royal responsibility is also a major factor: if the king is unrighteous, all the people will suffer, and the people are responsible because they requested a monarch (Deuteronomy 17:14; 1 Samuel 8:5). The biblical view of justice is grounded, especially in Deuteronomy, in a strong collective sense of "you" and a vivid sense of divine reward or punishment for collective behavior. Drawing these disparate elements together, Kaminsky argues that the biblical concept of justice is a coherent idea, even though it is a complex mixture of many elements. Accordingly, one need not conclude that the God of biblical justice is arbitrary or unfair. God's wrath and anger may be unleashed, especially for a violation of holiness, even if the transgression is inadvertent.

Amulek understood and invoked many of these elements that played a role in shaping the ancient concept of collective responsibility. He explicitly mentioned divine justice: that God cries by the voice of his angels that he will come down "with equity and justice in my hands" (Alma 10:21). He referred to God's anger: that "in his fierce anger he will come out against you" (v. 23). Amulek cited the group's choice as a source of collective responsibility, warning that destruction will follow "if the time should come that the voice of this people should choose iniquity" (v. 19). He based the people's culpability on the group's "iniquities" (v. 20) and cited the fact that they were collectively warned: "Well doth [God] cry" (v. 20). Moreover, Amulek argued forcefully that the people of Ammonihah were collectively responsible because they had chosen those leaders who "pervert the ways of the righteous" and "bring down the wrath of God upon your heads" (v. 18). Because all of the people together had appointed their judges and lawyers, they were communally responsible for the conduct of those men. Indeed, King Mosiah had made the people vicariously liable for the wrongs of their leaders, not under the old concepts of kingship, but because the new leaders were to be chosen "by the voice of the people" (Mosiah 29:26–27; Alma 10:19). Thus, in a matter of only a few succinct words, Amulek connected virtually all of the elements that were typically associated with the ancient concept of corporate responsibility and thereby boldly formulated his verdict of collective punishment upon the people of Ammonihah as if they lived "in the days of Noah" and the flood (Alma 10:22).

Fortunately, the doctrine of corporate responsibility[21] and its attendant utter destruction has a favorable reciprocal side, namely, collective preservation. Just as the wickedness of a few may lead to the destruction of the entire community, so the righteousness of a few may preserve the whole. Thus Amulek also declared that the prayers of a few righteous people in the city of Ammonihah were all that were preventing the Ammonihahites from already being condemned to "utter destruction" (Alma 10:22–23; see 62:40). Amulek's words may well have drawn to mind the image of Abraham searching and praying to find but ten righteous souls in the cities of Sodom and Gomorrah (Genesis 18). Only because of the prayers of Abraham were those wicked cities temporarily spared. The implicit comparison with Sodom and Gomorrah would not have been flattering to the people of Ammonihah. Even more devastating were the days of Noah, when all flesh was destroyed in divine punishment for the general state of wickedness. But this time, Amulek prophesied that Ammonihah would be destroyed not by flood but by "famine, and by pestilence, and the sword" (Alma 10:22).

Amulek Accused of Reviling and Lying

As soon as he finished his speech, Amulek was accused by the people of "revil[ing] against our laws which are just, and our wise lawyers whom we have selected" (Alma 10:24; 14:2). Unfortunately, we do not have a record of all that Amulek said on this occasion (11:46; 9:34), and from the record we have it is difficult to see why he was accused of reviling against the laws of this people. Whatever he may have said about the laws in general, it would seem that he must have said something aimed at a unique

---

21. For more information on collective responsibility, see Zeʾev W. Falk, "Collective Responsibility in the Bible and the Aggada" (in Hebrew), *Tarbiz* 30 (1960): 16–20; Julien Harvey, "Collectivisme et individualisme (Ez. 18, 1–32 et Jer. 31, 29)," *Sciences Ecclesiastiques* 10 (1958): 167–202; Barnabas Lindars, "Ezekiel and Individual Responsibility," *Vetus Testamentum* 15, no. 4 (1965): 452–67; Dale Patrick, "Collective Address in Deuteronomic Law," in *American Academy of Religion and Society of Biblical Literature*, comp. F. O. Francis (Missoula, MT: American Academy of Religion, 1974), 1–13; Dale Patrick, "The Rhetoric of Collective Responsibility in Deuteronomic Law," in *Pomegranates and Golden Bells: Studies in Biblical, Jewish, and Near Eastern Ritual, Law and Literature in Honor of Jacob Milgrom*, ed. David P. Wright, David Noel Freedman, and Avi Hurvitz (Winona Lake, IN: Eisenbrauns, 1995), 421–36; Anthony Phillips, "Double for All Her Sins," *Zeitschrift für die alttestamentliche Wissenschaft* 94, no. 1 (1982): 130–32; Stanislav Segert, "Bis in das dritte und vierte Glied (Ex 20, 5)," *Communio Viatorum* 1 (1958): 37–39; and Zeʾev W. Weisman, "The Place of the People in the Making of Law and Judgment," in Wright, Freedman, and Hurvitz, *Pomegranates and Golden Bells*, 407–20. On horizontal and vertical reciprocity relating to corporate responsibility that also includes natural disasters as responses to human culpability as well as the responses of nature to human virtue, see Joseph P. Schultz and Lois Spatz, *Sinai and Olympus: A Comparative Study* (Lanham, MD: University Press of America, 1995), 131–73.

aspect of law authorized only in Ammonihah. Perhaps Amulek targeted the way in which they had contrived to pay lawyers in this city. It appears that the law of Mosiah had contemplated the compensation only of judges: "It was in the law of Mosiah that every man who was a *judge* of the law . . . should receive wages" (11:1); "and the *judge* received for his wages according to his time—a senine of gold for a day" (v. 3). But in Ammonihah it had become "the object of these *lawyers* . . . to get gain; and they got gain according to their employ" (10:32). Apparently the law of Mosiah had been expanded in Ammonihah to include "lawyers" within the ambit of the law authorizing compensation of judicial functionaries (v. 27).

In addition, Amulek reviled against these lawyers themselves and by implication reviled the people who had selected those lawyers (Alma 10:24). He accused them of "laying the foundations of the devil," of "laying traps and snares to catch the holy ones of God," and of "laying plans to pervert the ways of the righteous" (vv. 17–18). Amulek's denunciation of the lawyers was tantamount to cursing them or accusing them of adopting a premeditated plot to trap him like an animal in a net or snare. As in the case of "lying in wait" under the law of homicide (Exodus 21:13–14), plotting to expose a person to wrongful harm through a miscarriage of justice would have been seen as a serious element of intentional perversion of the justice system.

Evidently, however, some people in Ammonihah felt very strongly about the justice and validity of their legal system. Their rules were based on significant provisions in the law reform of Mosiah that were crucially important to the less empowered groups in Nephite society. Those provisions protected minority parties and guaranteed that every man would have "an equal chance" (Mosiah 29:38). The fact that the people of Ammonihah had selected their own legal officials and arranged their affairs presumably by the voice of the people gave legitimacy to their public conduct and system (following v. 39). Because Amulek's accusations effectively challenged the freedom and correctness of the legal and religious system in the land of Ammonihah, over which liberty this people only a few years earlier had "exceedingly rejoiced" (v. 39), it is at least understandable that the people of Ammonihah would object and claim that Amulek was wrongfully "reviling" against them at this time. Amulek's accusations must have raised fundamental questions in the minds of these people about the degree to which populations like the Ammonihahites would enjoy freedom from insult and condemnation at the hands of leaders from the dominant Nephite culture. Moreover, although Amulek was a resident of the land of Ammonihah, his background and genealogy would have made it plain to all involved that his predispositions and ultimate loyalties all along were on the side of the Nephites (Alma 10:3).

In response, Amulek adamantly denied the charge that he had reviled their law (Alma 10:26). He claimed, instead, to have spoken in favor of their law, although to their condemnation, by reminding the people that they were indeed free to govern themselves by their own voice, but that Mosiah had also said that "if the time should come that the voice of this people should choose iniquity, . . . they would be ripe for destruction" (v. 19). Amulek admitted, however, that he meant what he had said about "the unrighteousness of [the] lawyers and [the] judges" (v. 27).

Amulek was then accused of lying for claiming that he had not spoken against the law when in fact he had (Alma 10:28). This charge of lying seems to have subsumed the prior accusation of reviling the law, for in the next verse the people seem to drop or diminish the reviling charge, which may have simply transmuted into the charge of reviling the lawyers, and now they accused Amulek of reviling not only "our lawyers" but also now "our judges" (v. 29).

Money in Ammonihah

At this point in the narrative, the text introduces a man named Zeezrom and gives a remarkable explanation of the Nephite system of weights and measures.[22] This system was "established" by King Mosiah (Alma 11:4), apparently as an integral part of his great legal reform. The economic interlude provided in Alma 11 serves several rhetorical purposes in helping readers appreciate various details in Alma's account. By dwelling so long on gold and silver, the text subtly highlights Zeezrom's crass motives, and by pointing out the fact that these weights and measures had been decreed by King Mosiah, the account implicitly corroborates Amulek's point that the people of Ammonihah were bound by all of Mosiah's words, not only some of them. Moreover, this information prepares the reader to assess the value of the bribe (v. 22), which amounted to the equivalent of a judicial salary for about two months' time (vv. 11–13). But perhaps most of all, this interruption shifts the momentum in the debate in favor of Amulek. His devotion to eternal treasures and divine truths shines in contrast with the love of money that motivates Zeezrom.

---

22. For a comparative examination of royal standardization of weights and measures, mathematical fractions and ratios, and the use of weights before coins in the ancient Near East, the laws of Eshnunna, and in Alma 11, see John W. Welch, "Weighing and Measuring in the Worlds of the Book of Mormon," *Journal of Book of Mormon Studies* 8, no. 2 (1999): 36–46.

Paying Judges for Judicial Services

The immediate reason for Mormon's detour into the Nephite system of weights and measures was the need to explain the fact that, under the new law of Mosiah, Nephite judges had become entitled to be paid a daily sum for their service (Alma 11:3). This arrangement had contributed to judicial corruption and bribery in the city of Ammonihah. Significantly, this particular system of weights and measures was somewhat new, having been established ten years earlier by King Mosiah. This innovation among the Nephites accompanied the change from kingship to judgeship and was a radical departure from past judicial practice.

Under the ancient theory of kingship in the Old World, the monarch was generally responsible to ensure the equitable administration of justice throughout his kingdom.[23] If officers were needed to administer court procedures, or law books or tablets were required, or agents were necessary to carry out decrees or judgments, these goods and services either had to be provided voluntarily by the people in the kingdom or the king would need to conscript or pay people to perform these tasks. In a small kingdom, especially where the population was culturally homogeneous and socially coherent, town elders and priests probably provided most of the judicial machinery needed to keep the customary rules of the community operating smoothly.[24] But with the abandonment of kingship at the end of the book of Mosiah, and with the increased diversity of competing social interests that arose at this time among the Nephites, Zoramites, Nehorites, Limhites, Amlicites, and the covenant congregations of Alma, the legal system in the land of Zarahemla became much more complex.

Under Israelite law in ancient times, priests, town elders, or officers of the king served as judicial officials (2 Chronicles 19:8–11).[25] Prior to the law reform introduced by King Mosiah around 91 BC (Mosiah 27:4–5; 29:40–41), it is unlikely that any judges were paid for their services in Nephite society. There is no evidence in the Bible that Israelite towns or cities paid judges or judicial administrators,[26] and the only parties who would

---

23. Keith W. Whitelam, *The Just King: Monarchical Judicial Authority in Ancient Israel* (Sheffield, England: JSOT Press, 1979), 37; and Hans Jochen Boecker, *Law and the Administration of Justice in the Old Testament and Ancient East*, trans. Jeremy Moiser (Minneapolis: Augsburg, 1980), 40–49.

24. Falk, *Hebrew Law in Biblical Times*, 34, 36–50.

25. Falk, *Hebrew Law in Biblical Times*, 36; and Boecker, *Law and the Administration of Justice*, 25–26.

26. See Ruth 4:1–2; Harold B. Clark, *Biblical Law* (Portland, OR: Binfords & Mort, 1943), 260n19, "Originally the judges were not paid"; Haim H. Cohn, "Bribery," in Elon, *Principles of Jewish Law*, 510, "[Judges] are urged to be impartial, and not susceptible to bribes (2 Chronicles

have had a financial interest in paying judges would have been the litigants themselves, and they were forbidden to do so because any such payment was viewed as a form of bribery.[27] The law of Moses strongly prohibited judges from receiving gifts that might in any way influence their opinions (Exodus 23:8). The traditional understanding of this rule held that it precluded the payment of judges in any form, even the giving of gifts of appreciation by a winning litigant long after a case had been closed.[28]

As he fashioned his reform, Mosiah must have realized that his judges would need to be paid in some way if his new system was going to have any chance of succeeding. Switching to a reign of judges involved enormous risks. Who would the judges be? How would they learn their job? Where would they find the time to investigate facts thoroughly and judge righteously according to the law? Sensing the political problems brewing in his own kingdom, and appreciating as an insider the great difficulty and importance of justice in all public affairs, Mosiah chose to provide generously for the new judges: "And the judge received for his wages according to his time—a senine of gold for a day, or a senum of silver, which is equal to a senine of gold; and this is according to the law which was given" (Alma 11:3).

As well-intentioned as Mosiah's program was, it was quickly subject to abuse. Many people who, in all probability, had never served as judges or legal assistants soon realized that for every day they spent working on a case, they could claim a senine (worth one full measure of grain) as a

---

19:7) and reminded that judicial services should be given free (Bek. 29a)"; Herbert Lockyer, *All the Trades and Occupations of the Bible: A fascinating Study of Ancient Arts and Crafts* (Grand Rapids, MI: Zondervan, 1969), 125, "Fees for judgment were not allowed but were regarded as bribery"; Aaron M. Schreiber, *Jewish Law and Decision Making* (Philadelphia: Temple University Press, 1979), 346, citing Babylonian Talmud (TB) *Bekhorot*, chap. 4, Mishnah chap. 6. See also Jacob Bazak, "Judicial Ethics in Jewish Law," *Jewish Law Association Studies III: The Oxford Conference Volume*, ed. A. M. Fuss (Atlanta: Scholars Press, 1987): 27–40.

27. Cohn, "Bribery," 510, "The injunction not to take [or give] bribes is several times repeated in the Bible, twice with the reason given that 'bribes blind the clear-sighted and upset the pleas of the just' (Ex. 23:8; Deut. 16:19). . . . Bribery seems to have been rather widespread (cf. 1 Samuel 8:3), or else the prophets would hardly have denounced it so vehemently (Isa. 1:23; 5:23; 33:15; Ezek. 22:12; Amos 5:12; Micah 7:3)." See Bernard S. Jackson, "Ideas of Law and Legal Administration: A Semiotic Approach," in *The World of Ancient Israel: Sociological, Anthropological and Political Perspectives*, ed. R. E. Clements (Cambridge: Cambridge University Press, 1989), 187–88.

28. Moses Maimonides, *The Code of Maimonides: Book Fourteen, the Book of Judges*, trans. Abraham M. Hershman (New Haven, CT: Yale University Press, 1949), 68–69. See also Clark, *Biblical Law*, 260n19, "Even manifestation of unusual kindness on the part of a judge was frowned upon." Cohn, "Bribery," 511, "Other talmudic jurists carried the rule against bribery to extremes by refusing to sit in judgment over any person who had shown them the slightest courtesy, such as helping them to alight from a boat (Ket. 105a)."

daily wage guaranteed by statute. It is unclear who paid these wages. Perhaps the losing litigants were charged, perhaps the local village took this amount out of common storehouses, or perhaps the central government in the land of Zarahemla had to foot the bill.[29] But whatever the source of the wages was, it would not have taken a genius to figure out that more litigation equaled more personal gain (Alma 11:20). Moreover, though the law itself seemed to contemplate that only a judge would receive wages, the practice soon emerged "that every man who was a judge of the law" and in addition all "those who were appointed to be judges" or lawyers were claiming entitlement to payment (10:32–11:1). Thus it appears that all men involved with the administration of the law (including elected judges, appointed officers, and lawyers) were able to get gain "according to their employ" in these litigations (10:32).[30]

Lawyers in Ammonihah

In this interlude, the narration also mentions briefly the presence of lawyers in the legal system in Ammonihah. Because lawyers are mentioned

---

29. According to Cohn, in the Second Temple period, "originally judges were remunerated from Temple revenues (Ket. 105a), which furnished the legal basis for their remuneration, in later periods, from communal funds. As all members were required to contribute to the communal funds, so were litigants later—as today in the rabbinical courts in Israel—required to pay court fees, not to any particular judge but into a general fund out of which all court expenses were defrayed." Cohn, "Bribery," 511. Maimonides writes that "Karna [a judge of the exile] used to take one *istira* from the innocent party and one *istira* from the guilty party and then informed them of his decision. . . . Karna took [the two *istira*] as a fee . . . [as] compensation for loss of work." Maimonides, *The Code of Maimonides*, 69, cited in Cohn, "Bribery," 511.

30. The Old Testament does not mention lawyers (nor attorneys or advocates), and lawyers are mentioned in the Book of Mormon only after Mosiah's legal reforms (see Mosiah 29), the first mention being in Alma 10:14. Originally, allowing the appointment of judges posed little threat to the government or the society because cases were brought to the judges by the people. But expanding the system so that officials could initiate lawsuits created a blatant conflict of interest. Mosiah probably should have guarded against such distortion and corruption that certainly runs contrary to the spirit of the law of Moses, which prohibits judges from taking bribes or gifts: "Thou shalt take no gift: for the gift blindeth the wise, and perverteth the words of the righteous" (Exodus 23:8; see Deuteronomy 16:19). Jewish law interpreted this provision as prohibiting judges from receiving any compensation at all for serving as a judge, considering any payment or gift to any judge to be equivalent to a bribe. Although Mosiah's judicial program seems to have gotten off to a rocky start, corrections were evidently made quickly enough for the system to endure. After the judicial tragedy in Ammonihah (Alma 14:23–28), the reign of judges became more stabilized. Perhaps the law was clarified so that only the highest-ranking judges received wages and their appointees received less than the full statutory wage, or perhaps some officials were not paid at all. Whatever the reason, there are no further references in the Book of Mormon to unethical lawyers or judicial corruption as such (although in the heyday of the Gadianton robbers, politicians sought power in order to get gain, and perhaps it was by means of exploiting this system or one similar to it that they were able to extort riches from the system; see Alma 60).

rarely in the Book of Mormon (3 Nephi 6:11), it is impossible to determine who these lawyers were, how they were educated, and specifically how they functioned. It does not appear, however, that they were lawyers in the modern sense of that term. The lawyers in Ammonihah were not likely private advocates or independent professional counsel. In the ancient Israelite world, there were no attorneys as we know them today who represented clients in court. The parties were required to appear *pro se*.[31] No evidence indicates that the lawyers in Ammonihah represented clients or served as advocates for clients.

Rather, they were unique officers or officials of the state skilled in the study of the law. What little we know simply says that they were skilled and clever, and their role is described very briefly. They were "hired or appointed by the people *to administer the law* at their times of trials, or at the trials of the crimes of the people before the judges" (Alma 10:14). As state officials, quasi-judges, or rulers, they would have been protected under the principles of the law of Moses from those reviling them (Exodus 22:28).

From the information in Alma 11, it is evident that three groups of judicial functionaries operated in the legal system in the land of Zarahemla: judges, lawyers (Alma 10:14–15), and officers. One can assume that the "officers" mentioned in Alma 11:2 were different from the lawyers and judges (Alma 14:17; 30:29; 3 Nephi 6:11; compare *shoterim* in Exodus 5:6; Deuteronomy 16:18), and thus one might conclude that the officers did not receive the statutory wages paid to judges.[32] Likewise, the "lawyers" were not judges, for at this time they only administered the law at trials before the judges (Alma 10:14).[33]

One wonders whether the lawyers were paid by the state or by the losing party. In 3 Nephi 12:26, Jesus says that the losing defendant will have to pay the "uttermost senine," perhaps implying that the losing party would have to pay the judge's wage as well as any damages. As mentioned above, while the law of Mosiah contemplated that some judges would be elected by the voice of the people and that others could be appointed, it seems clear that Mosiah intended that only those who actually served as judges would be paid (at least Alma 11:1 mentions only "judges" who

31. "For one's own behalf." Haim H. Cohn, "Attorney," in Elon, *Principles of Jewish Law*, 573–74. Cohn explains that this practice changed over time and that the talmudic law allowed attorneys to represent parties in order to avoid injustice.

32. Perhaps these officers performed the same functions as those mentioned in Matthew 5:25; Luke 12:58; John 7:32, 45–46; and Acts 5:22, 26.

33. A century later, lawyers in the land of Zarahemla were powerful players in the process of condemning people, but it appears that they would have needed, even then, to present their condemnation to the governor, either directly or through a judge or high priests (3 Nephi 6:21–22).

should receive wages). In Ammonihah, however, not only the judges but also the lawyers were getting paid, which seems to have been the result of an expansive reading of the intent of the law of Mosiah. Thus it seems that the people in Ammonihah innovatively appointed many lawyers and took the liberty of paying them like judges. Those administrators then corruptly exploited the situation by instigating and encouraging lawsuits so they could charge more in court costs and fees (Alma 11:20). All this is consistent with the important plank in the Nehorite platform that every priest or teacher "ought to be supported by the people" (1:3).

Zeezrom's Interrogation

After the detour into Mosiah's system of weights and measures, the account turns to accusatory questioning by one Zeezrom, who was "the foremost" and "one of the most expert" of the accusers (Alma 10:31). Zeezrom's strategy, reflecting his Nehorite tendencies, was to require Amulek to answer specific questions regarding the nature of God. He gave Amulek little opportunity at first to explain himself or to clarify the apparent contradictions inherent in his answers to Zeezrom's questions.

Before Zeezrom began, he offered Amulek, a man of considerable wealth, a substantial bribe of six onties (Alma 11:22). This was a very large bribe—worth forty-two days of professional labor—large enough that it might not have been taken seriously. Amulek generously discounted Zeezrom's ploy as a disingenuous offer and did not accuse Zeezrom of having made a serious attempt at bribery, but rather accused him of lying (v. 25).

Zeezrom's questions involved the existence of a true God, the coming of the Son of God, and the redemption of sinful people (vv. 26–37). Evidently, Zeezrom was trying to set up a case that Amulek had violated the commandment "Thou shalt have no other gods before me" (Exodus 20:3) when he had Amulek admit that "there is but one God, yet . . . the Son of God shall come" (Alma 11:35). And when he led Amulek to say that Christ would come and that God would not save his people (v. 35), it seems that Zeezrom was promoting two of the main Nehorite doctrines, namely, that Christ would not come (Mosiah 26:2) and that God would surely save all men (Alma 1:4).

When Zeezrom finished, Amulek again accused Zeezrom of lying (Alma 11:36), and Amulek then delivered a detailed statement about the basic elements in the plan of redemption and divine judgment as taught by the Nephites. His points were directly responsive to Zeezrom's stances: God will redeem his people if they will believe and repent; the Son is indeed the "very Eternal Father of heaven and of earth" (v. 39; compare "the

Father of heaven and earth," Mosiah 3:8); and the Son and God the Father, along with the Holy Spirit, are "one Eternal God" (Alma 11:44). Amulek's direct and penetrating response caused the people to be astonished and Zeezrom to tremble, conscious that he was guilty of lying (11:46–12:1).

Alma Accuses Zeezrom of Lying to God

Alma then reentered the proceeding. He accused Zeezrom of lying not only to men but also to God (Alma 12:3–6). This accusation reflects the fact that the underlying purpose of most serious judicial proceedings in the ancient world was to determine the will of God on the subject.[34] Thus all false statements made under an oath sworn in the name of a god and all dishonest declarations pertinent to an investigation through which the divine will would be determined were considered to be tantamount to lying to God.

In response, Zeezrom asked to know more about the resurrection and the judgment (Alma 12:8). However, his questioning took a different tone; given his later defense of Alma and Amulek (14:6–7), he likely asked out of sincere desire to understand. Zeezrom's point of departure makes good sense, coming from a follower of Nehor who "did not believe what had been said concerning the resurrection of the dead" (Mosiah 26:2) and did not understand the need for divine judgment (Alma 1:4).

In answer to Zeezrom's questions, Alma delivered one of his most profound discourses (Alma 12:9–13:20) and called the people of Ammonihah to repentance or, in the alternative, consigned them to destruction (13:20–21). Alma discoursed on the mysteries of God, the creation, the fall of Adam and Eve, the first death, the plan of redemption and happiness, the second death, the priesthood after the order of the Son, ordinances allowing for the remission of sin, repentance, righteousness, and many other sacred themes.[35] Because Alma must have known that many of the people in Ammonihah would not comprehend or accept his message, the point of his elaborate statement must have been to strengthen Amulek and the other faithful men in the audience, to instruct Zeezrom, and simply to warn the rest. Biblical and Jewish law requires that a person be given a full warning before he can be held liable for a transgression (2 Chronicles 19:10; Ezekiel 3:19).[36] Alma's declaration certainly gave

---

34. See the discussion of divine judgment in Falk, *Hebrew Law in Biblical Times*, 50–56.

35. For a discussion of the sacred elements in this speech, see John W. Welch, "The Temple in the Book of Mormon," in *Temples of the Ancient World: Ritual and Symbolism*, ed. Donald W. Parry (Salt Lake City: Deseret Book and FARMS, 1994), 364–67.

36. Cohn, "Penal Law," 473; and "Evidence," 599–600.

everyone present a clear and full understanding of the plan and will of God so that each became fully accountable for any subsequent conduct contrary to the word of the Lord.

Moreover, one of the main themes of Alma's discourse concerned the true nature of the priesthood (Alma 13).[37] The relevance of this subject to the circumstances at hand remains obscure until one realizes that priesthood authority and the nature of priesthood service had been made a major issue by the Nehorites. The people of Ammonihah followed priests after the "order" of Nehor; Alma spoke exclusively of priests after God's holy "order." The people denied Alma's authority over them; his reply in Alma 13 affirmed that he had true authority over them by virtue of his divine calling. The Ammonihahites had fostered their own order of popular priests; Alma in effect repudiated their entire priesthood order and urged them to replace it with the order that Alma represented, the order of the Son of God typified by the most noteworthy ancient high priest, Melchizedek.[38]

Apprehension and Indictment

Following Alma's profound and eloquent oration, however, the majority of the people remained resolute; the priests in Ammonihah were probably especially resentful at Alma's delineation of a priesthood order that supplanted their own. Some of the Ammonihahites repented (Alma 14:1), but most of them took Alma and Amulek, bound them, and delivered them to the chief judge of the land of Ammonihah (v. 4). There a number of witnesses appeared against them (v. 5, see 10:13) who testified of Alma and Amulek's words, which Zeezrom had told them to remember (11:35). Alma and Amulek were taken into custody and held in prison.

Zeezrom's Change of Heart

Upon hearing his own arguments rehearsed and analyzed critically before the chief judge, Zeezrom became "astonished" (Alma 14:6). This cannot mean that he was surprised at what the witnesses said, for Zeezrom himself had expertly crafted the arguments (10:31). What shocked Zeezrom must have been the stark consequences of his shrewdness. He

---

37. Discussed further in John W. Welch, "The Melchizedek Material in Alma 13:13–19," in *By Study and Also by Faith*, ed. John M. Lundquist and Stephen D. Ricks (Salt Lake City: Deseret Book, 1990), 2:238–72. See also Robert L. Millet, "The Holy Order of God," in *The Book of Mormon: Alma, the Testimony of the Word*, ed. Monte S. Nyman and Charles D. Tate Jr. (Provo, UT: Religious Studies Center, Brigham Young University, 1992), 61–88.

38. See, for example, Margaret Barker, "The Great High Priest," *BYU Studies* 42, nos. 3–4 (2003): 65–84.

knew that he had been too clever and manipulative in his debate with Amulek (11:21–46), that he had lied (14:6), and that he himself had been silenced by Amulek's bold response (12:1). To his eternal credit, Zeezrom knew that he could not join the other witnesses in accusing Alma and Amulek, for as one of the accusers he would have to be among those to carry out the punishment or execution (Deuteronomy 17:7).

Zeezrom's reversal was even more dramatic than Alma the Elder's in the trial of Abinadi, for the young priest Alma had probably not taken a leading role in accusing Abinadi but had attentively listened, knowing all along of the iniquity of which Abinadi spoke (Mosiah 17:2). Alma was converted because he knew that Abinadi spoke the truth; Zeezrom changed when he honestly saw that he had perverted justice and had been party to a false accusation. He openly confessed his own legal culpability before the chief judge ("behold, I am *guilty*," Alma 14:7; emphasis added); he testified on behalf of Alma and Amulek ("these men are spotless before God," v. 7) and began to plead their case before the judges and his former cohorts.

Expulsion of the Faithful Men

For their support of Alma and Amulek, all the men of Ammonihah (including Zeezrom) who believed their words were cast out of the city, and other men were sent to "cast stones at them" as they left (Alma 14:7). Why were these men not put to death? Probably because the use of capital punishment had been sharply curtailed under the law of Mosiah. Only for murder, it appears, could a man under ordinary civil conditions be "punished unto death" (30:10). For a man's beliefs, however, he could not be punished (1:17; 30:9). Since it is clear that the Ammonihahites ostensibly operated their legal system under the authority of the law of Mosiah, to which they owed their separate "equality" and right to appoint and pay their own local judges, they would not have dared to repudiate that law by putting these men to death for their beliefs. That would have brought down upon these judges the political powers of the nation from Zarahemla. Instead, they ostracized and expelled these men from their community under a severe ban, or *ḥerem*.[39]

Burning of the Women, Children, and Books

Under that law, however, the women, children, or property of these banished men were even less protected. The law was primarily concerned with the conduct of men: "If a *man* murdereth . . . ," the law read

---

39. For a discussion of *ḥerem*, see Haim H. Cohn, "*ḥerem*," in Elon, *Principles of Jewish Law*, 539–44.

(Alma 34:11; emphasis added).[40] While women and children were highly valued in biblical society, their status was secondary in Israelite law.[41] Women, for example, could not generally serve as witnesses[42] or inherit property equally with their brothers,[43] and their civil rights were in many ways dependant upon the status and situation of their men.[44] Obviously, in Ammonihah the women and children who believed or had been taught to believe in Alma's doctrines were not given the protections of the law of Mosiah ensuring them the freedom of belief. In what must be seen as another perversion of the intent of the law by the men in Ammonihah, the law as it was applied in that city apparently granted no rights to women and children in this regard. They were taken and, along with the men's books, were burned (14:8).

Because women in biblical societies had great potential to teach and influence religious beliefs in the home (e.g., the concerns expressed about marrying women outside the tribes of Israel in Exodus 34:16 and Deuteronomy 7:4), perhaps the people of Ammonihah saw total destruction of the women as the most sure method of guaranteeing that the teachings of Alma and Amulek would not be perpetuated in the community. With the men already expelled from the city, perhaps the people were concerned that, should these women marry again, or should they be allowed to remain and to raise their children to believe in the words of Alma and Amulek, they would—like the wives of Solomon—turn away the hearts of the people "after other gods" (1 Kings 11:4) or walk in ways not favored by the Ammonihahites.

The burning of these women, children, and "holy scriptures" (Alma 14:8) is reminiscent of the expunging of Achan and his property from the camp of Israel in Joshua 7:24–25 and also belongs to the genre of religious war.[45] For his crime, Achan was burned and buried under a great heap of

---

40. The significance that should be given to the fact that "the whole Torah always uses the masculine form" was a subject debated in Jewish law; Cohn, "Witness," 606. Some medieval scholars concluded, for example, that this grammatical detail was not trivial but played a controlling role in defining the legal rights of women. Similar implications may have been drawn by the Nephites regarding application of provisions in their law to women and children.

41. See Carol Pratt Bradley, "Women, the Book of Mormon, and the Law of Moses," *Studia Antiqua* (Summer 2003): 125–71; and Hannah Clayson Smith, "Protecting the Widows and the Fatherless in the Book of Mormon," *Studia Antiqua* (Summer 2003): 173–80.

42. Cohn, "Witness," 606; and Falk, *Hebrew Law in Biblical Times*, 110.

43. Falk, *Hebrew Law in Biblical Times*, 112.

44. "The law, for instance, treated women harshly, whereas custom operated in her favor. . . . While socially the wife was considered her husband's partner ('God said unto *them*' Genesis 1:27–28), assistant ('helper' Genesis 2:18), and mistress of the household (Proverbs 31:10–28), in law she was accorded a lower status." Falk, *Hebrew Law in Biblical Times*, 110.

45. Falk, *Hebrew Law in Biblical Times*, 75.

stones, along with his children, his animals, tents, and property (for some reason his wife is not mentioned), in order to remove evil from the community. One major difference between Achan's day and Alma's, however, was the greater observance in Zarahemla of the rule that "the fathers shall not be put to death for the children, neither shall the children be put to death for the fathers: every man shall be put to death for his own sin" (Deuteronomy 24:16). This rule was evidently a major plank in the doctrines of Nehorism, and it continued to play a part in Korihor's sophistry in arguing that the fall of Adam could not have had a negative moral impact on mankind: "Ye say that this people is a guilty and a fallen people, because of the transgression of a parent. Behold, I say that a child is not guilty because of its parents" (Alma 30:25). Thus it is significant that the Ammonihahites did not burn the women and children in Ammonihah under some theory of vicarious liability for the crimes of their husbands and fathers, but because they had believed or had been contaminated by having been taught to believe in Alma's preaching of the word of God (14:8).

Alma and Amulek as Witnesses

Alma and Amulek were forced to watch the burning at "the place of martyrdom, that they might witness the destruction of those who were consumed by fire" (Alma 14:9). The wicked people of Ammonihah may have wanted them to watch this gruesome scene to intimidate them into retracting the prophecy that the Ammonihahites as a hard-hearted and unbelieving people would "be cast into a lake of fire and brimstone" (14:14; see 12:17). Thus the burning of the women and children was a perverse form of talionic punishment, fashioned to mirror the very words spoken by Alma and Amulek.[46] These two witnesses, however, would not be swayed, and saw in the deaths of these martyrs a different purpose. They watched and became witnesses[47] in order "that [God's] judgments which he shall exercise upon them in his wrath may be just; and the blood of the innocent shall stand as a witness against them" (14:11). This scene was particularly "awful" for Amulek (v. 10). Amulek had "many kindreds" and family in Ammonihah (v. 4). It is possible (even likely, given Alma's sojourn in his house) that a number of those women and children listened to and were converted by Alma. While the men who followed Alma and

---

46. See the discussion of talionic punishments in chapter 13 below.

47. The Hebrew word for witness, *ʿēd*, has at least three meanings: (1) one "who is able to say publicly something of another," (2) an accuser, and (3) one "officially present at an act." J. P. M. van der Ploeg, "Studies in Hebrew Law: The Terms," *Catholic Biblical Quarterly* 12, no. 3 (1950), 257. The third concept of witnessing is present in Alma 14:11; the term is used in the first and second senses in Alma 10:12 and 19, respectively.

Amulek were chased out of the city (v. 7), the women and children—quite possibly Amulek's own wife and children—were burned unspeakably in front of Amulek's eyes.

With this atrocity, the case against Ammonihah, the apostate city, was completed and sealed. The people had been warned, the high priest had made a diligent investigation, and all the righteous men had been driven out of town and their righteous women and children killed. Those left in the city were ripe for destruction. God could thus utterly destroy the city without reservation.

Smiting on the Cheek

After the burning of the innocents, the chief judge approached Alma and Amulek and "smote them with his hand upon their cheeks" several times (Alma 14:14, 15, 17, 20). He returned the next day and "smote them again on their cheeks" and many others did the same, each one taunting, accusing, and threatening Alma and Amulek (v. 20). Many days later, the chief judge and the accusers again returned, each one smiting the prisoners on the cheek and "saying the same words, even until the last" (vv. 24–25).

It would seem that something formulaic was occurring here. Every judge and witness did and said exactly the same thing, one at a time. Although there is no precedent that absolutely confirms this practice in the ancient world, it appears that the slap on the cheek was used in Ammonihah as a form of ritual indictment. Alma and Amulek were slapped on the face and challenged to a legal duel: "Will ye stand again and judge this people, and condemn our law" (Alma 14:20); "If ye have the power of God deliver yourselves from these bands, and then we will believe that the Lord will destroy this people according to your words" (v. 24). Like throwing down the gauntlet, the slap on the face appears to have been the equivalent of the modern notion of "service of process," a legal step in giving notice and obtaining jurisdiction over a defendant. No text displays this more vividly than this incident in Alma 14.

Although it is a novel thesis that the slap on the cheek had procedural, legal significance in this ancient context,[48] there is support for this idea. Physical gestures often accompanied the making of serious oaths and

---

48. For example, most biblical commentators see the slapping or smiting of Jeremiah only as an insult, a beating, or an expression of impatience and improper anger. Gwilym H. Jones, *New Century Bible Commentary* (Grand Rapids, MI: Eerdmans, 1984), 2:368; Carl Friedrich Keil, *Biblical Commentary on the Prophecies of Ezekiel*, trans. James Martin (Edinburgh: T. and T. Clark, 1857), 1:312; George A. Butterick and others, eds., *The Interpreter's Bible* (New York: Abingdon, 1956), 5:969; and William L. Holladay, *A Commentary on the Book of the Prophet Jeremiah* (Philadelphia: Fortress, 1986), 542.

the incurring of legal obligations.[49] Although the symbolic function of this slapping remains obscure, it is significant that smiting on the cheek is mentioned four times in the Old Testament in connection with judicial process or legal punishment: the prophet Micaiah was smitten on the cheek before being sentenced to prison by Zedekiah (1 Kings 22:24–27); Jeremiah was smitten perhaps on the face by Pashur and put in the stocks as the officer of the temple in Jerusalem tried to maintain order there (Jeremiah 20:2); in a twist of irony against the judges who imposed such sanctions, Micah wrote, "They shall smite the judge of Israel with a rod upon the cheek" (Micah 5:1); and Isaiah spoke of turning his back to smiters and his cheeks to those who plucked out the hair, being shamed and spit upon but knowing that God would justify the righteous against those who contend against them and accuse them (Isaiah 50:6–9).

An eighth-century BC Aramaic treaty curse likewise reads, "[and just as this wax woman is taken] and one strikes her on the face, so may the [wives of Matiʾel] be taken [and . . .]."[50] Jesus also was smitten while he was being accused before the Sanhedrin (John 18:23). The slap on the cheek was not just an extreme form of insult,"[51] but a "deadly affront."[52]

---

49. Oaths were often sworn in Israel while laying on hands or making physical contact, as, for example, in Genesis 24:9. See David P. Wright, "The Gesture of Hand Placement in the Hebrew Bible and in Hittite Literature," *Journal of the American Oriental Society* 106, no. 3 (1986): 433–46. Gestures of legal and ritual importance in sacrificing, incurring indebtedness, or appointing an agent are mentioned by Falk, *Hebrew Law in Biblical Times*, 53, 55–56, 96, 97, 98–99.

50. Joseph Fitzmyer, *The Aramaic Inscriptions of Sefire* (Rome: Pontifical Biblical Institute, 1967), 17, 57, brackets in original. I am grateful to Jo Ann Hackett for drawing this inscription to my attention, agreeing that there is a judicial background to at least some of the cases of smiting on the cheek. Compare Jo Ann Hacket and John Huchnergard, "On Breaking Teeth," *Harvard Theological Review* 77, nos. 3–4 (1984): 259–75, discussing the ancient legal context of a different but comparable practice.

51. See Job 16:10; Psalm 3:7–8; Lamentations 3:30; Micah 5:1. Martha T. Roth, "Mesopotamian Legal Traditions and the Laws of Hammurabi," *Chicago-Kent Law Review* 71 (1995): 13–39, shows that slapping on the cheek was viewed as a serious tort in the ancient Near East because the face was "a part most susceptible to shame" (p. 29). In the Old Babylonian period, an Amorite infantryman was accused of striking an important man on the cheek; the case went to the viceroy and judges, who sent the accused to the Gate of Ishtar; he was eventually required to pay three and a half shekels of silver. See James B. Pritchard, ed., *Ancient Near Eastern Texts Relating to the Old Testament*, 3rd ed. (Princeton: Princeton University Press, 1969), 545, document 11. Daube interprets Jesus's statement of turning the other cheek in terms of the law of *boshet*. See David Daube, *The New Testament and Rabbinic Judaism* (London: Athlone, 1956), 254. *Boshet* allowed for "humiliation" damages to be assessed for personal injuries. See Elon, *Principles of Jewish Law*, 332–34. For the similar insult of plucking off a beard, see Edward J. Kissane, *The Book of Isaiah: Translated from a Critically Revised Hebrew Text with Commentary* (Dublin: Browne and Nolan, 1943), 2:150.

52. Heinrich L. E. Luering, "Cheek," in *The International Standard Bible Encyclopedia*, ed. Geoffrey W. Bromiley et al. (Grand Rapids, MI: Eerdmans, 1979), 1:639.

The Lord, then, was asking the ultimate when he told his disciples to turn the other cheek (Matthew 5:39; 3 Nephi 12:39).

In Babylonia smiting on the cheek also had ritual as well as grave legal consequences. In the Babylonian year rite, the high priest slapped the king on the cheek until he cried as a part of his humiliation and confession in their New Year festival: "He shall strike the king's cheek. If, when [he strikes] the king's cheek, the tears flow, (it means that) the god Bel is friendly."[53] Under the law codes of Eshnunna and Hammurabi it was actionable to slap another person on the cheek.[54] "The oriental guards with jealous care his cheek from touch or defilement, therefore a stroke on the cheek was, and is to this day, regarded as an act of extreme rudeness of behavior, a deadly affront."[55] The slap on the cheek was also a sign of repudiating the authority of another person of formerly higher status. Thus, if a son wished to disavow his legal relationship to the wife of his deceased father, he would "say, '(She is) not my mother,'" and she would "strike his cheek" and then leave the household empty.[56] This is not to say that every slap on the cheek was a ritual or formal act, but that such a blow was a very serious act with many meanings, some of which had legal implications.

The slap on the cheek certainly had great significance to the descendants of Lehi.[57] Abinadi cursed the people of Noah that they would be "smitten on the cheek, . . . and slain" (Mosiah 12:2);[58] among these people this was a symbol of humiliation, subjugation, and exercising of authority (21:3). The sons of Mosiah were smitten "upon [their] cheeks; . . . stoned, and taken and bound with strong cords, and cast into prison" (Alma 26:29). Among the Nephites, smiting upon the cheek is also mentioned in the list of wrongs committed by members of the church (Helaman 4:12) in violation of the laws they had been taught to obey (Alma 1:32; 16:18), whereas one of the signs of righteousness was to suffer such humiliation: "I gave my back to the smiter, and my cheeks to them that plucked off the hair. I hid not my face from shame and spitting" (2 Nephi 7:6, quoting Isaiah 50:6).

---

53. Pritchard, *Ancient Near Eastern Texts*, 334. Slapping the face is also discussed in Jonathan Z. Smith, *Imagining Religion: From Babylon to Jonestown* (Chicago: University of Chicago Press, 1982), 90–92 (the slap was a symbolic threat to strip the king of his kingship if he acted like foreign kings).

54. Laws of Eshnunna 42 (the penalty was ten shekels of silver, the same as the penalty for daytime trespass or housebreaking); Code of Hammurabi sections 202–205 (the penalties were comparable to those imposed for putting out another's eye); In Roman law, see Aulus Gellius, *Attic Nights*, 20:1.12; Twelve Tables 8:2–4.

55. Luering, "Cheek," 1:639.

56. See the Emar testament discussed in Roth, "Mesopotamian Legal Traditions," 32–33.

57. Quite parenthetically, the word for cheek in Hebrew is *lehi*.

58. Compare Fitzmyer, *Aramaic Inscriptions of Sefire*, 16–17.

Remaining Silent

In response to the insulting challenges and threats of the chief judge and witnesses, Alma and Amulek simply remained silent (Alma 14:17, 18, 19). For many days they refused to say anything. They had already said enough.

For the accused in an ancient Israelite court of law, however, there was no right to remain silent.[59] Silence was viewed as an admission of guilt or capitulation to the charges, and apparently a person's silence in the face of his accusers could be held against him.[60] Thus, by refusing to reply to the charges, Alma and Amulek exposed themselves to whatever sentence the chief judge in Ammonihah dared, in the purported name of justice, to impose.

Imprisonment and Abuse in Ammonihah

The decision of the chief judge was not to burn or kill Alma and Amulek but to hold them in prison under extremely severe, torturous conditions (Alma 14:17, 22), undoubtedly hoping that they would die of "natural" causes. Prolonged imprisonment was mentioned as an option that was considered by the Ammonihahites from the time Amulek finished speaking (10:13); and in the end, Alma and Amulek were held in prison for "many days" (perhaps as many as forty days), during which they were bound with cords, taunted, stripped, and starved; food and water were withheld (14:22).[61] The clear intention was that they would not be supported by God and would die (compare Jeremiah 38:9; 52:11). Unlike the three-day imprisonment of Abinadi,[62] the treatment of Alma and Amulek was conducted more as an ordeal than as mere detention. Testing the veracity of a witness or the guilty of an accused by subjecting him to some form of water or fire ordeal was a well-established practice in ancient Near Eastern and biblical law, as is evident in Numbers 5:12–31, Deuteronomy 32:34–36, Daniel 3:17–27, and elsewhere.[63] Subjecting Alma and Amulek to the rigors of starvation and physical privation, along with scaring them with the prospect of "delivering [them] up unto the flames"

---

59. Compare Falk, *Hebrew Law in Biblical Times*, 59. See the discussion above of Abinadi and remaining silent.

60. Allison A. Trites, *The New Testament Concept of Witness* (Cambridge: Cambridge University Press, 1977), 46–47, 83, 176, citing, among others, Isaiah 41:21–23; 43:9; 44:7. See also Bovati, *Re-Establishing Justice*, 335–36, 341–43.

61. Similar treatment was given to the sons of Mosiah in the city of Middoni (Alma 20:29).

62. See the discussion of the brief imprisonment of Abinadi pending trial, in chapter 6 above.

63. See, for example, P. Kyle McCarter, "The River Ordeal in Israelite Literature," *Harvard Theological Review* 66, no. 4 (1973): 403–12; K. van der Toorn, "Ordeal Procedures in the Psalms and the Passover Meal," *Vetus Testamentum* 38, no. 4 (1988): 427–45.

(Alma 14:19), constitutes a prototypical use of physical ordeals in ancient judicial settings.[64] Willing to see their survival as a manifestation of God's judgment (v. 29), the chief judge was able to expose Alma and Amulek to extreme conditions without actually rendering a verdict against them and carrying out their execution. If they were to have died as a result of the ordeal, the chief judge and his judicial officers would not have been guilty of murder. Indeed, at least as a general principle of later Jewish law, "starving a man to death, or exposing him to heat or cold or wild beasts, or in any other way bringing about his death by the anticipated—and however certain—operation of a supervening cause, would not be capital murder."[65] Evidently, the chief judge in Ammonihah was operating under similar concepts of ordeal and exposure to extreme conditions.

Just as the Ammonihahites had burned the women and children because Alma had preached of fire and brimstone, they came into the prison, smote Alma and Amulek on their cheeks, "gnashed their teeth upon" them (compare Psalm 35:16) and demanded to know, "How shall we look when we are damned?" (Alma 14:21), doing this because Alma had said they would be punished by God. This abusive treatment, however, came to an abrupt halt as the prison walls split in two at the word of Alma (vv. 26–29), and Alma and Amulek departed out of the city (15:1).

Aftermath

Less than four months later (Alma 16:1), the city of Ammonihah was destroyed (vv. 2–4; 25:2). It was obliterated by the Lamanites who were seeking their own revenge against the Amalekites and Amulonites, who, like the people of Ammonihah, were also after the order of the Nehors (24:28; 25:2). As a result of this invasion, "every living soul of the Ammonihahites was destroyed, and also their great city" (16:9), thus completing the judgment of God upon them in a single day.

The carcasses of those who were slain were "heaped up upon the face of the earth" and were given the token burial of "a shallow covering" (Alma 16:11). In other words, no grave was dug and a small amount of dirt was thrown on top of them. Receiving some kind of burial was considered of great importance in the ancient world ("If a man beget a hundred

---

64. This topic has been capably explored by one of my students, Ammon Sutherland, in his paper "Alma 14 as a Trial by Ordeal," (2006, paper in the Howard W. Hunter Law Library, Brigham Young University). See also Eric E. Vernon, "Illegal Speech: Blasphemy and Reviling," *Studia Antiqua* (Summer 2003): 123 ("The ruling, again given by divine intervention, is that Amulek spoke the truth.")

65. Haim H. Cohn, "Homicide," in Elon, *Principles of Jewish Law*, 476, citing Maimonides, Yad, *Roze'ah* 3:10–13. Compare also 1 Nephi 7:16.

children, and live many years, ... [yet] his soul be not filled with good, and also that he have no burial; I say, that an untimely birth is better than he," Ecclesiastes 6:3); any burial was better than no burial at all, even if it consisted only of a small symbolic act. One thinks readily of the Greek case of Antigone, who risked her life to sneak out at night to give her brother a token burial so that his soul would not suffer the fate of wandering over the face of the earth interminably.[66] Less well known is the case of the Athenian admirals who chose to pursue their vanquished enemies' ships and not to return into dangerous stormy waters to recover the bodies of some of their sailors who had died at sea in the Battle of Arginusae (406 BC) so that they could be given a proper burial; upon returning to Athens, these admirals were executed for not giving the dead a proper burial and for not attempting to rescue the survivors.[67] While it cannot be determined how the people in Ammonihah felt about burials and the afterlife of the soul,[68] it would appear that the purpose behind the "shallow covering" of earth involved in the burials in Ammonihah was not hygienic, but rather was some kind of token collective gesture showing a minimal degree of honor to those who had been slain, for the covering of earth was not sufficient to cover the bodies for very long. Soon, "so great was the scent" that people did not return to the land of Ammonihah for many years, and the bodies were "mangled by dogs and wild beasts of the wilderness" (Alma 16:10), a noted fate of those who pervert justice (1 Kings 21:23–24; Mosiah 12:2).

The city of Ammonihah was left desolate, becoming known as the "Desolation of Nehors" (Alma 16:11). Just as the law of Moses required, under Deuteronomy 13:12–17, the city of Ammonihah became a "heap" and "the people did not go in to possess the land of Ammonihah for many years. . . . And their lands remained desolate" (Alma 16:11). These lands were deemed untouchable for just over seven years (there are eight years, nine months, and five days between Alma 16:1, which gives the date of the destruction, and Alma 49:1–3, where mention is made of the rebuilding of the city), which would seem to be some kind of ritual cleansing period.[69]

66. Sophocles, *Antigone* 21–77, 407–40.

67. Diodorus, *Historical Library* 13.14.1–2. Xenophon, *Hellenica* 1.6.34–1.7.35, gives the impression that the admirals could have rescued some of these men still alive and that they were executed for wronging the people of Athens by disobeying orders to pick up the shipwrecked (1.7.20), not mentioning the issue of burial emphasized by Diodorus.

68. For a general discussion of various burial customs in the First and Second Temple periods in Israel, see Elizabeth Bloch-Smith and Rachel Hachlili, "Burials," in *Anchor Bible Dictionary*, 1:785–94.

69. A seven-year ban on occupation was placed on the island of Cyprus after it had been annihilated in the Christian patristic era. Constantinus Prophyrogentius, *De Administrando Imperio*

The Law of Apostate Cities

Deuteronomy 13:12–18	Ammonihah (Alma 9–16)
certain men gone out from among you	Nehorites had gone out from Zarahemla (Alma 1:15; 15:15)
withdrawn the inhabitants of their city	they had withdrawn their city from Nephite leadership (9:6; 14)
serve other gods	turned from God (11:24)
children of Belial	Satan had great hold (8:9; 9:28; 11:21)
inquire and search diligently	Alma visits personally (8:8)
smite all inhabitants with the sword	everyone killed (16:9; 25:2)
destroy utterly	everything destroyed (16:9–10)
a heap forever	bodies heaped up (16:11)
abomination	desolation of Nehors (16:11)

Underlying this desolation was the systematic miscarriage of justice. The case of Alma and Amulek in Ammonihah stands as a dominant social marker of Alma's and God's righteous judgment against a people who persisted in judging unrighteously in spite of Alma's repeated warnings, his extraordinarily full declarations of principles and doctrines, and his extension of ample opportunities to correct past violations and misjudgments. In light of the numerous infractions of the prevailing code of judicial ethics in Exodus 23 (see chapter 3 above), the disastrous outcome of this case for the city of Ammonihah is easily justified. The account in Alma 14 shows violations, in order, point by point, of most of the commandments required of Israelite judges. These judges and officers brought false accusations against Alma and Amulek, claiming that they had intentionally lied (Alma 14:2; compare Exodus 23:1). The accusers "went forth and witnessed against them" (Alma 14:5), thus combining with others to "raise a false report" (Exodus 23:1). They clearly "follow[ed] a multitude to do evil" (v. 2). They turned against Zeezrom when he righteously attempted to "speak in a cause to decline after many to wrest [pervert] judgment" (v. 2; see Alma 14:7). They denied justice to defenseless women and children (compare Exodus 23:6). They went on to "execute [those] innocent and righteous" women and children (Alma 14:8; compare Exodus 23:7), and in the end their own women and children will consequently also be

47, in *Patrologia Graeca* 113:366.

killed. They openly offered to "take a bribe" (v. 8; see Alma 11:22). And if the people of Ammonihah were of Mulekite descent, and if they thus considered Alma and Amulek to be foreigners in their midst because of their Nephite ancestry (Alma 10:3), these people even succeeded in breaking the final commandment in the Israelite code of judicial justice, "Thou shalt not oppress a resident stranger" (Exodus 23:9). Indeed, the only part of the code not violated—namely, "neither shalt thou countenance [be partial toward] a poor man in his cause" (v. 3)—was inapplicable, because Amulek was not poor, but well-to-do (Alma 10:4). Thus the case rightly becomes a paradigmatic case of judging unrighteously.

A number of immediate legal precedents flowed directly from Alma's courageous victory in Ammonihah. For example, the use of "lawyers" in administering judicial affairs and the abuse of the system that provided for the payment of judges are not mentioned again in subsequent Nephite history. Sympathy for those who had been persecuted because of their faith was also certainly strengthened, paving the way for the ready acceptance in Zarahemla of those Ammonite converts who had managed to survive execution at the hands of other Nehorites in the land of Nephi. When those fortunate survivors were brought to Zarahemla by Ammon, they were immediately given land, granted exemption from active military duty,[70] and afforded other privileges (Alma 27:22), perhaps due in large part to the feeling of sympathy that must have prevailed among the Nephites in response to the tragic pain and loss suffered by the faithful women and children less than four years earlier in Ammonihah.

For the Nephites, however, the broadest long-term legal value of this overt display of God's judgment against the order of the Nehors resided in the fact that this result put an end to overt, organized religious opposition to the Church of Christ among the Nephites. Soon enough, other religious dissenters, such as Korihor, would still surely come, but they would function mainly as individual operators, not as an alternative church within the land of Zarahemla. Likewise, political opposition would also continue to arise, but these opponents were forced to hide and work essentially underground in the mode of secret combinations and robber bands. After the destruction of Ammonihah, outright, blatant priestcraft (whether enforced by the sword or not) or competitor churches ceased to be a factor in the city of Zarahemla. Apparently, the legal and religious messages emerging from the destruction of Ammonihah were strong and clear enough that people took heed and avoided the appearance of organized apostasy within the lands

70. John W. Welch, "Exemption from Military Duty," in *Reexploring the Book of Mormon*, 189–92.

under the influence of Alma's leadership or jurisdiction. Accordingly, the Zoramites (who like the followers of Nehor also refused to keep the law of Moses, to "observe the performances of the church," or to supplicate God in daily prayer, Alma 31:9–10) found it necessary to withdraw from Zarahemla and thus "gathered themselves together in a land which they called Antionum" (v. 3), where they built their own style of synagogue and worshipped in their own unusual way upon their Rameumptom. Only seven years after the destruction of Ammonihah, that very separatist and somewhat guarded conduct of these Zoramites and of Korihor (who will eventually die in the Zoramite city of Antionum) will give rise to the next major trial in Nephite legal history, the case of Korihor.

CHAPTER NINE

THE TRIAL OF KORIHOR

Fifty years after King Benjamin's unifying covenant speech and seventeen years after King Mosiah's legal reforms, a man named Korihor appeared in the land of Zarahemla. The text gives no indication whatever of his ethnic or tribal origin, his city or land of residence, or his religious or political affiliations. All these omissions cannot be accidental. Indeed, the text wants readers to see Korihor as an isolated individual defying the foundation of collective responsibility that undergirded the concepts of justice, ethics, prosperity, and well-being in Nephite and Israelite societies. In the Book of Mormon array of typologies, Korihor represents the radical individual thinker, detached from community and unconcerned about the consequences of his ideas, who is bound and determined above all to speak his mind. Speech was his stock-in-trade.

As encountered above in the trial of Nehor and in the case of Alma and Amulek, the law reform of Mosiah included several provisions against which the righteousness of a judgment could be measured. The trial of Korihor tested particularly, for the first time, the limits of free speech under the system of justice established by King Mosiah's reforms.

For many reasons (not the least of which was to ensure broad popular support for the new regime), the new law had promised that everyone would have "an equal chance," granting all people "liberty" but also making them accountable (Mosiah 29:38–39). This guarantee was actualized initially in the legal maxim that "the law could have no power on any man for his belief" (Alma 1:17), and eighteen years into the reign of judges it was stated, "There was no law against a man's belief; for it was strictly contrary to the commands of God that there should be a law which should bring men on to unequal grounds. . . . If [a man] believed in God it was his privilege to serve him; but if he did not believe in him there was no law to punish him" (30:7–9). More than creating social or economic equality, the law of Mosiah made all people under its jurisdiction equal in the sense that they could not be punished for what they believed. While it was clear that "if [a man] murdered he was punished unto death; and if he robbed he was also punished; and if he stole he was also punished; and if he committed adultery he was also punished . . . nevertheless, there was no law against a man's belief; therefore, a man was punished only for the crimes which he had done; therefore all men were on equal grounds" (vv. 10–11).

The case of Korihor put to the test the question of what it meant to be "equal" under Nephite jurisprudence. Did equality mean that a person could not only believe whatever he wanted but also say whatever he wanted? If a person did not believe that Jehovah was God, could he be punished for profaning the name of Jehovah or speaking insolently against him? In other words, did freedom of belief (or disbelief) entail freedom of expression specifically articulating or reflecting that belief? This important question had been neither contemplated nor addressed in the law originally established by King Mosiah a generation earlier.

It was a difficult question. As a result, Alma 30:1–60 contains a relatively lengthy and detailed account of the trial of Korihor. In many ways, the outcome of this fascinating case established a crucial precedent in Nephite religious and legal history, involving important issues concerning religious freedom, blasphemy, and leading others into apostasy.

Did Korihor Have Nehorite or Other Such Connections?

The record does not disclose the place of Korihor's personal or intellectual origins (Alma 30:6). He may, however, have been associated with people in Ammonihah, since some of his arguments seem to build upon those of the radical Nehorites of that city as well as upon the teachings of Nehor that were still being promoted by the Amulonites, the former priests of Noah who had become affiliated with the order of Nehor (21:5–6). For example:

- The people in Ammonihah had a fundamental, but unspecified, antipathy toward the Nephite political system, as a result of which they did "study . . . [to] destroy the liberty of [the] people [of Alma]" (Alma 8:17). Korihor similarly opposed the Nephite rulers (30:31–32), claiming that Alma's people were in political subjection, not liberty (vv. 23–24).
- Nehor taught that it ultimately did not matter what people did, since all would be saved in the afterlife (Alma 1:4; 21:6); still they "durst not" commit actual crimes (1:17–18). Korihor went one step further, insisting that "whatsoever a man did was no crime" (30:17), denying any afterlife.

- Nehorism apparently rejected the doctrine of the fallen state of mankind (Alma 1:4). Korihor did likewise (30:25). While Alma had called the people in Ammonihah "a lost and a fallen people" (9:32), Korihor raised a similar charge against the Nephite leaders but broadened it to a theological argument in opposition to the fall of Adam, criticizing the Nephites for saying that their own people are "a guilty and a fallen people, because of the transgression of a parent" (30:25).

- Although Nehor declared belief in God the Creator (Alma 1:3–4), Zeezrom (who represented the leaders in Ammonihah) claimed to reject "the existence of a Supreme Being" and offered Amulek a bribe to deny the existence of an all-powerful God (11:22). Korihor agreed, not only rejecting the idea of an omnipotent God but also denying the possibility of any human knowledge about God, "a being who never has been seen or known, who never was nor ever will be" (30:28).

Since Ammonihah had been left desolate by the war that had ended only a few years before Korihor entered the land of Zarahemla (Alma 16:9–11), his base of operation or closest allies may well have been destroyed by the Lamanite invasion that left Ammonihah in ruins. That loss could explain Korihor's apparent homelessness as he moved from city to city, from Zarahemla to Jershon to Gideon. The similarity between the names Nehor and Korihor might also suggest, even if only faintly, some group connection between them as well.[1] If Korihor was somehow associated with Nehorism and if he had even intensified and radicalized Nehor's teachings, that would also account, to some extent, for his rapid success in Zarahemla. Nehor had attracted a following there only seventeen years earlier, and strong currents of religious and social dissension were gathering strength among the Zoramites that would soon bring about further factional wars led by local rebels such as Zerahemnah (43:3–5) and Amalickiah (46:3). Those tensions, together with certain wickedness or indifference among the people, the difficulty of the law getting hold of him, or the possibility that Korihor, like Nehor, could become yet another martyr to an infamous cause, explain much of the reticence of the people in Zarahemla to press charges against Korihor.

---

1. It may be more than coincidental that another Corihor once lived in the land of Nehor, where Corihor drew away many people after him (Ether 7:4). To a Nephite audience familiar with this detail in Jaredite history, the connection between the later Korihor and the man Nehor may have gone without saying.

Korihor's case, as a legal matter, arose in the latter part of the seventeenth year of the reign of the judges, when he went from the city of Zarahemla into the land of Jershon. It is unclear why Korihor went to Jershon. Jershon had recently been settled by the ultrafaithful Ammonites, some of whose fellow converts had been put to death in the land of Nephi at the instigation of the Amulonites, who, ironically enough, were "after the order of Nehor" (Alma 21:4; 24:8–9). Perhaps Korihor was unaware of this background, or perhaps he believed that these converts might be vulnerable because they were a displaced people and were young in the gospel. It is also possible that he believed that, as former Lamanites, the Ammonites would be as receptive to his message as some of their former kinsmen had been to Nehorism (21:4, 24:28). In any event, spurred on by his unchallenged success in the city of Zarahemla, Korihor went to Jershon and began preaching there against the prophecies about the coming of Christ (30:6, 19), a long-standing plank in the platform of the Nephite dissenters (Mosiah 26:2). Korihor, however, went further, speaking out sharply against the commandments of the Lord, the religious leaders of the people, and the very being of God.

Legal Backgrounds and Political Challenges

Before the institution of the reign of judges, Nephite law punished false prophets, false preachers, and false teachers "according to their crimes" (Words of Mormon 1:15). There is no reason to think that sincerity could exonerate an accused false teacher during Benjamin's time. Legal support for taking action against such speakers before the time of Mosiah was probably drawn from provisions in the law of Moses that forbid several forms of impious speech, including false prophecy (Deuteronomy 13:1–5; 18:20–22), blasphemy (Exodus 20:7; Leviticus 24:10–16), reviling the gods (Exodus 22:28), and leading people into apostasy or idolatry (Deuteronomy 13:1–18). Hebrew prophets placed a curse on those worthless shepherds who do not take care of the people but will eat of the meat of the best sheep (Zechariah 11:16–17).[2]

With the reforms of Mosiah and the shift to the reign of the judges, however, came several changes in the Nephite legal system—innovations that particularly accommodated the needs of a society that had become

---

2. These early Hebrew passages decrying such inappropriate conduct came to be seen in later Jewish circles as the behavior of the anti-Christ, as discussed by G. W. Lorein, *The Antichrist Theme in the Intertestamental Period* (London: T&T Clark, 2003); and L. J. Lietaert Peerbolte, *The Antecedents of the Antichrist: A Traditio-Historical Study of the Earliest Christian Views on Eschatological Opponents* (Leiden: Brill, 1996).

home to Mulekites, Nephites, Zoramites, Nehorites, king-men, the followers of Alma, and Limhi's refugees. These reforms, as discussed above, brought some significant changes in both the substantive and the procedural Nephite law. Because the law of Mosiah had been promulgated only seventeen years before Korihor began preaching in Zarahemla, his case would have arisen at a time when Nephite judges and society were still working out the practical implications of those changes. Indeed, it appears that Korihor's case, like Nehor's case, raised some legal issues that arose for the first time in interpreting the meaning of the law of Mosiah. For example, who was to have jurisdiction over cases of false preaching and blasphemy—the chief judge or the high priest? Was unruly or erroneous speech ever to be punishable under the new law, or could a person only be punished for his overt actions? Without prior experience to direct the judgment of the court, these questions became an issue of first impression for the highest courts in Gideon and Zarahemla.

After briefly reporting the principal themes of Korihor's preaching, the account of his trial begins by stating the main provisions in Nephite law "established" (Alma 1:1) by Mosiah that were relevant to Korihor's case:

> Now there was no law against a man's belief; for it was strictly contrary to the commands of God that there should be a law which should bring men on to unequal grounds. For thus saith the scripture: Choose ye this day, whom ye will serve. Now if a man desired to serve God, it was his privilege; or rather, if he believed in God it was his privilege to serve him; but if he did not believe in him there was no law to punish him. (Alma 30:7–9)

As stated at the beginning of the book of Alma, with respect to legal conditions in the first year of the reign of judges eighteen years earlier, "now the law could have no power on any man for his beliefs" (Alma 1:17). Nevertheless, "liars were punished" if it were known that they were prevaricating; and as a result, "for fear of the law" some speakers "pretended" to believe what they preached (v. 17). This set of new rules in particular must have spawned several questions in Nephite civil law. How would such terms as *belief* or *liar* be defined? What was the underlying rationale behind this new law? How was this law to be understood and applied?

The picture is further complicated by the fact that the Nephites divided human conduct into three categories: words, actions, and thoughts (Mosiah 4:30). Alma's teachings made it clear that God would impose punishments on people with respect to all three of these categories (Alma 12:14). The right of humans to inflict punishment on others, however, was limited. While people could be punished under the law for their actions (30:10),[3] it was unlawful for the government to punish people for their sincere beliefs (1:17; 30:7, 11).

That much was straightforward. Much more difficult, however, were two problems that had to be faced sooner or later under the law of Mosiah. One problem was evidentiary: how should a court determine whether a person sincerely believed what he taught? In other words, what evidence would be required to prove a person guilty? The second issue was conceptual: how were speech acts to be treated? Should speech be considered merely to be an assertion of one's *beliefs* and therefore protected under the civil law and punishable only by divine justice, or should some speech acts be viewed as a type of overt *action* punishable by civil or religious authorities? Speech is a hybrid between thoughts and actions, and the law of Mosiah did not provide a ready answer for how some of the old laws, such as prohibitions against blasphemy or leading people into apostasy, should be treated under the new regime.

Korihor was clever. He was smart enough to understand these issues and bold enough to assert his right to "equality" under the law (Alma 30:7, 11). Moreover, unlike Nehor, Korihor scrupulously avoided acting in any way that was expressly forbidden. All he did was preach. But this had disturbing consequences for the Nephites, for thus it seemed that "the law could have no hold upon him" (v. 12). Korihor exploited this situation to the limit: he preached openly (v. 12), encouraging others to commit sins (v. 18); he went "about perverting the ways of the Lord" and taught "people that there shall be no Christ," seeking thereby "to interrupt their rejoicings" (v. 22). Eventually he was found to be reviling, falsely accusing, and blaspheming public figures (vv. 30–31). Yet still the civil law took no hold upon him. Had the law of Mosiah gone too far in allowing people to speak openly about their beliefs? Under the new law, were no forms of speech punishable? The trial of Korihor would supply God's answers to these questions.

Another background factor that seems to have complicated this case was an issue of jurisdiction. Before the time of the reign of judges, the king and his priests worked closely together on legal problems like the ones created by Korihor, as evidenced by the collaboration of Benjamin

3. Jewish law typically requires an overt, completed action before punishment can be imposed; see Haim H. Cohn, "Penal Law," in *The Principles of Jewish Law*, ed. Menachem Elon (Jerusalem: Keter, 1975), 471. "Mere talk does not amount to an overt act"; see Cohn, "Slander," in Elon, *Principles of Jewish Law*, 513. See generally Bernard S. Jackson, "Liability for Mere Intention in Early Jewish Law," in *Essays in Jewish and Comparative Legal History* (Leiden: Brill, 1975), 202–34.

and "the holy prophets who were among his people" (Words of Mormon 1:16–18) and of Noah and his priests (Mosiah 12–17). With the establishment of a church and a separate civil administration in Zarahemla, priests were no longer involved in civil matters,[4] which were instead heard by the judges. This, of course, raised the question of whether Korihor's case should be considered a church matter or a public matter. He had directly attacked the teachings of the church, repudiating the prophecies concerning the coming of the Messiah (Alma 30:6), and thus he may well have been an apostate member of the church (speaking to Korihor, Alma called the righteous Nephites "thy brethren," 30:44; but when speaking himself, Korihor disowned close connections with the Nephites, speaking of "your fathers," vv. 14, 16). Should he thus be taken to the high priest? On the other hand, he had also created a public disruption and incited others to break the civil law. Should he thus be taken to a civil judge? The fact that he was eventually taken to both may indicate that this point remained a preliminary issue in such a case.

Those Nephites who contemplated apprehending Korihor in Zarahemla were probably also inhibited by at least two additional factors. First, memories of the civil strife and violent encounters with Nehor's followers five years after his trial and execution (Alma 2–3) must have made the Nephites in Zarahemla wary of confronting Korihor, since making him another martyr would perhaps fan the flames of smoldering political animosities and controversies.[5] Second, under the law of Moses, witnesses had to take the initiative and responsibility of bringing a case before the priests or judges. Accusing someone under such a system was a risky proposition because of the burden it placed on the accuser, who would normally have needed to buttress his claim with a true oath; losing the case could lead people to view his oath as false, thus exposing him to the same consequences he had intended for the accused (Deuteronomy 19:15–19).

Thus, considering the difficult legal and political issues that Korihor's case would have necessarily involved, as well as the courage and righteous determination it would have required to stand up against this potent

---

4. Alma the Elder, for example, was given authority "over the church" (Mosiah 26:8), but Mosiah retained power over the affairs of the state. Similarly, Alma the Younger gave legal authority to Nephihah (Alma 4:17) but retained authority to ordain priests and elders "to preside and watch over the church" (6:1). As discussed above, even the people of Ammonihah recognized the jurisdictional divide between political and religious leaders (8:11–12).

5. It was important in ancient law to do justice, "but at the same time" to maintain "social unity." Robert R. Wilson, "Israel's Judicial System in the Preexilic Period," *Jewish Quarterly Review* 74, no. 2 (1983): 235–36, stating that if "unhappy individuals or groups . . . refuse to accept the verdict, . . . the result will be a split . . . that may ultimately endanger the entire social structure."

demagogue, it is hardly surprising that no one in Zarahemla came forward to take the risk of accusing Korihor of violating the law.

Korihor's Expulsion from the Land of Jershon

After enjoying a fair amount of success in the land of Zarahemla, Korihor carried his preaching to the Ammonites in the land of Jershon, "who were once the people of the Lamanites" (Alma 30:19). As he did so, however, they "took him, and bound him, and carried him before Ammon, who was a high priest over that people," and "he caused that he should be carried out of the land" (vv. 20–21).[6] In essence, Korihor was apprehended by members of the general population, as would have been normal under their law; he was tied up, taken to the priest by these witnesses, and then banished from the territory by their high priest.

Because the Ammonites had taken this action, Alma praised them and called them "more wise than many of the Nephites" (Alma 30:20). Since it would have been unusual for Alma to praise the scrupulously righteous people of Jershon for doing anything that was in violation of the law or that ran roughshod over Korihor's civil rights (even in the name of religion), it is reasonable to assume that these people in Jershon acted in a perfectly legal manner by turning Korihor away. This legal episode prompts several prospects and considerations.

First, it is significant that Korihor was taken to the high priest over the Ammonites. No civil judge is mentioned here at all, as happens when Korihor is prosecuted in Gideon and in Zarahemla (Alma 30:21, 29). In other words, the Ammonites perspicaciously framed this case as a religious matter and took Korihor directly to their high priest. In retrospect that was a wise move, since the case was eventually resolved primarily as a religious matter.

Second, it is also possible that the legal system of the Ammonites in Jershon was somewhat different or somewhat independent from the laws in the land of Zarahemla.[7] Nothing in the record indicates that the

---

6. The exercise of jurisdiction over an offender from outside a community is known in Hebrew as *ḥerem bet din*. In ancient Hebrew law, this right applied only to the Sanhedrin and other high courts. It seems the Nephites, like their Old World counterparts, extended this right to local communities. See Isaac Levitats, "Herem Bet Din," in *Encyclopaedia Judaica*, ed. Fred Skolnik and Michael Berenbaum, 2nd ed. (Jerusalem: Keter, 2007), 9:16.

7. The Ammonites stood apart from those in the land of Zarahemla because of their distinctive oath against taking up arms and their rare but legally justifiable exemption from military duty. Moreover, when the land of Jershon was given to the Ammonites (Alma 27:22), the conveyance was conditioned only upon the Ammonites' commitment to "give . . . a portion of their substance" (v. 24) to help support the Nephite armies; it was not combined with any overt moves by the people in Zarahemla to annex this group. See John W. Welch, "Law and War in the Book

Ammonites ever agreed to be bound by the law of Mosiah. Formal popular adoption of that law, essential for it to become binding upon the people, had occurred several years before the Ammonites arrived in Zarahemla (Alma 1:14). It follows that the Ammonites may not have been bound by the progressive law of Mosiah and that, in carrying Korihor out of their independent land of inheritance, they were simply exercising a typical, traditional prerogative of excluding Korihor, as a foreigner, from taking up residence in their city without some local patron host.[8] The Nephites, by contrast, would not have had that option of denying him residence if he had been a lifetime citizen of part of their land.

Taking yet another tack, perhaps the Ammonites were subject to the law of Mosiah but argued that expulsion or banishment was not a form of punishment that was prohibited by that law. In other words, they may have held that a person could be ostracized or banished, but not beaten or executed, for disruptive speech.

Taken, Bound, and Carried to the Priest and Judge in Gideon

After his expulsion from the land of Jershon, Korihor continued his preaching in the land of Gideon. As had happened in the land of Jershon (Alma 30:20), Korihor was "*taken* and *bound* and *carried*" before the highest officials in the land of Gideon (v. 21; emphasis added).[9] The consistent repetition of the three terms in Nephite arrests has been noted above.[10] Because the people of Limhi had entered into a public agreement to take "upon themselves the name of Nephi, that they might be called the children of Nephi and be numbered among those who were called Nephites" (Mosiah 25:12), the legal practice in the city of Gideon would have undoubtedly followed the same rules and regulations as were found generally in the land of Zarahemla.

Korihor was taken before two officials in the land of Gideon: the high priest, named Giddonah, and the chief judge (Alma 30:21). This duality

---

of Mormon," in *Warfare in the Book of Mormon*, ed. Stephen D. Ricks and William J. Hamblin (Salt Lake City: Deseret Book and FARMS, 1990), 63–65; and "Exemption from Military Duty," in *Reexploring the Book of Mormon*, ed. John W. Welch (Salt Lake City: Deseret Book and FARMS, 1992), 189–92.

8. Without hotels or other public accommodations for travelers in ancient towns, foreigners typically needed to have a local patron who would house them, vouch for their integrity, and represent them in the local courts. Christiana van Houten, *The Alien in Israelite Law* (Sheffield, England: JSOT Press, 1991), 36–42.

9. The seizure of offenders sometimes constituted the formal initiation of legal proceedings against them in the ancient Near East. Raymond Westbrook, *A History of Ancient Near Eastern Law* (Leiden: Brill, 2003), 1:31–32.

10. See the treatment of arrest in the trial of Abinadi, in chapter 6 above.

again seems to reflect uncertainty over who (if anyone) had power to do anything to restrain Korihor.

Reviling God

Neither the high priest nor the chief judge in Gideon, however, had any desire to reply to Korihor's words. As Giddonah and the chief judge in Gideon interrogated Korihor, it became clear that Korihor "would revile even against God" (Alma 30:29). At that point "they would not make any reply to his words" (v. 29). Perhaps they viewed his language as so impious and irreverent that they did not want to hear or be contaminated by his words profaning Deity. Such conduct was clearly against the law of Moses given centuries before: "Thou shalt not revile the gods" (Exodus 22:28).[11]

Apparently it was unclear whether this rule had been overridden by the law of Mosiah; otherwise one would assume that Giddonah and the chief judge would simply have found Korihor guilty of reviling God and would have handled the case without further delay (as in the cases of the blasphemer in Leviticus 24 and Naboth in 1 Kings 21:10). The question of whether the grant of equal status and freedom of belief under the law of Mosiah had superseded the law of Moses in this regard, however, would have been a significant issue, and on this ground I would conclude that Korihor's case needed to be referred to higher legal and ecclesiastical authorities.

Transferal to the Authorities in Zarahemla

"They [the high priest and chief judge in the land of Gideon] caused that he should be bound; and they delivered him up into the hands of the officers, and sent him to the land of Zarahemla" (Alma 30:29). The reference to "officers" here is a clear but rare reference in an actual legal proceeding to the functioning of officers in a Nephite court. The law of Mosiah had called for the establishment of officers to transport people in custody (11:2). Here those officers are seen in action, performing their legal duty (compare 14:17). One may assume that their functions, in addition to their title, were somewhat similar to the "officers" (*shoterim*) of the Deuteronomic courts: "Judges and officers shalt thou make thee in all thy gates" (Deuteronomy 16:18), although little is known about those officers.[12]

It is apparent, however, that Korihor's case was not sent to the higher authorities for judicial review in a modern legal sense. The officials in Gideon did not reach a decision and so had no ruling to send for review

---

11. See the treatment of reviling in the trial of Abinadi, in chapter 6 above.

12. Haim H. Cohn, "Practice and Procedure," in Elon, *Principles of Jewish Law*, 581; and Ludwig Köhler, "Justice in the Gate," in *Hebrew Man* (New York: Abingdon, 1956), 127–50.

by another body of judges. Alma and the chief judge in Zarahemla took original jurisdiction over the case and initiated their own inquiry de novo, beginning the case from scratch and not merely reviewing the decision of the lower court. The law of Mosiah provided that the lower judges be judged of a higher judge if the lower judges "do not judge you according to the law which has been given" (Mosiah 29:28). From that language, which gave the higher judges authority to judge *the lower judges* (not their judgments), as well as from the fact that no decision regarding Korihor was actually reached by the lower court in the city of Gideon, one may conclude that the Nephite reign of judges did not utilize substantive appellate review as such, but rather used impeachment or discipline of judges for misconduct or capriciousness. Allowing appeals would have been inconsistent with the ancient idea that God's will was manifested through the judicial process, and therefore once a verdict had been reached, second-guessing the decision itself would have been problematic.[13]

The idea of not getting a second hearing on judicial determinations of law or fact is consistent with what is known about the court system in ancient Israel, which featured no practice of judicial review.[14] The local courts were expected to handle routine matters and to refer the hard cases directly to the central authorities. For example, during the period of the exodus, important cases could be referred directly to Moses (Exodus 18:22; Leviticus 24:11); in such cases, the popular courts did not reach a decision that would then have been sent to Moses for affirmation or reversal. Similarly, it appears that Jehoshaphat's central courts in Jerusalem were established to hear hard cases referred to them from the cities of Judah in order to decide "between blood and blood, between law and commandment, statutes and judgments" (2 Chronicles 19:10); but one assumes that the local courts had sole jurisdiction over common disputes or causes of action.

Korihor's case was apparently viewed as a difficult one, arising out of an alleged conflict or uncertainty between the law of Mosiah and the

---

13. "Guilt cannot be negotiated, and a divine oracle cannot be appealed." Wilson, "Israel's Judicial System in the Preexilic Period," 237.

14. "Special judges appear to have been commissioned by the central authorities to sit as courts of first instance." Ze'ev W. Falk, *Hebrew Law in Biblical Times: An Introduction*, ed. John W. Welch, 2nd ed. (Provo, UT: Brigham Young University Press; Winona Lake, IN: Eisenbrauns, 2001), 58. "There was no possibility of appeal to a court superior to or other than the local one, because there was no such court." Hans Jochen Boecker, *Law and the Administration of Justice in the Old Testament and Ancient Near East*, trans. Jeremy Moiser (Minneapolis: Augsburg, 1980), 40. See Raymond Westbrook, "Punishments and Crimes," in *The Anchor Bible Dictionary*, ed. David Noel Freedman et al., 6 vols. (New York: Doubleday, 1992), 5:546–56.

commandments of God, and so this matter was referred without any further proceedings to the two most prestigious authorities in the land. Moreover, by taking Korihor both to Alma the high priest and to Nephihah, the chief judge (Alma 30:30), the people of Gideon finessed the issue of whether this case should be viewed as a "matter of the Lord" or as a "matter of the king"—a distinction that influenced the procedures in the trial of Abinadi and was as old as the reforms of Jehoshaphat (2 Chronicles 19:11).

Blasphemy and Further Reviling

Appearing before Alma and Nephihah, Korihor actually "went on to blaspheme" (Alma 30:30).[15] He may have flagrantly defamed, cursed, or uttered the sacred name of Jehovah (Leviticus 24:11), or his crime may have been a more general act of irreverence or disrespect, such as denying the existence of God.[16] Either way, Korihor's language now became even more offensive, escalating his conduct from reviling to blasphemy, the latter traditionally being a capital offense (v. 16). Once again, at least to some extent, it must have been unclear to this new set of judges in Zarahemla to what extent, if at all, the law of Mosiah had changed the traditional law of blasphemy. Absent some uncertainty of that nature, one would have expected the judges to have simply executed Korihor at this point in the trial.

In addition, Korihor also "did revile against the priests and teachers" (Alma 30:31). This created issues similar to those regarding his blasphemy and reviling of God. The ancient law required "Thou shalt not . . . curse the ruler of thy people" (Exodus 22:28). Since Korihor had launched an attack in the city of Gideon against the established rulers in Zarahemla, accusing them of "usurp[ing] power and authority" and of extorting and oppressing the people (Alma 30:23, 27), it was clear that he had reviled the rulers of the people. In Zarahemla, Korihor went further to "revile against the priests and teachers, accusing them of leading away the people after the silly traditions of their fathers, for the sake of glutting on the labors of the people" (v. 31). Nephite priests and teachers were consecrated as officials "over the land" (2 Nephi 5:26); and though their functions were religious, it would appear that they would qualify as "rulers" entitled to

---

15. This might have put Korihor beyond forgiveness because, under ancient Hebrew law, an offender who "persist[ed] in claiming to be in the right and carrie[d] on with arrogant and overbearing behavior" would have to be subject to a court in order to protect the "unjustly oppressed." Pietro Bovati, *Re-Establishing Justice: Legal Terms, Concepts and Procedures in the Hebrew Bible* (Sheffield, England: JSOT Press, 1994), 169.

16. See the sources on blasphemy, discussed in connection with the cases of Sherem and Abinadi, in chapters 5 and 6 above.

protection against reviling, although this point may have been somewhat unclear. Once again, however, it must also have been fundamentally unclear whether such repeated and cumulous contemptuous speech was punishable at all under the law of Mosiah. Otherwise the chief judge could have readily disposed of Korihor's case on the additional basis of reviling.

Korihor Accuses the Priests and Teachers of Priestcraft

In addition to reviling against the priests and teachers, Korihor specifically accused them of teaching falsehoods in order to get gain—a sort of priestcraft. By making such an accusation, Korihor took legal initiative against the Nephite priests and teachers, assuming the conventional composite role of accuser, plaintiff, and witness. Such accusers, as has been seen consistently in biblical and Book of Mormon cases, bore the burden of supporting their claims—or facing serious consequences (Deuteronomy 19:15–21).

Alma's Refutation

Alma began by denying the accusations that Korihor had made against the Nephite priests and teachers. He rebuffed the notion that Nephite leaders had glutted themselves "upon the labors of this people" (Alma 30:32) with his own testimony that he had never received payment for his labors in the church (v. 33), thus disproving Korihor's argument that Alma had preached to get gain (v. 35). Then he probed Korihor's statement about the alleged "silly traditions" (v. 31) taught by Nephite priests. He asked Korihor if he believed in the existence of God. Korihor said he did not. In this way, Alma strategically laid the groundwork for accusing Korihor of two offenses: (1) initiating false accusations against the Nephite priests and teachers, and (2) lying about the nonexistence of God.

Warning Korihor

After Korihor denied the existence of God, Alma gave him a final chance to withdraw his claim. Alma warned him by naming the witnesses that would stand against him: Alma himself was a witness, testifying that he knew "there is a God, and also that Christ shall come" (Alma 30:39); and in order to give further evidence in support of that testimony, Alma asserted that "all things [are] a testimony that these things are true" (v. 41),[17] and he also cited the testimonies "of all these thy brethren" (v. 44). By contrast,

---

17. Bovati, *Re-Establishing Justice*, 40n12, 81–82, cites times when mountains, the cosmos, heaven, and earth have been called upon as witnesses. Haim Hermann Cohn, "Witness," in *Encyclopaedia Judaica*, 21:115, explains that "lasting inanimate objects, such as stones (Gen. 31:48) [and] the moon (Ps. 89:38), . . . [could] be invoked as witnesses."

Korihor lacked any support for his accusations (v. 40), a serious deficiency. Alma also expressly warned Korihor that by denying the existence of God, he was lying, being "possessed with a lying spirit" (v. 42), thus putting Korihor on notice that he could be punished under the law of Mosiah, which required people to believe sincerely what they taught (1:17).

By warning Korihor, Alma fulfilled one of the traditional legal duties of a priest in Israel. Centuries before Alma's time, Jehoshaphat had commanded the priests and judges whom he installed in Jerusalem during his reforms in the eighth century BC to "warn [the people] that they trespass not against the Lord" (2 Chronicles 19:10). Similarly, the Lord told Ezekiel that if he failed "to warn the wicked from his wicked way, . . . the same wicked man shall die in his iniquity; but his blood will I require at thine hand" (Ezekiel 3:17–19). Thus an affirmative duty rested upon Alma to warn Korihor properly one final time.

Such warnings were essential so that the wicked could not use ignorance of the law as a defense. By the time of the Mishnah, the necessity of warning was so firmly embedded in Jewish law that it was "incumbent upon the prosecution to show that the accused was, immediately before the commission of the offense, expressly warned by two competent witnesses that it would be unlawful for him to commit it, and that if he committed it he would be liable to that specific penalty provided for it by law."[18] One school of rabbis even taught that a good judge should ask a prosecuting witness, among other things, "Did ye warn him? Did he accept your warning?"[19] Korihor seems to have eventually been somewhat sobered by the warning, and Alma cautioned him concerning what the exact punishment would be if he denied God again: "If thou shalt deny again, behold God shall smite thee, that thou shalt become dumb" (Alma 30:45–48).

The Problem of a Sole Accuser

As part of the substantive warning to Korihor that he was lying, Alma also pointed out to him that he had only one witness for his position, namely, Korihor himself. In contrast, Alma had rebutted Korihor's assertions and called a host of witnesses: "Behold, I have all things as a testimony that these things are true" (Alma 30:41). By doing this, Alma rhetorically showed that Korihor had failed, even nominally, to produce the minimum number of witnesses required by law—two (Deuteronomy 19:15). Alma's query, "What evidence have ye that there is no God, or that Christ cometh not?" effectively turned the tables on Korihor, who

---

18. Cohn, "Penal Law," 473; and Babylonian Talmud (hereafter TB) *Sanhedrin* 8b, 9b, and 40a.
19. TB *Sanhedrin* 40b.

suddenly found himself running the risk of being convicted of bearing false witness under Deuteronomy 19:16–21. In this way, Alma was able to expose an objectively provable defect in Korihor's case. Alma's legal logic is based implicitly on the reasonable presumption that bearing sole witness was a form of judicial speech that Nephite law could still punish and, thus, was an act not insulated from prosecution by the law of Mosiah. In addition, Alma's strategy throws at Korihor the same argument that the Nehorite lawyers and judges in Ammonihah had thrown at Alma a decade earlier: "Suppose ye that we shall believe the testimony of one man?" (Alma 9:2). Especially if Korihor had Nehorite ties, this turnabout was, more than ironically, fair play.

Diligent Inquisition

The law regarding false witnesses and accusers, found in Deuteronomy 19, most literally applies to cases in which only one witness (namely, the plaintiff himself) testifies on the side of the plaintiff.[20] The law of Moses required that the two opposing parties in such a controversy "stand before the Lord" so that the accusation could be settled after diligent questioning by the priests and the judges. It seems that this procedure applied exactly to Korihor's situation, for Alma next conducted an inquisition as required by Deuteronomy 19:17–18, asking Korihor a series of questions. Alma's inquiry fully satisfied the spirit of Israelite and Jewish jurisprudence. Later Jewish jurists required that, in order to refute the testimony of a false witness, the challenged position had to be tested by seven inquiries, a requirement that the Talmud implied from the text of Deuteronomy.[21] The refuting witnesses were to pose questions to the accused false witness such as, "How can you assert that you have seen the accused commit this act . . . when at that very time you were with us at such-and-such a place?"[22] Alma asked Korihor similarly phrased questions—twelve of them (Alma 30:34–45).[23] To these questions Korihor responded adamantly and incorrigibly (vv. 36, 38, 43, 45).

---

20. Haim H. Cohn, "Perjury," in Elon, *Principles of Jewish Law*, 517, points out that under talmudic law "no single witness could be convicted of perjury," but this relates to witnesses, not accusers.

21. Hyman E. Goldin, *Hebrew Criminal Law and Procedure* (New York: Twayne, 1952), 119n4: "That the number of these inquiries must be seven, is derived in the Talmud (*Gemara*, 40a) from the seven Biblical words or expressions used in connection with the examination of witnesses in matters involving capital punishment." The seven questions sought specification regarding the time and place of the alleged offense.

22. Goldin, *Hebrew Criminal Law*, 119n4.

23. Five of them seem to be rhetorical questions: Alma 30:34 (What doth it profit us?), 35a (Why sayest thou that we preach to get gain when thou knowest that we receive no gain?), 44a (Will ye tempt your God?), 44b (Will ye say, show me a sign?), and 45a (Yet do ye go about leading

Korihor's Request for a Sign

Korihor probably realized that the weight of evidence was stacking up against him. As in the case of Sherem, his request for a sign was an extraordinary step, a last resort, and a sort of voluntary request for an ordeal.[24] Korihor, who found himself on the defensive, was now willing to submit the matter to God, who he claimed, of course, did not exist. Korihor's overall position basically compelled him to assume that this was a low-risk tactic and that he would survive the judgment of God, a being who he believed was nonexistent. After Alma and Korihor challenged each other's testimonies, and after Alma finally accepted Korihor's challenge, the outcome of the case rested entirely in God's hands.[25]

Better One Should Perish

Quoting the words of the angel to Nephi five hundred years earlier (1 Nephi 4:13), Alma affirmed that Nephite justice was not offended by the prospect that God should smite Korihor: "But behold, it is better that thy soul should be lost than that thou shouldst be the means of bringing many souls down to destruction by thy lying and by thy flattering words" (Alma 30:47).

The idea that it is better for one to perish than an entire city to be destroyed runs sharply contrary to modern liberal jurisprudence but was part of biblical law. Among the Old Testament narratives that presuppose or utilize this principle, 2 Samuel 20 is pivotal, involving the killing of the rebel Sheba in order to preserve the city of Abel. Likewise, Jehoiakim, the king of Judah, was turned over to Nebuchadnezzar by the Jews in order to save Jerusalem from destruction.[26] Over the years, striking a proper bal-

---

away the hearts of this people testifying?). These five questions expected and received no answer. The other seven questions were more specific interrogatories addressing Korihor's beliefs (three times), evidence (once), and denials (three times): Alma 30:35b (Believest thou?), 37 (Believest thou?), 39 (Will ye deny?), 40 (What evidence have ye?), 41a (Will ye deny?), together with 41b (Believest thou?), and 45b (Will ye deny?). These seven questions either received answers from Korihor or were supplied answers by Alma. See Bovati, *Re-Establishing Justice,* 77–79, which discusses the function of dialogue in the *rîb.*

24. Ironically, making this request, Korihor was both appealing and subjecting himself to a being he claimed did not exist; see Herbert Chanan Brichto, "Blessing and Cursing," in *Encyclopaedia Judaica* 3:750–51 (referring to a man-invoked curse as a "prayer" and explaining that "such invocation is implicitly an acknowledgment of the Deity's sovereignty"). Ordeals were a "widespread method of ascertaining God's judgment" in Hebraic law. Haim Hermann Cohn, "Ordeal," in *Encyclopaedia Judaica,* 15:462 (citing examples). Compare the request for signs and the role of ordeals in the cases of Sherem and Abinadi, discussed in chapters 4 and 5 above.

25. For the use of divine judgment at a similar impasse in the case of Sherem, see chapter 4 above.

26. *Genesis Rabbah* 94:9 on 46:26; see also 2 Chronicles 36:6–10.

ance between the rights of the individual and the needs of the community was debated in Jewish law,[27] but it is not hard to see why Alma would have invoked this basic rubric of Israelite jurisprudence to remind Korihor of the vulnerability of his position.

Alma, however, did not anticipate that Korihor would "perish" in death (1 Nephi 4:13), but rather that his "soul should be lost" (Alma 30:47). Just as Korihor had threatened to lead people into sin and spiritual damnation, so his punishment would likewise be at the hands of God unto the destruction of his soul. God's curse upon Korihor, taking away his soul or spoken breath (in Hebrew, *nefesh* is the word for both soul and breath), would be a definitive sign to the people that Korihor was guilty.

Korihor Struck with Speechlessness

Alma invoked a curse upon Korihor: "If thou shalt deny again, behold God shall smite thee, that thou shalt become dumb" (Alma 30:47). This follows the typical ancient formula for pronouncing such a curse: "God do so to thee, and more also, if . . ." (e.g., 1 Samuel 3:17). Such a curse has been called "an oath to do evil."[28]

In addition to evidencing divine approval of Alma's position, Korihor's punishment provides another good example of divinely executed talionic justice: his curse befits his crime. Because he had spoken evil, he was punished by being made unable to speak. Even more literally than those whose mouths had uttered false doctrines during the time of Benjamin (Words of Mormon 1:15), Korihor's mouth was physically shut. In the ancient Near East, talionic justice was the rule: Assurbanipal once boasted that, in a case where two men had spoken gross blasphemy against the god Assur, "I ripped out their tongues and skinned them alive."[29]

Interestingly, Korihor's punishment was considerably lighter than Nehor's. Of course, Korihor had not tried to enforce his beliefs with the sword and had not killed anyone, and in addition, perhaps Alma had grown more patient after seventeen years of the reign of judges. No doubt

27. TJ *Terumot* 8:10, 46b; and Roger David Aus, "The Death of One for All in John 11:45–54 in Light of Judaic Traditions," in *Barabbas and Esther and Other Studies in the Judaic Illumination of Earliest Christianity*, ed. Jacob Neusner et al. (Atlanta: Scholars Press, 1992), 29–63. See also TB *Terumot*, 8:12; TB *Makkot*, 11a; *Genesis Rabbah* 94:9; *Leviticus Rabbah* 19:6; Saul Lieberman, *Tosefta ki-feshutah: A Comprehensive Commentary on the Tosefta* (New York: Jewish Theological Seminary, 1955), 422n141; and David Daube, *Collaboration with Tyranny in Rabbinic Law* (London: Oxford University Press, 1965), 18–27.

28. Falk, *Hebrew Law in Biblical Times*, 52, citing Leviticus 5:4; Psalm 15:4.

29. Ernst F. Weidner, "Assyrische Beschreibungen der Kriegs-Reliefs Aššurbânaplis," *Archiv für Orientforschung* 8 (1932–33): 184:28, quoted in Shalom M. Paul, "Daniel 3:29—A Case Study of 'Neglected Blasphemy,'" *Journal of Near Eastern Studies* 42, no. 4 (1983): 293.

he would want to avoid any repetition of the aftermath of Nehor's execution. In any event, the Nephite government was more secure now during Korihor's time than it had been during its first, shaky years, and so Alma and his colleagues could well afford to wait on the Lord and allow divine justice to take its own course.

Cursing a Party with Speechlessness

When Alma pronounced a curse on Korihor, "In the name of God, ye shall be struck dumb, that ye shall no more have utterance" (Alma 30:49), he utilized a venerable ancient practice. When the curse materialized, divine disapproval was so clear that Korihor was compelled to yield the case.

While the use of such a curse may seem somewhat unusual or sensational to modern readers, the pronouncing of curses or spells was common in the ancient Mediterranean world,[30] and their most frequent use was in fact in the legal sphere. In recent decades more than one hundred Greek and Latin "binding spells"—curses inscribed on small lead sheets that were folded up and pierced through with a nail—have been recovered from tombs, temples, and especially wells near the law courts, where they were placed in hopes that a deity from the underworld would receive them.[31]

These spells are known as *defixiones* because their words and powers were intended to "defix"—to restrain or hinder—an opponent. The opponent targeted by these quasi-religious petitions or incantations in ancient Greece could be a commercial, athletic, or romantic rival or one's adversary in litigation.[32]

The largest body of these Greek binding spells deals with litigation, with sixty-seven different defixiones having been discovered containing pleas that curses fall on a legal opponent.[33] These lead curse tablets "became popular in the fifth century B.C. and continued in use in Mediter-

---

30. For more information on curses, see Douglas Stuart, "Curse," in *Anchor Bible Dictionary*, 1:1218–19.

31. Such texts have been studied most recently by Christopher A. Faraone; see his study "The Agonistic Context of Early Greek Binding Spells," in *Magika Hiera: Ancient Greek Magic and Religion*, ed. Christopher A. Faraone and Dirk Obbink (New York: Oxford University, 1991), 3–32. I am grateful to James V. Garrison for assisting me in this area of research.

32. Faraone, "Early Greek Binding Spells," 11.

33. See R. Wünsch, *Defixionum Tabellae Atticae*, in *Inscriptiones Graecae*, vol. 3.3 (Berlin: Reimer, 1897), numbers 25, 38–39, 63, 65–68, 81, 88, 94, 95, 103, 105–7, and 129; A. Audollent, *Defixionum Tabellae* (Paris: Fontemoing, 1904), numbers 18, 22–35, 37, 39, 43–44, 49, 60, 62–63, 77, and 87–90; and D. R. Jordan, "A Survey of Greek Defixiones Not Included in the Special Corpora," *Greek, Roman, and Byzantine Studies* 26, no. 2 (1985): 151–97, numbers 6, 9, 19, 42, 49, 51, 61, 68, 71, 89, 95, 99, 100, 108, 133, 162–64, 168, 169, 173, 176, and 179.

ranean lands" for at least a millennium.[34] Of the more than a thousand "judicial defixiones," thirteen, most of which come from Cyprus, ask the gods specifically to bind the tongue of a legal opponent in such a way that the speechless adversary would lose the case. They employ such language as "make him cold and voiceless and without breath," "make him cold and dumb," "seize control of his voice," "muzzle/silence my opponents," and "bind his tongue" or "put his tongue to sleep."[35] An additional twenty-one known curses from Cyprus, Attica, and Epirus make reference to the voice, tongue, or words of the legal opponent, and many of these probably imply complete silencing of the accuser as well.[36] Similar curses are also found in Hellenistic Jewish texts: "Silence . . . the mouth of all people who stand against me";[37] "Let none of the children of Adam and Eve be able to speak against me."[38]

Evidence shows that people believed that these curses were sometimes actually fulfilled. A third-century BC stele from Delos expresses the gratitude of a victorious litigant who had been helped in court by a god: "For you bound the sinful men who had prepared the lawsuit, secretly making the tongue silent in the mouth, from which (tongue) no one heard a word or an accusation, which is the helpmate in a trial. But as it turned out by divine providence, they confessed themselves to be like god-stricken statues or stones."[39] Other evidence of divinely induced speechlessness is found in ancient literature. Aristophanes, in his play *The Wasps*, speaks of a litigant who became speechless:

> Bdelycleon: Come forward and defend yourself. What means this silence?
> Philocleon: No doubt he has nothing to say.
> Bdelycleon: Not at all, I think he has got what happened once to Thucydides in court; his jaws suddenly set fast.[40]

---

34. Jordan, "Survey of Greek Defixiones," 151. See also Faraone, "Early Greek Binding Spells," 16. The use of curses and spells in general has roots that run much earlier throughout the ancient Near East.

35. Audollent, *Defixionum Tabellae*, numbers 22–24, 26–29, 31, 33, 34, and 37.

36. Wünsch, *Defixionum Tabellae Atticae*, numbers 49, 50, 68, 88, 94–95, and 105–107; Audollent, *Defixionum Tabellae*, numbers 30, 32, 35, 49, and 87; and Jordan, "Survey of Greek Defixiones," numbers 51, 95, 99, 100, 107, 108, and 164.

37. Israel Museum, bowl, item no. 8.1.2.

38. *Sepher ha-Razim*, First Firmament, lines 134–41.

39. Faraone, "Early Greek Binding Spells," 19.

40. Aristophanes, *The Wasps* 946–48.

A scholiast attributes the silence to magic.[41] Libanius tells of a time when he fell mute and could not be cured until a dead chameleon was found in his classroom with its mouth bound shut. When the chameleon was removed, his voice returned.[42] The famous Roman jurist Cicero speaks of a number of times when his legal opponents either fell dumb or lost their memory at the moment of trial, some attributing the affliction to magic potions or incantations.[43]

Obviously, the speechlessness of Korihor—and to an extent also the stunning of Sherem—was precisely the kind of sign or restraint that people in the ancient world expected a god to manifest in a judicial setting, especially in the face of false accusations, as in the cases of Korihor and Sherem, or when one party to a lawsuit was placed at a distinct disadvantage by some unfair ploy of his opponent. In such cases, resorting to curses or appealing to supernatural intervention was perfectly acceptable and perhaps even expected. Indeed, what was most important to avoid when calling down a curse on another was invoking the power of the wrong god. Leviticus 19:31 and 20:5–6 were a reminder to the Israelites that there was only one power to which they should subscribe: "I am the Lord your God." Thus, although there were strong scriptural prohibitions against the Israelites using magic by invoking the names of other gods or powers, under biblical law Jews were permitted to properly and appropriately invoke the power of the one true God against their enemies (see the curses invoked in Deuteronomy 27:14–26, the curse of bitter waters in Numbers 5:21, and the sign called down from heaven by Elijah in 1 Kings 18:38). Although Israelites were religiously and legally restricted in the use of evil incantations to impose spells upon people, the overall objective of any judicial proceeding in Hebrew society was to silence one of the parties, one way or the other. As Bovati clearly explains, silence means defeat: "The keeping silent . . . is the prosecution's (or defence's) inability to carry on the debate, which is equivalent to saying there are no more arguments and therefore one's adversary is right."[44]

When a litigant was stricken by the gods in such cases, it was not uncommon for that person to erect a confession stele. These confession inscriptions appear to have served several purposes. One was "a confession

41. Fr. Dübner, *Scholia Graeca in Aristophanem* (Hildesheim: Verlag, 1969), 156, discussed in Christopher A. Faraone, "An Accusation of Magic in Classical Athens (Ar. *WASPS* 946–48)," *Transactions of the American Philological Association* 119 (1989): 149–60.

42. Libanius, *Autobiography* 245–50, discussed in Faraone, "Early Greek Binding Spells," 15–16, and 16n70.

43. Cicero, *Brutus* 217; *Orator* 128–30; and Faraone, "Early Greek Binding Spells," 15.

44. Bovati, *Re-Establishing Justice*, 342.

of guilt, to which the author has been forced by the punishing intervention of the deity, often manifested by illness or accident."[45] In addition, these inscriptions appeased the god who had taken action against the confessor, who would often include a clear profession of his newly admitted faith in the god and would warn others not to disdain the gods.[46]

In the same manner, Sherem's confession revoked what he had previously taught, confessed the truth of the god who had intervened against him, admitted his error, and expressed concern that he would never be able to appease God (Jacob 7:17–19). In Korihor's case, the chief judge turned immediately to the task of obtaining a confession from Korihor acknowledging the power of God, probably in part to ensure that the curse would not afflict any others, as well as to terminate the dispute (Alma 30:51). Such reactions are similar to the typical responses of others in the ancient world whose judicial perfidy or false accusations had been exposed and quashed by the intervention of a god responding to a restraining curse invoked by a beleaguered litigant.

Korihor's Confession

After Korihor was struck dumb, the chief judge asked him if he was now convinced of the power of God or if he would dispute further. Evidently, the extraction of the legally required confession was viewed at this time as a duty of the chief judge, for Alma the high priest plays no official role in the concluding phases of this trial. The chief judge asked four specific questions:

1. Art thou convinced of the power of God?
2. In whom did ye desire that Alma should show forth his sign?
3. Would ye that he should afflict others, to show unto thee a sign?
4. Behold, he has showed unto you a sign; and now will ye dispute more? (Alma 30:51)

In reply Korihor wrote the following:

> I know that nothing save it were the power of God could bring this upon me; yea, and I always knew that there was a God. But

45. H. S. Versnel, "Beyond Cursing: The Appeal to Justice in Judicial Prayers," in Faraone and Obbink, *Magika Hiera*, 75.

46. Versnel, "Judicial Prayers," 75. See also Bernard S. Jackson, "Ideas of Law and Legal Administration: A Semiotic Approach," in *The World of Ancient Israel: Sociological, Anthropological and Political Perspectives*, ed. R. E. Clements (Cambridge: Cambridge University Press, 1989), 189–92; and Paul Douglas Callister, "Law's Box: Law, Jurisprudence and the Information Ecosphere," *University of Missouri–Kansas City Law Review* 74, no. 2 (2005): 263–334, for more on the ancient use of monuments and steles and on the physical dimensions of legal records.

behold, the devil hath deceived me; for he appeared unto me in the form of an angel, and said unto me: Go and reclaim this people, for they have all gone astray after an unknown God. And he said unto me: There is no God; yea, and he taught me that which I should say. And I have taught his words; and taught them because they were pleasing unto the carnal mind; and I taught them, even until I had much success, insomuch that I verily believed that they were true; and for this cause I withstood the truth, even until I have brought this great curse upon me. (Alma 30:52–53)

As discussed above, the law of Moses emphasized the importance of confession after conviction. For example, Leviticus 5:5 requires, "When he shall be guilty in one of these things, that he shall confess that he hath sinned in that thing." Joshua required Achan to "make confession unto [God]; and tell me now what thou hast done" (Joshua 7:19; see Leviticus 26:40; Numbers 5:6–7; Psalm 32:5, 51:3; Proverbs 28:13). Facilitating and obtaining a confession of guilt was so important that later Jewish law even required judges to assist the convict in making his confession.[47]

As in the case of Sherem, Korihor's confession was somewhat specific as to his crimes, and his statement was appropriately made a matter of public record.[48] First he openly acknowledged the power of God, an issue that had become a main point of contention in his trial; and he added that he "always knew that there was a God," thus admitting that he had deliberately lied (Alma 30:52). Under biblical law, a confession had to "be verbalized because it is the act that counts, not just its intention."[49] Korihor further confirmed Alma's accusations by admitting that he had been misled by the devil and was carnally motivated in his teachings. Indeed, confession is not required under biblical law "for inadvertencies, but only for deliberate sins."[50] By confessing in such a manner, Korihor undoubtedly fulfilled the court's hopes that his statement would deter the people from engaging in such conduct in the future and that he might help himself spiritually as much as possible.

The fact that Korihor's confession was taken down in writing is interesting. The chief judge assisted Korihor by writing his questions and by

---

47. For discussions of confession, see the analysis of the trials of Sherem and Nehor in chapters 5 and 7 above.

48. "The biblical postulate seems to have been that confession is made to the injured party." Jacob Milgrom, *Leviticus 1–16*, (New York: Doubleday, 1991), 303. Here Korihor's sin was against both God and the public, so his confession could not be silent, before God alone.

49. Milgrom, *Leviticus 1–16*, 301.

50. Milgrom, *Leviticus 1–16*, 301.

allowing Korihor to write back in reply. Korihor was probably not deaf
and could have heard the questions of the chief judge, but by putting his
questions in writing, the chief judge created a full and precise written record of what he had asked and of how Korihor had responded. The words
of that official document could be read, posted, or broadcast by messengers throughout the land.

Although confessions were strongly desired under Nephite law, confessing did not stay the execution of the punishment—in this case, divine
punishment. Moreover, in Korihor's case there is no reason to believe that
his confession was complete or sincere. While he responded in detail to
the chief judge's first question, Korihor glaringly ignored the other three:
Korihor's confession does not disclose the identity of the person upon
whom he had wanted the sign of God's judgment to fall, it is silent on
whether he had harbored evil designs that Alma should afflict someone
else, and it makes no explicit promise that Korihor would cease and desist from further disputations. Moreover, Korihor's confession rational-
izes his misconduct rather than taking responsibility for it: he blames his
errors on the devil and on the people who encouraged him by acclaim-
ing him a success. His confession, therefore, was not entirely satisfactory,
even though he went so far as to admit, "I have brought this great curse
upon me" (Alma 30:53). Accordingly, when he appropriately asked the
high priest if he would take the curse off him, Alma refused, noting that
if the Lord removed the curse, Korihor would "again lead away the hearts
of this people" (v. 55).[51] Confession was "the legal device . . . to convert
deliberate sins into inadvertencies, thereby qualifying them for sacrificial
expiation,"[52] but the confession needed to be genuine for Alma to inter-
cede in his priestly capacity. Korihor's insincerity in connection with his
confession also gave the chief priest ample reason to doubt that Korihor's
preaching had been motivated by a sincere belief. Moreover, even if it was
sincere, it was not always appropriate to forgive an offender to the point of
staying a punishment.[53]

Korihor's Punishment

The curse was not taken from Korihor, and he was "cast out" (Alma
30:56), which may mean at least two things: (1) Korihor could have been

51. "Sometimes it is wiser to punish than to tolerate, because forgiveness may encourage the
habit of evil." Bovati, *Re-Establishing Justice*, 169–70.

52. Milgrom, *Leviticus 1–16*, 301–2.

53. Such an act of forgiveness in these circumstances might have "ma[de] light of the crime
committed." Bovati, *Re-Establishing Justice*, 169.

physically transported from the land, just as he had been deported from Jershon and forbidden to return, or (2) he could simply have been socially ostracized and banned from engaging commercially with anyone in the land, which might explain why he had to beg for food from house to house.

A severe penal option available to judges in antiquity was to banish or expel the offender from the community.[54] In many ways, this was a fate worse than death, for an ancient person could not easily relocate in another city, and life outside settled lands was rugged. A severe banishment (or *ḥerem*) was pronounced publicly, with a "warning not to associate with the anathematized."[55] According to Josephus, outcasts often died miserable deaths.[56]

Evidence of the use of banishment can be found in "the records of all ancient nations,"[57] and the Israelites and Nephites are no exception. The basic principle behind the practice of banishment was a desire to purge the people of contagious iniquities. Such separation of unrighteous and impure people and things from pure and sacral ones can be traced, in the Hebrew mind, back to the beginning when God drove Adam and Eve out of the Garden of Eden (Genesis 3:23–24). In Old Testament times, *ḥerem* occurred in widely varying forms ranging from complete annihilation to a mere seven-day separation from the community. Jeremiah appears to have been pronouncing a *ḥerem* on behalf of the Lord when he cursed the fallen prophet Hananiah, who had falsely prophesied unto the people: "Therefore thus saith the Lord; Behold, I will cast thee from off the face of the earth: this year thou shalt die, because thou hast taught rebellion against the Lord" (Jeremiah 28:16). Hananiah died within the year. A milder form of expulsion from God's people was imposed upon Moses's sister, Miriam, when she spoke against Moses: "Let her be shut out from the camp seven days, and after that let her be received in again" (Numbers 12:14). This incident is the first recorded instance in the Bible of a person being separated from the community but being allowed to

---

54. For more information, see Adela Y. Collins, "The Function of 'Excommunication' in Paul," *Harvard Theological Review* 73, nos. 1–2 (1980): 251–63; and Moshe Weinfeld, "The Ban of the Canaanites and Its Development in Israelite Law," *Zion* 53, no. 2 (1988): 135–48.

55. Haim H. Cohn, "Ḥerem," in Elon, *Principles of Jewish Law*, 544.

56. Flavius Josephus, *The Wars of the Jews* 2.143 ("But for those that are caught in any heinous sins, they cast them out of their society; and he who is thus separated from them, does often die after a miserable manner; for as he is bound by the oath he hath taken, and by the customs he hath been engaged in, he is not at liberty to partake of that food that he meets with elsewhere, but is forced to eat grass, and to famish his body with hunger till he perish").

57. William D. Morrison and Janet I. Low, "Banishment," in *Encyclopaedia of Religion and Ethics*, ed. James Hastings, John A. Selbie, and Louis H. Gray (New York: Charles Scribner's Sons, 1981), 2:346.

live. This temporary banishment was later termed *niddui*, meaning the "punishment of an offender by his isolation from, and his being held in enforced contempt by, the community at large."[58] Other forms of social and religious banishment (resembling ostracism and excommunication) appear to have first developed at the time of Ezra in the fourth century BC to meet the needs of Israel at that time, when they lived in a heterogeneous world and needed to reestablish and maintain their religious identity in a pluralistic society.

It is unclear from Alma 30:56 whether Korihor began begging in Zarahemla and then, seeing no success there, went among the Zoramites or whether he started to beg outside the land of Zarahemla. But whether by physical deportation or social anathematization, the effect was the same: Korihor was banned from the community, a commensurate punishment for one who had effectively rejected the community by reviling so openly against the integrity of its leaders and values.

Proclamation of Sentence and Warning to Others

The result of Korihor's trial "was immediately published throughout all the land; yea, the proclamation was sent forth by the chief judge to all the people in the land, declaring unto those who had believed in the words of Korihor that they must speedily repent, lest the same judgments would come unto them" (Alma 30:57). This action by the chief judge completed the process outlined in Deuteronomy 19:16–21 regarding the case of a false witness or false accuser: "And those which remain shall hear, and fear, and shall henceforth commit no more any such evil among you." This provision was the basis of the rabbinic rule requiring that the outcome of notorious cases, such as Korihor's, be publicly heralded.[59] By publicly announcing the verdict in such a case, the local officials fulfilled their obligation, imposed explicitly in the historical record of the law reform of Jehoshaphat, to "warn [the people] that they trespass not against the Lord" (2 Chronicles 19:10).

In addition to issuing a general warning to the people against committing the same sins that Korihor had committed, the chief judge may have been making his people aware that Korihor had been stigmatized. Just as one of the main purposes of punishment in biblical times was to "put the evil away from among you" (Deuteronomy 19:19), so likewise in later Jewish law in Europe "the proclamation [of a *ḥerem*] contained

---

58. Cohn, "Ḥerem," 540.
59. TB *Sanhedrin* 6:2, 43a.

a public warning not to associate with the anathematized and concluded with a plea for the welfare of the congregation of the faithful."[60]

Korihor's Rejection among the Zoramites

Korihor's outcast status forced him to go to another land where the anathema would have no force, and Antionum was apparently the only place open to him. Korihor had been expelled from Jershon, Gideon, and Zarahemla; the followers of Nehor had been ejected from the land of Nephi (Alma 24:28; 25:8); and the city of Ammonihah had been destroyed. The Zoramites who inhabited Antionum, on the other hand, "had separated themselves from the Nephites" (30:59) and would not have considered themselves bound by any proclamation from the Nephite chief judge. Korihor also might have hoped for a sympathetic reception in Antionum, since the Zoramites also denied Christ and rejected the law of Moses (31:16). Nevertheless, Korihor's antiestablishment political views undoubtedly would have been unwelcome among the leaders of the truly oppressive oligarchy in Antionum, who burdened the poor mercilessly and notoriously. Accordingly, "as he went forth amongst [the Zoramites], behold, he was run upon and trodden down, even until he was dead" (30:59).

Korihor's death may have been accidental. Mishaps were often viewed anciently as a manifestation of God's judgment.[61] However, God's justice, it would seem, had been fully satisfied by the silencing of Korihor. There was also probably no legal basis for a judge to require Korihor's death at that time. Therefore, it seems more likely that Korihor's death was extralegally caused by the Zoramites. As the text says, he was "run upon . . . until he was dead" (Alma 30:59). Elsewhere, when the Book of Mormon text uses passive verbs to say that Korihor was "carried out" or "bound," it is obvious that human agents were actively involved. If Korihor's death was deliberately caused, then one may assume that the people of Antionum intentionally rejected Korihor, either (1) because he was a political agitator, (2) because he was a Nephite, or (3) because he had been cursed by a god and was therefore a pariah, or one marked with evil spirits. When trampling or treading is mentioned in the Old Testament, it usually has to do with trampling an evil or wicked person (2 Kings 7:17; 9:33; Job 40:12;

---

60. Cohn, "Ḥerem," 544.

61. For example, Abimelech was mortally wounded when a woman threw a piece of millstone and it broke his skull, and "thus God rendered the wickedness of Abimelech" (Judges 9:53, 56). In later times, "people were warned that premature death (at the age of 50), or death without leaving issues, were signs of the divine *karet*, . . . and that every undetected murderer would meet with 'accidental' death at the hands of God." See Haim H. Cohn, "Divine Punishment," in Elon, *Principles of Jewish Law*, 524.

Isaiah 14:19; 28:3, 18; 63:3–6; Malachi 4:3), lending credence to the likelihood that Korihor's death was more than merely accidental and was based on a concern or fear about receiving into the city someone who had been cursed by God.

Legal Outcomes

Two powerful precedents were set by the trial of Korihor. First, this proceeding established that some forms of speech were still punishable under the law of Mosiah. Korihor had lied, falsely accused the leaders of Zarahemla, reviled against the priests and teachers, and blasphemed against God, and for his words he was divinely smitten (revealing God's will regarding such cases) and then cast out by the people.

Second, it became the law that any person who persisted in believing in the words of Korihor was equally subject to such punishments: the proclamation of the chief judge made it clear that any of Korihor's followers who would not change their minds would be subject to both of "the same judgments" (Alma 30:57), namely, divine punishment and human banishment. In effect, no longer could anyone honestly claim to believe the words or ideologies of Korihor, and therefore those who persisted in promulgating such beliefs could be punished as liars under the law (1:17). This is a significant exception to the law of Mosiah that protected people from being punished for their beliefs (1:17; 30:7, 11). Indeed, the rule in Korihor's case was apparently observed in Nephite law from that time forward, for his case is the last time that such sophism or doctrinal errors surface in Nephite history as far as the Book of Mormon indicates. The record itself concludes with the strong assertion that this case "put an end" not only to Korihor himself but also "to the iniquity after the manner of Korihor" (30:58).

This case also reinforced several long-standing principles of righteous judgment among the Nephites. The wisdom and patience of Alma and the Nephite judges yielded good results, promoting the cause of human and divine justice, protecting the well-being of the community, dutifully warning possible transgressors, and allowing persistent offenders ample opportunities to change.

CHAPTER TEN

Comparing Sherem, Nehor, and Korihor

⤾

In chapters 5, 7, and 9, we examined the cases of Sherem, Nehor, and Korihor separately, which now puts us in a good position to compare and contrast these three proceedings in greater detail than ever before. The following review and comparative analysis allow us to go beyond the obvious similarities and to solidify our understanding of these cases. The fuller picture now brought to light answers the questions about these archetypal accounts that Elder B. H. Roberts raised in 1922.

Although the cases of Sherem, Nehor, and Korihor share certain features with one another, these three actions involving Nephite dissenters have less in common than one might assume based on casual familiarity or superficial comparison. The similarities are not materially greater than one would expect to find in any series of precedent-setting cases coming out of a single culture. Moreover, the differences are case-specific and distinctive, as one finds in real-life legal experience, in which no two cases are factually or procedurally identical. The salient, distinguishing facts of these cases make the legal value and the historical significance of each one truly unique.

Similarities

Some readers and commentators have given the similarities in these cases primary attention, leading them to conclude that these proceedings are mere stereotypes or caricatures and are not historical, actual legal narratives. The most extensive articulation of the idea that the degree of "repetition or parallelism" between these three cases is so strong that one might doubt their historicity was written by Roberts in his long-unpublished "Book of Mormon Study." There Roberts set out to identify the main problems that he thought critics of the Book of Mormon might someday raise.[1] He spelled out these issues not because he lacked faith or

---

1. B. H. Roberts, *Studies of the Book of Mormon*, ed. Brigham D. Madsen (Urbana: University of Illinois, 1985), 264–71. The original, handwritten document is in Special Collections, box 15, folder 21, J. Willard Marriott Library, University of Utah.

confidence in the Book of Mormon,[2] but because he hoped that future defenders of the faith would benefit from his exploration of problems.[3]

Roberts described all three of these dissidents as "Anti-Christs," even though the Book of Mormon applies that term only to Korihor (Alma 30:6). With respect to Sherem, Roberts noted that he was a "learned" man who was a powerful and flattering speaker (Jacob 7:2, 4). After quoting most of Jacob 7, Roberts suggested that some people might see "a certain 'raw'ness" or "a certain amateurishness" in this account.[4] The legal and literary treatment of Sherem's case offered above in chapter 5, however, would certainly suggest otherwise and, I think, would have satisfied and pleased Roberts. Turning to the trial of Nehor, Roberts wondered if in its viewpoint the "confession of error by the Anti-Christ, an ignominious death, [and] the triumph of the orthodox faith" might reflect the same amateurish spirit.[5] After discussing how the Amalekites mocked Aaron in the land of Jerusalem (Alma 21),[6] Roberts quoted at length from the case of Korihor in Alma 30, pointing out that he preached in various parts of the land "in a manner strongly reminiscent of the controversy between Jacob and Sherem."[7] In reality, these cases are significantly divergent, as is discussed below and as the accompanying table demonstrates.

Accounting for the Similarities

Roberts outlined twelve alleged similarities between the cases of Sherem and Korihor: the two cases both involve (1) denying Christ,

2. John W. Welch, "B. H. Roberts: Seeker after Truth," *Ensign*, March 1986, 56–62. Roberts's 1927–28 theological treatise *The Truth, The Way, The Life: An Elementary Treatise on Theology*, which was reprinted by BYU Studies in 1994 (John W. Welch, ed.), was unavailable for examination when the cloud was raised in the 1980s about his testimony of the Book of Mormon, but the words and logic of that treatise now seem to have dispelled any lingering residue of that shadow. I discuss this issue in the introduction to that volume, pp. xxiv–xxvii, and also in "Roberts Affirms Book of Mormon Antiquity," in *Pressing Forward with the Book of Mormon*, ed. John W. Welch and Melvin J. Thorne (Provo, UT: FARMS, 1999), 289–92.

3. Letter of Roberts to Richard R. Lyman, October 24, 1927, in Roberts, *Studies of the Book of Mormon*, 60.

4. Roberts, *Studies of the Book of Mormon*, 266.

5. Roberts, *Studies of the Book of Mormon*, 266–67.

6. This Book of Mormon episode did not result in a legal proceeding in which anyone was convicted or punished; rather, Aaron was simply rejected, and he voluntarily departed out of that land (Alma 21:11). As Aaron and his brethren then came into the land of Middoni, they were cast into prison (v. 13); but it appears that they were imprisoned simply as trespassers or intruders (compare Mosiah 7:7), not because of anything they had said or done or believed. They were eventually freed from prison by Ammon and King Lamoni (Alma 21:14). Accordingly, what Roberts suggested might possibly be viewed by some as only a "slight variation" (*Studies of the Book of Mormon*, 267) within these cases actually involves completely different facts, circumstances, and procedures.

7. Roberts, *Studies of the Book of Mormon*, 268.

(2) charging the established ministry with misleading the people, (3) rejecting prophetic knowledge of the future, (4) denying the scriptures, (5) questioning the accuser, (6) the accuser hesitating to answer directly, (7) the accuser demanding a sign, (8) the accused hesitating to involve the power of God, (9) the accuser being stricken, (10) the accuser confessing his error, (11) the accuser sensing the futility of his repentance, and (12) restoring righteousness and justice among the people.[8]

These similarities can be put into perspective in several ways. First is to recognize that a similar degree of uniformity can be found in recorded legal cases throughout the ancient world. Stylistic similarities can be found in the stock manner in which legal proceedings were recorded in the ancient Near East, even though these cases were separated from each other by long periods of time. Likewise, legal cases in the Old Testament—for example, the case of the blasphemer in Leviticus 24:10–23 and the case of the Sabbath wood gatherer in Numbers 15:32–36—are also reported with a high degree of uniformity. In those two Old Testament cases, conduct occurred that seemed to violate the rules protecting the sacred name of God and the sanctity of the Sabbath, and so the people brought the potential offender to Moses, they put the accused in ward, the Lord declared to Moses what should be done, and the man was taken outside the camp and put to death by stoning, the whole congregation participating as the Lord commanded. The Old Testament trials of Naboth (1 Kings 21) and Jeremiah (Jeremiah 26) and the New Testament trials of Jesus (Matthew 26; Mark 14; Luke 22; John 18) and Stephen (Acts 6–7) also have several salient features in common: false witnesses, accusations of blasphemy and false prophecy, corrupt elders and judges, innocent defendants, and so on.[9] Ancient historiography (consider the writer of Chronicles in the Old Testament or the historian Herodotus) is frequently characterized by its employment of standard formulas and repeated patterns to a considerable extent, even when reporting distinctive, independent incidents.[10]

---

8. Roberts, *Studies of the Book of Mormon*, 270–71. For a discussion of the ancient concept of restoring justice, see generally Pietro Bovati, *Re-Establishing Justice: Legal Terms, Concepts and Procedures in the Hebrew Bible* (Sheffield, England: JSOT Press, 1994), related to the juridical dispute between Sherem and Jacob above. The element of reconciliation is always the ultimate goal of the *rib*.

9. For a detailed comparison of the trial of Jeremiah with the trial of Jesus, see Bernard S. Jackson, "The Prophet and the Law in Early Judaism and the New Testament," *Cardozo Studies in Law and Literature* 4, no. 2 (1992): 123–66.

10. Alan Goff, "Historical Narrative, Literary Narrative—Expelling Poetics from the Republic of History," *Journal of Book of Mormon Studies* 5, no. 1 (1996): 50–102. Robert Alter, *The World of Biblical Literature* (New York: BasicBooks, 1992), 117.

Second, one may also turn to general legal experience. The reporting of most legal cases will have certain elements in common. In modern judicial practice, two different contract cases or two different securities fraud cases, especially if they are decided and reported by the same judge or court, will often have several stylistic and formulaic points in common. For example, most decisions handed down by the United States Supreme Court follow fairly consistent patterns in reporting the procedural posture, issues, facts, analysis, and holding of the case. Almost all trial court cases involve common factors such as establishing jurisdiction over the accused, lodging the complaint, presenting evidence, interrogating the parties, introducing witnesses, reaching a verdict, and carrying out the consequences of the decision. Against this background of uniform procedures, rules, and judicial practices, the particular facts and circumstances of each case come to light and are legally evaluated, and judicial decisions finally play themselves out.

Third, the alleged similarities are not always very remarkable. It is common enough in almost all litigations for an accuser (such as Sherem) or an accused (such as Korihor) to try to discredit or to draw into question the knowledge or point of view of the opposing parties. All defendants in all legal systems are prone to question or challenge their accusers, and accusers are typically hesitant to answer those objections any more directly than necessary. Post-conviction confessions may often be offered by all convicts, but usually these last-ditch efforts prove futile and inconsequential. The element of restoring peace and righteousness among the people was always the primary goal of every legal action in biblical times (as discussed in chapter 5 above). Furthermore, the relative degree of noteworthy similarity between the cases of Sherem and Korihor diminishes when the trial of Nehor and the variety of legal cases throughout the Book of Mormon are brought back into the picture.

Finally, as will be pointed out in detail below, the alleged similarities between the cases of Sherem and Korihor (let alone between them and Nehor) are not always clear or demonstrable. As the following discussion shows, these three opponents are very diverse. Their cases arose in different ways, on different legal grounds, and for different political and religious purposes. They do not all deny the scriptures, their confessions vary widely, and they were not all stricken or punished in the same way.

Seeing the Differences

Seldom have commentators, however, focused on the numerous differences that are found in the reports of the three cases of Sherem, Nehor, and Korihor. While legal cases are, by their very nature, somewhat repetitive and formulaic, each of these cases involves particular distinguishing facts, as the accompanying table illustrates.

	Sherem	Nehor	Korihor
Date	c. 500 BC	91 BC	c. 74 BC
Location	City of Nephi	Land/City of Zarahemla	Zarahemla, Jershon, Gideon, Antionum
Labeled an anti-Christ?	No	No	Yes
Source of power	Power of speech	Popular and physical strength	Power of devil
Basic theology	Theist, traditionalist	Theist, universalist	Atheist
Religion	Pro law of Moses	All law irrelevant	Anti law of Moses
Political stance	Reactionary, royalist	Populist, oppositionist	Radical, dissident
View on priests	Should keep law	Should be paid	Oppress the poor
Openly opposed the "foolishness" of leaders and among the people	No	No	Yes
Can anyone know the future?	Not if too far in the future	Probably, at least that all will have eternal life	Not at all
Impact of preaching	Led away hearts, no actions of followers mentioned	Many believed, followers gave money	Led away hearts, many committed sin and whoredoms
Nature of legal action or offense	Falsely accused Jacob of 1) causing apostasy 2) blasphemy 3) false prophecy	Killed Gideon, was convicted of enforcing priestcraft with the sword	Reviled both priests and God, committed blasphemy
Was arrested?	No	Yes	Yes
Status in legal proceedings	Plaintiff	Defendant with defenses	Defendant with counterclaims
Nature of court	Divine justice	One judge	Several judges
Interrogated by the court?	About Christ	No	About God's existence

	Sherem	Nehor	Korihor
Accepted the scriptures?	Yes	In part	No
Denial of Christ	Evasive	No	Clear
Was warned?	Indirectly	No	Yes
Requested a sign?	Yes	No	Yes
Was the sign-giver hesitant?	Yes, for fear of tempting God	Not applicable	No, better that one should perish
Reason for sign	Confirm revelation by Holy Ghost	Not applicable	Confirm existence of God
What divine sign was given?	Smitten to earth but still could speak	None	Struck dumb but could still write and walk
Was there a judicial verdict?	No	Yes	No
Confession	Sincere, complete	Involuntary	Incomplete
Role of devil	Impersonal, deceived by devil's power	None	Personal, visited and taught by devil
Penalty	Divine justice	Capital punishment	Divine justice, ostracism, trampled
Cause of death	Nonhuman causes	Human, legal	Human, probably extralegal
Publicity	Public confession	Ignominious death	Result heralded
Effect on people	Fell to earth, love restored	Priestcrafts continued	End of this wickedness, all converted
Precedential value of the holding	Legitimized Nephite Christianization of law of Moses	Gave original jurisdiction to chief judge under new reign of judges	Some speech acts still punishable under law of Mosiah

The facts and circumstances of these cases, which were of utmost importance in leading to their respective verdicts or outcomes, are also key factors in our evaluation of the meanings of those outcomes. Consider how these cases differ:

The three cases arise in different lands and involve different kinds of courts and judges. The political and social situation in the land of Nephi during Jacob's lifetime involved a fragile, fledgling community; Jacob probably had little political power with which to counter the attacks of Sherem. Alma, while also a new and therefore somewhat insecure judge at the time that Nehor's case arose, held in his own hands a coalition of judicial, religious, military, and administrative powers that enabled him to carry out a death sentence against a very popular local leader. A few years later, however, Korihor could take advantage of a deliberate separation of religious and civil functions in the government of Zarahemla; by exercising his right of equality, he was able at first to speak openly and to incite change in several neighborhoods and lands in the region, almost with impunity.

Of the three challengers, only Korihor is called "Anti-Christ" (Alma 30:6). Each is said to draw his power and effectiveness from different sources: Sherem from his power of speech (Jacob 7:4), Nehor from his physical strength and popularity (Alma 1:2–3), and Korihor from the tutelage by the devil (30:53).

While they were certainly united in their opposition to the Nephite regime in Zarahemla, they differed widely and significantly in their theology, religion, and political agendas. They held different views on the law and about priests, and they advocated different degrees of change. Sherem was in favor of traditional views of the law of Moses (Jacob 7:7) and appears to have been a royalist and, if not a reactionary, at least a conservative (vv. 9–13). His strategy focused on a narrow theological concern— protecting and conserving traditional understanding of the law of Moses (vv. 6–7). Nehor was a theist who definitely believed in God and universal salvation (Alma 1:4); thus for him, law was essentially irrelevant (Alma 1:6–9). He catered to the popular masses and sought to establish a church with a paid ministry (1:3), and he was the leader of a new movement that offered a peaceful alternative to Alma's church (vv. 5–6), at least until he killed Gideon in a fight (v. 9). Korihor was an atheist who adamantly denied the existence of God and all knowledge of him or of the future (30:12–16). He did not attempt to establish a church (v. 18) but was an iconoclastic, itinerant skeptic or cynic with a radical political agenda. His campaign was based on a bundle of ideologies and philosophies; he was far more subtle, radical, and sophisticated than Sherem, whose argument fundamentally accepted God and presupposed the validity of the scriptures. In contrast, Korihor openly rejected the scriptures and adamantly denied not only Christ but also God (vv. 12–15), while Nehor's ideology allowed people to believe or do almost anything they wanted.

The social impact of their teachings was different, and the legal actions involved in these cases were varied. Even the postures of the parties were totally different: Jacob found himself the accused defendant; Sherem was the accuser (Jacob 7:6). Nehor was a criminal defendant who raised defenses (Alma 1:13–14). Korihor, though also a defendant, was accused of religious offenses only and was aggressive in raising counterclaims and counterattacks (30:22–55).

In addition, each of these three committed or were accused of different crimes, and they raised different legal issues or political accusations against their opponents. The case of Sherem involved accusations of blasphemy, false prophecy, and leading people into apostasy (Jacob 7:19); Nehor was convicted of enforcing priestcraft with the sword (Alma 1:12–14); Korihor reviled the priests and eventually blasphemed God (30:22–55).

The three cases feature different procedural aspects dealing with such elements as whether the accused was arrested or not, and whether the case was tried and decided under divine justice, before a secular judge, or by an ecclesiastical body. The procedures differ in terms of the nature and unfolding of the interrogation, the extent of the warnings given, the use of the sign or ordeal to determine guilt or innocence, the presence or absence of a formal verdict, the purpose and type of confession, the authority imposing the penalty, the nature of the punishment, the actual cause of death, the announcement of the outcome, the people's reaction, and the long-term meaning of the case in Nephite legal history. For example, Sherem's guilt was not announced by officers to the general public, but instead he spoke his confession directly to the general population in the city of Nephi (Jacob 7:16–21). On the other hand, Korihor did not speak or write directly to the general population in the city of Zarahemla; rather, his verdict was heralded by public messengers throughout the land (Alma 30:57–58).

Thus, on careful inspection, the accounts of the cases of Sherem, Nehor, and Korihor differ in many respects; and given their times and circumstances, they differ precisely in the ways one could expect them to differ. Each proceeding was tailored to the individual facts and circumstances of the case. Some surprising and unique twists and turns occurred, and different legal issues were encountered in each case. Above all, the historical or jurisprudential value of each case was to establish different results: each proceeding raised legal problems of first impression that were of pressing importance for that particular moment in Nephite legal and religious history. When they are read with sensitivity toward their legal technicalities and jurisprudential principles, these cases can now clearly be seen to be subtly nuanced, historically plausible, and legally credible.

CHAPTER ELEVEN

THE CASE OF PAANCHI

Just as the trial of Korihor raised a difficult legal question about the point at which speech became conduct that was actionable under the law of Mosiah, the trial of Paanchi concerned a similar question that also presented difficulties under ancient law: At what point does conspiracy or incitement to commit treason become punishable? This complex legal question raised several interrelated issues. Was it illegal under Nephite law to criticize the chief judge or, worse, to talk about overthrowing the government? Or did a person have to call for—or worse yet, actually commit—some specific overt action before the inciter could be tried and convicted of treasonous conspiracy? In other words, could a person be punished according to the law for expressing mere intent? Where was the line between intending to commit a crime (which was presumably not actionable) and actually planning with others to commit a crime (which was overtly demonstrable and more likely criminal)?

In all societies, the crimes of conspiracy and incitement are difficult to define and even harder to enforce. Given the serious difficulties that the Nephites experienced as a result of the secret combinations of the Gadianton robbers in the fifty years preceding the appearance of Christ, this legal concept likely became a key point in Nephite law during the years covered by the book of Helaman and the first few chapters of 3 Nephi. Perhaps for this reason, among others, the writers and abridgers of the book of Helaman positioned the case of Paanchi at the very outset of that book. As the leading motif of the book of Helaman, this legal issue confronts readers over and over during this period of Nephite history.

Out of the sedition of Paanchi grew the principal Nephite precedent that legally defined conspiracy. The brief but intriguing account of this case, which occurred in the fortieth year of the reign of the judges (51 BC), is found in Helaman 1:7–8. This case arose out of civil strife resulting from the selection of a successor to the Nephite chief judgeship (transition points in Nephite politics, when power was passed from one ruler to another, often gave rise to rebellion or turmoil).[1] Three of the sons of Pahoran were contenders for the office, each having his own popular constituency (Helaman 1:4). When Pahoran was appointed, Pacumeni accepted the result but Paanchi did not. Paanchi incited a rebellion, which led to his apprehension, trial, and execution by the people: "But behold, Paanchi, and that part of the people that were desirous that he should be their governor, was exceeding wroth; therefore he was about to flatter away those people to rise up in rebellion against their brethren. And it came to pass as he was about to do this, behold, he was taken, and was tried according to the voice of the people, and condemned unto death; for he had raised up in rebellion and sought to destroy the liberty of the people" (vv. 7–8).

The record of these events is relatively brief. The Nephites were evidently careful to give as little press as possible to their political opponents in order to keep the ways of seditious conspirators out of the public eye. Indeed, when Alma passed the Jaredite records on to his son Helaman twenty years earlier, he commanded him to "retain all their oaths, and their covenants, and their agreements in their secret abominations; yea, and all their signs and their wonders ye shall keep from this people, that they know them not, lest peradventure they should fall into darkness also and be destroyed" (Alma 37:27). The book of Helaman, written by Alma's grandson, was true to this commission. Never is anything said about the words or contents of these seditious oaths and covenants.

The headnote for the book of Helaman makes it clear that the dominant organizing purpose behind this book is to tell about the "wars and contentions, and . . . dissensions . . . and the wickedness and abominations of the Nephites" and to contrast that state of affairs with the "conversion . . . and righteousness of the Lamanites." Along the way, the prophetic powers of Nephi, the son of Helaman, and also of Samuel the Lamanite are spotlighted (Helaman 10, 13–15). Thus the tone for the entire book is set by openly and unapologetically recounting the embarrassing jockeying for power that occurred at the highest levels of Nephite government and society. Twice, in what can only be seen as an understatement, these

---

1. Compare the strife that ensued shortly after Alma the Younger became chief judge (Alma 2), the instability that followed his departure in Alma 45 (even though at that time he was not the chief judge), and the turmoil that arose when Nephi became the chief judge (Helaman 4). The causes of war in the Book of Mormon are discussed in my introduction to *Warfare in the Book of Mormon*, ed. Stephen D. Ricks and William J. Hamblin (Salt Lake City: Deseret Book and FARMS, 1990), 6–16. "Warring parties consistently picked opportune moments to strike" (p. 16).

affairs are called "serious": "In the commencement of the fortieth year of the reign of the judges over the people of Nephi, there began to be a serious difficulty among the people of the Nephites. . . . There began to be a serious contention concerning who should have the judgment-seat" (1:1, 2). The seriousness of these matters is underscored by the book of Helaman's bleak final verses: "Satan did stir them up to do iniquity continually; yea, he did go about spreading rumors and contentions upon all the face of the land. . . . Satan did get great hold upon the hearts of the people upon all the face of the land. . . . And thus ended the book of Helaman, according to the record of Helaman and his sons," Nephi and Lehi (16:22, 23, 25).

Although Mormon interjected a few of his own comments in his abridgment of the book of Helaman (see, most notably, his editorial anticipation in Helaman 3:12–14 that the problems of conspiracy and secret combinations would eventually prove to be "the overthrow, yea, almost the entire destruction of the people of Nephi"), Helaman and his sons recognized the seriousness of the legal and political problem of how to punish conspiracy right from the first appearance of sedition instigated by Paanchi. His incitement to rebellion threatened the fragile existence of the Nephite reign of judges to the core. If a legal system is to operate openly, in the public sphere and by the voice of the people, nothing destroys the trust and confidence of the people in that system more than secret manipulations and covert dealings to subvert or obstruct justice.

The Crime of Inciting to Rebellion

Interestingly, Paanchi's crime was merely that of being *about to* incite a rebellion. The text says twice that he was "about to" set his plan into action: "He was *about* to flatter away those people to rise up in rebellion; . . . as he was *about* to do this . . ." (Helaman 1:7–8; emphasis added). Apparently he was apprehended and stopped just after he went beyond some critical point of preparation to set his plan into action. He had laid specific plans to call the people to rebellion. He may have been in a public place, just about to call the people to revolt. Thus it seems evident that Nephite law recognized the imminent incitement of rebellion as a completed crime; at least this point of law was clearly established by Paanchi's arrest, conviction, and execution, if for some reason it had not been quite so clear before. If there had been any doubt about this point of law under the law reform of Mosiah, there is every reason to believe that the Nephites had learned from the awful civil war started by Amlici in the fifth year of the reign of the judges forty-five years earlier (Alma 2:1), and also from the extensive bloodshed that followed the vicious defection of Amalickiah a generation before Paanchi (Alma 46–51), that a stronger stand needed to be taken more quickly to quell incipient rebellions before they generated a head of steam.

Other instances from early antiquity can be cited in which it was considered a capital offense to plan and actually prepare to incite a rebellion or to be on the brink of setting a plan of rebellion into action. The oldest sources indicate that staging a rebellion was itself a capital offense, even if the plot never got off the ground. The earliest case of this nature comes from an Egyptian account of a trial in 1164 BC concerning a conspiracy and plotted rebellion. The Judicial Papyrus of Turin records the trial and execution of one Pai-bak-kamen. Like Paanchi, he was the leader of a group whom he incited, calling them to "gather people and stir up enemies to make rebellion against their lord"; many others who had colluded with him, and some who were only remotely implicated, were also executed, mutilated, or left to commit suicide.[2]

Reflecting similar precautions, some very early ancient Near Eastern treaties required vassals to prevent conspiracies against the overlord. A third-century BC treaty between the cities of Ebla and Abarsal placed heavy legal burdens on the rulers of Abarsal, including the obligation "to denounce any conspiracy against the ruler of Ebla."[3] Disloyalty to or conspiring against a king could always land the perpetrators in serious trouble.

During the early Israelite monarchy, conspiracy was severely punished. The case of the priest Ahimelech, who had unwittingly given bread and a sword to David, shows that King Saul could treat even such incidental conduct as treasonous. Saul executed Ahimelech and all of the members of his family, together with eighty-five priests (1 Samuel 22:13–18) on the ground that they had "conspired against [the king]" (v. 8), even though (as one must presume) most of those executed people themselves had taken no specific action against Saul.

Another pre-exilic Israelite case of conspiracy is described in 2 Chronicles 33, where servants of King Amon, the son of Manasseh, "conspired against him, and slew him in his own house" (v. 24). Here, too, all people who were in any way part of the conspiracy were killed. "The people of the land slew all them that had conspired against king Amon" (v. 25), even

2. John A. Wilson, trans., "Results of a Trial for Conspiracy," in *Ancient Near Eastern Texts Relating to the Old Testament*, ed. James B. Pritchard, 3rd ed. (Princeton: Princeton University Press, 1969), 214–16.

3. Jerrold Cooper, "International Law in the Third Millennium," in *A History of Ancient Near Eastern Law*, ed. Raymond Westbrook (Leiden: Brill, 2003), 1:245, 247.

though some of those victims probably had not done more than given their encouragement or acquiescence to the perpetrators. The assassination of Amon, which occurred in Jerusalem in 640 BC, would have been well known to the prophet Lehi, who was an Israelite youth at that time. Following the assassination and these executions, "the people of the land" selected Josiah as the new king of Judah (v. 25).

Following these old Israelite rules, the first-century AD school of Shammai imposed criminal "liability for [mere] incitement" (i.e., where there was instruction or encouragement but no active help by the inciter). Shammai drew authority for his view from the pre-exilic prophet Haggai: "If [someone] says to his agent, Go forth and slay a soul, . . . [the] sender is liable, for [Haggai] said, 'Thou hast slain him with the sword of the children of Ammon.'"[4] Shammai particularly accepted the idea that a person could be held criminally liable for incitement to murder.[5]

From the time of the founding of Rome, Roman law also aggressively suppressed treason and seditious speech. Under the laws of the Twelve Tables, anyone "who shall have roused up a public enemy . . . must suffer capital punishment."[6] The common Roman crime of *maiestas* (which encompassed high treason, sedition, or attacking a magistrate) condemned all types of treasonous conversations or libelous speech, including "spreading slanderous stories in the army with a seditious intent," and the potential penalty for any form of *maiestas* was death.[7] For example, the infamous conspiracy of Cataline was detected by Cicero in 63 BC when he intercepted a written oath given by Cataline's co-conspirators enlisting a group of Gauls to join Cataline's army to attack Rome. Denied a trial, the conspirators were strangled by vote of the Senate while they were held in prison at Rome. Although the Senators felt fully justified in executing the conspirators, Cicero and the leaders of the Senate would pay a high political price a few years later because they had not given these conspirators,

---

4. Bernard S. Jackson, "Liability for Mere Intention in Early Jewish Law," *Hebrew Union College Annual* 42 (1971): 197–225, reprinted in and cited here from Bernard S. Jackson, *Essays in Jewish and Comparative Legal History* (Leiden: Brill, 1975), 202–34, quotation on p. 231 (emphasis in original).

5. Jackson, "Liability for Mere Intention," 225n109. Also, on plotting a murder, see Douglas MacDowell, "Unintentional Homicide in the *Hippolytos*," *Rheinisches Museum für Philologie* 111, no. 2 (1968): 156–58.

6. Table IX.5, reproduced in E. H. Warmington, ed., *Remains of Old Latin*, vol. 3, *Lucilius, The Twelve Tables* (Cambridge, MA: Harvard University Press, 1979), 497.

7. Robert Samuel Rogers, *Criminal Trials and Criminal Legislation under Tiberius* (Middletown, CT: American Philological Association, 1935), 79–99, quotation on p. 91.

who were Roman citizens, a trial and an opportunity to appeal any adverse verdict, as legal procedure normally would have required.[8]

Roman jurisprudence, however, soon adopted a different policy, one requiring that the inciter must have given some form of help or advice along with the incitement before he could be tried and punished: "If one aided another by giving him both advice and active help, one came within the principle [of culpability for incitement], which was applied in cases of theft, *iniuria* [defamation], treason, and procuring."[9] Some Roman jurists argued that a special case was presented by "inciting a dispossession by a force of armed men," holding that this was a crime even without "active help" being rendered by the inciter; but the prevailing opinion in Roman law went against this position.[10] Under this view, liability was not imposed for a simple expression of intent, but only for "an actual instruction to someone else to carry out one's intention."[11]

During the first century AD, the old Israelite view also gave way to the eventually prevailing view in Jewish law, represented by the rabbinic school of Hillel, that opposed the school of Shammai. Like the emerging consensus in Roman law, the opinion of Hillel and his followers went against the idea that a person could be punished merely for intending or planning to commit a crime. Thus Josephus at this time comments: "Merely to plan a thing without actually doing it is not deserving of punishment."[12] This dictum is consistent with a proposition that generally prevails even today in Jewish law: that a person cannot be punished in human courts for thoughts alone.[13] Thus it has been observed that the "concept of incitement is lacking in Jewish Law."[14]

With this background in mind, one can see that Paanchi's case presented its own share of legal difficulties. Under the approach of the old, commonsense Israelite law, Paanchi, as an inciter to rebellion, would have been summarily executed. Just about the same time as Roman and Jewish law on this point was changing in the Old World, similar legal pressures were apparently also being felt in Nephite legal history, even if not quite so potently. In particular, under the law inaugurated by King Mosiah, it

---

8. Frank Richard Cowell, *Cicero and the Roman Republic*, 2nd ed. (New York: Pelican, 1956), 233–34.

9. Jackson, "Liability for Mere Intention," 232.

10. Jackson, "Liability for Mere Intention," 232–33.

11. Jackson, "Liability for Mere Intention," 230.

12. Josephus, *Antiquities of the Jews*, 12:358 (author's translation).

13. Jackson, "Liability for Mere Intention," 212–13; compare Alma 1:17: "The law could have no power on any man for his belief."

14. Jackson, "Liability for Mere Intention," 232.

had become clear that a person could not be punished for his thoughts or beliefs alone (Alma 1:17; 30:7). That principle would seem to make it impossible for a judge in Zarahemla to convict a person merely on the basis of belief or intent alone. At least this question (and related ones) may well have arisen in some minds: Had the law of Mosiah modified in any way the old law regarding conspiracy or incitement? How much aid, help, or action needed to be involved in the case before the inciter could be executed? Did an actual rebellion need to begin, or was it enough (as in Paanchi's case) for the accused to have been on the very cusp of calling for armed rebellion?

Paanchi's case resolved this legal uncertainty by reaching a decision that was consistent with the older, more traditional Israelite conduct. Paanchi was apprehended and executed as he was "about to" incite the people to rebellion. We are left to wonder, How much had he actually done up to the point of his arrest? Had he talked to many people beforehand? Had he given specific instructions to others to carry out his orders? Had they formed a pact to go forward with the rebellion? Had Paanchi given help and aid to the insurgents? If he had done any of these things, the holding of the case does not seem to turn on those factors. Rather, it appears that the people ruled that Paanchi had gone far enough—even if only slightly—beyond mere intent and thus could be convicted. The historical report of the case concludes that Paanchi's incitement was legally tantamount to completed rebellion. The verdict was not just that he was "about to" commit rebellion but (going beyond the stated facts) that he, actually, for legal purposes, "*had raised up* in rebellion and sought to destroy the liberty of the people" (Helaman 1:8; emphasis added).

The Voice of the People

Significantly, the report of this case goes out of its way to emphasize that Paanchi was tried "according to the voice of the people" (Helaman 1:8).[15] Why should this have been the case when the trial of Paanchi took place during the reign of the judges? Had not Pahoran, the newly installed governor and chief judge, the right and the duty to judge all such cases? (Mosiah 29:25).

First, as argued above, it may well have been that the law of conspiracy was not clearly settled under Nephite law at the time when this case arose. Seeing the possible conflict between legal action on conspiracy and the rights afforded people to believe and to think what they wanted, the

---

15. See Pietro Bovati, *Re-Establishing Justice: Legal Terms, Concepts and Procedures in the Hebrew Bible* (Sheffield, England: JSOT Press, 1994), 228–30.

chief judge Pahoran may have determined that this case needed to be submitted to the people for their determination. King Mosiah had made "it [their] law—to do [their] business by the voice of the people" (Mosiah 29:26). By turning the case of Paanchi over to the ultimate legal authority still vested in the people, Pahoran would have insulated himself from the inevitable charges that could easily have been brought against him if he had proceeded against Paanchi on shaky judicial grounds. For example, certain factions in the society might have claimed that he had acted out of self-interest or that he lacked jurisdiction in the matter.

Second, Paanchi's case created problems because of its political timing and the nature of the case. Since Pahoran's very appointment was the cause of the rebellion, there may have been some potential argument that no chief judge had yet been definitively and authoritatively installed; and accordingly, in the case of such a contested appointment, jurisdiction and legal authority would have reverted back to the voice of the people in their basic political groups. Legitimizing the political superstructure of judges and chief judges in the land of Zarahemla was the voice of the people (Mosiah 29:26). Their voices were "cast in" and heard "in bodies" that were assembled throughout the land (v. 39). Those collective bodies may have reflected the kinship or lineage-group organization of this society that began in Lehi's day (Jacob 1:13) and that remained down to the end of Nephite civilization (Mormon 1:8)—even when the central government collapsed (3 Nephi 7:1–4)—and from which governing officials in Zarahemla ultimately derived their authority.

Similarly, ancient Near Eastern courts of law and judicial assemblies derived their authority from popular sources. Democracy was not, in this sense, a later creation of the Greeks or Americans.[16] Thorkild Jacobsen gives an account from one Old Babylonian letter of a man who, like Paanchi, was arrested for "seditious utterances" and was placed before the popular assembly, rather than before the king, where he was tried and convicted. Jacobsen concludes: "The judiciary organization here outlined is democratic in essence. . . . These judiciary institutions represent a last stronghold, a stubborn survival, of ideas rooted in earlier ages."[17] Similarly, popular judicial institutions were deeply rooted in Nephite society,

---

16. Thorkild Jacobsen, "Primitive Democracy in Ancient Mesopotamia," in *Toward the Image of Tammuz and Other Essays on Mesopotamian History and Culture*, ed. Wiliam L. Moran (Cambridge, MA: Harvard University Press, 1970), 157–72; see also G. d'Ercole, "The Juridical Structure of Israel from the Time of Her Origin to the Period of Hadrian, " in *Populus Dei: Studi in onore de Card. Alfredo Ottaviani per il cinquantesimo di sacerdozio 18 marzo 1966*, ed. I. Israel (Rome: Comunio, 1969), 389–461.

17. See Jacobsen, "Primitive Democracy in Ancient Mesopotamia," 161–62.

and thus from this case we see that even during the reign of judges the Nephites continued to look to the voice of the people in difficult cases of first impression. Pahoran was wise to refer this case back to the people, thus avoiding the political fallout that Cicero and the Roman senators encountered by executing the five Catalinian conspirators without following the normal rules of public law.

The Aftermath

In spite of the involvement of the public in this proceeding, the execution of Paanchi evoked a powerful objection among his followers. They enlisted Kishkumen to kill the chief judge Pahoran (Helaman 1:9). One may assume that Pahoran had been instrumental in seeking for justice in the case against Paanchi before the people. If the Nephite law on conspiracy was even somewhat vague before this trial, it becomes even more understandable why Paanchi's followers would have been so incensed by the holding in Paanchi's case. This verdict had serious political ramifications and clearly eliminated Paanchi as a contender for office and power in the Nephite government.

The aftermath of Paanchi's execution, however, was unfortunate. Kishkumen approached the judgment seat in disguise and murdered Pahoran. With Paanchi and Pahoran both dead, their brother Pacumeni was appointed chief judge and governor by the voice of the people "to reign in the stead of" Pahoran, "according to his right" (Helaman 1:13).[18] Kishkumen and his confederates then "entered into a covenant, yea swearing by their everlasting Maker, that they would tell no man that Kishkumen had murdered Pahoran" (v. 11). Because Kishkumen and his band of covenanters then intermingled with the population, they could not be easily identified and prosecuted, although "as many as were found" were summarily "condemned unto death" (Helaman 1:12). Apparently, these oath-swearing conspirators—like robbers or outlaws who had placed themselves outside the law and therefore were not entitled to its protections (compare the summary execution of the robber Zemnarihah in 3 Nephi 4:28)—were held incontestably guilty upon arrest. Once again, the law that required more than mere intent must have been satisfied by the element of the conspirator's oath. Further legal support justifying the execution of those who had sworn an oath of treason could well have been drawn from the long-standing biblical provision "Thou shalt not . . . curse the

---

18. It is unclear whose right is being spoken of here, either Pacumeni standing as the legal representative of his murdered brother's right to rule or Pacumeni's own right to assume office since he had been appointed by the voice of the people.

ruler of thy people" (Exodus 22:28; compare Mosiah 17:12 in the trial of Abinadi). After the precedent set by the case of Paanchi, no further legal question existed under Nephite law concerning the culpability of these oath-swearing covenanters as guilty co-conspirators, although apparently very few of them could actually be apprehended and executed.

As the Nephite government struggled in its campaign against these terrorists at home, matters grew worse because of external pressures. Within a single year, surely sensing a moment of weakness in the shaky leadership of the Nephite government, a Lamanite army invaded Zarahemla, and amidst the violence Pacumeni was killed by Coriantumr (Helaman 1:21). Coriantumr was none other than "a descendant of Zarahemla" (v. 15). As a descendant of the Mulekite king of the land of Zarahemla, Coriantumr could plausibly stake a legal claim to kingship, and he had little trouble being appointed leader of a Lamanite army to invade the land of Zarahemla (vv. 16–17).

Meanwhile, with Pacumeni now dead, another "contention" arose among the Nephites "concerning who should fill the judgment-seat" because there was no one from Pahoran's family who could do so (Helaman 2:1). The populace turned back to the family of Alma for leadership, and Helaman, the son of Helaman and the grandson of Alma the Younger, was appointed "by the voice of the people" to serve as the new chief judge (v. 2).

Thus the case of Paanchi and the deaths of Pahoran and Pacumeni served to establish the continuing legal right of the people to regulate their important judicial affairs "by the voice of the people." This case, which stands as a prologue to the book of Helaman, establishes the clear illegality of the very kinds of secret activities that continuously plagued the Nephites throughout the book of Helaman and into the first parts of 3 Nephi. In addition, recounting these catastrophic dissensions also shows that the Nephite leaders from the house of Alma were the only rulers during this era who could sustain their positions as governors, that they did not usurp the chief judgeship wrongfully, and that, indeed, they had not even sought that office.

The record of Helaman and his sons gives no hint that anyone in Zarahemla ever challenged the right of Helaman to rule. Nevertheless, dissidents in the Book of Mormon were always quick to challenge the rights of rulers to rule, a timeworn practice that began with Laman and Lemuel (1 Nephi 16:37) and continued down through the centuries (Mosiah 10:15). Undercurrents of dissent undoubtedly continued to fester in Zarahemla. But unlike the "robbers" who within about twenty-five years would gain "sole management of the government" by secret murders and combinations (Helaman 6:38–39), Helaman and his successors took charge openly, legally, and by the voice of the people.

In the face of immediate risks of assassination, Helaman magnanimously took this position of leadership because "there was no one to fill the judgment-seat," and he held that position until his son Nephi eventually delivered that political office to Cezoram twenty years later (Helaman 5:1). All of this legal clarification and political reshuffling, leading to the demise of the house of Pahoran, began with the verdict reached in the case of Paanchi. That righteous judgment, which reasserted traditional values, was certainly justifiable enough (especially from the point of view of Pahoran and his sympathizers). The judgment of the people reaffirmed the traditional, broad definition of the crime of incitement or conspiracy with intent to commit treason. The swiftness of this judicial decision explains not only why the immediate reaction of some people in this society was so violent, but also why the Nephite legal system continued to encounter so many difficulties in the ensuing decades in trying to seize and prosecute those who formed seditious, oath-swearing secret combinations.

Socially and politically, the trial of Paanchi left in its wake feelings of alienation and hostility on the part of some people in the land of Zarahemla. Conditions very similar to these have given rise to the phenomenon of "social banditry"[19] in several other times and places in world history. Typically included among those conditions are the disruptions caused by prolonged wars, famines, economic inequality, administrative inefficiencies, sharp social divisions, and political marginalization of minorities.[20] The main factor listed by social scientists regarding the conditions that have consistently produced social banditry in many traditional pretechnical societies, however, is a sense of indignity and injustice: "Social banditry emerges from circumstances and incidents in which what is dictated by the state or the local rulers is felt to be unjust or intolerable."[21] Thus the outcomes and repercussions of the trial of Paanchi, which must

---

19. For a good summary of several sources on social banditry, see Richard A. Horsley, "Josephus and the Bandits," *Journal for the Study of Judaism* 10 (1979): 42–52. See also Eric Hobsbawm, *Primitive Rebels: Studies in Archaic Forms of Social Movement in the Nineteenth and Twentieth Centuries* (1959; reprint, New York: Norton, 1965); *Bandits* (New York: Delacorte, 1969); Anton Blok, "The Peasant and the Brigand: Social Banditry Reconsidered," *Comparative Studies in Society and History* 14, no. 4 (1972): 494–503; Ramsay MacMullen, *Enemies of the Roman Order* (Cambridge, MA: Harvard University Press, 1966), 192–241, 255–68; and John W. Welch, "Legal and Social Perspectives on Robbers in First-Century Judea," in *Masada and the World of the New Testament*, ed. John F. Hall and John W. Welch (Provo, UT: BYU Studies, 1997), 141–53.

20. Horsley, "Josephus and the Bandits," 43–45.

21. Horsley, "Josephus and the Bandits," 43. See also John W. Welch, "Legal and Social Perspectives on Robbers in First-Century Judea," *BYU Studies* 36, no. 3 (1997): 141–53; reprinted

have been perceived as unjust in the minds of Paanchi's followers and others who would have felt threatened by the precedent set by this case, surely contributed to other conditions that were plentiful in Nephite society in the middle of the first century BC that incubated the rise of the militant Gadianton robbers and the other bands of social brigands that became such a sore curse among the Nephites for the next seventy-five years.

in *Masada and the World of the New Testament*, ed. John F. Hall and John W. Welch (Provo, UT: BYU Studies, 1997), 141–53.

CHAPTER TWELVE

THE TRIAL OF SEANTUM

About thirty years after the rebellion and execution of Paanchi, legal difficulties arose in the life of Nephi, the son of Helaman. Helaman had become the chief judge after all three of the sons of Pahoran had been killed within two years (Helaman 1:8, 9, 21), and Nephi succeeded his father after he had ruled for a dozen years (3:37). At the time of the trial of Seantum, Nephi was no longer serving as chief judge over the Nephites (5:1), having become "weary because of their iniquity," for they "could not be governed by the law nor justice, save it were to their destruction" (5:3–4). The text specifically associates their unrighteousness with abrogating the commandments of God and altering or rescinding the laws of King Mosiah (4:21–22).

In response to these legal changes, Nephi and his brother Lehi had left their seat of power in the capital city of Zarahemla and (much as Alma the Younger and the four sons of King Mosiah had done half a century earlier) proselytized for one year, going city by city, first among the Nephites in the north and then to the Lamanites in the south (Helaman 5:15–17). Their greatest success was among the Lamanites, some of whom returned with Nephi and Lehi and tried to sway the Nephites to return to their previous ways of faith, obedience, and repentance. Six years later, Nephi would make one more effort to prophesy and preach to the people in the north, but he was unequivocally rejected and "could not stay among them" (7:3).

Upon his return to the city of his birth, Nephi found conditions utterly lamentable. He describes the situation in terms that epitomize a complete state of unrighteous judgment, for the Gadianton robbers had corruptly usurped the judgment seats and spawned all sorts of corruption. They had laid "aside the commandments of God," had failed to act right before God even in small ways, had done "no justice unto the children of men," had condemned "the righteous because of their righteousness," had let "the guilty and the wicked go unpunished because of their money," and had taken personal advantage of their power in office "to rule and do according to their wills, that they might get gain and glory," and especially to commit adultery, to steal, and to kill (Helaman 7:4–5). One cannot overlook the obvious allusions here in Nephi's bill of particulars to the apodictic commandments in the biblical code of righteous judgment in Exodus 22–23. The judicial system in Zarahemla had deteriorated into a complete disregard of the express standards of righteous judgment: the corrupt judges had condemned and killed the poor and "the innocent and righteous" (as condemned in Exodus 23:3, 6, 7), they had favored the rich (prohibited by 23:3, 8), and they had failed utterly to be "holy men unto [God]" (as required by 22:31).

Seeing this terrible state of judicial depravity, Nephi took refuge on a tower in the garden of his ancestral residence (Helaman 7:10), where he began to mourn and loudly lament the wickedness and apostasy of the Nephites as if he were at a funeral (v. 11).[1] Nephi told them that unless they would repent, God would scatter them forth and they would "become meat for dogs and wild beasts" (v. 19). This, of course, could very well have been recognized by these people as precisely the same shockingly notorious fate that had befallen the city of Ammonihah about sixty years earlier (where the people's "carcases were mangled by dogs and wild beasts of the wilderness," Alma 16:10), and also as the same curse that had been placed on Noah's people by the martyr-prophet Abinadi a century before (that "the vultures of the air, and the dogs, yea, and the wild beasts, shall devour their flesh," Mosiah 12:2). In the ancient world generally, one of the most disgraceful things that could be done to a human corpse was to deny it a proper burial or leave it exposed to the elements and wild animals (1 Kings 16:4; 21:19, 23; Jeremiah 26:23). In a classic prophetic judgment speech, Nephi pronounced curses on the people three times: "Yea, wo be unto you," "Yea, wo shall come unto you," "Yea, wo be unto you." Twice he prophesied that they would be "utterly destroyed" and "destroyed from off the face of the earth," and finally he solemnly testified that "these things are true because the Lord God has made them known unto me" (Helaman 7:24–29).

---

1. John W. Welch, "Was Helaman 7–8 an Allegorical Funeral Sermon?" in *Reexploring the Book of Mormon*, ed. John W. Welch (Salt Lake City: Deseret Book and FARMS, 1992), 239–41. See especially Helaman 7:11, 15. In a typical funeral, family members would wail and cry, tear part of their clothing, veil their faces, cut their beards, put on sackcloth, and sit in ashes. See John W. Welch and Robert D. Hunt, "Culturegram: Jerusalem 600 B.C.," in *Glimpses of Lehi's Jerusalem*, ed. John W. Welch, David Rolph Seely, and Jo Ann H. Seely (Provo, UT: FARMS, 2004), 36–37 and sources cited at 40n41.

Thus it is not surprising that Nephi's audience in Zarahemla reacted sharply to his piercing condemnation. If Nephi had not been able to produce a prophetic sign validating the truthfulness of his testimony against them, the people would certainly have commenced definitive legal action against him, just as quickly and as sharply as Noah had rejected Abinadi and the people of Ammonihah had recoiled against Alma and Amulek.

The Limited Power of the Nephite Judges

In an effort to mobilize the populace against Nephi, the corrupt judges in the crowd began encouraging the people to take action, prodding and asking them, "Why do ye not seize upon this man and bring him forth, that he may be condemned according to the crime which he has done?" (Helaman 8:1). The crime named by the agitators was reviling the people and the law (v. 2). That the judges did not bring an action against Nephi themselves indicates quite clearly that judges in Zarahemla did not have authority in the law of Mosiah to initiate ordinary lawsuits, perhaps because of the obvious conflict of interest that judges would probably have if they were also involved as prosecutors or otherwise interested parties. Apparently only a private party—one or some of the people—could do this. Consistently in the Nephite legal cases, only the people had standing or the right to appear as plaintiffs: this was the case with Nehor (a group of church members had initiated the action against him; Alma 1:10), Abinadi, Alma and Amulek, Korihor, and Paanchi (a broad popular consensus supported the case against the accused; Mosiah 12:9; Alma 11:20; 30:20–21; Helaman 1:8), but most explicitly and definitely in the present case. It seems unlikely that the wicked judges who opposed Nephi were reluctant to act against him for political reasons, for they protested in public against him. Thus they probably would have accused him themselves if they had had the legal power or procedural standing to do so. This limitation on the power of the Nephite judges seems to be a constraint carried over from Israelite and Nephite restrictions on the powers of kings, who likewise under ancient law could not (or at least did not) act as judges on their own initiative.[2]

---

2. As discussed in connection with King Noah's role in the trial of Abinadi, kings in Israel did not function as judges in day-to-day civil or criminal matters; see Hans J. Boecker, *Law and the Administration of Justice in the Old Testament and Ancient Near East* (Minneapolis: Augsburg, 1980), 40–49. And under Jewish law, the king exercised no ordinary judicial powers whatever; see Babylonian Talmud (hereafter TB) *Sanhedrin* 2:1, 18a. Extending this principle separating judicial roles from administrative powers, the law of Mosiah seems to have given judges the power to judge but not the power to initiate legal actions (Mosiah 29:28–29; Alma 11:2).

One wonders how many people were required to participate in order to commence an action under Nephite law. Requiring a majority of the enfranchised population to commence every judicial proceeding would have been impractical, and so it appears that something less than a majority probably had standing in this regard. Indeed, the vocal opposition against Nephi did not subside on account of insufficient numbers, but rather because of "fear" (Helaman 8:4, 10). In any event, no policemen, public prosecutors, or state attorneys general existed in this civilization who could file a complaint at the behest of the judges, on behalf of the people, or in the name of the city or land of Zarahemla.

Instead, the judges agitated the people, suggesting to them that they had ample grounds to arrest Nephi since they had seen and heard "him revile against this people and against our law" (Helaman 8:2). Nephi's complete innocence, however, is assured from the outset, at least under the higher commandments of God and in the eyes of the writers or abridgers of the book of Helaman: "Nothing did he speak which was contrary to the commandments of God" (v. 3). This editorial exoneration appears to have been inserted as an irrefutable exculpation from any charge of reviling or as a defense against any future criticism of Nephi's conduct.

A Public Matter

Nephi's condemnation of "all this people, even unto destruction" (Helaman 8:5) resulted in an emotionally charged set of spontaneous debates and "contentions" (v. 7).[3] Some argued vehemently against Nephi, while others spoke up in his defense (vv. 5–9). This turbulent scene is reminiscent of the typical public setting of ancient Israelite trials: "There is nothing private about [the ancient Israelite] trial, for it is taking place in the public market-place, and many of the town's inhabitants are there watching the proceedings with intense interest."[4]

The result of the ensuing debate was that Nephi's supporters eventually prevailed, and he was not taken to the judges for trial. He continued his speech and in the end gave the people evidence of their own wickedness by disclosing details of treachery in their own midst: "Behold [destruction] is now even at your doors; yea, go ye in unto the judgment-seat, and search; and behold, your judge [Seezoram] is murdered, and he lieth in his blood; and he hath been murdered by his brother, who seeketh to sit

---

3. On the use of "contentions," *rîb*, in a legal context, see the discussion above regarding the case of Sherem.

4. Donald A. McKenzie, "Judicial Procedure at the Town Gate," *Vetus Testamentum* 14, no. 1 (1964): 102.

in the judgment-seat" (Helaman 8:27). Hearing these words, five runners were immediately dispatched by the people to see if Nephi had spoken the truth (9:1, 12). At the sight of the assassinated chief judge, the five men fell to the earth overcome. Other people, hearing the cry of the servants of the assassinated chief judge, arrived on the scene and, discovering the five men, concluded that they were the murderers and "laid hold on them, and bound them and cast them into prison" (v. 9).

A public proclamation was then sent out by messengers to announce the murder and to herald the apprehension of the suspects. One purpose served by this unusual announcement seems to have been the calling of a day of fasting and mourning (Helaman 9:10). The day after the death of a political leader was traditionally a day of fasting and burial in the Near East (1 Samuel 31:13; 2 Samuel 1:12; 3:35; 12:16–23).[5] The calling of a special fast may also have set the stage for the inevitably ensuing legal investigations and pious procedures to detect and punish the culprit. King Ahab was able to create an aura of false solemnity at the outset of the trial of Naboth by proclaiming a fast (1 Kings 21:12), so the day of fasting in the case of Seezoram's assassination may have served that purpose as well.

The Inadmissibility of Circumstantial Evidence

Following the burial of the murdered chief judge, the ruling parties wasted no time investigating the killing. On that same day, the five suspects were brought to the judges.[6] The five suspects, however, could not be convicted on circumstantial evidence under a legal system in which the often-invoked two-witness rule was as inviolate as it was in the Israelite system: "Circumstantial evidence seems to be ruled out by the scriptural law since every fact must be substantiated by the testimony of two witnesses."[7]

---

5. Roland de Vaux, *Ancient Israel: Its Life and Institutions* (New York: McGraw-Hill, 1965), 1:59–61; H. A. Brongers, "Fasting in Israel in Biblical and Post-Biblical Times," in *Instruction and Interpretation: Studies in Hebrew Language, Palenstinain Archaeology, and Biblical Exegesis*, ed. A. S. van der Woude (Leiden: Brill, 1977), 3–7; and Stephen D. Ricks, "Fasting in the Book of Mormon and the Bible," in *The Book of Mormon: The Keystone Scripture*, ed. Paul R. Cheesman (Provo, UT: Religious Studies Center, Brigham Young University, 1988), 129–30, showing that fasting in connection with mourning and burial was a pre-exilic Israelite practice expressing both grief and homage. As recently as with the death of Sadat in Egypt (1981), the day after his death was proclaimed a day of national mourning and fasting.

6. In the commotion, the five who had been sent were not identified as being the same as the five suspects until after the burial of the chief judge: "They were brought, and behold they were the five who were sent" (Helaman 9:13).

7. Boaz Cohen, "Evidence in Jewish Law," *Recueils de la Societé Jean Bodin* 16 (1965): 107. "Two witnesses is a *sine qua non* of any conviction and punishment." Haim H. Cohn, "Evidence," in *The Principles of Jewish Law*, ed. Menachem Elon (Jerusalem: Keter, 1975), 599. See also Pietro Bovati, *Re-Establishing Justice: Legal Terms, Concepts and Procedures in the Hebrew Bible*

"No circumstantial evidence is ever sufficient to support a conviction."[8] As Irene and Yale Rosenberg have argued, "Even in cases like the bloody sword wielder in which accuracy might not really be a concern, the no conjecture requirement [of biblical and talmudic law] still precludes conviction because receipt of the evidence would violate the formal procedural rules established for ascertainment of guilt."[9] Presumably, divine retribution would deal with cases where the factually guilty were not convicted and cannot be convicted because of the lack of admissible, direct evidence of their secret or covert crimes (e.g., Deuteronomy 27:15, 24).

In this case, all of the evidence was circumstantial. No one had witnessed the killing of the chief judge, for Seantum had killed his brother Seezoram "by a garb of secrecy" (Helaman 9:6). Even the servants did not know who had committed the crime, for the judges had to press Nephi to "make known . . . the true murderer of this judge" (v. 17).

A Case of an Unobserved Murder

The case of an unwitnessed murder presented special problems under the law of Moses, requiring special rituals and oaths of innocence.[10] If a person was "found slain in the land which the Lord thy God giveth thee to possess it, lying in the field, and it be not known who hath slain him" (Deuteronomy 21:1), then the law of Moses required the elders and the judges of the nearest city, in the presence of priests, to kill a heifer and ceremoniously wash their hands over the heifer and solemnly swear, "Our hands have not shed this blood, neither have our eyes seen it" (v. 7).[11] The procedure in Seantum's case never reached the stage of ritually expiating the blood of Seezoram, since the identify of the murderer was soon discovered. Nevertheless, at the time the five messengers were interrogated, the identity of the murderer was still unknown, and in this context these five men solemnly testified and declared their innocence before the judges, saying, "As for the murder of this man, we know not who has done it" (Helaman 9:15). Because these five men had been arrested, "cast into prison" (v. 12), and subpoenaed by the judges and were now making their

---

(Sheffield, England: JSOT Press, 1994), 268–75; and Robert R. Wilson, "Israel's Judicial System in the Preexilic Period," *Jewish Quarterly Review* 74, no. 2 (1983): 237.

8. Haim H. Cohn, "Practice and Procedure," in Elon, *Principles of Jewish Law*, 582; and TB *Sanhedrin* 37b.

9. Irene Merker Rosenberg and Yale L. Rosenberg, "'Perhaps What Ye Say Is Based Only on Conjecture'—Circumstantial Evidence, Then and Now," *Houston Law Review* 31, no. 5 (1995): 1387.

10. For more on unobserved crimes and witnesses in the Bible, see Bovati, *Re-Establishing Justice*, 273.

11. M. Athidiyah, "Scapegoat" (Hebrew), *Beit Mikra* 6 (1961): 80.

statement in a judicial setting, one may assume that they swore an oath or were required to wash their hands in some solemn gesture of innocence. In any event, the testimony that they gave, "As for the murder of this man, we know not who has done it," was formally consistent with the particular exculpatory statement called for in Deuteronomy 21:7, "Our hands have not shed this blood, neither have our eyes seen it."

Legal Issues Regarding Collusion

Nephi was immediately suspected of being a "confederate" (Helaman 9:20)—in other words, of having colluded with the murderer so that he could pretend to prophesy the death of the chief judge. The suspicious people apprehended Nephi and caused that he "should be taken and bound and brought before the multitude" (v. 19).[12] Again the decision whether to press charges rested with the people—not the judges, who despite their strong (but perhaps self-interested) suspicions (v. 16) could not commence a legal action against Nephi themselves to negate his criticism of their political corruption and wickedness.

It appears significant that the people next began to urge Nephi to acknowledge his "fault" (Helaman 9:20; see v. 17), as opposed to admitting any guilt. While nothing in the written texts of biblical law addresses this issue, under traditional oral Jewish law, conspirators and confederates were not considered equally culpable with the actual perpetrator of a crime:

> As a general rule, only the actual perpetrator of an offense is criminally responsible in Jewish law. Thus no responsibility attaches to procurers, counselors, inciters, and other such offenders who cause the offense to be committed by some other person. . . . Where a person hires another to commit a crime, criminal responsibility attaches only to the agent who actually commits it, and not to the principal who made him commit it, . . . [unless] the agent is not capable of criminal responsibility . . . or, where the actual perpetrator is an innocent agent. . . . However, the blameworthiness of the procurer did not escape the talmudic jurists: everybody agrees that he is liable to some punishment, lesser (*dina zuta*) or greater (*dina rabba*), and the view generally taken is that he will be visited with divine punishment.[13]

---

12. The familiar pattern is discussed in several chapters above, although this time the suspect was taken first to the people for interrogation rather than to the judge.

13. Haim H. Cohn, "Penal Law," in Elon, *Principles of Jewish Law*, 469–70. Ze'ev W. Falk, *Hebrew Law in Biblical Times* (Jerusalem: Wahrmann, 1964), 70, argues that the case of David and Uriah supports the idea that the law "held a man responsible for the acts of his servants

Under such legal principles, Nephi would not have been punishable as a confederate for the murder of the chief judge unless he was somehow extraordinarily involved as an accomplice or exceptionally liable as a principal. Accordingly, the record merely states that the judges hoped that Nephi would "confess his *fault* [not his guilt] and make known unto [them] the true murderer of this judge" (Helaman 9:17; emphasis added). Thus the judges probably never hoped to accuse Nephi successfully and to put him to death as a confederate in the crime.

Still, when he refused to admit any fault before the judges, those in control had Nephi taken, bound, and brought before the people (Helaman 9:19). In an effort to find evidence against him, the multitude pressed the case further against Nephi and aggressively interrogated him "in divers ways that they might cross him, that they might accuse him to death" (v. 19). Apparently they hoped to convict him of crimes such as false prophecy, reviling, or conspiracy even if they could not convict him as a direct perpetrator of unmitigated homicide. Indeed, if Nephi were truly guilty of homicide and not just of moral turpitude due to collusion, the death penalty would have been mandatory under Nephite and Israelite law (Genesis 9:6; Exodus 21:12; Alma 30:10; 34:11). Offering to drop or reduce other charges, the people offered Nephi immunity from prosecution if he would tell who his agent had been and if he would implicate the agent through disclosure of the agreement between himself and the agent ("acknowledge thy fault; . . . here is money; and also we will grant unto thee thy life if thou wilt tell us, and acknowledge the agreement which thou has made with him," Helaman 9:20), indicating that the people must have realized that they were not in a strong legal position to pursue capital charges of homicide against Nephi.

Bribery

The offer of money drew an outburst from Nephi: "O ye fools, ye uncircumcised of heart, ye blind, and ye stiffnecked people" (Helaman 9:21). Of course, it is hard to imagine Nephi considering a bribe under any circumstances. As was discussed in connection with Zeezrom's half-hearted attempt to bribe Amulek with his six onties, receiving a bribe in any form was strictly denounced by the law of Moses as one of the most salient characteristics of judging unrighteously: "And thou shalt take no gift: for the gift blindeth the wise, and perverteth the words of

---

performed under his orders," but David's case is better understood as falling in the domain of divine punishment and blameworthiness, not legal liability.

the righteous" (Exodus 23:8; see Deuteronomy 16:19; 27:25),[14] although "there is no penalty and no non-penal sanction prescribed in the Bible for taking bribes; . . . it was in the nature of unethical misconduct rather than of a criminal offense."[15] Still, the giving or receiving of bribes was condemned vehemently and repeatedly by the prophets and sages in Israel (e.g., 1 Samuel 8:1–3; Proverbs 17:23; Isaiah 1:23; 5:23; 33:15; Jeremiah 5:28; 2 Nephi 15:23), as it was also harshly condemned in other ancient cultures. For example, changing a final judgment, possibly under the influence of a bribe or some other personal benefit, resulted in removal from office under section 5 of the Laws of Hammurabi. Especially in cases of homicide, the payment of money (*kofer*) to the victim's heirs, let alone to the government, to exculpate oneself from the just imposition of capital punishment was strictly prohibited under the law of Moses: "Ye shall take no satisfaction for the life of a murderer, which is guilty of death" (Numbers 35:31).[16]

Detection of the Transgressor by Revelation

In response to the people, Nephi revealed other things to them, specifically that Seantum was the murderer, that they would find blood on the skirts of his cloak, and that he would confess his crime and would affirm Nephi's veracity when they would say to him, "We know that thou are guilty" (Helaman 9:34–36). Elsewhere in biblical law, other guilty parties were detected by various forms of revelation or divination. The casting of lots, for example, was often used to put an end to disputes and separate powerful men from each other (Proverbs 18:18). "In important cases the lot-casting was performed 'before Yahweh' or 'before the face of Yahweh', [i.e.,] at a holy place."[17] In the case of Achan, Joshua detected the offender by a form of revelation in which the Lord first identified the tribe, then the clan, then the family, and then the man who was the culprit (Joshua 7:14–15).

Whether by casting lots or some other means of selection, "the procedure in question had the character of a sacral act"[18] because divine indicators were brought to bear in the legal process not to judge as man

---

14. Tikva Frymer-Kenski, "Israel," in *A History of Ancient Near Eastern Law*, ed. Raymond Westbrook (Leiden: Brill, 2003), 2:992–93; and Haim H. Cohn, "Bribery," in Elon, *Principles of Jewish Law*, 510–11.

15. Cohn, "Bribery," 510; and Bovati, *Re-Establishing Justice*, 198.

16. Falk, *Hebrew Law in Biblical Times*, 73.

17. Johannes Lindblom, "Lot-Casting in the Old Testament," *Vetus Testamentum* 12, no. 2 (1962): 169.

18. Lindblom, "Lot-Casting in the Old Testament," 169. See Proverbs 16:33.

judges but to see justice and to reach proper judgment consonant with God's mind and will.

Execution Based on Self-Incriminating Confession

Just as Achan confessed his guilt in Joshua 7 as soon as he was detected by the oracle of God as the soldier in the camp of Israel who had hidden the contraband booty under the carpet of his tent, so Seantum immediately confessed his guilt, having been exposed by the glance of God's all-searching eye: "According to the words [of Nephi] he did deny; and also according to the words he did confess. And he was brought to prove that he himself was the very murderer" (Helaman 9:37–38).[19] Nephi and the five investigators were then liberated. All this transpired on the day of the burial of Seezoram (vv. 18, 38), which was the day after the murder. One can only assume that Seantum was soon put to death, although the record gives no further details about his demise.

The precipitous judicial use of Seantum's self-incriminating admission may strike modern readers as unceremoniously abrupt, and it may also seem out of line with the legal requirement that a conviction must be based on the testimony of two eyewitnesses. Yet this Book of Mormon account is in harmony with another technicality of righteous judgment that can be found in the early biblical period. While it is true that it was commonly held in the rabbinic period that no man could be put to death on the strength of his own testimony alone, for "no man may call himself a wrongdoer,"[20] especially in a capital case,[21] there was an arcane exception to this rule known from earlier times. In the Old Testament are found four episodes that support the idea that self-incriminating confessions could be used under certain circumstances in justifying punishment for unobserved criminal acts. The four cases are (1) the detection and execution of Achan (Joshua 7); (2) the man put to death for admitting that he had killed Saul (2 Samuel 1:10–16); (3) the two assassins of Ishbosheth, the son of Saul, who were similarly executed (2 Samuel 4:8–12); and (4) Micah, the son who voluntarily confessed stealing from his mother

---

19. Bovati, *Re-Establishing Justice*, 94; and Wilson, "Israel's Judicial System," 238.

20. TB *Sanhedrin* 9b; and Haim H. Cohn, "Confession," in Elon, *Principles of Jewish Law*, 614. Jewish law worried about the unreliability of confessions made by emotionally distressed persons or that confessions would be extracted by torture or other abuse. Cohn, "Confession," 614–15. Bernard Susser, "Worthless Confessions: The Torah Approach," *New Law Journal* 130, no. 5976 (1980): 1056–57.

21. "No man may be allowed to forfeit his life (as distinguished from his property)," but lesser punishments could be imposed by self-incriminating confessions or admissions of liability. Haim H. Cohn, "Admission" and "Confession," in Elon, *Principles of Jewish Law*, 612–14, quotation on p. 614.

(Judges 17:1–4). How the ancients reconciled these four cases with the rigid rule that required two witnesses has long been a subject of jurisprudential attention.[22] The rabbis explained that the four early biblical cases did not violate the two-witness rule, on several possible grounds: because they were confessions outside of court, because they came "after [the] trial and conviction [and were] made for the sole purpose of expiating the sin before God," or because they were "exceptions to the general rule . . . [since they were] related to proceedings before kings or rulers" instead of before judges.[23] These distinctions seem valid especially, as Falk points out, in the case of Achan, whose conviction was "corroborated by an ordeal [the casting of lots]" and whose confession was confirmed "by the production of the *corpus delicti* [the illegal booty under his tent floor]."[24]

Thus one can conclude with reasonable confidence that, in the biblical period, the two-witness rule could be overridden in the case of a self-incriminating confession, but not easily, and only if (1) the confession occurred outside the court or the will of God was evidenced in the detection of the offender, and (2) corroborating physical evidence was produced proving who committed the crime. Quite remarkably, Seantum's self-incriminating confession was precisely such a case on all counts, and thus his execution would not have been legally problematic. His confession was spontaneous and occurred outside of court. The evidence of God's will was supplied through Nephi's prophecy. The tangible evidence was present in the blood found on Seantum's cloak. The combination of these circumstances would have overridden the normal concerns in biblical jurisprudence about using self-incriminating confessions to obtain a conviction.

Given the complicated and important ancient legal issues presented by the case of Seantum, it is little wonder that the text makes special note of the fact that Seantum "was brought to prove that he himself was the very murderer" (Helaman 9:38). No further evidence was legally needed to convict him, and one may assume that it was proper that he was summarily executed.

---

22. Kirschenbaum finds the evidence inconclusive: "Whether this pentateuchal requirement of two witnesses, adopted as standard Israelite criminal procedure (1 Kings 21:10, 13), was construed loosely, as an alternative or supplement to confession—as would appear from David's judicial decisions—or whether it was interpreted strictly, as excluding confession—as taught by the Oral Tradition . . . —must remain an open question to the critical scholar." Aaron Kirschenbaum, *Self-Incrimination in Jewish Law* (New York: Burning Bush Press, 1970), 33. Cohn is not so tentative: "The rule against self-incrimination dates only from talmudic times." Cohn, "Confession," 614.

23. Cohn, "Confession," 614.

24. Falk, *Hebrew Law in Biblical Times*, 60.

Although the case of Seantum was quite unusual and therefore probably did not serve to establish an evidentiary precedent that was used in many legal cases in subsequent Nephite history, this outcome was significant in several other ways. It certainly drew a vivid distinction between the unrighteous judgments that were being handed down by the self-serving Gadianton judges and the self-effacing righteous judgment effectuated by Nephi. At this time in Nephite history, when the influence of the church was in steep decline in the city of Zarahemla, God's entrance into this proceeding demonstrated that he was aware of the corruption of political officials to the point of openly sustaining and validating the words of his prophets. In this case especially, righteous judgment equates with God's judgment, and at least for a few years many of the people were convinced that Nephi was "a prophet" (Helaman 9:40), and some even thought he was "a god" (v. 41). While most of these people soon reverted to their wicked ways, the case had been made that God knew well and condemned the wickedness and unrighteous judgments of the robbers and assassins who continued to plague the Nephites.

Thus the case of Seantum would have sustained and encouraged the righteous few in this society in their adamant determination to resist civil corruption, to challenge and expose secret combinations, to induce confessions of secret wrongdoings, and to judge courageously and righteously themselves. Because of Nephi's ability to prophesy correctly in the case of Seantum, several people would find themselves more inclined fifteen years later to believe the prophecy given at that time by Samuel the Lamanite (that the sign of the Messiah's birth would be given within a five-year window); and a few of those people would be willing to believe in that prophecy even up to its final day of expiration, even to the point of risking their lives in order to maintain their belief in the power of Samuel's prophecy (3 Nephi 1:9). Perhaps for these reasons, the righteous historians at the end of this era looked back on the trial of Seantum as an important highpoint. They placed this episode at the very center of the book of Helaman, featuring it as a salient victory by God's prophets over the factions of the wicked.

CHAPTER THIRTEEN

JUDICIAL PUNISHMENTS:
TYPES AND RATIONALES

To bring this study of the legal cases in the Book of Mormon to closure, the ultimate subject of judicial punishments deserves attention. Every legal case that ended with a guilty verdict saw the infliction of some form of punishment, and judging righteously required, in the end, the application of an appropriate (sometimes legally prescribed) type and level of punishment. Picking up where the general discussion of court procedures left off in chapter 4, and consolidating the specific information about individual case results presented in chapters 5–12, this chapter considers which forms of legal punishments were typically available to judges in biblical times and when, how, and why those punishments were used by Nephite jurists.

The legal cases reported in the Book of Mormon most often resulted in the death of the convicted party. The cases of Abinadi, Nehor, Pachus (Alma 62:9–10), Paanchi, Seantum, and Zemnarihah (3 Nephi 4:28) all ended with the accused being executed under official orders. The cases of Sherem and Korihor concluded with forms of divine judgment or punishment that led to death, while Ammon (Mosiah 7:16), Alma, Amulek, Aaron (Alma 21:12–14), Nephi, and Lehi (Helaman 5:21–22) were delivered from prison before their cases had resulted in their conviction. The possibility of capital punishment was indeed common enough in all ancient legal systems, but it was not the only option open to ancient courts. In fact, actual executions may have been fairly rare, although meaningful statistical evidence in this regard is unfortunately completely lacking.

Ancient legal rules for punishing convicted offenders were often quite specific, even formulaic. Some laws included provisions about what should happen if those laws were broken. In Babylonian law, for example, section 2 in the Laws of Hammurabi provides that if a person is accused of sorcery, the accused "shall go to the holy river; he shall leap into the holy river and, if the holy river overwhelms him, his accuser shall take and keep his house." Likewise in biblical law, Leviticus 24:14 spells out the punishment for one who blasphemes the name of the Lord: "Let all that heard him lay their hands upon his head [apparently to transfer the impurity back to the culprit], and let all the congregation stone him." When such legal specificity existed, it was important for ancient courts and officers to impose the prescribed form of punishment at the conclusion of a trial. Under such circumstances, little latitude was left for judicial discretion in the imposition of the conventional sanctions. Plea bargaining or grants of immunity were even less possible. Whether or not it was possible during some early eras of biblical law for convicted offenders to pay ransom (*kofer*) at the discretion of the next of kin in order to avoid capital punishment, as has been debated, even that escape route was "banned at a late stage in the development of biblical literature (represented by Numbers 35)," as Bernard Jackson explains and allows.[1] In any event, by the time of Lehi and the Book of Mormon the ban on *kofer* in Numbers 35:31–32 may have already been in place, and indeed there is no indication in the Book of Mormon that a righteous judge could give a convict the option of buying his freedom. Nehor, Paanchi, and Seantum were offered no such way out.

Over the years, ancient Near Eastern legal practice increasingly coupled specific infractions with correlative punishments. Because custom strengthened the association of certain consequences with particular transgressions, if a person committed a certain crime or caused a particular injury, society expected the respective punishment to follow, and this outcome was viewed as just. At the end of this process, rabbinic commentary became quite specific about which penalties would be appropriate for most crimes. During Book of Mormon times, however, sentencing guidelines had not yet become entirely rigid, as the novel execution of Abinadi and the extraordinary detention of Alma and Amulek tend to show.

Even where the law attempts to be precise, it will always be impossible for any legal system to enumerate every way in which people may violate the law (as King Benjamin soberly acknowledges in Mosiah 4:29) or to formulate in advance a suitable punishment for every case. Thus logic and analogy also played important roles in the development of ancient penal concepts throughout the ancient Near East and also in the Book of Mormon. Wherever possible, punishments were fashioned so as to relate logically and symbolically to the crime. Thus, under the Code of Hammurabi, a housebreaker would be hanged in the exact place where he broke in (section 21), a looter of a burning house would himself in turn be burned

---

1. Bernard S. Jackson, *Wisdom-Laws: A Study of the Mishpatim of Exodus 21:1–22:16* (Oxford: Oxford University Press, 2006), 133.

(section 25), the offending tongue of an adopted son who disowned his parents was to be cut out (section 192), the breasts of a wet nurse who wrongfully replaced a child for one who died were to be cut off (section 194), the hand of a son that struck his father or that embezzled seed or fodder was cut off (sections 195, 253), and a person who was supposed to plant seed in a field but failed to do so was to be tied behind two oxen and dragged through the field unless he could pay the prescribed fine (section 256). Many more examples of "mirroring punishments" could be listed.

Ancient law often applied this balancing principle, along with other principles of justice, to fashion specific remedies in cases where no explicit form of punishment was stated. Thus, even when a court was not given the equivalent of statutory direction on what punishment to impose, the decision was not an arbitrary or unprincipled one, for the choices open to the court were limited by both conceptual and practical factors. In theory, principles such as those mentioned above provided controlling guidance, while in practice, only certain options were physically feasible or culturally acceptable in these societies.

A wide variety of punishments are mentioned in the Babylonian, Hittite, Middle Assyrian, and other Near Eastern legal corpora, many of which are completely absent in, and were presumably unauthorized under, biblical law. These include modes of execution (e.g., capital punishment by drowning, impalement, and dragging) and punishments (e.g., fines paid to the palace of the king, long-term imprisonment, branding, and extensive beating).

By contrast, far fewer options seem to have been available to courts and judges operating under biblical law and likewise in the Book of Mormon. Torture, brutality, mutilation, and prolonged incarceration are either wholly absent or only vestigially present in the biblical law codes and narratives. Compared with Assyrian practices, which could be very brutal (including impalement, cutting off noses, tearing out eyes, or castration), the Israelite system of justice appears to have been far more humane, even though Israelite law demanded strict enforcement and required that "thine eye shall not pity; but life shall go for life, eye for eye, tooth for tooth, hand for hand, foot for foot" (Deuteronomy 19:21).

According to Zeʾev Falk, the laws in the Pentateuch established "fixed forms of punishment"[2] for the main offenses that those laws recognized. By the time of Lehi, those forms were probably well established by several years of custom and legal experience under the judicial practices instituted

---

2. Zeʾev W. Falk, *Hebrew Law in Biblical Times: An Introduction*, ed. John W. Welch, 2nd ed. (Provo, UT: Brigham Young University Press; Winona Lake, IN: Eisenbrauns, 2001), 73.

during the monarchy and shaped further by the rules found in the priestly regulations and in the book of Deuteronomy. The punishments discussed below were known and utilized in the Near East around the time of Lehi and are congruently evident in Lehite societies in the Book of Mormon.

Talionic Punishments

As Jacques Mikliszanski has rightly observed, probably no Old Testament passage is more commonly associated with the law of Moses and more frequently misunderstood as endorsing barbaric vengeance than is Exodus 21:23–25: "If any mischief follow, then thou shalt give life for life, eye for eye, tooth for tooth, hand for hand, foot for foot, burning for burning, wound for wound, stripe for stripe."[3] Even in cases under the law of Moses where this *lex talionis* (talionic law) was literally prescribed as punishment, scholars disagree on how this rubric was actually applied.[4] The least ambiguous and most important use of the talionic formula can be found in the concept of divine justice—the "ultimate justice, or the effect of a cause from which one simply could not escape"[5]—and in the teachings of prophets about that justice. Warnings that God will adhere to this principle when judging human conduct are plentiful in both the Old Testament and the Book of Mormon, and it is fair to say that no principle is more fundamental to the concept of justice in biblical times than the requirement that the punishment should somehow match, relate to, or balance out the nature of the crime or wrongdoing itself. Talionic justice

---

3. Jacques Koppel Mikliszanski, "The Law of Retaliation and the Pentateuch," *Journal of Biblical Literature* 66, no. 3 (1947): 295–303.

4. For some of the main studies of talion in biblical law, see Calum M. Carmichael, "Biblical Laws of Talion," *Hebrew Annual Review* 9 (1985): 107–26, reprinted in *Witnesses in Bible and Talmud*, ed. David Daube (Oxford: Oxford Centre for Postgraduate Hebrew Studies, 1986), 21–39. Richard Haase, "Talion und spiegelnde Strafe in den keilschriftlichen Rechtscorpora," *Zeitschrift für Altorientalische und Biblische Rechtsgeschichte* 3 (1997): 195–201; Bernard S. Jackson, *Studies in the Semiotics of Biblical Law* (Sheffield, England: Sheffield Academic Press, 2000), 271–97; Hans-Winfried Jüngling, "'Auge für Auge, Zahn für Zahn.' Bemerkungen zu Sinn und Geltung der alttestamentlichen Talionsformeln," *Theologie und Philosophie* 59, no. 1 (1984): 1–38; Philip J. Nel, "The Talion Principle in Old Testament Narratives," *Journal of Northwest Semitic Language* 20, no. 1 (1994): 21–29; Eckart Otto, "Die Geschichte der Talion im Alten Orient und Israel," in *Ernten, was man Sät: Festschrift für Klaus Koch*, ed. Dwight R. Daniels, Uwe Gleßmer, and Martin Rösel (Neukirchen-Vluyn: Neukirchener Verlag, 1991), 101–30, reprinted in *Kontinuum und Proprium: Studien zur Sozial- und Rechtsgeschichte des Alten Orients und des Alten Testaments* (Wiesbaden: Harrassowitz, 1996), 224–45; Stuart A. West, "The *Lex Talionis* in the Torah," *Jewish Bible Quarterly* 21, no. 3 (1993): 183–88; and Raymond Westbrook, "Lex Talionis and Exodus 21:22–25," *Revue Biblique* 93, no. 1 (1986): 52–69.

5. James E. Priest, *Governmental and Judicial Ethics in the Bible and Rabbinic Literature* (New York: KTAV, 1980), 155.

achieved a sense of poetic justice, rectification of imbalance, relatedness between the nature of the wrong and the fashioning of the remedy, and appropriateness in determining the measure or degree of punishment. Both divine and human actions, as well as natural consequences, can conform to these talionic principles, so it is often difficult to determine in a given case whether divine, human, or natural justice is involved.[6] It is important to understand talionic prescriptions in the law of Moses against the broader legal context of the time.[7] First, the *lex talionis* originated much earlier than the law of Moses. It is not a creation of biblical law. Its roots can probably be traced into the practices of ancient nomadic tribes[8] and into a pre-legal, "independent, oral existence."[9] All legal codes from the ancient Near East contain provisions that impose talionic-type punishments, even if the biblical formulation is not exactly paralleled there.[10] In addition to the talionic punishments mentioned in the Laws of Hammurabi above, this code prescribes that if a physician's hand causes death or loss of an eye, his hand is to be cut off (section 218); and if a slave does not obey (listen to) his master, his ear is to be cut off (sections 205, 282). Under the Laws of Ur-Nammu, if a female slave speaks insolently to her mistress, her mouth is to be scoured with salt (section 25). Under the Middle Assyrian Laws, if a man kisses another man's wife, an ax blade is to be drawn across his lip (tablet A9). Under the Hittite Laws, if a man steals bees, he is to be exposed to a swarm of stinging bees (section 92). Under

---

6. Klaus Koch and T. A. Boogaart argue that the talion embodies a natural law in which God plays no active role. They describe acts as having "a tangible, independent existence and an efficacy all their own. Once launched, these acts return to surround the agent and determine his fate." T. A. Boogaart, "Stone for Stone: Retribution in the Story of Abimelech and Shechem," *Journal for the Study of the Old Testament* 32 (1985): 47, discussing Klaus Koch, "Gibt es ein Vergeltungsdogma im Alten Testament," *Zeitschrift für Theologie und Kirche* 52 (1955): 1–42. This position seems extreme. The Book of Mormon and the Old Testament both support Towner when he says, "Like it or not, there is a notion of divine retribution in the Old Testament which presents God as one who intervenes in human affairs to punish those who anger him." W. Sibley Towner, "Retributional Theology in the Apocalyptic Setting, Daniel 7–12," *Union Seminary Quarterly Review* 26, no. 3 (1971): 204–5.

7. Raymond Westbrook, "Mesopotamia: Old Babylonian Period," in *A History of Ancient Near Eastern Law*, ed. Raymond Westbrook (Leiden: Brill, 2003), 1:414 ("An underlying principle of punishment appears to have been its symbolic association with the crime, especially by talion, either in like means of death or like member of family killed [vicarious talion]"); and Tikva Frymer-Kenski, "Anatolia and the Levant: Israel," in Westbrook, *History of Ancient Near Eastern Law*, 2:1033 (discussing talionic punishments in Israel).

8. Hans J. Boecker, *Law and the Administration of Justice in the Old Testament and Ancient Near East*, trans. Jeremy Moiser (Minneapolis: Augsburg, 1980), 174.

9. Jackson, *Wisdom-Laws*, 188.

10. Jackson, *Wisdom-Laws*, 188–89n87.

the Roman Twelve Tables, if a person maims another's limb, his limb is to be maimed unless he pays damages,[11] and so on.

Second, the law of Moses may have actually taken a step forward in the history of civilization by applying talionic punishments (as brutal as they may well seem) to all people equally. Except in Israel, where slavery was sharply curtailed (Exodus 21:1–11; Leviticus 25:39–55) and talionic principles applied universally, slavery and class distinctions pervaded the ancient world and the rules of talionic justice applied only "between members of the same social class."[12] For example, under the Laws of Hammurabi (sections 198, 199, and 201), if a member of the upper class injured a person of a lower class, the offender was not required to suffer comparable injury as a judicial punishment; he only had to pay damages. In contrast, a main point in the case of the blasphemer holds that the same law should be applied to Israelites and to resident aliens alike (Leviticus 24:16, 22). Thus biblical law made all people equal in this regard before the law.

Third, any legal system that allowed retaliation in kind was undoubtedly open to abuse. Vengeance was usually carried out privately and probably unjustly in many cases (as the boast of Lamech in Genesis 4:23–24 reflects). Under biblical law, however, talionic punishment was imposed by those judging the case. Thus Israel's version of the talion "was a tremendous improvement over earlier vendetta law or differential penalties depending on the social status of aggressor and victim."[13] Scholars generally view Israel's application of the talion as "an amplification of the public punishment of crimes as opposed to private revenge, and inseparable from it is an intensification of equality before the law."[14]

Finally, it may well have been the case that the purpose of the "eye for an eye" formula was not . . . to "*inflict* injury (as it might sound to us today) but to *limit* injury," particularly by preventing a "spiraling of revenge."[15] Hence, Boecker and others point out that the famous talionic phrase restrictively means "only *one* eye for an eye."[16] At least in noncapital cases, scholars support the idea that the "eye for eye" punishment was probably subject to financial settlement if the injured person was willing to accept money.[17]

---

11. Jackson, *Wisdom-Laws*, 192.

12. Boecker, *Law and the Administration of Justice*, 123. See Code of Hammurabi 196, 197, 200.

13. Priest, *Governmental and Judicial Ethics*, 147n11.

14. Boecker, *Law and the Administration of Justice*, 132.

15. Boecker, *Law and the Administration of Justice*, 174–75.

16. Boecker, *Law and the Administration of Justice*, 175; and Jackson, *Wisdom-Laws*, 190n98.

17. Jackson, *Wisdom-Laws*, 192–93.

Talionic punishments have been described as identical to, mirroring, or equivalent to the crime committed.[18] An identical talion was one in which the exact kind of injury or atrocity that had been committed was inflicted back upon the offender. For example, a murderer's blood would be shed because he had shed blood (Genesis 9:6). When Adoni-bezek, a Canaanite king, was captured by Judah and Simeon, they "cut off his thumbs and his great toes" precisely because he had cut off the thumbs and big toes of seventy kings whom he had reduced to servitude (Judges 1:6–7). After Samuel chastised Saul for failing to destroy Agag, the king of the Amalekites, the prophet fulfilled the very commandment that the king had been unwilling to carry out. Samuel commanded that the Amalekite king be brought before him, and he gave an explanation of the penalty before executing it: "As thy sword hath made women childless, so shall thy mother be childless among women" (1 Samuel 15:33). After Ahab arranged for the death of the innocent Naboth so that he might inherit his vineyard, the prophet Elijah prophesied that in "the place where dogs licked the blood of Naboth shall dogs lick thy blood," which cursing came to pass (1 Kings 21:19; 22:38). These kings suffered exactly the same atrocities they had inflicted upon others.

In cases of talionic mirroring punishment, the offending part of the wrongdoer's body was punished (e.g., cutting off an offending hand in Deuteronomy 25:11–12; compare Matthew 5:30). On other occasions, the punishment was designed to mimic the offender's own behavior in order to make complete compensation (e.g., if a man let his animals eat in another man's field, he had to make restitution out of the best of his own field, according to Exodus 22:5).

An equivalent talionic punishment was one that involved some characteristic of the crime or wrongdoing but did not need to mete it out as an exact retribution.[19] Forms of equivalent talionic justice were less exact but no less poetic than were identical talions. Sometimes they gave effect (or opposite effect) to the offender's intent, now applied to the offender himself. Often they were the result of divine justice. Thus Haman was hanged on the gallows he had prepared for Mordecai, even though Mordecai was not ever hanged (Esther 7:9–10). Elisha's servant Gehazi experienced a form of

---

18. Haim H. Cohn, "Talion," in *The Principles of Jewish Law*, ed. Menachem Elon (Jerusalem: Keter, 1975), 525; and Priest, *Governmental and Judicial Ethics*, 147. Falk, *Hebrew Law in Biblical Times*, 73; and Raymond Westbrook, "Punishments and Crimes," in *The Anchor Bible Dictionary*, ed. David Noel Freedman and others, 6 vols. (New York: Doubleday, 1992), 5:555. Jackson, *Wisdom-Laws*, 191n100, emphasizes the distinction between "literal" *talio* and mirroring consequences.

19. Cohn, "Talion," 525. See Deuteronomy 25:12.

equivalent talion because he had accepted a gift for a miracle that Elisha had performed but for which Elisha had not accepted a reward: Elisha had cured Naaman, captain of the Syrian host, of leprosy; because of his greediness, Gehazi was told that the "leprosy . . . of Naaman shall cleave unto thee, and unto thy seed for ever" (2 Kings 5:27). Abimelech, an ambitious Israelite who had killed seventy of his brothers "upon one stone" in order to become king, was killed not upon a stone but by a piece of a millstone: "Thus God rendered the wickedness of Abimelech, which he did unto his father, in slaying his seventy brethren" (Judges 9:56).[20] The sense of justice epitomized in these cases runs deeply throughout biblical law. Thus if a person afflicts any widow or fatherless child in any way, then "your wives shall be widows, and your children fatherless" (Exodus 22:22–24).

Similarly, the Book of Mormon records incidents of God punishing the wicked by afflicting them with the evil (or an equivalent and associated punishment) that they have inflicted upon others. Some of these occasions arise out of judicial settings; others surface in narrative contexts. For example, the prison walls fell upon those who unjustly imprisoned Alma and Amulek (Alma 14:27). After speaking against God, Korihor was cursed so that he could no longer speak (30:50). As Abinadi was being burned, he prophesied unto those who burned him, "Ye shall suffer, as I suffer, the pains of death by fire" (Mosiah 17:18); this came to pass when Noah suffered death by fire at the hands of his own men (19:20). Zemnarihah, the treasonous leader of the Gadianton robbers, "was taken and hanged upon a tree, yea, even upon the top thereof," after which that tree was symbolically felled to the earth, representing the way that God will fell to the earth all those who elevate themselves and try to bring down the people of God (3 Nephi 4:28–29). Mormon observed that "the judgments of God will overtake the wicked; and it is by the wicked that the wicked are punished" (Mormon 4:5). Following this remark, Mormon recorded a stream of atrocious acts that wicked Nephites and Lamanites committed against each other (vv. 11–18).

Prophets in both the Old Testament and the Book of Mormon taught that the talionic principle was especially part of divine justice. A remarkable chiastic[21] statement of this concept of retributive justice is found in Leviticus 24:17–21:

---

20. See Boogaart, "Stone for Stone," for a detailed analysis of the talionic principle in this story.

21. The entire case of the blasphemer is chiastically structured, with verses 17–21 at the heart of this elegant and meaningful composition. See my discussion in "Chiasmus in Biblical Law: An Approach to the Structure of Legal Texts in the Hebrew Bible," in *Jewish Law Association*

And he that killeth any *man* shall surely be put to death.
> And he that killeth a *beast* shall make it good, beast for beast.
>> And if a man cause a *blemish* in his neighbor as he hath done
>> so shall it be done to him.
>>> Breach for breach
>>> Eye for eye
>>> Tooth for tooth
>> As he hath caused a *blemish* in a man,
>> so shall it be done to him again
> And he that killeth a *beast,* he shall restore it.
And he that killeth a *man,* he shall be put to death.

The inverted symmetry, or reverse parallelism, of this balanced literary passage is worth special attention because it so impressively and fully conveys the balancing principle of talionic justice. Two Hebrew words here are especially important as markers of talionic texts: *kaʾasher* ("as that," as in "*kaʾasher* he has done") and *taḥat* ("for," as in "fracture *taḥat* fracture"). If these two words were at one time associated with different legal traditions (with the one word applicable to intentional injury, the other to any actual conduct whether intentional or not), by the time of Leviticus 24 and perhaps other related legal texts, this legal distinction had been "unified" into a single concept,[22] potentially covering all actions (planned or implemented, intentional or merely negligent). Completed actions remained of paramount concern: "As (*kaʾasher*) thou hast done, it shall be done unto thee: thy reward shall return upon thine own head," preached Obadiah (Obadiah 1:15). But intentions were also an important consideration in fashioning talionic punishments in ancient Israel.[23] It was considered just and fitting for a person to suffer the same as he had planned for another, even if the plan had not materialized. Thus the rationale for punishing the false witness was to "do unto him as he had thought to have done unto his brother" (Deuteronomy 19:19). Likewise, Jeremiah wrote: "I the Lord search the heart, I try the reins, even to give every man according to his ways, and according to the fruit of his doings" (Jeremiah 17:10).

King Benjamin and Alma similarly taught that men would be judged and rewarded not only according to their actions but also according to their thoughts or intentions (Mosiah 3:24–25; Alma 12:14). The talionic

---

Studies IV: The Boston Conference Volume, ed. Bernard S. Jackson (Atlanta: Scholars Press, 1990), 7–12; discussed in Jackson, *Wisdom-Laws,* 195, 201–7.

   22. Jackson, *Wisdom-Laws,* 206–7.

   23. Priest, *Governmental and Judicial Ethics,* 148–49.

principle is evident in Benjamin's teaching that "if ye judge the man who putteth up his petition to you for your substance that he perish not, and condemn him, how much more just will be your condemnation for withholding your substance, which doth not belong to you but to God, to whom also your life belongeth; and yet ye put up no petition, nor repent of the thing which thou hast done" (Mosiah 4:22).

There is no better illustration in the Book of Mormon of a prophet's explanation of the literal talionic nature of God's justice than Alma's admonition to his son Corianton in Alma 41:13–15:

> The meaning of the *word restoration* is to bring back again
> >evil for evil, or
> >carnal for carnal, or
> >devilish for devilish
>
> >>(a) *good* for that which is (a') *good*,
> >>>(b) *righteous* for that which is (b') *righteous*,
> >>>>(c) *just* for that which is (c') *just*,
> >>>>>(d) *merciful* for that which is (d') *merciful*;
> >>>>>>therefore my son
> >>>>>>>(d') see that you are *merciful* unto your
> >>>>>>>brethren,
> >>>>>>(c') deal *justly*,
> >>>>>(b') judge *righteously*,
> >>>>(a') and do *good* continually.
>
> >>>And if ye do all these things
> >>>then shall ye receive your reward;
> >>>>(d) Yea, ye shall have *mercy* restored unto you again;
> >>>(c) Ye shall have *justice* restored unto you again;
> >>(b) Ye shall have a *righteous* judgment restored to you again
> >(a) And ye shall have *good* rewarded unto you again.
>
> >For that which ye do send out
> >Shall return unto you again
> >And be restored
> Therefore the *word restoration* more fully condemneth the sinner
> and justifieth him not at all.

As in the passage from Leviticus 24 discussed above, an elaborate and elegant chiastic structure embodies the very notion of the talion, an important teaching in the words of Alma.[24] And here too the text reflects a confluence of the *taḥat* formula (evil *for* evil, good *for* good) and also the *kaʾasher* formula (*for that which* ye do send out).

Although most uses of the talionic formula are found in passages expressing statements of divine justice, the formula was also employed as a juridical principle. The law of Moses, however, prescribed it expressly in only three cases, and even there its meaning and operation have been the subject of much debate. The crimes for which biblical law required judges to be guided by this rubric in fashioning identical punishments were murder (Genesis 9:6; Exodus 21:23; Leviticus 24:17, 21), false witness (Deuteronomy 19:19), and bodily injury (Exodus 21:24–25; Leviticus 24:19–20).

There is little dispute that talionic retribution was applied literally in the case of murder in Lehi's day.[25] This becomes clear when the scriptural passages cited above are combined with Numbers 35:31, which prohibits the accepting of compensation for murder in lieu of the execution of the murderer. The reason for this is outlined later in the same passage: "So ye shall not pollute the land wherein ye are: for blood it defileth the land: and the land cannot be cleansed of the blood that is shed therein, but by the blood of him that shed it" (v. 33).[26] In order that the land might be cleansed, the law assigned an "avenger of blood" the task of slaying the murderer (vv. 12, 19). The English term *avenger* is somewhat misleading; it is "more accurately to be rendered as a redeemer of blood,"[27] which demonstrates that the talion in this case was more redemptive than vengeful in nature.[28]

---

24. See Alma 9:28 and 11:44 for other talionic teachings.

25. Even Mikliszanski, who otherwise maintains that literal application of the talion was absent in ancient Israel as a juridical principle, admits that the law of Moses prescribes life-for-life retribution in the case of intentional murder. Mikliszanski, "Law of Retaliation and the Pentateuch," 296–97.

26. According to Greenberg, "killing in self-defense and the judicial execution of criminals are explicitly exempted (Exodus 22:2; Leviticus 20:9, etc.)." Priest, *Governmental and Judicial Ethics*, 159, citing Moshe Greenberg, "Bloodguilt," *Interpreter's Dictionary of the Bible*, ed. George Arthur Buttrick (New York: Abingdon, 1962), 1:449.

27. Haim H. Cohn, "Blood-Avenger," in Elon, *Principles of Jewish Law*, 530.

28. As noted earlier, however, those guilty of manslaughter (i.e., killing a man unintentionally) were not condemned to death by the law. The distinction between murder and manslaughter, particularly in the eyes of the blood avenger (who was the next of kin of the victim), was often quite blurry (Cohn, "Blood-Avenger," 530); for this reason cities of refuge were provided for those who had killed unintentionally (Numbers 35:26–28; Deuteronomy 19:4–6). If there was a dispute concerning the guilt of one who had taken refuge in such a city (Cohn, "Blood-Avenger," 531–32), there was a public trial and a judgment by the congregation "between the slayer [manslaughterer] and the revenger of blood" (Numbers 35:24–25; Deuteronomy 19:11–13).

Perhaps the most striking prescription of the talion was in the case of false witness. "If a false witness rise up against any man to testify against him that which is wrong . . . then shall ye do unto him, as he had thought to have done unto his brother" (Deuteronomy 19:16, 19). In other words, if a person falsely accused someone of murder—for which the punishment was death—then the accuser would be executed instead. This seemingly harsh penalty for perjury undoubtedly stems from the nature of Israelite trial law. As Dale Patrick points out, "The Israelite trial depended heavily on testimony; evidence played a much smaller role than it does in modern trial procedure. Consequently, trials were vulnerable to dissembling witnesses."[29] To deter Israelites from abusing this system,[30] the law provided a stiff penalty against false accusers. The story of Susanna and the two elders offers a literary case in point. The elders falsely accused Susanna of adultery, for which she was nearly executed before Daniel proved that her accusers were lying. The elders were then put to death "to fulfill the law of Moses" (Daniel 13:62).[31] This, however, is the only apparent instance of the talion being applied against false witnesses; it is unclear how often and in what manner the talion was generally implemented in actual cases of perjury, let alone in lesser cases of honest mistakes of judgment or memory.[32] But at a minimum, this story reflects a widespread cultural expectation.

The practical application of the rules that prescribe talionic punishment in cases of personal injury (Exodus 21:24–25; Leviticus 24:19–20) has been the subject of much discussion.[33] The debate centers around whether the verses call for the literal application of the talion (i.e., if one had poked out another's eye, his own eye was poked out) or merely the administration of penalties commensurate to the crime or tort (i.e., fines or ransom). Haim Cohn, James Priest, and others tend to believe that literal application of the talion was at least an option sometimes used in ancient Israelite law,[34] while other scholars, such as Dale Patrick, view

---

29. Dale Patrick, *Old Testament Law* (Atlanta: John Knox Press, 1985), 125.

30. See 1 Kings 21 for a case in which this vulnerability was successfully exploited.

31. In the Old Testament Apocrypha, Daniel 13.

32. Mikliszanski argues that *lex talionis* was only literally applied in the case of murder and that consequently perjurers in other cases were only penalized commensurately (i.e., they paid fines instead of receiving the physical punishment) because that is the punishment the accused would have received. Mikliszanski, "Law of Retaliation and the Pentateuch," 299–300.

33. See Boecker, *Law and the Administration of Justice*, 172–73; Mikliszanski, "Law of Retaliation and the Pentateuch," 295–303; Patrick, *Old Testament Law*, 180–81; and Bernard S. Jackson, *Wisdom Laws*, 196–208.

34. Cohn, "Talion," 526; and Priest, *Governmental and Judicial Ethics*, 149–50.

"biblical *lex talionis* as a poetic expression of equivalence applied literally for murder but figuratively for injury."[35] In the Hebrew Bible there is no record of *lex talionis* being applied literally in a legal case involving personal injury. While evidence concerning the matter is inconclusive, the arguments that literal application of the talion was absent or infrequent in cases of personal injury seem more convincing than those to the contrary. By talmudic times, any literal application of the talionic formula was reserved to God; commensurate compensation, complete with an elaborate formula for calculating the amount of the fine, became the norm among the rabbis.[36]

Thus, while talionic formulas are found mostly in cases of divine justice in the biblical period, the talionic principle guided judges in certain cases as well. The same was the case in Book of Mormon law and society.

The clearest application of the talion in the Book of Mormon was for murder.[37] The law of Mosiah prescribed death as the penalty for murder (Alma 1:14; 30:10),[38] and at least part of the rationale behind this provision was similar to the explanation given in Numbers 35. Nehor, who had killed Gideon, was told, "Thou hast shed the blood of a righteous man, yea, a man who has done much good among this people; and were we to spare thee his blood would come upon us for vengeance" (1:13). As Nehor had shed blood, his blood was shed in the belief that doing so would cleanse the land and the people and the judges of any guilt.

Talionic principles also figure prominently in the Book of Mormon cases of false witnessing. Abinadi was put on trial because of his prophecies that King Noah would burn "as a garment in a hot furnace" and that the people would "have burdens lashed upon their backs" (Mosiah 12:3, 5). He was accused of and punished for lying or reviling the king (v. 14; 17:12). In an apparent application of the talionic punishment for being a false accuser, the priests of King Noah applied as a punishment the very things that he had prophesied would come upon the king and the people:

---

35. Patrick, *Old Testament Law*, 180; and Roland de Vaux, *Ancient Israel: Its Life and Cultures* (New York: McGraw Hill, 1965), 1:149–50.

36. Priest, *Governmental and Judicial Ethics*, 149–52. Other ancient Near Eastern cultures, such as the Hittites, also had compensation schemes. Richard Haase, "Anatolia and the Levant: The Hittite Kingdom," in Westbrook, *History of Ancient Near Eastern Law*, 1:652 ("Compensation is paid in two forms: replacement of the object . . . or pecuniary payment equal to the loss").

37. This was also known in the ancient Near East. Haase, "Anatolia and the Levant: The Hittite Kingdom," 1:644.

38. Indeed, murder is the only crime listed in Alma 30:10 for which capital punishment is expressly given as the penalty. This was narrower in scope than capital punishment under Hebrew law, which included adultery and "(other) religious infractions." Frymer-Kenski, "Anatolia and the Levant: Israel," 2:1027–28, 1034, 1037.

Abinadi was bound and "scourged [and/or scorched] . . . with faggots" (bundles of sticks) and burned. Abinadi's testimony, however, was not false—the people soon had heavy burdens placed on their backs (21:3), and the king suffered death by fire (19:20).[39]

In a similar case of perverted justice, the Ammonihahite judges and lawyers mocked Alma and Ammon by "gnashing their teeth upon them, and spitting upon them, and saying: How shall we look when we are damned?" (Alma 14:21). Alma and Amulek had just warned the people about the consequences of their sins if they did not repent. Perhaps it was in response to these perceived false accusations that the judges and lawyers treated Alma and Amulek in a manner similar to that which they had predicted their Ammonihahite antagonists would encounter in hell.

The Book of Mormon is silent concerning punishments imposed or compensation extracted in cases of personal injury.

In summary, the talionic principle—that one will or should be treated as he treats others—is applied in the Book of Mormon in the same pattern as in ancient Israel. Prophets taught that it was an integral part of God's justice; divine intervention in human affairs brought about talionic justice on several occasions, and the Nephite legal system clearly acknowledged the talion in the case of murder and probably applied it against those who had falsely testified or sworn false accusations in commencing legal actions.

Stoning

Another form of punishment evident in both biblical law and the Book of Mormon is stoning, the most common mode of inflicting capital punishment in ancient Israel.[40] Stoning is prescribed as the requisite form of punishment for eighteen different crimes in the Bible. Nevertheless, it was not the only method of execution used, nor was its use limited to those eighteen offenses.[41] Indeed, the mode of execution of a murderer in the early biblical period was often "left to the discretion" of the next of kin of the victim who was acting as the "redeemer of blood."[42] But in general, "persons put to death for public crimes were mostly stoned and then hanged."[43] The stoning resulted in the death of the criminal. Hanging the

39. For an extended discussion of the trial and execution of Abinadi, see chapter 6 above.

40. Westbrook, "Punishments and Crimes," 5:555; and Elon, *Principles of Jewish Law*, 526. See, for example, Leviticus 24:23; Numbers 15:36; 1 Kings 21:13; 2 Chronicles 24:21.

41. Jackson, *Wisdom-Laws*, 261–63; Haim H. Cohn, "Capital Punishment," in Elon, *Principles of Jewish Law*, 527; and Maimonides, Yad, Sanhedrin 15:10.

42. Falk, *Hebrew Law in Biblical Times*, 73.

43. Falk, *Hebrew Law in Biblical Times*, 73.

body was a method of publicly humiliating and making an example of the executed person (Deuteronomy 21:22).

Several theories have been proposed to rationalize the use of stoning. For example, Julius Finkelstein argues that all cases of stoning involved crimes that were "insurrections against the cosmic order itself."[44] Anthony Phillips sees stoning as most applicable to infractions of the Decalogue, perhaps, as Jackson suggests, because stoning was ordained in Exodus 19:13 as the punishment "for the offence of breaking the sanctity of the mountain at the time of the revelation of these laws."[45] But none of these theories explain all of the cases of stoning. More significant than the nature of the wrong being punished is the public dimension of stoning. Stoning was always the collective responsibility of the community and was carried out to drive away from the village the evil that had been committed. "Stoning was the instinctive, violent expression of popular wrath. . . . All the people had to pelt the guilty one with stones until he died."[46] The accusers and witnesses upon whose initiative and testimony the culprit was convicted were required to cast the first stones: "The hands of the witnesses shall be first upon him to put him to death" (Deuteronomy 17:7). Then "all the people" were required to join in the stoning (Leviticus 24:14; Numbers 15:35; Deuteronomy 17:7; 21:21).[47] In this way, "so shalt thou put evil away from among you" (Deuteronomy 17:7; 21:21). The essence of this punishment is to cast out, or exterminate (*ba'ar*), the wickedness by casting the stones, whether spontaneously or after judicial determination of guilt.[48] In the talmudic period, several legal reforms rendered this procedure perhaps somewhat more humane and less of a public spectacle—the culprit could be thrown down upon the rocks at the "stoning place," which was a quicker form of death than having stones thrown at him.[49] But this mode of execution still retained its public character.

A few Book of Mormon texts mention stoning. From their scriptural records, Nephites knew that Zenock and other ancient Israelite prophets

44. Julius J. Finkelstein, "The Ox That Gored," *Transactions of the American Philosophical Society* 71, no. 2 (1981): 28.

45. Anthony Phillips, "The Decalogue—Ancient Israel's Criminal Law," *Journal of Jewish Studies* 34, no. 1 (1983): 1–20; discussed in Jackson, *Wisdom-Laws*, 263.

46. Cohn, "Capital Punishment," 526.

47. Boecker, *Law and the Administration of Justice*, 40; Priest, *Governmental and Judicial Ethics*, 124–25; and Hyman E. Goldin, *Hebrew Criminal Law and Procedure* (New York: Twayne, 1952), 31.

48. Bernard Jackson, "The Goring Ox Again," *Journal of Juristic Papyrology* 18 (1974): 55–93; reprinted in Jackson, *Essays in Jewish and Comparative Legal History* (Leiden: Brill, 1975), 112–13, which seeks to distinguish between stoning as an early method of lynching and stoning as a mode of judicial execution, perhaps reflected in the two terms ṣaḳeil and rāgam, respectively.

49. Cohn, "Capital Punishment," 527; and Goldin, *Hebrew Criminal Law and Procedure*, 32.

had been stoned (1 Nephi 1:20; Alma 33:17). Nephi also prophesied that the wicked in the New World would "cast out the prophets, and the saints, and stone them, and slay them; wherefore the cry of the blood of the saints shall ascend up to God from the ground against them" (2 Nephi 26:3). The fulfillment of that prophecy occurred when God destroyed the cities of Laman, Josh, Gad, and Kishkumen because of their wickedness "in casting out the prophets and stoning those whom [God] did send to declare unto them concerning their wickedness and their abominations . . . that the blood of the prophets and the saints whom [God] sent among them might not cry unto [God] from the ground against them" (3 Nephi 9:10–11; see Helaman 13:33; 3 Nephi 8:25). Apparently the people of these communities apprehended those prophets as unwelcome intruders and then executed them by stoning. The fact that this was a community activity is evident from 3 Nephi 7:19, reporting that Nephi's brother was stoned and suffered death "by the people."

Several cases during the reign of the Nephite judges are reported in which stoning was used as an extrajudicial, community means of harassing a person or driving him out of a city, but not to the point of putting him to death. The men of Ammonihah who accepted Alma and Amulek were "cast out and stoned" by those who were sent "to cast stones at them," but these converts survived to hear from Alma and Amulek how their wives and children had been burned (Alma 14:7; 15:1–2). The sons of King Mosiah were "stoned and taken and bound" in the cities of the Lamanites (26:29). Alma's son Shiblon was stoned but not killed by the Zoramites (38:4), and the people of Zarahemla drove Samuel the Lamanite away by throwing stones at him, as well as by shooting arrows (Helaman 16:2; compare Exodus 19:13, which calls for either stoning or shooting arrows). In these instances, stoning was used to expel, injure, or terrify the victim, but apparently the assailants lacked the judicial power or motivation to carry out the stoning to the point of death. In the land of Zarahemla, the law of Mosiah removed from the people the legal "power to condemn any one to death" (3 Nephi 6:22),[50] and the sons of Mosiah may have been pro-

---

50. The final say over capital punishment in the ancient Near East, as in the Book of Mormon, often rested with the king. Kathryn Slanski, "Mesopotamia: Middle Babylonian Period," in Westbrook, *History of Ancient Near Eastern Law*, 1:489 ("As in other periods, the king is the highest judge in the land and sits on cases concerning loss of life"); and Ignacio Márquez Rowe, "Anatolia and the Levant," in Westbrook, *History of Ancient Near Eastern Law*, 1:705, 716, 739 ("A crime [*arnu*] that carried the death penalty of the evildoer . . . [was] in all likelihood decided by [the king.] . . . It seems clear that execution was supervised by the king. . . . In all likelihood execution was within the exclusive competence of the king").

tected somewhat by their royal status. Among the Lamanites, no instances of stoning as a legal punishment are mentioned.

Hanging on a Tree (and Crucifixion)

Hanging presents another close parallel. At the outset, it is important to note that "hanging" could be used either as a means of execution or as a way of displaying the body of an executed criminal. The mode of hanging could vary. It might involve tying a rope around the neck of the victim and hanging him until he died of strangulation or of a broken neck.[51] In other cases, the culprit or his corpse might have been strapped onto the tree (*ʿl-ʿetz*, Deuteronomy 21:22) or "upon the top thereof" (3 Nephi 4:28), with death then occurring mainly by exhaustion and asphyxiation.[52]

As a form of punishment used in ancient Israelite society, hanging was sometimes coupled with stoning. Under certain circumstances, the body of the convicted criminal would be hung following the execution by stoning. The purpose of hanging the corpse was to publicly humiliate the offender and deter others from committing similar offenses. When hanging was used as a method for displaying the corpse of an executed criminal, it was done to ensure that the criminal was dead and to expose the corpse infamously to the world. This method of exposing the corpse for public humiliation and warning was practiced by many ancient cultures. For example, as mentioned above, the Code of Hammurabi required that if a man had broken into a house, he was to be put to death and then hung before the breach that he had caused. A similar punishment, that of execution followed by a public hanging of the corpse, was required if a man caused the removal of the identifying marks on another's slave so that the slave could not be traced.[53]

On other occasions, however, hanging was the method chosen for the execution itself. Deuteronomy 21:22–23 is the key text: "And if a man have committed a sin worthy of death, and he be to be put to death, and thou hang him on a tree: his body shall not remain all night upon the tree, but thou shalt in any wise bury him that day; (for he that is hanged is accursed

---

51. The case involving Haman and Mordecai (Esther 5:14; 7:9–10) apparently followed Persian practices. Haman, a Persian, had secretly planned to kill Mordecai, a Jew. When the Persian king discovered Haman's treachery, he caused Haman to be hanged on the gallows that Haman had built. The gallows, "fifty cubits high," was probably used to hang Haman with a rope around his neck, but the record does not clearly state the details.

52. For a medical analysis of death by hanging or crucifixion, see W. Reid Litchfield, "The Search for the Physical Cause of Jesus Christ's Death," *BYU Studies* 37, no. 4 (1997–98): 93–109.

53. Code of Hammurabi 227.

of God;) that thy land be not defiled, which the Lord thy God giveth thee for an inheritance."

A graphic case of hanging as a method of execution is found in 3 Nephi 4:28–33. It is one of the most complete accounts of an execution ceremony found in any ancient record. This text gives, in considerable detail, an account of the execution of Zemnarihah, the captured leader of the defeated Gadianton robbers. The account begins with the stark statement "And their leader, Zemnarihah, was taken and hanged upon a tree, yea, even upon the top thereof until he was dead" (3 Nephi 4:28). In Zemnarihah's case, it is clear that he was not executed by stoning or otherwise before his body was hung on the tree; instead, he was "hanged . . . until he was dead," apparently dying by strangulation or suffocation. This suggests that the Nephites understood Deuteronomy 21:22 to allow execution by hanging—a reading the rabbis also saw as possible. While the rabbis generally viewed hanging only as a means in their day of exposing the dead body after it had been stoned,[54] they were aware of an archaic penalty of "hanging until death occurs."[55] For example, they mention an occasion when a number of women were "hung" to death as witches in Ashkelon in the first century BC, and Josephus tells of one occasion when eight hundred Pharisees were crucified (a form of hanging) by Alexander Jannaeus, one of the Maccabean high priests in Jerusalem (103–76 BC).[56] The rabbis, however, rejected hanging as an obsolete means of execution, since this was "as the government does."[57] This reasoning implies that they had no objection to hanging as a legally and historically possible form of execution, but they rejected it because it had become too closely identified with Roman practices from which the rabbis sought to distance themselves.

Crucifixion is often thought of only as a Roman or Persian mode of punishment; but execution by hanging a person on a tree is now found in the Dead Sea Scrolls, especially as a mode of execution for traitors or people involved illegally in wonder-working.[58] In the Temple Scroll from Qumran, the prescribed penalty for one who "informs against [or slan-

---

54. "Persons put to death for public crimes were mostly stoned and then hanged." Falk, *Hebrew Law in Biblical Times*, 73.

55. Cohn also acknowledges strangulation by hanging as an extraordinary remedy. Cohn, "Capital Punishment," 529. See also Babylonian Talmud (hereafter TB) *Sanhedrin* 6:6.

56. Josephus, *Wars*, I, 97.

57. TB *Sanhedrin* 6:6–7.

58. John W. Welch, "Miracles, *Maleficium*, and *Maiestas* in the Trial of Jesus," in *Jesus and Archaeology*, ed. James H. Charlesworth (Grand Rapids, MI: Eerdmans, 2006), 381–82. See generally John C. Robison, "Crucifixion in the Roman World: The Use of Nails at the Time of Christ," *Studia Antiqua* 2, no. 1 (Brigham Young University, 2002): 25–59.

ders] his people, and delivers his people up to a foreign [pagan] nation," or one who "has defected into the midst of nations, and has cursed his people, [and] the children of Israel," is that he shall be "hung on a tree."[59] It should be noted that the Temple Scroll's description of the kinds of cases that deserve hanging fits Zemnarihah's case exactly. As a robber who had defected away from his people, who had been party to threatening demands that the Nephites deliver up their lands and possessions (3 Nephi 3:6), and who had attacked his people, Zemnarihah was a most notorious and despicable traitor. He received nothing short of the most humiliating public hanging.

The execution of Zemnarihah closely followed ancient customs of ceremony and law. The Book of Mormon text goes on to say that after he was dead, "they did fell the tree to the earth" (3 Nephi 4:28). Quite clearly, the main reason for hanging Zemnarihah on the *top* of the tree was to make the greatest spectacle of his death and also of his fall when the tree was chopped down. Upon the felling of the tree, the people chanted together "with a loud voice, saying: May the Lord preserve his people in righteousness and in holiness of heart, that they may cause to be felled to the earth all who shall seek to slay them because of power and secret combinations, even as this man hath been felled to the earth" (vv. 28–29). Next they exulted and rejoiced and cried out "with one voice" for God to "protect this people in righteousness, so long as they shall call upon the name of their God for protection" (v. 30). Then they "broke forth, all as one, in singing and praising their God for the great thing which he had done for them, in preserving them from falling into the hands of their enemies" (v. 31). They also shouted "Hosanna!" (literally "Save us now!"),[60] which fittingly here, as in Psalm 118:25, "expresses the prayer that God will grant help and success."[61] Although the usage and history of the word *hosanna* is puzzling in many instances, it has been suggested that Jewish liturgical usage dating to at least 163 BC understood the word as having "political, as

---

59. 11QT 64:6–11. See also Otto Betz, "The Temple Scroll and the Trial of Jesus," *Southwestern Journal of Theology* 30, no. 3 (1988): 5–8; Max Wilcox, "'Upon the Tree'—Deut 21:22–23 in the New Testament," *Journal of Biblical Literature* 96, no. 1 (1977): 85–99; J. Massyngberde Ford, "'Crucify him, Crucify him' and the Temple Scroll," *Expository Times* 87, no. 9 (1976): 275–78; Joseph M. Baumgarten, "Does *tlh* in the Temple Scroll Refer to Crucifixion?" *Journal of Biblical Literature* 91, no. 4 (1972): 472–81; Yigael Yadin, "Pesher Nahum (4Q pNahum) Reconsidered," *Israel Exploration Journal* 21, no. 1 (1971): 1–12; and Samuel Rosenblatt. "The Crucifixion of Jesus from the Standpoint of Pharisaic Law," *Journal of Biblical Literature* 75, no. 4 (1956): 315–21.

60. On the meaning of *hosanna*, see Eduard Lohse, "Hosanna," in *Theological Dictionary of the New Testament*, ed. Gerhard Kittel and Gerhard Friedrich (Grand Rapids, MI: Eerdmans, 1974), 9:682–84.

61. Lohse, "Hosanna," 9:682.

well as . . . religious, implications. . . . It is a one-word prayer with potential political impact to unsettle oppressors everywhere."[62] The Nephite usage on this occasion appears to have served identical purposes. Finally, they blessed the name of the Lord and wept profusely in a great and joyous celebration (3 Nephi 4:32–33). This outburst may have been spontaneous, but it seems more likely that the people were repeating customary or ritualistic words, since they all shouted and sang out in unison.

Several factors indicate the antiquity of the execution of Zemnarihah. First, no trial is mentioned; the people took him straightaway and executed him. This treatment can be explained by Zemnarihah's status as a robber. Robbers in the ancient world were more than common thieves; they were outsiders and enemies to society itself. As such, the ancients reasoned, they were outlaws, outside the law, and not entitled to legal process. Against bandits and brigands, "the remedies were military, not legal."[63]

It is also significant that the tree on which Zemnarihah was hung was chopped down. This appears to have been done consciously in accordance with ancient legal custom. Although the practice cannot be documented as early as the time of Lehi, Jewish practice shortly after the time of Christ expressly required that the tree upon which the culprit was hung had to be buried with the body.[64] Hence the tree had to be chopped down. The rabbis understood that this burial should take place immediately, and thus the Babylonian Talmud[65] recommends hanging the culprit on a detached tree or a post. This way, the eminent medieval Jewish scholar Maimonides explains, "no felling is needed."[66] Unfortunately, the origins of this particular practice in Israelite legal history are obscure. Only these rabbinic instructions and the execution of Zemnarihah have survived as evidences of this unusual practice. The rather striking similarities between these two sources, however, bespeak a common historical base. Accordingly, one

---

62. Marvin H. Pope, "Hosanna—What It Really Means," *Bible Review* 4, no. 2 (April 1988): 16–25, quotations on 25. Much has also been written propounding various theories about the word *hosanna* and why the people shouted "hosanna to the Son of David" when Jesus entered Jerusalem (Matthew 21:8–9; Mark 11:7–10; Luke 19:35–38; John 12:12–15). For example, see Eric Werner, "'Hosanna' in the Gospels," *Journal of Biblical Literature* 65, no. 2 (1946): 97–122; and J. Spencer Kennard Jr., "'Hosanna' and the Purpose of Jesus," *Journal of Biblical Literature* 67, no. 2 (1948): 171–76. See generally Bjørn Sandvik, *Das Kommen des Herrn beim Abendmahl im Neuen Testament* (Zürich: Zwingli, 1970).

63. Jackson, *Wisdom-Laws*, 306; and *Theft in Early Jewish Law*, 180, 251–60.

64. TB Sanhedrin 6:7, 46b.

65. TB Sanhedrin 6:7, 46b.

66. *Code of Maimonides*, Sanhedrin 15:9. See Moses Maimonides, *The Code of Maimonides: Book Fourteen, the Book of Judges*, trans. Abraham M. Hershman (New Haven CT: Yale University Press, 1949), 43.

may assume that the formalities observed in 3 Nephi 4 were brought to the New World by Lehi's people, from which one may plausibly infer that these practices were known in pre-exilic Israel.

The rationale for chopping down the tree seems to relate to the idea of removing all traces and recollections of the executed criminal from the face of the earth, as well as expunging any impurities that the dead body would have caused. According to Maimonides, the tree should be removed "in order that it should not serve as a sad reminder, people saying: 'This is the tree on which So-and-so was hanged.'"[67]

This concern reflected by Maimonides shows that, in the minds of the people, the tree upon which the criminal had been hung was associated with the person who was executed. Similarly, the Nephites expressly identified the tree upon which Zemnarihah was hung with him and all those like him. As mentioned above, the people saw the felling of Zemnarihah's tree as a symbolic act, figuratively representing the downfall and elimination of this infamous robber. They cried out: "May [the Lord's people] cause to be felled to the earth all who shall seek to slay them . . . even as this man hath been felled to the earth" (3 Nephi 4:29).

In addition, the ancient idea of fashioning the punishment to fit the crime was carried out here.[68] The punishment of Zemnarihah was related symbolically to his offense. He was hung in front of the very nation he had tried to destroy,[69] and he was felled to the earth much as he had tried to bring that nation down.

Finally, the chanting of the people, proclaiming the wickedness of Zemnarihah, is reminiscent of the ancient practice requiring a notorious execution to be heralded. Deuteronomy 19:20, speaking of the punishment of those convicted of being false accusers, demands that "those which remain shall hear, and fear, and shall henceforth commit no more any such evil among you." In other words, the punishment of an offender was to serve, at least in one respect, as an example and as a warning to others. This was accomplished by immediate publication of the punishment. Commenting on this ancient practice, Rabbi Jeudah explained: "He is executed immediately and a proclamation is written and sent to all places."[70] In particular, all public matters, such as the execution of a rebelling judge, had to be heralded.[71]

---

67. *Code of Maimonides*, Sanhedrin, 15:9.

68. See generally the discussion of talion above.

69. Compare Code of Hammurabi 21, where the hanging was "in front of the place where he broke in." Similarly, Zemnarihah was hung in front of the nation he had offended.

70. TB Sanhedrin 10:6, 89a.

71. TB Sanhedrin 10:6, 89a.

Thus it is consistent that the execution of Zemnarihah, a notorious public offender, was proclaimed long and loud in immediate connection with his death. Much the same occurred with the prompt heralding of the outcome of Korihor's case (Alma 30:57). Lying behind both these cases were obvious political and religious motivations seeking to ensure that all those who remained would "hear and fear" and not follow the ways of these men who had radically opposed the central government. Thus the fear of God was specifically instilled in the people by an incantation against "all who shall seek to slay [the righteous]" (3 Nephi 4:29).

Burning

Burning represents a Book of Mormon expansion on Near Eastern practice since it was rarely employed as a means of execution or punishment in the Bible.[72] Burning is first mentioned in the patriarchal period, when Judah said of his daughter-in-law Tamar, "Bring her forth, and let her be burnt" (Genesis 38:24). Fire was also used, after execution by stoning, to exterminate the household of Achan, who had "sinned against the Lord God" by secreting booty under his tent (Joshua 7:20, 25).[73] These two early accounts typify the two kinds of offenders for whom burning was prescribed or mandated: first, it was used in cases involving "grave sexual offenses," such as the man who has sexual relations with his mother-in-law (Leviticus 20:14) or the daughter of a priest who becomes a whore (21:9);[74] and second, it "was applied as a penalty for grave offenses against the divinity,"[75] as in the case of Achan.[76] In situations where God had been

---

72. Burning as punishment was not unknown in other ancient cultures. For example, in Egypt it appears that "the Tod Inscription of Sesostris I may mandate burning as a legal punishment." Richard Jasnow, "Egypt: Middle Kingdom and Second Intermediate Period," in Westbrook, *History of Ancient Near Eastern Law*, 1:256; see also Richard Jasnow, "Egypt: New Kingdom," in Westbrook, *History of Ancient Near Eastern Law*, 1:343 ("Death through burning is apparently attested in the New Kingdom"). It also appears in Mesopotamia: "The edicts encourage informing, threatening witnesses who fail to report a breach of the rules with severe punishments, even burning at the stake (Edict 19)." Sophie Lafont, "Mesopotamia: Middle Assyrian Period," in Westbrook, *History of Ancient Near Eastern Law*, 1:535.

73. Frymer-Kenski, "Anatolia and the Levant: Israel," 2:1014 ("The reason [for the stoning and burning was] the nature of *ḥerem*: the presence of a *ḥerem* object turned the whole household into a *harem*. They were stoned for violation of the *ḥerem* and were then burned to get rid of all traces of *ḥerem* contamination").

74. Falk, *Hebrew Law in Biblical Times*, 73–74.

75. Falk, *Hebrew Law in Biblical Times*, 75.

76. Burning was also involved in the case of an apostate city: "A town that commits apostasy is to be put to the sword. The cattle are to be killed; all the town and spoil are to be burned with nothing spared and the town is not to be rebuilt (Deut. 13:13–19)." Frymer-Kenski, "Anatolia and the Levant: Israel," 2:1041.

offended, it has been suggested that the offender was being "devoted" to God as a burnt offering from which there was no "redemption," there being no way for the victim to offer other forms of sacrifice or compensation to exculpate himself. "No devoted thing, . . . both of man and beast, and of the field . . . , shall be redeemed, but shall surely be put to death" (27:28–29). After the time of Lehi, cases of burning include the Babylonians' attempted execution of Shadrach, Meshach, and Abednego outside Israel for their refusal to serve pagan gods (Daniel 3:6, 15) and Herod's order that those who had incited others to defile the temple should be burned alive.[77] However, these later cases go beyond the precedents in biblical law, which did not allow a person to be punished by burning merely for his beliefs.

Burning is mentioned in similar contexts in the Book of Mormon, especially during an exceptional period between 150 BC and 75 BC. First and foremost, Abinadi was burned alive, his skin being scourged and/or scorched with faggots as he stood bound (Mosiah 17:13, 20). He had been accused of speaking of God sacrilegiously (v. 8), for which burning could have been an appropriate remedy. In the end, however, he was sentenced to die for reviling the king (v. 12), and his punishment by fire was apparently fashioned according to talionic principles. Abinadi went down in Nephite history as "the first that suffered death by fire because of his belief in God" (Alma 25:11).

About seventy years later, the wives, children, and followers of several men who were ostracized from the city of Ammonihah were also burned, along with their religious records (Alma 14:8). Much like the eradication of Achan and his family and possessions from the camp of Israel, the expulsion or annihilation of these people and their religious texts was motivated ostensibly by religious concerns, if not by superstitions. Presumably, however, their obliteration was not complete; since no mention is made of their cattle or other property being destroyed by fire (v. 8), that property may have been confiscated by their persecutors.

Eventually, descendants of the priests who had executed Abinadi and Noah by burning were found among the Lamanite soldiers, who soon after the burnings of the women and children in Ammonihah invaded and destroyed that city (Alma 25:4). When some of their Lamanite cohorts began to believe what had been preached to them by the sons of Mosiah, those descendants of the priests of Noah punished them "by fire because

---

77. Cohn, "Capital Punishment," 528; and Josephus, *Wars*, 1:655. "That burnings may also have taken place at the stake appears from midrashic sources (compare Gen. R. 65:22; Mid. Ps. 11:7)." Cohn, "Capital Punishment," 528.

of their belief" (v. 5). This fulfilled another prophecy of Abinadi—that the seed of the priests, like their fathers, would "cause that many shall suffer . . . even the pains of death by fire" (Mosiah 17:15), and for this those descendants were hunted "even as a wild flock is driven by wild and ferocious beasts" (v. 17; see Alma 25:12).

These cases of burnings, however, went beyond the customary law. Human agents rarely had authority to impose death by fire. Perhaps this expansion of the law seemed justifiable because the word *ba'ar*, meaning "to exterminate, put away, or cast out 'the evil from among you'" in such passages as Deuteronomy 17:7, 19:11–13, 21:21, 22:22, 24:7, also means "to burn" as well as "to be stupid."[78]

More typically, burning was viewed as God's mode of purifying the earth. By fire he would cleanse from sin (2 Nephi 31:17), destroy wicked cities (Jacob 5:7, 47, 77; 3 Nephi 9:3, 9–10), impose final judgment upon the world (Jacob 5:77; 3 Nephi 25:1), and actually or figuratively punish the wicked in the eternities (Mosiah 2:38; 27:28; Mormon 8:17).

Slaying by the Sword

Several instances of slaying by the sword occur in the Book of Mormon, but none are strictly legal in nature. The destruction of Ammonihah "by the sword" (Alma 10:22–23; 16:9–11) at the hands of the Lamanite army conforms closely with the ancient Israelite law regarding the annihilation of apostate cities found in Deuteronomy 13:12–16.[79] This is the only place in the law of Moses that calls for execution "by the sword." Apparently, the reason why Alma carefully recorded and documented the fact that the inhabitants of Ammonihah had satisfied every element of the crime of being an apostate city was so that when the justice of God destroyed that city, it was clear that this fate was in accordance with divine law. In light of the fact that *apostates* were to be executed by the sword, it is ironic that the crime for which Nehor was executed was trying to enforce an apostate priestcraft "by the sword" (Alma 1:12). The slaying of Laban specifically by the sword in order to prevent the apostasy of an entire nation (1 Nephi 4:13, 18) may be associated here as well.

Flogging

Beating was the main penalty imposed under biblical law for minor offenses or other infractions where no form of punishment was expressly

---

78. Helmer Ringgren, "*b'r*," in *Theological Dictionary of the Old Testament*, ed. Johannes G. Botterweck, Helmer Ringgren, and Heinz-Josef Fabry (Grand Rapids, MI: Eerdmans, 1975), 2:201–5.

79. See the discussion of the case of Alma and Amulek in Ammonihah in chapter 8.

provided.[80] Biblical law specifically limited the number of lashes that might be inflicted, and its purpose was primarily to correct rather than to exact retribution. Parents could discipline or chastise children by beating them (Deuteronomy 8:5; 21:18). First offenders in simple legal cases would be flogged;[81] those slandering a virgin were beaten (22:18), and masters could whip disobedient slaves (Exodus 21:20, 26). The key text in this regard is in Deuteronomy, which prescribes flogging as a possible general punishment for any losing litigant: "If there be a controversy between men, and they come unto judgment that the judges may judge them; then they shall justify the righteous and condemn the wicked. And it shall be, if the wicked man be worthy to be beaten, that the judge shall cause him to lie down and to be beaten before his face, according to his fault, by a certain number; forty stripes he may give him, and not exceed" (Deuteronomy 25:1–3).[82] Flogging could also be combined with other forms of social punishment such as banishment or isolation, as is attested at least in later periods in Jewish history. For example, in post-talmudic times some argued that serious offenders were to be "flogged and ostracized."[83] Nevertheless, it was usually the case that only one punishment would be inflicted upon an offender for each ordinary guilty action. Thus, for example, "where reparation must be made by money, as for the crime of stealing (Exodus 20:13; Deuteronomy 5:17), the payment of damages and fines is preferred to flogging; . . . the rule is that he who pays is not flogged."[84]

Flogging is mentioned several times in the Book of Mormon. The most notable passage is in Alma 11:2. Very much like Deuteronomy

---

80. For example, in Egypt, beating was the punishment for nonpayment of taxes. Richard Jasnow, "Egypt: Old Kingdom and First Intermediate Period," in Westbrook, *History of Ancient Near Eastern Law*, 1:131.

81. Falk, *Hebrew Law in Biblical Times*, 74. See also Frymer-Kenski, "Anatolia and the Levant: Israel," 2:1028 ("Where flogging was prescribed, the number of lashes could vary 'according to his wickedness' but could not exceed forty lashes, for the sake of the culprit's dignity [Deut. 25:3]"). Flogging was also known elsewhere in the ancient Near East. Joachim Oelsner, Bruce Wells and Cornelia Wunsch, "Mesopotamia: Neo-Babylonian Period," in Westbrook, *History of Ancient Near Eastern Law*, 2:966 ("One text mentions flogging and the pulling out of men's beards and hair").

82. The interpretation of this provision has been the subject of considerable debate. Some rabbis limited its application to cases of assault (reading *controversy* in a narrow sense) or perjury (or having falsely testified in losing the case). But remedies in cases of assault are specifically prescribed (as in Exodus 21:22), and the punishment of a false accuser is handled pursuant to Deuteronomy 19:16–21. Thus the instruction in Deuteronomy is best understood, as Cohn has stated, "as a self-contained exhortation to do justice in civil cases as well as in cases of mutual criminal accusations (compare Mid. Tan. to 25:1)." Haim H. Cohn, "Flogging," in Elon, *Principles of Jewish Law*, 533.

83. Haim H. Cohn, "Homicide," in Elon, *Principles of Jewish Law*, 477.

84. Cohn, "Flogging," 534.

25:1–3, Alma 11:2 gives instructions to judges on how to handle private controversies. It provides, "Now if a man owed another, and he would not pay that which he did owe, he was complained of to the judge; . . . and he judged the man according to the law and the evidences which were brought against him, and thus the man was compelled to pay that which he owed, or be striped, or be cast out from among the people." This summary of Nephite civil procedure seems to indicate that a Nephite judge had three alternatives open to him in resolving a case of a delinquent debtor: first, the judge could compel the debtor to pay what he owed, which would certainly be the preferred outcome of the case; second, if the offender could not or would not pay, he would be "striped"[85] (i.e., flogged) to discipline and reform him; third, the more severe option of banishment was also open, but this was quite certainly reserved as a last resort for repeated violators or recalcitrants. Also consistent with Jewish jurisprudence generally, it appears that these remedies were alternative punishments, since they are connected with the word *or*; the offender would not be given multiple sanctions for the relatively petty offense of nonpayment.

Flogging and other forms of beating also occur often in the Book of Mormon as general means of discipline. For example, Nephi's elder brothers spoke many hard words to him and Sam, trying to persuade them to abandon their efforts to obtain the plates of brass, and in these efforts they beat them "even with a rod" (1 Nephi 3:28–29). Specific mention of the rod may be significant since the usual form of beating in later Jewish law was with a whip made of calfskin,[86] whereas a rod was used in earlier times by the Assyrians[87] and is mentioned in the Bible (Exodus 21:20–21; Proverbs 13:24).

Morianton was known as a man of passion who once grew angry with one of his maid servants and "fell upon her and beat her much" (Alma 50:30). His right to flog his servant even quite excessively, so long as the servant did not die within a day or two (Exodus 21:21), cannot be contested; but by beating her severely he contravened the spirit of Deuteronomy 25:3, which prohibited excessive beating.

---

85. The printer's manuscript, along with the 1830, 1837, 1841, 1852, and RLDS 1908 editions of the Book of Mormon, read "striped." Other editions read "stripped." If the guilty party was "stripped," the penalty was confiscation, discussed further below.

86. Cohn, "Flogging," 534.

87. Middle Assyrian Laws Tablet A7: "If a woman has laid hand on a man and a charge has been brought against her, she shall pay 30 manehs of lead and shall be beaten 20 stripes *with rods*" (emphasis added). Reuben Yaron comments on "rod" as the correct translation in "The Middle Assyrian Laws and the Bible," *Biblica* 51 (1970): 549, 552.

In 2 Nephi, the prophet Nephi warns people who believe that God will treat their offenses lightly. They wrongly believed that his punishment would only be token: "God will beat us with a few stripes, and at last we shall be saved in the kingdom of God" (2 Nephi 28:8). As the lightest form of punishment in his legal system, flogging is the obvious example of punishment for Nephi to use in this context.

Banishment, Ostracism, or Excommunication

Another option available to ancient courts was to banish or expel the offender from the land.[88] Some people, such as Socrates, preferred death over banishment. Most people saw themselves as being inseparably connected with their families, their villages, and their lands. Evidence of the use of banishment can be found "in the records of all ancient nations,"[89] and the Israelites and Nephites were no exception.

The basic principle behind the practice of banishment, or forced separation, was to purge the people of contagious iniquities. Such separation of unrighteous and impure people and things from that which is pure and righteous can be traced, in the Hebrew mind, back to the beginning when God drove Adam and Eve out of the Garden of Eden (Genesis 3:23–24). In Old Testament times, such punishments ranged from complete annihilation to a mere seven-day separation from the community. An uncircumcised male (Genesis 17:14) or one who flouted the observance of Passover (Exodus 12:15, 19; Numbers 9:13) was to be excluded from the assembly. Lighter infractions of purity laws calling for *karet*, however, "could not possibly have been punished by exile [from the land, but] would be adequately punished by temporary seclusion or excommunication."[90] "Utter destruction"[91] was the severest form of *ḥerem*. Through this punishment the community purged itself and preserved its purity by eradicating the transgressor as completely as possible.[92] This extreme form of excision

---

88. This punishment was generally reserved for offenses against the gods, such as witchcraft and adultery, which "were thought to cause 'pollution' of the surrounding area." Raymond Westbrook, "Introduction: The Character of Ancient Near Eastern Law," in Westbrook, *History of Ancient Near Eastern Law*, 1:76. It was often an alternative to capital punishment; see Ignacio Márquez Rowe, "Anatolia and the Levant: Ugarit," in Westbrook, *History of Ancient Near Eastern Law*, 1:734.

89. William D. Morrison and Janet I. Low, "Banishment," in *Encyclopaedia of Religion and Ethics*, ed. James Hastings, John A. Selbie, and Louis H. Gray (New York: Charles Scribner's Sons, 1981), 2:346–47.

90. Mayer Sulzberger, "The Ancient Hebrew Law of Homicide," *Jewish Quarterly Review* 5, no. 4 (1915): 594.

91. See Exodus 22:20; Leviticus 27:29; Numbers 21:2–3; Deuteronomy 7:2; 13:16–17; 20:17–18.

92. Haim H. Cohn, "Ḥerem," in Elon, *Principles of Jewish Law*, 540.

could be pronounced not only upon individuals and all their family and property (as in the case of Achan),[93] but upon entire apostate cities as well (Deuteronomy 13:13–17).

Jeremiah appears to have pronounced a *ḥerem* when he cursed the false prophet Hananiah: "Therefore thus saith the Lord; Behold, I will cast thee from off the face of the earth: this year thou shalt die, because thou hast taught rebellion against the Lord" (Jeremiah 28:16). Because Hananiah posed a danger to the spiritual welfare of the community, he was to be separated from it completely. Hananiah died within the year.

A milder form of expulsion from God's people was imposed upon Moses's sister, Miriam, when she spoke against Moses and became leprous: "Let her be shut out from the camp seven days, and after that let her be received in again" (Numbers 12:14). She was separated from the community but was allowed to live. This temporary removal was later termed *niddui*, meaning the "punishment of an offender by his isolation from, and his being held in enforced contempt by, the community at large."[94]

Thus the pre-exilic texts recognize banishment or removal options as ranging from mild to severe and as being imposed by either God or man. Later Jewish law refined and developed these options in great detail. Following the return from Babylon, Ezra recognized expulsion from the religious community as a form of punishment (Ezra 7:26). *Ḥerem* was reintroduced in rabbinic times as a harsher form of *niddui* (both being compulsory), while *nezifah*, a voluntary form of dissociation usually lasting a week, developed even later. In the rabbinic writings there is much discussion about how long these different forms of separation should last, who could pronounce them, and who could renounce them. For example, with *niddui* a transgressor was allowed social intercourse "for purposes of study and of business," whereas with *ḥerem* a transgressor "had to study alone . . . and find his livelihood from a small shop he was permitted to maintain." In both cases the transgressor could not, among other things, wear shoes, wash (except for his face, hands, and feet), cut his hair, or wash his laundry; he had to "live in confinement with his family only, no outsider being allowed to come near him, eat and drink with him, greet him, or give him any enjoyment." In the Talmud, such punishments are sometimes referred to as "civil death" or "the utter loneliness"; yet *niddui*

---

93. The idea of inflicting punishment unto the third, fourth, or tenth generation (Deuteronomy 5:9; 23:2, 3, 8) may mean to "wipe out the memory of the guilty person, even to the point of executing the person's family as well." Patrick, *Old Testament Law*, 85, although Patrick declines to endorse this position.

94. Cohn, "Ḥerem," 540.

was still considered a "relatively light penalty, . . . perhaps because it could so easily be lifted." A severe *herem* was pronounced publicly, with a "warning not to associate with the anathematized."[95] As might be imagined, the lot of outcasts was often extremely miserable.

Having left Jerusalem before the exile, Lehi would have been familiar at least with the early Israelite practices of *herem*, as well as with Miriam's temporary quarantine. Lehi himself had been forced to flee from Jerusalem, in effect an extralegal form of banishment. As with the post-exilic Jewish experience, which saw the addition of rules regarding banishment and ostracism in the Old World, other rules and forms of excommunication also arose in the Book of Mormon.

The first appearance in the Nephite record of a form of rooting out occurs in the case of Sherem. Jacob pronounced the curse of God upon Sherem, much as Jeremiah had done to Hananiah. Both Hananiah and Sherem were seen by the prophets as deceivers. Hananiah had made the people in Jerusalem "trust in a lie" (Jeremiah 28:15), while Sherem "preached many things which were flattering" and "did lead away many hearts" (Jacob 7:2–3). As with Hananiah, the consequence that befell Sherem was executed by God. Sherem was smitten and never recovered.

Events in Ammonihah involved an extreme form of *herem* as well. When the judges and lawyers in Ammonihah burned the wives, children, and religious writings of the converts of Alma and Amulek, they were practicing their own version of *herem* to eradicate them from their city.[96] In a talionic twist of fate, a stronger form of *herem* soon returned to Ammonihah when the Lamanite armies attacked it: "Yea, every living soul of the Ammonihahites was destroyed" (Alma 16:9), fulfilling Alma's prophecy that the Ammonihahites would suffer "utter destruction" (9:18).

Because the Nephite faithful needed to differentiate themselves from sinners and apostates, the Book of Mormon speaks of the rise of the more common practice of cutting off, or excommunication. This practice was introduced during the late second century BC. At that time, the Nephites were a minority group in control of Zarahemla (Mosiah 25:2). As they came under increasing social and political pressures from competing groups such as the followers of Nehor, the Nephites responded by drawing their own ranks closer together. Alma was given authority to maintain seven groups and to enforce membership requirements (vv. 19, 23; 26:28–32). Whoever would repent would be allowed in, but "whosoever will not repent of his sins the same shall not be numbered among my

---

95. Cohn, "Ḥerem," 540, 541, 544.
96. See note 73 above.

people; and this shall be observed from this time forward" (26:32). This form of excommunication preserved this group's identity and purity, and covenant-breaking members simply reentered the mainstream society.

Procedural guidelines for dealing with offending members of the church were introduced at this time. Impenitent transgressors were first "admonished by the church" (Mosiah 26:6). The teachers of the church then brought them to the priests, who took them to Alma, the high priest. "Many witnesses" called from among the people "stood and testified of [the transgressors'] iniquity in abundance" (vv. 6–9). Alma, "troubled in spirit" by the severity and implications of these cases (v. 10), first implored King Mosiah to judge these cases, but Mosiah refused (v. 12). Alma then "poured out his whole soul to God" concerning the matter. It was revealed to him that he was to judge the people according to the commandments of God, and the names of the unrepentant offenders "were blotted out" (v. 36).

Being "blotted out" or "cast out" of the group had severe religious, social, political, economic, and legal consequences. In the Pentateuch, "the Lord said unto Moses, Whosoever hath sinned against me, him will I blot out of my book" (Exodus 32:33; see Deuteronomy 9:14; 29:20). In the Psalms, the weak and the poor ask that when their wicked persecutors are judged, "let [their] posterity be cut off; and in the generation following let their name be blotted out" (Psalm 109:13). Although this type of expulsion was seen primarily as a form of divine judgment (v. 15; 2 Kings 14:27), it is also possible that written or oral lists of names were created and that when a person was cast off (as was Achan), his and his children's names were effectively removed from the group roster.[97]

Around 100 BC, Benjamin took down the names of all those who had entered into the covenant he administered (Mosiah 6:1), and "numbering" serves to define righteous groups—either for religious, political, military, or legal purposes—throughout the Book of Mormon.[98] The typical form of excommunication among the Nephites apparently involved blotting the

---

97. Such lists may have been created on census days or New Year festivals, when the people were "numbered" for religious, civic, and military purposes. See Ephraim A. Speiser, "Census and Ritual Expiation in Mari and Israel," in *Oriental and Biblical Studies*, ed. J. J. Finkelstein and Moshe Greenberg (Philadelphia: University of Pennsylvania Press, 1967), 171–86, esp. 183–84.

98. See, for example, 2 Nephi 4:11 (Sam to be numbered with Nephi's seed); Mosiah 25:12 (the children of Amulon "took upon themselves the name of Nephi" and are numbered among the Nephites); Mosiah 25:13 (the Mulekites are numbered with the Nephites); Alma 27:27 (after entering into the covenant, the Ammonites are numbered among the Nephites and are given land); 3 Nephi 2:14–16; 3:14 (the righteous Lamanites are numbered among the Nephites, especially for military purposes); 3 Nephi 21:22 (Gentiles who repent and come in unto the covenant shall be numbered among the remnant of Jacob, to whom the land has been given for an inheritance).

wicked person's name off such a list (26:36; Alma 1:24; 6:3; Moroni 6:7). The people expelled in this fashion "were remembered no more among the people of God" (Alma 1:24; compare Deuteronomy 25:19), for it had been given as a "word of God" that "the names of the wicked shall not be mingled with the names of my people" (Alma 5:57; compare Psalm 69:28, "Let them be blotted out of the book of the living, and not be written with the righteous"). Apparently, the Nephites understood and applied this concept literally—not just theologically or figuratively—at least during the time of Alma.

Blotting a person's name out of the religious and civic community had severe connotations. Not only was the person removed from the congregation of Israel on earth, but "the remembrance" of the wicked person was also blotted out "from under heaven" (Deuteronomy 25:19). The full extent of ostracism of one expelled from society in ancient Israel during the early biblical period is not fully known. However, among the Nephites, excommunication was a severe sanction. Church members were instructed to forgive transgressors, but until there was repentance on the transgressors' part, the faithful were to come "out from the wicked, and be ye separate, and touch not their unclean things" (Alma 5:57). The righteous remained separate from and probably refrained from social and perhaps business dealings with those whose names had been blotted out. Such harsh treatment of apostates would be consistent with later Jewish practices, and it may well account for the resentment and persecution of church members by those who were expelled. In fact, persecutions occurred immediately after the main instances of expulsion during this era (e.g., Mosiah 26:38; Alma 1:25).

Korihor's case illustrates the severity of banishment among the Nephites. Korihor was first physically expelled from Jershon by the religious authorities (Alma 30:21). After his trial in Zarahemla, he "was cast out, and went about from house to house begging for his food" (v. 56). Heralds were sent out by the chief judge proclaiming this banishment "to all the people in the land" (v. 57). Though not precisely clear, Korihor was apparently forbidden from engaging in business transactions to earn a living, since he was reduced to begging for food. In any case, he soon was deported to, or left to go voluntarily among, the Zoramites in Antionum, who had voluntarily "separated themselves from the Nephites" (v. 59); and so Korihor's banishment would not have precluded him from associating with the Zoramites. However, his fate was miserable there as well: "As he went forth among them, behold, he was run upon and trodden down, even until he was dead" (v. 59). Thus Korihor's banishment appears to have been more severe than that of those who had simply been excommunicated from the church. He had been cursed by God (v. 54) and condemned by the chief judge (v. 57), not merely reprimanded or anathematized by the high priest.

As mentioned above in connection with flogging, banishment was an option open to the judges when dealing with delinquent debtors under the law of Mosiah. They could be "cast out from among the people" (Alma 11:2). In a somewhat similar way, under post-talmudic law, creditors could impose *niddui* on defaulting debtors, and in some Jewish loan documents borrowers were expressly required to stipulate "in writing beforehand to be placed under *niddui* by the creditor in the event of non-payment."[99]

In addition, several apparently extrajudicial instances of expulsion also occurred during this time period. Alma the Elder and his followers were forced into the wilderness by King Noah and his priests (Mosiah 18:34; 23:1).[100] The converts of Alma the Younger and Amulek were driven away from the city of Ammonihah (Alma 14:7). About eight years later, the Zoramites banished the poor who believed the words of Alma; they "were cast out of the land" (35:6). Later, the Nephites cast out Samuel the Lamanite, who never returned to the land of Zarahemla (Helaman 16:2, 8). These may or may not have been formal actions, but either way they show a pervasive concern at this time of maintaining the integrity of these communities by regulating who was let in and who was kept out.[101]

Nephite law regarding excommunication for both civil and religious purposes changed in 3 Nephi. Speaking to the Nephites at Bountiful, the resurrected Jesus Christ taught that while an unrepentant member should "not be numbered among my people, that he may not destroy my people," the faithful were not to cast such a person "out of your synagogues, . . . for unto such shall ye continue to minister" (3 Nephi 18:31–32).

At the end of Nephite civilization, Moroni recorded that the believers "were strict to observe that there should be no iniquity among them; and whoso was found to commit iniquity and three witnesses of the church did condemn them before the elders, and if they repented not, and confessed not, their names were blotted out, and they were not numbered among the people of Christ" (Moroni 6:7). This procedure is basically the

---

99. Cohn, "Herem," 542.

100. Perhaps Alma the Elder was later motivated to deal directly with the excommunication process because he had personally suffered the injustice of this expulsion.

101. Consider also restrictions on travel and expatriation in my discussion in "Law and War in the Book of Mormon," in *Warfare in the Book of Mormon*, ed. Stephen D. Ricks and William J. Hamblin (Salt Lake City: Deseret Book and FARMS, 1990), 57–59. Apparently people were not always free to travel outside of their homeland.

same as the one established by Alma the Elder in Mosiah 26:29–32; both required sincere repentance and confession of guilt for exoneration. But the rules in Moroni's day specifically required three witnesses (compare Deuteronomy 19:15), and jurisdiction was now given to the elders. In all cases, "as oft as they repented and sought forgiveness, with real intent, they were forgiven" and reinstated (Moroni 6:8; Mosiah 26:30–31).

Shaming

Another punishment connected with ostracism and excommunication was that of public shaming. This was a strong factor in coercing compliance with the law and also in contributing to the odiousness of judicial punishments in biblical Israel and in ancient societies generally.[102] The most salient example is found in Deuteronomy 25:5–10, where a widow is permitted to bring her brother-in-law before the elders for not fulfilling his duty of taking her to wife to raise seed for his dead brother. The widow was allowed to take the sandal off the brother-in-law's foot, spit in his face, and have the derisive epithet "the man who had his sandal pulled off" attached to his family name. Although such actions might appear innocuous today, they were extremely shameful for several reasons: they were done in public, the "dominant" man was shamed by the usually "submissive" woman, the spitting rendered a person ritually unclean, the removal of the sandal represented the removal of the priestly privilege, and the family's reputation would be perpetually scarred in Israel.[103] Such public shaming was a serious matter because the Israelites saw themselves as a collective whole, so if one member was shamed, everyone was shamed.[104] There are several other instances of shaming in the Old Testament, and the fear of shame was used as an effective way of preventing wrongdoing.[105]

Shame is mentioned often enough in the Book of Mormon to prove that a strong culture of honor and shame operated in Nephite society. For

---

102. See generally Lyn M. Bechtel, "Shame as a Sanction of Social Control in Biblical Israel: Judicial, Political, and Social Shaming," *Journal for the Study of the Old Testament* 49 (1991): 47–76.

103. Bechtel, "Shame as a Sanction of Social Control in Biblical Israel," 57–61; comprehensive list of various shaming techniques on p. 72. See Johannes Pedersen, "Honour and Shame," in *Israel: Its Life and Culture* (London: Oxford University Press, 1973), 1:213–44; and David Daube, "The Culture of Deuteronomy," *Orita* (Ibadan, Nigeria) 3, no. 1 (1969): 27–52.

104. Bechtel, "Shame as a Sanction of Social Control in Biblical Israel," 51–53. At least one ancient Near Eastern culture employed collective punishment under a similar rationale. "Hittite law applied collective punishment in certain circumstances; thus if a person rejects a judgment of the royal court of justice, his 'house' (his whole family) is destroyed." Haase, "Anatolia and the Levant: The Hittite Kingdom," 1:651.

105. For a comprehensive list of various shaming techniques, see Bechtel, "Shame as a Sanction of Social Control in Biblical Israel," 72. See also Isaiah 20:3–5; 2 Samuel 10:1–5; Job 12:4; 19:2–5; 21:3.

example, Jacob used a heavy dose of shame in castigating the men in the city of Nephi for their sexual infidelity and greed, berating them because their actions had wounded their wives and children and even caused himself "to shrink with shame" (Jacob 2:6–9). Alma tried to sway his accusers in Ammonihah by telling them that eventually they would have to acknowledge before God to their "everlasting shame that all his judgments are just" (Alma 12:15).

Imprisonment

Unlike most modern legal systems, which employ imprisonment as their principal form of long-term punishment for criminal acts, ancient Near Eastern courts used prisons more temporarily, in the spirit of the Roman jurist Ulpian's dictum "Prison is intended for the confinement, and not punishment, of people."[106] Biblical law does not mention imprisonment as a judicial penalty.[107] The first solid legal evidence that incarceration was sanctioned in a punitive or coercive sense comes from the time of Ezra. When he reestablished the law of Moses in Jerusalem upon the return of the Jews from Babylon, Ezra brought a decree from the king of Persia providing that those who "will not do the law of God" will be subject to punishment, "whether it be unto death, or to banishment, or to confiscation of goods, or to imprisonment" (Ezra 7:25–26). This use of imprisonment as a punitive device was unusual in the Israelite experience; it was also absent from the Greek and Roman legal systems.[108] Prisons, however, were well known to the Jews from their experiences and contacts with other cultures in Egypt (Genesis 40:3) and Mesopotamia (Jeremiah 52:11); and several words for prisons, pits,

---

106. Menachem Elon, "Imprisonment," in Elon, *Principles of Jewish Law*, 536. See Bertrand Lafont and Raymond Westbrook, "Mesopotamia: Neo-Sumerian Period (Ur III)," in Westbrook, *History of Ancient Near Eastern Law*, 1:221 ("Imprisonment is mentioned but not specifically as a punishment. It applied to debtors and criminals pending payment of penalties"); Jasnow, "Egypt: Middle Kingdom and Second Intermediate Period," 1:266 ("Imprisonment in the sense of our 'jails' or prisons does not figure very prominently in the sources," though it was not unknown). The practice in some ancient Near Eastern cultures is not as clear, but it appears that prisons were used for punishment to some extent. See Ignacio Márquez Rowe, "Anatolia and the Levant: Alalakh," in Westbrook, *History of Ancient Near Eastern Law*, 1:716 ("Another kind of punishment consisted in being placed in prison or in the 'workhouse,' an institution which is also known at Nuzi. Unfortunately, our text only records the final confinement of two men and does not refer to the grounds for the penalty"); Oelsner, Wells, and Wunsch, "Mesopotamia: Neo-Babylonian Period," 2:967 ("There is ample evidence that prisons were in use, but their exact nature and purpose remains unclear. They were used for those guilty of theft, fraud, and, presumably, other offenses").

107. Falk, *Hebrew Law in Biblical Times*, 74.

108. Elon, "Imprisonment," 536.

stocks, or other places of detention or confinement are used in pre-exilic Hebrew texts.[109]

In ancient Israel, imprisonment was primarily employed for two purposes: first, to detain alleged transgressors during their trial and pending their execution; and second, as a purely political measure,[110] with troublemakers being "shut up by police action, often arbitrarily."[111] Two Old Testament incidents demonstrate that the typical use of prisons in pre-exilic Israel was for temporary confinement. In both the case of the man who gathered sticks on the Sabbath and that of the son of the Egyptian who blasphemed the name of the Lord, the witnesses apprehended the alleged transgressor and took him to Moses, who "put him in ward, that the mind of the Lord might be shewed" (Leviticus 24:12; see Numbers 15:34). Upon learning what should be done, Moses issued the sentence—in both cases stoning—which the people immediately carried out (Leviticus 24:13–14; Numbers 15:35). Incarceration served merely to hold the accused until his fate could be determined.

The use of imprisonment for political detention occurs at least three times in the Old Testament, and each incident involves a prophet and a king. King Ahab commanded that the prophet Micaiah be carried to Joash, the king's son,[112] to be cast into prison because Micaiah's prophecies displeased the king (1 Kings 22:26–27). Micaiah's confinement was worse than that of the Sabbath breaker's, for Micaiah was to be fed "with the bread of affliction and with the water of affliction" (v. 27), but the purpose of his imprisonment seems to have been to silence him rather than punish him for a crime. King Asa similarly sentenced the seer Hanani to "a prison house: for he was in a rage with him" because of what he had prophesied (2 Chronicles 16:10).

Jeremiah was also held "in the court of the prison," which was in the king's palace (Jeremiah 32:2). His case differs slightly from the other two since he was at least given the appearance of a judicial proceeding, for the princes charged him with sedition, treason,[113] or false prophecy and

---

109. Sulzberger, "The Ancient Hebrew Law of Homicide," 598, arguing that this evidence works against the assumption that "the ancient Hebrews did not know deprivation of liberty as a punishment for crime." See further David L. Blumenfeld, "The Terminology of Imprisonment and Forced Detention in the Bible" (PhD diss., New York University, 1977).

110. Elon, "Imprisonment," 536.

111. De Vaux, *Ancient Israel*, 1:160. See 1 Kings 22:27; Jeremiah 37:15–18.

112. Both King Ahab and King Zedekiah had their sons act as the keepers of the prison (1 Kings 22:26; Jeremiah 38:6).

113. John Bright, *Jeremiah: A New Translation with Introduction and Commentary* (Garden City, NY: Doubleday, 1965), 232.

sought his execution (38:4). However, this passage does not clearly establish that Jeremiah's imprisonment resulted from a judicial decision, since Zedekiah relinquished the case to the princes to do as they wished (v. 5). They lowered Jeremiah into a dungeon of mire, apparently hoping he would starve to death. Since such a judicial penalty for treason is unprecedented, it appears that the main reason Jeremiah was confined was not because it was the result of a legal proceeding, but because he was being silenced from making disturbing prophecies. Jeremiah's treatment, along with that of other prophets confined pursuant to administrative prerogatives, was worse than the treatment of those imprisoned in the course of judicial procedures.

The judicial and governmental use of prisons in the Book of Mormon needs to be approached in three different categories: (1) practices among the Nephites, which closely parallel those of their ancient Israelite ancestors; (2) inhumane practices of the Lamanites and the Nehorites; and (3) the long-term use of prisons among the Jaredites.

Among Lehi's descendants, the use of imprisonment was limited. As in ancient Israel before Lehi left Jerusalem, prisons were used only for temporary detainment, in arbitrary police actions, and on rare occasion for political detentions under martial law.[114]

Ammon and his scouting party, for example, upon discovering the people of King Limhi in the city of Nephi, were promptly bound and cast into prison (Mosiah 7:6–16, about 120 BC). Ammon and three of his men had come too close to the city walls when the king and his guards were outside the gate. The king took them into custody, bound them, and held them in prison, having mistaken them for the priests of King Noah, who had stolen daughters of the Lamanites. Two days later, Ammon and his companions were brought before the king, who soon determined they were not the priests of Noah and released them. Ammon's company had been imprisoned pending interrogation concerning crimes they were suspected of committing. Once their innocence was established, they were liberated. Had their guilt been determined, they would have been executed (vv. 7–11; 21:23). Limhi's father, the corrupt King Noah, had also used prisons in much the same way. Abinadi was held in prison three days during his trial (Mosiah 12:17; 17:5–6).

The suspected murderers of Pahoran were similarly cast into prison in the city of Zarahemla, only to be freed when their innocence was promptly proved (Helaman 9:9, 18). In such cases imprisonment served as

---

114. The case of imprisoning captives of war is considered in my chapter on martial law in Ricks and Hamblin, *Warfare in the Book of Mormon*, 75–82.

a temporary detainment measure during the judicial process rather than a lasting punishment imposed on a convicted criminal. There is no hint here that sentencing the convict to imprisonment was a penal option open to the court. The one case of prolonged incarceration among the Nephites, namely, the imprisonment of the leaders of the rebel king-men (about 67 BC), was justified under martial law on the asserted grounds that "there was no time for their trials at this period" (Alma 51:19).

Among the Lamanites, other incidents of imprisonment are somewhat less informative, primarily because divine intervention ended these periods of imprisonment before their cases were heard; yet it appears that the Lamanites used prisons for prolonged periods to humiliate or torture their enemies or undesirable intruders. In the case of Nephi and Lehi (Helaman 5:21–22, about 30 BC), an army of Lamanites cast them in prison in the city of Nephi (the same prison that had held Ammon and his companions ninety years earlier). There they were held for "many days without food," but the intent was not to confine them indefinitely, for the Lamanites "went forth into the prison to take them that they might slay them" (v. 22). Although angelic intervention prevented the Lamanites from carrying out the execution, the incident demonstrates that this imprisonment was temporary in nature.

Though not clear, it is likely that the Lamanites had used prisons in a similar manner approximately sixty years earlier when they confined Aaron and his brethren "for many days" at Middoni and caused them to suffer nakedness, "hunger, thirst, and all kinds of affliction" (Alma 20:29–30; 21:13). They were liberated when King Lamoni "found favor in the eyes of the king of the land" (20:28). There is no indication what otherwise would have happened to them.

Alma and Amulek's imprisonment in the Nehorite city of Ammonihah also deviated from the normal pre-exilic Israelite uses of imprisonment. Though Alma and Amulek were held in prison while their trial was in progress (a normal practice), it appears that imprisonment was also a punitive option available to the judges in Ammonihah. Those who attempted to snare Alma and Amulek in their words hoped to see the prophets arrested and "judged according to the law, . . . that they might be slain or *cast into prison*, according to the crime which they could make appear or witness against them" (Alma 10:13; emphasis added). That Alma and Amulek remained in prison somewhat longer than usual (about four to six weeks)[115]

---

115. Although Alma and Amulek were held in prison "many days" before the city's miraculous destruction (Alma 14:22–29), it is clear that they could not have been held there more than a few months. Since Amulek first met Alma on the fourth day of the seventh month of the tenth year (10:6), and since they were miraculously delivered from the prison three months and eight days

and received very poor treatment[116] by the officials finds negative precedent in the Old Testament experiences of Jeremiah, Hanani, and Micaiah. The asserted allowance of imprisonment as a post-judicial part of the Ammonihahite penal system, however, is unprecedented in the pre-exilic Israelite legal texts,[117] although imprisonment would have been known to these people either from stories on the plates of brass or from the Jaredite record, which had been translated in Zarahemla only ten years earlier. The adoption of incarceration as a form of judicial punishment by the Ammonihahites may be another example of how that society had stretched the law in order to prolong litigation and increase legal fees.[118]

The Jaredite experience differs even further from Israelite practice. While no incident of long-term imprisonment is ever recorded among the Lehites, the Jaredites regularly imprisoned political rivals for life and even made their posterity "serve many years in captivity" for generations thereafter (Ether 8:3; 10:15, 30). The Jaredites left Mesopotamia centuries before the time of Moses, so their traditions and legal customs were undoubtedly different from those of the Nephites. Hugh Nibley describes the background of Jaredite traditions: "Moving back to the earliest records of all, we find a large class of legends all over the ancient world telling how the victorious god in the beginning bound and imprisoned his rebellious relatives—not killing them, since they partook of his own divine nature; the earliest myths of Zeus and Osiris at once come to mind."[119] The book of Ether contains several accounts of kings imprisoning their sons, brothers, and even fathers. Akish did this when he became jealous of his son, eventually starving him to death (Ether 9:7). This is the only case in

later on the twelfth day of the tenth month in the tenth year (14:23), and since they had also spent "many days" together before beginning to preach (8:27), it is reasonable to estimate that they were held in the prison about four to six weeks.

116. The similarity between the treatment received by Alma and Amulek and that received by Aaron and his brethren is striking. Both parties were stripped and bound with strong cords and denied food and drink while in prison (Alma 14:22; 20:29).

117. It is doubtful that imprisonment would have been a long-term disposition of this case open to the court. It is hard to imagine the city of Ammonihah holding a Nephite dignitary like Alma for very long. As with Nephi and Lehi in Helaman 5, the intended outcome of that process is unknown because the trial was halted by divine intervention.

118. Other possible explanations of this anomaly in Ammonihah are that Alma 10:13 has oversimplified the legal complexities involved or that the threatened imprisonment was not asserted as a punishment under law but rather as a police measure available to the judges. It seems more likely, however, that the legal system in Ammonihah was corrupted, and thus the use of prisons there as a form of judicial punishment does not represent legitimate Nephite legal practices in general.

119. Hugh Nibley, *Lehi in the Desert; The World of the Jaredites; There Were Jaredites* (Salt Lake City: Deseret Book and FARMS, 1988), 207.

the Jaredite record of imprisonment accompanied by repressive measures leading to death. Most other rivals to the throne were made to serve and were allowed to beget children while imprisoned (10:13–14; 11:18–19, 23); one family earned the dubious honor of begetting five generations while imprisoned (10:30–31). Of such practices Nibley writes, "It seems to us a perfectly ridiculous system, yet it is in accordance with the immemorial Asiatic usage."[120] Nibley cites several examples of relatives imprisoning one another but allowing the imprisoned royalty to enjoy surprising degrees of freedom.[121]

King Riplakish employed imprisonment in an unparalleled way when he imposed heavy taxes and imprisoned all subjects who could not or would not pay them. To incarcerate so many people he needed "many prisons," and he caused all those in prison to "labor continually for their support"; whoever refused to work was put to death. Not only did Riplakish cause these prisoners to labor for their own support, but "all manner of fine workmanship he did cause to be wrought in prison" (Ether 10:5–7). No other cases of widespread imprisonment of common citizens appear in Ether's account. The practice of holding prisoners in a form of house arrest and requiring them to work at a craft solved the major problem that made imprisonment unfeasible in most ancient societies. It was enormously expensive to hold and care for prisoners otherwise (even in some form of work detention; see Mosiah 23–24), making long-term imprisonment an unattractive judicial option in ancient Israel as well as among the Nephites.

Jurisprudential Rationales for Judicial Punishment

Finally, although only a few examples of actual punishments are found in the Book of Mormon, sufficient information yields insights into the theological, religious, social, and jurisprudential principles that stood behind those punishments. The following discussion of various punishments moves from most to least important, with importance measured by the number of references found in the Book of Mormon, the explicit nature of the references, and the status of the lawgiver or enforcer.[122]

---

120. Nibley, *Lehi in the Desert*, 206.

121. Nibley, *Lehi in the Desert*, 205–10.

122. It should be noted that the various punishments described in the Book of Mormon can be discussed under several headings because they were often influenced by several factors. For example, Nehor's execution served not only as a public deterrent but also as a way of avenging Gideon's death, purging the people of an evil influence, and atoning for breaking God's commandments. This should not be surprising since modern executions are also based on several of the same principles,

Public Deterrence. One of the most dominant reasons behind Book of Mormon punishments is the theory of public deterrence. It is not surprising that this would be the case. Such a principle has held wide appeal through the centuries and in various societies. From the Roman crucifixions outside town gates to the public French guillotine decapitations and the lynchings in the American West, the purpose was to scare people into obeying the law: Don't step out of line or this will happen to you. Such punishments almost always took place before large audiences and were usually for heinous crimes such as murder. It was important that as many people as possible be able to view the punishments as a deterrent to further crimes.

A prominent example is Nehor, one of the most notorious criminals in the Book of Mormon. Nehor had been preaching false doctrines (Alma 1:3–4) and had established a profitable ministry to support himself (vv. 5–6). When confronted by Gideon about his practices, Nehor became "wroth," so much so that he inflicted several sword blows, enough to kill the aged Gideon (vv. 8–9). Nehor was brought in and arraigned before Alma and formally charged with priestcraft and the murder "of a righteous man," a charge that merited death (vv. 12–14). His "ignominious" execution took place on top of the hill Manti (v. 15). This was not a private execution carried out in secrecy, but rather a humiliating and disgraceful public display. In order to deter any potential criminals, Alma wanted as many people as possible to see what becomes of murderers. The record specifically records that the execution was "ignominious," and although we do not know exactly what that entailed, the chief judges probably felt that such was the only way to deter any further practice of murder and priestcraft. In any event, the nature of Nehor's execution was in line with ancient Hebrew capital punishments that were intended to be public deterrents.[123]

Another example of the public deterrent rationale is found in the trial and execution of Abinadi, which was certainly meant by King Noah to keep anyone else from challenging him about his ways. King Noah appears to have wanted to show that he was the potentate and that anyone

---

mainly deterrence, rehabilitation, and retribution. See generally David M. Adams, *Philosophical Problems in the Law*, 4th ed. (Belmont, CA: Wadsworth Learning, 2005), 442–66.

123. Falk, *Hebrew Law in Biblical Times*, 73. Deterrence was also a major consideration of other ancient Near Eastern cultures, in which capital punishment, for instance, was often imposed for treason. See Westbrook, "Introduction," 1:76; Amalia Catagnoti, "Anatolia and the Levant: Elba," in Westbrook, *History of Ancient Near Eastern Law*, 1:236; Jasnow, "Egypt: Middle Kingdom and Second Intermediate Period," 1:282; Rowe, "Anatolia and the Levant: Alalakh," 1:716; Ignacio Márquez Rowe, "Anatolia and the Levant: Canaan," in Westbrook, *History of Ancient Near Eastern Law*, 1:742; and Oelsner, Wells, and Wunsch, "Mesopotamia: Neo-Babylonian Period," 2:965.

who disapproved or disagreed with him would meet a violent death. He reinstituted the gruesome death-by-fire penalty in order to make a statement and keep silent any other critics (Alma 25:11).[124] It was probably a fairly effective deterrent.

King Noah's fiery mode of execution seems to have achieved some degree of popularity among the more wicked people in the Book of Mormon. Following successful missionary efforts by Alma and Amulek in Ammonihah, the government leaders became violently upset due to the many conversions (Alma 14:1–2). The judges who saw this missionary activity as social upheaval wanted to show Alma and Amulek, along with everyone else, who really had the power and authority in Ammonihah. Following a speedy trial, those who "believed or had been taught to believe in the word of God . . . [were] cast into the fire" along with all of their scriptures (v. 8). For purposes of intimidation, Alma and Amulek were allowed to watch: the judges wanted to make clear the fate of those who opposed the government and were involved in supposedly subversive behavior (v. 9). The gruesome spectacle certainly would have made all people in the city extremely wary of listening to the missionaries. However, the public deterrent did not have long to take effect since the city was destroyed soon after (16:9–11).

A series of executions appear to have been instituted as public deterrents in Alma 62. While the Nephites were crumbling under the persistent attacks from the Lamanites, the men of Pachus and the king-men were involved in some type of civil disobedience linked with treason: they "would not take up arms in the defense of their country, but would fight against it" (Alma 62:9). Pahoran had to take quick action or face his government's internal collapse. He had all persons who were found "denying their freedom" and who were not true to the cause of freedom executed (vv. 10–11). Such measures were evidently effective in deterring any further acts of treachery because peace was restored to the land of Zarahemla (v. 11).

The execution of Zemnarihah is another example of public deterrence (3 Nephi 4:28–32). Zemnarihah was responsible for much bloodshed because of his involvement as leader of the Gadianton robbers (v. 17). Following some successful maneuvering by the Nephite armies, the Gadianton robbers were captured and given the choice of becoming prisoners of war or being slain (v. 27). Zemnarihah, who was apparently not given the choice of becoming a prisoner of war, was subsequently executed in

---

124. Abinadi's execution seems even more heinous in light of the fact that burnings were usually reserved for those guilty of "grave sexual offenses," a charge that did not even come up at the trial. Compare Falk, *Hebrew Law in Biblical Times*, 73–74.

an elaborate manner. In front of the entire Nephite nation, he was hung on the top of a tree "until he was dead" (v. 28).[125] A ritualistic celebration followed with the chopping down of the tree and chanting in celebration of the failed attempts of the wicked (vv. 28–32). The Nephites wanted all to see the fate of vicious criminals such as Zemnarihah.

In a few cases, divinely enforced punishments served as public deterrents. The punishments of Sherem and Korihor, for example, deterred false preaching and sign seeking. At the beginning of Alma 30, the laws concerning freedom of religion are explicitly set forth, under none of which could Korihor be indicted for his false preaching (Alma 30:7–12). Similar laws probably protected Sherem as well. However, both Sherem and Korihor knew they were trying to get around the law. After wrongly accusing Jacob and asking for a divine sign, Sherem died within a few days (Jacob 7:13–20). Korihor became mute after his trial, was cast out, and died in rather unclear circumstances: he was "run upon and trodden down, even until he was dead" by some Zoramites (Alma 30:58–59). The news of the unusual fates of Sherem and Korihor would certainly have become well known, especially to any false preachers, and probably would have made any sign seeker wary of asking for a sign from a Nephite judge. Korihor is the last example of such a person in the Book of Mormon, so it is probable that others were successfully deterred.

The destruction of the city of Ammonihah certainly served as a public deterrent (Alma 16:2–3).[126] Such a quick and total destruction by the Lamanites would have sent a clear message to the rest of the Nephite nation that God would not tolerate cities awash in sin. This evidence of divine judgment probably prompted repentance among other Nephites, frightened by the possibility of a similar impending doom.

Purging the Nation. The second most prevalent reason for punishment in the Book of Mormon is the desire to keep the nation pure. Whereas public deterrence is a preventative measure, purging is more remedial in nature. It was believed that if heinous offenders were not cast out, the whole society would remain contaminated. Nehor's story provides insight into this aspect. In addition to being charged with murder, Nehor was charged with priestcraft (Alma 1:12–13). Alma saw Nehor's priestcraft as a serious threat to civilization, stating that "were priestcraft to be enforced

---

125. Under Hebrew law, "persons put to death for public crimes were mostly stoned and then hanged." Falk, *Hebrew Law in Biblical Times*, 73.

126. In the Old Testament "the idolatrous city . . . [was] put to death by the sword, like the enemy killed in battle." Falk, *Hebrew Law in Biblical Times*, 74. Such was the fate of Ammonihah at the hands of the Lamanites.

among this people it would prove their entire destruction. . . . Therefore thou art condemned to die" (vv. 12, 14). This was the first time priestcraft had been introduced among the Nephites. Alma knew that this new evil had to be eradicated as soon as possible, and he determined it could be done most effectively by getting rid of the source. Though the record implicitly indicates that Nehor's removal was intended to stop the priestcraft, "nevertheless, this did not put an end to the spreading of priestcraft" (v. 16). Alma's efforts to keep the nation pure did not succeed.

The trials and subsequent sentences of Abinadi and Alma and Amulek also represent a desire to keep society pure. The recalcitrant individuals who conducted these trials were motivated by a perceived need (misplaced though it was) to eradicate evil from their societies. Abinadi was charged with causing contention and strife among the people (Mosiah 11:28), while Alma and Amulek were charged with contempt of the law and legal system and with causing upheaval among the populace (Alma 14:2–5). Their trials represent a correct principle wrongly applied.

Zemnarihah's ritualistic execution also demonstrates a desire to purge wickedness from society. As leader of the Gadianton robbers, Zemnarihah had caused the deaths of "tens of thousands" and was executed by being hung on the top of a tree "until he was dead" (3 Nephi 4:21, 28). The tree was then cut down, and the people praised the Lord for protecting them. A man as wicked as Zemnarihah could not be permitted to live, even as a prisoner of war (an option offered to his soldiers). Society had to be purged of him.

The cases of Sherem and Korihor, although examples of divine punishments, can be included as punishments intended to purge the nation of evil. Sherem had been preaching false doctrine, leading others to sin, and denying the Christ (Jacob 7:1–3, 7–9, 19). When confronted with these charges, Sherem asked for a divine sign and was promptly given one (vv. 13–15). He became physically incapacitated and was unconscious for several days and then became conscious only long enough to confess his sins before he died. Obviously the Lord felt that Sherem needed to be removed or he would cause much damage to the Nephites. Once he was gone, "peace and the love of God was restored again among the people" (v. 23). Society had been purged and righteousness restored.

Korihor's case is similar. He too had preached false doctrines, had encouraged many people to commit sexual sin, and had blasphemed (Alma 30:6, 12, 18, 29–30). He was banished from the lands of Jershon and Gideon: the inhabitants wanted to keep their lands pure (v. 21). But he was allowed to dwell, and was even listened to, in Zarahemla (vv. 6, 18).

When Korihor was brought before Alma, he denied God, accused Alma of priestcraft, and finally asked for a sign (vv. 31–43). Korihor became mute, confessed in writing that he had preached falsely, and asked for the curse of muteness to be removed (vv. 49–50, 56). Alma denied his request, reasoning that "if this curse should be taken from thee thou wouldst again lead away the hearts of this people" (v. 55) and furthermore that "it is better that thy soul should be lost than that thou shouldst be the means of bringing many souls down to destruction, by thy lying and by thy flattering words" (v. 47). Korihor suffered a pathetic end begging for food as an outcast and being trodden to death. Alma clearly understood the danger that Korihor posed to Zarahemlan society and rendered him incapable of causing further damage.

Vengeance. Although considered inappropriate in a strictly rational legal system, vengeance is a natural human response; instinctively, people want to "get even" after being wronged. Vengeance is usually motivated more by personal desire than by an institutional desire for deterrence. Vengeance is often understood to be revenge, which generally carries a negative connotation, but it can also mean *avenge*. This is the interpretation the ancients would have understood, for they felt a duty to their wronged departed friends and family members who, they believed, were still alive in the spirit world. It would have been inexcusable for the living not to avenge a wrongful death. It is interesting to note that in the Book of Mormon there are punishments that served to avenge deaths as well as those that sought revenge. The examples of avenging death occur under righteous governments, while the examples of getting revenge occur under corrupt governments. Avenging Gideon's death was the primary reason for Nehor's execution. Apparently priestcraft was not a crime punishable by death, but capital punishment for murder had been reaffirmed by Mosiah not long before Nehor's trial (Alma 1:14; see also 2 Nephi 9:35). The principle of avengement is clearly stated by Alma: "Were we to spare thee his [Gideon's] blood would come upon us for vengeance. Therefore thou art condemned to die, according to the law" (Alma 1:13–14). If Nehor had not been executed, the people would have been held responsible for Gideon's death. The acceptable retribution was taking the life of the murderer in place of the murdered.

Avengement also brought about the execution of Zemnarihah described in 3 Nephi 4:26–32. As the leader of the murderous band of outlaws known as the Gadianton robbers, Zemnarihah was one of the most evil men alive. When he was finally captured and executed, the Nephites were evidently seeking to avenge not only the deaths of the bloody battle of year 19, in which Zemnarihah was undoubtedly highly involved, but also the "tens of thousands" who were killed during the siege of year 21 (3 Nephi 4:21). The Nephites who died in these conflicts with the Gadianton robbers were certainly the brothers, fathers, and sons of those still living. It would have been unacceptable not to have punished the man responsible for so much carnage. The principle of avengement helps to explain the symbolic meaning of cutting down the tree on which Zemnarihah was hung and of the celebration that followed.

Some punishments were promulgated for revenge's sake, as in the execution of Abinadi. He had caused quite a disturbance with his preaching (Mosiah 11:27–29). Just before he was finally sentenced, Abinadi warned that if Noah executed him it would stand as a testimony against Noah at the last day (17:10). The record states that Noah "feared" Abinadi's word and was "stirred up in anger against him" (vv. 11, 12). Then, with the urging of the priests, Noah ordered execution by burning, the first burning among the Nephites (Alma 25:11). It appears that because Abinadi had frightened him and questioned his authority as king, Noah handed down a much harsher judgment than would normally have been given. He wanted to get back at Abinadi in a severe manner for the embarrassment he experienced.

Revenge also appears as a theme in the trial of Alma and Amulek. While preaching in Ammonihah, they had been charged with reviling the law, the lawyers and judges, and the people, all very serious charges (Alma 14:5). The casting out of Zeezrom when he sided with Alma and the burning of the believers and their scriptures indicate that the Ammonihahites wanted harsh revenge for such disturbances to their society (vv. 7–8). If the objective was to quiet Alma and Amulek, the people of Ammonihah could have simply expelled them from the city. On the other hand, in the cases of Sherem and Korihor it appears that they could not be punished for false preaching since it was treated as an expression of religious belief, for which no punishment was allowed under the law (30:7–12). Although Abinadi, Alma, and Amulek were all charged with the identical crime of false preaching, they were given extremely harsh sentences best explained by a factor of revenge.

Atonement. One theory of punishment that is all but absent from most modern societies is atonement. In ancient societies acts of atonement, or reconciliation, were of utmost importance, required for any deed believed to be a sin or offense against God. If God had been offended, the situation needed to be remedied or the nation would pay the price. Nehor's execution is a clear example of Alma enforcing God-given commandments, evident when he declared, "Thou hast shed the blood of a righteous man [Gideon], yea, a man who has done much good among this people; and were we to spare thee his blood would come upon us for vengeance" (Alma 1:13). Alma had no choice but to execute Nehor as God had prescribed (2 Nephi 9:35). Under Hebrew law, capital punishment was seen as a form of atonement.[127]

The celebration following Zemnarihah's execution also indicates that the people killed Zemnarihah as an atonement for the numerous deaths he had caused. They praised God for preserving them "from falling into the hands of their enemies" and surely were encouraged in their belief that, pursuant to Zemnarihah's atoning execution, God would "protect this people in righteousness" in the future (3 Nephi 4:30–31). There appears to have been an understanding that they were keeping the commandments of God by executing Zemnarihah and that had they not done so they would have been destroyed. The Nephites shouted upon Zemnarihah's death, "May the Lord preserve his people . . . that they may cause to be felled to the earth all who shall seek to slay them" (vv. 28–29). Zemnarihah's life had to be taken in exchange for his crimes.

The punishments given to Sherem and Korihor also indicate a need to enforce God's rules. These punishments are quite self-evident: God will not tolerate false preaching and priestcraft and will enforce his commandments.

Monetary Fines. In certain circumstances in various cultures, it has been considered appropriate to make monetary compensation in lieu of corporeal punishment.[128] There is some direct evidence in the Book of Mormon that a criminal could buy his way out of punishment for a civil offense (*kofer*), as well as a few instances indicating that money did enter the judicial process from time to time. In Alma 11 there is record of a specific debtor's law, which was apparently part of the corpus of law created by Mosiah. After a complaint was made to a judge concerning a debtor and proper evidence submitted, the debtor was either "compelled to pay that which he owed, or be stripped, or be cast out from among the people as a thief and a robber" (Alma 11:1–2). This payment should probably be understood as a form of restitution since it appears that the

---

127. Falk, *Hebrew Law in Biblical Times*, 73; also Frymer-Kenski, "Anatolia and the Levant: Israel," 2:1027–28 ("Capital punishment is never imposed for property offenses, but is reserved for homicide, adultery, and [other] religious infractions").

128. See Westbrook, "Mesopotamia: Old Babylonian Period," 1:416 (discussing fines for injury offenses); and Haase, "Anatolia and the Levant: The Hittite Kingdom," 1:645–46, 651–52 (discussing fines among the Hittites).

debtor was required to pay back only what he owed. Apparently that was the preferred punishment. Only if he was unwilling or unable to pay back the money did the debtor suffer the other punishments. However, technically speaking, if the debtor did pay he was buying his way out of being stripped naked, flogged, or cast out, and so this kind of settlement can be considered a *kofer*.

The other references to money in legal disputes are instances of bribery. Zeezrom was one of those corrupt judges or lawyers who "did stir up the people to riotings . . . that they might have more employ, that they might get money" (Alma 11:20). While contending with Alma and Amulek, Zeezrom offered Amulek "six onties of silver" if he would "deny the existence of a Supreme Being" (v. 22). The fact that Zeezrom would try to bribe a party in a legal proceeding indicates that judicial officers in this system were probably not immune from accepting money for a favorable decision. After all, these judges were trying to increase their personal wealth. This type of bribery shows up again when Nephi was accused of killing a chief judge. The tribunal offered him money and a plea bargain if he would confess his presumed confederate villain (Helaman 9:20). These two examples, of course, are the opposite of *kofer* since the judge was offering money in order to extract a confession, rather than an accused seeking to obtain leniency. Perhaps these were corruptions of the use of *kofer* since we know that Mosiah's sound law system was still in effect, at least during the time of the encounter with Zeezrom.

Closing Statement

Many things can be said at this juncture about the legal cases in the Book of Mormon. Above all, I hope this book has caused readers to think about things they have not considered before. Those previously unfamiliar with the Book of Mormon have probably encountered for the first time names such as Sherem, Korihor, Paanchi, and Seantum, to say nothing of the details of their words and deeds. Beyond that, they, as with those who have grown up with the Book of Mormon, may have been exposed for the first time to concepts such as Jehovah's Covenant Code, talionic justice, collective responsibility, and the religious beliefs behind practices such as pre-execution confession and the forensic use of oaths, oracles, and ordeals, together with a dose of arcane legal terminology. In many respects, I hope that all readers have found this examination and their reflection on Nephite jurisprudence in light of biblical law traditions to be informative and rewarding.

I also hope that this study, as a groundbreaking effort, is only the beginning of further studies to follow. Just as David Daube's 1947 *Studies in Biblical Law* led out in showing biblical scholars the value of reading Old Testament narratives with ancient legal concepts and procedures in mind, the present study has tried to show the same for the Book of Mormon. Since much of the Book of Mormon is explicitly grounded on Hebrew law, it makes sense to draw on that cultural background in analyzing the legal cases in the Book of Mormon.

Seven main goals were set out at the end of the first chapter: (1) to examine the literary and historical background of each legal case in the Book of Mormon, (2) to compare the legal terms and procedures found in the Nephite record with those in the Hebrew Bible and the ancient world in general, (3) to understand the facts and legal issues raised by each case in the Book of Mormon, (4) to utilize all available tools to illuminate these passages, (5) to appreciate the judicial and historical uniqueness of each case, (6) to highlight the various modes of persuasion and judgment in these cases, and (7) to extract ethical and religious values from each of these precedent-setting cases. Although more can yet be said to further enlarge our understanding of these cases, I submit that enough has been included to accomplish these goals and to make clear sense of these interesting texts, not only in terms of their broad judicial sweep but also in their use of technical legal terminology that otherwise tends to escape notice in the course of regular reading.

Following the methods and approaches discussed and adopted in chapter 2, it now seems clear that each legal case in the Book of Mormon can be amply understood in the context of pre-exilic Israelite law. Although one cannot always be certain about the precise state of the law in Jerusalem shortly before Lehi's departure and the Babylonian conquest, it is evident that the legal principles in these cases fit comfortably in the developing biblical law tradition at that time.

Viewed this way, the legal cases in the Book of Mormon make for very interesting reading. Paying careful attention to the narrative contexts and legal backgrounds of these cases brings their original meanings even more to life. Moreover, these stories are told with style, care, and sophistication befitting the particular purposes and personal experiences of their authors, compilers, and abridgers. The fact that these cases are more complicated than readers have previously noted makes the Book of Mormon all the more intriguing and respectable.

Through this legal reading, it has become evident that the authors of the Book of Mormon were experienced in the law, especially Alma, who served professionally for nine years as the Nephite chief judge. All these writers appear to have been fully conversant with their legal system. We see them consciously striving to judge righteously, being guided by the precepts of professional ethics that were set in legal stone by the judicial decalogue in Exodus 23:1–3, 6–9. They made accurate use of legal rules, jurisprudential principles, and judicial practices. They assumed that their readers would somehow understand the normal operation of their legal system, which they take for granted.

In sum, the following substantive laws have been found to surface most prominently in these seven cases: laws against blasphemy, leading others into apostasy, false prophecy, idolatry, becoming an apostate city, reviling the law, conspiring to commit treason, cursing the king, and shedding innocent blood. It is significant that most of these laws deal essentially with offenses against God, indicating that maintaining their covenant relationship with God was of utmost importance to the Nephites.

This study has also shown that the Nephite administration of justice, like the Israelite system upon which it was based, featured various modes of adjudication and dispute resolution, ranging from private contentions to formal divisions of jurisdiction between priests and the king. Having adopted the legal and political reforms of King Mosiah, the Nephite legal system became more structured with the establishment of a system of lower and higher judges known as the reign of judges. Under this regime, which lasted about 150 years, answers to several legal issues produced rules and practices concerning the number of judges involved in various proceedings, the transfer of difficult cases to higher judges, the public locations of trials, the importance of judgment seats, and the miscarriage of justice through political corruption and bribes. These and other developments in Nephite law are understandable reflections of authentic experiences within Nephite civilization as its leaders met challenges, made decisions, and lived with the consequences of their actions.

Over the course of Nephite history, most of the basic judicial procedures, however, remained stable. Little change is seen concerning such procedural particularities as the populace's obligation to initiate judicial actions; taking, binding, and carrying an indicted party before a judge; smiting on the cheek as a form of humiliation and indictment; judging one's accountability based on degree of knowledge; requiring parties to appear personally without advocates or representatives; insisting on the two-witness rule; the swearing of oaths and the predominance of oral testimony; diligent inquisition or examination of parties; severe consequences for false accusation or perjury; construing silence as an admission of guilt; the acceptance of self-incrimination under certain conditions; resolving deadlocked cases by ordeal, signs, or oracular detection of culprits; accepting unequivocally the divine determination of innocence or guilt; the absence of courts of appeal on the merits; heralding judicial outcomes; using certain types of punishments; justifying the death penalty on certain rationales and in prescribed modes of execution; using post-judgment and pre-execution confessions; using the accusers as executioners; and ensuring that the operation of the legal system resulted in the establishment of justice and the restoration of peace in the society.

The significant number of legal principles found in these cases shows that the Book of Mormon cannot be fully appreciated without seeing it through many lenses, including the lenses of law, justice, equity, and mercy. Understood in the broad Israelite sense, law (*torah*), with its judgments, statutes, customs, and testimonies, was fundamental to Nephite culture and religion. The Nephite prophets strictly honored both the letter and the meaning of the law. The legal cases in the Book of Mormon reflect the importance of revealed law in Nephite society and convey significant truths about judging righteously.

By way of overview, these cases can now be headnoted and characterized as follows:

- The case of Sherem stands as a classic case of an overconfident critic who seriously misjudges the situation and makes unsustainable accusations of blasphemy, apostasy, and false prophecy. This episode should give pause to any would-be plaintiff or political opponent. Pride and hubris blur righteous judgment. It is unclear what Sherem had to gain by accusing the aged Jacob of these capital offenses, but what he tried to impose on Jacob eventually came back upon himself.

- The trial of Abinadi is an archetypal case of abuse of power that resulted when King Noah took umbrage at Abinadi's remonstrations. The case swirls around a king's unwillingness to be corrected and his priests' obsequious interest in currying favor. Yielding more than a case about a gadfly who got swatted, the death of the prophet Abinadi will haunt King Noah, whose execution by his priests shows that those who play with fire themselves get burned.

- The trial of Nehor is a classic case of an angry member of a minority religious and political party who lost his temper, feeling oppressed, frustrated, or insulted by the controlling government. Probably assuming that his popular power base was strong enough, Nehor figured he could use force with impunity. In his way stood only the novice judge Alma, who had to make a politically difficult decision in order to reinforce and stand up for important legal values and against the use of violence and physical force.

- The accusation and imprisonment of Alma and Amulek is a shocking case of local pride on the part of a schismatic group that got carried away in its rejection of its previous leaders. Their tactics included perversion of the legal system, bribery, self-justification, torture, humiliation, censorship, and killing innocent women and children. This horrific miscarriage of justice soon ended in the complete demise of the perpetrators.

- The trial of Korihor presents a remarkable case of a radically independent thinker. Ultimately, his case asks, at what point does the individual's right to speak jeopardize the welfare of the community as a whole? Is speech more like thought (which is necessarily protected) or like action (which is therefore publicly punishable)? Each society must determine the limits of free speech and when it will hold people responsible not only for what they do but also, in some cases, for what they say.

- The case of Paanchi is a lamentable case of a raw thirst for power among three brothers, all of whom end up dead.
- The matter of Seantum is an all-too-familiar case of corruption, cowardice, and trying to get others to do the dirty work under the cloak of secrecy. In this case, all was eventually revealed, for God sees and knows all things, and this ultimately leaves nowhere to hide.

Collectively, these cases help significantly to establish key precedents that support the stated purposes of the Book of Mormon, namely, to convince readers that Jesus is the Christ, the Messiah of whom the prophets have spoken, and that God remembers the covenants that he has made and sustains his righteous followers. The case of Sherem proves that prophesying of Christ was neither inconsistent with nor incorrect under the law of Moses. The validated testimony of Abinadi establishes that true prophets bear good tidings of Christ, through whose redemption and resurrection all mankind may have eternal life. The ignominious deaths of Nehor, of his followers in Ammonihah, and of the anti-Christ Korihor show that teachers and leaders who deny Christ and aggressively reject the priesthood order of the Son of God are not to be sustained, while the true and accurate prophecy of Nephi in the detection of Seantum shows that God will sustain his covenant keepers.

While integral to the Book of Mormon's broad purposes, these cases were also significant to the individual writers who were personally involved with them, another perspective that readers can now more fully appreciate. All these authors saw this mortal life as a time for all people to prepare to stand resurrected before God to be judged according to their works (1 Nephi 15:32–33; 2 Nephi 9:44; 25:22; Mosiah 3:23–24; 16:10; Alma 12:12; 34:32; 40:21; Mormon 3:18). The theme of God's judgment runs throughout the Book of Mormon, even down to its concluding line in which Moroni says: "I bid unto all farewell . . . until my spirit and body shall again reunite, and I am brought forth triumphant through the air, to meet you before the pleasing bar of the great Jehovah, the Eternal Judge of both quick and dead" (Moroni 10:34). No doubt Moroni and his predecessors envisioned the future judgment as comparable to their own judicial tribunals: the facts would be clear, the parties would know of their guilt or innocence, and God's justice would dispense righteous judgment. This will be pleasingly triumphant for some, but it will be especially unfortunate for those who have not judged righteously. Indeed, the legal cases in the Book of Mormon offer a unanimous warning in this regard.

Although much ground has been covered in this volume, many other legal topics remain to be addressed concerning Nephite law as a whole. Other volumes planned to build on this one will discuss homicide, robbery, family law, property law, martial law, social justice, festival laws, and many other legal topics. Considerable research, however, already indicates that the Nephite understanding of those subjects is also compatible with an ancient Israelite origin for the Nephite legal system, just as with the procedural laws that have been the focus of this volume.

Also remaining to be considered are other questions such as, How much would or could Joseph Smith have known about ancient Israelite law from his reading of the Bible or from his surrounding culture? Could Joseph have grasped the nature and operation of biblical law as a young reader of the Bible? (He was twenty-three when he dictated the text of the Book of Mormon.) Although a few biblical scholars in the 1820s were aware of certain legal features of the Old Testament, they were mainly interested in the New Testament. Disciplined study of early biblical law only began much more recently. There is no evidence that Joseph Smith conducted any study along these lines, and even if he had somehow acquired a full understanding of biblical law on his own, one wonders how he could have seamlessly woven all these legal principles into these narratives as he dictated the entire book in the short period of time between April 7 and June 30, 1829. Although a full discussion of early American law must be left for another day, present results show that the Book of Mormon is accurate in its use of such terms as *contend* and *robber*, which precisely correspond with their Hebrew counterparts *rîb* and *gedud*, and that its texts present a coherent picture of an actual legal system that is quite different from the New York legal system that Joseph had encountered as a material witness as early as 1819 and as an accused in 1826.

For the time being, I mention the subject of Book of Mormon origins because this question legitimately arises in all serious discussions of this book. For many skeptical readers, of course, the Book of Mormon is too extraordinary to be plausible. But there are answers to these detractions, even if they require a few crucial assumptions about holy scripture, historiography, salvation history, and the possibility of divine revelation.

This is not to say that hard evidences, for or against the Book of Mormon, are unimportant. As I have discussed elsewhere, evidence plays important roles in the nurturing of faith. As theologian Austin Farrer has written, "Though argument does not create conviction, lack of it destroys belief. What seems to be proved may not be embraced; but what no one shows that ability to defend is quickly abandoned. Rational argument does not create belief, but it maintains a climate in which belief may flourish."[1] One may hope, in any religious quest, that the fruits of earnest inquiry and positive experience will eventually lead sincere people to ask God to impart to the honest in heart a needed measure of inspiration, wisdom, truth, and goodness.

In the end, the Book of Mormon simply invites people to give it a chance. It may be just as hard to explain the existence of this book as it is to deny the validity of its claims. The book should not be simply brushed aside, but taken seriously, at least as one of the most remarkable instances of raw religious creativity to come out of America if not as one of the vanguards in the parade of long-lost ancient texts that began to come forth in the mid-nineteenth century.

I sincerely hope that the Book of Mormon might be taken seriously as an instrument in improving the condition of people everywhere throughout the world. As one can now see, a large part of its mission is to inspire people to judge righteously, something that the world urgently needs now. One could hope that the legal precedents contained in the Book of Mormon, reaching back into the roots of Judeo-Christian-Islamic civilization, might curb abuses of justice and offer effective models for establishing peace and harmony. In today's society, which is more potentially violent than any before, the tempering virtues of righteous judgment are more needed than ever: telling the truth; following God, not the crowd; shunning bribes and their equivalents; not persecuting or killing the innocent; and not oppressing others just because they come as strangers from other lands or traditions.

Rules for judging righteously are legally exemplified in the Bible and Book of Mormon. These books extend to the world vivid and poignant invitations to "judge righteously between every man and his brother, and the stranger that is with him" (Deuteronomy 1:16); to be "merciful unto your brethren"; and to "deal justly, judge righteously, and do good continually" (Alma 41:14).

---

1. Austin Farrer, "Grete Clerk," in *Light on C. S. Lewis*, comp. Jocelyn Gibb (New York: Harcourt and Brace, 1965), 26, discussed in my chapter "The Power of Evidence in the Nurturing of Faith," in *Echoes and Evidences of the Book of Mormon*, ed. Donald W. Parry, Daniel C. Peterson, and John W. Welch (Provo, UT: FARMS, 2002), 17–53.

LEGAL PROCEEDINGS IN THE OLD TESTAMENT

Laban's Confrontation against Jacob (Genesis 31:25–55)

25 Laban caught up with Jacob as he was camped in the hill country of Gilead, and Laban set up his camp not far from Jacob's. 26 And Laban came and said to Jacob, "Why did you slip away secretly and carry off my daughters—the heart of me!—like you were taking prisoners of war? 27 Why did you not tell me you were leaving? I would have made a great feast for you, sending you off with harp and tambourine music! 28 This is all your fault, you fool! You did not even let me kiss my daughters and grandchildren good-bye! 29 I have the means to harm you—even to kill you—but I will not, because your father's God appeared to me last night and warned me not to say anything, good or bad, to you. 30 I understand why you left—you are homesick and long to see your father's home again—but why did you steal my gods?"

31 And Jacob answered and said to Laban, "I left in such a hurry because I was afraid that you would take your daughters from me by force if you knew. 32 If anyone in my camp is found with your gods, that person will die for stealing them. And if you find anything else that belongs to you, point it out in the presence of these relatives of ours and you can have it back." (Jacob said this because he did not know that it was Rachel who had stolen her father's gods.)

33 So Laban went searching, first in Jacob's tent, then in Leah's tent and the tent of the two slave girls, but he did not find his gods, or anything else. Finally, he searched Rachel's tent. 34 Before he arrived, though, Rachel had taken the images and put them in her camel saddle and was now sitting on them. Laban searched everything in the tent but did not find what he was looking for. 35 While Laban was searching, Rachel said to him, "I am sorry,

---

The English version of these texts has been created with the collaboration of John Nielsen, drawing upon several Bible translations and rephrasing them with legal connotations in mind.

Father, that I cannot stand up for you, but I am on my monthly period." For all his searching, Laban could not find his household gods.

36 Jacob now became angry and began to dispute again with Laban, answering Laban's accusations, saying, "What is my crime? What have I done to justify you to come after me in hot pursuit as if I were a common criminal, or to hunt me down like a thieving animal? 37 You have rummaged through everything I own—did you find anything? If you have, please point it out! Set it here before our relatives—let them judge between us! 38 In all my twenty years in your house, not once did your ewes and she-goats miscarry! Not once did I eat any animal from your flock! 39 Not once did I bring you an animal carcass that was mangled by wild animals! I bore the loss of it myself because you required me to; it did not even matter whether something was taken in broad daylight or in the dark of night! 40 I worked for you through the scorching heat of day and through cold and sleepless nights! 41 I worked like a slave in your house for twenty years—fourteen for your daughters, six more for your flock—and yet you changed my wages ten times! 42 If the God of my father, the fearsome God of Abraham and of Isaac, had not been with me, you would have sent me away empty-handed. But, thankfully, God has seen all my hard work and rebuked you last night."

43 Now Laban answered Jacob, "These daughters are my daughters, and these children are my children, and these cattle are my cattle; in fact, everything that you see is mine. But what can I do now about my daughters and their children? 44 So come, let us make a covenant—something to witness our commitment to each other."

45 And so Jacob took a stone and set it upright as a sacred pillar, a monument to their agreement. 46 Then Jacob said to his relatives, "Gather up some stones," which they did, piling them in a heap. Jacob and Laban then sat next to the sacred monument they had made and ate a covenant meal together. 47 Laban called it Jegar-sahadutha, and Jacob called it Galeed, both of which mean "witness pile," the first in Aramaic, the second in Hebrew. 48 These names came from something Laban had said: "This heap is a witness between us today." 49 However, it was also called Mizpah, which means "watchtower," because Laban also said, "May the Lord watch between us to make sure we keep this covenant when we are apart from each other. 50 If you mistreat any of my daughters, or if you take other wives besides them, God will see it, even if no one else does, because he is our witness of this covenant."

51 And Laban said to Jacob, "Look at this heap and this pillar that I have set up between us. 52 This heap and pillar—this monument—is also

a witness that neither of us will pass by here with the intent to harm the other. 53 I call on the God of Abraham, and the God of Nahor, the God of their father, to judge between us."

And Jacob swore by the fearsome God of his father Isaac to respect the boundary that they had set up. 54 Then Jacob offered a sacrifice on the hill and invited everyone to a covenant feast. 55 Early the next morning, Laban got up, kissed and blessed his daughters and grandchildren, and left, returning to his home.

The Trial of the Blasphemer (Leviticus 24:10–23)

10 One day, a man who was the son of an Israelite mother and an Egyptian father came out of his tent and got into a fight with a man of pure Israelite descent. 11 During the brawl, the son of the Egyptian man blasphemed the holy name of the Lord by using it as a curse word. So those who heard it brought the blasphemer to Moses 12 and kept him in custody until the Lord's will on the matter was made clear. 13 The Lord then spoke to Moses, 14 "Take the man who blasphemed out of the camp, and tell all that heard him curse to lay their hands on his head. Then let the whole community stone him to death. 15 Afterwards, say to the Israelites, 'Anyone who curses God will bear his sin. 16 Anyone who blasphemes the Lord's name, Israelite or foreigner, must be stoned to death by the whole community of Israel. 17 Anyone who murders any man must also be put to death. 18 Anyone who kills his neighbor's animal shall restore a live animal for the one that he killed. 19 And if a man injures and disfigures another, he must bear the same: 20 bone fracture for bone fracture, eye for eye, tooth for tooth. Whatever anyone does to injure another person will be done to him in kind. 21 Whoever kills an animal, he will have to restore it. Whoever murders a man shall be put to death. 22 The same standard applies to both native Israelites and the foreigners among you, for I am the Lord your God.'" 23 Moses gave these instructions to the Israelites, and they took the blasphemer out of the camp and stoned him to death, as the Lord commanded Moses.

The Trial of the Sabbath-Day Wood Gatherer (Numbers 15:32–36)

32 During the time that the Israelites were in the desert, they found a man gathering wood on the Sabbath day. 33 Those who caught him in the act brought him before Moses and Aaron and all the community. 34 They kept him in custody because it was not clearly known what should be done with him. 35 And the Lord said to Moses, "This man must be put to death. The whole community must stone him outside the camp." 36 So the whole

community took him outside the camp and all stoned him to death, as the Lord commanded Moses.

A Ruling on the Inheritance of the Daughters of Zelophehad (Numbers 27:1–11)

1 A claim was presented by the daughters of Zelophehad, the son of Hepher, the son of Gilead, the son of Machir, the son of Manasseh, who belonged to the tribe of Manasseh the son of Joseph. Their names were Mahlah, Noah, Hoglah, Milcah, and Tirzah. 2 They appeared at the entrance of the tabernacle in front of Moses, Eleazar the priest, the rulers of the Israelites, and all the community and said: 3 "Our father died in the wilderness. He was not one of Korah's followers who organized a rebellion against the Lord, but rather died because of his own sins. He had no sons, 4 but is it right that our father's name should disappear from his tribe just because he did not have a son? We, his daughters, should receive his property on the same footing with other survivors of our father's family." 5 And Moses brought their cause before the Lord.

6 And the Lord spoke unto Moses, 7 "The daughters of Zelophehad have a legitimate claim: you must give them a portion of land as to the other members of their father's surviving family. Assign them the property that would have gone to their father. 8 Then tell the children of Israel that if a man dies and has no son, then you must give his inheritance to his daughter or daughters. 9 And if he does not have a daughter, then you must give his inheritance to his surviving family. 10 And if he has no surviving family, then ye shall give his inheritance to his father's surviving family. 11 And if his father have no surviving family, then ye shall give his inheritance to his next of kin, and he will inherit it. This will be the legally required procedure in matters of inheritance for the Israelites, as the Lord commanded Moses."

A Ruling on the Marriages of the Daughters of Zelophehad (Numbers 36:1–13)

1 And the leaders of the Gilead clans (who were descendants of Machir, son of Manasseh, who was one of the sons of Joseph) approached Moses and the other Israelite leaders with a petition. 2 And they said, "Sir, the Lord commanded you to divide up this land to the Israelite tribes by lot, but he also commanded you to give Zelophehad's grant of land to his daughters. 3 Now, if any of them marry an Israelite from another tribe, then their portion of land will be taken from our clan and go with them to the tribe into which they marry. Our clan and tribe will lose that land

forever 4 because when the fifty-year jubilee comes around, it will go to the tribe they married into."

5 So Moses, instructed by the Lord, gave the Israelites this ruling: "The tribe of the sons of Joseph is right; they have a legitimate claim. 6 This is the Lord's command regarding the daughters of Zelophehad: 'They may marry whom they will, but they must marry within their tribe.' 7 In this way, the land grants to the tribes will be preserved and not shift around, because the land given to each tribe must remain as the Lord allotted. 8 Whenever an Israelite woman is in line to inherit her father's land, she must marry within her tribe so that all the tribes will retain their ancestral land grants. 9 No land grants may pass from one tribe to another; each tribe of Israel must keep its allotted portion of land."

10 Just as the Lord had commanded Moses, the daughters of Zelophehad 11 (Mahlah, Tirzah, Hoglah, Milcah, and Noah) all married men from their own tribe, 12 men who were descendants of Manasseh the son of Joseph, and their property remained in their tribe. 13 These are the commandments, regulations, and decrees that the Lord gave the Israelites through Moses while they were camped on the plains of Moab beside the Jordan River, across from Jericho.

The Case of Achan (Joshua 7:1–26)

1 But the Israelites defied the ban placed on things dedicated to the Lord. A man named Achan (who was the son of Carmi, son of Zabdi, son of Zerah, of the tribe of Judah) took some of the things set apart for the Lord, and the Lord became very angry with the Israelites.

2 Joshua sent men from Jericho to Ai (which is located near Beth-aven, to the east of Beth-el) and ordered them: "Go up and spy on that land," which they did.

3 When they returned, they said to Joshua, "There is no need for the whole Israelite army to go attack Ai; two or three thousand men should be plenty because there are so few of them." 4 So three thousand Israelite warriors went up to attack Ai, but they were soundly defeated; 5 the men of Ai killed some thirty-six of them and chased them all the way to the stone quarries as far as the city gate.

Because of this, the Israelites' courage melted away and they were paralyzed with fear. 6 Joshua and the other leaders tore their clothes in dismay, threw dust on their heads, and prostrated themselves in front of the ark of the Lord until the evening came. 7 And Joshua cried out, "O Lord God, why did you ever bring us across the Jordan River, only to have the Amorites kill us? If only we had been content to settle on the other side of the river! 8 O Lord, what can I say now that we Israelites have been routed by our enemies? 9 What will happen when the Canaanites and other native people of the land hear of this? They will come swarming around us and wipe us out! And what will then become of your great name?"

10 And the Lord said to Joshua, "Stand up. Why are you lying on your face like that? 11 Israel sinned and broke my covenant. They took what was set apart to me. Not only that, but they have hid it among their own things and lied to cover it up! 12 This is why the Israelite army was so soundly defeated by their enemies. Unless they destroy every forbidden thing, I will no longer be with them as a people. 13 Get up, and command the people to purify themselves. Tell them that the Lord says: 'You have forbidden things hidden among you, Israelites. Until you rid yourselves of all of them, you will never defeat your enemies.' 14 Then in the morning, assemble yourselves by tribe, and the Lord will point out the tribe to which the guilty man belongs. Then that tribe will assemble by family clan, and the Lord will point out the guilty clan. Finally, that family must come forward one by one. 15 The one who stole the forbidden things will be burned, together with all he owns, because he has broken the Lord's covenant and done a disgraceful outrage in Israel."

16 So Joshua arose early in the morning and brought Israel by their tribes; and the tribe of Judah was singled out. 17 And he brought the family clans of Judah, and the Zarhite clan was singled out. And he brought the Zarhite clan one by one, and the Zabdi family was singled out. 18 And he brought his family man by man; and Achan (who was the son of Carmi, son of Zabdi, son of Zerah, of the tribe of Judah) was singled out. 19 And Joshua said to Achan, "My son, I implore you, give glory to the Lord God of Israel, and confess to him. Tell me now what you have done; do not hide it from me!"

20 And Achan answered Joshua, "It is true! I have sinned against the Lord God of Israel. Here is what I did: 21 I saw among the plunder a very fine piece of clothing, a mantle from Babylon, two hundred shekels of silver, and a bar of gold weighing fifty shekels. I coveted them and took them. You will find it all buried under my tent, with the silver buried deepest."

22 So Joshua sent messengers, and they ran to the tent and found all these things, with the silver buried deepest. 23 And they brought them to Joshua, and unto all the Israelites, and spread them out in front of the Lord. 24 And Joshua, and all Israel with him, took Achan, Zerah's son—and the silver, the clothing, the bar of gold, his sons and his daughters, his oxen, his donkey, his sheep, his tent, and all that he had—and brought them unto the valley of Achor. 25 And Joshua said, "As you brought disaster on us, the

Lord will bring disaster on you." Then all the Israelites stoned Achan and his family to death and burned their bodies. 26 They then put a pile of stones over Achan's corpse, which is still there today. The Lord's anger was abated that day, which is why the place is called the Valley of Achor.

Boaz v. Kinsman of Naomi (Ruth 4:1–12)

1 Now Boaz went to the gate of the city and sat down there. Just then, the family redeemer, or next of kin, he had mentioned passed by, so Boaz called out to him by name, saying, "Here, come over here and sit down! I want to talk with you." The man came and sat down. 2 Then Boaz stopped ten elders of the town and asked them to sit as witnesses, which they did. 3 Boaz said to the family redeemer, "You remember the piece of land that belonged to our relative Elimelech? Naomi has returned from Moabite country and is selling it. 4 I thought I should make you aware of it so you can redeem it if you wish. If you are going to do your duty as next of kin, then buy the land here, in the presence of these witnesses; but if you do not want it, then let me know right away, because I am next in line to redeem it after you."

The man replied, "All right, I will redeem it."

5 Then Boaz responded, "Well, just remember that if you buy Naomi's land, you are required to marry Ruth, the Moabite widow, so that she can have children in order to carry on her husband's name and keep the land in the family."

6 And the man said, "In that case, I cannot redeem the land, because I do not want to endanger my own estate. You redeem it. I cannot do it."

7 Now in those days it was customary in Israel for anyone selling land to take off his sandal and hand it to the purchasing party. This served to validate the transaction, making it legally binding. 8 So the family redeemer took off his sandal as he said to Boaz, "You buy the land and redeem it as next of kin."

9 And Boaz said to the witnesses and everyone else present, "You are all witnesses today that I have bought all that belonged to Elimelech, Chilion, and Mahlon, as it belonged to Naomi. 10 With the land I have acquired Ruth, a Moabite widow of Mahlon, to be my wife. This way she can have a son to carry on the family name of her dead husband and to inherit the family property here in his hometown. You are all witnesses of this today."

11 And all the people that were present, including the formal witnesses, said, "We are witnesses. May the Lord make this woman who is coming into your home like Rachel and like Leah, the two from whom all of

Israel descends. May you prosper greatly in Ephratah and be famous in Beth-lehem. 12 And may the Lord give you descendants through this young woman also, who will be like those of Pharez, the son of Tamar and Judah."

Saul v. Ahimelech (1 Samuel 22:6–23)

6 The news of David's return to Judah reached Saul as he sat beneath a tamarisk tree in Gibeah with a spear in his hand, surrounded by his officers. 7 "Listen here, Benjamites," Saul said to his officers when he heard the news. "Has David promised to give you all lands and vineyards and to make you high-ranking officers in his army? 8 Is that why all of you have conspired against me? Not one of you told me when my own son made a pact with him—you did not even give it a thought!—yet my son has encouraged David to lie in wait and kill me! Even as we speak, he plans to do it!"

9 Then Doeg the Edomite, who was standing there with Saul's men, spoke up: "When I was at Nob, I saw David talking to the priest Ahimelech, son of Ahitub. 10 Ahimelech consulted the Lord on his behalf and then gave him provisions and the sword of Goliath the Philistine."

11 Then Saul immediately sent for Ahimelech and all his family (who served as priests at Nob). They all came. 12 As soon as they arrived, Saul said to Ahimelech, "Listen here, son of Ahitub!"

And he answered, "What is it, my king?"

13 And Saul said to him, "Why have you conspired against me—you and David? Why did you give him provisions and a sword and consult God for him? Why have you encouraged him to kill me, which he plans to do, even as I speak?"

14 Then Ahimelech answered the king, "Who among all your servants has been as loyal as your son-in-law David? He is appointed to your staff, the captain of your bodyguard, and a highly honored member of your household—he does whatever you ask him to do. 15 Was I the first one to consult the Lord for him? No, I was not. I know nothing about any plot against you, small or great, my king; neither me nor my family. I trust that you will not accuse us in this matter."

16 And the king said, "You will certainly die, Ahimelech, you and all your family." 17 And the king ordered the footmen who stood next to him, "Turn around, and kill the priests of the Lord because they are allies and co-conspirators with David—they knew he was a fugitive but did not tell me." But Saul's men refused to kill the Lord's priests. 18 And the king said to Doeg, "You do it, then!" And Doeg the Edomite turned around and faced the priests. He attacked them and killed eighty-five of them, even

though they were still wearing their priestly clothing. 19 Then he attacked their city, Nob, and killed every living thing: men and women, children and nursing babies, cattle, donkeys, sheep, and goats. 20 Only Abiathar, one of the sons of Ahimelech, escaped and joined David. 21 He told David how Saul had killed the Lord's priests.

22 And David said to Abiathar, "I knew it! When I saw Doeg the Edomite there that day, I knew he was sure to tell Saul. I am responsible for the death of your entire family! 23 Stay here with me, and do not be afraid. The same man seeks to kill us both, but you will be safe with me."

The False Petition of the Woman of Tekoah (2 Samuel 14:4–11)

4 And when the woman from Tekoah spoke to the king, she prostrated herself before him as a sign of deep respect and said, "Help me, O your majesty!"

5 And the king said to her, "What is the matter?"

And she answered, "I am a widow; my husband is dead. 6 I had two sons, and they got into a fight in the field. Because no one was there to separate them, one of them struck the other and killed him! 7 Now, Sir, the rest of the family has demanded that I hand him over. They said to me, 'Hand over the brother that smote and killed his brother, so that we may execute him for his murder! We will also kill his heir!' If they do this, then they will extinguish the last ember of my husband's name, and he will have no one to carry on his name in the earth!"

8 And the king said to the woman, "Go to your home, and I will issue an order for you, and see to it that no one touches your son."

9 And the woman of Tekoah said to the king, "My lord, O king, may the guilt for this fall on me and my family, and not on your throne, for you will be innocent of this!"

10 And the king said, "If anyone objects, then bring him to me. I can assure you he will never complain again."

11 Then the woman said, "Swear to me by the Lord your God that you will not allow anyone to take vengeance on my son."

And the king said, "As surely as the Lord lives, not a hair of your son's head will fall to the ground."

The Petition of the Two Harlots before Solomon (1 Kings 3:16–28)

16 Now two women, who were prostitutes, stood in front of the king to present their dispute to him. 17 And one woman said, "Please, my lord, this woman and I live in the same house. While she still lived with me, I had a baby. 18 Three days after my baby was born, this woman also had a baby. It was just us in the house; we were alone. 19 Her son died because

she rolled over on him at night as she slept. 20 In the middle of the night, she got up and took my son from my side while I was asleep. She laid down with my child in her arms and put her dead baby in my arms. 21 When I got up the next morning to nurse my baby, I found him dead. But when I looked closer in the morning light, I saw that it was not my son at all!"

22 Then the other woman interrupted and said, "That's not true! The living son is mine, and the dead son is yours!"

And the other said, "No! Your son is dead, and my son is alive!" So they argued back and forth in front of the king.

23 Then the king said, "Let us get the matter straight: one of you says, 'This is my son that is alive, and your son is dead'; the other says, 'No! Your son is dead, and my son is alive!'" 24 Then the king said, "Bring me a sword." So they brought him a sword. 25 And the king said, "Cut the living child in half, and give one half to each woman."

26 Then the mother of the living child, moved with love for her son, said, "O my lord, give her the living child—whatever you do, do not kill him!"

But the other said, "All right; it will belong to neither of us; go ahead and divide it."

27 Then the king answered and said, "Give the living child to the woman who wants him alive, for she is the real mother!" 28 When all Israel heard about the king's verdict, they were in awe of him because they saw that God's wisdom was in him and that he would administer justice.

The Trial of Naboth (1 Kings 21:1–16)

1 Naboth from Jezreel owned a vineyard in Jezreel, right next to the palace of Ahab, king of Samaria. 2 One day, Ahab said to Naboth, "Your vineyard is so close to my palace—let me have it for a garden; I will give you an even better vineyard in return. If you prefer, I will pay you for it instead."

3 And Naboth said to Ahab, "Far be it from me to disobey the Lord's word. He forbids me from parting with my ancestral land."

4 So Ahab went home angry and sullen because Naboth had said, "I will not give you my ancestral land!" And Ahab lay down on his bed, covered his face, and refused to eat.

5 But Jezebel his wife came to him and said, "What is the matter? Why are you so upset that you refuse to eat?"

6 And he said to her, "Because I spoke unto Naboth the Jezreelite and said to him, 'Sell me your vineyard, or, if you like, trade it to me for another.' And he answered, 'I will not give you my vineyard.' He refused me!"

7 And his wife Jezebel said to him, "Are you or are you not king of Israel? Get up and eat! Cheer up! I will get Naboth's vineyard for you." 8 So she wrote letters in Ahab's name, sealed them with his royal seal, and sent the letters to the elders and nobles living in the city. 9 And she wrote in the letters, "Call everyone in town together for fasting and prayer, and give Naboth the seat of honor. 10 But seat two scoundrels opposite him who will testify against him, accusing him of cursing God and the king. Then take him outside of town and stone him to death!"

11 So the elders and nobles of the city did just as Jezebel directed them in the letters that she sent them. 12 They called everyone together for public fasting and prayer and gave Naboth the seat of honor. 13 And they seated two scoundrels opposite him, who testified against him, accusing him in the presence of the people of blasphemy, saying, "Naboth cursed God and the king!" Then the people carried him outside of town and stoned him to death.

14 Then they sent word to Jezebel, saying, "Naboth is dead; we stoned him." 15 As soon as Jezebel heard that Naboth was stoned to death, she said to Ahab, "Get up and take possession of Naboth's vineyard, which he refused to sell to you. Naboth is dead!" 16 As soon as Ahab heard that Naboth was dead, he got up and went down to take possession of Naboth's vineyard.

The Trial of Jeremiah (Jeremiah 26:1–24)
The Precedent of Micah (Jeremiah 26:18–19)
The Precedent of Urijah ben Shemaiah (Jeremiah 26:20–23)

1 In the early days of the reign of Jehoiakim (who was the son of Josiah, king of Judah), Jeremiah received this message from the Lord: 2 "This is what the Lord says: 'Go stand in the courtyard of my house, the temple, and speak to the people who have come here from all over Judah to worship there—tell them everything I say, not leaving out a single word. 3 Perhaps they will listen to you and turn from their evil ways so that I can revoke the disaster I am planning to bring on them because of their evil deeds. 4 And you will say unto them, "This is what the Lord says: 'If you will not listen to me, to follow my law, which I have set before you, 5 and listen to the words of my servants the prophets—whom I took great pains to send to you, but you never listened— 6 then I will destroy this temple as I destroyed Shiloh, and will make Jerusalem an object of ridicule to all the nations of the earth.'"'" 7 So the priests and the prophets and all the people heard Jeremiah speaking these words in the temple.

8 Now, as Jeremiah finished speaking all that the Lord had commanded him to speak, the priests and the prophets and all the people grabbed him and said, "You must die! 9 Why have you prophesied in the name of the Lord, saying, 'This temple will be destroyed like Shiloh, and Jerusalem will be a desolate, uninhabited waste'?" And all the people crowded around Jeremiah in the temple. 10 When the royal officials of Judah heard what was happening, they came up from the royal palace to the temple and took their places at the new temple gate, sitting down in the entry to hold court. 11 Then the priests and the prophets said to the royal officials and to all the people, "This man must die! You have heard yourselves that he is a traitor—he prophesied against Jerusalem!"

12 Then Jeremiah said to all the royal officials and all the people, "The Lord sent me to prophesy against this temple and against Jerusalem—he gave me every word. 13 If you will change your ways and obey the voice of the Lord your God, then the Lord will change his mind about this disaster that he has decreed against you. 14 As for me, look and see—I am in your hands: do with me what you will. 15 But know for certain, that if you put me to death, you will bring innocent blood on yourselves, and on this city, and on every soul that lives here, because the Lord has truly sent me to you to speak all these words to you."

16 Then the royal officials and all the people said to the priests and to the prophets, "This man must not die, because he has spoken to us in the name of the Lord our God."

17 Then some of the wise old men stood up and said to all the people assembled there, 18 "In the time of Hezekiah, king of Judah, Micah the Morasthite prophesied to all the people of Judah, 'This is what the Lord of heaven's armies says: "Zion will be plowed like a field, and Jerusalem will be reduced to ruins, and a thicket will grow on the heights where the temple now stands!"' 19 But did Hezekiah and the people put him at all to death for saying this? Did not Hezekiah fear the Lord, and seek after him, so that the Lord relented and changed his mind about the destruction that he had decreed against them? Now we are the ones bringing such calamity on ourselves!

20 "And there was also another man that prophesied in the name of the Lord, Urijah the son of Shemaiah, who came from Kirjath-jearim. He prophesied against Jerusalem and against this land of Judah, just like Jeremiah has done. 21 Now, when Jehoiakim the king and all his officers royal officials heard his words, the king sought to put him to death. But when Urijah heard about their plan, he feared for his life and escaped to Egypt. 22 Jehoiakim the king sent men to Egypt to hunt Urijah down, such as

Elnathan the son of Achbor, and others like him. 23 And they took Urijah prisoner, brought him out of Egypt, and delivered him to Jehoiakim the king. The king then had him killed with a sword, and threw his dead body into the graves of the common people."

24 But Ahikam, the son of Shaphan, stood up for Jeremiah and used his influence to persuade the court not to turn him over to the mob to be killed.

The Trial of Susanna (Daniel 13:1–62)[1]

1 Now there was a man that lived in Babylon, and his name was Joakim. 2 He married a woman named Susanna, the daughter of Helcias. She was a very beautiful woman, and one that feared God. . . . 4 Now Joakim was very rich and had an orchard near his house: the Jews often came to him to resolve disputes because he was the most honorable man among them. 5 And there were two of the elders of the people appointed as judges that year. . . . 6 These men, however, often went to the house of Joakim, and they learned much about righteous judgment there. 7 And when the people left at noon, Susanna went in and walked in her husband's orchard. 8 And the elders saw her going in every day and walking around and were inflamed with lust towards her: 9 this lust turned their eyes and minds from judging righteously. . . .

15 One day as they watched, she went in the orchard at the agreed time, as she had the previous two days, with two servant girls. She wanted to wash herself in the orchard because the weather was very hot. 16 She and the two men who had hidden themselves and were watching her were the only ones there. 17 So she said to the servant girls, "Bring me oil and soap, and shut the doors of the orchard so I can wash myself." 18 The servant girls did as she asked, shutting the doors of the orchard and going out by a back door to get what she had commanded them. They did not know that the two men were hidden inside.

19 Now when the servant girls left, the two men got up and ran to her, and said: 20 "Look, the orchard doors are shut—nobody can see us! We are both in love with you! Please agree to have sex with us! 21 If you do not, we will testify against you and say that you sent away your servant girls because you had a young man with you."

22 Susanna sighed and said, ". . . 23 It is better for me to fall into your hands without doing it than to sin in the sight of the Lord." 24 Then Susanna cried out loudly, and the elders also cried out, accusing her. 25 And one of them ran to the door of the orchard and opened it. 26 So

---

1. Text based on the LXX Apocrypha, Douay-Rheims Version.

when the servants of the house heard the cry in the orchard, they rushed in by the back door to see what was the matter. 27 But after the men had made their accusation, the servants were greatly ashamed because nothing like it had ever been said about Susanna.

And on the next day, 28 when the people came to Joakim her husband, the two elders also came full of evil intent against Susanna, desiring to put her to death. 29 And they accused her in front of everyone, saying, "Go get Susanna, daughter of Helcias, the wife of Joakim!" So they did. 30 And she came with her parents and children and all her relatives. 31 Now Susanna was a very delicate woman and beautiful to look upon. 32 But those wicked men forced her to uncover her face (which was veiled) so that at least they might please themselves with her beauty. 33 Because of this, all her friends and all her acquaintances wept.

34 But the two elders, rising up to accuse her in the middle of the people, put their hands upon her head. 35 And she, weeping, looked up to heaven because her heart trusted in the Lord. 36 And the elders said: "While we were walking in the orchard alone, this woman came in with two servant girls, shut the doors of the orchard, and then sent her servant girls away. 37 Then a young man who was hidden in the orchard came to her and had sex with her. 38 But we that were in another corner of the orchard, seeing this great sin, ran up to them, and we saw them having sex. 39 We were unable to catch and hold him, because he was stronger than us and escaped. 40 We were able to detain this woman, but when we asked who the young man was, she would not tell us. This is what we saw!"

41 The crowd of people believed them since they were prominent men, their elders and judges, and they all condemned her to die.

42 Then Susanna cried out in a loud voice, saying, "O eternal God, who knows hidden things, who knows all things before they happen, 43 you know that they have borne false witness against me, yet I am going to die. I have done none of the things that they have maliciously fabricated to accuse me of!"

44 And the Lord heard her voice. 45 And when she was led away to be put to death, the Lord raised up the holy spirit of a young boy whose name was Daniel. 46 And he cried out with a loud voice, "I am clear from the blood of this woman."

47 Then all the people turned around and faced him, and said, "What do you mean?"

48 He replied, as he stood in the middle of them all, "Are ye so foolish, you Israelites, that without examination or knowledge of the truth, you

have condemned a daughter of Israel? 49 Go back to her trial, for the two men have borne false witness against her."

50 So all the people immediately turned around, and the old men said to him, "Come, and sit down with us, and show us righteous judgment, seeing that the Lord has made you venerable."

51 And Daniel said to the people: "Separate these two men far from one another, and I will examine them, asking them questions." 52 So when they were thus separated, he called one of them and said, ". . . 53 You have judged unjust judgments, oppressed the innocent, and let the guilty go free, contrary to the Lord's word, which says, 'The innocent and the just you shall not kill' [Exodus 23:7]. 54 Now then, if you saw her, tell me under what tree you saw them lying together."

The judge replied, "Under a mastic tree."

55 And Daniel said, "Then truly you have lied against your own head, for the angel of God having received the sentence from God himself, shall cut you in two."

56 And after he was sent away, Daniel commanded that the other should come, and he said to him, "You are a Canaanite, and not from Judah! You have been deceived by beauty and perverted by lust! 57 And you did it to Israelite girls, who only lay with you out of fear! But a daughter of Judah would not stand for your wickedness. 58 Now therefore tell me, under what tree didst thou take them lying together?"

And he answered, "Under a holm tree."

59 And Daniel said to him, "Then truly you have also lied against your own head, for the angel of the Lord waits with a sword to cut you in two and to destroy you."

60 With that, all the assembly cried out with a loud voice, and they blessed God, who saves them that trust in him. 61 And they rose up against the two elders (for Daniel had convicted them of false witness by their own mouth), and they did to them as they had maliciously dealt against their neighbour, 62 thus fulfilling the law given to Moses. They put them to death, and innocent blood was saved that day.

Legal Proceedings in the Book of Mormon

The Case of Sherem (Jacob 7:1–23)

1 And now it came to pass after some years had passed away, there came a man among the people of Nephi, whose name was Sherem. 2 And it came to pass that he began to preach among the people, and to declare unto them that there should be no Christ. And he preached many things which were flattering unto the people; and this he did that he might overthrow the doctrine of Christ. 3 And he labored diligently that he might lead away the hearts of the people, insomuch that he did lead away many hearts; and he knowing that I, Jacob, had faith in Christ who should come, he sought much opportunity that he might come unto me. 4 And he was learned, that he had a perfect knowledge of the language of the people; wherefore, he could use much flattery, and much power of speech, according to the power of the devil. 5 And he had hope to shake me from the faith, notwithstanding the many revelations and the many things which I had seen concerning these things; for I truly had seen angels, and they had ministered unto me. And also, I had heard the voice of the Lord speaking unto me in very word, from time to time; wherefore, I could not be shaken.

6 And it came to pass that he came unto me, and on this wise did he speak unto me, saying: "Brother Jacob, I have sought much opportunity that I might speak unto you; for I have heard and also know that thou goest about much, preaching that which ye call the gospel, or the doctrine of Christ. 7 And ye have led away much of this people that they pervert the right way of God, and keep not the law of Moses which is the right way; and convert the law of Moses into the worship of a being which ye say shall come many hundred years hence. And now behold, I, Sherem, declare unto you that this is blasphemy; for no man knoweth of such things; for he cannot tell of things to come." And after this manner did Sherem contend against me.

8 But behold, the Lord God poured in his Spirit into my soul, insomuch that I did confound him in all his words. 9 And I said unto him: "Deniest thou the Christ who shall come?"

And he said: "If there should be a Christ, I would not deny him; but I know that there is no Christ, neither has been, nor ever will be."

10 And I said unto him: "Believest thou the scriptures?"

And he said, "Yea."

11 And I said unto him: "Then ye do not understand them; for they truly testify of Christ. Behold, I say unto you that none of the prophets have written, nor prophesied, save they have spoken concerning this Christ. 12 And this is not all—it has been made manifest unto me, for I have heard and seen; and it also has been made manifest unto me by the power of the Holy Ghost; wherefore, I know if there should be no atonement made all mankind must be lost."

13 And it came to pass that he said unto me: "Show me a sign by this power of the Holy Ghost, in the which ye know so much."

14 And I said unto him: "What am I that I should tempt God to show unto thee a sign in the thing which thou knowest to be true? Yet thou wilt deny it, because thou art of the devil. Nevertheless, not my will be done; but if God shall smite thee, let that be a sign unto thee that he has power, both in heaven and in earth; and also, that Christ shall come. And thy will, O Lord, be done, and not mine."

15 And it came to pass that when I, Jacob, had spoken these words, the power of the Lord came upon him, insomuch that he fell to the earth. And it came to pass that he was nourished for the space of many days.

16 And it came to pass that he said unto the people: "Gather together on the morrow, for I shall die; wherefore, I desire to speak unto the people before I shall die." 17 And it came to pass that on the morrow the multitude were gathered together; and he spake plainly unto them and denied the things which he had taught them, and confessed the Christ, and the power of the Holy Ghost, and the ministering of angels. 18 And he spake plainly unto them, that he had been deceived by the power of the devil. And he spake of hell, and of eternity, and of eternal punishment. 19 And he said: "I fear lest I have committed the unpardonable sin, for I have lied unto God; for I denied the Christ, and said that I believed the scriptures; and they truly testify of him. And because I have thus lied unto God I greatly fear lest my case shall be awful; but I confess unto God." 20 And it came to pass that when he had said these words he could say no more, and he gave up the ghost.

21 And when the multitude had witnessed that he spake these things as he was about to give up the ghost, they were astonished exceedingly; insomuch that the power of God came down upon them, and they were overcome that they fell to the earth. 22 Now, this thing was pleasing unto me, Jacob, for I had requested it of my Father who was in heaven; for he had heard my cry and answered my prayer. 23 And it came to pass that peace and the love of God was restored again among the people; and they searched the scriptures, and hearkened no more to the words of this wicked man.

The Trial of Abinadi (Mosiah 11–17)

11:20 And it came to pass that there was a man among them whose name was Abinadi; and he went forth among them, and began to prophesy, saying: "Behold, thus saith the Lord, and thus hath he commanded me, saying, 'Go forth, and say unto this people, "Thus saith the Lord—'Wo be unto this people, for I have seen their abominations, and their wickedness, and their whoredoms; and except they repent I will visit them in mine anger. 21 And except they repent and turn to the Lord their God, behold, I will deliver them into the hands of their enemies; yea, and they shall be brought into bondage; and they shall be afflicted by the hand of their enemies. 22 And it shall come to pass that they shall know that I am the Lord their God, and am a jealous God, visiting the iniquities of my people. 23 And it shall come to pass that except this people repent and turn unto the Lord their God, they shall be brought into bondage; and none shall deliver them, except it be the Lord the Almighty God. 24 Yea, and it shall come to pass that when they shall cry unto me I will be slow to hear their cries; yea, and I will suffer them that they be smitten by their enemies. 25 And except they repent in sackcloth and ashes, and cry mightily to the Lord their God, I will not hear their prayers, neither will I deliver them out of their afflictions'"'"; and thus saith the Lord, and thus hath he commanded me." 26 Now it came to pass that when Abinadi had spoken these words unto them they were wroth with him, and sought to take away his life; but the Lord delivered him out of their hands.

27 Now when king Noah had heard of the words which Abinadi had spoken unto the people, he was also wroth; and he said: "Who is Abinadi, that I and my people should be judged of him, or who is the Lord, that shall bring upon my people such great affliction? 28 I command you to bring Abinadi hither, that I may slay him, for he has said these things that he might stir up my people to anger one with another, and to raise contentions among my people; therefore I will slay him." 29 Now the eyes of

the people were blinded; therefore they hardened their hearts against the words of Abinadi, and they sought from that time forward to take him. And king Noah hardened his heart against the word of the Lord, and he did not repent of his evil doings.

12:1 And it came to pass that after the space of two years that Abinadi came among them in disguise, that they knew him not, and began to prophesy among them, saying: "Thus has the Lord commanded me, saying—'Abinadi, go and prophesy unto this my people, for they have hardened their hearts against my words; they have repented not of their evil doings; therefore, I will visit them in my anger, yea, in my fierce anger will I visit them in their iniquities and abominations. 2 Yea, wo be unto this generation!' And the Lord said unto me: 'Stretch forth thy hand and prophesy, saying: "Thus saith the Lord, 'It shall come to pass that this generation, because of their iniquities, shall be brought into bondage, and shall be smitten on the cheek; yea, and shall be driven by men, and shall be slain; and the vultures of the air, and the dogs, yea, and the wild beasts, shall devour their flesh. 3 And it shall come to pass that the life of king Noah shall be valued even as a garment in a hot furnace; for he shall know that I am the Lord. 4 And it shall come to pass that I will smite this my people with sore afflictions, yea, with famine and with pestilence; and I will cause that they shall howl all the day long. 5 Yea, and I will cause that they shall have burdens lashed upon their backs; and they shall be driven before like a dumb ass. 6 And it shall come to pass that I will send forth hail among them, and it shall smite them; and they shall also be smitten with the east wind; and insects shall pester their land also, and devour their grain. 7 And they shall be smitten with a great pestilence—and all this will I do because of their iniquities and abominations. 8 And it shall come to pass that except they repent I will utterly destroy them from off the face of the earth; yet they shall leave a record behind them, and I will preserve them for other nations which shall possess the land; yea, even this will I do that I may discover the abominations of this people to other nations.'"'" And many things did Abinadi prophesy against this people.

9 And it came to pass that they were angry with him; and they took him and carried him bound before the king, and said unto the king: "Behold, we have brought a man before thee who has prophesied evil concerning thy people, and saith that God will destroy them. 10 And he also prophesieth evil concerning thy life, and saith that thy life shall be as a garment in a furnace of fire. 11 And again, he saith that thou shalt be as a stalk, even as a dry stalk of the field, which is run over by the beasts and trodden under foot. 12 And again, he saith thou shalt be as the blossoms

of a thistle, which, when it is fully ripe, if the wind bloweth, it is driven forth upon the face of the land. And he pretendeth the Lord hath spoken it. And he saith all this shall come upon thee except thou repent, and this because of thine iniquities. 13 And now, O king, what great evil hast thou done, or what great sins have thy people committed, that we should be condemned of God or judged of this man? 14 And now, O king, behold, we are guiltless, and thou, O king, hast not sinned; therefore, this man has lied concerning you, and he has prophesied in vain. 15 And behold, we are strong, we shall not come into bondage, or be taken captive by our enemies; yea, and thou hast prospered in the land, and thou shalt also prosper. 16 Behold, here is the man, we deliver him into thy hands; thou mayest do with him as seemeth thee good."

17 And it came to pass that king Noah caused that Abinadi should be cast into prison; and he commanded that the priests should gather themselves together that he might hold a council with them what he should do with him. 18 And it came to pass that they said unto the king: "Bring him hither that we may question him"; and the king commanded that he should be brought before them. 19 And they began to question him, that they might cross him, that thereby they might have wherewith to accuse him; but he answered them boldly, and withstood all their questions, yea, to their astonishment; for he did withstand them in all their questions, and did confound them in all their words.

20 And it came to pass that one of them said unto him: "What meaneth the words which are written, and which have been taught by our fathers, saying: 21 'How beautiful upon the mountains are the feet of him that bringeth good tidings; that publisheth peace; that bringeth good tidings of good; that publisheth salvation; that saith unto Zion, "Thy God reigneth"; 22 thy watchmen shall lift up the voice; with the voice together shall they sing; for they shall see eye to eye when the Lord shall bring again Zion; 23 break forth into joy; sing together ye waste places of Jerusalem; for the Lord hath comforted his people, he hath redeemed Jerusalem; 24 the Lord hath made bare his holy arm in the eyes of all the nations, and all the ends of the earth shall see the salvation of our God'?"

25 And now Abinadi said unto them: "Are you priests, and pretend to teach this people, and to understand the spirit of prophesying, and yet desire to know of me what these things mean? 26 I say unto you, wo be unto you for perverting the ways of the Lord! For if ye understand these things ye have not taught them; therefore, ye have perverted the ways of the Lord. 27 Ye have not applied your hearts to understanding; therefore, ye have not been wise. Therefore, what teach ye this people?"

28 And they said: "We teach the law of Moses."

29 And again he said unto them: "If ye teach the law of Moses why do ye not keep it? Why do ye set your hearts upon riches? Why do ye commit whoredoms and spend your strength with harlots, yea, and cause this people to commit sin, that the Lord has cause to send me to prophesy against this people, yea, even a great evil against this people? 30 Know ye not that I speak the truth? Yea, ye know that I speak the truth; and you ought to tremble before God. 31 And it shall come to pass that ye shall be smitten for your iniquities, for ye have said that ye teach the law of Moses. And what know ye concerning the law of Moses? Doth salvation come by the law of Moses? What say ye?"

32 And they answered and said that salvation did come by the law of Moses.

33 But now Abinadi said unto them: "I know if ye keep the commandments of God ye shall be saved; yea, if ye keep the commandments which the Lord delivered unto Moses in the mount of Sinai, saying: 34 'I am the Lord thy God, who hath brought thee out of the land of Egypt, out of the house of bondage. 35 Thou shalt have no other God before me. 36 Thou shalt not make unto thee any graven image, or any likeness of any thing in heaven above, or things which are in the earth beneath.'"

37 Now Abinadi said unto them, "Have ye done all this? I say unto you, Nay, ye have not. And have ye taught this people that they should do all these things? I say unto you, Nay, ye have not."

13:1 And now when the king had heard these words, he said unto his priests: "Away with this fellow, and slay him; for what have we to do with him, for he is mad." 2 And they stood forth and attempted to lay their hands on him; but he withstood them, and said unto them: 3 "Touch me not, for God shall smite you if ye lay your hands upon me, for I have not delivered the message which the Lord sent me to deliver; neither have I told you that which ye requested that I should tell; therefore, God will not suffer that I shall be destroyed at this time. 4 But I must fulfil the commandments wherewith God has commanded me; and because I have told you the truth ye are angry with me. And again, because I have spoken the word of God ye have judged me that I am mad."

5 Now it came to pass after Abinadi had spoken these words that the people of king Noah durst not lay their hands on him, for the Spirit of the Lord was upon him; and his face shone with exceeding luster, even as Moses' did while in the mount of Sinai, while speaking with the Lord. 6 And he spake with power and authority from God; and he continued his words, saying: 7 "Ye see that ye have not power to slay me, therefore I finish my

message. Yea, and I perceive that it cuts you to your hearts because I tell you the truth concerning your iniquities. 8 Yea, and my words fill you with wonder and amazement, and with anger. 9 But I finish my message; and then it matters not whither I go, if it so be that I am saved. 10 But this much I tell you, what you do with me, after this, shall be as a type and a shadow of things which are to come." [Abinadi then recites the rest of the Ten Commandments, says that salvation does not come by the law alone, asserts that God himself shall make an atonement for the sins of his people, quotes and explains Isaiah 53, and explicates the meaning of Isaiah 52:7–10 and the plan of redemption.]

17:1 And now it came to pass that when Abinadi had finished these sayings, that the king commanded that the priests should take him and cause that he should be put to death. 2 But there was one among them whose name was Alma, he also being a descendant of Nephi. And he was a young man, and he believed the words which Abinadi had spoken, for he knew concerning the iniquity which Abinadi had testified against them; therefore he began to plead with the king that he would not be angry with Abinadi, but suffer that he might depart in peace. 3 But the king was more wroth, and caused that Alma should be cast out from among them, and sent his servants after him that they might slay him. 4 But he fled from before them and hid himself that they found him not. And he being concealed for many days did write all the words which Abinadi had spoken.

5 And it came to pass that the king caused that his guards should surround Abinadi and take him; and they bound him and cast him into prison. 6 And after three days, having counseled with his priests, he caused that he should again be brought before him.

7 And he said unto him: "Abinadi, we have found an accusation against thee, and thou art worthy of death. 8 For thou hast said that God himself should come down among the children of men; and now, for this cause thou shalt be put to death unless thou wilt recall all the words which thou hast spoken evil concerning me and my people."

9 Now Abinadi said unto him: "I say unto you, I will not recall the words which I have spoken unto you concerning this people, for they are true; and that ye may know of their surety I have suffered myself that I have fallen into your hands. 10 Yea, and I will suffer even until death, and I will not recall my words, and they shall stand as a testimony against you. And if ye slay me ye will shed innocent blood, and this shall also stand as a testimony against you at the last day."

11 And now king Noah was about to release him, for he feared his word; for he feared that the judgments of God would come upon him.

12 But the priests lifted up their voices against him, and began to accuse him, saying: "He has reviled the king." Therefore the king was stirred up in anger against him, and he delivered him up that he might be slain.

13 And it came to pass that they took him and bound him, and scourged his skin with faggots, yea, even unto death. 14 And now when the flames began to scorch him, he cried unto them, saying: 15 "Behold, even as ye have done unto me, so shall it come to pass that thy seed shall cause that many shall suffer the pains that I do suffer, even the pains of death by fire; and this because they believe in the salvation of the Lord their God. 16 And it will come to pass that ye shall be afflicted with all manner of diseases because of your iniquities. 17 Yea, and ye shall be smitten on every hand, and shall be driven and scattered to and fro, even as a wild flock is driven by wild and ferocious beasts. 18 And in that day ye shall be hunted, and ye shall be taken by the hand of your enemies, and then ye shall suffer, as I suffer, the pains of death by fire. 19 Thus God executeth vengeance upon those that destroy his people. O God, receive my soul."

20 And now, when Abinadi had said these words, he fell, having suffered death by fire; yea, having been put to death because he would not deny the commandments of God, having sealed the truth of his words by his death.

The Trial of Nehor (Alma 1:1–15)

1 Now it came to pass that in the first year of the reign of the judges over the people of Nephi, from this time forward, king Mosiah having gone the way of all the earth, having warred a good warfare, walking uprightly before God, leaving none to reign in his stead; nevertheless he had established laws, and they were acknowledged by the people; therefore they were obliged to abide by the laws which he had made.

2 And it came to pass that in the first year of the reign of Alma in the judgment-seat, there was a man brought before him to be judged, a man who was large, and was noted for his much strength. 3 And he had gone about among the people, preaching to them that which he termed to be the word of God, bearing down against the church; declaring unto the people that every priest and teacher ought to become popular; and they ought not to labor with their hands, but that they ought to be supported by the people. 4 And he also testified unto the people that all mankind should be saved at the last day, and that they need not fear nor tremble, but that they might lift up their heads and rejoice; for the Lord had created all men, and had also redeemed all men; and, in the end, all men should have eternal life. 5 And it came to pass that he did teach these things so

much that many did believe on his words, even so many that they began to support him and give him money. 6 And he began to be lifted up in the pride of his heart, and to wear very costly apparel, yea, and even began to establish a church after the manner of his preaching.

7 And it came to pass as he was going, to preach to those who believed on his word, he met a man who belonged to the church of God, yea, even one of their teachers; and he began to contend with him sharply, that he might lead away the people of the church; but the man withstood him, admonishing him with the words of God. 8 Now the name of the man was Gideon; and it was he who was an instrument in the hands of God in delivering the people of Limhi out of bondage. 9 Now, because Gideon withstood him with the words of God he was wroth with Gideon, and drew his sword and began to smite him. Now Gideon being stricken with many years, therefore he was not able to withstand his blows, therefore he was slain by the sword.

10 And the man who slew him was taken by the people of the church, and was brought before Alma, to be judged according to the crimes which he had committed. 11 And it came to pass that he stood before Alma and pleaded for himself with much boldness.

12 But Alma said unto him: "Behold, this is the first time that priestcraft has been introduced among this people. And behold, thou art not only guilty of priestcraft, but hast endeavored to enforce it by the sword; and were priestcraft to be enforced among this people it would prove their entire destruction. 13 And thou hast shed the blood of a righteous man, yea, a man who has done much good among this people; and were we to spare thee his blood would come upon us for vengeance. 14 Therefore thou art condemned to die, according to the law which has been given us by Mosiah, our last king; and it has been acknowledged by this people; therefore this people must abide by the law."

15 And it came to pass that they took him; and his name was Nehor; and they carried him upon the top of the hill Manti, and there he was caused, or rather did acknowledge, between the heavens and the earth, that what he had taught to the people was contrary to the word of God; and there he suffered an ignominious death.

The Trial of Alma and Amulek (Alma 14)

1 And it came to pass after [Alma] had made an end of speaking unto the people many of them did believe on his words, and began to repent, and to search the scriptures. 2 But the more part of them were desirous that they might destroy Alma and Amulek; for they were angry with

Alma, because of the plainness of his words unto Zeezrom; and they also said that Amulek had lied unto them, and had reviled against their law and also against their lawyers and judges. 3 And they were also angry with Alma and Amulek; and because they had testified so plainly against their wickedness, they sought to put them away privily.

4 But it came to pass that they did not; but they took them and bound them with strong cords, and took them before the chief judge of the land. 5 And the people went forth and witnessed against them—testifying that they had reviled against the law, and their lawyers and judges of the land, and also of all the people that were in the land; and also testified that there was but one God, and that he should send his Son among the people, but he should not save them; and many such things did the people testify against Alma and Amulek. Now this was done before the chief judge of the land.

6 And it came to pass that Zeezrom . . . 7 . . . began to plead for them from that time forth; but they reviled him, saying: "Art thou also possessed with the devil?" And they spit upon him, and cast him out from among them, and also all those who believed in the words which had been spoken by Alma and Amulek; and they cast them out, and sent men to cast stones at them.

8 And they brought their wives and children together, and whosoever believed or had been taught to believe in the word of God they caused that they should be cast into the fire; and they also brought forth their records which contained the holy scriptures, and cast them into the fire also, that they might be burned and destroyed by fire.

9 And it came to pass that they took Alma and Amulek, and carried them forth to the place of martyrdom, that they might witness the destruction of those who were consumed by fire. 10 And when Amulek saw the pains of the women and children who were consuming in the fire, he also was pained; and he said unto Alma: "How can we witness this awful scene? Therefore let us stretch forth our hands, and exercise the power of God which is in us, and save them from the flames."

11 But Alma said unto him: "The Spirit constraineth me that I must not stretch forth mine hand; for behold the Lord receiveth them up unto himself, in glory; and he doth suffer that they may do this thing, or that the people may do this thing unto them, according to the hardness of their hearts, that the judgments which he shall exercise upon them in his wrath may be just; and the blood of the innocent shall stand as a witness against them, yea, and cry mightily against them at the last day."

12 Now Amulek said unto Alma: "Behold, perhaps they will burn us also."

13 And Alma said: "Be it according to the will of the Lord. But, behold, our work is not finished; therefore they burn us not."

14 Now it came to pass that when the bodies of those who had been cast into the fire were consumed, and also the records which were cast in with them, the chief judge of the land came and stood before Alma and Amulek, as they were bound; and he smote them with his hand upon their cheeks, and said unto them: "After what ye have seen, will ye preach again unto this people, that they shall be cast into a lake of fire and brimstone? 15 Behold, ye see that ye had not power to save those who had been cast into the fire; neither has God saved them because they were of thy faith." And the judge smote them again upon their cheeks, and asked: "What say ye for yourselves?" 16 Now this judge was after the order and faith of Nehor, who slew Gideon.

17 And it came to pass that Alma and Amulek answered him nothing; and he smote them again, and delivered them to the officers to be cast into prison. 18 And when they had been cast into prison three days, there came many lawyers, and judges, and priests, and teachers, who were of the profession of Nehor; and they came in unto the prison to see them, and they questioned them about many words; but they answered them nothing.

19 And it came to pass that the judge stood before them, and said: "Why do ye not answer the words of this people? Know ye not that I have power to deliver you up unto the flames?" And he commanded them to speak; but they answered nothing.

20 And it came to pass that they departed and went their ways, but came again on the morrow; and the judge also smote them again on their cheeks. And many came forth also, and smote them, saying: "Will ye stand again and judge this people, and condemn our law? If ye have such great power why do ye not deliver yourselves?" 21 And many such things did they say unto them, gnashing their teeth upon them, and spitting upon them, and saying: "How shall we look when we are damned?"

22 And many such things, yea, all manner of such things did they say unto them; and thus they did mock them for many days. And they did withhold food from them that they might hunger, and water that they might thirst; and they also did take from them their clothes that they were naked; and thus they were bound with strong cords, and confined in prison. 23 And it came to pass after they had thus suffered for many days, (and it was on the twelfth day, in the tenth month, in the tenth year of the reign of the judges over the people of Nephi) that the chief judge over the

land of Ammonihah and many of their teachers and their lawyers went in unto the prison where Alma and Amulek were bound with cords. 24 And the chief judge stood before them, and smote them again, and said unto them: "If ye have the power of God deliver yourselves from these bands, and then we will believe that the Lord will destroy this people according to your words." 25 And it came to pass that they all went forth and smote them, saying the same words, even until the last; and when the last had spoken unto them the power of God was upon Alma and Amulek, and they rose and stood upon their feet.

26 And Alma cried, saying: "How long shall we suffer these great afflictions, O Lord? O Lord, give us strength according to our faith which is in Christ, even unto deliverance." And they broke the cords with which they were bound; and when the people saw this, they began to flee, for the fear of destruction had come upon them. 27 And it came to pass that so great was their fear that they fell to the earth, and did not obtain the outer door of the prison; and the earth shook mightily, and the walls of the prison were rent in twain, so that they fell to the earth; and the chief judge, and the lawyers, and priests, and teachers, who smote upon Alma and Amulek, were slain by the fall thereof.

28 And Alma and Amulek came forth out of the prison, and they were not hurt. . . . 29 Now the people having heard a great noise came running together by multitudes to know the cause of it; and when they saw Alma and Amulek coming forth out of the prison, and the walls thereof had fallen to the earth, they were struck with great fear, and fled from the presence of Alma and Amulek even as a goat fleeth with her young from two lions.

The Trial of Korihor (Alma 30:6–60)

6 But it came to pass in the latter end of the seventeenth year, there came a man into the land of Zarahemla, and he was Anti-Christ, for he began to preach unto the people against the prophecies which had been spoken by the prophets, concerning the coming of Christ. 7 Now there was no law against a man's belief; for it was strictly contrary to the commands of God that there should be a law which should bring men on to unequal grounds. 8 For thus saith the scripture: "Choose ye this day, whom ye will serve." 9 Now if a man desired to serve God, it was his privilege; or rather, if he believed in God it was his privilege to serve him; but if he did not believe in him there was no law to punish him. 10 But if he murdered he was punished unto death; and if he robbed he was also punished; and if he stole he was also punished; and if he committed adultery he was also

punished; yea, for all this wickedness they were punished. 11 For there was a law that men should be judged according to their crimes. Nevertheless, there was no law against a man's belief; therefore, a man was punished only for the crimes which he had done; therefore all men were on equal grounds.

12 And this Anti-Christ, whose name was Korihor, (and the law could have no hold upon him) began to preach unto the people that there should be no Christ. And after this manner did he preach, saying: 13 "O ye that are bound down under a foolish and a vain hope, why do ye yoke yourselves with such foolish things? Why do ye look for a Christ? For no man can know of anything which is to come. 14 Behold, these things which ye call prophecies, which ye say are handed down by holy prophets, behold, they are foolish traditions of your fathers. 15 How do ye know of their surety? Behold, ye cannot know of things which ye do not see; therefore ye cannot know that there shall be a Christ. 16 Ye look forward and say that ye see a remission of your sins. But behold, it is the effect of a frenzied mind; and this derangement of your minds comes because of the traditions of your fathers, which lead you away into a belief of things which are not so."

17 And many more such things did he say unto them, telling them that there could be no atonement made for the sins of men, but every man fared in this life according to the management of the creature; therefore every man prospered according to his genius, and that every man conquered according to his strength; and whatsoever a man did was no crime. 18 And thus he did preach unto them, leading away the hearts of many, causing them to lift up their heads in their wickedness, yea, leading away many women, and also men, to commit whoredoms—telling them that when a man was dead, that was the end thereof.

19 Now this man went over to the land of Jershon also, to preach these things among the people of Ammon, who were once the people of the Lamanites. 20 But behold they were more wise than many of the Nephites; for they took him, and bound him, and carried him before Ammon, who was a high priest over that people. 21 And it came to pass that he caused that he should be carried out of the land.

And he came over into the land of Gideon, and began to preach unto them also; and here he did not have much success, for he was taken and bound and carried before the high priest, and also the chief judge over the land. 22 And it came to pass that the high priest said unto him: "Why do ye go about perverting the ways of the Lord? Why do ye teach this people that there shall be no Christ, to interrupt their rejoicings? Why do ye speak against all the prophecies of the holy prophets?" 23 Now the high priest's name was Giddonah.

And Korihor said unto him: "Because I do not teach the foolish traditions of your fathers, and because I do not teach this people to bind themselves down under the foolish ordinances and performances which are laid down by ancient priests, to usurp power and authority over them, to keep them in ignorance, that they may not lift up their heads, but be brought down according to thy words. 24 Ye say that this people is a free people. Behold, I say they are in bondage. Ye say that those ancient prophecies are true. Behold, I say that ye do not know that they are true. 25 Ye say that this people is a guilty and a fallen people, because of the transgression of a parent. Behold, I say that a child is not guilty because of its parents. 26 And ye also say that Christ shall come. But behold, I say that ye do not know that there shall be a Christ. And ye say also that he shall be slain for the sins of the world— 27 and thus ye lead away this people after the foolish traditions of your fathers, and according to your own desires; and ye keep them down, even as it were in bondage, that ye may glut yourselves with the labors of their hands, that they durst not look up with boldness, and that they durst not enjoy their rights and privileges. 28 Yea, they durst not make use of that which is their own lest they should offend their priests, who do yoke them according to their desires, and have brought them to believe, by their traditions and their dreams and their whims and their visions and their pretended mysteries, that they should, if they did not do according to their words, offend some unknown being, who they say is God—a being who never has been seen or known, who never was nor ever will be."

29 Now when the high priest and the chief judge saw the hardness of his heart, yea, when they saw that he would revile even against God, they would not make any reply to his words; but they caused that he should be bound; and they delivered him up into the hands of the officers, and sent him to the land of Zarahemla, that he might be brought before Alma, and the chief judge who was governor over all the land.

30 And it came to pass that when he was brought before Alma and the chief judge, he did go on in the same manner as he did in the land of Gideon; yea, he went on to blaspheme. 31 And he did rise up in great swelling words before Alma, and did revile against the priests and teachers, accusing them of leading away the people after the silly traditions of their fathers, for the sake of glutting on the labors of the people.

32 Now Alma said unto him: "Thou knowest that we do not glut ourselves upon the labors of this people; for behold I have labored even from

the commencement of the reign of the judges until now, with mine own hands for my support, notwithstanding my many travels round about the land to declare the word of God unto my people. 33 And notwithstanding the many labors which I have performed in the church, I have never received so much as even one senine for my labor; neither has any of my brethren, save it were in the judgment-seat; and then we have received only according to law for our time. 34 And now, if we do not receive anything for our labors in the church, what doth it profit us to labor in the church save it were to declare the truth, that we may have rejoicings in the joy of our brethren? 35 Then why sayest thou that we preach unto this people to get gain, when thou, of thyself, knowest that we receive no gain? And now, believest thou that we deceive this people, that causes such joy in their hearts?"

36 And Korihor answered him, "Yea."

37 And then Alma said unto him: "Believest thou that there is a God?"

38 And he answered, "Nay."

39 Now Alma said unto him: "Will ye deny again that there is a God, and also deny the Christ? For behold, I say unto you, I know there is a God, and also that Christ shall come. 40 And now what evidence have ye that there is no God, or that Christ cometh not? I say unto you that ye have none, save it be your word only. 41 But, behold, I have all things as a testimony that these things are true; and ye also have all things as a testimony unto you that they are true; and will ye deny them? Believest thou that these things are true? 42 Behold, I know that thou believest, but thou art possessed with a lying spirit, and ye have put off the Spirit of God that it may have no place in you; but the devil has power over you, and he doth carry you about, working devices that he may destroy the children of God."

43 And now Korihor said unto Alma: "If thou wilt show me a sign, that I may be convinced that there is a God, yea, show unto me that he hath power, and then will I be convinced of the truth of thy words."

44 But Alma said unto him: "Thou hast had signs enough; will ye tempt your God? Will ye say, 'Show unto me a sign,' when ye have the testimony of all these thy brethren, and also all the holy prophets? The scriptures are laid before thee, yea, and all things denote there is a God; yea, even the earth, and all things that are upon the face of it, yea, and its motion, yea, and also all the planets which move in their regular form do witness that there is a Supreme Creator. 45 And yet do ye go about, leading away the hearts of this people, testifying unto them there is no God? And yet will ye deny against all these witnesses?"

And he said: "Yea, I will deny, except ye shall show me a sign."

46 And now it came to pass that Alma said unto him: "Behold, I am grieved because of the hardness of your heart, yea, that ye will still resist the spirit of the truth, that thy soul may be destroyed. 47 But behold, it is better that thy soul should be lost than that thou shouldst be the means of bringing many souls down to destruction, by thy lying and by thy flattering words; therefore if thou shalt deny again, behold God shall smite thee, that thou shalt become dumb, that thou shalt never open thy mouth any more, that thou shalt not deceive this people any more."

48 Now Korihor said unto him: "I do not deny the existence of a God, but I do not believe that there is a God; and I say also, that ye do not know that there is a God; and except ye show me a sign, I will not believe."

49 Now Alma said unto him: "This will I give unto thee for a sign, that thou shalt be struck dumb, according to my words; and I say, that in the name of God, ye shall be struck dumb, that ye shall no more have utterance."

50 Now when Alma had said these words, Korihor was struck dumb, that he could not have utterance, according to the words of Alma. 51 And now when the chief judge saw this, he put forth his hand and wrote unto Korihor, saying: "Art thou convinced of the power of God? In whom did ye desire that Alma should show forth his sign? Would ye that he should afflict others, to show unto thee a sign? Behold, he has showed unto you a sign; and now will ye dispute more?"

52 And Korihor put forth his hand and wrote, saying: "I know that I am dumb, for I cannot speak; and I know that nothing save it were the power of God could bring this upon me; yea, and I always knew that there was a God. 53 But behold, the devil hath deceived me; for he appeared unto me in the form of an angel, and said unto me: 'Go and reclaim this people, for they have all gone astray after an unknown God.' And he said unto me: 'There is no God'; yea, and he taught me that which I should say. And I have taught his words; and I taught them because they were pleasing unto the carnal mind; and I taught them, even until I had much success, insomuch that I verily believed that they were true; and for this cause I withstood the truth, even until I have brought this great curse upon me."

54 Now when he had said this, he besought that Alma should pray unto God, that the curse might be taken from him. 55 But Alma said unto him: "If this curse should be taken from thee thou wouldst again lead away the hearts of this people; therefore, it shall be unto thee even as the Lord will."

56 And it came to pass that the curse was not taken off of Korihor; but he was cast out, and went about from house to house begging for his food. 57 Now the knowledge of what had happened unto Korihor was immediately published throughout all the land; yea, the proclamation was sent forth by the chief judge to all the people in the land, declaring unto those who had believed in the words of Korihor that they must speedily repent, lest the same judgments would come unto them. 58 And it came to pass that they were all convinced of the wickedness of Korihor; therefore they were all converted again unto the Lord; and this put an end to the iniquity after the manner of Korihor. And Korihor did go about from house to house, begging food for his support. 59 And it came to pass that as he went forth among the people, yea, among a people who had separated themselves from the Nephites and called themselves Zoramites, being led by a man whose name was Zoram—and as he went forth amongst them, behold, he was run upon and trodden down, even until he was dead. 60 And thus we see the end of him who perverteth the ways of the Lord; and thus we see that the devil will not support his children at the last day, but doth speedily drag them down to hell.

The Case of Paanchi (Helaman 1:1–10)
1 And now behold, it came to pass in the commencement of the fortieth year of the reign of the judges over the people of Nephi, there began to be a serious difficulty among the people of the Nephites. 2 For behold, Pahoran had died, and gone the way of all the earth; therefore there began to be a serious contention concerning who should have the judgment-seat among the brethren, who were the sons of Pahoran. 3 Now these are their names who did contend for the judgment-seat, who did also cause the people to contend: Pahoran, Paanchi, and Pacumeni. 4 Now these are not all the sons of Pahoran (for he had many), but these are they who did contend for the judgment-seat; therefore, they did cause three divisions among the people.

5 Nevertheless, it came to pass that Pahoran was appointed by the voice of the people to be chief judge and a governor over the people of Nephi. 6 And it came to pass that Pacumeni, when he saw that he could not obtain the judgment-seat, he did unite with the voice of the people.

7 But behold, Paanchi, and that part of the people that were desirous that he should be their governor, was exceedingly wroth; therefore, he was about to flatter away those people to rise up in rebellion against their brethren. 8 And it came to pass as he was about to do this, behold, he was taken, and was tried according to the voice of the people, and condemned

unto death; for he had raised up in rebellion and sought to destroy the liberty of the people.

9 Now when those people who were desirous that he should be their governor saw that he was condemned unto death, therefore they were angry, and behold, they sent forth one Kishkumen, even to the judgment-seat of Pahoran, and murdered Pahoran as he sat upon the judgment-seat. 10 And he was pursued by the servants of Pahoran; but behold, so speedy was the flight of Kishkumen that no man could overtake him.

The Trial of Seantum (Helaman 7–9)

7:1 Behold, now it came to pass in the sixty and ninth year of the reign of the judges over the people of the Nephites, that Nephi, the son of Helaman, returned to the land of Zarahemla from the land northward.... 4 And seeing the people in a state of such awful wickedness, and those Gadianton robbers filling the judgment-seats—having usurped the power and authority of the land; laying aside the commandments of God, and not in the least aright before him; doing no justice unto the children of men; 5 condemning the righteous because of their righteousness; letting the guilty and the wicked go unpunished because of their money; and moreover to be held in office at the head of government, to rule and do according to their wills, that they might get gain and glory of the world, and, moreover, that they might the more easily commit adultery, and steal, and kill, and do according to their own wills— 6 . . . his heart was swollen with sorrow within his breast; and he did exclaim in the agony of his soul: "... 24 ... Thou shalt be utterly destroyed except thou shalt repent. 25 Yea, wo be unto you because of that great abomination which has come among you. . . . 28 And except ye repent ye shall perish; yea, even your lands shall be taken from you, and ye shall be destroyed from off the face of the earth. 29 Behold now, I do not say that these things shall be, of myself, because it is not of myself that I know these things; but behold, I know that these things are true because the Lord God has made them known unto me, therefore I testify that they shall be."

8:1 And now it came to pass that when Nephi had said these words, behold, there were men who were judges, who also belonged to the secret band of Gadianton, and they were angry, and they cried out against him, saying unto the people: "Why do ye not seize upon this man and bring him forth, that he may be condemned according to the crime which he has done? 2 Why seest thou this man, and hearest him revile against this people and against our law?" 3 For behold, Nephi had spoken unto them concerning the corruptness of their law; yea, many things did Nephi speak which cannot be written; and nothing did he speak which was contrary to the commandments of God.

4 And those judges were angry with him because he spake plainly unto them concerning their secret works of darkness; nevertheless, they durst not lay their own hands upon him, for they feared the people lest they should cry out against them. 5 Therefore they did cry unto the people, saying: "Why do you suffer this man to revile against us? For behold he doth condemn all this people, even unto destruction; yea, and also that these our great cities shall be taken from us, that we shall have no place in them. 6 And now we know that this is impossible, for behold, we are powerful, and our cities great, therefore our enemies can have no power over us."

7 And it came to pass that thus they did stir up the people to anger against Nephi, and raised contentions among them; for there were some who did cry out: "Let this man alone, for he is a good man, and those things which he saith will surely come to pass except we repent; 8 yea, behold, all the judgments will come upon us which he has testified unto us; for we know that he has testified aright unto us concerning our iniquities. And behold they are many, and he knoweth as well all things which shall befall us as he knoweth of our iniquities; 9 yea, and behold, if he had not been a prophet he could not have testified concerning those things."

10 And it came to pass that those people who sought to destroy Nephi were compelled because of their fear, that they did not lay their hands on him; therefore he began again to speak unto them, seeing that he had gained favor in the eyes of some, insomuch that the remainder of them did fear. 11 Therefore he was constrained to speak more unto them saying: ". . . 26 Yea, even at this time ye are ripening, because of your murders and your fornication and wickedness, for everlasting destruction; yea, and except ye repent it will come unto you soon. 27 Yea, behold it is now even at your doors; yea, go ye in unto the judgment-seat, and search; and behold, your judge is murdered, and he lieth in his blood; and he hath been murdered by his brother, who seeketh to sit in the judgment-seat. 28 And behold, they both belong to your secret band, whose author is Gadianton and the evil one who seeketh to destroy the souls of men."

9:1 Behold, now it came to pass that when Nephi had spoken these words, certain men who were among them ran to the judgment-seat; yea, even there were five who went, and they said among themselves, as they went: 2 "Behold, now we will know of a surety whether this man be a prophet and God hath commanded him to prophesy such marvelous things unto us. Behold, we do not believe that he hath; yea, we do not believe that he is a prophet; nevertheless, if this thing which he has said concerning the chief judge be true, that he be dead, then will we believe that the other words which he has spoken are true."

3 And it came to pass that they ran in their might, and came in unto the judgment-seat; and behold, the chief judge had fallen to the earth, and did lie in his blood. 4 And now behold, when they saw this they were astonished exceedingly, insomuch that they fell to the earth. . . .

6 Now, immediately when the judge had been murdered—he being stabbed by his brother by a garb of secrecy, and he fled, and the servants ran and told the people, raising the cry of murder among them; 7 and behold the people did gather themselves together unto the place of the judgment-seat—and behold, to their astonishment they saw those five men who had fallen to the earth.

8 And now behold, the people knew nothing concerning the multitude who had gathered together at the garden of Nephi; therefore they said among themselves: "These men are they who have murdered the judge, and God has smitten them that they could not flee from us."

9 And it came to pass that they laid hold on them, and bound them and cast them into prison. And there was a proclamation sent abroad that the judge was slain, and that the murderers had been taken and were cast into prison.

10 And it came to pass that on the morrow the people did assemble themselves together to mourn and to fast, at the burial of the great chief judge who had been slain. 11 And thus also those judges who were at the garden of Nephi, and heard his words, were also gathered together at the burial. 12 And it came to pass that they inquired among the people, saying: "Where are the five who were sent to inquire concerning the chief judge whether he was dead?"

And they answered and said: "Concerning this five whom ye say ye have sent, we know not; but there are five who are the murderers, whom we have cast into prison."

13 And it came to pass that the judges desired that they should be brought; and they were brought, and behold they were the five who were sent; and behold the judges inquired of them to know concerning the matter, and they told them all that they had done, saying: 14 "We ran and came to the place of the judgment-seat, and when we saw all things even as Nephi had testified, we were astonished insomuch that we fell to the earth; and when we were recovered from our astonishment, behold they cast us into prison. 15 Now, as for the murder of this man, we know not

who has done it; and only this much we know, we ran and came according as ye desired, and behold he was dead, according to the words of Nephi."

16 And now it came to pass that the judges did expound the matter unto the people, and did cry out against Nephi, saying: "Behold, we know that this Nephi must have agreed with some one to slay the judge, and then he might declare it unto us, that he might convert us unto his faith, that he might raise himself to be a great man, chosen of God, and a prophet. 17 And now behold, we will detect this man, and he shall confess his fault and make known unto us the true murderer of this judge."

18 And it came to pass that the five were liberated on the day of the burial. Nevertheless, they did rebuke the judges in the words which they had spoken against Nephi, and did contend with them one by one, insomuch that they did confound them. 19 Nevertheless, they caused that Nephi should be taken and bound and brought before the multitude, and they began to question him in divers ways that they might cross him, that they might accuse him to death— 20 saying unto him: "Thou art confederate; who is this man that hath done this murder? Now tell us, and acknowledge thy fault; saying, Behold here is money; and also we will grant unto thee thy life if thou wilt tell us, and acknowledge the agreement which thou hast made with him."

21 But Nephi said unto them: "O ye fools, ye uncircumcised of heart, ye blind, and ye stiffnecked people, do ye know how long the Lord your God will suffer you that ye shall go on in this your way of sin? 22 O ye ought to begin to howl and mourn, because of the great destruction which at this time doth await you, except ye shall repent. 23 Behold ye say that I have agreed with a man that he should murder Seezoram, our chief judge. But behold, I say unto you, that this is because I have testified unto you that ye might know concerning this thing; yea, even for a witness unto you, that I did know of the wickedness and abominations which are among you. 24 And because I have done this, ye say that I have agreed with a man that he should do this thing; yea, because I showed unto you this sign ye are angry with me, and seek to destroy my life. 25 And now behold, I will show unto you another sign, and see if ye will in this thing seek to destroy me. 26 Behold I say unto you: Go to the house of Seantum, who is the brother of Seezoram, and say unto him— 27 'Has Nephi, the pretended prophet, who doth prophesy so much evil concerning this people, agreed with thee, in the which ye have murdered Seezoram, who is your brother?' 28 And behold, he shall say unto you, 'Nay.' 29 And ye shall say unto him: 'Have ye murdered your brother?' 30 And he shall stand with fear, and wist not what to say. And behold, he shall deny unto you; and he

shall make as if he were astonished; nevertheless, he shall declare unto you that he is innocent. 31 But behold, ye shall examine him, and ye shall find blood upon the skirts of his cloak. 32 And when ye have seen this, ye shall say: 'From whence cometh this blood? Do we not know that it is the blood of your brother?' 33 And then shall he tremble, and shall look pale, even as if death had come upon him. 34 And then shall ye say: 'Because of this fear and this paleness which has come upon your face, behold, we know that thou art guilty.' 35 And then shall greater fear come upon him; and then shall he confess unto you, and deny no more that he has done this murder. 36 And then shall he say unto you, that I, Nephi, know nothing concerning the matter save it were given unto me by the power of God. And then shall ye know that I am an honest man, and that I am sent unto you from God."

37 And it came to pass that they went and did, even according as Nephi had said unto them. And behold, the words which he had said were true; for according to the words he did deny; and also according to the words he did confess. 38 And he was brought to prove that he himself was the very murderer, insomuch that the five were set at liberty, and also was Nephi.

Bibliography

Adams, David M. *Philosophical Problems in the Law*. 4th ed. Belmont, CA: Wadsworth Learning, 2005.

Adams, William James, Jr. "Nephi's Written Language and the Standard Biblical Hebrew of 600 B.C." In Welch, Seely, and Seely, *Glimpses of Lehi's Jerusalem*, 245–58.

Ahlström, G. W. *Royal Administration and National Religion in Ancient Palestine*. Leiden: E. J. Brill, 1982.

Albright, W. F. "The Judicial Reform of Jehoshaphat." In *Alexander Marx Jubilee Volume on the Occasion of His Seventieth Birthday*, edited by Rebekah Kohut, 61–82. New York: Jewish Theological Seminary of America, 1950.

Alexander, John B. "New Light on the Fiery Furnace." *Journal of Biblical Literature* 69, no. 4 (1950): 375–76.

Alt, Albrecht. "The Origins of Israelite Law." In *Essays on Old Testament History and Religion*, translated by R. A. Wilson, 79–132. Oxford: Blackwell, 1966.

Alter, Robert. *The World of Biblical Literature*. New York: Basic Books, 1992.

Althann, Robert. "The Psalms of Vengeance against Their Ancient Near Eastern Background." *Journal of Northwest Semitic Languages* 18 (1992): 1–11.

Anderson, Gary A. "Intentional and Unintentional Sin in the Dead Sea Scrolls." In Wright, Freedman, and Hurvitz, *Pomegranates and Golden Bells*, 49–64.

Anderson, Jeff S. "The Social Function of Curses in the Hebrew Bible." *Zeitschrift für die alttestamentliche Wissenschaft* 110, no. 2 (1998): 233–37.

Aristotle. *The Athenian Constitution*. Translated by Frederic G. Kenyon. Adelaide: eBooks, 2004.

Athidiyah, M. "Scapegoat" [in Hebrew]. *Beit Mikra* 6 (1961).

Aus, Roger David. *Barabbas and Esther and Other Studies in the Judaic Illumination of Earliest Christianity*. Edited by Jacob Neusner, William Scott Green, James Strange, Darrell J. Fasching, and Sara Mandell. Atlanta: Scholars Press, 1992.

Avalos, Francisco. "An Overview of the Legal System of the Aztec Empire." *Law Library Journal* 86, no. 2 (1994): 259–76.

Avalos, Hector. *Illness and Health Care in the Ancient Near East: The Role of the Temple in Greece, Mesopotamia, and Israel*. Atlanta: Scholars Press, 1995.

———. *Health Care and the Rise of Christianity*. Peabody, MA: Hendrickson, 1999.

Barker, Margaret. "The Great High Priest." *BYU Studies* 42, nos. 3–4 (2003): 65–84.

———. "Joseph Smith and Preexilic Religion." In *The Worlds of Joseph Smith: A Bicentennial Conference at the Library of Congress*, edited by John W. Welch, 69–82. Provo, UT: BYU Press, 2006.

———. "What Did King Josiah Reform?" In Welch, Seely, and Seely, *Glimpses of Lehi's Jerusalem*, 523–42.

Barmash, P. "The Narrative Quandary: Cases of Law in Literature." *Vetus Testamentum* 54, no. 1 (2004): 1–16.

Baumgarten, Joseph M. "Does *tlh* in the Temple Scroll Refer to Crucifixion?" *Journal of Biblical Literature* 91, no. 4 (1972): 472–81.

———. "The Duodecimal Courts of Qumran, Revelation, and the Sanhedrin." *Journal of Biblical Literature* 95, no. 1 (1976): 59–78.

———. "On the Testimony of Women in 1QSa." *Journal of Biblical Literature* 76, no. 4 (1957): 266–69.

Bazak, Jacob. "Judicial Ethics in Jewish Law." In *Jewish Law Association Studies III: The Oxford Conference Volume*, edited by A. M. Fuss, 27–40. Atlanta: Scholars Press, 1987.

Beard, Mary, John North, and Simon Price. *Religions of Rome*. 2 vols. Cambridge, England: Cambridge University Press, 1998.

Beattie, D. R. G. "The Book of Ruth as Evidence for Israelite Legal Practice." *Vetus Testamentum* 24, no. 3 (1974): 251–67.

Bechtel, Lyn M. "Shame as a Sanction of Social Control in Biblical Israel: Judicial, Political, and Social Shaming." *Journal for the Study of the Old Testament* 49 (1991): 47–76.

Bellefontaine, Elizabeth. "Customary Law and Chieftainship: Judicial Aspects of 2 Samuel 14:4–21." *Journal for the Study of the Old Testament* 38 (1987): 47–72.

Bendor, S. *The Social Structure of Ancient Israel: The Institution of the Family* (Beitʾab) *from the Settlement to the End of the Monarchy.* Jerusalem: Simor, 1996.

Bennett, Harold V. *Injustice Made Legal: Deuteronomic Law and the Plight of Widows, Strangers, and Orphans in Ancient Israel.* Grand Rapids, MI: Eerdmans, 2002.

Benson, Ezra Taft. *A Witness and a Warning: A Modern-day Prophet Testifies of the Book of Mormon.* Salt Lake City: Deseret Book, 1988.

Betz, Otto. "The Temple Scroll and the Trial of Jesus." *Southwestern Journal of Theology* 30, no. 3 (1988): 5–8.

Bickerman, Elias J. "The Warning Inscriptions of Herod's Temple." *Jewish Quarterly Review* 37, no. 4 (1947): 387–405.

Bienkowski, Piotr. "Education." In Bienkowski and Millard, *Dictionary of the Ancient Near East*, 101.

Bienkowski, Piotr, and Alan Millard, eds. *Dictionary of the Ancient Near East.* Philadelphia: University of Pennsylvania Press, 2000.

Black, Susan Easton, ed. *Expressions of Faith: Testimonies of Latter-day Saint Scholars.* Salt Lake City: Deseret Book and FARMS, 1996.

Bloch, Abraham P. *The Biblical and Historical Background of Jewish Customs and Ceremonies.* New York: KTAV, 1980.

———. *The Biblical and Historical Background of the Jewish Holy Days.* New York: KTAV, 1978.

Blok, Anton. "The Peasant and the Brigand: Social Banditry Reconsidered." *Comparative Studies in Society and History* 14, no. 4 (1972): 494–503.

Blumenfeld, David L. *The Terminology of Imprisonment and Forced Detention in the Bible.* PhD diss., New York University, 1977.

Bock, Darrell L. *Blasphemy and Exaltation in Judaism: The Charge against Jesus in Mark 14:53–65.* Grand Rapids, MI: Baker Books, 2000.

Boecker, Hans J. *Law and the Administration of Justice in the Old Testament and Ancient East.* Translated by Jeremy Moiser. Minneapolis: Augsburg, 1980.

———. *Redeformen des Rechtslebens im Alten Testament.* Neukirchen-Vluyn: Neukirchener Verlag, 1964. Revised edition, 1970.

Boogaart, T. A. "Stone for Stone: Retribution in the Story of Abimelech and Shechem." *Journal for the Study of the Old Testament* 32 (1985): 45–56.

Botterweck, Johannes G., Helmer Ringgren, and Heinz-Josef Fabry, eds. *Theological Dictionary of the Old Testament.* Translated by John T. Willis. 15 vols. Grand Rapids, MI: Eerdmans, 1974–2004.

Bovati, Pietro. *Re-Establishing Justice: Legal Terms, Concepts and Procedures in the Hebrew Bible*. Translated by Michael J. Smith. Sheffield, England: JSOT Press, 1994.

Bradley, Carol Pratt. "Women, the Book of Mormon, and the Law of Moses." *Studia Antiqua: The Journal of the Student Society for Ancient Studies* (Brigham Young University) (Summer 2003): 125–71.

Brichto, Herbert Chanan. "The Worship of the Golden Calf: A Literary Analysis of a Fable on Idolatry." *Hebrew Union College Annual* 54 (1983): 1–44.

———. *The Problem of "Curse" in the Hebrew Bible*. Journal of Biblical Literature Monograph Series 13. Philadelphia: Society of Biblical Literature, 1963.

Bright, John. *Jeremiah: A New Translation with Introduction and Commentary*. Garden City, NY: Doubleday, 1965.

Brongers, H. A. "Fasting in Israel in Biblical and Post-biblical Times." In *Instruction and Interpretation: Studies in Hebrew Language, Palestinian Archaeology and Biblical Exegesis*, edited by A. S. van der Woude, 1–21. Leiden: E. J. Brill, 1977.

Bruckner, James K. *Implied Law in the Abraham Narrative: A Literary and Theological Analysis*. New York: Sheffield Academic Press, 2001.

Buchanan, George Wesley. "The Courts of the Lord." *Vetus Testamentum* 16, no. 2 (1966): 23–32.

———. "Some Vow and Oath Formulas in the New Testament." *Harvard Theological Review* 58, no. 3 (1965): 319–26.

Büchler, Adolf. *Studies in Sin and Atonement in the Rabbinic Literature of the First Century*. London: Oxford University Press, 1928.

Bushman, Richard L. *Joseph Smith and the Beginnings of Mormonism*. Urbana: University of Illinois Press, 1984.

Buttenwieser, Moses. *The Prophets of Israel from the Eighth to the Fifth Century: Their Faith and Their Message*. New York: Macmillan, 1914.

Butterick, George Arthur, ed. *The Interpreter's Bible: The Holy Scriptures in the King James and Revised Standard Versions with General Articles and Introduction, Exegesis, Exposition for Each Book of the Bible*. 12 vols. New York: Abingdon, 1952–1957.

Callister, Paul Douglas. "Law's Box: Law, Jurisprudence and the Information Ecosphere." *University of Missouri-Kansas City Law Review* 74, no. 2 (2005): 263–334.

Cannon, Andrew G. "We're All in the Same Boat: Old Testament and Book of Mormon Concepts of Corporate Responsibility as a Complement to Individual Responsibility for Describing Our World." Unpublished paper, 2006. Howard W. Hunter Law Library, Brigham Young University.

Carmichael, Calum. "Biblical Laws of Talion." *Hebrew Annual Review* 9 (1985): 107–26. Reprinted in *Witnesses in Bible and Talmud*, edited by David Daube, 21–39. Oxford: Oxford Centre for Postgraduate Hebrew Studies, 1986.

———, ed. *Collected Works of David Daube*. 3 vols. Berkeley: Robbins Collection, 1992–2003.

———. *The Spirit of Biblical Law*. Athens, GA: University of Georgia Press, 1996.

Casson, Lionel. *Travel in the Ancient World*. London: George Allen and Unwin, 1974.

Cassuto, U. *The Documentary Hypothesis and the Composition of the Pentateuch*. Jerusalem: Magnes Press, 1983.

Catagnoti, Amalia. "Anatolia and the Levant: Ebla." In Westbrook, *A History of Ancient Near Eastern Law*, 1:225–39.

Cheesman, Paul R. *The Book of Mormon: The Keystone Scripture, Papers from the First Annual Book of Mormon Symposium*. Assisted by S. Kent Brown and Charles D. Tate Jr. Provo, UT: Religious Studies Center, Brigham Young University, 1988.

Chin, Catherine. "Job and the Injustice of God: Implicit Arguments in Job 13.17–14.12." *Journal for the Study of the Old Testament* 64 (1994): 91–101.

Chirichigno, Gregory C. *Debt-Slavery in Israel and the Ancient Near East*. Sheffield, England: JSOT, 1993.

Christensen, Kevin. "The Temple, the Monarchy, and Wisdom: Lehi's World and the Scholarship of Margaret Barker." In Welch, Seely, and Seely, *Glimpses of Lehi's Jerusalem*, 449–522.

Clark, Harold B. *Biblical Law*. Portland, OR: Binfords and Mort, 1943.

Coggins, Richard. "On Kings and Disguises." *Journal for the Study of the Old Testament* 50 (1991): 55–62.

Cohen, Boaz. "Art in Jewish Law." *Judaism* 3, no. 2 (1954): 165–76.

———. "Evidence in Jewish Law." *Recueils de la Société Jean Bodin* 16 (1965): 103–15.

Cohn, Haim H. "The Proof in Biblical and Talmudical Law." In *La Preuve en Droit*, edited by C. Perelman and P. Foriers, 77–98. Bruxelles: Bruylant, 1981.

Collier, Jane Fishburne. *Law and Social Change in Zinacantan*. Stanford: Stanford University Press, 1973.

Collins, Adela Yarbro. "The Function of 'Excommunication' in Paul." *Harvard Theological Review* 73, nos. 1–2 (1980): 251–63.

Conkling, J. Christopher. "Alma's Enemies: The Case of the Lamanites, Amlicites, and Mysterious Amalekites." *Journal of Book of Mormon Studies* 14, no. 1 (2005): 108–17.

Cooper, Jerrold. "International Law in the Third Millennium." In Westbrook, *A History of Ancient Near Eastern Law*, 1:241–51.

Cowell, F. R. *Cicero and the Roman Republic*. 2nd ed. New York: Pelican, 1956.

Crüsemann, Frank. *The Torah: Theology and Social History of Old Testament Law*. Translated by Allan W. Mahnke. Minneapolis: Fortress, 1996.

Danby, Herbert. *Tractate Sanhedrin: Mishnah and Tosefta—The Judicial Procedure of the Jews as Codified towards the End of the Second Century A.D.* New York: Macmillan, 1919.

Daube, David. *Ancient Jewish Law: Three Inaugural Lectures*. Leiden: E. J. Brill, 1981.

———. *Civil Disobedience in Antiquity*. In Carmichael, *Collected Works of David Daube*, 3:565–679.

———. *Collaboration with Tyranny in Rabbinic Law*. London: Oxford University Press, 1965.

———. "The Culture of Deuteronomy." *Orita* (Ibadan, Nigeria) 3, no. 1 (1969): 27–52.

———. "Direct and Indirect Causation in Biblical Law." *Vetus Testamentum* 11, no. 3 (1961): 246–69.

———. *The New Testament and Rabbinic Judaism*. London: Athlone, 1956.

———. " 'One from among Your Brethren Shall You Set King over You.' " *Journal of Biblical Literature* 90, no. 4 (1971): 480–81.

———. "The Scales of Justice." *Juridical Review* 63, no. 2 (1951): 109–29.

———. *Sin, Ignorance and Forgiveness in the Bible*. London: The Liberal Jewish Synagogue, 1960.

———. "Some Forms of Old Testament Legislation." In *Abstract of Proceedings for the Academic Year 1944–1945*, 36–46. Oxford: Oxford Society of Historical Theology, 1945.

———. *Studies in Biblical Law*. 1947. Reprint, New York: KTAV, 1969.

———. *Witnesses in Bible and Talmud*. In Carmichael, *Collected Works of David Daube*, 1:401–23.

Davies, Philip R. *In Search of "Ancient Israel."* Sheffield, England: JSOT Press, 1992.

Derby, Josiah. "The Daughters of Zelophehad Revisited." *Jewish Bible Quarterly* 25, no. 3 (1997): 169–71.

D'ercole, G. "The Juridical Structure of Israel from the Time of Her Origin to the Period of Hadrian." In *Populus Dei: Studi in onore del Card. Alfredo Ottaviani per il einquantesimo di sacer dozio: 18 marzo 1966*, edited by I. Israel, 389–461. Rome: Communio, 1969.

deSilva, David A. "The Wisdom of Ben Sira: Honor, Shame, and the Maintenance of the Values of a Minority Culture." *Catholic Biblical Quarterly* 58, no. 3 (1996): 433–55.

de Vaux, Roland. *Ancient Israel: Its Life and Institutions.* 2 vols. New York: McGraw-Hill, 1965.

Dion, Paul E. "Deuteronomy 13: The Suppression of Alien Religious Propaganda in Israel during the Late Monarchial Era." In Halpern and Hobson, *Law and Ideology in Monarchic Israel*, 147–216.

Dohmen, Christoph. *Das Bilderverbot: Seine Entstehung und seine Entwicklung im Alten Testament.* Bonner Biblische Beiträge 62. Frankfurt: Athenäum, 1987.

Dorff, Elliot N., and Arthur Rosett. *A Living Tree: The Roots and Growth of Jewish Law.* Albany: State University of New York Press, 1988.

Driver, G. R., and John C. Miles. "Ordeal by Oath at Nuzi." *Iraq* 7 (1940): 132–38.

———, eds. *The Assyrian Laws.* Oxford: Clarendon Press, 1935.

Dübner, Friedrich. *Scholia Graeca in Aristophanem.* Hildesheim: Verlag, 1969.

Elon, Menachem. *The Principles of Jewish Law.* Jerusalem: Keter, 1975.

Elwin, Warwick. *Confession and Absolution in the Bible: A Study of the Evidence of Holy Scripture upon the Doctrine of Penance; Its Progressive Revelation and Subsequent Practice.* London: J. T. Hayes, 1883.

Epstein, Isidore, trans. and ed. *Soncino Talmud.* 18 vols. London: Soncino, 1948.

Epsztein, Léon. *Social Justice in the Ancient Near East and the People of the Bible.* Translated by John Bowden. London: SCM Press, 1986.

Essig, Fred, and H. Daniel Fuller. "Nephi's Slaying of Laban: A Legal Perspective." FARMS Preliminary Report. Provo, UT: FARMS, 1981.

Falk, Ze'ev W. "Collective Responsibility in the Bible and the Aggada" [in Hebrew]. *Tarbits* 30 (1960): 16–20.

———. "Forms of Testimony." *Vetus Testamentum* 11, no. 1 (1961): 88–91.

———. *Hebrew Law in Biblical Times: An Introduction.* Jerusalem: Wahrmann Books, 1964.

———. *Hebrew Law in Biblical Times.* Edited by John W. Welch. 2nd ed. Provo, UT: Brigham Young University Press; Winona Lake, IN: Eisenbrauns, 2001.

———. "Hebrew Legal Terms." *Journal of Semitic Studies* 5, no. 4 (1960): 350–54.

———. *Introduction to Jewish Law of the Second Commonwealth.* Part 1. Leiden: E. J. Brill, 1972.

———. *Law and Religion: The Jewish Experience.* Jerusalem: Mesharim, 1981.

———. "On Talmudic Vows." *Harvard Theological Review* 59, no. 3 (1966): 309–12.

———. "Oral and Written Testimony." *Iura* 19 (1968): 113–19.

———. "Ruler and Judge" [in Hebrew]. *Leshonenu* 30 (1965–66): 243–47.

———. "Spirituality and Jewish Law." In Firmage, Weiss, and Welch, *Religion and Law,* 123–38.

———. "Testate Succession in Jewish Law." *Journal of Jewish Studies* 12, nos. 1–2 (1961): 67–77.

Falkenstein, Adam. *Die Neusumerischen Gerichtsurkunden II.* Philosophisch-Historische Klasse Abhandlungen 40. Munich: Bayerische Akademie der Wissenschaften, 1956.

Faraone, Christopher A. "An Accusation of Magic in Classical Athens (Ar. *WASPS* 946–48)." *Transactions of the American Philological Association* 119 (1989): 149–60.

———. "The Agonistic Context of Early Greek Binding Spells." In Faraone and Obbink, *Magika Hiera,* 3–32.

Faraone, Christopher A., and Dirk Obbink, eds. *Magika Hiera: Ancient Greek Magic and Religion.* New York: Oxford University Press, 1991.

Farber, Walter. "Wehe, wenn . . . !" *Zeitschrift für Assyriologie* 64, no. 2 (1975): 177–79.

Fensham, F. Charles. "The Battle between the Men of Joab and Abner as a Possible Ordeal by Battle?" *Vetus Testamentum* 20, no. 3 (1970): 356–57.

———. "The Judges and Ancient Israelite Jurisprudence." *Ou Testamentiese Werkgemeenskap in Suid-Afrika* (Potchefstroom, South Africa) 2 (1959): 15–22.

———. "Malediction and Benediction in Ancient Near Eastern Vassal-Treaties and the Old Testament." *Zeitschrift für die alttestamentliche Wissenschaft* 74 (1962): 1–9.

Finkelstein, J. J. "The Ox That Gored." *Transactions of the American Philosophical Society* 71, no. 2 (1981): 1–89.

Finsterbusch, Karin. "Christologie als Blasphemie: Das Hauptthema der Stephanusperikope in lukanischer Perspektive." *Biblische Notizen* 92 (1998): 38–54.

Firmage, Edwin B., Bernard G. Weiss, and John W. Welch, eds. *Religion and Law: Biblical-Judaic and Islamic Perspectives.* Winona Lake, IN: Eisenbrauns, 1990.

Fitzmyer, Joseph A. *The Aramaic Inscriptions of Sefire.* Rome: Pontifical Biblical Institute, 1967.

Fitzpatrick-McKinley, Anne. *The Transformation of Torah from Scribal Advice to Law.* Sheffield, England: Sheffield Academic Press, 1999.

Ford, Lewis S. "The Divine Curse Understood in Terms of Persuasion." *Semeia: An Experimental Journal for Biblical Criticism* 24 (1982): 81–87.

Ford, J. Massyngberde. "'Crucify him, Crucify him' and the Temple Scroll." *Expository Times* 87, no. 9 (1976): 275–78.

Forte, David F. "Apostasy and Blasphemy in Pakistan." *Connecticut Journal of International Law* 10, no. 1 (1994): 27–68.

Foxe, John. *Foxe's Book of Martyrs.* Edited and abridged by G. A. Williamson. Boston: Little, Brown, 1965.

Fraenkel, Jonah. "Ma'aseh be-R. Shila." *Tarbits* 40 (October 1970): 33–40.

Freedman, David Noel, Gary A. Herion, David F. Graf, John David Pleins, and Astrid B. Beck, eds. *The Anchor Bible Dictionary.* 6 vols. New York: Doubleday, 1992.

Freedman, David Noel, with Jeffrey C. Geoghegan and Michael M. Homan. *The Nine Commandments: Uncovering the Hidden Pattern of Crime and Punishment in the Hebrew Bible.* Edited by Astrid B. Beck. New York: Doubleday, 2000.

Friedrich, Gerhard, ed. *Theological Dictionary of the New Testament.* Translated by Geoffrey W. Bromiley. 10 vols. Grand Rapids, MI: Eerdmans, 1974. Reprint, 1999.

Frick, Frank S. *The City in Ancient Israel.* Missoula, MT: Scholars Press, 1977.

———. *The Formation of the State in Ancient Israel: A Survey of Models and Theories.* Decatur, GA: Almond, 1985.

Friend, James A. "Do Not Testify according to the Majority" [in Hebrew]. *Bibliotechka Mezhdunarodnika* 26 (1981): 129–36.

Frimer, Dov I. "The Role of the Lawyer in Jewish Law." *Journal of Law and Religion* 1, no. 2 (1983): 297–305.

Frimer, Norman. "A Midrash on Morality or When Is a Lie Permissible." *Tradition: A Journal of Orthodox Jewish Thought* 13, no. 4; 14, no. 1 (1973): 23–34.

Frymer-Kenski, Tikva. "Anatolia and the Levant: Israel." In Westbrook, *A History of Ancient Near Eastern Law*, 2:973–1046.

———. *The Judicial Ordeal in the Ancient Near East.* 2 vols. PhD diss., Yale University, 1977.

———. "The Strange Case of the Suspected Sotah (Numbers V 11–31)." *Vetus Testamentum* 34, no. 1 (1984): 11–26.

Gardner, Brant. "Scourged with Faggots." *Insights* (FARMS, Brigham Young University) 21, no. 7 (2001): 2–3.

Garnier, Colonel J. *The Worship of the Dead or the Origin and Nature of Pagan Idolatry and Its Bearing upon the Early History of Egypt and Babylonia.* London: Chapman and Hall, 1904.

Gee, John. "Egyptian Society during the Twenty-sixth Dynasty." In Welch, Seely, and Seely, *Glimpses of Lehi's Jerusalem,* 277–98.

Gemser, Berend. "The *rib* or Controversy-Pattern in Hebrew Mentality." In *Wisdom in Israel and in the Ancient Near East,* edited by M. Noth and D. Winton Thomas, 120–37. Supplements to Vetus Testamentum, vol. 3. Leiden: E. J. Brill, 1955.

Gerhardsson, Birger. *Memory and Manuscript: Oral Tradition and Written Transmission in Rabbinic Judaism and Early Christianity.* Grand Rapids, MI: Eerdmans, 1998.

Gervitz, S. "On Hebrew *sebet* = Judge." In *The Bible World: Essays in Honor of Cyrus H. Gordon,* edited by Gary Rendsburg and Cyrus H. Gordon, 61–66. New York: KTAV, 1980.

Gevirtz, Stanley. "West-Semitic Curses and the Problem of the Origins of Hebrew Law." *Vetus Testamentum* 11, no. 2 (1961): 137–58.

Goff, Alan. "Abinadi's Disguise and the Fate of King Noah." *Insights* (FARMS, Brigham Young University) 20, no. 12 (December 2000): 2.

———. "Historical Narrative, Literary Narrative—Expelling Poetics from the Republic of History." *Journal of Book of Mormon Studies* 5, no. 1 (1996): 50–102.

———. "Uncritical Theory and Thin Description: The Resistance to History." *Review of Books on the Book of Mormon* 7, no. 1 (1995): 170–207.

Goitein, Hugh. *Primitive Ordeal and Modern Law.* London: Allen and Unwin, 1923. Reprint, Littleton, CO: Rothman, 1980.

Goldin, Hyman E. *Hebrew Criminal Law and Procedure.* New York: Twayne, 1952.

Goldman, E. A., ed. *Jewish Law Association Studies VIII: The Jerusalem 1994 Conference Volume.* Atlanta: Scholars Press, 1996.

Good, Edwin M. "Capital Punishment and Its Alternatives in Ancient Near Eastern Law." *Stanford Law Review* 19, no. 5 (1967): 947–77.

Gordis, Robert. "Love, Marriage, and Business in the Book of Ruth: A Chapter in Hebrew Customary Law." In *A Light unto My Path: Old*

Testament Studies in Honor of Jacob M. Myers, edited by Howard N. Bream, Ralph D. Heim, and Carey A. Moore, 241–64. Philadelphia: Temple University Press, 1974.

Greenberg, Moshe. "Biblical Attitudes toward Power: Ideal and Reality in Law and Prophets." In Firmage, Weiss, and Welch, *Religion and Law*, 101–12.

Greengus, Samuel. "A Textbook Case of Adultery in Ancient Mesopotamia." *Hebrew Union College Annual* 40–41 (1969–1970): 33–44.

Gutmann, Joseph. "The 'Second Commandment' and the Image in Judaism." *Hebrew Union College Annual* 32 (1961): 161–74.

Haas, Peter. "'Die He Shall Surely Die': The Structure of Homicide in Biblical Law." *Semeia* 45 (1989): 67–87.

Haase, Richard. "Anatolia and the Levant: The Hittite Kingdom." In Westbrook, *A History of Ancient Near Eastern Law*, 1:619–56.

———. "Talion und spiegelnde Strafe in den keilschriftlichen Rechtscorpora." *Zeitschrift für Altorientalische und Biblische Rechtsgeschichte* 3 (1997): 195–201.

Hackett, Jo Ann, and John Huehnergard. "On Breaking Teeth." *Harvard Theological Review* 77, nos. 3–4 (1984): 259–75.

Hall, John F., and John W. Welch, eds. *Masada and the World of the New Testament*. Provo, UT: BYU Studies, 1997.

Halpern, Baruch. "Yhwh's Summary Justice in Job XIV 20." *Vetus Testamentum* 28, no. 4 (1978): 472–74.

Halpern, Baruch, and Deborah W. Hobson, eds. *Law and Ideology in Monarchic Israel*. Sheffield, England: Sheffield Academic Press, 1991.

Harris, R. Laird, Gleason L. Archer Jr., and Bruce K. Waltke. *Theological Wordbook of the Old Testament*. 2 vols. Chicago: Moody Press, 1980.

Harvey, Julien. "Collectivisme et individualisme: Éz. 18, 1–32 et Jér. 31, 29." *Sciences Ecclésiastiques* 10 (1958): 167–202.

Hastings, James, John A. Selbie, and Louis H. Gray, eds. *Encyclopaedia of Religion and Ethics*. 12 vols. and index. New York: Charles Scribner's Sons, 1980.

Hecht, Neil S., Bernard S. Jackson, Stephen M. Passamaneck, Daniela Piatelli, and Alfredo Mordechai Rabello, eds. *An Introduction to the History and Sources of Jewish Law*. Oxford: Clarendon Press, 1996.

Hempel, Johannes. *Die israelitische Anschauungen von Segen und Fluch im Lichte altorientalischer Parallelen*. Beiheft zur Zeitschrift für die alttestamentliche Wissenschaft 81. Berlin: de Gruyter, 1961.

Hillers, Delbert R. *Treaty-Curses and the Old Testament Prophets*. Rome: Pontifical Biblical Institute, 1964.

Hobsbawm, Eric. *Primitive Rebels: Studies in Archaic Forms of Social Movement in the Nineteenth and Twentieth Centuries*. 1959. Reprint, New York: W. W. Norton, 1965.

———. *Bandits*. New York: Delacorte, 1969.

Hocherman, Y., M. Lahav, and Z. Zemarion, eds. *Yaacov Gil Jubilee Volume*. Jerusalem: Rubin Mass, 1979.

Hoenig, Sidney B. *The Great Sanhedrin: A Study of the Origin, Development, Composition and Functions of the* Bet Din ha-Gadol *during the Second Jewish Commonwealth*. Philadelphia: Dropsie College, 1953.

Hoffner, Harry Angier, Jr. *The Laws of the Hittites: A Critical Edition*. Leiden: E. J. Brill, 1997.

Hoftijzer, J. "David and the Tekoite Woman." *Vetus Testamentum* 20, no. 4 (1970): 419–44.

Holladay, William L. *Jeremiah 1: A Commentary on the Book of the Prophet Jeremiah, Chapters 1–25*. Edited by Paul D. Hansen. Philadelphia: Fortress Press, 1986.

Holmes, Oliver Wendell. *The Path of the Law*. Bedford, MA: Applewood Books, n.d.

Horine, Steven. "A Study of the Literary Genre of the Woe Oracle." *Calvary Baptist Theological Journal* 5, no. 2 (1989): 74–97.

Horowitz, George. *The Spirit of Jewish Law*. New York: Bloch, 1953.

Horsley, Richard A. "Josephus and the Bandits." *Journal for the Study of Judaism* 10, no. 1 (1979): 37–63.

Hossfeld, F. L., and I. Meyer. "Der Prophet vor dem Tribunal. Neuer Auslegungsversuch von Jer 26." *Zeitschrift für die alttestamentliche Wissenschaft* 86, no. 1 (1974) 30–50.

Hoyles, J. Arthur. *Punishment in the Bible*. London: Epworth, 1986.

Hutton, Rodney R. "Narrative in Leviticus: The Case of the Blaspheming Son (Lev 24:10–23)." *Zeitschrift für Altorientalische und Biblische Rechtsgeschichte* 3 (1997): 145–63.

———. "The Case of the Blasphemer Revisited, Lev XXIV: 10–23." *Vetus Testamentum* 49, no. 4 (1999): 532–41.

Jackson, Bernard S. "The Concept of Religious Law in Judaism." In *Aufstieg und Niedergang der römischen Welt*, edited by Hildegard Temporini and Wolfgang Haase, II.19.1: 33–52. Berlin: de Gruyter, 1979.

———. *Essays in Jewish and Comparative Legal History*. Leiden: E. J. Brill, 1975.

———. "The Goring Ox Again." *Journal of Juristic Papyrology* 18 (1974): 55–93. Reprinted in Jackson, *Essays in Jewish and Comparative Legal History*, 112–13. Leiden: E. J. Brill, 1975.

———. "Ideas of Law and Legal Administration: A Semiotic Approach." In *The World of Ancient Israel: Sociological, Anthropological and Political Perspectives*, edited by R. E. Clements, 185–202. Cambridge: Cambridge University Press, 1989.

———, ed. *Jewish Law Association Studies II: The Jerusalem Conference Volume*. Atlanta: Scholars Press, 1986.

———, ed. *Jewish Law Association Studies IV: The Boston Conference Volume*. Atlanta: Scholars Press, 1990.

———. "Legalism and Spirituality: Historical, Philosophical, and Semiotic Notes on Legislators, Adjudicators, and Subjects." In Firmage, Weiss, and Welch, *Religion and Law*, 243–61.

———. "Liability for Mere Intention in Early Jewish Law." In Jackson, *Essays in Jewish and Comparative Legal History*, 202–34.

———. "Liability for Mere Intention in Early Jewish Law." *Hebrew Union College Annual* 42 (1971): 197–225.

———. "The Prophet and the Law in Early Judaism and the New Testament." *Cardozo Studies in Law and Literature* 4, no. 2 (1992): 123–66.

———. "Reflections on Biblical Criminal Law." *Journal of Jewish Studies* 24, no. 1 (1973): 8–38.

———. Review of *The Laws of Deuteronomy*, by Calum M. Carmichael. *Journal of Jewish Studies* 27, no. 1 (1976): 84–87.

———. *Semiotics and Legal Theory*. London: Routledge, 1987.

———. "Structuralism and the Notion of Religious Law." *Investigaciones Semióticas* 2 (1982–83): 1–43.

———. *Studies in the Semiotics of Biblical Law*. Sheffield, England: Sheffield Academic Press, 2000.

———. "Susanna and the Singular History of Singular Witnesses." *Acta Juridica* (1977): 37–54.

———. "*Testes Singulares* in Early Jewish Law and the New Testament." In Jackson, *Essays in Jewish and Comparative Legal History*, 172–201.

———. *Theft in Early Jewish Law*. Oxford: Clarendon Press, 1972.

———. "Towards an Integrated Approach to Criminal Law: Fletcher's Rethinking Criminal Law." *Criminal Law Review* (October 1979): 621–29.

———. "Two or Three Witnesses." In Jackson, *Essays in Jewish and Comparative Legal History*, 153–71.

———. *Wisdom-Laws: A Study of the Mishpatim of Exodus 21:1–22:16*. Oxford: Oxford University Press, 2006.

Jacobsen, Thorkild. "Primitive Democracy in Ancient Mesopotamia." In *Toward the Image of Tammuz and Other Essays on Mesopotamian*

History and Culture, edited by William L. Moran, 157–72. Cambridge: Harvard University Press, 1970.

Jasnow, Richard. "Egypt: New Kingdom." In Westbrook, *A History of Ancient Near Eastern Law*, 1:289–359.

———. "Middle Kingdom and Second Intermediate Period." In Westbrook, *A History of Ancient Near Eastern Law*, 1:255–88.

Johnson, Roy. "A Comparison of the Use of the Oath in the Old Testament and the Book of Mormon." FARMS Preliminary Report. Provo, UT: FARMS, 1982.

Jones, Gwilym H. *New Century Bible Commentary: 1 and 2 Kings*. Grand Rapids, MI: Eerdmans, 1984.

Jordan, D. R. "A Survey of Greek Defixiones Not Included in the Special Corpora." *Greek, Roman, and Byzantine Studies* 26, no. 2 (1985): 151–97.

Josephus, Flavius. *The Antiquities of the Jews*. In *The Works of Josephus*, 27–542.

———. *The Wars of the Jews*. In *The Works of Josephus*, 543–772.

———. *The Works of Josephus*. Translated by William Whiston. Rev. ed. Peadbody, MA: Hendrickson, 1987.

Juarros, Don Domingo. *A Statistical and Commercial History of the Kingdom of Guatemala in Spanish America*. London: John Hearne, 1823.

Jüngling, von Hans-Winfried. " 'Auge für Auge, Zahn für Zahn.' Bemerkungen zu Sinn und Geltung der alttestamentlichen Talionsformeln." *Theologie und Philosophie* 59, no. 1 (1984): 1–38.

Kahn, Charles H. *The Art and Thought of Heraclitus: An Edition of the Fragments with Translation and Commentary*. Cambridge: Cambridge University Press, 1979.

Kaminsky, Joel S. *Corporate Responsibility in the Hebrew Bible*. Sheffield, England: Sheffield Academic Press, 1995.

Keil, Carl Friederich. *Biblical Commentary on the Prophecies of Ezekiel*. Translated by James Martin. Edinburgh: T and T Clark, 1857.

Keim, Paul, "'Cursed Be . . .': Mundane Malediction and Sacral Sanction in Biblical Law." Paper presented at the annual Society of Biblical Literature convention in the Biblical Law Section. 1994.

Kenik, Helen Ann. "Code of Conduct for a King: Psalm 101." *Journal of Biblical Literature* 95, no. 3 (1976): 391–403.

Kennard, J. Spencer, Jr. " 'Hosanna' and the Purpose of Jesus." *Journal of Biblical Literature* 67, no. 2 (1948): 171–76.

King, Philip J., and Lawrence E. Stager. *Life in Biblical Israel*. Louisville: Westminster John Knox Press, 2001.

Kirschenbaum, Aaron. *Self-Incrimination in Jewish Law.* New York: Burning Bush Press, 1970.

Kissane, Edward J. *The Book of Isaiah: Translated from a Critically Revised Hebrew Text with Commentary.* Dublin: Browne and Nolan, 1943.

Kitchen, K. A. *On the Reliability of the Old Testament.* Grand Rapids, MI: Eerdmans, 2003.

Kline, Meredith G. "Oath and Ordeal Signs." *Westminster Theological Journal* 27 (1964–65): 115–39.

Klingenberg, Eberhard. "Judgment and Settlement in Court in Jewish and Comparative Legal History." *Jewish Law Annual* 8 (1989): 135–45.

Knierim, Rolf, P. "Customs, Judges, and Legislators in Ancient Israel." In *Early Jewish and Christian Exegesis: Studies in Memory of William Hugh Brownlee*, edited by Craig A. Evans and William F. Stinespring, 8–15. Atlanta: Scholars Press, 1987.

Koch, Klaus. "Der Spruch 'Sein Blut bleibe auf seinem Haupt' und die israelitische Auffassung vom vergossenen Blut." *Vetus Testamentum* 12, no. 4 (1962): 396–416.

———. "Gibt es ein Vergeltungsdogma im Alten Testament." *Zeitschrift für Theologie und Kirche* 52 (1955): 1–42.

Köhler, Ludwig. *Hebrew Man: Lectures Delivered at the Invitation of the University of Tübingen, December 1–16, 1952.* Translated by Peter R. Ackroyd. New York: Abingdon, 1956.

Lafont, Bertrand, and Raymond Westbrook. "Mesopotamia: Neo-Sumerian Period (Ur III)." In Westbrook, *A History of Ancient Near Eastern Law*, 1:183–226.

Lafont, Sophie. "Mesopotamia: Middle Assyrian Period." In Westbrook, *A History of Ancient Near Eastern Law*, 1:521–63.

Lahav, M. "Jehoshaphat's Judicial Reform." In Hocherman, Lahav, and Zemarion, *Yaacov Gil Jubilee Volume*, 141–48.

Laney, J. Carl. "The Role of the Prophets in God's Case against Israel." *Bibliotheca Sacra* 138, no. 552 (1981): 313–25.

Lattimore, Richmond, trans. *Greek Lyrics.* 2nd ed., rev. Chicago: University of Chicago Press, 1960.

Leclerc, Thomas L. *Yaheweh Is Exalted in Justice: Solidarity and Conflict in Isaiah.* Minneapolis: Fortress, 2001.

Lehmann, Manfred R. "Biblical Oaths." *Zeitschrift für die alttestamentliche Wissenschaft* 81, no. 1 (1969): 74–92.

Levine, Baruch A. "In Praise of the Israelite *Mišpāhâ*: Legal Themes in the Book of Ruth." In *The Quest for the Kingdom of God: Studies in Honor of George E. Mendenhall*, edited by H. B. Huffmon, F. A. Spina, and A. R. W. Green, 95–106. Winona Lake, IN: Eisenbrauns, 1983.

Levinson, Bernard M. "The Right Chorale: From the Poetics to the Hermeneutics of the Hebrew Bible." In *"Not in Heaven": Coherence and Complexity in Biblical Narrative*, edited by Jason P. Rosenblatt and Joseph C. Sitterson Jr., 129–53. Bloomington: Indiana University Press, 1991.

———. "The Case for Revision and Interpolation within the Biblical Legal Corpora." In *Theory and Method in Biblical and Cuneiform Law: Revision, Interpolation and Development*, edited by Bernard M. Levinson, 37–59. Sheffield, England: Sheffield Academic Press, 1994.

Levmore, Saul. "Rethinking Group Responsibility and Strategic Threats in Biblical Texts and Modern Law." *Chicago-Kent Law Review* 71, no. 1 (1995): 85–121.

Levy, Leonard W. *Treason against God: A History of the Offense of Blasphemy*. New York: Schocken Books, 1981.

Lewis, C. S. *Reflections on the Psalms*. London: Fontana Books, 1961.

Lewy, Immanuel. "The Puzzle of DT. XXVII: Blessings Announced, but Curses Noted." *Vetus Testamentum* 12, no. 2 (1962): 207–11.

Lieberman, Saul. Tosefta ki-fshutah: *A Comprehensive Commentary on the Tosefta*. New York: Jewish Theological Seminary, 1955.

Light, Alfred R. "Civil Procedure Parables in the First Year: Applying the Bible to Think Like a Lawyer." *Gonzaga Law Review* 37, no. 2 (2001–2002): 283–313.

Lindars, Barnabas. "Ezekiel and Individual Responsibility." *Vetus Testamentum* 15, no. 4 (1965): 452–67.

Lindblom, Jon. "Lot-Casting in the Old Testament." *Vetus Testamentum* 12, no. 2 (1962): 164–78.

Litchfield, W. Reid. "The Search for the Physical Cause of Jesus Christ's Death." *BYU Studies* 37, no. 4 (1997–98): 93–109.

Livingston, Dennis H. "The Crime of Leviticus XXIV 11." *Vetus Testamentum* 36, no. 3 (1986): 352–54.

Lockyer, Herbert. *All the Trades and Occupations of the Bible: A Fascinating Study of Ancient Arts and Crafts*. Grand Rapids, MI: Zondervan, 1969.

Lorein, G. W. *The Antichrist Theme in the Intertestamental Period*. London: T and T Clark, 2003.

Ludlow, Daniel H., ed. *Encyclopedia of Mormonism*. 5 vols. New York: Macmillan, 1992.

Luering, Heinrich L. E. "Cheek." In *The International Standard Bible Encyclopedia*, edited by James Orr. Rev. ed. Grand Rapids, MI: Eerdmans, 1960.

Lundquist, John M., and Stephen D. Ricks, eds. *By Study and Also by Faith: Essays in Honor of Hugh W. Nibley on the Occasion of His Eightieth Birthday, 27 March 1990.* 2 vols. Salt Lake City: Deseret Book and FARMS, 1990.

Lutz, Henry Frederick. *The Verdict of a Trial Judge in a Case of Assault and Battery.* U. C. Publications in Semitic Philology. Berkeley: University of California Press, 1930.

Mabee, Charles. "Jacob and Laban: The Structure of Judicial Proceedings (Genesis XXXI 25–42)." *Vetus Testamentum* 30, no. 2 (1980): 192–207.

MacDowell, Douglas. "Unintentional Homicide in the *Hippolytos.*" *Rheinisches Museum für Philologie* 111, no. 2 (1968): 156–58.

Macholz, Georg Christian. "Die Stellung des Königs in der israelitischen Gerichtsverfassung." *Zeitschrift für die alttestamentliche Wissenschaft* 84, no. 2 (1972): 157–82.

MacMullen, Ramsay. *Enemies of the Roman Order: Treason, Unrest, and Alienation in the Empire.* Cambridge, MA: Harvard University Press, 1966.

Maimonides, Moses. *The Code of Maimonides: Book Fourteen, the Book of Judges.* Translated by Abraham M. Hershman. New Haven, CT: Yale University Press, 1949.

Malchow, Bruce V. *Social Justice in the Hebrew Bible.* Collegeville, MN: Liturgical Press, 1996.

Malina, Bruce J., and Richard L. Rohrbaugh. *Social-Science Commentary on the Synoptic Gospels.* Minneapolis: Augsburg Fortress, 1992.

Malul, Meir. *The Comparative Method in Ancient Near Eastern and Biblical Legal Studies.* Neukirchen-Vluyn: Butzon and Bercker Kevelaer, 1990.

Manning, Joseph G. "Egypt: Demotic Law." In Westbrook, *A History of Ancient Near Eastern Law,* 2:817–62.

Marshall, Jay W. *Israel and the Book of the Covenant: An Anthropological Approach to Biblical Law.* Atlanta: Scholars Press, 1993.

Matthews, Robert J. "Abinadi: Prophet and Martyr." *Ensign,* April 1992, 25–30.

———. "Abinadi: The Prophet and Martyr." In *The Book of Mormon: Mosiah, Salvation Only through Christ,* edited by Monte S. Nyman and Charles D. Tate Jr., 91–112. Provo, UT: Religious Studies Center, Brigham Young University, 1991.

Matthews, Victor H. "Kings of Israel: A Question of Crime and Punishment." In *SBL Seminar Papers*, 517–26. Baltimore: Scholars Press, 1998.

———. *Manners and Customs in the Bible*. Rev. ed. Peabody, MA: Hendrickson, 1991.

———. "The Social Context of Law in the Second Temple Period." *Biblical Theology Bulletin* 28 (1998): 7–15.

Matthews, Victor H., and Don C. Benjamin. *Social World of Ancient Israel, 1250–587* B.C.E. Peabody, MA: Hendrickson, 1993.

Maxwell, Neal A. " 'By the Gift and Power of God.' " In Parry, Peterson, and Welch, *Echoes and Evidences of the Book of Mormon*, 1–15.

Mays, James Luther. "The Place of the Torah-Psalms in the Psalter." *Journal of Biblical Literature* 106, no. 1 (1987): 3–12.

McCarter, P. Kyle. "The River Ordeal in Israelite Literature." *Harvard Theological Review* 66, no. 4 (1973): 403–12.

McConville, J. G. *Law and Theology in Deuteronomy*. Sheffield, England: JSOT Press, 1984.

McFadden, Patrick M. *A Student's Guide to Legal Analysis: Thinking Like a Lawyer*. Gaithersburg, MD: Aspen Law and Business, 2001.

McGuire, Richard. "Prophetic Lawsuits in the Hebrew Bible and the Book of Mormon." FARMS Preliminary Report. Provo, UT: FARMS, 1982.

McKane, W. "Poison, Trial by Ordeal and the Cup of Wrath." *Vetus Testamentum* 30, no. 4 (1980): 474–92.

McKay, J. W. "Exodus XXIII 1–3, 6–8: A Decalogue for the Administration of Justice in the City Gate." *Vetus Testamentum* 21, no. 3 (1971): 311–25.

McKenzie, Donald A. "The Judge of Israel." *Vetus Testamentum* 17, no. 1 (1967): 118–21.

———. "Judicial Procedure at the Town Gate." *Vetus Testamentum* 14, no. 1 (1964): 100–104.

McKenzie, John L. "The Elders in the Old Testament." *Biblica* 40 (1959): 522–40.

McNamara, Martin. *Targum and Testament: Aramaic Paraphrases of the Hebrew Bible: A Light on the New Testament*. Grand Rapids, MI: Eerdmans, 1972.

Mikliszanski, J. K. "The Law of Retaliation and the Pentateuch." *Journal of Biblical Literature* 66, no. 3 (1947): 295–303.

Milgrom, Jacob. "The Ideological and Historical Importance of the Office of Judge in Deuteronomy." In *Isac Leo Seeligmann Volume: Essays on the Bible and the Ancient World*, edited by Alexander Rofé and

Yair Zakovitch, 129–39. Jerusalem: E. Rubinstein's Publishing House, 1983.

———. *Leviticus 1–16: A New Translation with Introduction and Commentary*. The Anchor Bible. New York: Doubleday, 1991.

———. *Leviticus 17–22: A New Translation with Introduction and Commentary*. The Anchor Bible. New York: Doubleday, 2000.

Milikowsky, Chaim. "Law at Qumran. A Critical Reaction to Lawrence H. Schiffman, *Sectarian Law in the Dead Sea Scrolls: Courts, Testimony, and the Penal Code*." *Revue de Qumrân* 12, no. 2 (1986): 237–49.

Millet, Robert L. "The Holy Order of God." In *The Book of Mormon: Alma, the Testimony of the Word*, edited by Monte S. Nyman and Charles D. Tate Jr., 61–88. Provo, UT: Religious Studies Center, Brigham Young University, 1992.

———. "Sherem the Anti-Christ." In *The Book of Mormon: Jacob Through Words of Mormon, To Learn with Joy*, edited by Monte S. Nyman and Charles D. Tate Jr., 175–91. Provo, UT: Religious Studies Center, Brigham Young University, 1990.

Mittwoch, H. "The Story of the Blasphemer Seen in a Wider Context." *Vetus Testamentum* 15, no. 3 (1965): 386–89.

Moran, William L. "New Evidence from Mari on the History of Prophecy." *Biblica* 50, no. 1 (1969): 15–56.

Morgenstern, Julian. "Trial by Ordeal among the Semites and in Ancient Israel." In *Hebrew Union College Jubilee Volume (1875–1925)*, edited by David Philipson, H. G. Enelow, K. Kohler, Jacob Z. Lauterbach, Jacob Mann, Julian Morgenstern, and William Rosenau, 113–43. Cincinnati: n.p., 1925.

Morisse, Mark J. "Simile Curses in the Ancient Near East, Old Testament, and Book of Mormon." FARMS Preliminary Report. Provo, UT: FARMS, 1981. Also in *Journal of Book of Mormon Studies* 2, no. 1 (1993): 124–38.

Morris, Leon. "Judgement and Custom." *Australian Biblical Review* 7 (1959): 72–74.

Morrison, William Douglas, and Janet I. Low. "Banishment." In Hastings, Selbie, and Gray, *Encyclopaedia of Religion and Ethics*, 2:346–47.

Nardoni, Enrique. *Rise Up, O Judge: A Study of Justice in the Biblical World*. Peabody, MA: Hendrickson, 2004.

Nel, Philip J. "The Talion Principle in Old Testament Narratives." *Journal of Northwest Semitic Language* 20, no. 1 (1994): 21–29.

Neusner, Jacob. " 'By the Testimony of Two Witnesses' in the Damascus Document IX, 17–22 and in Pharisaic-Rabbinic Law." *Revue de Qumrân* 8, no. 2 (1973): 197–217.

Nibley, Hugh. *An Approach to the Book of Mormon.* Edited by John W. Welch. The Collected Works of Hugh Nibley, vol. 6. Salt Lake City: Deseret Book and FARMS, 1988.

———. *Approaching Zion.* Edited by Don E. Norton. The Collected Works of Hugh Nibley, vol. 9. Salt Lake City: Deseret Book and FARMS, 1989.

———. "How to Get Rich." In Nibley, *Approaching Zion,* 178–201.

———. *Lehi in the Desert; The World of the Jaredites; There Were Jaredites.* Edited by John W. Welch, Darrell L. Matthews, and Stephen R. Callister. The Collected Works of Hugh Nibley, vol. 5. Salt Lake City: Deseret Book and FARMS, 1988.

———. *The Prophetic Book of Mormon.* Edited by John W. Welch. The Collected Works of Hugh Nibley, vol. 8. Salt Lake City: Deseret Book and FARMS, 1989.

———. *Teachings of the Book of Mormon, Semester 2.* Provo, UT: FARMS, 1993.

Niehr, Herbert. "Grundzüge der Forschung zur Gerichtsorganisation Israels." *Biblische Zeitschrift* 31, no. 2 (1987): 206–27.

Nielsen, Kirsten. *Yahweh as Prosecutor and Judge: An Investigation of the Prophetic Lawsuit (Rîb-Pattern).* Journal for the Study of the Old Testament Supplement Series 9. Sheffield, England: JSOT, 1978.

North, Christopher R. *The Essence of Idolatry.* Beiheft zur Zeitschrift für die alttestamentliche Wissenschaft 77. Berlin: de Gruyter, 1958.

Nyman, Monte S., and Charles D. Tate Jr., eds. *The Book of Mormon: Alma, the Testimony of the Word.* Provo, UT: Religious Studies Center, Brigham Young University, 1992.

———, eds. *The Book of Mormon: Second Nephi, the Doctrinal Structure.* Provo, UT: Religious Studies Center, Brigham Young University, 1989.

Oaks, Dallin H. "Opening Remarks." 27 August 1973. http://www.law2.byu .edu/law_school/foundingdocumentsnew/index.php (accessed June 11, 2008).

Oelsner, Joachim, Bruce Wells, and Cornelia Wunsch. "Mesopotamia: Neo-Babylonian Period." In Westbrook, *A History of Ancient Near Eastern Law,* 2:911–74.

Otto, Eckart. "Die Geschichte der Talion im Alten Orient und Israel." In *Ernten, was man Sät: Festschrift für Klaus Koch,* edited by Dwight R.

Daniels, Uwe Gleßmer, and Martin Rösel, 101–30. Neukirchen-Vluyn: Neukirchener Verlag, 1991. Reprinted in *Kontinuum und Proprium: Studien zur Sozial- und Rechtsgeschichte des Alten Orients und des Alten Testaments*, edited by E. Otto and S. Uhlig, 224–45. Wiesbaden: Harrassowitz, 1996.

———. "Interdependenzen zwischen Geschichte und Rechtsgeschichte des antiken Israels." *Rechtshistorisches Journal* 7 (1988): 347–68.

———. *Theologische Ethik des Alten Testaments*. Stuttgart: Kohlhammer, 1994.

———. *Wandel der Rechtsbegründungen in der Gesellschaftsgeschichte des antiken Israel: Eine Rechtsgeschichte des "Bundesbuches" Ex XX 22–XXIII 13*. Leiden: E. J. Brill, 1988.

———. "Zur Stellung der Frau in den ältesten Rechtstexten des Alten Testament (Ex 20:14; 22, 15f)—wider die hermeneutische Naivität im Umgang mit dem Alten Testament." *Zeitschrift für Evangelische Ethik* 26, no. 3 (1982): 279–305.

Parry, Donald W. "Hebraisms and Other Ancient Peculiarities in the Book of Mormon." In Parry, Peterson, and Welch, *Echoes and Evidences of the Book of Mormon*, 155–89.

———, ed. *Temples of the Ancient World: Ritual and Symbolism*. Salt Lake City: Deseret Book and FARMS, 1994.

Parry, Donald W., Daniel C. Peterson, and John W. Welch, eds. *Echoes and Evidences of the Book of Mormon*. Provo, UT: FARMS, 2002.

Parry, Donald W., and Emanuel Tov, eds. *The Dead Sea Scrolls Reader*. 6 parts. Leiden: E. J. Brill, 2004–2005.

Parry, Donald W., and John W. Welch, eds. *Isaiah in the Book of Mormon*. Provo, UT: FARMS, 1998.

Patai, Raphael. *Family, Love and the Bible*. London: MacGibbon and Kee, 1960.

Patrick, Dale. *Old Testament Law*. Atlanta: John Knox Press, 1985.

———. "The Rhetoric of Collective Responsibility in Deuteronomic Law." In Wright, Freedman, and Hurvitz, *Pomegranates and Golden Bells*, 421–36.

———. "Studying Biblical Law as a Humanities." *Semeia* 45 (1989): 27–47.

Patterson, Richard D. "The Widow, the Orphan, and the Poor in the Old Testament and the Extra-Biblical Literature." *Bibliotheca Sacra* 130, no. 519 (1973): 223–34.

Paul, Shalom M. "Daniel 3:29—A Case Study of 'Neglected' Blasphemy." *Journal of Near Eastern Studies* 42, no. 4 (1983): 291–94.

————. "Unrecognized Biblical Legal Idioms in the Light of Comparative Akkadian Expressions." *Revue Biblique* 86, no. 2 (1979): 231–39.

Peck, Debra. "The Trial of Naboth as a Violation of the Covenant Code." Unpublished paper, 2006. Howard W. Hunter Law Library, Brigham Young University.

Pedersen, Johannes. "Honour and Shame." In Pedersen, *Israel: Its Life and Culture*, 1:213–44. London: Oxford University Press, 1973.

Peerbolt, L. J. Lietaert. *The Antecedents of Antichrist: A Traditio-Historical Study of the Earliest Christian Views on Eschatological Opponents*. Leiden: E. J. Brill, 1996.

Person, Raymond F., Jr. *The Deuteronomic School: History, Social Setting, and Literature*. Atlanta: Society of Biblical Literature, 2002.

Pesch, Rudolf. *Die Vision des Stephanus*. Stuttgart: Katholisches Bibelwerk, 1966.

Phillips, Anthony. "The Decalogue—Ancient Israel's Criminal Law." *Journal of Jewish Studies* 34, no. 1 (1983): 1–20.

————. " 'Double for All Her Sins.' " *Zeitschrift für die alttestamentliche Wissenschaft* 94, no. 1 (1982): 130–32.

————. *Essays on Biblical Law*. London: Sheffield, England Academic Press, 2002.

Piattelli, Daniela, and Bernard S. Jackson. "Jewish Law during the Second Temple Period." In Hecht et al., *An Introduction to the History and Sources of Jewish Law*, 19–56.

Pike, Dana M. " 'How Beautiful upon the Mountains': The Imagery of Isaiah 52:7–10 and Its Occurrences in the Book of Mormon." In Parry and Welch, *Isaiah in the Book of Mormon*, 249–91.

————. "Israelite Inscriptions from the Time of Jeremiah and Lehi." In Welch, Seely, and Seely, *Glimpses of Lehi's Jerusalem*, 193–244.

Plescia, Joseph. *The Oath and Perjury in Ancient Greece*. Tallahassee: Florida State University Press, 1970.

Pope, Marvin H. "Hosanna—What It Really Means." *Bible Review* 4, no. 2 (1988): 16–25.

Porten, Bezalel. "Structure and Chiasm in Aramaic Contracts and Letters." In Welch, *Chiasmus in Antiquity*, 169–82.

Potts, Geoffrey. "Communal Liability and Joint and Several Liability." Unpublished paper, 1989. Howard W. Hunter Law Library, Brigham Young University.

Priest, James E. *Governmental and Judicial Ethics in the Bible and Rabbinic Literature*. New York: KTAV, 1980.

Pritchard, James B. *The Ancient Near East: An Anthology of Texts and Pictures*. Princeton: Princeton University Press, 1958.

———, ed. *Ancient Near Eastern Texts Relating to the Old Testament*. 3rd ed. Princeton: Princeton University Press, 1975.

Radday, Yehuda T. "Chiasmus in Hebrew Biblical Narrative." In Welch, *Chiasmus in Antiquity*, 50–117.

Radday, Yehuda T., and John W. Welch. "Structure in the Scroll of Ruth." *Beth Mikra* 77 (1979): 180–87.

Radner, Karen. "Mesopotamia: Neo-Assyrian Period." In Westbrook, *A History of Ancient Near Eastern Law*, 2:883–910.

Rakover, Nahum. "The One vs. the Many in Life and Death Situations." In *Jewish Law Association Studies VIII: The Jerusalem 1994 Conference Volume*, edited by E. A. Goldman, 129–53. Atlanta: Scholars Press, 1996.

Rasmussen, James L. "Blood Vengeance in the Old Testament and Book of Mormon." FARMS Preliminary Report. Provo, UT: FARMS, 1981.

Redfield, Sarah E. *Thinking Like a Lawyer: An Educator's Guide to Legal Analysis and Research*. Durham, NC: Carolina Academic Press, 2002.

Reviv, Hanoch. "The Traditions Concerning the Inception of the Legal System in Israel: Significance and Dating." *Zeitschrift für die alttestamentliche Wissenschaft* 94, no. 4 (1982): 566–75.

Reynolds, Noel B, ed. *Book of Mormon Authorship Revisited: The Evidence for Ancient Origins*. Provo, UT: FARMS, 1997.

———, "Book of Mormon, Government and Legal History in the." In Ludlow, *Encyclopedia of Mormonism*, 1:160–62.

———. "The Coming Forth of the Book of Mormon in the Twentieth Century." *BYU Studies* 38, no. 2 (1999): 6–47.

Ricks, Stephen D. "Fasting in the Book of Mormon and the Bible." In Cheesman, *The Book of Mormon: The Keystone Scripture*, 127–36.

Ricks, Stephen D., and William J. Hamblin, eds. *Warfare in the Book of Mormon*. Salt Lake City: Deseret Book and FARMS, 1990.

Roberts, B. H. *New Witnesses for God*. 3 vols. Salt Lake City: Deseret News, 1909.

———. *Studies of the Book of Mormon*. Edited by Brigham D. Madsen, with a bibliographic essay by Sterling M. McMurrin. Urbana: University of Illinois Press, 1985.

———. *The Truth, the Way, the Life: An Elementary Treatise on Theology*. Edited by John W. Welch. Provo, UT: BYU Studies, 1994.

Robertson, John F. "Temples and Sanctuaries: Mesopotamia." In Freedman et al., *The Anchor Bible Dictionary*, 6:372–76.

Robinson, Gnana. "The Prohibition of Strange Fire in Ancient Israel: A New Look at the Case of Gathering Wood and Kindling Fire on the Sabbath." *Vetus Testamentum* 28, no. 3 (1978): 301–17.

Robison, John C. "Crucifixion in the Roman World: The Use of Nails at the Time of Christ." *Studia Antiqua: The Journal of the Student Society for Ancient Studies* (Brigham Young University) 2, no. 1 (2002): 25–59.

Robinson, Olivia. "Private Prisons." *Revue Internationale des Droits de l'Antiquité* 15 (1968): 389–98.

Rofé, Alexander. "Methodological Aspects of the Study of Biblical Law." In Jackson, *Jewish Law Association Studies II: The Jerusalem Conference Volume*, 1–16.

Rogers, Robert Samuel. *Criminal Trials and Criminal Legislation under Tiberius*. Middletown, CN: American Philological Association, 1935.

Romantz, David S., and Kathleen Elliott Vinson. *Legal Analysis: The Fundamental Skill*. Durham, NC: Carolina Academic Press, 1998.

Rosenberg, Irene Merker, and Yale L. Rosenberg. "In the Beginning: The Talmudic Rule Against Self-Incrimination." *New York University Law Review* 63, no. 5 (1988): 955–1050.

———. " 'Perhaps What Ye Say Is Based Only on Conjecture'—Circumstantial Evidence, Then and Now." *Houston Law Review* 31, no. 5 (1995): 1371–427.

Rosenblatt, Samuel. "The Crucifixion of Jesus from the Standpoint of Pharasaic Law." *Journal of Biblical Literature* 75, no. 4 (1956): 315–21.

———. "The Relations between Jewish and Muslim Laws concerning Oaths and Vows." *American Academy for Jewish Research* 7 (1936): 229–44.

Roth, Martha T. *Law Collections from Mesopotamia and Asia Minor*. Edited by Piotr Michalowski. Atlanta: Scholars Press, 1995.

———. "Mesopotamian Legal Traditions and the Laws of Hammurabi." *Chicago-Kent Law Review* 71, no. 1 (1995): 13–39.

Rowe, Ignacio Márquez. "Anatolia and the Levant: Alalakh." In Westbrook, *A History of Ancient Near Eastern Law*, 1:693–717.

———. "Anatolia and the Levant: Canaan." In Westbrook, *A History of Ancient Near Eastern Law*, 1:737–43.

———. "Anatolia and the Levant: Ugarit." In Westbrook, *A History of Ancient Near Eastern Law*, 1:719–35.

Rushdoony, Rousas John. *The Institutes of Biblical Law*. N.p.: Presbyterian and Reformed Publishing, 1973.

Rutter, Irvin C. "Law, Language, and Thinking Like a Lawyer." *University of Cincinnati Law Review* 61 (1993): 1303–60.

Ruwet, J. "Misericordia et Iustitia Dei in Vetere Testamento." *Verbum Domini* 25 (1947): 35–42, 89–98.

Salmon, John M. *Judicial Authority in Early Israel: An Historical Investigation of Old Testament Institutions.* PhD diss., Princeton Theological Seminary, 1968.

Sandvik, Bjørn. *Das Kommen des Herrn beim Abendmahl im Neuen Testament.* Zürich: Zwingli, 1970.

Sassoon, John. *Ancient Laws and Modern Problems.* London: Third Millennium Publishing, 2001.

Schade, Aaron P. "The Kingdom of Judah: Politics, Prophets, and Scribes in the Late Preexilic Period." In Welch, Seely, and Seely, *Glimpses of Lehi's Jerusalem,* 299–336.

Schiffman, Lawrence H. "The Law of Vows and Oaths (*Num.* 30, 3–16) in the *Zadokite Fragments* and the *Temple Scroll.*" *Revue de Qumrân* 15, nos. 1–2 (1991): 199–214.

———. "The Qumran Law of Testimony." *Revue de Qumrân* 8, no. 4 (1975): 603–12.

———. *Sectarian Law in the Dead Sea Scrolls: Courts, Testimony, and the Penal Code.* Chico, CA: Scholars Press, 1983.

Schottroff, Willy. *Der altisraelitische Fluchspruch.* Neukirchen-Vluyn: Neukirchener Verlag, 1969.

Schreiber, Aaron M. *Jewish Law and Decision-Making.* Philadelphia: Temple University Press, 1979.

Schroer, Silvia. *In Israel gab es Bilder: Nachrichten von darstellender Kunst im Alten Testament.* Orbis Biblicus et Orientalis 74. Frieburg, Schweiz: Vandenhoeck und Ruprecht, 1987.

Schultz, Hermann. *Das Todesrecht im Alten Testament: Studien zur Rechtsform der Mot-Jumat-Sätze.* Beiheft zur Zeitschrift für die alttestamentliche Wissenschaft 114. Berlin: Töpelmann, 1969.

Schultz, Joseph P. "Max Weber and the Sociological Development of Jewish Law." *Diné Israel* 16 (1991–92): 71–82.

Schultz, Joseph P., and Lois Spatz. *Sinai and Olympus: A Comparative Study.* Lanham, MD: University Press of America, 1995.

Seely, David Rolph. "The Ten Commandments in the Book of Mormon." In Van Orden and Top, *Doctrines of the Book of Mormon: The 1991 Sperry Symposium,* 166–81.

Segal, Peretz. "The Divine Verdict of Leviticus X 3." *Vetus Testamentum* 39, no. 1 (1989): 91–95.

———. "The Penalty of the Warning Inscription from the Temple of Jerusalem." *Israel Exploration Journal* 39, nos. 1–2 (1989): 79–84.

Segert, Stanislav. "Bis in das dritte und vierte Glied (Ex 20, 5)." *Communio Viatorum* 1 (1958): 37–39.

Sharma, Arvind. "Satan." In *The Encyclopedia of Religion*, edited by Mircea Eliade, 13:81–84. New York: Macmillan, 1987.

Skolnik, Fred, and Michael Berenbaum, eds. *Encyclopaedia Judaica*. 22 vols. 2nd ed. Jerusalem: Keter, 2007.

Skousen, Royal. *Analysis of Textual Variants of the Book of Mormon: Part Three, Mosiah 17–Alma 20*. Provo, UT: FARMS, 2006.

———. "History of the Critical Text Project of the Book of Mormon." In *Uncovering the Original Text of the Book of Mormon*, edited by M. Gerald Bradford and Alison V. P. Coutts, 5–21. Provo, UT: FARMS, 2002.

———. " 'Scourged' vs. 'Scorched' in Mosiah 17:13." *Insights* (FARMS, Brigham Young University) 22, no. 3 (2002): 2–3.

———. "Towards a Critical Edition of the Book of Mormon." *BYU Studies* 30, no. 1 (1990): 51–53.

———. "Translating the Book of Mormon: Evidence from the Original Manuscript." In Reynolds, *Book of Mormon Authorship Revisited*, 61–93.

Slanski, Kathryn. "Mesopotamia: Middle Babylonian Period." In Westbrook, *A History of Ancient Near Eastern Law*, 1:486–520.

Smith, Hannah Clayson. "Protecting the Widows and the Fatherless in the Book of Mormon." *Studia Antiqua: The Journal of the Student Society for Ancient Studies* (Brigham Young University) (Summer 2003): 173–80.

Smith, James E. "How Many Nephites? The Book of Mormon at the Bar of Demography." In Reynolds, *Book of Mormon Authorship Revisited*, 255–93.

Smith, Jonathan Z. *Imagining Religion: From Babylon to Jonestown*. Chicago: University of Chicago Press, 1982.

Smith, Mark S. *The Origins of Biblical Monotheism: Israel's Polytheistic Background and the Ugaritic Texts*. Oxford: Oxford University Press, 2001.

Solon. "The Ten Ages of Man." In *Greek Lyrics*, translated by Richmond Lattimore, 23. 2nd ed. Chicago: University of Chicago Press, 1960.

Sorenson, John L. "The Composition of Lehi's Family." In Lundquist and Ricks, *By Study and Also by Faith*, 2:174–96.

———. *Images of Ancient America: Visualizing Book of Mormon Life.* Provo, UT: FARMS, 1998.

Speiser, Ephraim A. "Census and Ritual Expiation in Mari and Israel." In *Oriental and Biblical Studies,* edited by J. J. Finkelstein and Moshe Greenberg, 171–86. Philadelphia: University of Pennsylvania Press, 1967.

Sprinkle, Joe M. *'The Book of the Covenant': A Literary Approach.* Sheffield, England: JSOT Press, 1994.

Stock, Konrad. "Gott der Richter. Der Gerichtsgedanke als Horizont der Rechtfertigungslehre." *Evangelische Theologie* 40, no. 3 (1980): 240–56.

Sulzberger, Mayer. "The Ancient Hebrew Law of Homicide." *Jewish Quarterly Review* 5, no. 4 (1915): 559–614.

Susser, Bernard. "Worthless Confessions: The Torah Approach." *New Law Journal* 130, no. 5976 (1980): 1056–57.

Sutherland, Ammon. "Alma 14 as a Trial by Ordeal." Unpublished paper, 2006. Howard W. Hunter Law Library, Brigham Young University.

Sweeney, Marvin A. *King Josiah of Judah: The Lost Messiah of Israel.* Oxford: Oxford University Press, 2001.

Szink, Terrence L., and John W. Welch. "King Benjamin's Speech in the Context of Ancient Israelite Festivals." In Welch and Ricks, *King Benjamin's Speech,* 147–223.

Teichert, Jeffrey B. "The Principle of Collective Salvation in Ancient Israelite Law." Unpublished paper, 1994. Howard W. Hunter Law Library, Brigham Young University.

Thompson, John S. "Lehi and Egypt." In Welch, Seely, and Seely, *Glimpses of Lehi's Jerusalem,* 259–76.

Thompson, Thomas, and Dorothy Thompson. "Some Legal Problems in the Book of Ruth." *Vetus Testamentum* 18, no. 1 (1968): 79–99.

Towner, W. Sibley. "Retributional Theology in the Apocalyptic Setting." *Union Seminary Quarterly Review* 26, no. 3 (1971): 203–14.

Tozzer, Alfred M., ed. *Landa's Relación de las Cosas de Yucatán.* Papers of the Peabody Museum of American Archaeology and Ethnology, Harvard University, vol. 18. Cambridge, MA: Peabody Museum, 1941.

Trites, Allison A. *The New Testament Concept of Witness.* Cambridge: Cambridge University Press, 1977.

Tsevat, Matitiahu. "The Prohibition of Divine Images According to the Old Testament." In *Wünschet Jerusalem Frieden,* edited by Matthias Augustin and Klaus-Dietrich Schunck, 211–20. Frankfurt am Main: Verlag Peter Lang, 1988.

Tvedtnes, John A. " 'As a Garment in a Hot Furnace.' " *Journal of Book of Mormon Studies* 6, no. 1 (1997): 76–79.

Underwood, Richard H. "False Witness: A Lawyer's History of the Law of Perjury." *Arizona Journal of International and Comparative Law* 10, no. 2 (1993): 215–52.

van der Ploeg, J. "Studies in Hebrew Law." *Catholic Biblical Quarterly* 12, no. 3 (1950): 248–59.

van der Toorn, Karel. "Ordeal Procedures in the Psalms and the Passover Meal." *Vetus Testamentum* 38, no. 4 (1988): 427–45.

van der Woude, A. S. "The Book of Nahum: A Letter Written in Exile." In *Instruction and Interpretation: Studies in Hebrew Language, Palestinian Archaeology and Biblical Exegesis. Papers Read at the Joint British-Dutch Old Testament Conference Held at Louvain, 1976*, edited by H. A. Brongers, 108–26. Leiden: E. J. Brill, 1977.

van Houten, Christiana. *The Alien in Israelite Law.* Sheffield, England: JSOT Press, 1991.

Van Orden, Bruce A., and Brent L. Top, eds. *Doctrines of the Book of Mormon: The 1991 Sperry Symposium.* Salt Lake City: Deseret Book, 1992.

Van Seters, John. *A Law Book for the Diaspora: Revision in the Study of the Covenant Code.* Oxford: Oxford University Press, 2003.

van Vliet, Hendrik. *Did Greek-Roman-Hellenistic Law Know the Exclusion of the Single Witness?* Franeker, Netherlands: Wever, 1980.

———. *No Single Testimony: A Study on the Adoption of the Law of Deut. 19:15 par. into the New Testament.* Utrecht, Netherlands: Kemink and Zoon, 1958.

Veenhof, Klaas R. "Mesopotamia: Old Assyrian Period." In Westbrook, *A History of Ancient Near Eastern Law*, 2:431–83.

Vernon, Eric E. "Illegal Speech: Blasphemy and Reviling." *Studia Antiqua: The Journal of the Student Society for Ancient Studies* (Brigham Young University) (Summer 2003): 117–24.

Versnel, H. S. "Beyond Cursing: The Appeal to Justice in Judicial Prayers." In Faraone and Obbink, *Magika Hiera*, 60–106.

von Rad, Gerhard. *Old Testament Theology.* Transated by D. M. G. Stalker. 2 vols. London: Harper and Row, 1962–65.

von Waldow, Eberhard. *Der traditionsgeschichtliche Hintergrund der prophetischen Gerichtsreden.* Beiheft zur Zeitschrift für die alttestamentliche Wissenschaft 85. Berlin: Töpelmann, 1963.

Wacholder, Ben Zion. "Rules of Testimony in Qumranic Jurisprudence: CD 9 and 11Q Torah 64." *Journal of Jewish Studies* 40, no. 2 (1989): 163–74.

Warby, David. "The Book of Mormon Reveals the Forgotten Law of False Prophecy." Unpublished paper, 1981. Howard W. Hunter Law Library, Brigham Young University.

———. "The Book of Mormon Sheds Valuable Light on the Ancient Israelite Law of False Prophecy." *Studia Antiqua: The Journal of the Student Society for Ancient Studies* (Brigham Young University) (Summer 2003): 107–16.

Warby, David, and Lisa B. Hawkins. "The Crime of False Prophecy under Ancient Israelite Law." FARMS Preliminary Report. Provo, UT: FARMS, 1983.

Warmington, E. H., ed. *Remains of Old Latin.* Vol. 3, *Lucilius, The Twelve Tables.* Cambridge, MA: Harvard University Press, 1979.

Watts James W. *Reading Law: The Rhetorical Shaping of the Pentateuch.* Sheffield, England: Sheffield Academic Press, 1999.

Webster, Noah. *An American Dictionary of the English Language.* 2 vols. New York: S. Converse, 1828. Reprint, New York: Johnson Reprint, 1970.

Weidner, Ernst F. "Assyrische Beschreibungen der Kriegs-Reliefs Aššurbânaplis." *Archiv für Orientforschung* 8 (1932–33): 175–203.

Weinfeld, Moshe. "The Ban of the Canaanites and Its Development in Israelite Law." *Zion* 53, no. 2 (1988): 135–48.

———. "The Decalogue: Its Significance, Uniqueness, and Place in Israel's Tradition." In Firmage, Weiss, and Welch, *Religion and Law,* 3–47.

———. *Deuteronomy 1–11: A New Translation with Introduction and Commentary.* New York: Doubleday, 1991.

———. *Social Justice in Ancient Israel and in the Ancient Near East.* Jerusalem: Magnes Press; Minneapolis: Fortress Press, 1995.

Weingreen, J. "The Case of the Blasphemer (Leviticus XXIV10ff.)." *Vetus Testamentum* 22, no. 1 (1972): 118–23.

———. "The Case of the Daughters of Zelophchad." *Vetus Testamentum* 16, no. 4 (1966): 518–22.

———. "The Case of the Woodgatherer (Numbers XV32–36)." *Vetus Testamentum* 16, no. 3 (1966): 361–64.

Welch, John W. "Abinadi and Pentecost." In Welch, *Reexploring the Book of Mormon,* 135–38.

———. "Authorship of the Book of Isaiah in Light of the Book of Mormon." In Parry and Welch, *Isaiah in the Book of Mormon,* 423–37.

———. "B. H. Roberts: Seeker after Truth." *Ensign*, March 1986, 56–62.

———. "Benjamin's Speech: A Masterful Oration." In Welch and Ricks, *King Benjamin's Speech*, 55–88.

———. "Benjamin's Speech as a Prophetic Lawsuit." In Welch and Ricks, *King Benjamin's Speech*, 225–32.

———. *Biblical Law Cumulative Bibliography*. Winona Lake, IN: Eisenbrauns; Provo, UT: BYU Press, 2005. CD-ROM.

———. "Bibliography of Hebrew Law in the Book of Mormon." *Studia Antiqua: The Journal of the Student Society for Ancient Studies* (Brigham Young University) (Summer 2003): 181–86.

———. "The Calling of Lehi as a Prophet in the World of Jerusalem." In Welch, Seely, and Seely, *Glimpses of Lehi's Jerusalem*, 421–48.

———. "Chiasmus in Ancient Greek and Latin Literatures." In Welch, *Chiasmus in Antiquity*, 250–68.

———, ed. *Chiasmus in Antiquity: Structures, Analyses, Exegesis.* Hildesheim: Gerstenberg, 1981; Provo, UT: Research Press, 1999.

———. "Chiasmus in Biblical Law: An Approach to the Structure of Legal Texts in the Hebrew Bible." In Jackson, *Jewish Law Association Studies IV: The Boston Conference Volume*, 5–22.

———. "Chiasmus in the Book of Mormon." *BYU Studies* 10, no. 1 (1969): 69–84.

———. "Chiasmus in the New Testament." In Welch, *Chiasmus in Antiquity*, 211–49.

———. "Democratizing Forces in King Benjamin's Speech." In Welch and Thorne, *Pressing Forward with the Book of Mormon*, 110–26.

———. "The Destruction of Ammonihah and the Law of Apostate Cities." In Welch, *Reexploring the Book of Mormon*, 176–79.

———. "Doubled, Sealed, Witnessed Documents: From the Ancient World to the Book of Mormon." In *Mormons, Scripture, and the Ancient World*, edited by Davis Bitton, 391–444. Provo, UT: FARMS, 1998.

———. "The Execution of Zemnarihah." In Welch, *Reexploring the Book of Mormon*, 250–52.

———. "Exemption from Military Duty." In Welch, *Reexploring the Book of Mormon*, 189–92.

———. "Getting through Isaiah with the Help of the Nephite Prophetic View." In Parry and Welch, *Isaiah in the Book of Mormon*, 9–45.

———. "Good and True." In *Expressions of Faith: Testimonies of Latter-day Saint Scholars*, edited by Susan Easton Black, 231–42. Salt Lake City: Deseret Book and FARMS, 1996.

———. "How Much Was Known about Chiasmus in 1829 When the Book of Mormon Was Translated?" *FARMS Review* 15, no. 1 (2003): 47–80.

———. *Illuminating the Sermon at the Temple and Sermon on the Mount*. Rev. ed. Provo, UT: FARMS, 1999.

———. "Isaiah 53, Mosiah 14, and the Book of Mormon." In Parry and Welch, *Isaiah in the Book of Mormon*, 293–312.

———. "Judicial Process in the Trial of Abinadi." FARMS Preliminary Report. Provo, UT: FARMS, 1983.

———. "Law and War in the Book of Mormon." In Ricks and Hamblin, *Warfare in the Book of Mormon*, 46–102.

———. "The Law of Mosiah." In Welch, *Reexploring the Book of Mormon*, 158–61.

———. "Legal and Social Perspectives on Robbers in First-Century Judea." In Hall and Welch, *Masada and the World of the New Testament*, 141–53. Also printed in *BYU Studies* 36, no. 3 (1997): 141–53.

———. "Legal Perspectives on the Slaying of Laban." *Journal of Book of Mormon Studies* 1, no. 1 (1992): 119–41.

———. "Lehi's Last Will and Testament: A Legal Approach." In Nyman and Tate, *The Book of Mormon: Second Nephi, the Doctrinal Structure*, 61–82.

———. "The Melchizedek Material in Alma 13:13–19." In Lundquist and Ricks, *By Study and Also by Faith*, 2:238–72.

———. "Miracles, *Malficium*, and *Maiestas* in the Trial of Jesus." In *Jesus and Archaeology*, edited by James H. Charlesworth, 349–83. Grand Rapids, MI: Eerdmans, 2006.

———. "The Miraculous Translation of the Book of Mormon." In Welch, *Opening the Heavens*, 77–213.

———. "Number 24." In Welch, *Reexploring the Book of Mormon*, 272–74.

———, ed. *Opening the Heavens: Accounts of Divine Manifestations, 1820–44*. Provo, UT: Brigham Young University Press and Deseret Book, 2005.

———. "The Power of Evidence in the Nurturing of Faith." In Parry, Peterson, and Welch, *Echoes and Evidences of the Book of Mormon*, 17–53.

———, ed. *Reexploring the Book of Mormon*. Salt Lake City: Deseret Book and FARMS, 1992.

———. "Roberts Affirms Book of Mormon Antiquity." In Welch and Thorne, *Pressing Forward with the Book of Mormon*, 289–92.

———. "Sherem's Accusations against Jacob." *Insights* (FARMS, Brigham Young University) 11, no. 1 (January 1991): 2.

———. "A Steady Stream of Significant Recognitions." In Parry, Peterson, and Welch, *Echoes and Evidences of the Book of Mormon*, 331–87.

———. "The Temple in the Book of Mormon: The Temples at the Cities of Nephi, Zarahemla, and Bountiful." In Parry, *Temples of the Ancient World: Ritual and Symbolism*, 297–387.

———. "Theft and Robbery in the Book of Mormon and in Ancient Near Eastern Law." FARMS Preliminary Report. Provo, UT: FARMS, 1985.

———. "The Trial of Jeremiah: A Legal Legacy from Lehi's Jerusalem." In Welch, Seely, and Seely, *Glimpses of Lehi's Jerusalem*, 337–56.

———. "Unintentional Sin in Benjamin's Discourse." *Insights* (FARMS, Brigham Young University) 16, no. 4 (April 1996): 2.

———. "Was Heleman 7–8 an Allegorical Funeral Sermon?" In Welch, *Reexploring the Book of Mormon*, 239–41.

———. "Weighing and Measuring in the Worlds of the Book of Mormon." *Journal of Book of Mormon Studies* 8, no. 2 (1999): 36–46.

———, ed. *The Worlds of Joseph Smith: A Bicentennial Conference at the Library of Congress*. Provo, UT: BYU Press, 2006.

Welch, John W., and Robert D. Hunt. "Culturegram: Jerusalem 600 B.C." In Welch, Seely, and Seely, *Glimpses of Lehi's Jerusalem*, 1–40.

Welch, John W., and Kelsey D. Lambert. "Two Ancient Roman Plates." *BYU Studies* 45, no. 2 (2006): 55–76.

Welch, John W., and Heidi Harkness Parker. "Better That One Man Perish." In Welch and Thorne, *Pressing Forward with the Book of Mormon*, 17–19. Also published in *Insights* (FARMS, Brigham Young University) 18, no. 6 (June 1998): 2.

Welch, John W., and Stephen D. Ricks, eds. *King Benjamin's Speech: "That Ye May Learn Wisdom."* Provo, UT: FARMS, 1998.

Welch, John W., David Rolph Seely, and Jo Ann H. Seely, eds. *Glimpses of Lehi's Jerusalem*. Provo, UT: FARMS, 2004.

Welch, John W., and Melvin J. Thorne, eds. *Pressing Forward with the Book of Mormon: The FARMS Updates of the 1990s*. Provo, UT: FARMS, 1999.

Welch, John W., and J. Gregory Welch. *Charting the Book of Mormon: Visual Aids for Personal Study and Teaching*. Provo, UT: FARMS, 1999.

Wells, Bruce. *The Law of Testimony in the Pentateuchal Codes*. Wiesbaden: Harrassowitz, 2004.

Werner, Eric. " 'Hosanna' in the Gospels." *Journal of Biblical Literature* 65, no. 2 (1946): 97–122.

West, Stuart A. "The *Lex Talionis* in the Torah." *Jewish Bible Quarterly* 21, no. 3 (1993): 183–88.

Westbrook, Raymond. "Biblical and Cuneiform Law Codes." *Revue Biblique* 92, no. 2 (1985): 255–56.

———. "Biblical Law." In Hecht et al., *An Introduction to the History and Sources of Jewish Law*, 1–17.

———. "Cuneiform Law Codes and the Origins of Legislation." *Zeitschrift für Assyriologie* 79, no. 2 (1989): 201–22.

———. "Evidentiary Procedure in the Middle Assyrian Laws." *Journal of Cuneiform Studies* 55 (2003): 87–97.

———, ed. *A History of Ancient Near Eastern Law*. 2 vols. Leiden: E. J. Brill, 2003.

———. "Introduction: The Character of Ancient Near Eastern Law." In Westbrook, *A History of Ancient Near Eastern Law*, 1:1–89.

———. "Jubilee Laws." *Israel Law Review* 6 (1971): 209–26.

———. "The Laws of Biblical Israel," in *The Hebrew Bible: New Insights and Scholarship*, ed. Frederick E. Greenspahn. New York: New York University Press, 2008. pp. 99–119.

———. "Lex Talionis and Exodus 21, 22–25." *Revue Biblique* 93, no. 1 (1986): 52–69.

———. "Mesopotamia: Old Babylonian Period." In Westbrook, *A History of Ancient Near Eastern Law*, 1:361–430.

———. *Studies in Biblical and Cuneiform Law*. Paris: Gabalda, 1988.

———. "Witchcraft and the Law in the Ancient Near East." In *Recht gestern und heute*, edited by Joachim Hengstl and Ulrich Sick, 45–52. Wiesbaden: Harrassowitz, 2006.

Whitelam, Keith W. *The Just King: Monarchical Judicial Authority in Ancient Israel*. Sheffield, England: JSOT Press, 1979.

Wilcox, Max. " 'Upon the Tree'—Deut 21:22–23 in the New Testament." *Journal of Biblical Literature* 96, no. 1 (1977): 85–99.

Willis, Timothy M. "Yahweh's Elders (Isa 24,23): Senior Officials of the Divine Court." *Zeitschrift für die alttestamentliche Wissenschaft* 103, no. 3 (1991): 375–83.

Wilson, John A., trans. "Results of a Trial for Conspiracy." In *Ancient Near Eastern Texts Relating to the Old Testament*, edited by James B. Pritchard. 3rd ed., 214–16. Princeton: Princeton University Press, 1969.

Wilson, Robert R. "Israel's Judicial System in the Preexilic Period." *Jewish Quarterly Review* 74, no. 2 (1983): 229–48.

Wilson, William. *Old Testament Word Studies*. Grand Rapids, MI: Kregel Publications, 1978.

Woods, Fred E. "Elisha and the Children: The Question of Accepting Prophetic Succession." *BYU Studies* 32, no. 3 (1992): 47–58.

Wright, David P. "The Gesture of Hand Placement in the Hebrew Bible and in Hittite Literature." *Journal of the American Oriental Society* 106, no. 3 (1986): 433–46.

———. "The Laws of Hammurabi as a Source for the Covenant Collection (Exodus 20:23–23:19)." *Maarav* 10 (2003): 11–87.

Wright, David P., David Noel Freedman, and Avi Hurvitz, eds. *Pomegranates and Golden Bells: Studies in Biblical, Jewish, and Near Eastern Ritual, Law, and Literature in Honor of Jacob Milgrom.* Winona Lake, IN: Eisenbrauns, 1995.

Wyatt, N. "The Liturgical Context of Psalm 19 and Its Mythical and Ritual Origins." *Ugarit Forschungen* 27 (1995): 559–96.

Yadin, Yigael. "Pesher Nahum (4Q pNahum) Reconsidered." *Israel Exploration Journal* 21, no. 1 (1971): 1–12.

Yaron, Reuven. "Biblical Law: Prolegomena." In *Jewish Law in Legal History and the Modern World*, edited by Bernard S. Jackson, 27–44. Leiden: E. J. Brill, 1980.

———. "The Evolution of Biblical Law." In *La Formazione Del Diritto Nel Vicino Oriente Antico: Seminario svoltosi presso la Scuola di Perfezionamento in Diritto Romano e Diritti dell'Oriente Mediterraneo*, edited by Aristide Théodoridès, 77–108. Naples: Edizioni Scientifiche Italiane, 1988.

———. "Jewish Law and Other Legal Systems of Antiquity." *Journal of Semitic Studies* 4, no. 4 (1959): 308–31.

———. *The Laws of Eshunna*. 2nd ed. Jerusalem: Magnes: Leiden: E. J. Brill, 1988.

———. "The Middle Assyrian Laws and the Bible." *Biblica* 51, no. 4 (1970): 549–57.

Zahavy, Tzvee, trans. *The Talmud of the Land of Israel*. 35 vols. Chicago: University of Chicago Press, 1989.

Ziskind, Jonathan R. "When Two Men Fight: Legal Implications of Brawling in the Ancient Near East." *Revue Internationale des Droits de l'Antiquité* 44 (1997): 13–42.

CITATION INDEX

Subject Index

false prophecy tried in, 161
final verdict in, 203
God assumed to be in, 122
higher and lower judges in,
    222–23
number of priests in, 170–71
officers of, in Nephite
    civilization, 282
of King Noah, 139
proceedings in ancient Israel, 114
protection of holiness in, 195
removal from, 186
return to, multiple times, 198
royal as resource for local court,
    166
unanimous verdict in, 184
covenant
    fate of breakers of, 363
    made to keep the law, 97
    and Nephite community, 108
    obligations of, 61
    people of, 59
    people of Alma, 214, 218, 253
    people of Benjamin, 216–17, 364
    pillar as symbol of, 83
    practices of Alma, 149
    and secret combinations, 312,
        319–20
    transgression of, in
        Deuteronomy, 242
    with God, 118, 208, 384
Covenant Code, 27, 35, 57–58, 74,
    93, 133, 194, 383
    apodictic rules in, 59–76
criminal acts unobserved, 332
crucifixion, xix, 351–54, 374. *See
    also* hanging
curse/curses/cursing, 44, 66
    against Ahab by Elijah, 80
    against God, 77, 284

against Hananiah, 296, 362
against Korihor by Alma,
    289, 290–95, 342, 378. *See
    also* speechlessness
against shepherds, 276
against the political ruler, 159,
    199–201, 239, 284, 319–20, 384
as an oath, 96
as invocation of power of the
    wrong god, 292
as means of drawing divine
    directions, 123
bitter waters of, 292
blotting out of, 124
Gadianton robbers as, 322
hanging as, 351–56
in ancient laws, 111, 148
in Aramaic treaties, 264
in Psalms, 155
of Amulek against lawyers, 251
on tablets, 290–91
pronounced by Abinadi, 73,
    145–46, 152–57, 159–61,
    189–93, 204–6, 324
pronounced by Isaiah, 247
pronounced by Jacob, 149, 365
pronounced by Nephi, 324
ritual imposition of, 154
simile, 87
speechlessness, 290–92

dal (poor). *See* poor
Daube, David, v, 24–25, 27, 264,
    383
Day of Atonement, 37, 42
debtors, delinquent, 360, 366
Decalogue. *See* Ten Commandments
defendant
    challenge of, to a decision, 98
    challenging accusers by, 304

parties provided own, 92–93
physical, 93
scriptures as, 126
standards of, 95
expulsion, 22
  as divine judgment, 364
  as prelude to persecution, 365
  in the large plates, 366
  of Achan, 357
  of Alma, 185–86
  of faithful men, 260
  of Korihor, 64, 280–81
  of Miriam, 296
  of the people of Ammonihah, 357

Falk, Ze'ev W., v, xiii, 28, 112, 120,
    123, 135, 165, 283, 333, 337
false prophecy, 78–80, 200, 276,
    303, 384
  Abinadi accused of, 157–59,
    168–69, 185
  ancient jurisdiction over, 161
  Jacob accused of, 119–20,
    124–25, 305
  Jeremiah accused of, 25, 369
  Lehi accused of, 39
  punishment for, 176
false witness, 52, 60, 303
  against Naboth, 79
  and need for two witnesses, 242
  and talionic justice, 346–47
  a public crime, 159
  by Sherem, 131
  condemned in Book of
    Mormon, 69, 72
  in a judicial context, 72
  Korihor as, 287, 297
  punishment for, 93, 121–22, 136,
    343, 345
  refutation of, 287

family law in ancient cultures, 8
Feast of Tabernacles, 42, 240
Finkelstein, Julius J., 349
First Temple period, xiii, 110
flogging, 167, 173, 358–61, 381
  of Abinadi, 167, 203
  witnessed by convicting judge, 203
freedom of belief, 239, 273–74,
    277–78
free speech, 273, 387

Gadianton robbers, x, 26, 54, 62
  defeat of, 352
  in power in Zarahemla, 323, 334
  led by Zemnarihah, 342, 375–78
  oaths and idols of, 149
  rise of, 322
  secret combinations of, 311
  trials of defectors of, 100–101
gedud (robber), 388
Gideon, slaying of, 220–21, 224,
    307, 347, 374, 378
Greenberg, Moshe, viii

Haggai, Shammai school and, 315
Hammurabi, 30, 150
Hammurabi, laws of, 12, 31, 57
  and cheek slapping, 265
  calls for an ordeal, 121
  curses in, 148
  and false testimony, 135–36
  punishments specified by, 335,
    336, 339, 340, 351, 355
  unknown to Joseph Smith, 55
  warns judges against changing
    opinions, 185, 331
hanging, 167, 351–54, 355
  a dead body, 232, 348
  and felling of the tree, ix

and doubled, sealed, witnessed
documents, xii
held in prison, 369–70
pronounces simile curse, 153
purchase of family land by, xii
threatened with death, 194
trial of, 78, 87, 197, 223, 303
Jerusalem
Great Sanhedrin in, 173
in Lehi's time, 109–11, 160
prophecies concerning, 176
royal courts in, 166
temple in, 153, 156
Jesus Christ
birth of, 41
hosanna shouted to, 354
law of Moses and, 42–43, 43
legal disputes, pronouncement
on, 81, 256, 264, 366
Mormon's abridgment and, 49
proclaiming gospel of legally, 137
prophecies concerning, 109,
176–81, 207
trials of, ix–x, 62, 264, 303
Jethro, advice to Moses of, 84
Jewish law, relevance to Book of
Mormon, 32–33
Jewish Law Association, xi
Josephus, Flavius
on outcasts, 296
on planning an act, 316
on witchcraft, 352
Josiah, 37, 38, 87, 110, 150, 315
judge/judges, 83–88
appointed by the people, 249
appointment of, 216
at the town gate, 89
chief, corrects lower, 216, 223,
233, 283

chief, in Ammonihah, 237,
267–68
duties of, 165–67
executes punishment, 230
favor the rich, 70
God as, 83, 124
in ancient times, 6
in New Testament, 303
limited power of, 325–26
Nephite, 34
in case of Sherem, 116
number of, 78, 81, 85, 170–72,
281, 305
payment of, 217, 219, 251,
253–55, 254, 256
as profession of Alma the
Younger, 143
punishments available to, 335
qualifications of, 83–88, 92, 157
removal of, 185–86
required to warn offender, 221
responsibility of, 67–74
seating of, 173–75
unrighteous, 98, 101, 324
use of the law by, 3, 21, 52
voting of, 184
judgment seat, 140, 237, 238, 319,
326
judicial ideals, 3, 13, 52, 57–58, 63,
74–77
impartiality as, 70
Nephite, 212, 235
juridical procedures, 81, 89–99,
108, 111, 129
jurisdiction, 304
in cases of blasphemy, 277
in cases of false prophecy,
161–62
of elders, 159, 367
of God, 62

jurisdiction *(continued)*
  of judges, 84, 220, 223, 283
  of king, 86, 182, 318
  of priests, 21, 239
  plenary, 158
  slap as means to obtain, 263
justice, code of, 57–59
justice, social, 59
Justinian, 13

Kaminsky, Joel S., 248–49
karet (ostracism), 361
king
  appeal to, 98
  as supreme judge, 86
  charge of lying about, 159–61
  conspiring against, 77
  denied burial in Isaiah's
    prophecy, 232
  Hebrew word for (*melek*), 212
  judicial authority of, 91, 98,
    162–66
  judicial responsibility of, 253
  offenses against, 80, 119
  prerogative of, to kill, 160–61
  prohibitions applied to, 147–48
  responsibility for righteousness
    of, 249
  rights of, 150
  slapping on the cheek of, 265
kofer
  as compensation, 167, 331,
    380–81
  as ransom, 336
Korihor (see chapters 9, 10)
  as anti-Christ, 112, 302, 307
  as false witness, 287, 297
  as Nehorite, 274–76
  banishment of, 280–81, 296–98,
    365–66

banishment of followers of, 299
blasphemy, accused of, 284
confession of, 293–96
counterclaims of, 308
curse against by Alma, 289,
  290–95, 342, 378
expulsion of, 64, 280–81
request for trial by ordeal by, 288
righteous judgment in the trial
  of, 273
seven questions in Korihor's *rib*,
  287–88
talion and, 289
witness of, 285

Laban, case against Jacob, 81–83
  slaying of, xix
law
  and society, 3
  and wisdom literature, 15
  divine source of, 12–13
  Israelite meaning of, 14
  ongoing process, 4
  Psalms and, 13–14, 15, 118, 364
law of Moses, 207
  and atonement, 244
  and bribery, 330–31
  and compensation, 167
  and confession, 294
  and cursing, 239
  and false accusation, 346
  and gift-giving, 254–55
  and impious speech, 276, 282
  and Jesus Christ, 207
  and judicial responsibility, 181,
    183
  and justice at the city gates, 157
  and murder, 225
  and Nehor/Nehorites, 219, 243,
    271